—THE—
SAVE & PROSPER
RUGBY UNION
WHO'S WHO
1993/94

Compiled and edited by
Alex Spink

D1351039

CollinsWillow
An Imprint of HarperCollins*Publishers*

First published in 1993 by
Collins Willow
an imprint of HarperCollins*Publishers*
London

© Alex Spink 1993

A CIP catalogue record for this book
is available from the British Library

ISBN 0 00 218527 X

Photographs provided by Allsport

Printed in Great Britain by
Butler & Tanner Ltd, Frome and London

CONTENTS

PEP TALK

If you're looking to improve your investment performance then Save & Prosper is the team to come to for a PEP talk. Because Save & Prosper's Personal Equity Plan is an excellent way of investing up to £6,000 (£12,000 for a couple) a year in the stock market, with all your investment returns tax-free.

Save & Prosper, part of Flemings who manage £36 billion worldwide, are one of the leaders in the personal equity plan market with over 95,000 plans.

Talk to your financial adviser or ring us on our free Moneyline 0800 282 101 now.

CALL FREE 0800 282 101
9.00 a.m. – 5.30 p.m. ● 7 DAYS A WEEK

SAVE & PROSPER

■ THE INVESTMENT HOUSE ■
SPONSORS OF ENGLISH RUGBY

PREFACE

WELCOME to the naked world of rugby union as revealed by *The Save and Prosper Rugby Union Who's Who 1993/94*. You are cordially invited backstage to view the players free from the mud and grime, bumps and bruises – the greasepaint of their trade.

This year, in addition to our annual peek behind the scenes into the camps of England, France, Ireland, Scotland and Wales, we pay a maiden visit into the dens of Australia, New Zealand and South Africa. The characters who make the Big Eight huff and puff are all now at your fingertips.

The inclusion of the Southern Hemisphere triumverate, in this the fourth edition of the *RUWW*, is not before time. Australia and New Zealand are the premier global exponents of the game while South Africa, whatever their status, cannot be ignored.

However, acutely aware of the troubles in the Republic, the inclusion of the Springboks is dedicated to those waging the struggle against apartheid, and to those victims of it.

The 1992/93 season in international rugby was dominated by the Boys from Down Under. On the park, the world champion Wallabies preserved their pre-eminent status through the campaign and the born-again All Blacks edged past the Lions. Off it, too many diehard Corinthians continued to strive, Canute-like, to resist the tide of change.

Top grade rugby union is now a professional game, in all but name. The World Cup, Five Nations' Championship, overseas tours, even the Super-10 tournament, are neither for the faint-hearted nor the ill-committed. As Australia's Tim Gavin says: 'Gone are the days of twice-a-week training and playing on the Saturday with a few beers afterwards.'

Yet rugby continues to be played by men who are expected, basically, to fend for themselves financially. Is it not wrong, especially at a time when the pressure on meeting bills and feeding mouths grows ever greater, to expect players to give their all to the sport, which grows rich as a result, for little or no return?

Wallaby lock John Eales is in no doubt. He insists: 'If rugby is to continue to be as professional as it is, playing and training wise (we are on call for virtually 11 months of the year), it needs to give players

5

financial security. Many players have to give up a lot to go on tours.' Compatriot Richard Tombs adds: 'The daily tour allowance is not sufficient remuneration. A player should at least be reimbursed complete loss of wages.'

The players are expected to freely give of their time or their employers' time. One day, next year, next month, maybe next week even, the employers will say 'enough'. You want them, you support them. Who then will pick up the tab? However much the players are prepared to sacrifice for an international jersey, with zilch financial backing, the price might just become too high.

What compounds the irritation is the knowledge that certain players do benefit from the game: be they enticed abroad by lucrative covert payments, or sweetened by clubs to remain where they are and safeguard that all-important league status. Representative players do receive payments in South Africa, there is a Union-sanctioned All Black Club supporting the New Zealand Test stars, and the cosmopolitan influx to Italy each winter is, we can be assured, no culture-gaining excursion.

Where is the international policing, where is the consistency, where is the International Rugby Football Board? They are the game's overlords, from Auckland to Apia, Dublin to Durban, Twickenham to Tokyo, Nuku'alofa to the National Stadium, Cardiff. They must assert their authority on this subject. Many leading players feel they are being exploited and do not care for it. If the IRFB does not administer a one-for-all regulation relating to the amateurism question, they are doing the game a grave disservice.

'Being paid to play is not really the issue,' says Lions captain Gavin Hastings. 'All we want is a level playing field. Let's have the same rules for everyone.' If any one player is permitted the opportunity of making money from the game in whatever way, then so must everyone else. It is as simple as that.

International rugby players are not the blockheads they were once made out to be. A cauliflower ear does not make you a vegetable. England hooker Brian Moore, whom former Lions captain Finlay Calder reckons to be 'eloquent and well-versed', asks: 'Why is there no uniform interpretation of off-field activities? We should all be treated the same, irrespective of which hemsiphere we are located?'

He continues: 'The Aussies and New Zealanders might not necessarily be receiving broken time payments but their earnings out of sponsorship for off-the-field activities are far more liberally interpreted than ours.' A case of the whingeing Pom?

The failure of the IRFB to set down in black and white what exactly is permitted has led to resentment and confusion which could easily have been averted. 'Would someone please explain the off-the-field legislation, because I can't,' pleads England skipper Will Carling. 'Better communication is needed and everyone, regardless of hemisphere, should play by the same rules.' Poignantly, he adds: 'Players should be allowed to benefit from rugby-related activities because everything we do is naturally related to rugby.'

Well of course it is. To observe sport, in its purest form, is to holiday from life's humdrum. For that very reason its personalities stand out when thrust into an alien environment. Answer this. You see, say, Ieuan Evans on television dressed in plumber's overalls extolling the virtues of a new drainage system. What is your first reaction. Is it (a) 'Boy, that new drainage system looks just the job,' or (b) 'Hey, isn't that the Welsh rugby captain. That guy can sure move.'

Whatever Evans does and wherever he goes he is inextricably linked to rugby. Thus, whatever he does has, surely, to be rugby-related, whether plugging the latest drainage system or recommending a particular brand of rugby studs; whether standing in a sewer or on the halfway line at Cardiff Arms Park. To refer to an activity as non rugby-related is a nonsense.

While they wait in hope for the IRFB to paint over those grey areas, many players have spent time admiring another piece of the Board's handywork: last season's new turnover law. It met with virtually wholesale condemnation yet a fair proportion now want it to remain – simply because reverting to the previous version would disrupt another season.

Lions' prop Jason Leonard says: 'I don't like the ruck/maul law yet it is right to keep it for another year because the game can not continue being in a state of flux.' The Englishman asks: 'Why don't they just leave the laws alone? Rugby's biggest problem is that the law makers do not consult the players.'

England outside-half Stuart Barnes would raise a glass to that sentiment but stresses the need for a more positive approach towards such rule changes. He recalls: 'We remained positive at Bath and consequently our form held up. Having only a split-second to operate means that defenders only have a split-second to defend. To me, that is the essential concept of modern attacking rugby.'

The *Rugby Union Who's Who* is more than a store of opinions. It is a keepsake of the 1992/93 season and an essential reference for the 1993/94 campaign; be it through the comprehensive alphabetical player biographies (pp. 112–394) – a section which accommodates last season's Test players only – the Appendix (pp. 395–405) – which concisely details the borderline cases – the 1992/93 Reviews by each of the Big Eight captains (pp. 10–112), or the chronological results section (pp. 409–461) which starts with France against Romania in May 1992 and concludes with the Lions visit to New Zealand 15 months later on.

I am indebted to the national captains for their assistance in this production: to Michael Lynagh (Australia), Will Carling (England), Jean-Francois Tordo (France), Michael Bradley (Ireland), Sean Fitzpatrick (New Zealand), Gavin Hastings (Scotland), Naas Botha (South Africa) and Ieuan Evans (Wales). And to all the players included a big thank-you for your co-operation and your enthusiasm. May I also extend my gratitude to Greg Campbell, Wynne Gray (*The New Zealand Herald*), Chris Thau, Nick Cain, Westgate Sports, Michael Humphries & Partners, *Rugby World & Post*, *Rugby News*, each of the eight Unions, my colleagues in the British Rugby media, to my late godfather Douglas Harris for the inspiration and to Wallaby hero Nick Farr-Jones for his belter of a 'most embarrassing' revelation: 'Being photographed in the nude talking to the British Prime Minister John Major!'

My research was greatly helped by the following publications: *Rothmans Rugby Union Yearbooks* (1985–93, Queen Anne Press/ Headline, editor Stephen Jones), *The Guinness Rugby Union Fact Book* (Guinness, Chris Rhys), *Radio New Zealand Sport Rugby Annual* (21st and 22nd editions, Moa, Bob Howitt), *History of New Zealand Rugby Football, Volume 4, 1980–91* (Moa, R.H Chester & N.A.C McMillan), *McEwan's Rugby Record 1992–93* (IMA/Bill McMurtrie) and *Welsh Brewers Ltd Rugby Annual for Wales 1992–93* (Arwyn Owen).

Finally, to those whose lives are touched by this annual slog – Karen, Tom and Jenny – it's finished!

Alex Spink
July 1993

FOREWORD

PAUL BATEMAN
Chief Executive, Save & Prosper Group

This fourth edition of the *Save & Prosper Rugby Union Who's Who* breaks new ground in terms of coverage and value for money.

I am delighted that for the first time, players from Australia, New Zealand and South Africa are to be included. Thus from domestic beginnings, this booklet will now become an international reference manual. Despite this added value, the price remains the same.

Once again, the rugby world has become truly international. Save & Prosper was delighted to be able to sponsor the England versus South Africa game at Twickenham last November and many felt that this match was the official ending of South Africa's isolation.

During the 1992/93 domestic season, home advantage held sway and the end of England's successful run provided some enormously exciting and unpredictable results.

Save & Prosper looks forward enormously to another packed season of international rugby in 1993/94 and I trust this book will provide you with both formal and informal information about the participants.

THE CAPTAINS REVIEW
THE 1992/3 SEASON

 ## ENGLAND

Will Carling

THE International Board's decision to change the emphasis of the game prior to last season sounded the death knell for England's dominance of European rugby, at least temporarily. We did not know it at the time, but during the course of the campaign there was no doubt that we did not adapt to the new rules as well as others.

Sides would again have found it a lot harder to beat us under the old rules. We had developed a very successful gameplan around keeping a hold of the ball and taking it forward. Suddenly, with the new laws, it was not particularly important to be taking the ball forward. You have got to keep recycling and recycling. But we had built our strength up on set-pieces and we were very good at working ourselves into the area of the field in which we wanted to be. In one fell swoop that was taken away from us. It was most disappointing.

There will be new faces drafted in this season and they will probably find it easier to adapt than men who had been playing rugby all their lives under certain rules and become very successful. That said, I would still defend the selection of 16 Englishmen to tour with the British Lions. It was, I believe, a fair reflection of the strength of the English game. Although the year was not as successful as we would have wanted it to be, we have been the strongest side for three or four years. The English are now big-game players, we have enjoyed notable success, and Lions selection was a fitting reward.

Still, there were those who suggested certain players remained too long in the England team. I would have to disagree with that. If we had won a Grand Slam people would not have said that. All Test matches balance on a fine line. The difference this year was that we did not take our chances whereas, last year, we were very good at exploiting our opportunities. What caused us more problems than anything was not players going on too long, but the rule changes. As I have already said, these affected us far more than we anticipated.

To lose our Triple Grand Slam dream so early in the Championship was a major blow. I am not sure whether changing the team drastically after our 9–10 loss to Wales in Cardiff would have made a significant difference to our fortunes. It does not matter who you are if you do not take your chances.

'We had developed a very successful gameplan around keeping a hold of the ball and taking it forward. Suddenly, with the new laws, it was not particularly important to be taking the ball forward'

It was not too difficult to lift the lads after the Wales defeat. It was obviously acutely disappointing to have three Grand Slams taken away from us but you learn from your defeats and we will learn from what happened. Although our hat-trick ambition was dashed, all the players were realistic enough to know we were going to get beaten at some time. The other sides were not as weak as people were making out. They had taken a good look at England for two years and had learned.

To start the 1992/93 campaign at Wembley was slightly unreal. It was almost as though it was not a full international. All our home games are played at Twickenham and so it just felt like we were playing away. However, there were no excuses for our performance. We struggled on the day, though the Canadians had a very good pack of forwards who made it hard for us. It is very hard to play as well as you would

11

like, that early in the season.

That said, we should have read more into the performance than we did. We were struggling to adapt to the new rules, though more mentally than physically. Indeed, I do not think we placed enough significance on the problems we encountered in that game.

Returning to Twickenham, South Africa started very well against us and we went eight points down. They won a lot of good lineout ball and Naas Botha kicked unbelievably well, not only out of hand. They made very few mistakes in the first 30 minutes, while we did. We spilled ball, we missed tackles, we were not as efficient in the set-piece as we would have liked, and we were put under pressure. But we remained composed. And at half-time we decided that if we kept doing the basics and just made sure we did them better than we had in the first half, we would still win the game. That was what happened. Nothing different, we just cut out the mistakes and our superior fitness and technique showed as we finished very strongly.

Into the Five Nations' Championship and our win over France at Twickenham was branded 'lucky', with Ian Hunter converting a rebound off the crossbar into the winning try, by people quick to forget that the first French try was also fortuitous. The ball bounced rather nicely for them once Jon Webb had missed it. So it went both ways. By the second half we had control of the game. For whatever reason, we enjoy playing against the French. They seem to bring out the best in us these days and even when we were a few points down our self-belief remained intact. Our defence was very good and they never really looked that dangerous running the ball.

Rory Underwood leaves Scott Hastings groping thin air as he scorches over for the try of the 1993 Five Nations' Championship at Twickenham. England beat Scotland 26–12

However, we did again struggle to get any domination up front early on though, come the second half, we exercised a lot more control and Martin Johnson, on his debut, was superb. Whatever we might have lacked last season it was not character. That afternoon at Twickenham, we showed bucket loads of the stuff to come through and win, having started so badly.

Significantly, we do not feel that we are going to lose games at Twickenham now, certainly not in the Championship. We have not lost a Five Nations' game there since 1988. It takes a good side to come there and win, that's for sure. The support at HQ is so different now even from when I first started playing and the level of expectation is accordingly great.

That said, the rebuilding of the ground detracted from the atmosphere last season, which was a shame. When you have most of one side missing from a stadium, it cannot be quite the same. Hopefully, this season we will return to more of a cauldron-like atmosphere.

'There is no doubt Rob Andrew suffered from not being able to play club rugby on his enforced return from Toulouse. All season he struggled, by his standards, as a result of not playing regularly. It did not do him any good at all and the policy did not seem to serve any purpose'

Even though we still were not comfortable with the new rules going to Cardiff, I still felt we had players who were good enough to win the game, and I still believe that. We came up against a side who had done so much homework on us that they managed to stop us playing the game we wanted to play. And Ieuan (Evans) took their chance very well.

Their discipline was very good, they gave very few penalties away in the second half, but it was their defence, basically, that won the game for them. It was incredible. Our performance was frantic. Maybe we could have put more pressure on them. We ran a lot of ball and perhaps we should have put a few more balls up in the air. But we still made the chances, we still made the openings; we just did not take them. We did not seem to be able to get the same control on the game as we had enjoyed the previous year.

It was all the more frustrating when, against Scotland, we showed what we were capable. We have a potent back line and it was nice to remind people of the fact in the Calcutta Cup match. Stuart Barnes, who had come in for Rob Andrew at outside-half, managed to set it off on quite a few occasions.

I thought Rory Underwood's try, stemming from Stuart's darting break and Jerry Guscott's run, was one of the best I have seen at Twickenham. It was brilliant. Three tries of that calibre are rarely seen in the same game yet, Jerry and Tony Underwood also crossed for super scores. But still we did not dominate the game as we would have liked. Towards the end we gave far too many penalties away and, frankly, let the Scots, who were themselves no mugs, off the hook.

I felt terribly for Rob (Andrew), who watched from the bench. There is no doubt he suffered from not being able to play club rugby on his enforced return from Toulouse. All season he struggled, by his standards, as a result of not playing regular first-class rugby. It was a great shame that that happened. It did not do him any good at all and the policy did not seem to serve any purpose.

So to Dublin, where we had not lost since 1987. It sounds terrible to say, but I think Ireland had more to gain than we did from the game. There was obviously pride at stake for us but not a Grand Slam and however hard we tried to guard against it, players did have the thought of a forthcoming Lions tour which they hoped to make. For Ireland, it was a chance to win at home in the Championship for the first time since 1990 and they played with a fierce intensity. Having said that, we still managed to cope. Rory got over but the ball was stripped from his grasp. Mike Teague 'scored' but it was not given. So we still made the chances.

But the Irish never stopped driving forwards. When you are leading it is much easier to keep that intensity up. No excuses, though. We were well beaten by them and they deserved it. Psychologically, you always have to look for that edge in internationals, and we didn't find it. They did.

So, after two straight Grand Slams, we finished in mid-table with two wins and two losses. The end of an era? Yes, in the sense that a number of our stalwarts retired, but not in the sense that I see England enjoying less success in future. There are a lot of very good young players coming in which will give the team a different feel, a different edge, and I think they will bring different qualities to it. We will naturally evolve.

England's emphasis now will very much be on building a team for the next World Cup and, with the likes of Martin Johnson and numerous others in a strong B-side waiting in the wings, you have to remain confident. I do.

ENGLAND (P6 W4 D0 L2 F113 A83):
(H)	v	Canada (Wembley, 17.10.92)	won	26–13
(H)	v	South Africa (Twickenham, 14.11.92)	won	33–16

Five Nations' Championship
(H)	v	France (Twickenham, 16.1.93)	won	16–15
(A)	v	Wales (Cardiff, 6.2.93)	lost	9–10
(H)	v	Scotland (Twickenham, 6.3.93)	won	26–12
(A)	v	Ireland (Dublin, 20.3.93)	lost	3–17

England A (P7 W4 D0 L3 F230 A110):
(A)	v	New Zealand (Hamilton, 28.6.92)	lost	18–24
(A)	v	New Zealand (Pukekohe, 5.7.92)	lost	18–26
(H)	v	South Africa (Bristol, 7.11.92)	lost	16–20
(H)	v	France A (Leicester, 15.1.93)	won	29–17
(H)	v	Italy (Bath, 3.2.93)	won	59–0
(H)	v	Spain (Richmond, 5.3.93)	won	66–5
(A)	v	Ireland A (Dublin, 19.3.93)	won	22–18

Springboks in England (touring record: P4 W3 D0 L1 F87 A61):
(A)	v	Midlands (Leicester, 4.11.92)	won	32–9
(A)	v	England B (Bristol, 7.11.92)	won	20–16
(A)	v	Northern (Leeds, 10.11.92)	won	19–3

England XV (P1 W1 D0 L0 F18 A11):
(A)	v	Leicester (Welford Road, 5.9.92)	won	18–11

England U-21 (P3 W3 D0 L0 F107 A33):
(H)	v	Italy (Leicester, 5.9.92)	won	37–12
(H)	v	Ireland (Newc-Gosforth, 14.10.92)	won	39–28
(H)	v	F.A.F. (Twickenham, 1.5.93)	won	31–3

England Students (P8 W4 D0 L4 F233 A106):
(–)	v	Taiwan[+] (Naples, 1.7.92)	won	91–6
(–)	v	Argentina[+] (Naples, 5.7.92)	lost	6–9
(–)	v	South Africa[+] (Naples, 8.7.92)	won	20–13
(–)	v	France[+] (q/f: Cagliari, 11.7.92)	lost	6–9
(H)	v	France (Cambridge, 15.1.93)	won	20–9
(A)	v	Wales (Llanelli, 5.2.93)	lost	13–21
(H)	v	Scotland (Basingstoke, 5.3.93)	won	71–20
(A)	v	Ireland (Dublin, 19.3.93)	lost	6–19

[+] World Cup (in Italy: fifth)

English Universities (P3 W3 D0 L0 F130 A31):
(A)	v	Welsh (Newbridge, 5.2.93)	won	34–8
(H)	v	Scottish (London Welsh, 5.3.93)	won	52–13
(A)	v	Irish (Dublin, 21.3.93)	won	44–10

England Colts (P4 W3 D0 L1 F82 A85):
(H)	v	Italy (US Portsmouth, 13.3.93)	won	23–13
(H)	v	Wales (Bath, 27.3.93)	won	18–14
(A)	v	Scotland (Ayr, 10.4.93)	won	28–3
(A)	v	France (Nice, 24.4.93)	lost	13–52

England 18–Group (P4 W0 D0 L4 F27 A53):
(A)	v Wales (Pembroke, 24.2.93)	lost	7–8
(H)	v Scotland (Castlecroft, 3.4.93)	lost	3–10
(H)	v France (Camborne, 7.4.93)	lost	9–22
(A)	v Ireland (Belfast, 14.4.93)	lost	8–13

England 16-Group (P2 W2 D0 L0 F60 A15):
(H)	v Spain (Keswick, 4.4.93)	won	44–3
(H)	v Wales (Cambridge, 17.4.93)	won	16–12

England Women (P1 W1 D0 L0 F23 A5):
(H)	v Wales (Northampton, 13.2.93)	won	23–5

DOMESTIC RUGBY

COURAGE LEAGUES

Division One:	P	W	D	L	F	A	Pts
Bath	12	11	0	1	355	97	22
Wasps	12	11	0	1	186	118	22
Leicester	12	9	0	3	220	116	18
Northampton	12	8	0	4	215	150	16
Gloucester	12	6	0	3	173	151	12
Bristol	12	6	0	6	148	169	12
London Irish	12	6	0	6	175	223	12
Harlequins	12	5	1	6	197	187	11
Orrell	12	5	0	7	175	183	10
London Scottish	12	3	1	8	192	248	7
Saracens	12	3	0	9	137	180	6
West Hartlepool	12	3	0	9	149	236	6
Rugby	12	1	0	11	104	368	2

Division Two:	P	W	D	L	F	A	Pts
Newcastle Gosforth	12	10	0	2	241	106	20
Waterloo	12	10	0	2	228	138	20
Wakefield	12	8	1	3	186	123	17
Nottingham	12	8	0	4	249	145	16
Sale	12	7	1	4	237	102	15
Moseley	12	6	2	4	184	150	14
Bedford	12	6	2	4	186	188	14
Rosslyn Park	12	5	0	7	209	199	10
Richmond	12	5	0	7	204	196	10
Blackheath	12	4	2	6	142	231	10
Coventry	12	3	0	9	192	236	6
Fylde	12	0	3	9	108	290	3
Morley	12	0	1	11	112	374	1

Division 3 – Pro: Otley (c). **Rel:** Sheffield, Leeds, Liverpool St Helens, Clifton, Aspatria, Askeans, Broughton Park, Plymouth Albion
Division 4 North – Pro: Harrogate (c). **Rel:** Towcestrians
Division 4 South – Pro: Sudbury (c). **Rel:** Thurrock

ADT DIVISIONAL CHAMPIONSHIP

	P	W	D	L	F	A	Pts
South West	3	2	1	0	73	51	5
Midlands	3	1	1	1	50	57	3
London	3	1	0	2	70	66	2
North	3	1	0	2	46	65	2

CUP FINALS:

Pilkington Cup
Leicester 23, Harlequins 16 (Twickenham, 1.5.93)

ADT County Championship
Lancashire 9, Yorkshire 6 (Twickenham, 17.4.93)

U-21 County Championship
Buckinghamshire 22, Warwickshire 0 (Twickenham, 17.4.93)

Provincial Insurance Cup
Fleetwood 13, Hitchen 7 (Twickenham, 3.4.93)

UAU
Loughborough Univ 25, Bristol Univ 18 (aet; Twickenham, 17.3.93)

England scrum-half Dewi Morris splits the French cover mustered by hooker Jean-Francois Tordo (left) and wing-forward Laurent Cabannes. Peter Winterbottom is in support

17

1980:

I	W24–9	Twickenham	19 Jan	**t:** Scott, Slemen, SJ Smith **c:** Hare 3 **p:** Hare 2
F	W17–13	Paris	2 Feb	**t:** Carleton, Preston **p:** Hare **dg:** Horton 2
W	W 9–8	Twickenham	16 Feb	**p:** Hare 3
S	W30–18	Edinburgh	15 Mar	**t:** Carleton 3, Slemen, Smith **c:** Hare 2 **p:** Hare 2

1981:

W	L19–21	Cardiff	17 Jan	**t:** Hare **p:** Hare 5
S	W23–17	Twickenham	21 Feb	**t:** Davies, Slemen, Woodward **c:** Hare **p:** Hare 3
I	W10–9	Dublin	77 Mar	**t:** Dodge, Rose **c:** Rose
F	L12–16	Twickenham	21 Mar	**p:** Rose 4
Arg(1)	D19–19	Buenos Aires	30 May	**t:** Woodward 2, Davies **c:** Hare 2 **p:** Hare
Arg(2)	W12–6	Buenos Aires	6 Jun	**t:** Davies **c:** Hare **p:** Hare 2

1982:

A	W15–11	Twickenham	2 Jan	**t:** Jeavons **c:** Dodge **p:** Rose 3
S	D 9–9	Edinburgh	16 Jan	**p:** Dodge 2, Rose
I	L15–16	Twickenham	6 Feb	**t:** Slemen **c:** Rose **p:** Rose 3
F	W27–15	Paris	20 Feb	**t:** Woodward, Carleton **c:** Hare 2 **p:** Hare 5
W	W17–7	Twickenham	6 Mar	**t:** Carleton, Slemen **p:** Hare 3
US*	W59–0	Hartford	19 Jun	**t:** SJ Smith 2, Swift 2, Scott 2, Carleton, Rendall, Wheeler **c:** Hare 7 **p:** Hare 2 **dg:** Cusworth
Fj*	W60–19	Twickenham	16 Oct	**t:** Trick 3, Swift 2, Gadd 2, Scott, SJ Smith, Cusworth, Dodge, Colclough **c:** Hare 6

1983:

F	L15–19	Twickenham	15 Jan	**p:** Hare 4
				dg: Cusworth
W	D13–13	Cardiff	5 Feb	**t:** Carleton
				p: Hare 2
				dg: Cusworth
S	L12–22	Twickenham	5 Mar	**p:** Hare 3
				dg: Horton
I	L15–25	Dublin	19 Mar	**p:** Hare 5
NZ	W15–9	Twickenham	19 Nov	**t:** Colclough
				c: Hare
				p: Hare 3
C*	W27–0	Twickenham	15 Oct	**t:** Youngs, Winterbottom, penalty try
				c: Hare 3
				p: Hare 3

1984:

S	L 6–18	Edinburgh	4 Feb	**p:** Hare 2
I	W12–9	Twickenham	18 Feb	**p:** Hare 3
				dg: Cusworth
F	L18–32	Paris	3 Mar	**t:** R Underwood, Hare
				c: Hare 2
				p: Hare 2
W	L15–24	Twickenham	17 Mar	**p:** Hare 5
SA(1)	L15–33	Port Elizabeth	2 Jun	**p:** Hare 4
				dg: Horton
SA(2)	L9–35	Johannesburg	9 Jun	**p:** Hare 3
A	L3–19	Twickenham	3 Nov	**p:** Barnes

1985:

F	D 9–9	Twickenham	2 Feb	**p:** Andrew 2
				dg: Andrew
W	L15–24	Cardiff	20 Apr	**t:** Smith
				c: Andrew
				p: Andrew 2
				dg: Andrew
S	W10–7	Twickenham	16 Mar	**t:** Smith
				p: Andrew 2
I	L10–13	Dublin	30 Mar	**t:** R Underwood
				p: Andrew 2
NZ(1)	L13–18	Christchurch	1 Jun	**t:** Harrison, Teague
				c: Barnes
				p: Barnes
NZ(2)	L15–42	Wellington	8 Jun	**t:** Hall, Harrison
				c: Barnes 2
				dg: Barnes

1986:

W	W21–18	Twickenham	17 Jan	**p:** Andrew 6
				dg: Andrew
S	L6–33	Edinburgh	15 Feb	**p:** Andrew 2
I	W25–20	Twickenham	1 Mar	**t:** Richards 2, penalty try, Davies
				c: Andrew 3

				p: Andrew
F	L10–29	Paris	15 Mar	**t:** Dooley
				p: Barnes 2
J+	W39–12	Twickenham	11 Oct	**t:** R Underwood, Hall, Bailey, Richards, Rees, Salmon
				c: Rose 6
				p: Rose

1987:

I	L0–17	Dublin	7 Feb	
F	L15–19	Twickenham	21 Feb	**p:** Rose 4
				dg: Andrew
W	L12–19	Cardiff	7 Mar	**p:** Rose 4
S	W21–12	Twickenham	4 Apr	**t:** penalty try, Rose
				c: Rose 2
				p: Rose 3
A★	L6–19	Sydney	23 May	**t:** Harrison
				c: Webb
J★	W60–7	Sydney	30 May	**t:** R Underwood 2, Rees, Salmon, Richards, Simms, Harrison 3, Redman
				c: Webb 7
				p: Webb 2
US★	W34–6	Sydney	3 Jun	**t:** Winterbottom 2, Harrison, Dooley
				c: Webb 3
				p: Webb 4
W★	L3–16	Brisbane	8 Jun	**p:** Webb

1988:

F	L9–10	Paris	16 Jan	**p:** Webb 2
				dg: Cusworth
W	L3–11	Twickenham	6 Feb	**p:** Webb
S	W 9–6	Edinburgh	5 Mar	**p:** Webb 2
				dg: Andrew
I(a)	W35–3	Twickenham	19 Mar	**t:** Oti 3, R Underwood 2, Rees
				c: Webb, Andrew 3
				p: Webb
I(b)	W21–10	Dublin	23 Apr	**t:** R Underwood, Harding
				c: Webb 2
				p: Webb 3
A(a1)	L16–22	Brisbane	29 May	**t:** R Underwood, Bailey
				c: Webb
				p: Webb 2
A(a2)	L8–28	Sydney	12 Jun	**t:** Richards, R Underwood
Fj	W25–12	Suva	17 Jun	**t:** R Underwood 2, Barley
				c: Barnes 2
				p: Barnes 3
A(b)	W28–19	Twickenham	5 Nov	**t:** R Underwood 2, Morris, Halliday
				c: Webb 3
				p: Webb 2

1989:

S	D12–12	Twickenham	4 Feb	**p:** Andrew 2, Webb 2
I	W16–3	Dublin	18 Feb	**t:** Moore, Richards

				c: Andrew
				p: Andrew 2
F	W11–0	Twickenham	4 Mar	t: Carling, Robinson
				p: Andrew
W	L9–12	Cardiff	18 Mar	p: Andrew 2
				dg: Andrew
R	W58–3	Bucharest	13 May	t: Oti 4, Guscott 3, Probyn, Richards
				c: Hodgkinson 8
				p: Hodgkinson
				dg: Andrew
Fj	W58–23	Twickenham	4 Nov	t: R Underwood 5, Skinner, Bailey,
				Linnett, Ackford, Guscott
				c: Hodgkinson 5, Andrew
				p: Hodgkinson 2

1990:

I	W23–0	Twickenham	20 Jan	t: R Underwood, Probyn, Egerton,
				Guscott
				c: Hodgkinson 2
				p: Hodgkinson
F	W26–7	Paris	3 Feb	t: R Underwood, Guscott, Carling
				c: Hodgkinson
				p: Hodgkinson 4
W	W34–6	Twickenham	17 Feb	t: Carling, R Underwood 2, Hill
				c: Hodgkinson 3
				p: Hodgkinson 4
S	L7–13	Edinburgh	17 Mar	t: Guscott
				p: Hodgkinson
It[+]	W33–15	Rovigo	1 May	t: Oti, Buckton, Back, Andrew
				c: Hodgkinson 4
				p: Hodgkinson 2
				dg: Andrew
Arg(a1)	W25–12	Buenos Aires	28 Jul	t: Ryan, Oti
				c: Hodgkinson
				p: Hodgkinson 5
Arg(a2)	L13–15	Buenos Aires	4 Aug	t: Hodgkinson, Heslop
				c: Hodgkinson
				p: Hodgkinson
Ba+	W18–16	Twickenham	29 Sep	t: Richards, Hodgkinson
				c: Hodgkinson 2
				p: Hodgkinson 2
Arg(b)	W51–0	Twickenham	3 Nov	t: R Underwood 3, Guscott 2, Hill, Hall
				c: Hodgkinson 7
				p: Hodgkinson 3

1991:

W	W25–6	Cardiff	19 Jan	t: Teague
				p: Hodgkinson 7
S(a)	W21–12	Twickenham	16 Feb	t: Heslop
				c: Hodgkinson
				p: Hodgkinson 5
I	W16–7	Dublin	2 Mar	t: R Underwood, Teague

				c: Hodgkinson
				p: Hodgkinson 2
F	W21–19	Twickenham	16 Mar	t: R Underwood
				c: Hodgkinson
				p: Hodgkinson 4
				dg: Andrew
Fj	W28–12	Suva	20 Jul	t: Probyn, R Underwood, Andrew
				c: Webb 2
				p: Webb 2
				dg: Andrew 2
A(a)	L15–40	Sydney	27 Jul	t: Guscott
				c: Webb
				p: Webb 3
USSR*	W53–0	Twickenham	7 Sep	t: Oti 2, Guscott 2, R Underwood 2, Skinner 2, Andrew
				c: Andrew 4, Hodgkinson 3
				p: Hodgkinson
NZ★	L12–18	Twickenham	3 Oct	p: Webb 3
				dg: Andrew
It★	W36–6	Twickenham	8 Oct	t: R Underwood, Guscott 2, Webb
				c: Webb 4
				p: Webb 4
US★	W37–9	Twickenham	11 Oct	t: R Underwood 2, Carling, Skinner, Heslop
				c: Hodgkinson 4
				p: Hodgkinson 3
F★	W19–10	Paris	19 Oct	t: R Underwood, Carling
				c: Webb
				p: Webb 3
S(b)★	W 9–6	Edinburgh	26 Oct	p: Webb 2
				dg: Andrew
A(b)★	L6–12	Twickenham	2 Nov	p: Webb 2
1992:				
S	W25–7	Edinburgh	18 Jan	t: R Underwood, Morris
				c: Webb
				p: Webb 4
				dg: Guscott
I	W38–9	Twickenham	1 Feb	t: Webb 2, Morris, Guscott, R Underwood, Halliday
				c: Webb 4
				p: Webb 2
F	W31–13	Paris	15 Feb	t: Webb, R Underwood, Morris, penalty try
				c: Webb 3
				p: Webb 3
W	W24– 0	Twickenham	7 Mar	t: Carling, Skinner, Dooley
				c: Webb 3
				p: Webb 2
C†	W26–13	Wembley	17 Oct	t: Hunter 2, Guscott, Winterbottom
				p: Webb 2
SA	W33–16	Twickenham	14 Nov	t: T Underwood, Guscott, Morris,

				Carling
				c: Webb 2
				p: Webb 3

1993:

F	W16–15	Twickenham	16 Jan	**t:** Hunter
				c: Webb
				p: Webb 3
W	L9–10	Cardiff	6 Feb	**p:** Webb 2
				dg: Guscott
S	W26–12	Twickenham	6 Mar	**t:** Guscott, R Underwood,
				T Underwood
				c: Webb
				p: Webb 3
I	L3–17	Dublin	20 Mar	**p:** Webb
C(1)	L12–15	Vancouver	29 May	**p:** Pears 4
C(2)	W19–14	Ottawa	5 Jun	**t:** Challinor 2
				p: Challinor 2, Pears

* World Cup matches
⁺ Non-cap tests
† Five-point try introduced from this game onwards

IRELAND

Michael Bradley

I HAVE been asked by many people how we did it. How a side which had been beaten by virtually everyone for longer than we cared to remember could suddenly re-emerge as a potent force. Put simply, it was a case of bouncing up off the bottom of the barrel.

We had worked extremely hard at training but just could not get a result on the pitch. As the season developed we became more desperate for that one victory which the Irish people were willing us to have.

I remember a major turning point. The date was 6 March 1993, the venue was Cardiff Arms Park and there were 57 minutes on the clock. Ieuan Evans had just scored for Wales and our first winning position in ages was on the slide. We trooped back beneath the posts to await the conversion attempt and huddled together.

Twelve minutes earlier we had led 16–6, now it was 16–14 with the extra points-kick to come. Memories of our matches against Australia, in the 1991 World Cup quarter-final, and New Zealand, in the first Test during the summer, when we coughed up winning positions, came flooding back. When were we going to win again?

Then it happened. Normally myself and Terry Kingston, captain and vice-captain, would do the talking in such a situation. But on this occasion everyone had something to say. And it was all the same thing. 'This game is ours for the winning, we have it in our grasps, and we are not going to lose it.'

That, for me, was the moment when the fortunes of Irish rugby changed for the better. The moment when everybody took responsibility. You won't ever survive if there are only one or two people doing all the work and, as a team, we decided there and then that we had had enough of this losing crack, and that we were going to do something about it. Neil Jenkins missed the conversion and, minutes later, Eric Elwood slotted a penalty goal for us and we were on our way to a 19–14 win.

The roots of our revival were actually planted during the postmortem of our opening Championship game, a 15–3 defeat by Scotland at Murrayfield. Irish rugby, for quite a few years, has gone through a period where we reacted to teams rather than trying to dictate to them. The reason being that it is difficult to dictate when you don't understand your own pattern, and in the Scottish game we didn't play to a pattern.

We were bad on the day, but we were even worse tactically. The players would agree that we were headless chickens. Coach Gerry Murphy and assistant coach Willie Anderson sat down and discussed the situation with the players and we concluded that for a number of years we had not been playing an Irish game at all. We had been playing the recommended game by all the other countries who had

'Irish rugby, for quite a few years, has gone through a period where we reacted to teams rather than trying to dictate to them. The reason being that it's difficult to dictate when you don't understand your own pattern'

bigger, stronger and possibly even fitter players than us. We had certainly had no definable pattern the previous year, and the slow-handclapping and booing in the 1992 Scotland game at Lansdowne Road reflected the crowd's frustration.

We decided it was time to return a bit of what is good about Irish rugby into our game again. At least if we were going to lose we would then know why we lost. Before, we had tried to compete against, guys who were bigger and taller than us by trying to outjump them, which was not on at all.

The traditional Irish game, when control is involved, is a good hard rucking game. No matter who you are playing against it is a terribly difficult gameplan to counter if the opposition gets in amongst you.

You might go out with set positions in lineouts, set positions in scrums and rucks and mauls, but if there are two or three fellas hitting you every time you go to pick up the ball it gets a bit annoying and the mistakes start coming. If you start splitting any side when that happens, then you are onto a winner.

That was the theory anyway. And it was one we arrived at after the Scottish game when two defensive errors put us 15 points down before half-time. There was never a lack of commitment from us but it was desperately difficult to chase the game after that.

Come the France game in Dublin (lost 6–21) we had identified what we wanted to do and it was a question of putting it into effect. But we were still in a situation where only two or three players had featured on a winning Ireland side. So we still had a few barriers to knock down. First to decide on a gameplan, then go about trying to implement it, then go about trying to finish a team off. Our progressive performances in the last three games, against France, Wales and England, I think showed that slowly but surely we were getting there. What we needed was the one win that would lift everyone.

Such a result might have come at the most unlikely time, on our tour of New Zealand the previous summer, when we had just been walloped 62–7 by Auckland, at Eden Park. Their team performance was the best I had ever seen. They were absolutely outstanding. We played an orthodox game and they just hammered us. We simply could not get the ball, losing the first-half lineout count 19–2.

Dublin hero Mick Galwey thunders into the English rearguard again during his matchwinning display for Ireland at Lansdowne Road

The prospect of victory over the All Blacks at Dunedin was remote to say the least. Yet we worked on our lineout tactics – only when absolutely necessary kick the ball to touch – raced into a 12–0 lead and actually went in at half-time having secured more ball than they did. But, for all the encouraging signs the bottom line was that we lost 24–21, and the following week we were crushed 59–6.

To tour New Zealand, given the state of the national team, was always an ambitious move. It must be the toughest place to tour because you consistently come up against the toughest teams. We found it very difficult but a good learning process seeing how they prepared themselves physically as well as mentally for the game. We actually had a good tour, although not results-wise. All the players got to know each other very well and formed the nucleus of the side for the coming season. Even in defeat you learn and if you do that you achieve something.

The difference between the Australia World Cup game, the first Test in New Zealand and the England game, with which we brought down the curtain on the Five Nations' Championship, was that we won the latter. Against New Zealand we played very well, sticking to our gameplan, but when we got into a position to win we were not able to finish it off. Against Australia it was more of a defensive game in total and then in the last ten minutes we scored a breakaway try, but again left the door open at the back. But in the English game we put ourselves into a position to win and we exploited it.

'We diagnosed the game against England as a one-off. As far as we were concerned, everything was going against them psychologically'

In defeat by France we had seen that we could play rugby, that we could actually take people on who were bigger and stronger than us, especially in the pack, and that if our defence was organized properly, it was very difficult for people to score tries against us. France managed two late touchdowns and Wales just the one, so we were in a good frame of mind approaching England's visit.

We diagnozed the game as a one-off. We were playing the best side in Europe over the last five years. But they had a problem in that they were coming to Ireland to put a score on Ireland. Now, in the last three years that had not been a problem for them. But this time, in the back of their minds was the knowledge that they were virtually all going to be picked for the British Lions. So the worst possible scenario for any of them was to get injured. Add to that the fact that three of them were making their last appearances for England. As far as we were concerned, everything was going against them psychologically.

They may have been a better side results-wise and historically speaking but we considered that, with everything they had on their plate, we should be quietly confident going into the game.

All 15 players performed very well for the full 80 minutes that day. We tackled hard and closed the spaces down quickly. The crowd got behind the team at every opportunity to produce an electric atmosphere. We generated chances and we took them. We had played with control and confidence. It was truly a great Irish performance.

> 'Rugby is not necessarily the fastest and fittest running down the pitch and scoring tries. You have to want to do it as well. And while Ireland would not be the greatest producer of consistently outstanding players we are a great producer of players who are prepared to do extraordinary things for their country'

So we finished the Championship not with the Wooden Spoon, as had been widely anticipated, but in mid-table with a 50 percent record. We may still be an inexperienced side, in terms of caps won, but what experience we do have at least now includes some success. The likes of Ciaran Clarke, Eric Elwood and Peter Clohessy, young players with a good future, have seen that there are rewards for good performances and that is very heartening.

The past three years have illustrated how thin is the line between winning and losing. But we now have a squad who, as far as I am concerned, are good Irish international players. We have shown that we can compete, which is the main thing. And we can certainly build on this success, as we are a young side and we have confidence and belief.

Still, to have only had two players (Mick Galwey and Nick Popplewell) selected for the Lions was very disappointing. Possibly our good performances this year came too late to put our lads into serious contention. But I think Eric Elwood should have gone, and Peter Clohessy and Richard Wallace too.

Rugby is not necessarily the fastest and fittest running down the pitch and scoring tries. You have to want to do it as well. And while Ireland would not be the greatest producer of consistently outstanding players, we are a great producer of players who are prepared to do extraordinary things for their country. In that department, I would think we would rank right up there at the top.

Now, if we can get to the position where we can produce some of the outstanding athletes, that is when Irish rugby will really do well. We are becoming more up-to-date and realistic in our approach. Gerry Murphy and Willie Anderson have been working on a schedule to inform players what is going to happen up to the World Cup in 1995. Everyone, at last, seems to be pulling in the same direction.

IRELAND'S INTERNATIONAL SEASON 1992/93

IRELAND (P7 W2 D0 L5 F89 A178):

(A) v New Zealand (Dunedin, 30.5.92)	lost	21–24
(A) v New Zealand (Wellington, 6.6.92)	lost	6–59
(H) v Australia (Dublin, 31.10.92)	lost	17–42

Five Nations' Championship

(A) v Scotland (Edinburgh, 16.1.93)	lost	3–15
(H) v France (Dublin, 20.2.93)	lost	6–21
(A) v Wales (Cardiff, 6.3.93)	won	19–14
(H) v England (Dublin, 20.3.93)	won	17–3

Ireland in New Zealand (tour record: P8 W3 D0 L5 F156 A287):

(A) v South Canterbury (Timaru, 13.5.92)	won	21–16
(A) v Canterbury (Christchurch, 16.5.92)	lost	16–38
(A) v Bay of Plenty (Rotorua, 20.5.92)	won	39–23
(A) v Auckland (Auckland, 23.5.92)	lost	7–62
(A) v Poverty Bay/East Coast (Gisborne, 26.5.92)	won	22–7
(A) v Manawatu (Palmerston North, 2.6.92)	lost	24–58

Wallabies in Ireland (tour record: P5 W4 D0 L1 F123 A92):

(A) v Leinster (Dublin, 17.10.92)	won	38–11
(A) v Munster (Cork, 21.10.92)	lost	19–22
(A) v Ulster (Belfast, 24.10.92)	won	35–11
(A) v Connacht (Galway, 27.10.92)	won	14–6

Ireland A (P3 W2 D0 L1 F60 A72):

(H) v Scotland (Dublin, 28.12.92)	lost	13–22
(A) v Wales (Newport, 5.3.93)	won	29–28
(H) v England (Donnybrook, 19.3.93)	lost	18–22

Ireland U-21 (P3 W2 D0 L1 F68 A53):

(H) v Wales (Donnybrook, 28.10.92)	won	22–11
(A) v England (Gosforth, 14.10.92)	lost	28–39
(A) v Scotland (Murrayfield, 15.1.93)	won	18–3

Ireland Students (P6 W4 D0 L2 F192 A108):
(–)	v	Germany* (Rovigo, 2.7.92)	won	74–3
(–)	v	CIS* (Padua, 5.7.92)	won	35–16
(–)	v	Italy* (Rovigo, 8.7.92)	lost	6–17
(–)	v	New Zealand* (q/f: Cagliari, 12.7.92)	lost	9–53
(A)	v	Scotland (Edinburgh, 15.1.93)	won	49–13
(H)	v	England (Dublin, 19.3.93)	won	19–6

* World Cup (in Italy: eighth)

Irish Universities (P2 W0 D0 L2 F28 A64):
(A)	v	Welsh (Cross Keys, 5.3.93)	lost	18–20
(H)	v	English (Dublin, 21.3.93)	lost	10–44

Ireland Youth (P1 W0 D0 L1 F14 A20):
(A)	v	Scotland (Ayr, 10.4.93)	lost	14–20

Ireland Schools U-18 (P4 W3 D0 L1 F67 A44):
(A)	v	New Zealand (New Plymouth, 29.8.92)	lost	25–27
(A)	v	Wales (Ebbw Vale, 3.4.93)	won	8–0
(A)	v	Scotland (Glasgow, 10.4.93)	won	21–9
(H)	v	England (Belfast, 14.4.93)	won	13–8

Ireland Schools in New Zealand (tour record: P9 W7 D0 L2 F272 A154):
(A)	v	Southland (Invercargill, 1.8.92)	won	19–12
(A)	v	Canterbury (Christchurch, 5.8.92)	won	26–15
(A)	v	Seddon Shield (Blenholm, 8.8.92)	won	18–8
(A)	v	Hawke's Bay (Napier, 12.8.92)	lost	23–25
(A)	v	Taikawhata (Gisborne, 15.8.92)	won	30–11
(A)	v	Bay of Plenty (Rotorua, 19.8.92)	won	40–12
(A)	v	Wellington (Wellington, 22.8.92)	won	57–19
(A)	v	Horowhenua (Levin, 26.8.92)	won	34–25

DOMESTIC RUGBY

INSURANCE CORPORATION LEAGUE

Division One:	P	W	D	L	F	A	Pts
Young Munster	8	6	1	1	114	44	13
Cork Constitution	8	6	0	2	166	128	12
St Mary's College	8	5	1	2	170	94	11
Greystones	8	4	1	3	132	132	9
Old Wesley	8	4	0	4	107	151	8
Dungannon	8	3	0	5	144	172	6
Shannon	8	2	1	5	86	75	5
Garryowen	8	2	0	6	132	117	4
Ballymena	8	2	0	6	107	148	4

Division Two:	P	W	D	L	F	A	Pts
Lansdowne	9	9	0	0	209	118	18
Wanderers	9	7	0	2	168	121	14
Blackrock College	9	6	1	2	149	95	13
Dolphin	9	5	0	4	133	124	10
Terenure College	9	5	0	4	123	121	10
Instonians	9	5	0	4	124	126	10

	P	W	D	L	F	A	Pts
Old Crescent	9	3	0	6	130	166	6
Galwegians	9	1	2	6	97	143	4
Bangor	9	1	1	7	112	174	3
Clontarf	9	1	0	8	86	133	2

INTER-PROVINCIAL CHAMPIONSHIP

	P	W	D	L	F	A	Pts
Ulster	4	4	0	0	59	38	8
Exiles	4	2	0	2	63	57	4
Leinster	4	2	0	2	54	74	4
Munster	4	1	0	3	64	62	2
Connacht	4	1	0	3	56	65	2

CUP FINALS:

Connacht Cup
Corinthians 12, Ballina 5 (Galway, 25.4.93)

Leinster Cup
St Mary's 12, Old Wesley 6 (Lansdowne Road, 1.5.93)

Munster Cup
Garryowen 12, Young Munster 5 (Thomond Park, 25.4.93)

Ulster Cup
Ballymena 18, Dungannon 20 (Ravenhill, 25.4.93)

Eric Elwood ignores the attentions of Richard Webster, Neil Jenkins and Scott Gibbs to set up Ireland's try against Wales, scored by Brian Robinson

1980:

E	L9–24	Twickenham	19 Jan	**p:** Campbell 3
S	W22–15	Dublin	2 Feb	**t:** Keane, Kennedy
				c: Campbell
				p: Campbell 3
				dg: Campbell
F	L18–19	Paris	1 Mar	**t:** McLennan
				c: Campbell
				p: Cambell 3
				dg: Campbell
W	W21–7	Dublin	15 Mar	**t:** Irwin, O'Driscoll, C Fitzgerald
				c: Campbell 3
				p: Campbell
R+	D13–13	Dublin	18 Oct	**t:** F Quinn
				p: Campbell 3

1981:

F	L13–19	Dublin	7 Feb	**t:** MacNeill
				p: Campbell 3
W	L8–9	Cardiff	21 Feb	**t:** Slattery, MacNeill
E	L6–10	Dublin	7 Mar	**dg:** Campbell, MacNeill
S	L9–10	Edinburgh	21 Mar	**t:** Irwin
				c: Campbell
				p: Campbell
SA(1)	L15–23	Cape Town	30 May	**t:** McGrath, McLennan
				c: Campbell 2
				p: Campbell
SA(2)	L10–12	Durban	6 Jun	**t:** O'Brien
				p: Quinn 2
A	L12–16	Dublin	21 Nov	**p:** Ward 4

1982:

W	W20–12	Dublin	23 Jan	**t:** Ringland, Finn 2
				c: Campbell
				p: Campbell 2
E	W16–15	Twickenham	6 Feb	**t:** MacNeill, McLoughlin
				c: Campbell
				p: Campbell 2
S	W21–12	Dublin	20 Feb	**p:** Campbell 6
				dg: Campbell
F	L9–22	Paris	20 Mar	**p:** Campbell 3

1983:

S	W15–13	Edinburgh	15 Jan	**t:** Kiernan
				c: Campbell
				p: Campbell 3
F	W22–16	Dublin	19 Feb	**t:** Finn 2
				c: Campbell
				p: Campbell 4
W	L9–23	Cardiff	5 Mar	**p:** Campbell 2, MacNeill

E	W25–15	Dublin	19 Mar	t: Slattery, Campbell
				c: Campbell
				p: Campbell 5

1984:

F	L12–25	Paris	21 Jan	p: Campbell 4
W	L9–18	Dublin	4 Feb	p: Campbell 3
E	L9–12	Twickenham	18 Feb	p: Ward 3
S	L9–32	Dublin	3 Mar	t: Kiernan
				c: J Murphy
				p: J Murphy
A	L9–16	Dublin	10 Nov	p: Kiernan 3

1985:

S	W18–15	Edinburgh	2 Feb	t: Ringland 2
				c: Kiernan 2
				p: Kiernan
				dg: Kiernan
F	D15–15	Dublin	2 Mar	p: Kiernan 5
W	W21–9	Cardiff	16 Mar	t: Crossan, Ringland
				c: Kiernan 2
				p: Kiernan 3
E	W13–10	Dublin	30 Mar	t: Mullin
				p: Kiernan 2
				dg: Kiernan
J(1)*	W48–13	Osaka	26 May	t: Ringland 3, Matthews 2, Kiernan, MacNeill, C Fitzgerald
				c: Kiernan 5
				p: Kiernan 2
J(2)*	W33–15	Tokyo	2 Jun	t: Kiernan 2, Mullin, Anderson
				c: Kiernan 4
				p: Kiernan 3
Fj*	WJ6–15	Dublin	19 Oct	t: Bradley
				p: Kiernan 4

1986:

F	L9–29	Paris	1 Feb	p: Kiernan 3
W	L12–19	Dublin	15 Feb	t: Ringland
				c: Kiernan
				p: Kiernan 2
E	L20–25	Twickenham	1 Mar	t: Ringland, Mullin, McCall
				c: Kiernan
				p: Kiernan 2
S	L9–10	Dublin	15 Mar	t: Ringland
				c: Kiernan
				p: Kiernan
R	W60–0	Dublin	1 Nov	t: Crossan 3, Mullin 2, Dean 2, Anderson, Bradley, MacNeill
				c: Kiernan 7
				p: Kiernan 2

1987:

E	W17–0	Dublin	7 Feb	t: Kiernan, Matthews, Crossan

				c: Kiernan
				p: Kiernan
S	L12–26	Edinburgh	21 Feb	t: Lenihan
				c: Kiernan
				p: Kiernan
				dg: Kiernan
F	L13–19	Dublin	21 Mar	t: Ringland, Bradley
				c: Kiernan
				p: Kiernan
W(a)	W15–11	Cardiff	4 Apr	t: Dean, Mullin
				c: Kiernan 2
				p: Kiernan
W(b)*	L6–13	Wellington	25 May	p: Kiernan 2
C*	W46–19	Dunedin	30 May	t: Bradley, Crossan 2, Spillane, Ringland, MacNeill
				c: Kiernan 5
				p: Kiernan 2
				dg: Kiernan, Ward
T*	W32–9	Brisbane	3 Jun	t: MacNeill 2, Mullin 3
				c: Ward 3
				p: Ward 2
A*	L15–33	Sydney	7 Jun	t: MacNeill, Kiernan
				c: Kiernan 2
				p: Kiernan

1988:

S	W22–18	Dublin	16 Jan	t: Mullin, MacNeill, Bradley
				c: Kiernan 2
				p: Kiernan
				dg: Kiernan
F	L6–25	Paris	20 Feb	p: Kiernan 2
W	L9–12	Dublin	5 Mar	t: Kingston
				c: Kiernan
				p: Kiernan
E(a)	L3–35	Twickenham	19 Mar	dg: Kiernan
E(b)	L10–21	Dublin	23 Apr	t: S Smith, MacNeill
				c: Kiernan
WS	W49–22	Dublin	29 Oct	t: Crossan 2, Kiernan, Matthews, Mullin, Francis, McBride, Sexton
				c: Kiernan 4
				p: Kiernan 2
				dg: Sexton
It	W31–15	Dublin	31 Dec	t: Crossan 2, Matthews 2, Aherne
				c: Cunningham
				p: Danaher 2
				dg: Dean

1989:

F	L21–26	Dublin	21 Jan	t: Mullin
				c: Kiernan
				p: Kiernan 5
W	W19–13	Cardiff	4 Feb	t: Mannion, Dean

				c: Kiernan
				p: Kiernan 3
E	L3–16	Dublin	18 Feb	**p:** Kiernan
S	L21–37	Edinburgh	4 Mar	**t:** Mullin 2, Dunlea
				c: Kiernan 3
				p: Kiernan
C[+]	W24–21	Victoria	2 Sep	**t:** Dunlea, Sexton
				c: Kiernan 2
				p: Kiernan 4
US[+]	W32–7	New York	9 Sep	**t:** Dunlea, Mannion, Crossan, Bradley
				c: Kiernan 2
				p: Kiernan 3
				dg: B Smith
NZ	L6–23	Dublin	18 Nov	**p:** B Smith 2

1990:

E	L0–23	Twickenham	20 Jan	
S	L10–13	Dublin	3 Feb	**t:** J Fitzgerald
				p: Kiernan 2
F	L12–31	Paris	3 Mar	**p:** Kiernan 4
W	W14–8	Dublin	24 Mar	**t:** S Smith, McBride, Kingston
				c: Kiernan
Arg	W20–18	Dublin	27 Oct	**t:** Hooks, Kiernan
				p: Kiernan 4

1991:

F	L13–21	Dublin	2 Feb	**t:** S Smith
				p: Kiernan 3
W	D21–21	Cardiff	18 Feb	**t:** Clarke, Mullin, Geoghegan, Staples
				c: B Smith
				p: B Smith
E	L7–16	Dublin	2 Mar	**t:** Geoghegan
				p: B Smith
S	L25–28	Edinburgh	16 Mar	**t:** Crossan, Robinson, Geoghegan, Mullin
				c: B Smith 3
				dg: B Smith
Na(1)	L6–15	Windhoek	20 Jul	**t:** penalty try
				c: Mullin
Na(2)	L15–26	Windhoek	27 Jul	**t:** Staples, Cunningham
				c: Staples 2
				dg: Curtis
Z★	W55–11	Dublin	6 Oct	**t:** Robinson 4, Geoghegan, Popplewell 2, Curtis
				c: Keyes 4
				p: Keyes 5
J★	W32–16	Dublin	9 Oct	**t:** O'Hara, Mannion 2, Staples
				c: Keyes 2
				p: Keyes 4
S(b)★	L15–24	Edinburgh	12 Oct	**p:** Keyes 4
				dg: Keyes
A★	L18–19	Dublin	20 Oct	**t:** Hamilton

				c: Keyes
				p: Keyes 3
				dg: Keyes

1992:

W	L15–16	Dublin	18 Jan	t: Wallace
				c: Keyes
				p: Keyes 3
E	L9–38	Twickenham	1 Feb	t: Keyes
				c: Keyes
				p: Keyes
S	L10–18	Dublin	15 Feb	t: Wallace
				p: Keyes 2
F	L12–44	Paris	21 Mar	p: McAleese 4
NZ(1)	L21–24	Dunedin	30 May	t: Cunningham 2, Staples
				c: Russell 3
				p: Russell
NZ(2)	L6–59	Wellington	6 Jun	t: Furlong
				c: Russell
A†	L17–42	Dublin	31 Oct	t: Wallace
				p: Russell 4

1993:

S	L3–15	Edinburgh	16 Jan	p: Malone
F	L6–21	Dublin	20 Feb	p: Malone 2
W	W19–14	Cardiff	6 Mar	t: Robinson
				c: Elwood
				p: Elwood 3
				dg: C Clarke
E	W17–3	Dublin	20 Mar	t: Galwey
				p: Elwood 2
				dg: Elwood 2

⋆ World Cup matches
⁺ Non-cap tests
† Five-point try introduced from this game onwards

SCOTLAND

Gavin Hastings

WHEN Scottish rugby bade farewell to many of its most loyal servants at the start of last season, many believed that with them would go our chances of emulating the relative success we had enjoyed in recent years. But for a great deal of hard work by the players and coaches alike, that might have been the case.

Scotland have to progress rapidly just to stand still. So to lose David Sole, Derek White, John Jeffrey, Finlay Calder, Peter Dods, Sean Lineen and Iwan Tukalo in quick succession were heavy blows to withstand. Fortunately, though, I never subscribed to the sinking boat theory. With coach Ian McGeechan at the helm, anything was possible.

A quick appraisal of our resources after I had been appointed captain for the full season convinced me that we should go down Twickenham for the third leg of the Five Nations' Championship with a shot at the Triple Crown. That was not to say I believed we would end a 24-year drought in Paris by beating France at Parc des Princes, rather that I expected us to win our two home games against Ireland and Wales.

Even that notion appeared ambitious to some. Playing under the guise of a Scotland A XV, our first-choice team laboured to a 22–17 win over Italy at Melrose. There then followed an inconclusive National Trial conducted amid the reconstructed splendour of

Murrayfield. The signs were that we might welcome as many newcomers as when I was one of six debutants in the side which opened the 1986 Five Nations' Championship against France.

Ultimately four were selected for the initial test, against Ireland – GHK prop Alan Watt, Bath lock Andy Reed, London Scottish flanker Iain Morrison and Boroughmuir winger Derek Stark, who scored an early try – and each fully justified the faith placed in them as we ran-out considerably more emphatic winners than the 15–3 scoreline suggested.

> 'Scotland traditionally struggle in the first game of the Five Nations', simply because the standard of rugby in our club games and Inter-District matches is not high enough to really prepare us for going straight into a Championship where the pace of the game and the reaction time has to be so very much quicker'

It was an overwhelming relief to open the Championship with a win. I had been told that Ireland at home was the ideal game to start my reign as captain. Perhaps, but only if we won. To lose would have been disastrous.

To be fair, though, that never looked likely, not with us scoring ten points in as many minutes and a second try before half-time. As a first-up performance I was most encouraged; the more so, because I always feel we are a team that will improve throughout the Championship.

Scotland traditionally struggle in the first game, simply because the standard of rugby in our club games and Inter-District matches is not high enough to really prepare us for going straight into a Championship where the pace of the game and the reaction time has to be so very much quicker. Even in our 1990 Grand Slam campaign we struggled against Ireland first time out and, last season, certainly up to the England game, we did just that, building on each successive performance.

For my debut as Scotland captain I was probably the most relaxed I have ever been for an international, which was strange. I did not expect that. I guess I just had a good feeling about the day. It was blowing a gale but we could not do anything about that. Our preparations had gone as well as they possibly could have and there was an excellent team spirit, the new guys having settled down extremely well.

Significantly, in what was to be last his Five Nations' campaign, Geech (McGeechan) had put in extra effort as well, making it absolutely clear that everyone knew what was expected of them. And come the end of the day I do not think anyone was complaining about our manner of victory. We again had shown that you write off Scotland at your peril.

In fact, Northern Hemisphere rugby in general has had its detractors since the advent of the World Cup competition brought the Antipodean game into sharper focus. I personally do not think you can compare the two hemispheres on the basis of one-off games, simply because the respective styles of play are so different. It is no secret, to my mind, that the only team to have consistently beaten New Zealand over the past few years has been Australia. And that is because they play them so often.

'Ask any Southern Hemisphere Test player where he would like to play his rugby and I'm sure he will say the Five Nations' Championship because of its unique atmosphere. Games are played in front of far bigger crowds than the Wallabies and All Blacks enjoy'

As soon as you have teams playing against each other on a regular basis, competition becomes much more intense. I think Australia last summer were at the top of the game, when they defeated Scotland 27–12 and 37–13 in the two Tests. They were a tremendous side. So too New Zealand who, despite being in the process of rebuilding, were strong enough to come from behind and win the Centenary Series against a World XV of which I was fortunate to be a part. But I did not return home feeling in any way disheartened at the standards Down Under.

I disagreed with those observers who said that the Five Nations' Championship was adversely influenced by the new regulations. No matter how poor sides supposedly are on paper, by the time of a Five Nations' match both sides are thoroughly well prepared, the players are very fit and raring to go, and they are therefore very competitive occasions. There is a lot at stake.

You ask any Southern Hemisphere Test player where he would like to play his rugby and I'm sure he will say the Five Nations' Championship because of its unique atmosphere. Games are played in front of far bigger crowds than the Wallabies and All Blacks enjoy back home. There is also far more media attention. So the expectation and the pressure on the players is immense.

All those factors need to be borne in mind when assessing the Championship. And I certainly do not think that the Five Nations' teams are as poor as people have made out, though that is not to say one team cannot be a good deal better in any given game.

The new law changes presented the season's first challenge. It was frustrating in the early-season club matches, simply because while the referees were trying to get across that the new rules were being played, by and large, the players were not prepared to accept them. However, the message had got across by Christmas and we were not perhaps as slow as some players in other countries to adapt.

Following David Sole's retirement, we were all conscious of the new start which had to be made. What had happened in the past was largely irrelevant with so many newcomers to the national team. One major plus was the return of scrum-half Gary Armstrong, who had missed the 1992 Championship due to a knee ligament injury.

Without question Gary was one of the key players in the series. He is a very influential player when he is on top of his game and he was on top of it for most of the Championship, which was a tribute to his dedication in coming back from his serious injury and displacing Andy Nicol who had done remarkably well in his place; going as far as to be selected by the World XV for the Centenary Series.

An inconclusive Trial followed my first game in charge, against Italy A at the Greenyards. It is very difficult for established players to go in and gain anything from a trial. But it is a game you know you have to play. There is no getting round it and so you have just got to get on and make the most of it. That said, I do not think the SRU will hold another Trial.

With hindsight, the one benefit of the Trial was that it acclimatized us to the high winds which were also to blow when Ireland and Wales visited. After the Trial preparation it was perhaps no surprise that we fared reasonably well in the wind.

Having claimed the scalp of Ireland, we headed for the Parc des Princes where, astonishingly, Scotland has never won. We should have done this time. And what made the day so frustrating was the fact that we would not have needed to have played any better to have triumphed. Instead, we failed to take our chances and lost 3–11.

I would suggest the reason we did not score tries was our lack of finishing power, rather than the quality of the French defence. And I will praise the Welsh defence in the same way for the reason we did not score in the last 20 minutes against them at Murrayfield two weeks later. We had opportunities to score tries against the French and it was just bad passing, people being in the wrong position, a lack of killer instinct, that failed us on the day.

The quality of the pitch was a disgrace for an international rugby match and it was promptly relaid for Wales' visit the following month. My planting leg just gave way whenever I attempted a goalkick. The pitch was not soft, but there there was no substance to it. It was like sand, it just broke up.

Returning to Murrayfield, I thought we were capable of scoring a lot of tries against Wales. I was not worried that we had not scored any against France. What was required was an improvement in the final delivery of the pass to get over the try-line. In the event we managed only one, but we were not far off three or four.

> *'We would not have needed to have played any better against France to have won for the first time ever at Parc des Princes...where the quality of the pitch was a disgrace for an international rugby match'*

Wales were obviously on a tremendous high after beating England, but I was not prepared to even entertain the notion of losing to them. I felt we were without question the better side. And we showed that.

There are a lot of factors that combine to make a classy side. Against Wales, it was not the delivery of the final pass that blunted our attacking edge, it was lack of communication, lack of team work and lack of running in the right positions. What people do not understand is how good you have to be in all these attributes to score tries in international rugby. Even the easiest tries are a combination of all these skills.

The England try scored against us by Rory Underwood, for example, was magical. But people did not praise Stuart Barnes highly enough for the quality of his pass. If that pass had been half a yard behind where it was, my brother Scott would have intercepted it.

But the pass was magnificent; Guscott almost had to make an extra little stretch to reach the ball and with his pace we had no chance. I honestly thought that if we could play to our potential against England that we would have a very good chance. In the past, I have felt we would have to play out of our skins to threaten them because I think they were a really very much better side than Scotland were. You go back to the World Cup semi-final for instance. We were clinging on by our fingernails in that game even though we were not far away in the end.

Last season at Twickenham, England just about ran away with the game, after Craig Chalmers' departure, but I cannot praise the Scottish commitment too highly; the way we stuck in and came back in the last 20 minutes. I think it was a wonderful show of character because there was the potential there for a rout. Yet it was still disappointing that Geech had to bow out on a losing note.

> *'Wales were obviously on a tremendous high after beating England but I was not prepared to even entertain the notion of losing to them. I felt we were without question the better side. And we showed that'*

No-one can underestimate the amount of work and contribution that he has made to Scottish rugby. For a guy coming from Scotland to have achieved the acclaim he has is a great tribute to his qualities. Geech has given his all to Scottish rugby, he deserves a break and he should be left alone. If, after a year, he has a desire to come back in some capacity, I don't believe the Scottish Rugby Union would be foolish enough not to make a position for him.

Geech finished off with an unprecedented second term as British Lions coach and I was honoured to be appointed as his captain for the New Zealand trip. There are those who have suggested that with the World Cup tournament now the focus of international attention there is no longer a place for the Lions. I cannot agree.

Without question, Lions' selection represents the pinnacle of any rugby player's career in Britain and Ireland. You cannot live from World Cup to World Cup. Four years is too far apart. In athletics, there is the World Championships every two years and the Olympics every four. Long live the Lions.

As for Scotland, we have a long way to go before we can look to add to our two Grand Slams in the past decade. Without Geech, it will not be an easy journey either, but equally, without him, there is no danger of us taking anything for granted. That is vital as if Scotland become complacent about anything we will be away down the road to nowhere.

SCOTLAND'S INTERNATIONAL SEASON 1992/93

Scotland (P6 W2 D0 L4 F75 A104):
(A)	v	Australia (Sydney, 13.6.92)	lost	12–27
(A)	v	Australia (Brisbane, 21.6.92)	lost	13–37

Five Nations' Championship
(H)	v	Ireland (Edinburgh, 16.1.93)	won	15–3
(A)	v	France (Paris, 6.2.93)	lost	3–11
(H)	v	Wales (Edinburgh, 20.2.93)	won	20–0
(A)	v	England (Twickenham, 6.3.93)	lost	12–26

Scotland in Australia (tour record: P8 W2 D2 L4 F137 A140):
(A)	v	Northern Territory XV (Darwin, 28.5.92)	lost	16–17
(A)	v	Queensland (Brisbane, 31.5.92)	drew	15–15
(A)	v	Emerging Wallabies (Hobart, 3.6.92)	drew	24–24
(A)	v	New South Wales (Sydney, 6.6.92)	lost	15–35
(A)	v	NSW Country (Tamworth, 9.6.92)	won	26–10
(A)	v	Queensland Country (Toowoomba, 17.6.92)	won	29–12

Scotland A (P4 W3 D0 L1 F98 A73):
(A)	v	Spain (Madrid, 12.9.92)	won	35–14
(H)	v	Italy (Melrose, 19.12.92)	won	22–17
(A)	v	Ireland (Dublin, 28.12.92)	won	22–13
(H)	v	France (Aberdeen, 20.3.93)	lost	19–29

Scotland U-21 (P4 W0 D0 L4 F38 A130):
(H)	v	Italy (Kelso, 9.9.92)	lost	18–29
(H)	v	Ireland (Edinburgh, 15.1.93)	lost	3–18
(A)	v	France (Dijon, 5.2.93)	lost	9–67
(H)	v	Wales (Edinburgh, 19.2.93)	lost	8–16

Scottish Students (P7 W2 D0 L5 F118 A259):
(–)	v	Japan* (Genoa, 2.7.92)	won	21–16
(–)	v	Spain* (Genoa, 5.7.92)	won	25–4
(–)	v	France* (Genoa, 8.7.92)	lost	15–38
(–)	v	Argentina* (q/f: Cagliari, 12.7.92)	lost	18–29
(H)	v	Ireland (Duddingston, 15.1.93)	lost	13–49
(A)	v	France (La Voulte, 5.2.93)	lost	6–52
(A)	v	England (Basingstoke, 5.3.93)	lost	20–71

* World Cup (in Italy: sixth)

Scottish Universities (P2 W0 D1 L1 F31 A70):
(H)	v	Welsh (Peffermill, 19.2.93)	drew	18–18
(A)	v	English (London Welsh, 6.3.93)	lost	13–52

Scotland U-19 (P2 W0 D0 L2 F6 A48):
(H)	v	England (Ayr, 10.4.93)	lost	3–28
(A)	v	Wales (Cardiff, 24.4.93)	lost	3–20

Scotland U-18 (P2 W1 D0 L1 F48 A45)
(A)	v	Spain (Madrid, 3.4.93)	lost	28–31
(H)	v	Ireland (Ayr, 10.4.93)	won	20–14

Scotland Schools (P4 W1 D0 L3 F27 A66):

(A)	v	France (Castres, 19.12.92)	lost	5–37
(H)	v	Wales (Goldenacre, 4.1.93)	lost	3–5
(A)	v	England (Wolverhampton, 3.4.93)	won	10–3
(H)	v	Ireland (Balgray, 10.4.93)	lost	9–21

DOMESTIC RUGBY

McEWAN'S CLUB CHAMPIONSHIP

Division One:	P	W	D	L	F	A	Pts
Melrose	13	12	0	1	324	202	24
Edinburgh Acads	13	9	1	3	265	153	19
Gala	13	9	1	3	270	271	19
Currie	13	8	0	5	218	242	16
Jed-Forest	13	7	0	6	206	185	14
Boroughmuir	11	6	0	5	208	162	12
Hawick	12	5	1	6	197	170	11
Heriot's FP	13	5	0	8	295	285	10
Stirling County	13	5	0	8	179	179	10
Watsonians	13	5	0	8	196	278	10
Kelso	13	5	0	8	211	339	10
Selkirk	13	4	1	8	194	270	9
Glasgow H/K	13	4	0	9	291	252	8
Dundee HSFP	12	3	0	9	142	269	6

McEWAN'S INTER-DISTRICT CHAMPIONSHIP

Final table:	P	W	D	L	F	A	Pts
South	4	3	0	1	60	33	6
Edinburgh	4	2	1	1	93	69	5
North & Mids	4	2	0	2	60	101	4
Glasgow	4	1	1	2	44	59	3
Exiles	4	1	0	3	57	52	2

Alloa Brewery Cup final:
Dundee HSFP 16, Edinburgh Academicals 7 (Meggatland, 8.5.93)

Castlemaine XXXX Trophy final:
Duns 17, Greenock Wanderers 8 (Meggatland, 8.5.93)

SCOTLAND TEST RESULTS AND SCORERS SINCE 1980

1980:

I	L15–22	Dublin	2 Feb	t: Johnston 2
				c: Irvine
				p: Irvine
F	W22–14	Edinburgh	16 Feb	t: Rutherford, Irvine 2
				c: Irvine, Renwick
				p: Irvine 2
W	L6–17	Cardiff	1 Mar	t: Renwick
				c: Irvine
E	L18–30	Edinburgh	15 Mar	t: Tomes, Rutherford

44

| | | | | c: Irvine 2 |
| | | | | p: Irvine 2 |

1981:

F	L9–16	Paris	17 Jan	t: Rutherford
				c: Renwick
				p: Irvine
W	W15–6	Edinburgh	7 Feb	t: Tomes, penalty try
				c: Renwick 2
				p: Renwick
E	L17–23	Twickenham	21 Feb	t: Monro 2, J Calder
				c: Irvine
				p: Irvine
I	W10–9	Edinburgh	21 Mar	t: Hay
				p: Irvine
				dg: Rutherford
NZ(1)	L4–11	Dunedin	13 June	t: Deans
NZ(2)	L15–40	Auckland	20 Jun	t: Hay
				c: Irvine
				p: Irvine 2
				dg: Renwick
R	W12–6	Edinburgh	26 Sep	p: Irvine 4
A	W24–15	Edinburgh	19 Dec	t: Renwick
				c: Irvine
				p: Irvine 5
				dg: Rutherford

1982:

E	D 9–9	Edinburgh	16 Jan	p: Irvine 2
				dg: Rutherford
I	L12–21	Dublin	20 Feb	t: Rutherford
				c: Irvine
				p: Renwick 2
F	W16–7	Edinburgh	6 Mar	t: Rutherford
				p: Irvine 3
				dg: Renwick
W	W34–18	Cardiff	20 Mar	t: J Calder, Renwick, Pollock, White, Johnston
				c: Irvine 4
				dg: Renwick, Rutherford
A(1)	W12–7	Brisbane	3 Jul	t: Robertson
				c: Irvine
				p: Irvine
				dg: Rutherford
A(2)	L9–33	Sydney	10 Jul	p: Irvine 3
Fj⁺	W32–12	Edinburgh	25 Sep	t: Dods 2, Johnston, F Calder, Beattie
				c: Dods 3
				p: Dods
				dg: Rutherford

1983:

I	L13–15	Edinburgh	15 Jan	t: Laidlaw
				p: Dods 2

F	L15–19	Paris	5 Feb	**dg**: Renwick **t**: Robertson **c**: Dods **p**: Dods
W	L15–19	Edinburgh	19 Feb	**dg**: Gossman 2 **t**: Renwick **c**: Dods **p**: Dods 3
E	W22–12	Twickenham	5 Mar	**t**: Laidlaw, Smith **c**: Dods **p**: Dods 3
NZ	D25–25	Edinburgh	12 Nov	**dg**: Robertson **t**: Pollock **p**: Dods 5 **dg**: Rutherford 2

1984:

W	W15–9	Cardiff	21 Jan	**t**: Paxton, Aitken **c**: Dods 2 **p**: Dods
E	W18–6	Edinburgh	4 Feb	**t**: Johnston, Kennedy **c**: Dods 2 **p**: Dods 2
I	W32–9	Dublin	3 Mar	**t**: Laidlaw 2, penalty try, Robertson, Dods **c**: Dods 3 **p**: Dods 2
F	W21–12	Edinburgh	17 Feb	**t**: J Calder **c**: Dods **p**: Dods 5
R	L22–28	Bucharest	12 May	**t**: Leslie, Dods **c**: Dods **p**: Dods 3 **dg**: Robertson
A	L12–27	Edinburgh	8 Dec	**p**: Dods 4

1985:

I	L15–18	Edinburgh	2 Feb	**p**: Dods 4 **dg**: Robertson
F	L3–11	Paris	16 Feb	**p**: Dods
W	L21–25	Edinburgh	2 Mar	**t**: Paxton 2 **c**: Dods 2 **p**: Dods **dg**: Rutherford 2
E	L7–10	Twickenham	16 Mar	**t**: Robertson **p**: Dods

1986:

F	W18–17	Edinburgh	17 Jan	**p**: G Hastings 6
W	L15–22	Cardiff	1 Feb	**t**: Duncan, Jeffrey, G Hastings **p**: G Hastings
E	W33–6	Edinburgh	15 Feb	**t**: Duncan, Rutherford, S Hastings **c**: G Hastings 3

				p:'G Hastings 5
I	W10–9	Dublin	12 Mar	**t:** Laidlaw
				p: G Hastings 2
R	W33–18	Bucharest	30 Mar	**t:** Jeffrey, S Hastings, Deans
				c: G Hastings 3
				p: G Hastings 5

1987:

I	W16–12	Edinburgh	21 Feb	**t:** Laidlaw, Tukalo
				c: G Hastings
				dg: Rutherford 2
F(a)	L22–28	Paris	7 Mar	**t:** Beattie, S Hastings
				c: G Hastings
				p: G Hastings 4
W	W21–14	Edinburgh	21 Mar	**t:** Beattie, Jeffrey
				c: G Hastings 2
				p: G Hastings 2
				dg: Rutherford
E	L12–21	Twickenham	4 Apr	**t:** Robertson
				c: G Hastings
				p: G Hastings 2
Sp˙	W25–7	Edinburgh	19 Apr	**t:** Duncan, Tukalo, Deans, Paxton
				c: G Hastings 3
				p: G Hastings
F(b)*	D20–20	Christchurch	23 May	**t:** White, Duncan
				p: G Hastings 4
Z*	W60–21	Wellington	30 May	**t:** Tait 2, Duncan 2, Tukalo 2,
				Paxton 2, Oliver, G Hastings, Jeffrey
				c: G Hastings 8
R*	W55–28	Dunedin	2 Jun	**t:** G Hastings 2, Tukalo, Duncan,
				Tait 2, Jeffrey 3
				c: G Hastings 8
				p: G Hastings
NZ*	L3–30	Christchurch	6 Jun	**p:** G Hastings

1988:

I	L18–22	Dublin	16 Jan	**t:** Laidlaw, S Hastings
				c: G Hastings 2
				p: G Hastings 2
F	W23–12	Edinburgh	6 Feb	**t:** G Hastings, Tukalo
				p: G Hastings 4
				dg: Cramb
W	L20–25	Cardiff	20 Feb	**t:** F Calder, Duncan
				p: G Hastings 4
E	L 6–9	Edinburgh	5 Mar	**p:** G Hastings 2
A	L13–32	Edinburgh	19 Nov	**t:** G Hastings, Robertson
				c: G Hastings
				p: G Hastings

1989:

W	W23–7	Edinburgh	21 Jan	**t:** Armstrong, White, Chalmers
				c: Dods
				p: Dods 2

				dg: Chalmers
E	D12–12	Twickenham	4 Feb	**t:** Jeffrey
				c: Dods
				p: Dods 2
I	W37–21	Edinburgh	4 Mar	**t:** Tukalo 3, Jeffrey, Cronin
				c: Dods 4
				p: Dods 3
F	L3–19	Paris	19 Mar	**p:** Dods
Fj	W38–17	Edinburgh	28 Oct	**t:** Stanger 2, K Milne, Gray, G Hastings, Tukalo
				c: G Hastings 4
				p: G Hastings 2
R	W32–0	Edinburgh	9 Dec	**t:** Stanger 3, White, Sole
				c: G Hastings 3
				p: G Hastings 2

1990:

I	W13–10	Dublin	3 Feb	**t:** White 2
				c: Chalmers
				p: Chalmers
F	W21–0	Edinburgh	17 Feb	**t:** F Calder, Tukalo
				c: Chalmers 2
				p: Chalmers 2, G Hastings
W	W13–9	Cardiff	3 Mar	**t:** Cronin
				p: Chalmers 3
E	W13–7	Edinburgh	17 Mar	**t:** Stanger
				p: Chalmers 3
NZ(1)	L16–31	Dunedin	16 Jun	**t:** Lineen, Gray, Sole
				c: G Hastings 2
NZ(2)	L18–21	Auckland	23 Jun	**t:** Stanger, Moore
				c: G Hastings 2
				p: G Hastings 2
Arg	W49–3	Edinburgh	10 Nov	**t:** Stanger 2, K Milne 2, Moore, Armstrong, Gray, G Hastings, Chalmers
				c: G Hastings 5
				p: G Hastings

1991:

F	L9–15	Paris	19 Jan	**p:** Chalmers 2
				dg: Chalmers
W	W32–12	Edinburgh	2 Feb	**t:** Chalmers, White 2, Armstrong
				c: Chalmers, G Hastings
				p: Chalmers, G Hastings 2
				dg: Chalmers
E(a)	L12–21	Twickenham	16 Feb	**p:** Chalmers 4
I(a)	W28–25	Edinburgh	16 Mar	**t:** G Hastings, Stanger, S Hastings
				c: Chalmers 2
				p: Chalmers 3, G Hastings
R	L12–18	Bucharest	31 Aug	**t:** Tukalo
				c: Dods
				p: Dods 2

J*	W47–9	Edinburgh	5 Oct	**t:** S Hastings, Stanger, Chalmers, penalty try, White, Tukalo, G Hastings **c:** G Hastings 5 **p:** Chalmers, G Hastings 2
Z*	W51–12	Edinburgh	9 Oct	**t:** Tukalo 3, Turnbull, Stanger, S Hastings, Weir, White **c:** Dods 5 **p:** Dods 2 **dg:** Wyllie
I(b)*	W24–15	Edinburgh	12 Oct	**t:** Shiel, Armstrong **c:** G Hastings 2 **p:** G Hastings 3 **dg:** Chalmers
WS*	W28–6	Edinburgh	19 Oct	**t:** Jeffrey 2, Stanger **c:** G Hastings 2 **p:** G Hastings 4
E(b)*	L6–9	Edinburgh	26 Oct	**p:** G Hastings 2
NZ*	L6–13	Cardiff	30 Oct	**p:** G Hastings 2
1992:				
E	L7–25	Edinburgh	18 Jan	**t:** White **p:** G Hastings

Gary Armstrong, the world's best scrum-half, takes Welsh opposite number Robert Jones for a ride during Scotland's comprehensive 20–0 victory at Murrayfield

I	W18–10	Dublin	15 Feb	**t:** Stanger, Nicol
				c: G Hastings 2
				p: G Hastings 2
F	W10–6	Edinburgh	7 Mar	**t:** Edwards
				p: G Hastings 2
W	L12–15	Cardiff	21 Mar	**p:** G Hastings, Chalmers 2
				dg: Chalmers
A(1)	L12–27	Sydney	13 Jun	**t:** Wainwright
				c: G Hastings
				p: G Hastings 2
A(2)	L13–37	Brisbane	21 Jun	**t:** Lineen, Sole
				c: Chalmers
				p: Chalmers

1993:

I[†]	W15–3	Edinburgh	16 Jan	**t:** Stark, Stanger
				c: G Hastings
				p: G Hastings
F	L3–11	Paris	6 Feb	**p:** G Hastings
W	W20–0	Edinburgh	20 Feb	**t:** Turnbull
				p: G Hastings 5
E	L12–26	Twickenham	6 Mar	**p:** G Hastings 3
				dg: Chalmers
Fj[†]	W21–10	Suva	29 May	**t:** Hay, Logan
				c: Donaldson
				p: Donaldson 3
T[†]	W23–5	Nuka'Aloa	5 Jun	**t:** Weir, Logan, penalty try
				c: Townsend
				p: Townsend 2
WS[*]	L11–28	Apia	12 Jun	**t:** Nicol
				p: Townsend 2

[*] World Cup matches
[+] Non-cap tests
[†] Five-point try introduced from this game onwards

WALES

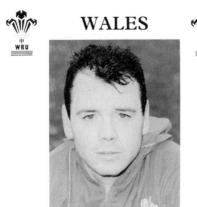

Ieuan Evans

NO-ONE said it would be easy and the 1992/93 season certainly was not. Frustrating doesn't begin to describe it. Anyone who placed a wager on us beating England and losing to everyone else will doubtless be as surprised as they are now wealthy.

To beat England, to then have bookies quoting prices for a Welsh Grand Slam, and to have more than 20,000 supporters flocking to Edinburgh for our next game, were highlights which will not be quickly forgotten. Nor, though, will the defeats which followed, leaving us with the Wooden Spoon.

International rugby is all about taking the chances that come your way and riding the pressure situations. We have to improve on both counts. We have got to be able to score when in favourable positions and to win when in favourable positions.

Furthermore, we must learn to wear the favourite's tag going into games. Last season it appeared to affect us. There is no doubt we played better as underdogs. We are a good team and we are going to get better, but that means we will find ourselves in situations where we are expected to win. We have got to be able to do so. It is all part of the learning process.

After our two Championship wins in 1992, over Ireland and Scotland, I warned that we could not afford to drop our guard, that we should still be under no illusions as to the size of the task still facing us.

Yet it seems to me that we put so much into beating England that we did not have enough left for the other challenges. I found that deeply frustrating.

The most encouraging aspect of the season for me was our defence. As Australia found when they came to Cardiff before Christmas (lost 6–23), our rearguard had improved dramatically over the last 12 months. I fervently believe that it is now as good as anybody else's in the world. Opponents really did struggle to score against us.

In contrast, our attack lacked a cutting edge. Save for the early-season match against Italy (won 43–12) under the Arms Park floodlights, when no caps were awarded and we ran in seven tries, we managed just three tries in five Tests. However good your defence, such a scoring ratio is just not acceptable.

Following on from the previous season's promise and September's successfully accomplished Italian job, expectation was high within the nation ahead of the visit of Australia, even though they were, and are still, the world champions. I do not feel this expectation was unrealistic either; after all, Swansea and Llanelli had both beaten the tourists.

But the Aussies were superbly organized. I actually felt the scoreline flattered them, as the contest had been fairly close up until the last minute when they scored a try, but the occasion gave us much food for

Welsh centre Mike Hall breaks a tackle, watched by team mate Mike Rayer and Australian legend David Campese. The Wallabies won 23–11

thought as we headed off to Lanzarote to prepare for the coming Five Nations' Championship.

The week went very well, except for the freak accident Michael Griffiths suffered while mountain biking which put him out of contention for a Test place. The time was spent well, uniting the players and focusing our minds totally for the match against England.

It was an especially valuable week as we had not toured in the summer of '92, the management choosing instead that we should recharge our batteries after a hectic schedule over the past few summers and I very much hope the Lanzarote experiment will be continued in future.

Back home, and the visit of England (won 10–9) brought a superb atmosphere; the best I have ever felt at the National Stadium. It was electric out there and provided the catalyst for a famous victory. In response, we produced a sterling performance, defensively in particular. And, for once, we took our chances.

'I am the eternal realist and, amid all the hysteria which surrounded our win over England, I saw that there were still weaknesses in our game. What won us the contest was a superb defence'

I was lucky enough to be the man who scored the winning try, chasing through onto a kick ahead by Emyr Lewis. I think the roar of the crowd hid the thud of my feet and Rory Underwood lost a little bit of concentration. At one point, I did not think I was going to get there. The closer I got I thought I might just have a chance if I could get my boot to the ball. From then on it was just a matter of racing for the line. There was still a long way to go after I had scored, but there was an incredible spirit among the team. We had 15 men of the match. Everyone tackled ferociously.

But I am the eternal realist and, amid all the hysteria which surrounded our win, I saw that there were still weaknesses in our game which we had to work on if we were going to achieve any honours throughout the season. The coaching staff also knew that. What won us the contest against England was a superb defence, and I was the first to admit that.

For many, beating England constitutes a successful season. I disagree. It is the biggest game, without a shadow of a doubt, but it is not everything. The players were still aware that the games to come were going to be very difficult, but we produced two unacceptably poor performances thereafter, against Scotland (lost 0–20) and Ireland (lost 14–19) which really set us back.

We were not helped, it has to be said, by the domestic schedule interwoven with the Five Nations' campaign. Between the England and Scotland games we had a vital round of Heineken League games. This concerned me. It is an extremely long season and January, February and March is basically just a constant peak. It is very difficult to maintain a level for eight to ten games, and it is asking an awful lot of players midway through the season to combine international matches with vital league and cup games.

Something needs to be done. At a time when we are united as an international squad we are expected to suddenly revert to club allegiances and knock seven bells out of each other. Put it this way, it is not the ideal preparation.

'It is asking an awful lot of players to combine international matches with vital league and cup games...At a time when we are united as an international squad we are expected to suddenly revert to club allegiances and knock seven bells out of each other'

A happy medium must be found and I would recommend completing the League programme before the international season, and then playing the Cup matches afterwards. But it is not for me to decide on how to do things. That said, something has to be done because the current arrangement is to the detriment of both the national team and the club sides. The clubs are not getting the best out of their players because they are tied up with the national side, and injuries sustained in domestic competition undermine the national effort.

Not that any of that is any excuse for our performance in Edinburgh. We travelled to Murrayfield with a high level of confidence and Scotland shattered it. It was a very disappointing game for us, but take nothing away from the Scots who really performed very well. Their pack in particular totally dominated us, plus they utilized the conditions to the full.

There was an amazing wind blowing around Murrayfield that

afternoon. We thought we had played into it in the first half until we turned around and Gary Armstrong put in a kick which went around 80 yards. What a blow to our morale that was. We were bemused as to how it could have travelled such a distance and our heads dropped a little bit.

Despite the defeat, and our failure to put a point on the board, we remained fairly confident going into the next game. We were returning to the Arms Park, where the memories of England's slaying were still fresh, and Ireland's form coming into the game was not good. What they did bring with them, however, was a proud record at Cardiff. That seemed to inspire them. They harried us, they pressurized us, and we turned in another poor performance.

It was a very below-average game as far as we were concerned. We made incorrect decisions in key areas which allowed Ireland a respite so they could take us back down the field. Their outside-half, Eric Elwood, had a superb game and the fact that we failed to capitalise on chances cost us dear. In contrast, they picked up their game marvellously.

What you have to do against Ireland is score when you get in certain areas because if you don't they get confident and the last thing you want coming at you is a bunch of confident Irishmen.

Returning to the National Stadium for the first time since beating England there might have been a slight feeling of overconfidence in the players, but I don't think that was the real reason. It was bad decision-making by ourselves in key areas. We were all aware of that afterwards in our debrief. And the fact that Ireland went out and beat England a fortnight later did not make us feel any better. We knew we should have beaten them.

The Five Nations' Championship was far more equal this year and I believe the best side were France, with whom we closed our programme (lost 10–26). They were undoubtedly the strongest outfit we came up against, and we played well ourselves, especially in the second half. What concerns me is that they were not only a very good side, but a very good side with a lot of good youngsters. So they will get even better.

Prior to the Paris match, the selectors made six changes to the team, but morale was not affected as the players coming in were already valued members of the squad anyway and had been on the bench prior to their call-up. The players knew, after the performance against Ireland, that alterations were likely but that did not lessen the disappointment for Robert Jones and Mike Rayer, in particular, whose

Lions aspirations were dealt a terminal blow. But a team was picked to perform and perform we did, with newcomers Rupert Moon and Andrew Lamerton having storming games.

After misfiring against Scotland and Ireland, our display in the Parc des Princes was very pleasing. We trailed 3–16 at half-time, but that did not reflect the balance of play. Thierry Lacroix kicked three monster penalties from halfway which gave the scoreline a misleading complexion.

> 'What you have to do against Ireland is score when you get in certain areas because if you don't they get confident and the last thing you want coming at you is a bunch of confident Irishmen'

The second half was a real slog, a real battle. In fact it must rate as one of the quickest halves of rugby I have ever played. We were all relieved to get off the field at the end, though again dispirited that the result had gone against us.

So one win from four Championship starts. Not good, but there is no time to rue what might have been. There is a summer tour to Zimbabwe and Namibia and a lot of work will be done out there. It was at this sort of time, four years ago, that England and Australia started to build-up a head of steam for the last World Cup. It is imperative that we do the same.

Looking back, the plus points for me were the number of young players who came on so superbly well. Mike Rayer, Scott Gibbs, Andrew Lamerton and Rupert Moon all shone. We must take heart from that as we must from our defence. The foundations are undoubtedly in place; we must now build on them.

WALES' INTERNATIONAL SEASON 1992/93

WALES (P6 W2 D0 L4 F83 A109):

(H)	v	Italy XV⁺ (Cardiff, 7.10.92)	won	43–12
(H)	v	Australia (Cardiff, 21.11.92)	lost	6–23
(H)	v	England (Cardiff, 6.2.93)	won	10–9
(A)	v	Scotland (Edinburgh, 20.2.93)	lost	0–20
(H)	v	Ireland (Cardiff, 6.3.93)	lost	14–19
(A)	v	France (Paris, 20.3.93)	lost	10–26

⁺ non-cap

Wallabies in Wales (tour record: P7 W5 D0 L2 F117 A91):

(A)	v	Swansea (St Helens, 4.11.92)	lost	6–21

(A)	v Wales B (Cardiff, 7.11.92)	won	24–11
(A)	v Neath (The Gnoll, 11.11.92)	won	16–8
(A)	v Llanelli (Stradey Park, 14.11.92)	lost	9–13
(A)	v Monmouthshire (Ebbw Vale, 17.11.92)	won	19–9
(A)	v Welsh Students (Bridgend, 24.11.92)	won	37–6

Wales A (P4 W2 D0 L2 F117 A78):
(H)	v North of England (Pontypool, 14.10.92)	won	21–13
(H)	v Australia (Cardiff, 7.11.92)	lost	11–24
(A)	v Netherlands (Den Bosch, 7.2.93)	won	57–12
(H)	v Ireland (Newport, 5.3.93)	lost	28–29

Wales U-21 (P2 W1 D0 L1 F27 A30):
(A)	v Ireland (Donnybrook, 28.10.92)	lost	11–22
(A)	v Scotland (Myreside, 19.2.93)	won	16–8

Wales Students (P7 W3 D0 L4 F127 A137):
(-)	v Holland* (Catania, 2.7.92)	won	49–7
(-)	v Romania* (Catania, 5.7.92)	lost	6–21
(-)	v New Zealand* (Catania, 8.7.92)	lost	7–15
(-)	v CIS* (Cagliari, 12.7.92)	won	27–9
(H)	v Australia (Bridgend, x.11.92)	lost	6–37
(H)	v England (Llanelli, 5.2.93)	won	21–11
(A)	v France (Nantes, 19.3.93)	lost	11–37

* World Cup (in Italy: ninth)

Welsh Universities (P3 W1 D1 L1 F46 A70):
(H)	v English (Newbridge, 5.2.93)	lost	8–34
(A)	v Scottish (Peffermill, 19.2.93)	drew	18–18
(H)	v Irish (Cross Keys, 5.3.93)	won	20–18

Wales U-19 (P1 W1 D0 L0 F20 A3):
(H)	v Scotland (Cardiff, 23.4.93)	won	20–3

Wales Youth (P5 W1 D0 L4 F86 A93):
(–)	v Wales 18-Group+ (Neath, 10.2.93)	lost	6–17
(A)	v Lupi+ (Rome, 23.2.93)	lost	10–26
(A)	v Italy (Milan, 27.2.93)	won	33–6
(H)	v France (Swansea, 13.3.93)	lost	21–27
(A)	v England (Bath, 27.3.93)	lost	16–17

+ non-cap

Wales Schools U-18 (P4 W2 D0 L2 F41 A46):
(–)	v Wales Youth+ (Neath, 10.2.93)	won	17–6
(H)	v England (Pembroke, 24.2.93)	won	8–7
(A)	v France (Lyon, 13.3.93)	lost	16–25
(H)	v Ireland (Ebbw Vale, 3.4.93)	lost	0–8

+ non-cap

Wales Schools U-16 (P2 W1 D0 L1 F64 A16):
(H)	v Spain (Builth Wells, 7.4.93)	won	52–0
(A)	v England (Cambridge, 17.4.93)	lost	12–16

Wales Women (P1 W0 D0 L1 F5 A23):
(H)	v England (Northampton, 13.2.93)	lost	5–23

DOMESTIC RUGBY

HEINEKEN LEAGUES

Division One:	P	W	D	L	F	A	Pts
Llanelli	22	19	1	2	901	254	39
Cardiff	22	18	0	4	636	260	36
Swansea	22	17	0	5	548	326	34
Neath	22	13	0	9	448	359	26
Pontypridd	22	11	2	9	400	353	24
Bridgend	22	11	1	10	402	400	23
Newport	22	11	0	11	513	512	22
Pontypool	22	10	0	12	489	508	20
Aberavon	22	7	0	15	271	501	14
Newbridge	22	6	0	16	258	536	12
Maesteg	22	3	1	18	278	632	7
SW Police	22	3	1	18	243	746	7

Division Two:	P	W	D	L	F	A	Pts
Dunvant	22	21	0	1	478	134	42
Cross Keys	22	16	1	5	474	268	33
Llanharan	22	16	1	5	435	202	33
Narbeth	22	15	1	6	358	209	31
Tenby Utd	22	12	1	9	432	234	25
Glamorgan W	22	11	0	11	357	409	22
Abertillery	22	11	0	11	366	355	22
Llandovery	22	7	0	15	285	345	14
Penarth	22	7	0	15	245	546	14
Ebbw Vale	22	7	0	15	183	355	14
Tredegar	22	3	2	17	200	406	8
Blaina	22	3	0	19	199	549	6

3 – Pro: Treorchy (c), Mountain Ash. **Rel:** Rumney, Wrexham

Swalec Cup final: *Llanelli 21, Neath 18 (Cardiff, 8.5.92) (* holders)

WALES TEST RESULTS AND SCORERS SINCE 1980

1980:

F	W18–9	Cardiff	19 Jan	**t:** E Rees, Holmes, D S Richards, G Price
				c: G Davies
E	L8–9	Twickenham	16 Feb	**t:** E Rees, Squire
S	W17–6	Cardiff	1 Mar	**t:** Holmes, Keen, D S Richards
				c: Blyth
				p: Fenwick
I	L7–21	Dublin	15 Mar	**t:** Blyth
				p: Fenwick
NZ	L3–23	Cardiff	1 Nov	**p:** Fenwick

1981:

E	W21–19	Cardiff	17 Jan	**t:** G Davies
				c: Fenwick

58

				p: Fenwick 4
				dg: G Davies
S	L6–15	Edinburgh	7 Feb	**dg:** Fenwick 2
I	W 9–8	Cardiff	21 Feb	**p:** G Evans 2
				dg: Pearce
F	L15–19	Paris	7 Mar	**t:** D S Richards
				c: G Evans
				p: G Evans 3
A	W18–13	Cardiff	5 Dec	**t:** R Moriarty
				c: G Evans
				p: G Evans 3
				dg: G Davies

1982:

I	L12–20	Dublin	23 Jan	**t:** Holmes
				c: G Evans
				p: G Evans
				dg: Pearce
F	W22–12	Cardiff	6 Feb	**t:** Holmes
				p: G Evans 6
E	L7–17	Twickenham	6 Mar	**t:** JR Lewis
				dg: G Davies
S	L18–34	Cardiff	20 Mar	**t:** Butler
				c: G Evans
				p: G Evans 4

1983:

E	D13–13	Cardiff	5 Feb	**t:** Squire
				p: Wyatt 2
				dg: Dacey
S	W19–15	Edinburgh	19 Feb	**t:** S Jones, E Rees
				c: Wyatt
				p: Wyatt 3
I	W23–9	Cardiff	5 Mar	**t:** Wyatt, Holmes, E Rees
				c: Wyatt
				p: Wyatt 3
F	L9–16	Paris	19 Mar	**t:** Squire
				c: Wyatt
				p: G Evans
J'	W29–24	Cardiff	22 Oct	**t:** Hadley, Brown, Dacey, Bowen, Giles
				c: Wyatt 3
				p: Wyatt
R	L6–24	Bucharest	12 Nov	**p:** G Evans 2

1984:

S	L9–15	Cardiff	21 Jan	**t:** Titley
				c: H Davies
				p: H Davies
I	W18–9	Dublin	4 Feb	**t:** Ackerman
				c: H Davies
				p: H Davies 2, Bowen 2
F	L16–21	Cardiff	18 Feb	**t:** H Davies, Butler
				c: H Davies

E	W24–15	Twickenham	17 Mar	**p:** H Davies 2
				t: Hadley
				c: H Davies
				p: H Davies 4
				dg: Dacey 2
A	L9–28	Cardiff	24 Nov	**t:** Bishop
				c: Wyatt
				p: Wyatt

1985:

S	W25–21	Edinburgh	2 Mar	**t:** Pickering 2
				c: Wyatt
				p: Wyatt 4
				dg: G Davies
I	L9–21	Cardiff	16 Mar	**t:** P Lewis
				c: G Davies
				p: G Davies
F	L3–14	Paris	30 Mar	**p:** Thorburn
E	W24–15	Cardiff	20 Apr	**t:** J Davies, Roberts
				c: Thorburn 2
				p: Thorburn 3
				dg: J Davies
Fj	W40–3	Cardiff	9 Nov	**t:** P Davies 2, Titley, Holmes, Hadley, James, Pickering
				c: Thorburn 3
				p: Thorburn 2

1986:

E	L18–21	Twickenham	17 Jan	**t:** Bowen
				c: Thorburn
				p: Thorburn 3
				dg: J Davies
S	W22–15	Cardiff	1 Feb	**t:** Hadley
				p: Thorburn 5
				dg: J Davies
I	W19–12	Dublin	15 Feb	**t:** P Lewis, P Davies
				c: Thorburn
				p: Thorburn 3
F	L15–23	Cardiff	1 Mar	**p:** Thorburn 5
Fj	W22–15	Suva	31 May	**t:** J Davies, Bowen
				c: Bowen
				p: Dacey 3
				dg: J Davies
T	W15–7	Nuku'alofa	12 Jun	**t:** P Moriarty
				c: Dacey
				p: Bowen 2, Dacey
WS	W32–14	Apia	14 Jun	**t:** Titley 2, Bowen, R Moriarty
				c: Dacey 2
				p: Dacey 3
				dg: J Davies

1987:

F	L9–16	Paris	7 Feb	**p:** Thorburn 3

E	W19–12	Cardiff	7 Mar	t: S Evans p: Wyatt 5
S	L15–21	Edinburgh	21 Mar	t: M Jones c: Wyatt p: Wyatt 2 dg: J Davies
I	L11–15	Cardiff	4 Apr	t: I Evans, Norster p: Wyatt
I(b)*	W13–6	Wellington	25 May	t: Ring p: Thorburn dg: J Davies 2
T*	W29–16	Palmerston North	29 May	t: Webbe 3, Hadley c: Thorburn 2 p: Thorburn 2 dg: J Davies
C*	W40–9	Brisbane	3 Jun	t: I Evans 4, Bowen, Hadley, Devereux, A Phillips c: Thorburn 4
E(b)*	W16–3	Brisbane	8 Jun	t: Roberts, Jones, Devereux c: Thorburn 2
NZ*	L6–49	Brisbane	14 Jun	t: Devereux c: Thorburn
A*	W22–21	Rotorua	18 Jun	t: Roberts, P Moriarty, Hadley c: Thorburn 2 p: Thorburn 2
US	W46–0	Cardiff	7 Nov	t: Bowen 2, Clement 2, Webbe, Young, P Moriarty, Norster c: Thorburn 4 p: Thorburn 2

1988:

E	W11–3	Twickenham	6 Feb	t: Hadley 2 dg: J Davies
S	W25–20	Cardiff	20 Feb	t: J Davies, I Evans, Watkins c: Thorburn 2 p: Thorburn dg: J Davies 2
I	W12–9	Dublin	5 Mar	t: P Moriarty c: Thorburn p: Thorburn dg: J Davies
F	L9–10	Cardiff	19 Mar	t: I Evans c: Thorburn p: Thorburn
NZ(1)	L3–52	Christchurch	28 May	p: Ring
NZ(2)	L9–54	Auckland	11 Jun	t: J Davies c: Ring p: Ring
WS	W24–6	Cardiff	12 Nov	t: N Davies 2, J Davies, C Davies c: Thorburn 4
R	L9–15	Cardiff	10 Dec	t: Devereux c: Thorburn

p: Thorburn

1989:

S	W23–7	Edinburgh	21 Jan	**t:** Hall
				p: Bowen
I	L13–19	Cardiff	4 Feb	**t:** M Jones
				p: Thorburn 3
F	L12–31	Paris	18 Feb	**p:** Thorburn 4
E	W12–9	Cardiff	18 Mar	**t:** Hall
				c: Thorburn
				p: Thorburn 2
NZ	L9–34	Cardiff	4 Nov	**p:** Thorburn 3

1990:

F	L19–29	Cardiff	20 Jan	**t:** Titley
				p: Thorburn 4
				dg: D Evans
E	L6–34	Twickenham	17 Feb	**t:** P Davies
				c: Thorburn
S	L9–13	Cardiff	3 Mar	**t:** Emyr
				c: Thorburn
				p: Thorburn
I	L8–14	Dublin	24 Mar	**t:** Ford, G O Llewellyn
Na(1)	W18–9	Windhoek	2 Jun	**t:** Thorburn, Bridges
				c: Thorburn 2
				p: Thorburn 2
Na(2)	W34–30	Windhoek	9 Jun	**t:** Emyr 2, O Williams, penalty try
				c: Thorburn 3
				p: Thorburn 3
				dg: Clement
Ba	L24–31	Cardiff	6 Oct	**t:** Thorburn
				c: Thorburn
				p: Thorburn 5
				dg: D Evans

1991:

E	L6–25	Cardiff	19 Jan	**p:** Thorburn, N Jenkins
S	L12–32	Edinburgh	2 Feb	**t:** Ford
				c: Thorburn
				p: Thorburn 2
I	D21–21	Cardiff	16 Feb	**t:** Arnold, N Jenkins
				c: Thorburn 2
				p: Thorburn 2
				dg: N Jenkins
F(a)	L3–36	Paris	2 Mar	**p:** Thorburn
A(a)	L6–63	Brisbane	21 Jul	**p:** Thorburn
				dg: A Davies
F(b)	L9–22	Cardiff	4 Sep	**t:** Collins
				c: Ring
				p: Ring
WS*	L13–16	Cardiff	6 Oct	**t:** Emyr, I Evans
				c: Ring
				p: Ring

Arg★	W16–7	Cardiff	9 Oct	**t:** Arnold
				p: Ring 3, Rayer
A(b)★	L3–38	Cardiff	12 Oct	**p:** Ring
1992:				
I	W16–15	Dublin	18 Jan	**t:** S Davies
				p: N Jenkins 3
				dg: C Stephens
F	L9–12	Cardiff	1 Feb	**p:** N Jenkins 3
E	L0–24	Twickenham	7 Mar	
S	W15–12	Cardiff	21 Mar	**t:** Webster
				c: N Jenkins
				p: N Jenkins 3
It[+][†]	W43–12	Cardiff	7 Oct	**t:** Clement, I Evans, Gibbs, C Stephens, Webster, S Davies, Rayer
				c: C Stephens 4
A	L6–23	Cardiff	21 Nov	**p:** C Stephens 2
1993:				
E	W10–9	Cardiff	6 Feb	**t:** I Evans
				c: N Jenkins
				p: N Jenkins
S	L0–20	Edinburgh	20 Feb	
I	L14–19	Cardiff	6 Mar	**t:** I Evans
				p: N Jenkins 3
F	L10–26	Paris	20 Mar	**t:** Walker
				c: N Jenkins
				p: N Jenkins
Z(1)	W35–14	Bulawayo	22 May	**t:** Moon, Hill, Proctor, P Davies
				c: N Jenkins 3
				p: N Jenkins 2
				dg: A Davies
Z(2)	W42–13	Harare	29 May	**t:** Llewellyn 2, Bidgood, J Davies, N Jenkins, S Davies
				c: N Jenkins 3
				p: N Jenkins 2
Na	W38–23	Windhoek	5 Jun	**t:** Lewis 2, Hill, Proctor, Moon
				c: N Jenkins 2
				p: N Jenkins 3

★ World Cup matches

[+] Non-cap tests

[†] Five-point try introduced from this game onwards

FRANCE

Jean-Francois Tordo
Speaking with Chris Thau

I HAVE to admit that it was a very satisfying feeling to sip champagne from the Five Nations' Trophy and be the first captain in the history of the Championship to do so. It was especially satisfying for me as five months earlier we had lost at home to South Africa and I had been dropped.

That October afternoon in Lyon (lost 15–20) was a disaster. We had been lulled into a sense of false confidence by our own media who had written off the Springboks. It is an old French malaise. We forgot we were dealing with a very knowledgeable, mature rugby side. We had become victims of our own propaganda.

Being relegated to the bench for the second Test in Paris (won 29–16) was a very frustrating experience but, in fairness to coach Pierre Berbizier, he did talk to me before announcing the changes, and told me that he must give everyone a chance to stake their claim. I agreed, but it did not make me any happier. The replacement bench is the worst place in the world for someone of my temperament.

Philippe Benetton had a cracking game and I was worried for my future, but the coach allayed my fears at the post-match function when he took me to one side and explained that, with Marc Cecillon having reached the end of his career, he was on the look-out for a new captain and I figured prominently in his plans. I appreciated those words from a man who I had played under in New Zealand in 1989, on a tour in which he had not only captained the side but been the playmaker and the inspiration. I liked his way of thinking and his attitude.

A telephone call the following week confirmed that I was back in the side for the visit of Argentina to Nantes and would I be interested in captaining France. At the time I did not fully appreciate the magnitude of what was on offer. I jumped at the offer, without much thinking and it only sunk in later when the emotion overwhelmed me. I immediately thought of my role model and inspiration, Jean-Pierre Rives. It was magic. Was I dreaming?

'Our historic home defeat by Argentina was certainly not Pierre Berbizier's fault. We had betrayed the man. I could not look him straight in the eye after the game but I told him that it was my fault, that I had let him down and that I was prepared to suffer the consequences. I was amazed that he did not ask me to step down as captain'

Unhappily, there followed a rude awakening against the Pumas (lost 20–24) in what was a bizarre game. We played textbook rugby for about 30 minutes and had them, or so we thought, sealed and delivered. We had scored two good tries to lead 15–3 but then became profligate, wasting chance after chance. Our pattern disintegrated. We started to play for ourselves, rather than for the team, and the unthinkable happened. France lost at home to Argentina for the first time ever.

I felt dreadful but knew that someone had to take responsibility for our historic defeat. It was certainly not Pierre Berbizier's fault. In fact, I said publicly at the time that we had betrayed the man. I could not look him straight in the eye after the game, but I told him that it was my fault, that I had let him down and that I was prepared to suffer the consequences.

I was amazed that he did not ask me to step down as captain. No-one would have blamed him for that. Instead, after the initial shock, he came back to me and said that we must work together to rebuild the fortunes of France.

Meanwhile, I had to concentrate on my club, Nice, of whom I have been captain for the past four years. I have played for them since I was a child, except for two seasons I spent at Toulon. I feel strongly attached to Nice, the city has a magic about it which makes me want to return every time I am elsewhere in France or abroad. That is the reason, in the build-up to the Five Nations' Championship, I invited the French forwards to Nice for a squad weekend to train together in this rather special atmosphere.

I was a bit worried that one or two would turn down the suggestion and the whole idea would have then collapsed. But they all came down and the weekend was a tremendous success. We trained together, ate and spent time together, under no pressure or media glare. We talked about the fundamentals that keep a side together, about humility, generosity and the pleasure of playing. The idea was to build an inner fabric, without which a side is not really a team.

> *'I invited the French forwards to Nice for a squad weekend to train together. We talked about the fundamentals that keep a side together, about humility, generosity and the pleasure of playing. The idea was to build an inner fabric, without which a side is not really a team'*

I told them that success starts with the individual, with one's own standards. You have to be very strict with yourself before you can expect anything similar from your team-mates. I also tried to convince them that we, France, had the potential to be the best, providing we all wanted it. These were not empty words manufactured for the occasion; rather my deeply held belief that we had not yet managed to express our remarkable potential. We could be a formidable side if all the aspects we discussed clicked together.

With France starting the Five Nations' Championship against England, the media kept trying to revive the issues thrown up in our unhappy game the previous year, when Gregoire Lascube and Vincent Moscato had been dismissed. I decided to set the record straight, regarding the Moscato incident, which led to his being sent off and banned for six months from the game. I pointed out that, in fact, I had been the chap who had engineered the charge that led to his dismissal. I hoped my confession would let the matter rest for good.

In the past my temperament has not been my best ally, and that is valid about most French players. The English, cool and methodic, are able to bring the worst out of us French. They will push us until we explode, and then they will play the injured party. This is not a complaint, but an admiration. Rugby is about control and concentration and I told my team-mates that there should not be any reason why we could not do the same. It is concentration that makes or breaks sides.

I have to admit that I used to have quite a reputation in French rugby. I had a very short fuse. The responsibility of captaincy has changed me profoundly. I used to push every confrontation to the limit, and beyond. Nowadays, I look at any source of conflict from a team's viewpoint. Will it serve our purpose or not?

In the wake of Nantes we decided to set ourselves a set of small targets. Regaining our credibility and self-esteem was the main objective. Before our game against England at Twickenham (lost 15–16), where I switched from flanker to hooker, our objective was not to win but to be able to all look each other in the eye and say we did our best. The better side might have won, but we did not let ourselves down. In the event we achieved that and, but for two divine crossbars – one blocking Jean-Baptiste Lafond's dropped goal attempt, the other gifting a try to Ian Hunter – we would have had the win.

> *'The English, cool and methodic, are able to bring the worst out of us French. They will push us until we explode, and then they will play the injured party. This is not a complaint, but an admiration. Rugby is about control and concentration'*

After that performance, the French media expected us to run riot against Scotland in Paris (won 11–3), where they had not won since 1969, and never at Parc des Princes. We were not yet prepared for that although in the last 20 minutes we played probably our best rugby of the season. I did not play well personally, but in rugby it is not always what you want that counts. It is what the opposition allows you to do. The Scots were by far the most accomplished side we played last season. They were a more balanced side than England and very resilient. They were knowledgeable and they were shrewd. In the scrum, for example, they lured us into a false sense of confidence for three scrums before shoving us back in the fourth. That said, we realized only about 65–70 per cent of our potential in that game.

We beat Ireland in Dublin (21–6), which a lot of people took for granted. When I expressed my view, after the game, that Ireland were about to become a formidable side, people thought I was trying to defend what was perceived as our limitations. Their subsequent results vindicated my point.

We finished our campaign against Wales (won 26–10) and it is hard to appreciate how much improvement they had made since I made my international debut against them the previous year. They were infinitely harder, stronger and more confident. Victory in that game, allied to England's failure in Dublin, gave us the title.

FRANCE'S INTERNATIONAL SEASON 1992/93

FRANCE (P11 W8 D0 L3 F259 A142):

(H)	v Romania (Le Havre, 28.5.92)	won	25–6
(A)	v Argentina (Buenos Aires, 4.7.92)	won	27–12
(A)	v Argentina (Buenos Aires, 11.7.92)	won	33–9
(H)	v South Africa (Lyon, 17.10.92)	lost	15–20
(H)	v South Africa (Paris, 24.10.92)	won	29–16
(H)	v Argentina (Nantes, 14.11.92)	lost	20–24
(A)	v Romania (Bucharest, xx.5.93)	won	37–20

Five Nations' Championship:

(A)	v England (Twickenham, 16.1.93)	lost	15–16
(H)	v Scotland (Paris, 6.2.93)	won	11–3
(A)	v Ireland (Dublin, 20.2.93)	won	21–6
(H)	v Wales (Paris, 20.3.93)	won	26–10

France in Argentina (tour record: P8 W5 D0 L3 F241 A136):

(A)	v Cordoba (Cordoba, 16.6.92)	won	62–20
(A)	v Buenos Aires (Buenos Aires, 20.6.92)	won	28–12
(A)	v Tucuman (San Miguel, 23.6.92)	lost	23–25
(A)	v Argentina B (San Juan, 27.6.92)	won	32–18
(A)	v Cuyo (Mendoza, 30.6.92)	lost	30–32
(A)	v Rosario * (Rosario, 7.7.92)	Abd	6–8

* Power-cut at half-time

Springboks in France (tour record: P9 W5 D0 L5 F210 A175):

(A)	v France Espoirs (Bordeaux, 3.10.92)	lost	17–24
(A)	v Aquitaine (Pau, 7.10.92)	won	29–22
(A)	v Midi-Pyrenees (Toulouse, 10.10.92)	won	18–15
(A)	v Provence-Cote D'Azur (Marseille, 13.10.92)	won	41–12
(A)	v Languedoc-Rousillon (Beziers, 20.10.92)	won	36–15
(A)	v French Universities (Tours, 28.10.92)	lost	13–18
(A)	v French Barbarians (Lille, 31.10.92)	lost	20–25

France B (P3 W2 D0 L1 F70 A65):

(H)	v South Africa (Bordeaux, 4.10.92)	won	24–17
(A)	v England (Leicester, 15.1.93)	lost	17–29
(A)	v Scotland (Aberdeen, 20.3.93)	won	29–19

France U-21 (P1 W1 D0 L0 F67 A9):

(H)	v Scotland (Dijon, 5.2.93)	won	67–9

France Students (P9 W8 D0 L1 F282 A116):

(–)	v Spain* (Imperia, 1.7.92)	won	57–3

(–)	v Japan★ (Finale L, 5.7.92)	won	34–25
(–)	v Scotland★ (Genoa, 8.7.92)	won	38–15
(–)	v England★ (q/f: Cagliari, 11.7.92)	won	9–6
(–)	v Italy★ (s/f: L'Aquila, 15.7.92)	won	25–21
(–)	v New Zealand★ (f: Rovigo, 19.7.92)	won	21–9
(A)	v England (Cambridge, 15.1.93)	lost	9–20
(H)	v Scotland (La Voulte, 5.2.93)	won	52–6
(H)	v Wales (Nantes, 19.3.93)	won	37–11

★ World Cup (in Italy: winners)

France Juniors (P2 W2 D0 L0 F79 A34):

(A)	v Wales Youth (Swansea, 13.3.93)	won	27–21
(H)	v England Colts (Nice, 24.4.93)	won	52–13

France Schools U–18 (P3 W3 D0 L0 F84 A30):

(H)	v Scotland (Castres, 19.12.92)	won	37– 5
(H)	v Wales (Lyon, 13.3.93)	won	25–16
(A)	v England (Camborne, 7.4.93)	won	22– 9

French Armed Forces (P1 W0 D0 L1 F3 A31):

(A)	v England U–21 (Twickenham, 1.5.93)	lost	3–31

DOMESTIC RUGBY

French Club Championship:

Semi–finals
Grenoble 21, Agen 15; Castres 17, Toulon 16.
Final
Castres 14, Grenoble 11 (Parc des Princes, Paris, 5.7.92)

FRANCE TEST RESULTS AND SCORERS SINCE 1980

1980:

W	L 9–18	Cardiff	19 Jan	t: Marchal
				c: Caussade
				dg: Caussade
E	L13–17	Paris	2 Feb	t: Averous, Rives
				c: Caussade
				p: Caussade
S	L14–22	Edinburgh	16 Feb	t: Gallion, Gabernet
				p: Gabernet
				dg: Caussade
I	W19–18	Paris	1 Mar	t: Gourdon 2
				c: Aguirre
				p: Aguirre 2
				dg: Pedeutour
SA	L15–37	Pretoria	8 Nov	t: Dintrans
				c: Vivies
				p: Vivies 3
R	L 0–15	Bucharest		

1981:

S	W16–9	Paris	17 Jan	**t:** Blanco, Bertranne
				c: Caussade
				p: Vivies, Gabernet
I	W19–13	Dublin	7 Feb	**t:** Pardo
				p: Laporte 2, Gabernet
				dg: Laporte 2
W	W19–15	Paris	7 Mar	**t:** Gabernet
				p: Laporte 3, Gabernet 2
E	W16–12	Twickenham	21 Mar	**t:** Lacans, Pardo
				c: Laporte
				dg: Laporte 2
A(1)	L15–17	Brisbane	5 Jul	**t:** Mesny
				c: Gabernet
				p: Blanco, Gabernet
				dg: Vivies
A(2)	L14–24	Sydney	11 Jul	**t:** Lacas, Elissalde
				dg: Elissalde, Sallefranque
R	W17–9	Narbonne		
NZ(1)	L9–13	Toulouse	14 Nov	**p:** Laporte 2
				dg: Gabernet
NZ(2)	L6–18	Paris	21 Nov	**p:** Laporte, Blanco

1982:

W	L12–22	Cardiff	6 Feb	**t:** Blanco
				c: Sallefranque
				p: Sallefranque, Martinez
E	L15–27	Paris	20 Feb	**t:** Pardo
				c: Sallefranque
				p: Sallefranque 2
				dg: Lescarboura
S	L7–16	Edinburgh	6 Mar	**t:** Rives
				p: Sallefranque
I	W22–9	Paris	20 Mar	**t:** Blanco, Mesny
				c: Gabernet
				p: Blanco 2, Gabernet 2
R	L9–13	Bucharest		
Arg(1)	W25–12	Toulouse	14 Nov	**t:** Sella 2, Esteve, Blanco
				p: Blanco, Camberabero
				dg: Camberabero
Arg(2)	W13–6	Paris	20 Nov	**t:** Begu, Blanco
				c: Camberabero
				p: Camberabero

1983:

E	W19–15	Twickenham	15 Jan	**t:** Esteve, Sella, Paparemborde
				c: Blanco 2
				p: Camberabero
S	W19–15	Paris	5 Feb	**t:** Esteve 2
				c: Blanco
				p: Blanco 3
I	L16–22	Dublin	19 Feb	**t:** Blanco, Esteve

				c: Blanco
				p: Blanco 2
W	W16–9	Paris	19 Mar	t: Esteve
				p: Blanco 3
				dg: Camberabero
A(1)	D15–15	Clermont-Ferrand	13 Nov	p: Lescarboura 3
				dg: Lescarboura, Lafond
A(2)	W15– 6	Paris	20 Nov	t: Esteve
				c: Lescarboura
				p: Gabernet, Lescarboura 2

1984:

I	W25–12	Paris	21 Jan	t: Gallion, Sella
				c: Lescarboura
				p: Lescarboura 4
				dg: Lescarboura
W	W21–16	Cardiff	18 Feb	t: Sella
				c: Lescarboura
				p: Lescarboura 4
				dg: Lescarboura
E	W32–18	Paris	3 Mar	t: Codorniou, Sella, Esteve, Bergu, Gallion
				c: Lescarboura 3
				p: Lescarboura
				dg: Lescarboura
S	L12–21	Edinburgh	17 Mar	t: Gallion
				c: Lescarboura
				p: Lescarboura
				dg: Lescarboura
NZ(1)	L9–10	Christchurch	16 Jun	t: Blanco
				c: Lescarboura
				p: Lescarboura
NZ(2)	L18–31	Auckland	23 Jun	t: Lescarboura 2, Bonneval
				p: Lescarboura 2
R	W18–3	Bucharest	11 Nov	t: Sella, Lescarboura
				c: Lescarboura 2
				p: Lescarboura 2

1985:

E	D9–9	Twickenham	2 Feb	dg: Lescarboura 3
S	W11– 3	Paris	16 Feb	t: Blanco 2
				p: Lescarboura
I	D15–15	Dublin	2 Mar	t: Esteve, Codorniou
				c: Lescarboura 2
				p: Lescarboura
W	W14–3	Paris	30 Mar	t: Esteve, Gallion
				p: Lescarboura 2
Arg(1)	L16–24	Buenos Aires	22 Jun	t: Blanco, Bonneval
				c: Lescarboura
				p: Lescarboura 2
Arg(2)	W23–15	Buenos Aires	29 Jun	t: Codorniou, Erbani, Berbizier, Blanco
				c: Lescarboura 2

				p: Lescarboura
J(1)[+]	W50–0	Dax	19 Oct	t: Lafond 4, Fabre, Cassagne, Codorniou, Rodriguez, Detrez, Dubroca
				c: Camberabero 5
J(2)[+]	W52–0	Nantes	26 Oct	t: Camberabero 2, Lafond 2, Charvet 2, Dintrans 2, Fabre, Rodriguez
				c: Camberabero 6

1986:

S	L17–18	Edinburgh	17 Jan	t: Berbizier, Sella
				p: Laporte 2
				dg: Laporte
I	W29–9	Paris	1 Feb	t: Berbizier, Marocco, Sella
				c: Laporte
				p: Laporte 3, Blanco
				dg: Lafond
W	W23–15	Cardiff	1 Mar	t: Sella, Lafond 2, Blanco
				c: Laporte 2
				dg: Laporte
E	W29–10	Paris	15 Mar	t: Sella, Blanco, penalty try, Laporte
				c: Laporte 2
				p: Laporte 3
R(a)	W25–13	Lille	xx xxx	t: Charvet, Bonneval, Sella, Erbani, Lagisquet
				c: Laporte
				p: Laporte
Arg(1)	L13–15	Buenos Aires	31 May	t: Bonneval
				p: Laporte 3
Arg(2)	W22–9	Buenos Aires	7 Jun	t: Lescarboura, Sella, Debroca
				c: Lescarboura 2
				p: Lescarboura 2
A	L14–27	Sydney	21 Jun	t: Blanco 2, Sella
				c: Lescarboura
NZ(a)	L9–18	Christchurch	28 Jun	dg: Lescarboura 3
R(b)	W20–3	Bucharest		t: Andrieu, Blanco, Berot
				c: Berot
				p: Berot 2
NZ(b1)	L7–19	Toulouse	8 Nov	t: Sella
				p: Berot
NZ(b2)	W16–3	Nantes	15 Nov	t: Charvet, Lorieux
				c: Berot
				p: Berot 2

1987:

W	W16–9	Paris	7 Feb	t: Mesnel, Bonneval
				c: Berot
				p: Berot 2
E	W19–15	Twickenham	21 Feb	t: Bonneval, Sella
				c: Berot
				p: Berot 2
				dg: Mesnel
S(a)	W28–22	Paris	7 Mar	t: Bonneval 3, Berot
				p: Berot 3

				dg: Mesnel
I	W19–13	Dublin	21 Mar	t: Champ 2
				c: Berot
				p: Berot 3
S(b)*	D20–20	Christchurch	23 May	t: Sella, Berbizier, Blanco
				c: Blanco
				p: Blanco 2
R(a)*	W55–12	Wellington	28 May	t: Charvet 2, Lagisquet 2, Sella, Andrieu,
				Camberabero, Erbani, Laporte
				c: Laporte 8
				p: Laporte
Z*	W70–12	Auckland	2 Jun	t: Modin 3, Camberabero 3, Charvet 2,
				Dubroca, Rodriguez 2, Esteve, Laporte
				c: Camberabero 9
Fj*	W31–16	Auckland	7 Jun	t: Lorieux, Rodriguez 2, Lagisquet
				c: Laporte 3
				p: Laporte 2
				dg: Laporte
A*	W30–24	Sydney	13 Jun	t: Lorieux, Sella, Lagisquet, Blanco
				c: Camberabero 4
				p: Camberabero 2
NZ*	L9–29	Auckland	20 Jun	t: Berbizier
				c: Camberabero
				p: Camberabero
S(c)+	L12–15	Galashiels	26 Sep	t: Mesnel
				c: Bianchi
				p: Bianchi 2
R(b)	W49–3	Agen	11 Nov	t: Berot, Lagisquet 2, Andrieu 2,
				Ondarts, penalty try
				c: Berot 6
				p: Berot 3

1988:

E	W10–9	Paris	16 Jan	t: Rodriguez
				p: Berot 2
S	L12–23	Edinburgh	6 Feb	t: Lagisquet
				c: Berot
				p: Berot
				dg: Lescarboura
I	W25–6	Paris	20 Feb	t: Blanco, Lagisquet, Sella,
				Camberabero, Carminati
				c: Camberabero
				dg: Berot
W	W10–9	Cardiff	19 Mar	t: Lescarboura
				p: Lafond 2
Arg(a1)	W18–15	Buenos Aires	18 Jun	t: Dintrans
				c: Berot
				p: Berot 4
Arg(a2)	L6–18	Buenos Aires	25 Jun	p: Berot 2
Arg(b1)	W29–9	Nantes	5 Nov	t: Blanco 2, Cecillon, Lagisquet,
				Rodriguez
				c: Berot 3

				p: Berot
Arg(b2)	W28–18	Lille	11 Nov	t: Sanz, Cecillon, Andrieu, Sella
				c: Berot 3
				p: Berot 2
R	W16–12	Bucharest	26 Nov	t: Blanco, Lagisquet
				c: Berot
				p: Berot 2

1989:

I	W26–21	Dublin	21 Jan	t: Lagisquet 2, Blanco, Lafond
				c: Lafond 2
				p: Lafond 2
W	W31–12	Paris	18 Feb	t: Blanco 2, Berbizier, Dintrans
				c: Lafond 3
				p: Lafond 2
				dg: Mesnel
E	L0–11	Twickenham	4 Mar	
S	W19–3	Paris	19 Mar	t: Berbizier, Blanco, Lagisquet
				c: Berot 2
				p: Berot
USSR	W18–16	Valence	20 May	t: Roumat
				c: Lafond
				p: Lafond 3, Camberabero
NZ(1)	L17–25	Christchurch	17 Jun	t: Blanco 2, Cecillon
				c: Berot
				p: Berot
NZ(2)	L20–34	Auckland	1 Jul	t: Rouge-Thomas, Cecillon
				p: Blanco 4
BL	L27–29	Paris	4 Oct	t: Blanco, Benetton, Camberabero
				c: Camberabero 3
				p: Camberabero 3
A(1)	L15–32	Strasbourg	4 Nov	p: Camberabero 4
				dg: Camberabero
A(2)	W25–19	Lille	11 Nov	t: Lagisquet, Andrieu
				c: Lacroix
				p: Lacroix 5

1990:

W	W29–19	Cardiff	20 Jan	t: Lafond, Sella, Camberabero, Lagisquet, Rodriguez
				c: Camberabero 3
				p: Camberabero
E	L7–26	Paris	3 Feb	t: Lagisquet
				p: Charvet
S	L0–21	Edinburgh	17 Feb	
I	W31–12	Paris	3 Mar	t: Mesnel 2, Lagisquet
				c: Camberabero 2
				p: Camberabero 5
R	L6–12	Auch	24 May	p: Lescarboura 2
A(1)	L9–21	Sydney	9 Jun	p: Camberabero 3
A(2)	L31–48	Brisbane	24 Jun	t: Blanco 2, Armary, Lacombe
				c: Camberabero 3

				p: Camberabero 3
A(3)	W28–19	Sydney	30 Jun	t: Camberabero, Mesnel
				c: Camberabero
				p: Camberabero 2, Blanco
				dg: Camberabero 3
NZ(1)	L3–24	Nantes	3 Nov	p: Camberabero
NZ(2)	L12–30	Paris	10 Nov	p: Camberabero 3
				dg: Camberabero

1991:

S	W15–9	Paris	19 Jan	p: Camberabero 2
				dg: Blanco, Camberabero 2
I	W21–13	Dublin	2 Feb	t: Lagisquet, Cabannes
				c: Camberabero 2
				p: Camberabero 3
W(a)	W36–3	Paris	2 Mar	t: Blanco, Saint–André, Mesnel, Roumat, Sella, Lafond
				c: Blanco, Camberabero 2
				p: Camberabero 2
E	L19–21	Twickenham	16 Mar	t: Saint-André, Camberabero, Mesnel
				c: Camberabero 2
				p: Camberabero
R(a)	W33–21	Bucharest	22 Jun	t: Blanco, Camberabero, Cecillon, Simon
				c: Camberabero
				p: Camberabero 5

Jean-Baptiste Lafond, who enjoyed a fine Test campaign in 1993, runs at Scotland wing Derek Stark in Paris during France's untidy 11–3 win

US(1)	W41–9	Denver	13 Jul	**t:** Blanco 2, Lafond, Saint–André, Champ, Courtiols, Cecillon, Mesnel **c:** Camberabero 3 **p:** Camberabero
US(2)	W10–3	Colorado Springs	20 Jul	**t:** Mesnel, Blanco **c:** Camberabero
W(b)	W22–9	Cardiff	4 Sep	**t:** Blanco, Camberabero, Saint–André **c:** Camberabero 2 **p:** Camberabero 2
R(b)★	W30–3	Beziers	4 Oct	**t:** penalty try, Saint–André, Roumat, Lafond **c:** Camberabero **p:** Camberabero 4
Fj★	W33–9	Grenoble	8 Oct	**t:** Lafond 3, Sella 2, Camberabero **c:** Camberabero 3 **p:** Camberabero
C★	W19–13	Agen	13 Oct	**t:** Lafond, Saint–André **c:** Camberabero **p:** Camberabero, Lacroix 2
E★	L10–19	Paris	19 Oct	**t:** Lafond **p:** Lacroix 2

1992:

W	W12–9	Cardiff	1 Feb	**t:** Saint–André **c:** Lafond **p:** Viars **dg:** Penaud
E	L13–31	Paris	15 Feb	**t:** Viars, Penaud **c:** Viars **p:** Viars
S	L 6–10	Edinburgh	7 Mar	**p:** Lafond 2
I	W44–12	Paris	21 Mar	**t:** Penaud 2, Viars 2, Cecillon, Cabannes, Sadourny **c:** Viars 5 **p:** Viars 2
R	W25–6	Le Havre	28 May	**t:** Saint–André, Cadieu, Galthie, penalty try **c:** Viars, Lacroix 2 **p:** Viars
Arg(a1)[†]	W27–12	Buenos Aires	4 Jul	**t:** Deylaud, Viars **c:** Deylaud **p:** Viars 4 **dg:** Penaud
Arg(a2)	W33–9	Buenos Aires	11 Jul	**t:** Saint–André, Viars, Hueber **c:** Viars 3 **p:** Viars 3 **dg:** Hueber
SA(1)	L15–20	Lyon	17 Oct	**t:** Penaud 2 **c:** Viars **p:** Viars
SA(2)	W29–16	Paris	24 Oct	**t:** Penaud, Roumat **c:** Lacroix 2

				p: Lacroix 5
Arg(b)	L20–24	Nantes	14 Nov	**t:** Gonzales, Galthie, Sella
				c: Viars
				p: Viars

1993:

E	L15–16	Twickenham	16 Jan	**t:** Saint–André 2
				c: Camberabero
				p: Camberabero
S	W11–3	Paris	6 Feb	**t:** Lacroix
				p: Camberabero 2
I	W21–6	Dublin	20 Feb	**t:** Saint–André, Sella
				c: Camberabero
				p: Camberabero 2
				dg: Camberabero
W	W26–10	Paris	20 Mar	**t:** Benetton 2, Lafond
				c: Lafond
				p: Lacroix 3
R	W37–20	Bucharest	20 May	**t:** Bernat-Salles 3, Cecillon
				c: Viars 4
				p: Viars 3
SA(1)	D20–20	Durban	26 Jun	**t:** Saint André
				p: Lacroix 3
				dg: Hueber, Penaud
SA(2)	W18–17	Johannesburg	3 Jul	**p:** Lacroix 4
				dg: Penaud, Lacroix

* World Cup matches
⁺ Non-cap tests
† Five-point try introduced from this game onwards

AUSTRALIA

Michael Lynagh
Speaking with Greg Campbell

TO retain our title of world champions throughout the 1992 season was a great feat. An arduous campaign saw us tackle two overseas tours, contest a total of eight Test matches, play under three captains and adjust to a mid-season change of laws. Yet we emerged with the Bledisloe Cup and the scalps of South Africa, Ireland and Wales.

We had worked hard to get into the position of being world champions and I would rather have gone into the season in the position of defending that crown rather than aspiring to it. I guess that was what the year was all about – living with the pressure of everyone wanting to knock us off our world champion perch.

It took a little while for the performances to get going. But that's the great thing about this Australia team. Once we got together before the Test series with Scotland we knew what we had to do. We know each other's game well and that's been the secret behind our success over the past few years. We haven't really had to develop a whole new range of combinations.

I had missed the beginning of the season because of my commitment to the Benetton club in Italy and it was great to get back to the Test match scene. There is always a great feeling among the guys and this time was no different, even though a few places had become vacant. From the World Cup winning team, Simon Poidevin had stepped down from representative rugby while Rob Egerton had moved to the United States for the year where his wife was studying at university. On the positive side, Tim Gavin had returned to fitness after missing the World Cup with a serious knee injury.

> *'We had only one week to play under the new laws before the First Test against New Zealand in Sydney. To my mind it was a stupid piece of timing introducing new laws midway through a season'*

Fortunately, the guys who replaced Poido and Rob, David Wilson and Paul Carozza, had both previously toured with the Wallabies and Paul had a couple of Tests behind him. This replacement scenario was not always the case with past Australian teams, but has been a positive feature of our touring commitments in recent years.

The Test series against Scotland was always one we were expected to win given the number of retirements the Scots had suffered following the World Cup. Still, we treated them with high respect rather than regard the series as a warm-up for the All Blacks. Scotland were a very good side and we did well to beat them (won 27–12 and 37–13), especially bearing in mind that the last time they toured Australia, in 1982, the series was squared at one Test apiece.

After the Scots departed, we had to quickly adapt to the new experimental laws. We had only one week to play under them before the first Test against New Zealand in Sydney. The New South Wales boys played a tour match against the All Blacks while Queensland played a club round in Brisbane. Looking back, it wasn't a great problem adjusting even though, at the time, it took a great deal of concentration and practice to make the switch. But to my mind it was a stupid piece of timing introducing new laws midway through a season.

For the Bledisloe Cup campaign, the All Blacks made several changes to their team, coaching staff and management but, despite this, we basically knew them well. There may have been a few new faces, but we were familiar with the surrounding players. It was also obvious the way they were going to play the game and that meant it would be very hard for us.

The series was also going to be a proving point. When you play New Zealand there is always a huge amount of pressure because so much is at stake. We knew this time that the outcome of the three-Test series would be seen as a measure of whether our World Cup victory was genuine or just a fluke.

We won the first Test 16–15 which was some achievement as we were required to come from behind several times before finally claiming victory, with tries by Campo and Tim Horan. The success really raised the confidence level within the team and set the ball rolling for the remainder of the series. Prior to the World Cup, the one thing Wallaby teams had been lacking was consistency. We could play a brilliant Test one week and then give a lacklustre performance the next. But when we played the second Test at Ballymore, it was fantastic to see that we could turn in a second good performance (won 19–17) and so clinch the series.

We were very clean to complete a 3–0 sweep when the series returned to Sydney. But this series followed the same pattern as in 1990 when New Zealand won the first two Tests before we took the third. This time the roles were reversed. They played very well and perhaps had more to play for, winning 26–23.

Soon after that series we toured South Africa and I for one did not enjoy the tour at all. I don't think many of the other players did either. It was a very hard and difficult two weeks, both on and off the field, and to get the results, which included a resounding 26–3 Test victory, was a terrific effort. We knew we needed to win to end any argument about the merit of our World Cup success. We kept on hearing that we weren't the real world champions until we had beaten South Africa. So to beat the Springboks when they had all the home advantages in their favour was a real gutsy effort.

'Prior to the World Cup the one thing Wallaby teams had been lacking was consistency. We could play a brilliant Test one week and then give a lacklustre performance the next'

We had heard a lot about South African rugby and I had read books on the South African game. Consequently, I perhaps expected the rugby to be much harder. The tour was tinged with controversy over the playing of the South African anthem when the Springboks played New Zealand at Ellis Park. Obviously we could not put this out totally of our minds, but as there was nothing we could do to sway the decision either way we just continued the tour as if the Test was going to be played. We were well rewarded for maintaining our concentration.

The Cape Town Test was Nick Farr-Jones' last as captain and I was honoured to be given the job for the tour to Ireland and Wales. I don't think it affected my game; when Nick had been there I still called the shots in the backs so that aspect had not changed. The tour was always going to be tough and physically demanding because we would be expected to win every game. but we focused on the two Tests which was what we were there to win. We had a few hiccups along the way – losing to Munster, Swansea and Llanelli – but we beat Ireland (42–17) and Wales (23–6) to round off a very satisfying year.

Personally speaking, it was strange taking to the field against Ireland without Nick as my half-back partner having played so many Tests together over so many years. But playing alongside Peter Slattery was hardly a new experience either since we had played so many games in tandem with Queensland and Queensland University. All the players have the highest respect for Peter.

> *'After assessing the team lists, we came to the conclusion that every player in our team was a better player than his opposite number in the Welsh team'*

It was a shame that I injured my shoulder at Lansdowne Road and that I was unable to finish the tour on the field. I was, though, very fortunate that the players, team management and Australian Rugby Union said they wanted me to return to the tour after my operation back home and continue in a non-playing captain's role.

The final Test, at Cardiff Arms Park, was immensely satisfying as we felt under a lot of pressure after our defeats by Swansea and Llanelli. But we stayed cool and after assessing the team lists, came to the conclusion that every player in our team was a better player than his opposite number in the Welsh team. That told us that we should win and, thanks to tries from Campo, Rod McCall and David Wilson, win we did.

AUSTRALIA'S INTERNATIONAL SEASON 1992

AUSTRALIA (P8 W7 D0 L1 F213 A109):
Scotland to Australia
(H) v Scotland (Sydney, 13.6.92)	won	27–12
(H) v Scotland (Brisbane, 21.6.92)	won	37–13

Bledisloe Cup
(H) v New Zealand (Sydney, 14.7.92)	won	16–15
(H) v New Zealand (Brisbane, 19.7.92)	won	19–17
(H) v New Zealand (Sydney, 25.7.92)	lost	23–26

Australia to South Africa
(A) v South Africa (Cape Town, 22.8.92)	won	26–3

Australia to Ireland and Wales
(A) v Ireland (Dublin, 31.10.92)	won	42–17
(A) v Wales (Cardiff, 21.11.92)	won	23–6

Wallabies in South Africa (tour record: P4 W4 D0 L0 F130 A41):
(A) v Western Transvaal (Potchefstroom, 11.8.92)	won	46–13
(A) v Northern Transvaal (Pretoria, 14.8.92)	won	24–17
(A) v Eastern Province (Port Elizabeth, 18.8.92)	won	34–8

Wallabies in Ireland and Wales (tour record: P13 W10 D0 L3 F312 A161):
(A) v Leinster (Dublin, 17.10.92)	won	38–11
(A) v Munster (Cork, 21.10.92)	lost	19–22
(A) v Ulster (Belfast, 24.10.92)	won	35–11
(A) v Connacht (Galway, 27.10.92)	won	14–6
(A) v Swansea (St Helens, 4.11.92)	lost	6–21
(A) v Wales B (Cardiff, 7.11.92)	won	24–11
(A) v Neath (The Gnoll, 11.11.92)	won	16–8
(A) v Llanelli (Stradey Park, 14.11.92)	lost	9–13
(A) v Monmouthshire (Ebbw Vale, 17.11.92)	won	19–9
(A) v Welsh Students (Bridgend, 24.11.92)	won	37–6
(A) v Barbarians (Twickenham, 28.11.92)	won	30–20

Australia U–21 (P1 W0 D0 L1 F10 A20):
(A) v New Zealand Colts (Brisbane, 19.7.92)	lost	10–20

1992 SUPER SIX TOURNAMENT

Canterbury 10, Auckland 22 (Christchurch)
Queensland 23, Wellington 6 (Brisbane)
Fiji 0, Auckland 29 (Suva)
Canterbury 31, Wellington 20 (Christchurch)
Fiji 9, Queensland 29 (Suva)
Wellington 18, New South Wales 35 (Wellington)
Fiji 38, Canterbury 17 (Suva)
Queensland 27, Auckland 15 (Brisbane)
Canterbury 14, New South Wales 35 (Christchurch)
Auckland 38, New South Wales 10 (Auckland)
Canterbury 10, Queensland 26 (Christchurch)

Auckland 33, Wellington 12 (Auckland)
New South Wales 52, Fiji 6 (Sydney)
Wellington 43, Fiji 10 (Wellington)
Queensland 23, New South Wales 18 (Sydney)

	P	W	D	L	F	A	Pts
Queensland	5	5	0	0	120	58	20
Auckland	5	4	0	1	136	59	16
New South Wales	5	3	0	2	150	99	13
Wellington	5	1	0	4	99	132	4
Canterbury	5	1	0	4	82	141	4
Fiji	5	1	0	4	63	162	4

Previous winners: 1988 – Auckland; 1989 – Auckland; 1990 – Auckland; 1991 – no competition (World Cup)

1992 DOMESTIC RUGBY

Interstate Series:
Queensland 23, New South Wales 18
Queensland 18, New South Wales 15
Queensland 33, ACT 0
New South Wales 30, ACT 17

Sydney Grand Final:
Randwick 28, Gordon 14

Brisbane Grand Final:
Southern Districts 44, Queensland University 10

AUSTRALIA TEST RESULTS AND SCORERS SINCE 1980

1980:

Fj	W22–9	Suva	24 May	t: Martin, Moon
				c: P E McLean
				p: P E McLean 3
				dg: P E McLean
NZ(1)	W13–9	Sydney	21 Jun	t: Hawker, Martin
				c: Gould
				dg: M Ella
NZ(2)	L9–12	Brisbane	28 Jun	t: Moon
				c: Gould
				p: Gould
NZ(3)	W26–10	Sydney	12 Jul	t: Grigg 2, O'Connor, Carson
				c: Gould 2
				p: Gould
				dg: M Ella

1981:

F(1)	W17–15	Brisbane	5 Jul	t: Poidevin, O'Connor, Moon
				c: P McLean
				p: Richards

F(2)	W24–14	Sydney	11 Jul	**t:** Hall, O'Connor **c:** P McLean 2 **p:** P McLean 4
I	W16–12	Dublin	21 Nov	**t:** O'Connor **p:** P McLean 3 **dg:** Gould
W	L13–18	Cardiff	5 Dec	**t:** Slack, M Cox **c:** P McLean **p:** P McLean
S	L15–24	Edinburgh	19 Dec	**t:** Poidevin, Moon, Slack **p:** P McLean

1982:

E	L11–15	Twickenham	2 Jan	**t:** Moon 2 **p:** P McLean
S(1)	L7–12	Brisbane	3 Jul	**t:** Hawker **p:** Hawker
S(2)	W33–9	Sydney	10 Jul	**t:** Gould 2, O'Connor **c:** P McLean 3 **p:** P McLean 5
NZ(1)	L16–23	Christchurch	14 Aug	**t:** Hawker, Campese **c:** Gould **p:** Gould 2
NZ(2)	W19–16	Wellington	28 Aug	**t:** G Ella, Campese **c:** Gould **p:** Gould 3
NZ(3)	L18–33	Auckland	11 Sep	**t:** Gould **c:** Gould **p:** Gould 3 **dg:** Hawker

1983:

US	W49–3	Sydney	9 Jul	**t:** Campese 4, Slack 2, Ross, Roche, Hanley **c:** Gould 4, Campese **dg:** M Ella
Arg(1)	L3–18	Brisbane	31 Jul	**dg:** Campese
Arg(2)	W29–13	Sydney	8 Aug	**t:** Moon 2, Roche, Campese, penalty try **c:** Campese 3 **p:** Campese
Fj	W16–3	Suva	xx Aug	**t:** Campese **p:** Lynagh 4
NZ	L8–18	Sydney	20 Aug	**t:** Slack, Poidevin
It	W29–7	Padova	22 Oct	**t:** Hawker 2, Moon, Williams, M Ella **c:** M Ella 3 **p:** M Ella
F(1)	D15–15	Clermont-Ferrand	13 Nov	**t:** Roche **c:** Campese **p:** Campese **dg:** M Ella, Hawker
F(2)	L6–15	Paris	20 Nov	**p:** Campese **dg:** M Ella

1984:

NZ(1)	W16–9	Sydney	21 Jul	t: Reynolds, Moon
				c: M Ella
				p: M Ella
				dg: Gould
NZ(2)	L15–19	Brisbane	4 Aug	t: M Ella
				c: M Ella
				p: M Ella 2, Campese
NZ(3)	L24–25	Sydney	18 Aug	t: Campese
				c: M Ella
				p: M Ella 5, Campese
E	W19–3	Twickenham	3 Nov	t: M Ella, Poidevin, Lynagh
				c: Lynagh 2
				p: Lynagh
I	W16–9	Dublin	10 Nov	t: M Ella
				p: Lynagh
				dg: M Ella 2, Lynagh
W	W28–9	Cardiff	24 Nov	t: Lawton, Tuynman, M Ella, Lynagh
				c: Gould 3
				p: Gould 2
S	W37–12	Edinburgh	8 Dec	t: Campese 2, Farr–Jones, M Ella
				c: Lynagh 3
				p: Lynagh 5

1985:

C(1)	W59–3	Sydney	15 Jun	t: Burke 2, Lane 2, Grigg 2, Calcraft, Farr-Jones, Kassulke
				c: Lynagh 7
				p: Lynagh 3
C(2)	W43–15	Brisbane	23 Jun	t: Burke 3, Grigg, Cutler, Tuynman, Farr-Jones
				c: Lynagh 3

David Campese takes the game to the Barbarians in his farewell-to-Twickenham match which Australia won 30–20

NZ	L9–10	Auckland	29 Jun	**p:** Lynagh 2
				dg: Lynagh
				t: Black
				c: Lynagh
				p: Lynagh
Fj(1)	W52–28	Brisbane	10 Aug	**t:** Farr-Jones 2, Reynolds, Cutler, Lawton, Papworth, Grigg
				c: Knox 3
				p: Knox 3
				dg: Knox 2, Campese
Fj(2)	W31–9	Sydney	17 Aug	**t:** Campese 2, Grigg, McIntyre, Cutler
				c: Knox
				p: Knox 3

1986:

It	W39–18	Brisbane	1 Jun	**t:** Campese 2, Tuynman, McIntyre, Moon, Burke
				c: Lynagh 6
				p: Lynagh
F	W27–14	Sydney	21 Jun	**t:** Campese
				c: Lynagh
				p: Lynagh 6
				dg: Lynagh
Arg(1)	W39–19	Brisbane	6 Jul	**t:** Papworth 2, Grigg, Campese
				c: Lynagh 4
				p: Lynagh 5
Arg(2)	W26–0	Sydney	12 Jul	**t:** Campese 2, Tuynman
				c: Lynagh
				p: Lynagh 4
NZ(1)	W13–12	Wellington	9 Aug	**t:** Campese, Burke
				c: Lynagh
				p: Lynagh
NZ(2)	L12–13	Dunedin	23 Aug	**p:** Lynagh 3
				dg: Lynagh
NZ(3)	W22–9	Auckland	6 Sep	**t:** Leeds, Campese
				c: Lynagh
				p: Lynagh 4

1987:

SK	W65–18	Brisbane	17 May	**t:** Burke 3, Grigg 2, Slack 2, Cook, Gould, B Smith, Miller, James, Farr-Jones
				c: Smith 5
				p: Smith
E★	W19–6	Sydney	23 May	**t:** Campese, Poidevin
				c: Lynagh
				p: Lynagh 3
US★	W47–12	Brisbane	31 May	**t:** penalty try, Smith, Slack, Leeds 2, Papworth, Campese, Codey
				c: Lynagh 6
				p: Lynagh
J★	W42–23	Sydney	3 Jun	**t:** Slack 2, Tuynman, Burke 2, Grigg, Hartill, Campese

				c: Lynagh 5
I*	W33–15	Sydney	7 Jun	t: McIntyre, Smith, Burke 2
				c: Lynagh 4
				p: Lynagh 3
F*	L24–30	Sydney	13 Jun	t: Campese, Codey
				c: Lynagh 2
				p: Lynagh 3
				dg: Lynagh
W*	L21–22	Rotorua	18 Jun	t: Burke, Grigg
				c: Lynagh 2
				p: Lynagh 2
				dg: Lynagh
NZ	L16–30	Sydney	25 Jul	t: Papworth
				p: Leeds 3
				dg: Hawker
Arg(1)	D19–19	Buenos Aires	31 Oct	t: Williams, Cutler, Lynagh
				c: Lynagh 2
				p: Lynagh
Arg(2)	L19–27	Buenos Aires	7 Nov	t: Williams 2
				c: Lynagh
				p: Lynagh 3

1988:

E(a1)	W22–16	Brisbane	29 May	t: Williams
				p: Lynagh 6
E(a2)	W28–8	Sydney	12 Jun	t: Campese, G Ella, Lynagh, Carter
				c: Lynagh 3
				p: Lynagh 2
NZ(1)	L7–32	Sydney	3 Jul	t: Williams
				p: Lynagh
NZ(2)	D19–19	Brisbane	16 Jul	t: Grant, Williams
				c: Leeds
				p: Leeds 3
NZ(3)	L9–30	Sydney	30 Jul	t: Walker
				c: Lynagh
				p: Leeds
E(b)	L19–28	Twickenham	5 Nov	t: Leeds, Campese, Grant
				c: Lynagh 2
				p: Lynagh
S	W32–13	Edinburgh	19 Nov	t: Lawton 2, Campese 2, Gourley,
				c: Lynagh 3
				p: Lynagh 2
It	W55–6	Milan	3 Dec	t: Campese 3, Niuqila 3, Leeds,
				Gourley, Lynagh
				c: Lynagh 8
				p: Lynagh

1989:

BL(1)	W30–12	Sydney	1 Jul	t: Walker, Gourley, Maguire, Martin
				c: Lynagh 4
				p: Lynagh
				dg: Lynagh
BL(2)	L12–19	Brisbane	8 Jul	t: Martin

				c: Lynagh
				p: Lynagh 2
BL(3)	L18–19	Sydney	15 Jul	t: Williams
				c: Lynagh
				p: Lynagh 4
NZ	L12–24	Auckland	5 Aug	t: Campese
				c: Lynagh
				p: Lynagh 2
F(1)	W32–15	Strasbourg	4 Nov	t: Horan 2, Williams, Campese
				c: Lynagh 2
				p: Lynagh 4
F(2)	L19–25	Lille	11 Nov	t: Kearns, Farr–Jones
				c: Lynagh
				p: Lynagh 3

1990:

F(1)	W21–9	Sydney	9 Jun	t: Martin
				c: Lynagh
				p: Lynagh 5
F(2)	W48–31	Brisbane	24 Jun	t: Carozza, Cornish, Gavin, Little, penalty try, Campese
				c: Lynagh 6
				p: Lynagh 4
F(3)	L19–28	Sydney	30 Jun	t: Campese, Daly
				c: Lynagh
				p: Lynagh 2
				dg: Lynagh
US	W67–9	Brisbane	8 Jul	t: Lynagh 2, Williams 2, Daly, McKenzie, Kearns, Gavin, Little, Farr-Jones, Slattery, Campese
				c: Lynagh 8
				dg: Campese
NZ(1)	L6–21	Christchurch	21 Jul	p: Lynagh 2
NZ(2)	L17–27	Auckland	4 Aug	t: Horan, Ofahengaue
				p: Lynagh 2
				dg: Lynagh
NZ(3)	W21–9	Wellington	18 Aug	t: Kearns
				c: Lynagh
				p: Lynagh 5

1991:

W(a)	W63–6	Brisbane	21 Jul	t: Lynagh 2, Kearns 2, Gavin 2, Ofahengaue, Horan, Roebuck, Campese, Egerton, Little
				c: Lynagh 6
				p: Lynagh
E(a)	W40–15	Sydney	27 Jul	t: Campese 2, Ofahengaue 2, Roebuck
				c: Lynagh 4
				p: Lynagh 4
NZ(a1)	W21–12	Sydney	10 Aug	t: Gavin, Egerton
				c: Lynagh 2
				p: Lynagh 3
NZ(a2)	L3–6	Auckland	24 Aug	p: Lynagh

Arg*	W32–19	Llanelli	4 Oct	t: Campese 2, Horan 2, Kearns
				c: Lynagh 3
				p: Lynagh 2
WS*	W 9–3	Pontypool	9 Oct	p: Lynagh 3
W(b)*	W38–3	Cardiff	12 Oct	t: Roebuck 2, Slattery, Campese, Horan, Lynagh
				c: Lynagh 4
				p: Lynagh 2
I*	W19–18	Dublin	20 Oct	t: Campese 2, Lynagh
				c: Lynagh 2
				p: Lynagh
NZ(b)*	W16–6	Dublin	27 Oct	t: Campese, Horan
				c: Lynagh
				p: Lynagh 2
E*	W12–6	Twickenham	2 Nov	t: Daly
				c: Lynagh
				p: Lynagh 2

1992:

S(1)	W27–12	Sydney	13 June	t: Campese 2, Carozza, Lynagh
				c: Lynagh
				p: Lynagh 3
S(2)	W37–13	Brisbane	21 Jun	t: Carozza 2, Horan 2, Eales
				c: Lynagh
				p: Lynagh 5
NZ(1)†	W16–15	Sydney	14 Jul	t: Campese, Horan
				p: Lynagh 2
NZ(2)	W19–17	Brisbane	19 Jul	t: Carozza 2
				p: Lynagh 3
NZ(3)	L23–26	Sydney	25 Jul	t: Farr-Jones, Herbert
				c: Lynagh 2
				p: Lynagh 3
SA	W26–3	Cape Town	23 Aug	t: Carozza 2, Campese
				c: Lynagh
				p: Lynagh 3
I	W42–17	Dublin	31 Oct	t: Campese, McKenzie, Little, Kelaher, Horan
				c: Roebuck 4
				p: Roebuck 3
W	W23–6	Cardiff	21 Nov	t: Wilson, McCall, Campese
				c: Roebuck
				p: Roebuck 2

1993:

T	W52-14	Brisbane	3 Jul	t: Campese 2, Morgan, Gavin, Little, Carozza, Johnstone
				c: Roebuck 3, Lynagh
				p: Roebuck 3
NZ	L10–25	Dunedin	17 Jul	t: Horan
				c: Kelaher
				p: Kelaher

* World Cup matches

⁺ Non-cap tests

† Five-point try introduced from this game onwards

NEW ZEALAND

Sean Fitzpatrick
Speaking with Wynne Gray
(*New Zealand Herald*)

IT became very obvious when the All Black national trial teams were announced last season (1992) that the new selectors wanted a different perspective.

Some of the old faces like Gary Whetton were missing and the panel consisting of coach Laurie Mains, Earle Kirton and Peter Thorburn, injected players they had seen after many years watching from the sidelines. They chose players they thought would help them in adapting to the new law changes brought into rugby.

From the outside they had also pinpointed problems in the All Blacks that others had commented on and which we on the inside were maybe finding difficult to detect.

Many of us were spoken to before the trials and I for one was given the message about the need for greater fitness and mobility. We were told no matter how many Tests we had played, we would not be picked if we were unfit. Some, like Va'aiga Tuigamala, were told to lose weight. Steve McDowell was warned about his contribution.

At that stage I had no inkling I would end up as the All Black captain, indeed I was even fairly reluctant to captain one of the All Black trial sides. Most conjecture was that Mike Brewer would be the new national skipper and undoubtedly that was Mains' plan until Brewer was injured and unable to play against the World XV.

When he was injured the first thought I had was that I would be captain and I didn't want to do it – I didn't want the responsibility and was just content to muddle along. In hindsight, though, it has been great because I needed some new challenges, an impetus to help my form. But it was a dramatic start because I obviously had some doubts about whether Mains really wanted me to be captain anyway.

But his hand was forced and it was all a bit uneasy and I imagine the players were even being a bit cautious about my appointment.

Things did not go so well leading up to our first Test together. We made a lot of mistakes at training and lost the first match with the World XV 28–14. We had won enough ball but fell down in our use of the possession, before we took the next two Tests, 54–26 and 26–15.

It was a series we all needed in trying to find combinations and sort out some positions for the visit of Ireland, followed by our tour to Australia and South Africa.

It gave many new faces exposure to international competition and all of us much needed groundwork with the changed laws. Mains had put a great deal of effort into making the laws work for us, he had a gameplan based on the Otago style of play which involved some of the hardest training sessions I have ever been involved in.

The players responded; we all knew it was a matter of adapting to the lineout, ruck and maul situations with selective use of possession.

Still, the first Test against Ireland (won 24–21) gave us a fright. Our play was sloppy, perhaps as a hangover from the Auckland game where we had beaten Ireland 62–7.

> 'The first Test against Ireland gave us a fright. Our play was sloppy…and coach Laurie Mains went through with his pre-match promise to drop players not performing'

We all got a shock and Mains went through with his pre-match promise to drop players not performing. Robin Brooke came in at lock and Olo Brown at tighthead prop in some very crucial changes in the pack. Straight away, before the next Test in Wellington, you could tell the difference and we gelled with a 59–6 victory.

While we had had mixed results at home, we left for Australia with great confidence. There were good selections and the management and players believed we would do well against the World Cup champions.

There was, therefore, some disappointment at the end of the series, with the Bledisloe Cup lost 1–2, but we had played some great rugby and there was no points differential between us at the end of three Tests. We should have won the first match in Sydney and perhaps even the second, but mistakes cost us dearly.

Lack of experience told a bit but some of the senior players had also made errors at crucial times, mistakes they would not normally make. But every game we were building and getting better, whereas we felt the Wallabies were stagnating.

That same feeling exists now because we think the Australians are at about the level the All Blacks were in 1989/90 and are starting to plateau out.

'Every game we were building and getting better, whereas we felt the Wallabies were stagnating. The Australians are at about the level the All Blacks were in 1989/90 and are plateauing out'

The idea of the tour was to get a hard core group of 20–25 players who could play test-match rugby. There was one major blemish, with the 17–40 loss to Sydney at Penrith, but those players responded well when they were asked to front up in South Africa.

Before that last section of the year they were perhaps average players, but most have been able to lift themselves to the next level. Some will drop out, but that leaves room for the next group to come through and push for places against the Lions and the tour to England and Scotland at the end of the year.

There was great controversy during Australia about two incidents featuring our loosehead prop Richard Loe. We believed the Aussies had orchestrated something against Loe through the media, and we felt rugby in Australia was the big loser because they wanted to concentrate on those issues rather than them winning the Bledisloe Cup.

The Loe controversy did not worry us too much. We all looked at the video replays and felt there was nothing conclusive about the incidents. What riled us more was Sam Scott-Young's comments slating the Haka and then his efforts to later write to our manager apologizing. That was stupid, but fortunately some other Wallabies were embarrassed by what he had done and told us so.

We are aware of the need for discipline and Mains is very firm on that point. When the tour of Australia finished, we set out for South Africa in the first official All Black visit for 16 years. For much of the Wallaby tour we were not sure whether the visit to the Republic would take place – events were changing daily so that eventually we put it out of our minds until we got the go-ahead.

We were a bit jaded but felt a great honour being the first official team back in South Africa once sanctions had been lifted. Drug testing had been a major issue before the tour, especially through our doctor John Mayhew, but for the players it was not so important – I am sure we have played against many players in the past who have been on drugs.

The passion of the welcome at Johannesburg was extraordinary and we knew we were in for a marvellous experience. The first game against Natal, the Currie Cup champions, was very important to the tour and our 43–25 win imperative for the tour's success.

We had been warned about the size of the forwards but they were not as huge as we expected and certainly not especially mobile.

It was also surprising how the bounce of the ball and the hardness of the grounds did not affect us. I always remember watching footage

'The Richard Loe controversy did not worry us too much...there was nothing conclusive about the incidents. What riled us more was Sam Scott-Young's comments slating the Haka and then his efforts to later write to our manager apologizing. That was stupid'

of previous All Black tours in '70 and '76 and seeing the ball doing acrobatics and players swathed in bandages after grass burns and the like.

By this stage our Test team was fairly settled and we decided to up the tempo of our game even further. We were confident that our grasp of the new laws, our combinations and South Africa's lack of exposure to recent international rugby would tell in our favour.

Refereeing was not good in matches outside the Tests and the South Africans had not adapted to the lineouts. Perhaps in the end, we conned them into trying to put on a good show when they had not practised enough for that strategy.

The 27–24 Test margin at Ellis Park did not really reflect our superiority, as we let in two late tries. It was a gruelling year, but the thing I enjoyed most and look forward to again this season is the younger players coming through, forwards like Jamie Joseph and Arran Pene – guys who at the start of the year were fairly average but

> *'Drug testing had been a major issue before the tour, but for the players it was not so important – I am sure we have played against many players in the past who have been on drugs'*

later made their mark. Grant Fox's steadiness and re-emergence as a potent force, the grunt of Olo Brown in the pack – the promise is there.

There is still more fine-tuning to be done, Mains has lots of other ideas to use with his base of 25 players, he is very organized and constantly thinking about ways to improve our performances.

His preparation and commitment is extraordinary, his flexibility is also a secret to his success. And Earle Kirton is a great foil when Mains gets too intense.

By the end of this year he will start looking towards the next World Cup in South Africa, but now the focus is the Lions, Western Samoa, getting back the Bledisloe Cup and touring England and Scotland. We got some leeway from critics last season but know there will be no such situation this year.

It was a strenuous year, one with plenty of surprises and, from a personal point of view, quite one of the most dramatic in my rugby career.

New Zealand centre Frank Bunce finds his way blocked by Lions Ieuan Evans, Andy Reed and Dewi Morris

NEW ZEALAND'S INTERNATIONAL SEASON 1992

NEW ZEALAND (P9 W6 D0 L3 F262 A178):
Centenary Series
(H)	v	World XV (Christchurch, 18.4.92)	lost	14–28
(H)	v	World XV (Wellington, 22.4.92)	won	54–26
(H)	v	World XV (Auckland, 25.4.92)	won	26–15

Ireland Tour
(H)	v	Ireland (Dunedin, 30.5.92)	won	24–21
(H)	v	Ireland (Wellington, 6.6.92)	won	59–6

Bledisloe Cup
(A)	v	Australia (Sydney,14.7.92)	lost	15–16
(A)	v	Australia (Brisbane,19.7.92)	lost	17–19
(A)	v	Australia (Sydney,25.7.92)	won	26–23
(A)	v	South Africa (Johannesburg, 15.8.92)	won	27–24

All Blacks in Australia (tour record: P11 W8 D0 L3 F400 A173)
(A)	v	W Australia (Perth, 21.6.92)	won	80–0
(A)	v	S Australia (Adelaide, 24.6.92)	won	48–18
(A)	v	NSW (Sydney, 28.6.92)	won	41–9
(A)	v	ACT (Canberra, 1.7.92)	won	45–13
(A)	v	Victoria (Melbourne, 8.7.92)	won	53–3
(A)	v	Queensland (Brisbane, 12.7.92)	won	26–19
(A)	v	Queensland B (Cairns, 15.7.92)	won	32–13
(A)	v	Sydney (Penrith, 22.7.92)	lost	17–40

All Blacks in South Africa (tour record: P5 W5 D0 L0 F167 A79)
(A)	v	Natal (Durban, 1.8.92)	won	43–25
(A)	v	OFS (Bloemfontein, 5.8.92)	won	33–14
(A)	v	Junior SA (Pretoria, 8.8.92)	won	25–10
(A)	v	Central Unions (Witbank, 10.8.92)	won	39–6

New Zealand XV (P2 W2 D0 L0 F50 A36):
(H)	v	England B (Hamilton, 29.6.92)	won	24–18
(H)	v	England B (Pukekohe, 5.7.92)	won	26–18

New Zealand Students (P6 W5 D0 L1 F238 A62):

World Cup (Italy: runners-up)
(–)	v	Romania (Cataia,1.7.92)	won	22–10
(–)	v	Holland (Cataia,4.7.92)	won	118–6
(–)	v	Wales (Catani,8.7.92)	won	15–7
(–)	v	Ireland (q/f: Cagliari, 12.7.92)	won	53–9
(–)	v	Argentina (s/f: Napoli, 16.7.92)	won	21–9
(–)	v	France (f: Rovigo, 19.7.92)	lost	9–21

New Zealand Colts (P1 W1 D0 L0 F20 A10):
(A)	v	Australia U–21 (Brisbane, 19.7.92)	won	20–10

New Zealand Colts in Australia (tour record: P3 W3 D0 L0 F139 A17):
(A)	v	Gold Coast (Brisbane, 12.7.92)	won	83–7
(A)	v	Darling Downs (Toowoomba, 16.7.92)	won	36–0

Super Six tournament: see pp 82–83

CANZ TOURNAMENT

North Auckland 7, North Harbour 29 (Whangarei)
North Harbour 9, Waikato 9 (Takapuna)
Otago 31, Canada 3 (Dunedin)
North Harbour 15, Canada 13 (Takapuna)
North Auckland 49, Canada 13 (Whangarei)
Waikato 47, Otago 15 (Hamilton)
North Auckland 6, Otago 27 (Whangarei)
Waikato 28, Canada 14 (Hamilton)
Otago 19, North Harbour 3 (Dunedin)
Waikato 49, North Auckland 6 (Hamilton)

	P	W	D	L	F	A	Pts
Waikato	4	3	1	0	133	44	14
Otago	4	3	0	1	92	59	12
North Harbour	4	2	1	1	56	48	10
North Auckland	4	1	0	3	68	118	4
Canada	4	0	0	4	43	123	1

Previous winners: 1989 – Waikato; 1990 – Otago; 1991 – no competition (World Cup)

DOMESTIC RUGBY

NATIONAL MUTUAL NATIONAL CHAMPIONSHIP
Division One:

	P	W	D	L	F	A	Pts
Auckland	8	7	0	1	253	127	28
Otago	8	6	0	2	203	147	25
North Harbour	8	6	0	2	222	157	24
Waikato	8	5	0	3	268	153	20
Wellington	8	4	0	4	183	182	18
King Country	8	3	0	5	144	245	12
Canterbury	8	2	0	6	197	198	10
Hawke's Bay	8	2	0	6	131	267	8
North Auckland	8	1	0	7	134	259	7

Semi–finals: Waikato 27, Auckland 21; Otago 26, North Harbour 23. Final: Waikato 40, Otago 5.

Division Two:

	P	W	D	L	F	A	Pts
Taranaki	8	7	0	1	317	150	29
Counties	8	7	0	1	317	91	29
Bay of Plenty	8	5	0	3	171	128	21
Manawatu	8	5	0	3	263	202	21
Southland	8	5	0	3	283	161	21
S Canterbury	8	4	0	4	216	230	17
Wairarapa Bush	8	2	0	6	143	325	8
Poverty Bay	8	1	0	7	100	382	4
Thames Valley	8	0	0	8	133	274	1

Semi–finals: Taranaki 29, Manawatu 18; Counties 31, Bay of Plenty 29. Final: Taranaki 12, Counties 0.

National Sevens: North Harbour 22, Wellington 15.

Ranfurly Shield: *Holders* – Auckland (57 games)
Marlborough 3, Auckland 55 Auckland 21, Otago 16 Hawke's Bay 9, Auckland 40 King
Country 15, Auckland 42 Auckland 49, North Auckland 3 Auckland 47, Canterbury 38
Counties 19, Auckland 24 Auckland 25, North Harbour 16

NEW ZEALAND TEST RESULTS AND SCORERS SINCE 1980

1980:

A(1)	L9–13	Sydney	21 Jun	**p:** Codlin 3
A(2)	W12–9	Brisbane	28 Jun	**t:** Reid
				c: Codlin
				p: Codlin 2
A(3)	L10–26	Sydney	12 Jul	**t:** Fraser
				p: Codlin 2
Fj(a)⁺	W30–6	Suva	23 Jul	**t:** Fraser 3, Allen, B Robertson
				c: Codlin 2
				p: Codlin 2
Fj(b)⁺	W33–0	Auckland	30 Sep	**t:** Osborne 2, K Taylor 2, Wylie, Woodman
				c: Valli 3
				p: Valli
C⁺	W43–10	Vancouver	11 Oct	**t:** M Shaw 3, Mourie, Haden, Osborne, S Wilson, Fraser
				c: Rollerson 4
				p: Rollerson
US⁺	W53–6	San Diego	Oct	**t:** Woodman 3, Osborne 2, Wilson, Allen, Old
				c: Codlin 6
				p: Codlin 3
W	W23–3	Cardiff	1 Nov	**t:** Mourie, Fraser, Allen, Reid
				c: Rollerson 2
				p: Rollerson

1981:

S(1)	W11–4	Dunedin	13 Jun	**t:** Wilson, Loveridge
				p: Hewson
S(2)	W40–15	Auckland	20 Jun	**t:** Wilson 3, Hewson 2, Robertson, Mourie
				c: Hewson 6
SA(1)	W14–9	Christchurch	15 Aug	**t:** Rollerson, Wilson, Shaw
				c: Rollerson
SA(2)	L12–24	Wellington	29 Aug	**p:** Hewson 4
SA(3)	W25–22	Auckland	12 Sep	**t:** Wilson, Knight
				c: Rollerson
				p: Hewson 3, Rollerson
				dg: Rollerson
R	W14–6	Bucharest	24 Oct	**t:** Salmon, Dalton
				p: Hewson
				dg: Rollerson
F(1)	W13–9	Toulouse	14 Nov	**t:** Wilson

				p: Hewson 2
				dg: Hewson
F(2)	W18–6	Paris	21 Nov	t: penalty try, Wilson
				c: Hewson 2
				p: Hewson 2

1982:

A(1)	W23–16	Christchurch	14 Aug	t: Mexted, Mourie, Pokere, Fraser
				c: Hewson 2
				p: Hewson
A(2)	L16–19	Wellington	28 Aug	t: Shaw, Fraser
				c: Hewson
				p: Hewson 2
A(3)	W33–18	Auckland	11 Sep	t: Hewson, Shaw
				c: Hewson 2
				p: Hewson 5
				dg: Hewson, Smith

1983:

BL(1)	W16–12	Christchurch	4 Jun	t: Shaw
				p: Hewson 3
				dg: Hewson
BL(2)	W9–0	Wellington	18 Jun	t: Loveridge
				c: Hewson
				p: Hewson
BL(3)	W15–8	Dunedin	2 Jul	t: Wilson
				c: Hewson
				p: Hewson 3
BL(4)	W38–6	Auckland	16 Jul	t: Wilson 3, Hewson, Hobbs, Haden
				c: Hewson 4
				p: Hewson 2
A	W18–8	Sydney	20 Aug	t: Taylor
				c: Hewson
				p: Hewson 4
S	D25–25	Edinburgh	12 Nov	t: Fraser 2, Hobbs
				c: Deans 2
				p: Deans 3
E	L9–15	Twickenham	19 Nov	t: Davie
				c: Deans
				p: Deans

1984:

F(1)	W10–9	Christchurch	16 Jun	t: Taylor
				p: Hewson 2
F(2)	W31–18	Auckland	23 Jun	t: B Smith, Dalton, Taylor
				c: Hewson 2
				p: Hewson 5
A(1)	L9–16	Sydney	21 Jul	p: Hewson 2
				dg: Hewson
A(2)	W19–15	Brisbane	4 Aug	t: Pokere
				p: Deans 5
A(3)	W25–24	Sydney	18 Aug	t: Clamp, Stone
				c: Deans

p: Deans 5

1985:

E(1)	W18–13	Christchurch	1 Jun	**p:** Crowley 6
E(2)	W42–15	Wellington	8 Jun	**t:** Green 2, Kirwan, Mexted, Hobbs, Shaw
				c: Crowley 3
				p: Crowley 3
				dg: Smith
A	W10–9	Auckland	29 Jun	**t:** Green
				p: Crowley 2
Arg(1)	W33–20	Buenos Aires	26 Oct	**t:** Kirwan 2, Hobbs, Crowley
				c: Crowley
				p: Crowley 4
				dg: Fox
Arg(2)	D21–21	Buenos Aires	2 Nov	**t:** Kirwan 2, Mexted, Green
				c: Crowley.
				p: Crowley

1986:

F(a)	W18–9	Christchurch	28 Jun	**t:** Brewer
				c: G Cooper
				p: G Cooper
				dg: Botica 2, G Cooper
A(1)	L12–13	Wellington	9 Aug	**t:** Brooke-Cowden
				c: G Cooper
				p: G Cooper 2
A(2)	W13–12	Dunedin	23 Aug	**t:** Kirk
				p: G Cooper 2
				dg: G Cooper
A(3)	L9–22	Auckland	6 Sep	**p:** Crowley 3
F(b1)	W19–7	Toulouse	8 Nov	**t:** Shelford
				p: Crowley 3
				dg: Stone, Crowley
F(b2)	L3–16	Nantes	15 Nov	**p:** Crowley

1987:

It*	W70–6	Auckland	22 May	**t:** Kirk 2, Kirwan 2, Green 2, M Jones, Taylor, McDowell, Stanley, A Whetton, penalty try
				c: Fox 8
				p: Fox 2
Fj*	W74–13	Christchurch	27 May	**t:** Green 4, Gallagher 4, Kirk, Kirwan, A Whetton, penalty try
				c: Fox 10
				p: Fox 2
Arg*	W46–15	Wellington	1 Jun	**t:** Kirk, Z Brooke, Stanley, Earl, Crowley, A Whetton
				c: Fox 2
				p: Fox 6
S*	W30–3	Christchurch	6 Jun	**t:** Gallagher, A Whetton
				c: Fox 2.
				p: Fox 6

W*	W49–6	Brisbane	14 Jun	**t:** Kirwan 2, Shelford 2, Drake, Brooke–Cowden, Stanley, A Whetton
				c: Fox 7
				p: Fox
F*	W29–9	Auckland	20 Jun	**t:** Kirk, Kirwan, M Jones
				c: Fox
				p: Fox 4
				dg: Fox
A	W30–16	Sydney	25 Jul	**t:** Fitzpatrick 2, Kirwan, Green
				c: Fox
				p: Fox 3
				dg: Fox

1988:

W(1)	W52–3	Christchurch	28 May	**t:** Kirwan 4, Wright 2, Gallagher, Deans, Shelford, G Whetton
				c: Fox 6
W(2)	W54–9	Auckland	11 Jun	**t:** Kirwan 2, Wright 2, Taylor, Deans, M Jones, McDowell
				c: Fox 8
				p: Fox 2
A(1)	W32–7	Sydney	3 Jul	**t:** Kirwan 2, McDowell, A Whetton, Schuster
				c: Fox 3
				p: Fox 2
A(2)	D19–19	Brisbane	16 Jul	**t:** M Jones, Wright, Kirwan
				c: Fox 2
				p: Fox
A(3)	W30–9	Sydney	30 Jul	**t:** Deans, Gallagher, Kirwan
				c: Fox 3
				p: Fox 4

1989:

F(1)	W25–17	Christchurch	18 Jun	**t:** Wright 2, A Whetton
				c: Fox 2
				p: Fox 3
F(2)	W34–20	Auckland	1 Jul	**t:** Stanley, Deans, Fitzpatrick, A Whetton
				c: Fox 3
				p: Fox 4
Arg(1)	W60–9	Dunedin	15 Jul	**t:** Gallagher 3, Kirwan 2, Wright 2, penalty try, M Jones 2
				c: Fox 7
				p: Fox 2
Arg(2)	W49–12	Wellington	29 Jul	**t:** Wright 2, Deans 2, Gallagher, Kirwan, A Whetton
				c: Fox 6
				p: Fox 3
A	W24–12	Auckland	5 Aug	**t:** Gallagher, Loe
				c: Fox 2
				p: Fox 4
W	W34–9	Cardiff	4 Nov	**t:** Innes 2, Bachop, Wright
				c: Fox 3

				p: Fox 4
I	W23–6	Dublin	18 Nov	t: Gallagher, Wright, Shelford
				c: Fox
				p: Fox 3

1990:

S(1)	W31–16	Dunedin	16 Jun	t: Kirwan 2, Crowley, I Jones, Fox,
				c: Fox 4
				p: Fox
S(2)	W21–18	Auckland	23 Jun	t: Loe
				c: Fox
				p: Fox 5
A(1)	W21–6	Christchurch	21 Jul	t: Fitzpatrick, Crowley, Innes, Kirwan
				c: Fox
				p: Fox
A(2)	W27–17	Auckland	4 Aug	t: Fitzpatrick, Z Brooke, G Bachop
				c: Fox 3
				p: Fox 2
				dg: Fox
A(3)	L9–21	Wellington	18 Aug	p: Fox 2
				dg: Fox
F(1)	W24–3	Nantes	3 Nov	t: Innes, A Whetton
				c: Fox 2
				p: Fox 3
				dg: Fox
F(2)	W30–12	Paris	10 Nov	t: Crowley, M Jones
				c: Fox 2
				p: Fox 6

1991:

Arg(1)	W28–14	Buenos Aires	6 Jul	t: Wright, Earl
				c: Fox
				p: Fox 5
				dg: Crowley
Arg(2)	W36–6	Buenos Aires	13 Jul	t: Z Brooke, M Jones, Kirwan, Wright
				c: Fox 4
				p: Fox 4
A(a1)	L12–21	Sydney	10 Aug	t: I Jones
				c: Fox
				p: Fox 2
A(a2)	W 6–3	Auckland	24 Aug	p: Fox 2
E*	W18–12	Twickenham	3 Oct	t: M Jones
				c: Fox
				p: Fox 4
US*	W46–6	Gloucester	8 Oct	t: Wright 3, Timu, Earl, Purvis, Tuigamala, Innes
				c: Preston 4
				p: Preston 2
It*	W31–21	Leicester	13 Oct	t: Z Brooke, Tuigamala, Hewitt, Innes
				c: Fox 3
				p: Fox 3
C*	W29–13	Lille	20 Oct	t: Timu 2, McCahill, Kirwan, Z Brooke

				c: Fox 3
				p: Fox
A(b)*	L6–16	Dublin	27 Oct	p: Fox 2
S*	W13–6	Cardiff	30 Oct	t: Little
				p: Preston 3

1992:

Wd(1)	L14–28	Christchurch	18 Apr	t: Turner, Tuigamala
				p: Fox 2
Wd(2)	W54–26	Wellington	22 Apr	t: G Cooper 2, Loe 2, Pene, Clarke 2, Tuigamala, Larsen, Strachan
				c: G Cooper 6, Fox
Wd(3)	W26–15	Auckland	25 Apr	t: Pene, Kirwan, Loe, Clarke
				c: G Cooper 2
				p: G Cooper 2
I(1)	W24–21	Dunedin	30 May	t: Henderson, Bunce 2, Clarke
				c: G Cooper 4
I(2)	W59–6	Wellington	6 Jun	t: Bunce 2, Pene 2, I Jones, Clarke, Timu, M Cooper 2, Kirwan, Strachan
				c: M Cooper 6
				p: M Cooper
A(1)†	L15–16	Sydney	14 Jul	t: Tuigamala, Bunce
				c: Fox
				p: Fox
A(2)	L17–19	Brisbane	19 Jul	t: Timu, Kirwan
				c: Fox 2
				p: Fox
A(3)	W26–23	Sydney	25 Jul	t: Bunce, Joseph
				c: Fox 2
				p: Fox 3
				dg: Fox
SA	W27–24	Johannesburg	15 Aug	t: Z Brooke, Kirwan, Timu
				c: Fox 3
				p: Fox 2

1993:

BL(1)	W20–18	Christchurch	12 Jun	t: Bunce
				p: Fox
BL(2)	L7–20	Wellington	26 Jun	t: Clarke
				c: Fox
BL(3)	W30–13	Auckland	3 Jul	t: Bunce, Fitzpatrick, Preston
				c: Fox 3
				p: Fox 3
A	W25–10	Dunedin	17 Jul	t: Fitzpatrick, Bunce
				p: Fox 5

* World Cup matches
' Non-cap tests
† Five-point try introduced from this game onwards

SOUTH AFRICA

Naas Botha
Speaking with Chris Thau

SOUTH Africa's failure on its return to international rugby was not unexpected. The South African media and public were hungry for success, but very few realized how badly the boycott had affected our sport. In 1992, the year of our comeback, we did very badly in the Olympics and we failed in both cricket and soccer. Rugby, they said, would be different. It was not.

The first mistake was to let the Currie Cup go ahead. During our years of isolation, the only meaningful rugby competition we had in South Africa was the Currie Cup, It had become the Holy Grail of South African rugby. For some players winning the Cup was more important than playing for the Springboks.

That is why we should have cancelled the tournament in 1992, to divert the focus back to the national cause. We should have sent the Springboks to Romania and Italy for an early build-up tour. We should have sent the best university side to the Students' World Cup. We should have sent the Under-21 side overseas, no matter where. Before embarking on the major challenges against the All Blacks and Wallabies, we should have tried to broaden our international experience.

That was our biggest mistake prior to a campaign in which we played five Tests and won just one – the first international against France in Lyon. Either side we were beaten by New Zealand and

Australia – results which, nonetheless, gave our people false expectations – and France (in Paris) and England.

Instead, the Currie Cup remained to further fuel provincial rivalries rather than unite a squad of provincial players under the South African banner. During the isolation years, the Springboks concept had lost its meaning, with players becoming attached to provincial values and traditions. This meant that when we came together there was discontent within the squad.

> '*The Currie Cup fuelled provincial rivalries rather than unite a squad of provincial players under the South African banner. During the isolation years the Springboks concept had lost its meaning, with players becoming attached to provincial values and traditions*'

In 1980 South Africa had played nine Tests so we were together in the national side more often than we were with our provinces, In 1981, our last season before the 11-year international boycott, we did not suffer from this problem either. When we went away on the tour to New Zealand we went as a team.

But on the French tour in October 1992 we were not a team; we were a squad of 30 individuals. You could see the factions: the Natal chaps would stick together, the Transvaal boys would be together, and so on. That was the divisive effect of the Currie Cup. There were guys in the squad who had left Northern Transvaal because of me: players who did not want to play with me, even hated me. Suddenly they had to play with me. It is impossible to change one's mentality overnight and decide 'now I like Naas Botha'. It's just impossible. So this was a very difficult problem to overcome.

Then there was the problem of the media. They have become a pressure group, rather than impartial observers. The game has a very high profile in South Africa but our media, unlike the players, do not seem capable of coming to terms with the fact that we are back on a learning curve. Besides, they have fallen into the same 'provincial' trap. They are not South African journalists some of them, but Natal, Transvaal or Northern Transvaal journalists.

After two games in France certain sections of the media were demanding my head. Our 20–15 Test win in Lyon quietened them down, but they were back in full voice after the second Test (lost

16–29). Matters improved in England, where the players felt more at ease. There was no language barrier, the food was similar, generally we felt better and our results improved.

> *'One of the chief problems was that there was no experience of touring. And at home we only set out on a Friday night and arrived back by Sunday morning. Suddenly the guys were being asked to come away for seven or eight weeks. It took about a quarter of the tour for some of them to get into stride'*

The French leg, by contrast, had been a failure statistically speaking, though a success story from a human viewpoint. I was delighted to have been chosen to take South Africa back into the international arena as I am a sports fanatic: be it rugby, golf, soccer, track and field or cricket. It is really great to be a part of the international fraternity again after so many years in the wilderness.

Ours was a very young side in terms of rugby experience. One of the chief problems was that there was no experience of touring. And at home we only set out on a Friday night and arrived back by Sunday morning. Suddenly the guys were being asked to come away for seven or eight weeks. It took about a quarter of the tour for some of them to get into stride. After two weeks one told me: 'I am only starting to relax now. The first week I was worried about the job, about the wife and about the children.'

It was a totally new experience: the beds were new, the hotels were new, the people, the food, even the language were all new. After a week in France all the players started to complain about the food. I personally loved it but for these guys, used to the staple South African diet of meat on the grill and potatoes, it was a problem. So given the chance we headed straight for the nearest McDonald's.

But for all the difficulties encountered I believe that the 1992 tour to France and England, no matter how maligned, will stand out as the turning point in the recent history of South Africa. Without it we would not have known how big was the gap, and how much work is needed to get back to the top. We lost so many matches. So what? It was not the end of the world. Let's look to the future. The foundations for success in the 1995 World Cup were, I believe, laid on that trip.

The Springboks will have to go forward without me, however. My international career is finished although I am still available for

Northern Transvaal. I belong to the generation of players whose careers have been cut short by the sporting boycott, but I have been lucky to have played a fair amount of international rugby.

> *'The tour to France and England, no matter how maligned, will stand out as the turning point in the recent history of South Africa. Without it we would not have known how big was the gap, and how much work is needed to get back to the top'*

I have to admit that it was not an easy decision, but I have been playing year-round rugby in South Africa and Italy for six seasons now and the time has come for me to slow down, especially with my wife Karen having our baby. I want to spend more time with her. But I will continue to coach Pretoria University – the Tukkies – together with Daan du Plessis.

In my six seasons in Italy, playing with Rovigo, we won two Championship titles and played in two other finals. Italy has been a tremendous experience, not only for myself, but for many other South African players unable to tour because of the boycott.

I had been invited to join Rovigo by the former Springbok coach Nellie Smith. It was not very difficult to get used to the new environment because we had Gerd Smal and Tito Lupini at the club. Italian clubs have long looked to well-known international players to increase the profile of the game in the country. They lured Michael Lynagh and John Kirwan to Treviso, Rob Louw to Aquila, David Campese to Milan, myself and Willie Ofahengaue to Rovigo and Zinzan Brooke to Rome. The policy has proved pretty successful. It is true that rugby does not enjoy the cult status of soccer, but it has developed a fairly significant public image, especially in the Venetian region and the north of Italy.

I have been playing continuously since March 1987 – one very long season. I used to play the game in Italy on a Sunday, train with the team on Tuesday and perhaps Thursday, fly to South Africa on Thursday or Friday, play for Northern Transvaal on Saturday, board a flight for Italy on Saturday night, and arrive back on Sunday morning ready for the next championship game. It was tough but I enjoyed it. It was a challenge and I have always enjoyed tough challenges.

I only hope that South Africa relishes equally the challenge of returning to the top of the world rugby order.

SOUTH AFRICA (P5 W1 D0 L4 F79 A130):

(H)	v	New Zealand (Johannesburg, 15.8.92)		lost	24–27
(H)	v	Australia (Cape Town, 22.8.92)		lost	3–26
(A)	v	France (Lyon, 17.10.92)		won	20–15
(A)	v	France (Paris, 24.10.92)		lost	16–29
(A)	v	England (Twickenham, 14.11.92)		lost	16–33

South Africa in France (touring record: P9 W5 D0 L5 F210 A175):

(A)	v	France Espoirs (Bordeaux, 3.10.92)	lost	17–24
(A)	v	Aquitaine (Pau, 7.10.92)	won	29–22
(A)	v	Midi-Pyrenees (Toulouse, 10.10.92)	won	18–15
(A)	v	Provence-Cote D'Azur (Marseille, 13.10.92)	won	41–12
(A)	v	Languedoc-Rousillon (Beziers, 20.10.92)	won	36–15
(A)	v	French Universities (Tours, 28.10.92)	lost	13–18
(A)	v	French Barbarians (Lille, 31.10.92)	lost	20–25

South Africa in England (touring record: P4 W3 D0 L1 F87 A61):

(A)	v	Midlands Division (Leicester, 4.11.92)	won	32–9
(A)	v	England B (Bristol, 7.11.92)	won	20–16
(A)	v	Northern Division (Leeds, 10.11.92)	won	19–3

All Blacks in South Africa (tourists' record: P5 W5 D0 L0 F167 A79):

(A)	v	Natal (Durban, 1.8.92)	won	43–25
(A)	v	Orange Free State (Bloemfontein, 5.8.92)	won	33–14
(A)	v	Junior South Africa (Pretoria, 8.8.92)	won	25–10
(A)	v	Central Unions (Witbank, 10.8.92)	won	39–6

Wallabies in South Africa (tourists' record: P4 W4 D0 L0 F130 A41):

(A)	v	Western Transvaal (Potchefstroom, 11.8.92)	won	46–13
(A)	v	Northern Transvaal (Pretoria, 14.8.92)	won	24–17
(A)	v	Eastern Province (Port Elizabeth, 18.8.92)	won	34–8

South Africa Students (P3 W1 D0 L2 F127 A35):

(–)	v	Argentina[+] (Naples, 2.7.2)	lost	6–15
(–)	v	Taiwan[+] (Naples, 4.7.92)	won	108–0
(–)	v	England[+] (Naples, 8.7.92)	lost	13–20

[+] World Cup (Italy: tenth)

DOMESTIC RUGBY

Currie Cup:
Final: Transvaal 13, Natal 14 (12 September 1992, Ellis Park, Johannesburg)

Transvaal: T van Rensburg; J Small, H Fuhls, J Thompson, P Hendriks; H le Roux, G Wright; H Rodgers, H Roberts, B Swart, K Wiese, L Labuschagne, F Pienaar, I McDonald, J Breedt (capt). *Scorers – Try:* Fuls. *Conversion:* Van Rensburg. *Penalty goals:* Van Rensburg 2.

Natal: H Reece-Edwards; K van der Westhuizen, P Muller, R Muir, A Watson; H Honiball, R du Preez; G Harding, J Allan, L Muller, S Atherton, S Platford, W Bartmann (capt), A Blakeway, G Teichmann. *Scorers – Try:* Teichmann. *Penalty goals:* Reece-Edwards 3.

Referee: F Burger (Western Province).

Urban Section:	P	W	D	L	F	A	Pts
Natal	10	8	1	1	246	175	17
Transvaal	10	6	2	2	373	267	14
Northern Transvaal	10	5	0	5	242	218	10
Western Province	10	4	0	6	205	280	8
Orange Free State	10	3	1	6	236	248	7
Eastern Province	10	2	0	8	152	266	4

Central A Section:	P	W	D	L	F	A	Pts
Western Transvaal	6	4	0	2	142	96	8
Border	6	4	0	2	114	86	8
Northern Free State	6	3	0	3	143	112	6
Eastern Transvaal	6	1	0	5	64	169	2

Central B Section:	P	W	D	L	F	A	Pts
Boland	8	6	0	2	189	132	12
Griqualand W	8	6	0	2	128	77	12
Far North	8	3	1	4	158	185	7
Vaal Triangle	8	3	0	5	140	144	6
SE Transvaal	8	1	1	6	141	218	3

Rural A Section:	P	W	D	L	F	A	Pts
Eastern OFS	6	5	1	0	194	92	11
Stellaland	6	4	1	1	218	76	9
SW Districts	6	4	0	2	162	105	8
NE Cape	6	3	0	3	157	93	6
Northern Natal	6	2	0	4	122	144	4
Lowveld	6	1	0	5	91	154	2
NW Cape	6	1	0	5	36	316	2

Currie Cup roll of honour (since 1980):
1980 Northern Transvaal 1981 Northern Transvaal 1982 Western Province 1983 Western Province 1984 Western Province 1985 Western Province 1986 Western Province 1987 Northern Transvaal 1988 Northern Transvaal 1989 Western Province 1990 Natal 1991 Northern Transvaal 1992 Natal

Lion Cup:
Quarter-finals (22.9.92): NE Cape 14, Northern Transvaal 29; Natal 15, Western Province 13; Orange Free State 34, Eastern Province 2 7; Stella 6, Transvaal 85. **Semi-finals** (29.9.92): Transvaal 21, Northern Transvaal 19; Natal 16, Orange Free State 26. **Final** (9.10.92): Transvaal 17, Orange Free State 12.

SOUTH AFRICA TEST RESULTS AND SCORERS SINCE 1980

1980:

SAm(a1)W24–9	Johannesburg	26 Apr	t: T du Plessis, Mordt, Germishuys
			c: Botha 3
			p: Botha
			dg: Botha
SAm(a2)W18–9	Durban	3 May	t: M du Plessis
			c: Botha
			p: Botha
			dg: Botha 3

BL(1)	W26–22	Cape Town	31 May	t: Louw, W du Plessis, Van Heerden, Germishuys, Serfontein c: Botha 3
BL(2)	W26–19	Bloemfontein	14 Jun	t: Louw, Stofberg, Germishuys, Pienaar c: Botha 2 p: Botha 2
BL(3)	W12–10	Port Elizabeth	28 Jun	t: Germishuys c: Botha p: Botha dg: Botha
BL(4)	L13–17	Pretoria	12 Jul	t: W du Plessis p: Pienaar 2, Botha
SAm(b1)	W22–13	Montevideo	18 Oct	t: Stofberg, Gerber, Berger c: Botha 2 p: Botha dg: Botha
SAm(b2)	W30–16	Santiago	26 Oct	t: Mordt 2, Germishuys 2, Gerber, M du Plessis c: Botha 3
F	W37–15	Pretoria	8 Nov	t: Pienaar, Germishuys, Serfontein, Stofberg, Kahts c: Botha 4 p: Botha 3

Springbok back row Tiaan Strauss in bullish form against France at Lyon; a match in which South Africa won 20–15

1981:

I(1)	W23–15	Cape Town	30 May	**t:** Gerber 2, Louw **c:** Botha **p:** Botha 3
I(2)	W12–10	Durban	6 Jun	**p:** Botha **dg:** Botha 3
NZ(1)	L9–14	Christchurch	15 Aug	**t:** Bekker **c:** Botha **dg:** Botha
NZ(2)	W24–12	Wellington	29 Aug	**t:** Germishuys **c:** Botha **p:** Botha 5 **dg:** Botha
NZ(3)	L22–25	Auckland	12 Sep	**t:** Mordt 3 **c:** Botha 2 **p:** Botha 2
US	W38–7	Glenville		**t:** Mordt 3, Geldenhuys, Germishuys 2, Beck, Berger **c:** Botha 3

1982:

SAm(1)	W50–18	Pretoria	27 Mar	**t:** Gerber 3, Mordt 2, Oosthuizen, C du Plessis, W du Plessis **c:** Botha 6 **p:** Heunis **dg:** Botha
SAm(2)	L12–21	Bloemfontein	3 Apr	**t:** Gerber **c:** Botha **p:** Botha 2

1984:

E(1)	W33–15	Port Elizabeth	2 Jun	**t:** Gerber, C du Plessis, Louw **c:** Heunis 3 **p:** Heunis 5
E(2)	W35–9	Johannesburg	9 Jun	**t:** Gerber 3, Stofberg, Sonnekus, Tobias **c:** Heunis 3, Tobias **p:** Heunis
SAm(1)	W32–15	Pretoria	20 Oct	**t:** Louw, Gerber, Serfontein, Heunis, Mallet **c:** Tobias 2, Gerber **p:** Tobias 2
SAm(2)	W22–13	Cape Town	27 Oct	**t:** C du Plessis, Ferreira, Mordt, Gerber **p:** Tobias 2

1986:

Cv(1)	W21–15	Cape Town	10 May	**t:** C du Plessis **c:** Botha **p:** Botha 3 **dg:** Botha 2
Cv(2)	L18–19	Durban	17 May	**t:** Reinach **c:** Botha **p:** Botha 4
Cv(3)	W33–18	Pretoria	24 May	**t:** Schmidt, Botha, Gerber, Reinach

				c: Botha 4
				p: Botha 3
Cv(4)	W24–10	Johannesburg	31 May	t: Wright
				c: Botha
				p: Botha 5
				dg: M du Plessis

1989:

Wd(1)	W20–19	Cape Town	26 Aug	t: Knoetze, Botha, Smal
				c: Botha
				p: Botha 2
Wd(2)	W22–16	Johannesburg	1 Sep	t: Heunis, M du Plessis
				c: Botha
				p: Botha 3
				dg: Botha

1992:

NZ[†]	L24–27	Johannesburg	15 Aug	t: Gerber 2, P Müller
				c: Botha 3
				p: Botha
A	L3–26	Cape Town	22 Aug	p: Botha
F(1)	W20–15	Lyon	17 Oct	t: Gerber, Small
				c: Botha 2
				p: Botha
				dg: Botha
F(2)	L16–29	Paris	24 Oct	t: Gerber
				c: Botha
				p: Botha 2
				dg: Botha
E	L16–33	Twickenham	14 Nov	t: Smit
				c: Botha
				p: Botha 2
				dg: Botha

1993:

F(1)	D20–20	Durban	26 Jun	t: Schmidt
				p: van Rensburg 5
F(2)	L17–18	Johannesburg	3 Jul	t: Small
				p: van Rensburg 4

* World Cup matches
' Non-cap tests
† Five-point try introduced from this game onwards

THE PLAYERS A-Z

KEY TO INDIVIDUAL STATISTICS

Take the case of Joe Bloggs (right) as an example*. Joe was first capped at senior level for Ireland in 1982, won 2 caps last season, and has 34 caps in all, with 61 points to his credit. He also played in the non-cap International against the Barbarians last season, landing a conversion. In 1993, Joe toured Africa with Ireland but did not play a Test. However, he played in the 1986 IRB Centenary match in Cardiff (Lions 7, The Rest 15) which has been included as a Lions cap. In 1992 he played one Test in the series against New Zealand.

Ireland (1982)		
Last Season	2 caps	3 pts
v Barbarians	1app	2 pts
1993		Tour to Africa
Career	34 caps	61 pts
Lions 1983		
1986		
1992	1 Test	0 pts

Caps (34): **1982** F, E, S, W **1983** NZ(1,2), E, F, W, S **1984** W, F, E, S, Fj **1987** S, E, W, wc–T, W, A **1989** W, S, E, F, Arg(1,2), Fj **1991** F, S, J, W **1993** E, F

Points (61 – 9t, 5c, 4p, 1dg) **1982** F(2t, 1p) S(1t), W(1t) **1983** NZ(1:1dg), E(2t) **1989** Fj(2p) **1991** F(1t), W(2t) **1993** F(1p)

Each player has his caps listed in order, plus a breakdown of his points tally, again in chronological order. For example, Joe marked his debut against France in 1982 with two tries and a penalty goal. If a nation is played more than once in the same year, the statistic is recorded in one of two ways. For a 3-match series against, say, Australia, the statistic reads: A(1,2,3). If our player has previously turned out against the Aussies in the same year, that statistic reads: A(a), followed by A(b1,b2,b3). This makes identification possible when it comes to points scored, e.g. A(b3:1t) means that our player has scored a try against Australia in the third Test of the second series.

---

* The qualification for entry in *The Save & Prosper Rugby Union Who's Who* is involvement in any Test match of any player from the Big Eight nations during the 1992/93 season (May 1992–July 1993). Players' statistics *do* include summer tours. Details of A-team players are logged in the Appendix section (pp 395–405)

Aherne, L. F. P.   Ireland

Full Name: Leslie Fergus Patrick Aherne
Club: Lansdowne
Position: Scrum-half
Height: 5ft 9in (1.76m)
Weight: 12st 10lb (82kg)
Occupation: Civil engineer with Project Management
Born: Cork, 16.3.63
Family: Elaine (wife)
Family links with rugby: Father (Gerald) played for Munster
Former clubs: University College Cork, Dolphin
International debut: Ireland 10, England 21, 1988
Five Nations' debut: Ireland 21, France 26, 1989
Best moment in rugby: Playing for Ireland against 1989 All Blacks
Most respected opponent: Robert Jones (Swansea & Wales)
Best memory last season: Earning Test recall against Australia
Suggestions to improve rugby:
On-field – Differentiate more between penalty and try. *Off-field* –

Ireland (1988)

Last Season	1 cap	0 pts
Career	16 caps	4 pts

Caps (16): **1988** E(b), WS, It **1989** F, W, E, S, NZ **1990** E, S, F, W(R) **1992** E, S, F, A

Points (4 – 1t): **1988** It(1t)

Remuneration for loss of earnings due to rugby – but guard against game going professional
Notable landmarks in rugby career: Represented University College, Cork for four seasons, captaining them to 1984/85 Munster Senior League title and wearing the colours of Irish Universities. Made his Provincial bow with Leinster, after breaking into Ireland team and returning with them from tour of France. Toured with Ireland to North America (1989) and captained Leinster in 1989/90 Irish Inter-Provincial Championship. Bench reserve for Ireland B in 27–12 win over Argentina in 1990/91 and toured Namibia (1991) without making the Test team (played against Namibia B and Namibia South Sub-Union). Included in 1991 World Cup squad, warming bench in all four matches, but returned to Test arena (first start for two years) for trip to Twickenham (1 February) in 1992 Five Nations Championship. After three Championship games, he toured New Zealand with Ireland, captaining the side against Canterbury (lost 13–38), scoring two tries in the 24–58 loss to Manawatu, and also turning out against Poverty Bay–East Coast (won 22–7)

and, as a replacement, Auckland (lost 7–62). Failed to make the Test side but did so on 31 October when winning 16th cap in 17–42 loss to Australia at Lansdowne Road
Touchlines: Golf

Andrew, C. R. England

Full Name: Christopher Robert Andrew
Club: Wasps
Position: Outside-half
Height: 5ft 9in (1.76m)
Weight: 12st 8lb (80kg)
Occupation: Associate director with Debenham, Tewson and Chinnock (chartered surveyors)
Born: Richmond, Yorkshire, 18.2.63
Family: Sara (wife) and Emily (daughter)
Family links with rugby: Brothers (Richard and David) play for Headingley
Former clubs: Middlesbrough, Cambridge University (Blues: 1982, 83, 84), Nottingham, Gordon (Sydney, Aus), Toulouse (Fr)
International debut: England 22, Romania 15, 1985
Five Nations' debut: England 9, France 9, 1985
Best moment in rugby: Beating France 21–19 at Twickenham to win 1991 Five Nations' Grand Slam
Worst moment in rugby: Losing 1990 Grand Slam decider 13–7 to Scotland – losing the World Cup final was disappointing but in a different way; losing England place (1992/93)
Most embarrassing moment: Missing 9 out of 10 kicks at goal for Nottingham at Beeston against London Welsh in fourth round of 1985 John Player Cup (lost 11–12)
Most respected opponent: Michael Lynagh (Australia)
Other sporting achievements: Played first-class cricket for Yorkshire 2nd XI and Cambridge Univ, 1984 and 1985 (as captain). Scored 101 n.o. for Univ against Notts at Trent Bridge (1984)
Best memory last season: Earning selection for British Lions having lost England place
Suggestions to improve rugby: *On-field* – Reduce number of offences for

which kicks at goal are permitted. Be careful not to go too far with rule changes designed to speed up game and make it more entertaining. XV-a-side needs to maintain a distinct identity from Sevens. End season with Five Nations (in March–April). Remove the ten-yard law for offside for players in front of ball (revert to old law). *Off-field* – Allow players to take advantage of commercial activities. RFU are moving in right direction. It's not about making fortunes out of the game – the sums, largely, are peanuts – it's the principal of being able to benefit from our massive commitment to rugby. The game is a multi-million pound industry and should be administered accordingly

Notable landmarks in rugby career: World's most capped outside-half (51 of his 52 caps in the No.10 jersey). Appeared on BBC's *Wogan* after setting then England records for points scored in an international (21: 6p,1dg) and penalties kicked in England's 21–18 win over Wales at Twickenham (17.1.86). Replaced injured Paul Dean (13.6.89) on triumphant Lions tour of Australia and played in last two Tests (1c,1p,1dg in Brisbane second Test). Either side of trip Down Under captained England to win 58–3 in Romania (13.5.89) and British Lions XV to 29–27 success over France (4.10.89) in French Revolution Bicentennial match. Most dropped goals by England international (14). Most capped England outside-half (51). Captained Wasps to 1989/90 Courage Championship and London to 1990 Divisional Championship (having represented North in 1985 and 1986). Non-cap England appearances at Twickenham against centenary Barbarians (29.9.90) and Soviet Union (7.9.91). Moved family, work and rugby to Toulouse after 1991 World Cup but returned with job early in 1992/93 season. Subject to 120-day re-qualification rule which prevented his playing League rugby and doubtless affected his form. Deposed by Stuart Barnes midway through 1993 Five Nations' Championship but regained upper hand on Lions' tour to New Zealand, playing in all three Tests

Touchlines: Gardening and DIY

England (1985)		
Last Season	4 caps	0 pts
Career	52 caps	148 pts
Lions 1989	2 Tests	8 pts
1993	3 Tests	3 pts

Caps (52): **1985** Ro, F, S, I, W **1986** W, S, I, F **1987** I, F, W, wc-J(R), US **1988** S, I(1,2), A(a1,a2), Fj, A(b) **1989** S, I, F, W, Ro, Fj. Lions–A(2,3) **1990** I, F, W, S, Arg(b) **1991** W, S, I, F, Fj, A(a) wc–NZ, It, US, F, S, A(b) **1992** S, I, F, W, C, SA **1993** F, W. Lions–NZ(1,2,3)

Points (148 – 1t,9c,28p,14dg): **1985** Ro(4p,2dg), F(2p,1dg), S(2p), I(2p), W(1c,2p,1dg) **1986** W(6p,1dg), S(2p), I(3c,1p) **1987** F(1dg) **1988** S(1dg), I(1:3c) **1989** S(2p), I(1c,2p), F(1p), W(2p,1dg), Ro(1dg), Fj(1c). Lions–A(2:1c,1p,1dg) **1991** F(1dg), Fj(1t,2dg) wc–NZ(1dg), S(1dg) **1993** Lions–NZ(2:1dg)

Andrews, K. S.   South Africa

Full Name: Keith Steven Andrews
Club: Villagers
Province: Western Province
Position: Tighthead prop
Height: 5ft 11in (1.80m)
Weight: 16st 7lb (105kg)
Occupation: Accountant
Born: Molteno, 3.5.62
International debut: England 33, South Africa 16, 1992
Notable landmarks in rugby career: Educated at Selbourne College in the South African district of East London, Keith played 95 times for Western Province before being selected to tour France and England with the Springboks. The Cape Town-based player appeared in eight of the 13 games – against France B (lost 17–24, Bordeaux, 4.11.92), Provence–Cote D'Azur (won 41–12, Marseille, 13.10.92), Languedoc–Roussillon (won 36–15, Beziers, 20.10.92), French Universities (lost 15–18, Tours 28.10.92) and French Barbarians

South Africa (1992)

Last Season	3 cap	0 pts
Career	3 cap	0 pts

Caps (3): **1992** E **1993** F(1,2)

Points Nil

(lost 20–25, Lille, 31.10.92) on the continental leg; followed by outings against the Midlands Division (won 32–9, Leicester, 4.11.92), England B (won 20–16, Bristol, 7.11.92) and, last but certainly not least, England (14.11.92). His Test debut ended in a 33–16 win for the home side in the first meeting of the two nations at Twickenham in almost 23 years. Keith added to his cap-tally with tighthead appearances in both Tests against France in the Summer of 1993

Armary, L.   France

Full Name: Louis Armary
Club: Lourdes
Position: Prop, hooker
Height: 6ft (1.83m)
Weight: 15st 12lb (101kg)
Occupation: Business executive
Born: Lourdes, 24.7.63
International debut: France 55, Romania 12, 1987
Five Nations' debut: Scotland 23, France 12, 1988
Notable landmarks in rugby career: Scored one and only international try for France in 48–31 second Test reversal at hands of Australia at Ballymore Oval, Brisbane (on 24 June 1990). Represented France in two different positions during 1991/92 season: at hooker against Wales in non-cap Test in Cardiff (4.9.91), and at loosehead prop at Murrayfield and in Paris against Ireland after first-choice Gregoire Lascube had been suspended for his dismissal against England. Last season, however, he remained at loosehead throughout the ten-match campaign and so has now played in 24 cap internationals at prop and 11 at hooker. France's

France (1987)

Last Season	12 caps	0 pts
Career	35 caps	4 pts

Caps (35): **1987** wc–Ro(a). Ro(b) **1988** S, I, W, Arg(b1,b2), Ro **1989** W, S, A(1,2) **1990** W, E, S, I, A(1,2,3), NZ(1) **1991** W(b) **1992** S, I, R, Arg(a1,a2), SA(1,2), Arg(b) **1993** E, S, I, W, SA(1,2)

Points (4 – 1t): **1990** A(2:1t)

most-capped prop is Robert Paparemborde with 55, so Louis still has some way to go yet. He was the only Frenchman to play in every Test in a 1992/93 campaign which ranged from the lows of a first ever home defeat by Argentina and the ignominy of being the only nation beaten by South Africa, to triumph in the 1993 Five Nations' Championship. In that spell the tighthead propping duties were shared between Philippe Gallart and Laurent Seigne. Louis was a member of France's 1991 World Cup squad but one who did not get off the bench. Also captained France B to 27–18 win over Scotland B in Albi. Former skipper of France A in FIRA Championship

Armstrong, G.   Scotland

Full Name: Gary Armstrong
Club: Jed-Forest
Position: Scrum-half
Height: 5ft 8in (1.73m)
Weight: 13st 10lb (87kg)
Occupation: Lorry driver with Mainetti (UK)
Born: Edinburgh, 30.9.66
Family: Shona (wife) and Darren James (son)
Family links with rugby: Father (Lawrence) played for Jed-Forest. Brother (Kevin) plays for Jed-Forest and, formerly, Scotland U-21s
Former club: Jed Thistle
International debut: Scotland 13, Australia 32, 1988
Five Nations' debut: Scotland 23, Wales 7, 1989
Best moment in rugby: Beating England to win 1990 Grand Slam
Worst moment in rugby: Knee injury suffered against Currie (11.1.92) which put me out of the Five Nations' Championship
Most repected opponent: Pierre Berbizier (Agen & France)
Biggest influence on career: Family – mum, dad and wife
Serious injuries: Torn knee, ankle ligaments, damaged elbow, three-quarter tear of medial ligament in left knee (v Currie, Riverside Park, 11.1.92)

Scotland (1988)

Last Season	4 caps	0 pts
Career	28 caps	16 pts
Lions 1989		

Caps (28): **1988** A **1989** W, E, I, F, Fj, Ro **1990** I, F, W, E, NZ(1,2), Arg **1991** F, W, E, I, Ro wc-J, I, WS, E, NZ **1993** I, F, W, E

Points (16 – 4t): **1989** W(1t) **1990** Arg(1t) **1991** W(1t) wc-I(1t)

Suggestions to improve rugby: *On-field* – Give players more time to learn new rules before changing them. Far too many new rules introduced, though happy that try was increased to five points. Still should increase conversion to three points to encourage even more open game. Scrap 90-degree wheel law. There needs to be a more unified interpretation of laws by referees. *Off-field* – Things moving slowly in right direction as regards player welfare. When I was injured in 1991/92 the SRU helped me out financially, but you should not have to go asking for everything. The player should be approached. It was a little embarrassing
Notable landmarks in rugby career: Made splendid recovery from torn knee ligament injury which had kept him out of 1992 Five Nations' campaign and

summer tour to Australia, and was widely considered the outstanding player in the 1993 Championship. Automatic choice for 1993 Lions but the cruel hand of fate touched him again and he was forced to withdraw with a groin injury sustained in the Five Nations' opener against Ireland. Represented Scotland at U-18, Youth, U-21 and twice at B level in 1988, v Italy (won 37–0) and France (won 18–12). Scored hat-trick of tries on B debut against Italians at Seafield, Aberdeen (1987). Selected to tour Australia with 1989 Lions, playing against Australia B (won 23–18), Queensland B (won 30–6), New South Wales B (won 39–19), Australian Capital Territory (won 41–25) and New South Wales Country (won 72–13), and accumulating five tries. But could not budge Wales' Robert Jones from the Test team. An integral part of Scotland's 1990 Five Nations' Grand Slam-winning side and was leading light in the '91 Murrayfield World Cup run to the semi-finals. Scotland A appearance last season was explained by fact that first-choice XV was given run-out in 22–17 win over Italy at Melrose (19.12.92)

Arnold, P. **Wales**

Full Name: Paul Arnold
Club: Swansea
Position: Lock
Height: 6ft 5in (1.95m)
Weight: 15st 9lb (99kg)
Occupation: Rugby development officer for Swansea RFC
Born: Morriston, 28.4.68
Family: Single
International debut: Namibia 9, Wales 18, 1990
Best moment in rugby: Going to Namibia after injured Gareth Llewellyn withdrew
Worst moment in rugby: Missing out on selection for 1992 Five Nations' squad
Most respected opponent: David Waters (Newport & Wales)
Biggest influence on career: Richard Moriarty (Swansea & Wales)
Best memory last season: Swansea's victory over Australia
Suggestions to improve rugby: On-field – Permit non-powered scrum if

Wales (1990)		
Last Season	2 cap	0 pts
Career	12 caps	8 pts

Caps (12): **1990** Na(1,2), Ba **1991** E, S, I, F, A(a) wc–Arg, A(b) **1993** F(R), Z(2)

Points (8 – 2t): **1991** I(1t). wc–Arg(1t)

team loses prop. Abandon new mauling rule – it is ridiculous. Permit support for jumpers in lineout. *Off-field* – Consider introducing win bonuses. Believe that game will go semi-professional by next World Cup. Keep encouraging the kids

Notable landmarks in rugby career: Toured with Wales to Zimbabwe and Namibia last summer, despite only having played 16 minutes of Test rugby during the 1992/93 season (as a 64th minute replacement for Mark Perego in the final game of the campaign, against France in Paris on 20 March). In sixth season at Swansea, having progressed through All Whites' youth set-up. Also gained experience playing in New Zealand (summer 1989). Quickly climbed up representative ladder after making Wales Under-21 debut in 24–10 defeat of Scotland at Ayr (28.4.90). Within five weeks had won a full cap, playing in the 18–9 first Test win over Namibia in Windhoek (2.6.90). Added a B cap in Leiden when helped down Netherlands 34–12 (2.12.90). Made Five Nations debut the following season against Grand Slam '91 England and scored first Test try later in the Championship in the 21st minute of the 21–21 draw with Ireland in Cardiff (16.2.91). Toured Australia in summer 1991 and played twice in World Cup, scoring the solitary Welsh try in a 16–7 win over Argentina (9.10.91). Overlooked for 1992 Championship. Helped Swansea beat touring Wallabies 21–6 last season (4.11.92) and one Wales A cap in 57–12 defeat of Holland at den Bosch (6.2.93)

Touchlines: Sunday soccer, indoor 5-a-side, indoor cricket, squash, swimming

Bachop, G. T. M. New Zealand

Full Name: Graeme Thomas Miro Bachop
Club: Linwood
Province: Canterbury
Position: Scrum-half
Height: 5ft 10in (1.77m)
Weight: 13st (82kg)
Occupation: Carpenter
Born: Christchurch, 11.6.67
Family links with rugby: Stephen (brother) plays for Otago and played four times for Western Samoa in 1991 World Cup, scoring tries against Argentina and Scotland. Switched allegiances to New Zealand and made seven appearances on 1992 tour of Australia and South Africa, though

failed to make Test side

International debut: Wales 9, New Zealand 34, 1989

Notable landmarks in rugby career: Toured Wales and Ireland with the All Blacks in 1989, two years after being a member of the New Zealand Colts team which beat their Australian counterparts 37–12. Indeed, in 1987, he had toured with the All Blacks to Japan, before even having made provincial bow for Canterbury, where he was only third choice. Selected ahead of Canterbury team mate Bruce Deans for first cap against Wales, at Cardiff, and celebrated with try in handsome win. That score was no surprise as he had bagged seven tries in six games on tour of Australia in 1988. Lost automatic place in national side to Auckland's Ant Strachan after World XV won the first Test 28–14 of the centenary series at Christchurch in April 1992. Only outing thereafter came against Australian Capital Territory in 45–13 win at Canberra in July 1992, where he was voted man of the match. It was his 42nd outing for the All Blacks

New Zealand (1989)

Last Season	1 cap	0 pts
Career	19 caps	8 pts

Caps (19): **1989** W, I **1990** S(1,2), A(1,2,3), F(1,2) **1991** Arg(1,2), A(a1,a2). wc-E, US, C, A, S **1992** Wd(1)

Points (8 – 2t): **1989** W(1t) **1990** A(2:1t)

Barnes, S.   England

Full Name: Stuart Barnes
Club: Bath
Position: Outside-half
Height: 5ft 6½in (1.69m)
Weight: 11st 12lb (75kg)
Occupation: Branch manager, Stroud & Swindon Building Society (Bath)
Born: Grays, Essex, 22.11.62
Family: Lesley (wife)
Former clubs: Oxford University, Bristol, Newport
International debut: England 3, Australia 19, 1984
Five Nations' debut: Scotland 33, England 6, 1986
Best moment in rugby: Dropped goal with last kick of extra-time to win 1992 Pilkington Cup final for Bath against Harlequins

Worst moment in rugby: Being dropped by England for first time

Most respected opponent: Peter Winterbottom (Harlequins & England)

Biggest influence on career: Bath coach Jack Rowell (for sustaining my club career after I was dropped from the national side)

Best memory last season: The Calcutta Cup game

Suggestions to improve rugby: *On-field* – Adopt a more positive approach towards rule-changes.

England (1984)

Last Season	2 caps	0 pts
Career	10 caps	34 pts
Lions 1993	Tour to New Zealand	

Caps (10): **1984** A **1985** Ro(R), NZ(1,2) **1986** S(R), F(R) **1987** I(R) **1988** Fj **1993** S, I

Points (34 – 5c,7p,1dg): **1984** A(1p) **1985** NZ(1:1c,1p), NZ(2:2c,1dg) **1986** F(R:2p) **1988** Fj(2c,3p)

There was such a negative approach shown last season, with people refusing to believe they would work. We remained positive at Bath – concentrating on crossing the gain-line and quickly recycling possession – and consequently our form held up. Be more positive. Having only a split-second to operate means that defenders only have a split-second to defend. To me that is the essential concept of modern, attacking rugby. *Off-field* – Something has to be done to help players who commit so much time to the sport. We have to earn a living and put a roof over our heads, yet the commitment sought from us to rugby is awesome. Somehow, the time given up to the game by us players has got to be recognized. Maintaining the amateur ethos is one thing but players will very soon ask whether they really need so much pressure without any reward. The RFU must look seriously at what they are asking of the players. I often train for one and a half hours at lunchtime which hardly leaves me in a fit state for my afternoon business commitments

Notable landmarks in rugby career: Played in three Varsity matches (1981–82–83) and finished on losing side each time. Strangely out of keeping with a playing career in which he has been closely associated with success throughout. In 1989 he made history by becoming the first player to captain a side (Bath) to the English League and Cup double. He has appeared in seven Cup finals at Twickenham – two with Bristol (1863–84), five with Bath (1986–87–89–90–92) – and only once (1984) played on the losing side. Ironically, on that occasion, Bath were the winners (10–9). His last outing of 1991/92 produced a match-winning moment of classic Barnes. With the last kick of extra-time in the Pilkington Cup final at Twickenham, he launched a 40-yard dropped goal which ensured a 15–12 win. Captained England B to a four-win Grand Slam in 1991/92: scoring seven points in 34–3 win over Spain (Madrid, 19.1.92), 11 in 47–15 defeat of Ireland B (Richmond, 31.1.92), 14 as France B were downed 22–18 (Paris, 15.2.92) and eight in a 16–10 close-call against Italy B (Rome, 7.3.92). He then led the B squad on tour in New Zealand (1992), playing in both Test defeats and, on his return, kicked two penalty goals as the B team lost a great contest to South Africa, 16–20 at Bristol (7.11.92). Also captained Barbarians in 16–16 draw with Scotland (Murrayfield, 7.9.91), landing two conversions. Despite being named in England's 33-man 1992 Five Nations' squad, he was not required to add to his cap-tally until the following season when drafted in for the Twickenham Calcutta Cup clash at the expense of Rob Andrew. Heralded as England's saviour, he responded with a magical display as England's back division sparked for the only time in the Championship. Retained his place for the Ireland defeat but again failed to add to his 34-point career contribution to the national cause, amassed since his debut against the Wallabies back in 1984 when he kicked a penalty goal. Ended season on high when selected for Lions tour to New Zealand

Touchlines: Prolific reader of serious literature and consumer of liquid substance from the Bordeaux region of France. Also enjoys horse-watching at Cheltenham

Bartmann, W. J. South Africa

Full Name: Wahl Justice Bartmann
Club: Harlequins (Durban)
Province: Natal
Position: Flanker
Height: 6ft 2in (1.88m)
Weight: 16st 7lb (105kg)
Occupation: Businessman
Born: Florida (RSA), 13.6.63
Former Province: Transvaal
International debut: South Africa 21, NZ Cavaliers 15, 1986
Notable landmarks in rugby career: Influential player who has inspired Natal to two Currie Cup triumphs in three years since switching provincial allegiances from Transvaal. Natal had not previously won South Africa's most prestigious tournament before beating Northern Transvaal 18–12 in 1990 (at Pretoria's Loftus Versfeld Stadium) and Transvaal 14–13 in 1992 (at Ellis Park, Johannesburg). It was in his days at Transvaal, where he played 93 times, that he made his Test debut, playing all four matches in the controversial 1986 series

South Africa (1986)

Last Season	4 caps	0 pts
Career	8 caps	0 pts

Caps (8): **1986** Cv(1,2,3,4) **1992** NZ, A, F(1,2)

Points Nil

against the rebel New Zealand Cavaliers. But he had to wait a further six years before adding to his haul when international sporting relations were restored in 1992. Caps against New Zealand and Australia at home were followed by appearances in both Internationals against France, in Lille and Paris. In all, he made five appearances on the tour of France and England although, unhappily, his English outings were confined to the 32–9 win over the Midlands Division at Leicester's Welford Road on 4 November. He captained the Springboks to a 29–22 defeat of Aquitaine (Pau, 7.10.92) and also turned out in the 18–15 win over Midi-Pyrenees (Toulouse 15.10.92)

Bayfield, M. C. England

Full Name: Martin Christopher Bayfield
Club: Northampton
Position: Lock
Height: 6ft 10in (2.08m)
Weight: 18st 2lb (115kg)
Occupation: Police constable with the Bedfordshire Constabulary
Born: Bedford, 21.12.66
Family: Single
Former clubs: Metropolitan Police, Bedford
International debut: Fiji 12, England 28, 1991
Five Nations' debut: Scotland 7, England 25, 1992
Best moment in rugby: Lions' selection
Worst moment in rugby: England's loss to Wales (1993) and Bedford's first division relegation season of 1989/90
Most respected opponent: Paul Ackford (Harlequins & England)
Suggestions to improve rugby:
On-field – Lifting should be permitted at the line-out. It is a bit of an art and, anyway, everyone does it.
Off-field – Put an end to confusion over amateurism. Personally I believe money spells bad news for rugby. But while there should be no financial reward for playing, there is no reason why players should not be reimbursed for loss of earnings and even given a free holiday with their family each year

England (1991)

Last Season	6 caps	0 pts
Career	12 caps	0 pts
Lions 1993	3 Tests	0pts

Caps (12): **1991** Fj, A **1992** S, I, F, W, C, SA **1993** F, W, S, I. Lions–NZ(1,2,3)

Points Nil

Notable landmarks in rugby career: The tallest forward to play for England, he played three games for England 18-Group, represented Midlands Division and British Police for three seasons, toured with British Police to Italy (1989) and broke into England B set-up during 1990/91 season, playing against Emerging Australians (12–12, Wasps 4.11.90) and Italy (12–9, Waterloo 27.3.91). Progressed to England squad for 1991 tour to Fiji and Australia, playing in both Tests after Wade Dooley sustained hand injury. Missed out on the World Cup squad but, following Paul Ackford's retirement, booked a permanent berth alongside Dooley in England's 1992 Grand Slam XV. Reverted to England B for summer of '92 tour to New Zealand, where he played in both 'Tests' losses to the All Black XV (lost 18–24, Hamilton, 28.6.92; lost 18–26, Pukekohe, 5.7.92). Returned to the senior side once back in Blighty and played the full season, doubling his cap-tally to a dozen, before being one of 16 Englishmen to tour with the British Lions in New Zealand

Touchlines: Weight training

Benazzi, A.   France

Full Name: Abdelatif Benazzi
Club: Agen
Position: No 8, flanker
Height: 6ft 6in (1.98m)
Weight: 17st 5lb (111kg)
Occupation: Sales representative
Born: Oujda, Morocco, 20.8.68
Former club: Cahors
International debut: Australia 21, France 9, 1990
Five Nations' debut: England 21, France 19, 1991
Notable landmarks in rugby career: Sent-off after 14 minutes of full debut in first Test against Australia in Sydney. But modest 14-day ban meant he was able to play in next two Tests of the series at flanker. Switched to second row for visit of All Blacks to Nantes (1990) and it was six internationals before he finally adopted his favoured No.8 berth. Came to France by way of Czechoslovakia where, while on tour with Morocco, he met up with a touring fourth division French club. On learning he wanted to play in France, they advised him to join

France (1990)

Last Season	7 caps	0 pts
Career	18 caps	0 pts

Caps (18): **1990** A(1,2,3), NZ(1,2) **1991** E, US(1R,2) wc–Ro, Fj, C **1992** SA(1R,2), Arg(b) **1993** E, S, I, W

Points Nil

Cahors. This he did before switching, a year later, to Agen, for whom he appeared in the 1990 French Cup final. Represented Morocco in the African zone of the 1991 World Cup qualifying rounds, against Belgium in Casablanca, and then France in the final stages. Became the first Moroccan to play at Twickenham when making Five Nations' debut for France in the 1991 Grand Slam decider. Suspended indefinitely during 1991/92 season by the French Federation after being sent-off for fighting with Eric Champ in an Agen–Toulon Cup match on 2 May 1991. The ban ruled him out of France's summer tour of Argentina but he was back in the engine room shortly afterwards, coming on as a 50th minute replacement for Jean-Marie Cadieu in the Test loss to South Africa, in Lyon on 17 October. Started the next six internationals, playing in historic home loss to Argentina but also in 1993 Championship triumph. Injury marred his 1993 Tour to South Africa

Benetton, P. France

Full Name: Philippe Benetton
Club: Agen
Position: Flanker, No 8
Height: 6ft 3in (1.90m)
Weight: 15st (95kg)
Occupation: Sports instructor with Agen council
Born: Cahors, 17.5.68
Former club: Cahors
International debut: France 27, British Lions 29, 1989
Five Nations' debut: England 16, France 15, 1993
Notable landmarks in rugby career: Marked his senior debut with a try against the 1989 British Lions, masquerading as a Home Unions XV, in the Paris floodlit international staged to mark the bicentenary of the French Revolution. In common with Abdel Benazzi, Michel Courtiols and Denis Charvet, he began his playing career with Cahors before switching to Agen in 1988. At international level Philippe graduated through the Under-21 and B set-ups. He missed out on the 1990 and 1991 Five

France (1989)

Last Season	11 caps	10 pts
Career	13 caps	14 pts

Caps (13): **1989** BL **1991** US(2) **1992** Arg(a1,a2R), SA(1R,2), Arg(b) **1993** E, S, I, W, SA(1,2)

Points (14 – 3t): **1989** BL(1t) **1993** W(2t)

Nations' Championships, unable in the latter to displace Xavier Blond from the blindside berth. However, he re-emerged on France's 1991 tour to North America, winning his second cap in the 10–3 second Test win over the US Eagles. The match, staged in Colorado Springs, was abandoned at half-time due to lightning. Although included in the 26-man World Cup squad, he remained redundant through France's four matches, and at first remained so after former club mate Pierre Berbizier had succeeded Jacques Fouroux as national coach. However, not only did he return to Test favour in 1992/93, he played in the last nine internationals. Having missed the contest with Romania at Le Havre in May '92, he toured Argentina and played in both Tests, the second as a 59th minute replacement for Jean-Marie Cadieu. He was benched for the next game – the defeat by South Africa at Lyon – but again came on in the second period, this time for Jean-Francois Tordo. From that time on he became first-choice blindside and finished the season on a high: France won the 1993 Championship and Philippe scored two tries in the title-clinching 26–10 defeat of Wales (Paris, 20.3.93). Played in both Tests on Summer tour to South Africa

---

Bernat-Salles, P.   France

Full Name: Philippe Bernat-Salles
Club: Pau
Position: Wing
Height: 5ft 11½in (1.81m)
Weight: 11st 8lb (74kg)
Occupation: Commercial agent
Born: 17.7.70
International debut: France 20, Argentina 24, 1992
Five Nations' debut: None
Notable landmarks in rugby career: Marked second cap with three-try show against Romania in 37–20 win (May 1993). Previously earned full international recognition against Argentina, not in South America as he would have initially hoped – having toured there with France in the summer of '92 (scoring tries against Cordoba,

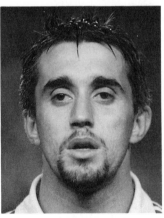

Buenos Aires and Cuyo) – but at Nantes, where the Pumas came, saw and historically conquered on 14 November 1992. France lost 20–24, their first ever home loss to the Pumas, and Philippe was one of many who paid the price for team failure. He was dropped down a notch on the representative ladder and turned out on the right wing for France B at Leicester, on 15 January 1993, where England A triumphed 29-17. Eleven months earlier, on 2 February 1992, he had made his B debut in the 27–18 win over Scotland B in Albi. He was reunited with Scotland in April 1993 as a member of the French team which contested the World Cup Sevens at Murray-field. Played both summer Tests to South Africa

France (1992)		
Last Season	4 cap	15 pts
Career	4 cap	15 pts
France VII 1993		World Cup

Caps (4): **1992** Arg(b) **1993** R,SA(1,2)

Points (15-3t): **1993** R(3t)

Berty, D. France

Full Name: David Berty
Club: Toulouse
Position: Wing
Height: 5ft 11in (1.80m)
Weight: 13st 5lb (85kg)
Occupation: PR representative
Born: 11.6.70
International debut: France 12, New Zealand 30, 1990
Five Nations' debut: None
Notable landmarks in rugby career: Flirted with international selection for the past three years since making his debut on the left wing against New Zealand on 10 November 1990. The All Blacks triumphed easily in the Parc des Princes and David subsequently lost his place in the squad for the 1991 Five Nations' Championship. However, he continued an association with the national A and B teams which had yielded B caps against Wales and Scotland in the 1989/90 season. It was not until 20 May 1992 that he returned to the senior XV, coming on as a 37th

France (1990)		
Last Season	1 cap	0 pts
Career	2 caps	0 pts
France VII 1993		World Cup

Caps (2): **1990** NZ(2) **1992** R(R)

Points Nil

minute replacement for Sebastien Viars in the 25–6 defeat of Romania at Le Havre. Thereafter, he was overlooked for the two-Test series against South

Africa, despite helping France B to a 24–17 win over the Springboks in Bordeaux on 4 October, the visit to Nantes of Argentina and the 1993 Five Nations' Championship, though he did represent France at Murrayfield in the inaugural World Cup Sevens

Bidgood, R. A.   Wales

Full Name: Roger Anthony Bidgood
Club: Newport
Position: Centre
Height: 6ft (1.83m)
Weight: 14st 4lb (91kg)
Occupation: Fireman at Whitchurch Fire Station
Born: Caerphilly, 15.9.65
Family: Deborah (wife)
Former clubs: Glamorgan Wanderers Youth, Pontypridd, Pontypool (two spells), Cardiff
International debut: Wales 15, Scotland 12, 1992
Five Nations' debut: As above
Best moment in rugby: Finally making Wales debut, five years after first selected
Worst moment in rugby: Missing potential debut (Wales 11, Ireland 15, Cardiff 1987) after match was postponed
Most embarrassing moment in rugby: Tackling a goal post and being taken to hospital with concussion

Wales (1992)		
Last Season	3 caps	5 pts
Career	4 caps	5 pts

Caps (4): 1992 S 1993 Z(1,2), Na

Points (5 – 1t): 1993 Z(2:1t)

Most respected opponent: Tony Bond (Sale, Askeans & England)
Biggest influence on career: Tom Hudson (Newport coach)
Serious injuries: Shoulder operation – tendon shortened (1988)
Best memory last season: Touring Africa with Wales and playing in all three Tests
Suggestions to improve rugby: *On-field*: Happy with five points for a try; promises to make the game more exciting for players and spectators alike. *Off-field*: As long as I keep my place in the Welsh team I am happy
Notable landmarks in rugby career: Thought his chances of a Wales cap had gone when freezing weather postponed Wales' 1987 Championship match against Ireland. Had been selected in place of the injured John Devereux but by

the time the match was rearranged Devereux was fit. Won two Wales Youth caps (v F,E) in 1984 whilst with Glamorgan Wanderers. During time at Pontypool, represented Wales B twice against France B – at Pontypridd in October 1986 (won 13–10) and at Begles in October 1987 (lost 0–26). Helped Newport win 1990/ 91 Heineken League division one title in his first season with the club and belatedly received his first full cap against Scotland (21.3.92). Roger, who has also represented Monmouthshire Counties, Crawshays and the Barbarians, took his cap-tally to four with appearances against Zimbabwe (two) and Namibia on tour last summer, scoring try in 42–13 second Test defeat of Zimbabwe in Harare (29.5. 93)

Touchlines: Snooker

Boobyer, N. Wales

Full Name: Neil Boobyer
Club: Llanelli
Position: Centre
Height: 5ft 10in (1.78m)
Weight: 12st (76kg)
Occupation: Student at Bridgend Technical College
Born: Bridgend, 11.6.72
Family: Single
Family links with rugby: Father (Brian) played for Tondu and Bridgend Sports
International debut: Zimbabwe 13, Wales 42, 1993
Five Nations' debut: None
Best moment in rugby: Making full Wales debut in Harare on 29 May 1993
Worst moment in rugby: Missing out on selection for Wales Youth against Italy
Most respected opponent: Mike Hall (Cardiff & Wales)
Best memory last season: Picking up two full caps in Zimbabwe and Namibia

Wales (1993)		
Last Season	2 caps	0 pts
Career	2 caps	0 pts

Caps (2): 1993 Z(2), Na

Points Nil

Suggestions to improve rugby: *On-field* – Reduce worth of penalty goal to two points. *Off-field* – Keep players together after Under-21, perhaps with a Wales Under-23 side
Notable landmarks in rugby career: Played a full and active role for Wales

130

Under-19s, turning out against Scotland and then touring to Canada and playing against that nation. There was also a Welsh Youth cap (won against Japan) for the family sideboard before, in 1991/92, Neil was selected to represent Wales Under-21s against Scotland Under-21s (17.4.92), a match in which the Welsh extended their monopoly in the fixture to six wins from six starts. Helped Scarlets to League and Cup double in 1992/93 before being selected for Wales' summer tour to Africa where made full international debut in 42–13 second Test win over Zimbabwe, partnering Newport's Roger Bidgood in midfield. Picked up second cap against Namibia (won 38–23, Windhoek, 5.6.93) in addition to turning out against Zimbabwe B (one try), Namibia B (two tries) and the South African Barbarians. Also represented Wales A against North of England (won 21–13, Pontypool, 14.10.92) and as a 14th minute replacement for clubmate Ian Jones in 11–24 loss to Australia (Cardiff, 7.11.92)

Touchlines: Golf, swimming, football

Botha, H. E.   South Africa

Full Name: Hendrik Egnatius (Naas) Botha
Club: Normaal College Pretoria
Province: Northern Transvaal
Position: Outside-half
Height: 5ft 10in (1.78m)
Weight: 12st 4lb (78kg)
Occupation: Businessman
Born: Breyten, 27.2.58
Family: Karen (wife) – represented South Africa in long-jump at 1992 Barcelona Olympics
International debut: South Africa 24, South America 9, 1980
Other sporting achievements: American football with Dallas Cowboys (1983); softball and baseball for Northern Transvaal
Notable landmarks in rugby career: One of the legends of the

game despite South Africa's limited involvement in international competition since his debut in 1980. His tally of 312 points places him fifth on the all-time list behind Australia's Michael Lynagh (760), New Zealand's Grant Fox (605), Scotland's Gavin Hastings (424) and France's Didier Camberabero (354). His haul includes a world record 18 dropped goals and his feat of landing three dropped goals in a Test (which he has performed twice) matches the world's

best. Even during the boycott he continued to travel, spending a brief spell in American football with the 1983 Dallas Cowboys, and rather longer with Rovigo in Italy, where he spends his winters playing against the likes of Lynagh and David Campese. On the domestic front he has picked up winners' medals in nine out of 11 Currie Cup finals playing in the colours of Northern Transvaal. His domination of the 1987 final, for instance, was absolute. The Blue Bulls beat Transvaal 24–18 with Naas kicking four penalties and four dropped goals
Touchlines: Golf (3-handicap)

South Africa (1980)

Last Season	5 caps	44 pts
Career	28 caps	312 pts

Caps (28): **1980** SAm(a1,a2), BL(1,2,3,4), SAm(b1,b2), F **1981** I(1,2), NZ(1,2,3), US **1982** SAm(1,2) **1986** Cv(1,2,3,4) **1989** Wd(1,2) **1992** NZ, A, F(1,2), E

Points (312 – 2t,50c,50p,18dg): **1980** Sam(a1:3c,1p,1dg), Sam(a2:1c, 1p,3dg), BL(1:3c), BL(2:2c,2p), BL(3:1c,1p,1dg), BL(4:1p), Sam (b1:2c,1p,1dg), Sam(b2:3c), F(4c,3p) **1981** I(1:1c,3p), I(2:1p, 3dg), NZ(1:1c,1dg), NZ(2:1c,5p, 1dg), NZ(3:2c,2p), US(3c) **1982** Sam(1:6c,1dg), Sam(2:1c,2p) **1986** Cv(1:1c,3p,2dg), Cv(2:1c, 4p), Cv(3:1t,4c,3p), Cv(4:1c,5p) **1989** Wd(1:1t,1c,2p), Wd(2:1c, 3p,1dg) **1992** NZ(3c,1p), A(1p), F(1:2c,1p,1dg), F(2:1c,2p,1dg), E(1c,2p,1dg)

Bradley, M. T.   Ireland

Full Name: Michael Timothy Bradley
Club: Cork Constitution
Position: Scrum-half
Height: 5ft 10in (1.78m)
Weight: 13st 2lb (83kg)
Occupation: Sales manager with Top Security (Cork)
Born: Cork, 17.11.62
Family: Gillian (wife)
Family links with rugby: Father (Austin) played for Cork Constitution; he also played amateur international soccer for Ireland
International debut: Ireland 9, Australia 16, 1984
Five Nations' debut: Scotland 15, Ireland 18, 1985
Best moment in rugby: Captaining

Cork Constitution to 1990/91 All-Ireland League victory and beating England in Dublin last season

Worst moment in rugby: Ireland losing 3–35 to England at Twickenham in 1988, having led 3–0 at half-time

Most respected opponent: Nick Farr-Jones (NSW & Australia)

Serious injuries: Torn ankle ligaments (1990)

Best memory last season: The look of delight on Noel Murphy's face when we beat England

Ireland (1984)
Last Season	6 caps	0 pts
Career	29 caps	16 pts

Caps (29): **1984** A **1985** S, F, W, E **1986** F, W, E, S, Ro **1987** E, S, F, W(a) wc–W(b), C, T, A **1988** S, F, W, E(a) **1990** W **1992** NZ(1,2) **1993** S, F, W, E

Points (16 – 4t): **1986** Ro(1t) **1987** F(1t) wc–C(1t) **1988** S(1t)

Suggestions to improve rugby: *On-field* – Happy with the new ruck/maul law because we won two games! I'm not about to advocate change now. *Off-field* – The respective Unions should listen to the players and, if they are having problems, actually act rather than paying homage to the notion. Players should receive bonus payments for International matches and reimbursement for loss of earnings. In my own work situation I have twice asked my employers whether they want me to get involved again. On each occasion they have said 'yes' but had their answer been 'no' then that would have been it. When it comes to promotion, rugby players who need time away often get passed over by others who are there all the time. There is reason for them to be to compensated for that or for the Unions, at the very least, to understand the situation that exists

Notable landmarks in rugby career: Succeeded Phil Danaher as Ireland captain during 1992 tour to New Zealand and retained the honour throughout the 1993 Five Nations' Championship, inspiring an upturn in Irish fortune. His finest hour came in the 17–3 win over Ireland at Lansdowne Road, an occasion he marked by becoming Ireland's most-capped scrum-half (29). Played four games for Irish Schools and captained them on 1980 tour of Australia. Captained Irish U-19s and U-21s. Completed journey up representative ladder with appearances for U-25s and B (1983 against Scotland). Chosen as replacement for Ireland in 1984 before having played provincial rugby for Munster. Played in Ireland's 1985 Triple Crown-winning side. Returned to Ireland's B team in 1990/91 and captained side to victories over Argentina (27–12, Limerick 20.10.90) and England (24–10, Old Belvedere 1.3.91). Scored try in defeat of touring Pumas. Unused replacement in Ireland's 20–18 win over Argentina (1990/91). Led Cork Constitution to 1990/91 All-Ireland League title. Played in both Tests on '92 New Zealand tour, taking over the captaincy for the second match, in Wellington. Ireland lost 6–59 and Michael lost his place for the next outing, against Australia in Dublin. However, he returned as skipper for the International Championship, leading the side to wins over Wales and England

Touchlines: Golf, landscaping in Robert Kennedy's garden (summer house)

Player to watch: Ciaran Clarke, Peter Clohessy and Eric Elwood (all Ireland)

Player of the year: Jean-Francois Tordo (France)

Breedt, J. C.   South Africa

Full Name: Jannie Breedt
Province: Transvaal
Position: No 8
Height: 6ft 4in (1.93m)
Weight: 15st 6lb (97kg)
Age: 34 years
International debut: South Africa 21, New Zealand Cavaliers 15, 1986
Notable landmarks in rugby career: An immediate success when given his international debut against the rebel New Zealand Cavaliers in 1986, Jannie was sorely missed by the Springboks six years later when he opted to renew his contract to coach and play in Italy while South Africa toured France and England. Even if Tiaan Strauss did flourish in his absence, there was little doubt the tourists missed Breedt's experience. After all, here was a man who had helped defeat the Cavaliers 3–1 in '86, then captained South Africa to a 2–0 Test series win over the IRB-sanctioned but still mighty controversial First National Bank World XV in 1989 (winning 20–19

South Africa (1986)		
Last Season	2 caps	0 pts
Career	8 caps	0 pts
Caps (8): **1986** Cv(1,2,3,4) **1989** Wd(1,2) **1992** NZ, A		
Points Nil		

in Cape Town and 22–16 in Johannesburg), and South Africa were heading into the big wide world without him. But having taken his cap tally to eight with appearances against New Zealand (lost 24–27, Johannesburg, 15.8.92) and Australia (lost 3–26, Cape Town, 22.8.92) he decided to forego the rigours of a 13-match tour itinerary. He finished the domestic 1992 season by captaining Transvaal to the 1992 Currie Cup final where, at Ellis Park, Johannesburg, they lost 13–14 to Natal. He had also been on the losing side in 1986 when Transvaal were beaten 22–9 by Western Province.

Brewer, M. R. New Zealand

Full Name: Michael Robert Brewer
Province: Otago
Position: Flanker, No 8
Height: 6ft 5in (1.95m)
Weight: 14st 13lb (95kg)
Born: Pukekohe, 6.11.64
International debut: New Zealand 18, France 9, 1986
Serious injuries: Damaged hip, foot, torn calf muscle
Notable landmarks in rugby career: Career ravaged by injury. Mike has been restricted to 19 Test appearances since marking his debut in Christchurch with a try against the beaten French. Two World Cups have passed him by while in 1992, on the day he was due to be named All Black captain, he was again crocked (torn calf muscle in final trial) and missed the three centenary Tests as well as the first test against Ireland. Captain of Otago in 1986 at the tender age of 21, Mike was also an everpresent in the New Zealand side that year, after making his debut for the baby All Blacks at No 8. He was transformed into a flanker on the 1987 tour to Japan. A hip injury

New Zealand (1986)

Last Season	2 caps	0 pts
Career	19 caps	4 pts

Caps (19): **1986** F(a), A(1,2,3), F(b1,b2) **1988** A(1) **1989** A, W, I **1990** S(1,2), A(1,2,3), F(1,2) **1992** I(2), A(1)

Points (4 – 1t): **1986** F(a:1t)

ruled him out of the 1987 World Cup, and thus robbed him of a winners' medal when the All Blacks beat France 29–9 in the Auckland final. Since then a combination of further injury and the competition for places with Michael Jones has severely limited his outings. Toured Australia in 1988 and, the following year, Ireland and Wales. His openside wing-forward play won a host of British admirers and it was little wonder that he featured in all seven Tests in 1990. Controversially omitted from the 1991 World Cup squad after failing an early fitness test ordered by the NZRU. Returned in 1992 for second Test against Ireland, a 59–6 thumping of the tourists in Wellington, before his progress was again interrupted by injury after 65 minutes of the first match in the Bledisloe Cup series against Australia. Prior to that he had skippered the side to wins over South Australia (scoring a try) and ACT. Captained Otago to 1991 national championship before, at the end of the 1992 campaign, his eighth year in charge, he relinquished the reins. Has made a total of 47 appearances for the All Blacks

Brooke, R. M.   New Zealand

Full Name: Robin Brooke
Province: Auckland
Position: Lock
Height: 6ft 5½in (1.96m)
Weight: 15st 12lb (101kg)
Born: 10.1.67
Family links with rugby: Zinzan (brother) plays for Auckland and New Zealand (20 caps); Martin (brother) a former New Zealand triallist
International debut: New Zealand 59, Ireland 6, 1992
Notable landmarks in rugby career: Settled remarkably easily into the New Zealand team in 1992 after being given his chance against Ireland in Wellington on 6 June. It might have come earlier for Robin had he not missed the national trials in favour of club commitments in Italy. As one of three All Black debutants that June day – along with Auckland prop Olo Brown and Waikato fullback Matthew Cooper – he partnered Ian Jones in the engine room as the Irish were routed 59–6.

New Zealand (1992)

Last Season	8 caps	0 pts
Career	8 caps	0 pts

Caps (8): **1992** I(2), A(1,2,3), SA **1993** BL(1,2,3)

Points Nil

His performance earned him a berth on the tour to Australia where he played alongside Jones in all three matches of the Bledisloe Cup series. But it was in Johannesburg on 15 August that Robin enjoyed his finest hour. With brother Zinzan, he was the star performer as New Zealand beat South Africa for the first time on African soil, 27–24. In addition to the Tests he turned out in the wins over Western Australia (80–0), New South Wales (41–9) and Queensland (26–19), while in South Africa he enjoyed that winning feeling against Junior South Africa (25–10) in Pretoria. A member of the New Zealand Maoris since 1988, Robin took part in their two tours during 1992: the first, an internal jaunt in May, took in wins against King Country (27–6) and a New Zealand President's XV (30–11). The second involved visits to the Pacific Islands (Rarotonga, Tonga, Western Samoa and Fiji) in October and November. First-choice lock in all three Tests against 1993 Lions

Brooke, Z. V.   New Zealand

Full Name: Zinzan Valentine
Brooke
Club: Marist
Province: Auckland
Position: No 8, flanker
Height: 6ft 3in (1.90m)
Weight: 15st 9lb (99kg)
Occupation: Courier
Born: Waiuku, 14.2.65
Family links with rugby: Martin
(brother) is a former New Zealand
triallist; Robin plays for Auckland,
Maoris and New Zealand (8 caps)
International debut: New Zealand
46, Argentina 15, 1987
Serious injuries: Broken ankle
(1991)
**Notable landmarks in rugby
career:** A product of the 1985 New
Zealand Colts team, Zinzan is
regarded as one of the world's
outstanding back row figures. He
has represented Auckland since
1986 and the All Blacks since
scoring one of their six tries in the
46–15 win over Argentina on his
debut in June 1987, at the inaugural
World Cup. Came to the fore when
succeeding captain Wayne Shelford
at No 8 after the Scotland series in
1990. But although he played in all

New Zealand (1987)

Last Season	6 caps	5 pts
Career	20 caps	25 pts

Caps (20): **1987** wc–Arg **1989** Arg(2R)
1990 A(1,2,3), F(1R) **1991**
Arg(2), A(a1,a2). wc–E, It, C,
A(b), S **1992** A(2,3), SA **1993**
BL(1,2,3R)

Points (25 – 6t): **1987** wc–Arg(1t) **1990**
A(2:1t) **1991** Arg(2:1t).
wc–It(1t), C(1t) **1992** SA(1t)

three Tests against Australia that year he was injured and replaced in the first
Test against France in Nantes and lost his place for the next International.
Returned strongly in 1991, after recovering from a broken ankle, and was the
All Black's first-choice No 8 through the World Cup, a personal campaign
which featured tries against Italy and Canada. An impressive Sevens player, he
captained New Zealand to victory in the 1989 and 1990 Hong Kong Sevens.
Auckland, too, have greatly benefited from his talents as he scored 74 tries for
them in his first 77 outings. Made ten appearances on the All Blacks' tour of
Australia and South Africa in 1992, playing in three of the four Tests and
captaining the side to a 53–3 win over a Victorian XV in Melbourne. Indeed, it
was his try-scoring performance that July day which was largely responsible for
returning him to the Test side after Arran Pene had been preferred to him for

the first Wallaby mission. A year which had begun in Italy where he and brother Robin chose to play club rugby rather than attend the key All Black trials in April, ended triumphantly with the Brooke brothers supreme in New Zealand's famous 27–24 defeat of South Africa in Johannesburg. The game, which included Zinzan's sixth Test try, marked his 50th All Black appearance

Brown, O. M. New Zealand

Full Name: Olo Brown
Province: Auckland
Position: Tighthead prop
Height: 6ft 0½in (1.85m)
Weight: 15st 11lb (100kg)
Born: Western Samoa, 24.10.67
International debut: New Zealand 59, Ireland 6, 1992
Notable landmarks in rugby career: First represented the All Blacks in 1990 when, having been flown out to join the tour of France as a replacement, he was thrust into the fray against France A in the Stade Marcel Deflandre, La Rochelle. The date was 6 November and the tourists won 22–15. Three months earlier he had helped Auckland beat the touring Australians 16–10 at Eden Park. Although overlooked for the Argentina tour and the World Cup in 1991, a fine display for the Saracens team which beat a New Zealand XV 20–15 in one of the national trial matches speeded his return to the big time. Having also

New Zealand (1992)

Last Season	8 caps	0 pts
Career	8 caps	0 pts

Caps (8): 1992 I(2), A(1,2,3), SA 1993 BL(1,2,3)

Points Nil

helped Auckland destroy Ireland 62–7 at Eden Park (23 May), weighing in with one of his team's 11 tries, his Test debut followed soon after (6 June) when selected in place of Richard Loe for the second International against the Irish in Wellington, which resulted in a 59–6 win for the host nation. Auckland team mate Robin Brooke and Waikato's Matthew Cooper also made their debuts that day. After that Olo was retained for the tour of Australia and South Africa, figuring as first-choice tighthead in the nine weekend engagements, including all four Test matches. He failed to score any points but his strength enabled the All Blacks to achieve an edge over their Wallaby rivals in the scrum

Bunce, F. E.   New Zealand

Full Name: Frank Eneri Bunce
Province: North Harbour
Position: Centre
Height: 6ft 1in (1.85m)
Weight: 14st 10lb (93kg)
Born: Auckland, 4.2.62
Family links with rugby: Steve (brother) plays for Western Australia
Former nation: Western Samoa
Former province: Auckland
Former club: Manukau
International debut (NZ): New Zealand 24, Ireland 21, 1992
Notable landmarks in rugby career: Six years after making his debut for Auckland in a Ranfurly Shield game against Horowhenua at Eden Park, coming on as a replacement and scoring a try, Frank finally hit the headlines in New Zealand. The occasion was the first Test against Ireland at Dunedin on 30 May 1992 and, aged 30 or not, he was the difference between the sides, scoring two tries as the All Blacks squeezed home 24–21. It was a timely performance by Bunce, who had made only 16 appearances for Auckland in those six seasons, as

Western Samoa (1991)		
Career	4 caps	4 pts
New Zealand (1992)		
Last Season	12 caps	36 pts
Career	12 caps	36 pts

Caps (12): **1992** Wd(1,2,3), I(1,2), A(1,2,3), SA **1993** BL(1,2,3)

Points (36 – 8t): **1992** I(1:2t), I(2:2t), A(1:1t), A(3:1t) **1993**(1:1t), BL(3:1t)

Ireland had been despatched 62–7 by Auckland only a week earlier. And he was rewarded with the selectors' faith thereafter. Mind you, Frank was no novice that day at Carisbrook. Frustrated at his lack of opportunities in the New Zealand national set-up he had declared his allegiance for Western Samoa in the 1991 World Cup and featured strongly in each of their four games – against Wales, Australia, Argentina and Scotland – and claiming a try in the 35–12 win over the Pumas. He had also represented the All Blacks in each leg of the three-Test centenary series against the World XV. Any notion that his Dunedin heroics were a flash in the pan was dispelled in the second Test when he weighed in within another try-brace. Frank has since gone from strength to strength, playing in ten of the All Blacks' fixtures on their tour of Australia and South Africa and scoring five tries: against Western Australia, New South Wales, Queensland, Orange Free State and the Wallabies in the first Test. A devastating defender, à la Joe Stanley, who combines a penatrative attacking game, it was little wonder that he was courted by Rugby League in 1991. Fortunately for the Union code, he resisted the overtures. Scored tries in the first and third Test wins against the 1993 Lions

Burnell, A. P. Scotland

Full Name: Andrew Paul Burnell
Club: London Scottish
Position: Prop
Height: 6ft (1.83m)
Weight: 16st 8lb (105kg)
Occupation: Sales director with Anglo-Scottish Finance (Reading)
Born: Edinburgh, 29.9.65
Family: Single
Former clubs: Marlow, Harlequins, Leicester
International debut: England 12, Scotland 12, 1989
Five Nations' debut: As above
Best moment in rugby: Beating England to win 1990 Grand Slam
Worst moments in rugby: Scotland losing 3-19 to France in 1989; London Scottish getting relegated from English Second Division (1988/89); missing 1992 tour to Australia due to torn knee medial ligament sustained in 12–15 defeat by Wales in '92 Five Nations Championship finale
Most respected opponent: David Sole (Edinburgh Acads & Scotland) – good scrummager, great ball player, superb captain
Serious injuries: Ruptured disc in back (1989, required surgery), acute tear in knee medial ligament (1992)
Best memory last season: Earning Lions selection
Suggestions to improve rugby: *On-field* – Clamp down on scrummage collapsing with penalty awarded if shoulder dips below hip. *Off-field* – Permit players to benefit from rugby-related activities. More recognition from the Unions to the amount of time required away from work to meet the standards required to play international rugby. Many clubs are outdated in their

Scotland (1989)

Last Season	4 caps	0 pts
Career	29 caps	0 pts
Lions 1993	Tour to New Zealand	

Caps (29): **1989** E, I, F, Fj, Ro **1990** I, F, W, E, Arg **1991** F, W, E, I, Ro wc-J, Z, I, WS, E, NZ **1992** E, I, F, W **1993** I, F, W, E

Points Nil

administration. Until more people who care about the game are recruited to run clubs financially, rather than committee men who treat the club as their own private 'club', then I am afraid junior and senior rugby will suffer

Notable landmarks in rugby career: Scored on first team debut for Leicester and Scotland B debut in 26–3 win over Italy in L'Aquila (1989). Twice helped London Scottish win promotion, as 1989/90 Third Division and 1991/92 Second Division champions, and featured in their triumphant 1990/91 Middlesex Sevens side. Toured with Scotland to Zimbabwe (1988) and New Zealand (1990), having been ever-present tighthead in Grand Slam campaign, but missed tours to Japan (1989) and Australia (1992) through injury. Prior to knee ligament tear against Wales (21.3.92) had played in 24 of Scotland's most recent 26 cap internationals, including all six World Cup games, one of which saw him switch to loosehead (v Zimbabwe). Recovered tighthead spot from Boroughmuir's Peter Wright, who had deputized on tour in Australia, and played throughout 1993 Five Nations' campaign. Both he and Wright were then selected to tour with the Lions to New Zealand. At A-level last season played in No 1 jersey in 35–14 win over Spain (12.9.92) and on opposite side of front row in 22–17 defeat of Italy (19.12.92)

Touchlines: Cinema-going

Cabannes, L. France

Full Name: Laurent Cabannes
Club: Racing Club de France
Position: Flanker
Height: 6ft 2in (1.88m)
Weight: 14st 2lb (89.5kg)
Occupation: Public relations officer
Born: Reims, 6.2.64
Former club: Pau
International debut: France 12, New Zealand 30, 1990
Five Nations' debut: France 15, Scotland 9, 1991
Notable landmarks in rugby career: One of the most mobile and effective loose forwards in the game, Laurent made his senior debut for Pau at the age of just 17. Last season, in addition to further enhancing his reputation with a hefty contribution to France's Five

Nations' triumph, he also turned out for France at Murrayfield in the World Cup Sevens tournament. In all, he made eight appearances – a sequence which

took in the '92 summer tour of Argentina (though he missed the first Test) and the two-Test visit of South Africa, but not the historic home defeat by the Pumas as skipper Jean-Francois Tordo was donning the No 7 jersey that day. Laurent, whose two international tries have come in spectacular style against Ireland, has travelled far in rugby pursuit, playing the club game in South Africa and in the south west region of France for

France (1990)
Last Season	8 caps	4 pts
Career	25 caps	8 pts
France VII 1993		World Cup Sevens

Caps (25): **1990** NZ(2R) **1991** S, I, W, E, US(2), W wc–Ro, Fj, C, E **1992** W, E, S, I, R, Arg(a2), SA(1,2) **1993** E, S, I, W, SA(1,2)

Points (8 – 2t): **1991** I(1t) **1992** I(1t)

Pau. But it was with Racing that his representative career burgeoned, scoring a try as the Paris side won the 1990 French Club Championship; their first success in 31 years. He had also been on the 1987 side which finished runners-up. In 1986 he had started playing France B rugby (against Wales B at Pontypridd) but it was only in November 1990 that he broke into the senior ranks as a replacement for Abdel Benazzi in the second Test against New Zealand in Paris

Cadieu, J. -M.   France

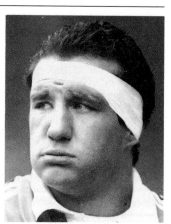

Full Name: Jean-Marie Cadieu
Club: Toulouse
Position: Lock
Height: 6ft 4in (1.93m)
Weight: 16st 1lb (102kg)
Occupation: PE/sports instructor
Born: Tulle, 16.10.63
Former club: Tulle
International debut: Romania 21, France 33, 1991
Five Nations' debut: Wales 9, France 12, 1992
Notable landmarks in rugby career: Broke his Test scoring duck last season when contributing one of four tries to France's 25–6 defeat of Romania, at Le Havre on 28 May 1992. He then toured Argentina, playing in both Test wins in Buenos Aires in July, but was one of the casualties after South Africa's 20–15 win in Lyon on 17 October. He was dropped to the bench for the second leg of the series in Paris and, with France

winning and replacement lock Abdel Benazzi faring well, Jean-Marie's international season was at a premature end. Benazzi retained the berth alongside Olivier Roumat through the remainder of the season. Previously, he had won three Championship medals with Toulouse (1985, 1986 and 1989) and been a regular in the France B team: turning out against the second strings of England and Scotland for three straight seasons: won 35–16 and lost 12–14 respectively in 1988/89, drew 15–15 and won 31–9 in 1989/90, won 10–6 and 31–10 in 1990/91. He did not contribute a point in those six games, nor against Scotland in 1985 and 1986 losses at Murrayfield and Villefranche-sur-Saône. An impressive performance for the French Barbarians against New Zealand in 1990 prompted his promotion to the senior team when he was one of six new caps blooded against Romania in Bucharest during the summer of '91. A permanent fixture during France's disappointing 1991 World Cup campaign, he lost his place after the equally unconvincing 1992 Five Nations' win over Wales in Cardiff, only to be recalled, after two games warming the bench, for the 44–12 rout of Ireland

France (1991)		
Last Season	4 caps	4 pts
Career	12 caps	4 pts

Caps (12): **1991** Ro, US(1) wc–Ro, Fj, C, E **1992** W, I, R, Arg(a1,a2), SA(1)

Points (4 – 1t): **1992** R(1t)

Camberabero, D.   France

Full Name: Didier Camberabero
Club: Beziers
Position: Outside-half
Height: 5ft 8½in (1.74m)
Weight: 11st 5lb (72kg)
Occupation: Public relations officer
Born: La Voulte, 9.11.61
Family links with rugby: Father (Guy) was capped 14 times for France between 1961–68; Brother (Gilles) is former captain of La Voulte
Former club: La Voulte
International debut: Romania 13, France 9, 1982
Five Nations' debut: England 15, France 19, 1983
Notable landmarks in rugby career: Caused much consternation

in the English camp last season when he was recalled for the 1993 Five Nations' Championship opener against them at Twickenham (one of eight changes to the side beaten by Argentina in Nantes) – such is the regard in which he is held. Little wonder when you consider his record. He is France's record points scorer in internationals with 354 (having surpassed Jean-Pierre Romeu's 265) and world record holder for most points scored in a single match, with 30 against Zimbabwe (3t,9c) in Auckland during 1987 World Cup. Made his France debut on the wing in Bucharest against Romania in 1982, having previously represented French Universities and France A in the FIRA Championship. Despite scoring 32 points (28 with the boot) in three World Cup-ties in 1991, he was not fond of the Adidas ball. 'It is a mixture between soap and a balloon ... it flies like a loose rocket... it's a flying object identified only by the International Rugby Board.' World Cup campaign ended prematurely for the son of Guy, with whom he shares the French record for most conversions in an international (nine), when he sustained a hairline rib fracture playing against Canada. His recall in January '93 helped create a Championship-winning French side and allowed them to pick up the inaugural Five Nations' Cup. Didier kicked five points against England (1c,1p), six points against Scotland (2p) and 11 points (1c,2p,1dg) against Ireland. The injury which kept him out of the Paris match prevented France from completing the entire Championship with an unchanged XV

France (1982)

Last Season	3 caps	22 pts
Career	36 caps	354 pts

Caps (36): **1982** Ro, Arg(1,2) **1983** E, W **1987** wc–Ro(R), Z, Fj(R), A, NZ **1988** I **1989** BL, A(1) **1990** W, S, I, Ro, A(1,2,3), NZ(1,2) **1991** S, I, W, E, Ro, US(1,2), W wc–Ro, Fj, C **1993** E, S, I

Points (354 – 12t,48c,59p,11dg): **1982** Ro(1c,1dg) Arg(1:1p,1dg), Arg(2:1c,1p) **1983** E(1p), W(1dg) **1987** wc–Ro(1t), Z(3t,9c), A(4c,2p), NZ(1c,1p) **1988** I(1t,1p) **1989** BL(1t,3c,3p), A(4p,1dg) **1990** W(1t,3c,1p), I(2c,5p), A(1:3p), A(2:3c,3p), A(3:1t,1c,2p,3dg), NZ(1:1p), NZ(2:3p,1dg) **1991** S(2p,2dg), I(2c,3p), W(2c,2p), E(1t,2c,1p), Ro(1t,1c,5p), US(1:3c,1p), US(2:1c), W(1t,2c,2p) wc–Ro(1c,4p), Fj(1t,3c,1p), C(1c,1p) **1993** E(1c,1p), S(2p), I(1c,2p,1dg)

Campese, D. I.   Australia

Full Name: David Ian Campese
Clubs: Randwick (Aus: since 1986),
Mediolanum Milan (It: since 1988)
State: New South Wales
Position: Wing, fullback
Height: 5ft 10in (1.77m)
Weight: 13st 5lb (85kg)
Occupation: Partner in Campo's
Sports Store
Born: 21.10.62
Family: Tony (father), Joan
(mother), Mario (brother), Lisa
(sister), Corinne (sister)
Former clubs: Queanbeyan (1980–
86), Petrarca (Padua, It: 1984–87)
International debut: New Zealand
23, Australia 16, 1982
Best moments in rugby: Debut in
first Test vs New Zealand 1982
when scored try; 1989 Hong Kong
Sevens Player of Tournament; 1991 World Cup.
Worst moment in rugby: Being dropped for first Test vs France in 1990
Most embarrassing moment: Dropping ball at Cardiff vs 1988 Barbarians
with try line in sight
Most respected opponent: Hugo Porta (Argentina)
Serious injuries: Dislocated shoulder (1985), ankle (1987), knee (1992)
Other sporting achievements: 1981 ACT Schools Golf Championship
Best memory last season: Beating South Africa and Wales
Suggestions to improve rugby: *On-field* – Allow playing the ball on the
ground. Stop locks marking wingers under current ruck and maul law. *Off-field*
– Install professional rugby administrators
Notable landmarks in rugby career: The world's leading Test try-scorer
with 52, Campo is also Australia's most-capped player, with 72 appearances to
his name. Shares with Greg Cornelsen the Aussie record for most tries scored
in a single Test, with his four against the United States Eagles in 1983. One of
a growing number of full-time rugby players, who follow the winter season
around the globe by playing their 'trade' in both hemispheres. Campo started
with Queanbeyan before joining Randwick in 1987. His State allegiance also
switched from Australian Capital Territory to New South Wales. Made his
international debut against arch-rivals New Zealand back in 1982 and has been
a thorn in opponents' flesh ever since; not least in the 1991 World Cup when
six tries in six appearances helped Australia win the Webb Ellis Cup and him
to be declared both the Player of the Tournament, the Australian Society of

Rugby Writers' Player of the Year and a similar accolade from the British Rugby Writers in the form of the Pat Marshall Memorial Award. Dropped only once, for the first Test against France in 1990, he was an ever-present throughout Australia's eight-Test campaign in 1992, adding to his try-tally against Scotland, New Zealand (first Test), South Africa (number 50), Ireland and Wales. His other Wallaby outings came against Western Transvaal, Northern Transvaal (two tries), Eastern Province, Leinster (two tries), Ulster, Connacht and, at Twickenham, the Barbarians

Tours: 1982 – New Zealand. 1983 – France and Italy. 1984 – Fiji, United Kingdom and Ireland. 1986 – New Zealand. 1987 – World Cup. 1988 – England, Scotland and Italy. 1989 – New Zealand, Canada and France. 1990 – New Zealand. 1991 – New Zealand, World Cup. 1992 – South Africa, Ireland and Wales

Touchlines: Golf

Player to watch: Terry Campese (my nephew)

Player of the Year: Willie Ofahengaue (Australia)

Australia (1982)

Last Season	8 caps	28 pts
Career	72 caps	255 pts

Caps (72): **1982** NZ(1,2,3) **1983** US, Arg(1,2), NZ, It, F(1,2) **1984** Fj, NZ(1,2,3), E, I, W, S **1985** Fj(1,2) **1986** It, F, Arg(1,2), NZ(1,2,3) **1987** wc-E, US, J, I, F, W. NZ **1988** E(1,2), NZ(1,2,3), E, S, It **1989** BL(1,2,3), NZ, F(1,2) **1990** F(2,3), US, NZ(1,2,3) **1991** W, E, NZ(1,2). wc–Arg, WS, W, I, NZ, E **1992** S(1,2), NZ(1,2,3), SA, I, W

Points (255 – 52t,8c,7p,2dg): **1982** NZ(1:1t), NZ(2:1t) **1983** US(4t,1c), Arg(1:1p), Arg(2:1t,3c,1p), It(3c,1p), F(1:1c,1p), F(2:1p) **1984** Fj(1t), NZ(2:1p), NZ(3:1t,1p), S(2t) **1985** Fj(1:1dg), Fj(2:2t) **1986** It (2t), F(1t), Arg(1:1t), Arg(2:2t), NZ(1:1t), NZ(3:1t) **1987** wc-E (1t), US(1t), J(1t), F(1t) **1988** E(a2:1t), E(b:1t), S(2t), I(3t) **1989** NZ(1t), F(1:1t) **1990** F(2:1t), F (3:1t), US(1t,1dg) **1991** W(a:1t), E(a:2t). wc-Arg(2t), W(b:1t), I (2t), NZ(b:1t) **1992** S(1:2t), NZ (1:1t), SA(1t), I(1t), W(1t)

Carey, R. W.   Ireland

Full Name: Ronald William Carey
Club: Dungannon
Position: Wing, centre
Height: 5ft 8in (1.73m)
Weight: 12st 6lb (79kg)
Occupation: Civil servant
Born: Dungannon, 6.8.65
Family: Single
International debut: New Zealand 24, Ireland 21, 1992
Five Nations' debut: None
Best moment in rugby: Winning first cap in Dunedin
Worst moment in rugby: Losing second Test to New Zealand 6–59 (1992)
Most embarrassing moment: Breaking collarbone diving to score a try v Malone (March 1986)
Most respected opponent: David Campese (Australia)
Biggest influence on career: Willie Anderson (Dungannon & Ireland)
Serious injuries: Broken collarbone
Other sporting achievements: Clocked 11.0s for 100m

Ireland (1992)

Last Season	2 caps	0 pts
Career	2 caps	0 pts

Caps (2): **1992** NZ(1,2)

Points Nil

Best memory last season: Scoring crucial try in 20–18 Ulster Senior Cup final win over Ballymena – Dungannon's first triumph for 17 years
Suggestions to improve rugby: *On-field* – Leave new regulations a while longer to see if players can adapt. Personally, however, I have suffered by them. I did not see half as much ball last season, as witnessed by the fact that I only scored five tries for Dungannon as compared with 25 in 1991/92. *Off-field* – Encourage more family involvement in rugby
Notable landmarks in rugby career: Worked way up Ulster representative ladder – Schools, U-18, U-19, U-20, senior cap – before embarking on an international career. Given Ireland B debut in 15–47 loss to England B at Richmond on 31 January 1992 before, rather against the odds, enjoying a closer tussle with New Zealand in Dunedin on 30 May when his full debut coincided with a narrow 21–24 loss; Ireland having led 12–0 at one stage. Retained his place on the tourists' right wing the following week in Wellington when the All Blacks, having reshuffled their side, stormed to a decisive 59–6 win. Considered number three in the wing rankings, behind Richard Wallace and Simon Geoghegan, on his return and consequently his outings were confined to

Ireland A appearances in the 29–28 defeat of Wales A at Newport (5 March 1993) and the 18–22 loss to England at Donnybrook (19 March 1993). On the latter occasion his disappointment at the result was tempered by a try-scoring performance

Carling, W. D. C. — England

Full Name: William David Charles Carling
Club: Harlequins
Position: Centre
Height: 5ft 11lb (1.81m)
Weight: 14st 2lb (89.5kg)
Occupation: Runs own management training/personal development company: 'Insight'
Born: Bradford-on-Avon, Wiltshire, 12.12.65
Family: Single
Family links with rugby: Father (Bill) played for Cardiff
Former club: Durham University
International debut: France 10, England 9, 1988
Five Nations' debut: As above
Best moments in rugby: England beating Australia 28-19 in my first game as captain; leading England to back-to-back Grand Slams; 1993 Lions' selection
Worst moment in rugby: Losing 1990 Grand Slam decider to Scotland
Most embarrassing moment: Not touching down try for Harlequins against Rosslyn Park at Twickenham after crossing line in 1990 Middlesex Sevens
Most respected opponent: Denis Charvet (Toulouse & France)
Serious injuries: Fracture of leg (1989)
Best memory last season: Rory Underwood's try against Scotland
Suggestions to improve rugby: *On-field* – Player involvement in law-changes

England (1988)

Last Season	6 caps	5 pts
Career	42 caps	29 pts
Lions 1993	1 Test	0pts

Caps (42): **1988** F, W, S, I(1,2), A(a2), Fj, A(b) **1989** S, I, F, W, Fj **1990** I, F, W, S, Arg(a1,a2), Arg(b) **1991** W, S, I, F, Fj, A(a) wc-NZ, It, US, F, S, A(b) **1992** S, I, F, W, C, SA **1993** F, W, S, I. Lions–NZ (1)

Points (29 – 7t): **1989** F(1t) **1990** F(1t), W(1t) **1991** wc-US(1t), F(1t) **1992** W(1t), SA(1t)

and in the administration of the game. It seems so logical to me yet the Powers-that-be ignore it. New rules should have an impact on the game by speeding it up. In turn, players will change to a more conformed 'flanker' body type. General level of coaching in English club rugby must be raised – still too stuck in our ways. We must learn from other countries. *Off-field* – Would someone please explain the off-the-field legislation. Because I can't. Better communication is needed and everyone, regardless of hemisphere, should play by the same rules. Players should be allowed to benefit from rugby-related activities because everything we do is naturally related to rugby. But we do not want to be paid to play

Notable landmarks in rugby career: England's most-capped centre (42) and holder of world record for most international wins as captain (26 in 35 games). Began playing career with Terra Nova School Under-11s as a six-year old. First fifth-former (15-year old) to play in Sedbergh's first XV (three years in team – experienced only two defeats), prior to captaining England 18-Group (1984) and moving on to Durham University on an Army scholarship (reading psychology) where switched to fullback. Northern Division selectors Geoff Cooke and Dave Robinson advised playing centre, where he has remained ever since. Rates a county performance for Durham against Lancashire as one of the most influential in shaping his future career. Bought himself out of Army (2nd Lt heading towards Royal Regiment of Wales) when told he would not be able to play representative rugby. Helped England B beat France B 22–9 (Bath, 20.2.87). England's youngest captain for 57 years (since P D Howard of Old Millhillians, 1931) when handed reins aged 22 years and 11 months for England's 28–19 win over Australia (5.11.88). Captain in two Grand Slams and 1991 run to World Cup final. Confessed, on Radio 4's *Desert Island Discs* (May 1992) that, if cast away, he would want with him Tolkein's book *The Hobbit*, Louis Armstrong's record *What a Wonderful World*, and a flotation tank. Toured New Zealand with 1993 Lions …'playing in first Test'…after six-match international season in Europe in which he had skippered side throughout and scored seventh Test try in 33–11 win over South Africa at Twickenham on 14 November 1992

Touchlines: Painting – sketching and inks, social golf

Carozza, P. V.   Australia

Full Name: Paul Vincent Carozza
Club: Western Districts
State: Queensland
Position: Wing
Height: 5ft 6in (1.66m)
Weight: 12st 8lb (80kg)
Occupation: School sports promotional officer with Queensland Department of Education
Born: 14.4.66
Family: Peter (father), Beryl (mother), John (brother), Maria (sister)
Former clubs: None
International debut: France 9, Australia 21, 1990
Best moment in rugby: 1992 Bledisloe Cup second Test – scoring both tries in 19-17 win over All Blacks
Worst moment in rugby: Missing 1991 World Cup selection
Most embarrassing moment: My cricket skills at an after-session cricket game
Most respected opponent: John Kirwan (Auckland & New Zealand)
Serious injuries: Groin (1991)
Other sporting achievements: GPS athletics competitor
Best memory last season: 1992 Bledisloe Cup series
Suggestions to improve rugby: *Off-field* – Compensate players for financial loss due to touring etc

Australia (1990)		
Last Season	8 caps	32 pts
Career	13 caps	36 pts

Caps	(13): **1990** F(1,2,3), NZ(2,3) **1992** S(1,2), NZ(1,2,3), SA, I, W

Points	(36 – 8t): **1990** F(2:1t) **1992** S(1:1t), S(2:2t), NZ(2:2t), SA(2t)

Notable landmarks in rugby career: Burst back onto the Test scene in 1992, after a one-off cap in 1990 against France (when David Campese was dropped for the only time in his Test career), by scoring three tries against the touring Scots in the Wallabies' 2–0 series win. From there he was voted the Chivas Regal Man-of-the-Series as Australia regained the Bledisloe Cup with a 2–1 series defeat of the All Blacks. He bagged two tries in the 19–17 second Test win at Brisbane – a series-clinching performance – and repeated the feat against South Africa, in Cape Town on 22 August, when the Springboks were handed their heaviest ever Test defeat (26–3). Whilst in the Republic he also played in the wins over Northern Transvaal and Eastern Province. Paul, who achieved the rare feat of representing his country before his State (Queensland), maintained his ever-present Test status in Ireland and Wales, on a tour in which he also turned out against Leinster, Ulster, Swansea and the Barbarians. First toured with the Wallabies (to South America) back in 1987, and appeared in England and Scotland on the 1988 trip

Tours: 1987 – South America. 1988 – England, Scotland and Italy. 1990 – New Zealand. 1991 – New Zealand. 1992 – South Africa, Ireland and Wales
Touchlines: Surfing
Player to watch: Tim Horan (Queensland)
Player of the Year: David Wilson (Australia)

Cecillon, M.   France

Full Name: Marc Cecillon
Club: Bourgoin-Jallieu
Position: No 8, flanker, lock
Height: 6ft 3in (1.90m)
Weight: 15st 2lb (96kg)
Occupation: Schoolmaster
Born: Bourgoin-Jallieu, 30.7.59
International debut: France 25, Ireland 6, 1988
Five Nations' debut: As above
Notable landmarks in rugby career: Indefatigable player who appeared in nine of France's ten Tests in 1992/93, missing only the nation's first ever defeat by Argentina on home soil, at Nantes on 14 November. Appointed captain for the summer and autumn Tests against Argentina (on tour in July) and South Africa (at Lyon and Paris in October) but was succeeded in that position by Jean-Francois Tordo thereafter. Still, Marc retained his place in the side at No 8 and played a full part in France's Championship triumph. Starting out, he had had to wait more than eight years between first representing France B – in December 1979 against Wales (won 33–12)in Bourg-en-Bresse – and

France (1988)

Last Season	11 caps	0 pts
Career	34 caps	28 pts

Caps (34): **1988** I, W, Arg(a2), Arg(b1,b2), Ro **1989** Ro, I, E, NZ(1,2), A(1) **1990** S, I, E(R) **1991** Ro,US(1), W wc–E **1992** W, E, S, I, R, Arg(a1,a2), SA(1,2) **1993** E, S, I, W, SA(1,2)

Points (28 – 7t): **1988** Arg(b1:1t), Arg(b2:1t) **1989** NZ(1:1t), NZ(2:1t) **1991** Ro(1t), US(1:1t) **1992** I(1t)

making his full debut against Ireland in Paris in 1988. In between he busied himself with regular tours of duty for France A in the FIRA Championship, before embarking on a cap-less world tour with France in 1986. A Jack of virtually all scrummage trades and master of a good many, Marc's 34 caps include 17 at No 8, 11 at flanker and three at lock. Before 1991 he appeared only sporadically, collecting four Championship caps in three seasons. All that changed in 1991/92 when he was recognized as a vital member of the French squad, as well as being the oldest. Indeed, so highly was he regarded that a place was made for him in the 26-man World Cup party despite then coach Jean Trillo knowing his torn thigh muscle would rule him out of the three Pool games. Last summer appeared in both Tests against South Africa

Chalmers, C. M. Scotland

Full Name: Craig Minto Chalmers
Club: Melrose
Position: Outside-half
Height: 5ft 10in (1.78m)
Weight: 13st 6lb (85kg)
Occupation: Marketing representative with Scottish Power
Born: Galashiels, 15.10.68
Family: Single
Family links with rugby: Father (Brian) coaches at Melrose
International debut: Scotland 23, Wales 7, 1989
Five Nations' debut: As above
Best moments in rugby: Winning 1990 Grand Slam by beating England; winning 1989/90, 1991/92 and 1992/93 Scottish Championships with Melrose

Worst moment in rugby: Being dropped by 1989 Lions, after playing in first Test against Australia (lost 12-30); breaking arm at Twickenham (6.3.93) to be ruled out of '93 Lions' selection
Most respected opponent: Grant Fox (New Zealand)/Michael Lynagh (Australia)
Biggest influence on career: Father, Ian McGeechan, Jim Telfer
Serious injuries: Torn knee cartilage, strained groin, dead leg, double break of right forearm (1993)
Best memory last season: Crushing Wales at Murrayfield
Suggestions to improve rugby: *On-field* – Play game without flankers (give

me more room to run). Reduce size of Scottish first division to 10 clubs. Make game more fluid, but not by decreasing worth of penalty goals as that would increase the number of infringements committed. *Off-field* – Introduce trust funds for international players, something per match, to be collected at the end of your career. I do not believe players should be directly paid to play, but why should we not be permitted to receive money for rugby-related activities; say, wearing a particular brand of boots? We are not doing anyone any harm

Notable landmarks in rugby career: Youngest player ever to represent Scotland B – as a 19-year old in the 18–12 defeat of France B at Chalon-sur-Saône (20.3.88) – having already turned out for Scottish Schools, Under-18, Under-19 and Under-21. Scored a try and dropped goal on full debut against Wales (21.1.89), having marked first XV debut for Melrose with three dropped goals against Harrogate. Earned selection to 1989 Lions tour of Australia and kicked six points in first Test before being replaced by Rob Andrew for remainder of series. Still, played in seven of the 12-match programme. Scotland's Grand Slam No.10 in 1990 who kicked three penalty goals in never-to-be-forgotten decider against England. Scored 46 points in 1991 Five Nations' Championship (9 v F, 12 v W, 12 v E, 13 v I) including 'grand slam' against Wales (1t,1c,1p,1dg); nine in 1992 campaign (all against Wales); and just three in 1993 (with dropped goal against England). Toured with Scotland to New Zealand (1990), North America (1991) and Australia (1992) and was relishing prospect of second Lions' tour of duty when he sustained a double break of his right forearm playing against England at Twickenham on 6 March – the last Test hurdle for Scotland before selection was made. The injury also meant he was a spectator as Melrose were crowned Scottish club champions for the third time in four seasons

Touchlines: Golf (12-handicap), ten-pin bowling

Scotland (1989)		
Last Season	11 caps	10 pts
Career	33 caps	117 pts
Lions 1989	1 Test	6 pts

Caps (33): **1989** W, E, I, F, Fj **1990** I, F, W, E, NZ(1,2), Arg **1991** F, W, E, I, Ro wc-J, Z, I, WS, E, NZ **1992** E, I, F, W, A(1,2) **1993** I, F, W, E

Points (117 – 4t,7c,23p,6dg): **1989** W(1t,1dg) **1990** I(1c,1p), F(2c,2p), W(3p), E(3p), Arg(1t) **1991** F(2p,1dg), W(1t,1c,1p,1dg), E(4p), I(2c,3p) wc-J(1t,1p), I(1dg) **1992** W(1dg,2p), A(2:1c,1p) **1993** E(1dg)

153

Clarke, B. B. — England

Full Name: Benjamin Bevan Clarke
Club: Bath
Position: No 8
Height: 6ft 5in (1.95m)
Weight: 16st 13lb (107kg)
Occupation: Sales, promotions and marketing official with Lordswood Dairy Farm, Longwell Green, Bristol
Born: Bishop's Stortford, 15.4.68
Family: Single
Family links with rugby: Father (Bevan) played for Bishop's Stortford and is now club chairman
Former clubs: Bishop's Stortford, Saracens
International debut: England 33, South Africa 16, 1992
Five Nations' debut: England 16, France 15, 1993
Best moment in rugby: Winning first cap against Springboks
Worst moment in rugby: Damaging shoulder and missing England XV's game against an Italy XV in Rovigo (1.5.90)
Most respected opponent: Dean Ryan (Wasps & England)

England (1992)		
Last Season	5 caps	0 pts
Career	5 caps	0 pts
Lions 1993	3 Tests	0 pts

Caps (5): 1992 SA 1993 F, W, S, I. Lions NZ(1,2,3)

Points Nil

Biggest influence on career: Tony Russ (ex-Saracens coach)
Serious injuries: Sprung shoulder joint, torn ligaments
Other sporting achievements: Swimming for Hertfordshire
Best memory last season: Learning of Lions' selection
Suggestions to improve rugby: *On-field* – Better policing of line-outs by referees. Sceptical of new mauling rule: no-one I know at Colts level, where they have experience of it, is in favour. *Off-field* – Compensate players or employers for time lost to rugby
Notable landmarks in rugby career: The great new hope of English rugby, being a forceful and dynamic runner as well as possessing the strength of an ox. Within five caps (v South Africa, France, Wales, Scotland and Ireland) of his England debut (14.11.92) last season the British Lions had snapped him up for their tour to New Zealand – a country he had visited 12 months earlier with England B, though he did not pick up a 'Test' scalp (lost 18–24, Hamilton, 28.6.92; lost 18–26, Pukekohe, 5.7.92). In his formative years Ben represented

Hertfordshire Colts, U-21 and full teams while with Bishop Stortford. On joining Saracens at start of 1990/91, he was selected for London Division, Public School Wanderers, Penguins, England Students and England B. Toured Australia (1991) with London, and was a member of the 1992 England B 'Grand Slam'-winning side which accounted for Spain, Ireland B, France B and Italy B (scored tries v Sp,I). Also played in England B's colours in thrilling 16–20 loss to South Africa at Bristol. Represented Bath at No.8 in sensational last-ditch 1992 Pilkington Cup triumph over Harlequins

Touchlines: Golf, squash, hockey

Clarke, C. P. Ireland

Full Name: Ciaran Paul Clarke
Club: Terenure College
Position: Fullback
Height: 6ft 1in (1.86m)
Weight: 14st 9lb (93kg)
Occupation: Sales executive with Pageboy
Born: Dublin, 8.3.69
Family: Single
Family links with rugby: brothers Scott and Brendan play for Terenure
International debut: Ireland 6, France 21, 1993
Five Nations' debut: As above
Best moment in rugby: Beating England (1993)
Worst moment in rugby: Breaking bone in back during club game and being told I would never play again
Most respected opponent: Jean-Baptiste Lafond (France)
Serious injuries: Broken bone in back (1989/90)
Other sporting achievements: Selected for 1989 Irish Cricket Panel
Best memory last season: Landing dropped goal vs Wales

Ireland (1993)		
Last Season	3 caps	3 pts
1993	Tour to Zim/Nam/SA	
Career	3 caps	3 pts

Caps (3): **1993** F, W, E

Points (3 – 1dg): **1993** W(1dg)

Suggestions to improve rugby: *On-field* – Amend ruck/maul law which is so frustrating. *Off-field* – Give players more for their semi-professional commitment. Reimburse us for what we are losing out on. Three or four days off for each match is costly for a sales rep

Notable landmarks in rugby career: Brought into Ireland side during 1993 Five Nations' Championship despite not having previously represented his country at any other level. Turned out for Leinster vs Australia last season but was injured midway through the Irish Inter-Provincial Championship, and instead had to make his case for Test inclusion in Division Two of the All-Ireland League. At the time of his selection he had made just eight appearances for Leinster. A stout defender, he impressed on his debut vs France and contributed a dropped goal to the emotional victory over Wales in Cardiff. The win over England completed his fairytale season at home and he was one of four full caps included in Ireland's development squad which toured Zimbabwe, Namibia and South Africa last summer

Touchlines: Cricket

Clarke, E. New Zealand

Full Name: Eroni Clarke
Province: Auckland
Position: Centre
Height: 6ft 1in (1.86m)
Weight: 14st 2lb (90kg)
Born: 31.3.69
International debut: New Zealand 54, World XV 26, 1992
Notable landmarks in rugby career: Eroni is another product of New Zealand's post-1991 World Cup revolution. Drafted into the squad for the centenary series, he was unleashed in the second Test at Wellington on 22 April and responded with two tries as the All Blacks triumphed 54–26 to make amends for their 14–28 loss in the opening match. His was the outstanding performance and he was deservedly retained for the series decider, in Auckland three days later, when he again made the try-sheet, with one of New Zealand's four in a 26–15 win. The man who had scored 40 points in 11 games for Auckland in 1991, as well as a try in a New Zealand XV's 60–30 win over Romania (Auckland, 9 June 1991),

New Zealand (1992)

Last Season	7 caps	25 pts
Career	7 caps	25 pts

Caps (7): **1992** Wd(2,3), I(1,2), SA(R) **1993** BL(1,2)

Points (25 – 6t): **1992** Wd(2:2t), Wd(3:1t), I(1:1t), I(2:1t) **1993** BL (2:1t)

was now on a roll and luckless Ireland were next in his path. Sure enough, a try in each Test against the Emerald Isle took his tally to five in four Tests. His own luck changed on the tour of Australia and South Africa. Although he made eight appearances – scoring tries against Western Australia, Australian Capital Territory (2) and the Victorian XV – he lost his Test place to North Harbour's Walter Little. Returned against Lions scoring try in 7–20 second Test loss in Wellington

Clarke, J. D. Ireland

Full Name: Jack David Clarke
Club: Dolphin
Position: Wing, centre
Height: 6ft (1.83m)
Weight: 13st 7lb (86kg)
Occupation: Pensions assistant with Standard Life (Dublin)
Born: Kisumu, Kenya, 2.9.68
Family: Single
Family links with rugby: Brother (Garoid) plays for Athlone and Irish Colleges
International debut: Wales 21, Ireland 21, 1991
Five Nations' debut: As above
Best moment in rugby: Running out onto Cardiff Arms Park for full debut
Worst moment in rugby: Losing to Australia at the death in 1991 World Cup quarter-final
Most embarrassing moment: Having to leave field after landing on boil on my backside when tackled
Serious injuries: Broken ankle (1984), torn hamstring
Other sporting achievements: Javelin for Irish Schools

Ireland (1991)

Last Season	1 cap	0 pts
Career	6 caps	4 pts

Caps (6): **1991** W, Na(1,2) wc–J, A **1993** NZ(2R)

Points (4 – 1t): **1991** W(1t)

Best memory last season: Ireland coming so close to beating New Zealand in first Test in Dunedin
Suggestions to improve rugby: *Off-field* – The game is heading in the right direction but there is still a long way to go
Notable landmarks in rugby career: Spent 12 years in Kenya before moving to Ireland and representing Irish Schools, Munster, Ireland Under-21s (won

10–9 v Italy, Treviso 30.9.89; drew 13–13 v New Zealand, Donnybrook 19.11.89), Ireland Under-25s (won 12–10 v US Eagles, Limerick 10.3.90; won 36–17 v Spain, Limerick 8.9.90) and Ireland B (won 27–12 v Argentina, Limerick 20.10.90; won 16–0 v Scotland B, Ravenhill 22.12.90; won 24–10 v England B, Old Belvedere 1.3.91). Scored try on full debut against Wales (16.2.91) prior to touring Namibia, where played in both Tests, and making two appearances in World Cup. Toured New Zealand with Ireland in the summer of '92, winning his sixth cap when entering the fray at Lancaster Park, Wellington, as a 43rd minute replacement for the injured Peter Russell. Unhappily, for Jack and Ireland, the All Blacks won 59–6. Also played against provincial opponents Canterbury (lost 13–38, Christchurch, 16 May), Auckland (routed 7–62, Auckland, 23 May) and Manawatu (lost 24–58, Palmerston North, 2 June)
Touchlines: Squash, swimming

Clement, A.   Wales

Full Name: Anthony Clement
Club: Swansea
Position: Outside-half, fullback
Height: 5ft 9in (1.75m)
Weight: 13st 8lb (86kg)
Occupation: Contract hire consultant with C.M. Day Ltd Swansea
Born: Swansea, 8.2.67
Family: Debra (wife)
Family links with rugby: Father (Malcolm) played for Bonymaen; brother (Michael) plays for Bonymaen
Former club: Morriston Youth
International debut: Wales 46, US Eagles 0, 1987
Five Nations' debut: England 3, Wales 11, 1988
Best moments in rugby: Scoring

two tries for Wales on debut. Helping Wales beat Australia 16–10 in quarter-finals of 1990 Hong Kong Sevens. Beating Scotland (21.3.92) to end three-year winless run at Arms Park. Call-up to '93 Lions
Worst moments in rugby: Being dropped by Wales for second time (before 1988/89 Five Nations' Championship) when playing well; having my name blackened for 48 hours during 1992/93 season by accusation of drug-involvement

Most respected opponent: Mike Rayer (Cardiff & Wales)

Serious injuries: Hamstring strain, shin fracture

Best memory last season: Swansea beating Australia at St Helens

Suggestions to improve rugby: *On-field* – Disagree with new maul ruling; encourages negative play. Sides struggling to win can too easily adopt a negative attitude. Referees to officiate more in the spirit of the game than to the letter of the law; as long as the ball is not in maul/ruck for too long, don't blow. Reduce worth of penalty goals (2), drop goals (2) and conversions (1). *Off-field* – Don't put to much store in tradition because it is a stumbling block to progress. There can be no hiding the fact that during the Five Nations Championship the game is semi-professional for those involved. Financial assistance is required for the commitment both of players and companies

Notable landmarks in rugby career: Stress fracture of left shin kept him out of early part of 1993 Five Nations' Championship which was a shame as he had started the season well, scoring one of Wales XV's seven tries against Italy, at the Arms Park on 7 October, and helping Swansea wallop the Wallabies 21–6, at St Helens on 14 November. Cardiff's Mike Rayer deputised and made favourable impression until losing place to Clement, who had also replaced him v Ireland, for Paris match. Spent last summer touring New Zealand with Lions, making seven appearances (scoring tries v North Auckland and Southland), having been a member of the 1989 series-winning squad in Australia. Toured South Africa with World XV in the same year. But it was not until 1991/92 season that he finally secured much-cherished fullback slot, after returning from Wales' horrible tour of Australia. Turned out against Western Samoa and Australia during 1991 World Cup and proved a major success in 1992 Five Nations Championship. Equally impressive for Swansea who won 1991/92 Heineken Championship. Joined All Whites in 1985, having played six games for Welsh Youth the previous year. Captained Wales U-20s and also represented Wales U-21s, B – twice against France (lost 0–26, Begles 17.10.87; lost 12–18, Brecon 29.10.88) and also against the Netherlands (won 34–12, Leiden 2.12.90)

Touchlines: Soccer, cricket

Wales (1987)		
Last Season	2 caps	0 pts
v Italy XV	1 app	5 pts
Career	21 caps	11 pts
Lions 1989		
1993		Tour to New Zealand

Caps	(21): **1987** US(R) **1988** E, NZ, WS(R), Ro **1989** NZ **1990** S(R), I(R), Na(1,2) **1991** S(R), A(a:R), F(b) wc–WS, A(b) **1992** I, F, E, S **1993** I(R), F

Points	(11 – 2t,1dg): **1987** US(R:2t) **1990** Na(2:1dg)

Clohessy, P. M. N.   Ireland

Full Name: Peter Martin Noel
Clohessy
Club: Young Munster
Position: Tighthead prop
Height: 5ft 11in (1.80m)
Weight: 16st (102kg)
Occupation: Company director
with TMM Ltd
Born: Limerick, 22.3.66
Family: Anna (wife)
Family links with rugby:
Grandfather (Peter O'Hallaran) won
Munster Senior Cup medal with
Garryowen
Former club: Garryowen
International debut: Ireland 6,
France 21, 1993
Five Nations' debut: As above
Best moment in rugby: Beating
England on first appearance at
Lansdowne Road
Worst moment in rugby: Young
Munster losing 9–7 to Shannon in
the 1992 Munster Cup final
Most embarrassing moment:
Dismissal against Old Wesley in an
All-Ireland League match

Ireland (1993)		
Last Season	3 caps	0 pts
Career	3 caps	0 pts

Caps (3): **1993** F, W, E

Points Nil

Most respected opponent: Mick Galwey (Shannon & Ireland)
Serious injuries: Slipped disc, broken leg and arm
Best memory last season: Helping Munster beat Australia 22–19 at
Thomond Park
Suggestions to improve rugby: *On-field* – Leave it alone. Happy with the
effect the new regulations have had on the game. *Off-field* – Likewise, no
problems
Notable landmarks in rugby career: Graduated through Irish Under-23
(1989 v Italy, Ravenhill) and B ranks to the full side last season, although he
had to wait three years for his first cap after playing in the 22–22 draw with
Scotland B at Murrayfield on 9 December 1989. Also last season helped Young
Munster win All-Ireland Championship and Munster to a bruising 22–19 win
over Australia in match labelled 'a shambles' by Wallaby coach Bob Dwyer.
Turned out in provincial colours v Ulster, Leinster and Connacht before
relieving Paul McCarthy of the national tighthead duties after Ireland's tame
defeat at Murrayfield. Retained No 3 jersey for the remainder of the

Championship and was considered a touch unfortunate to have missed out on Lions' selection to New Zealand last summer
Touchlines: Watersports, especially waterskiing

Coker, T.   Australia

Full Name: Troy Coker
Clubs: Southern Districts (Aus), Harlequins (Eng)
State: Queensland
Position: Lock, back row
Height: 6ft 6in (1.98m)
Weight: 17st 13lb (114kg)
Occupation: Industrial Relations Advocate with Carter Newell Solicitors
Born: 30.5.63
Family: Single
Former clubs: GPS (Brisbane: 1981–84), Western Districts (1985–91), Oxford University (1988–89)
International debut: Australia 19, England 6, 1987
Best moments in rugby: Winning 1991 World Cup and 1992 Bledisloe Cup series
Worst moment in rugby: Snapping cruciate ligament in right knee (Argentina 1987) after full recovery from left knee operation the previous year
Most embarrassing moment: Blocking attempted dropped goal with my groin region during club match in Brisbane

Australia (1987)		
Last Season	4 caps	0 pts
Career	13 caps	0 pts

Caps (13): **1987** wc–E, US, F, W **1991** NZ(a2). wc–Arg, WS, NZ(b), E(b) **1992** NZ(1,2,3), W(R)

Points Nil

Most respected opponent: Ian Jones (New Zealand)
Serious injuries: Left knee reconstruction (1986), right knee reconstruction (1987–88)
Other sporting achievements: Oxford rowing 1990–91
Best memories last season: Captaining Australia on tour of Ireland and Wales (v Connacht and Monmouthshire); captaining Australian sevens team to Uruguay
Suggestions to improve rugby: *On-field* – Get referees to realize that they have had a good game if people/players did not notice they were there. They

are there to administer the rules, not shove them down our throats!

Notable landmarks in rugby career: A familiar face to English audiences, having represented Oxford University (along with ex-Wallaby Brian Smith) in the 1988 and 1989 Varsity matches, and Harlequins since 1990 (helping them to a 1991 Pilkington Cup final victory over Northampton). First played for Australia in the 1987 World Cup, winning caps at No 8 against England, the United States, France and Wales. Thereafter despite touring in 1987 and 1990, did not add a fifth cap to his tally until 1991 when replacing Tim Gavin at No 8 against New Zealand in Auckland. Something of a utility forward in the Wallabies' triumphant World Cup campaign: employed at lock in the Pool victories over Argentina and Western Samoa, before reverting to No 8 for the semi-final defeat of New Zealand and the final win over England. His travels around the scrum continued when he opened 1992 at blindside in the 16–15 first Test defeat of the All Blacks in Sydney. From there he switched flanks to fill the openside berth for the remainder of the Bledisloe Cup-winning series. Displaced by a combination of Willie O and David Wilson thereafter, he nonetheless played against Wales in Cardiff (albeit as a 56th minute replacement for Wilson). Other Wallaby appearances in '92 came against Northern Transvaal, Eastern Province, Munster, Connacht (as skipper), Swansea, Neath, Llanelli, Monmouthshire (as skipper) and the Barbarians

Tours: 1987 – World Cup, South America. 1990 – New Zealand. 1991 – New Zealand, World Cup. 1992 – South Africa, Ireland and Wales

Touchlines: Rugby 12 months a year

Player to watch: Matthew Holt (Western Districts)

Player of the Year: John Eales (Australia)

Wallaby centre Jason Little takes man (Stuart Barnes) and ball during the 30–20 defeat of the Baa-baas at Twickenham

Cooksley, M. S.   New Zealand

Full Name: Mark Cooksley
Province: Counties
Position: Lock
Height: 6ft 7½in (2.02m)
Weight: 18st 2lb (115kg)
Born: 11.4.71
International debut: New Zealand 14, World XV 28, 1992
Notable landmarks in rugby career: The biggest man in New Zealand's squad for the 1992 tour of Australia and South Africa, Mark made his Test debut in the first match of the centenary series in Christchurch (18 April). The good news ended there as the All Blacks were beaten 28–14 and Mark, although teaming up with North Auckland's Ian Jones to get the better of Frenchmen Olivier Roumat and Marc Cecillon, sustained an injury. Fit for the aforementioned tour, he made seven appearances – against Western Australia (scored try), ACT, Victoria, Queensland B, Sydney, Natal and Central Unions –

New Zealand (1992)

Last Season	3 cap	0 pts
Career	3 cap	0 pts

Caps (3): 1992 Wd(1) 1993 BL(2,3R)

Points Nil

improving the longer the trip progressed. Graduated through the age-group ranks at second division Counties, developing into a strong lock and number four jumper, though also well versed in the front-jumping duties. Spent 1992 dominating his domestic opponents in second flight matches, and had the better of Gary Whetton as Counties led holders Auckland 13–6 midway through their Ranfurly Shield challenge at Pukekohe, before eventually succumbing 24–19. Represented New Zealand at Under-19 level and NZ Colts between 1990–91. One of his great memories is 11 August 1991 in Christchurch when he played on the Colts side which demolished their Australian counterparts 61–9. An All Black triallist in 1991, on the Possibles side beaten 40–22 by the Probables in Rotorua, he played in two of the three Trial matches the following season, including the Saracens team which deposed a New Zealand XV 20–15 at Napier. Selected as a reserve for the first Test against Ireland at Dunedin, but enjoyed greater exposure on the 1992 New Zealand Maoris' two tours: one internal, the other to the Pacific Islands.

Cooper, G. J. L.   New Zealand

Full Name: Greg Cooper
Province: Otago
Position: Fullback
Born: 10.6.65
Family links with rugby: Matthew
(brother) plays for Waikato and
New Zealand
Former province: Auckland
International debut: New Zealand
18, France 9, 1986
**Notable landmarks in rugby
career:** Greg was fullback for the
'Baby All Blacks' in 1986,
contributing eight points (one
conversion, one penalty and a
dropped goal) to the 18–8 defeat of
France, at Christchurch, on his
debut. With the unsanctioned New
Zealand Cavaliers in South Africa,
the NZRU had to dig deep into its
reserves and Greg was one of 11
uncapped players in the team on 28
June. Victory, for a team captained
by David Kirk, was a remarkable
achievement. With the 31 Cavaliers
under suspension, he retained his
place for the first two Tests against
Australia later that year, kicking
eight points in the 12–13 loss at
Wellington and, a fortnight later,

New Zealand (1986)

Last Season	4 caps	38 pts
Career	7 caps	63 pts

Caps (7): **1986** F(1),A(1,2) **1992**
       Wd(1,2,3),I(1)

Points (63 – 2t,14c,7p,2dg): **1986**
       F(1:1c,1p,1dg), A(1:1c,2p),
       A(2:2p,1dg) **1992** Wd(2:2t,6c),
       Wd(3:2c,2p), I(1:4c)

nine points (two penalty goals and a dropped goal) as the scoreline was reversed
at Dunedin. However, it was insufficient to keep him his place for the decisive
third Test in Auckland, his then home province, the fullback shirt going to
Kieron Crowley in a match Australia won 22–9. With the exception of two
bench appearances during the 1991 Bledisloe Cup series, he remained in the
international wilderness until last season when returning at fullback for the
centenary series. despite a 14–28 loss in the first Test at Christchurch, he
retained his place for the second leg of the series and responded with a 20-point
haul as the All Blacks rebounded to a 54–26 win. To that he added ten points
in Auckland as the deciding Test went with home advantage, 26–15. But
nothing is forever and he was one of the victims of the selectors purge, after the
first Test scare against Ireland. He was replaced for the 59–6 second Test win
in Wellington by brother Matthew, who proceeded to collect 23 points, a world

record for an International debutant. Kicked 16 points for New Zealand XV in 24–18 first Test win over England B in 1992. On a domestic note he was the top points scorer in New Zealand rugby last season with 291 points (8t,48c,51p,2dg), but campaign marred when he departed the national championship final prematurely, the victim of an alleged eye-gouging by Waikato prop Richard Loe

Cooper, M. J. A   New Zealand

Full Name: Matthew Cooper
Province: Waikato
Position: Fullback, centre
Height: 6ft 2in (1.88m)
Weight: 15st 4lb (96kg)
Born: 10.10.66
Family links with rugby: Greg (brother) plays for Otago and New Zealand
Former provinces: Otago, Hawke's Bay
International debut: New Zealand 59, Ireland 6, 1992
Notable landmarks in rugby career: Made record-breaking start to Test career when awarded his first cap in the second Test against Ireland at Wellington last season. The pressure was on, having displaced brother Greg at fullback, but he responded by contributing 23 points to New Zealand's 59–6 win. His tally, comprising two tries, six conversions and a penalty goal, consisted a world record for a Test debutant. Matthew, who finished second to his fraternal rival in the

New Zealand (1992)

Last Season	2 cap	23 pts
Career	2 cap	23 pts

Caps (2): 1992 I(2)

Points (23 – 2t,6c,1p): **1992** I(2:2t,6c,1p)
1993 BL(1R)

1992 New Zealand domestic charts, with 260 points (6t,59c,38p,1dg) to Greg's 291, at least had the satisfaction of taking national championship honours with Waikato, 40–5 against his brother's Otago side in front of 30,000 fans at Hamilton. In that game he kicked three penalty goals and converted all four tries. Matthew's national squad involvement began as far back as 1987, when he represented the All Blacks as a centre in Tokyo against Japan B, where the tourists triumphed 94–0, and in Kyoto in the 96–3 win over the Asian Barbarians. He scored a total three tries. Returned to set-up in 1992 after Trial in which he contributed 23 points to a winning cause. Took to 11 his total All Black appearances with eight outings during the 1992 tour of Australia and South Africa. Having kicked four conversions in the 80–0 rout of Western Australia, a disappointing showing against New South Wales cost him the chance of a Test place. Still, he was the tour party's second top scorer, behind Grant Fox (118), with 71 points; the bulk of them coming against Queensland B (17), Sydney (12), Orange Free State (13) and Central Unions (14). Came on for injured Walter Little in the first Test win over the 1993 British Lions

Copsey, A. H.   Wales

Full Name: Anthony Hugh Copsey
Club: Llanelli
Position: Lock
Height: 6ft 7in (2.01m)
Weight: 16st 7lb (105kg)
Occupation: Sales representative with Konica Peter Llewellyn (Swansea)
Born: Romford, Essex, 25.1.65
Family: Amanda (wife)
Family links with rugby: Brother (Peter) plays for Old Edwardians
Former clubs: Old Edwardians, Cardiff Institute
International debut: Ireland 15, Wales 16, 1992
Five Nations' debut: As above
Best moment in rugby: Winning first cap in Dublin
Worst moment in rugby: Every time I am on a losing side
Most embarrassing moment: Press finding out about the tattoo on my behind
Most respected opponent: Wade Dooley (Preston Grasshoppers & England)
Biggest influence on career: Andy Sankey and Steve Drake (school teachers)

Wales (1992)

Last Season	4 caps	0 pts
v Italy XV	1 app	0 pts
1993	Tour to Zimbabwe/Namibia	
Career	8 caps	0 pts

Caps (8): **1992** I, F, E, S, A **1993** E, S, I

Points Nil

Serious injuries: 48 stitches in all, dislocated collarbone, fractured ribs
Best memory last season: Winning League and Cup double with Llanelli
Suggestions to improve rugby: *On-field* – Help referees to get things right. Invite a second opinion. Give more power to the touch judges. *Off-field* – More

financial support for players and their employers from the Unions. As game continues to change more commitment is expected from players so they must at least be given freedom to earn from rugby-related activities

Notable landmarks in rugby career: Joined Llanelli (1989/90) via county rugby for Essex Colts and Eastern Counties Under-21s. Moved to work in Wales in 1986 and then enrolled at South Glamorgan Institute (Human Movements), allowing him to represent Welsh Colleges and England Students, with whom toured Namibia. Member of London Division squad. Selected for England Development squad before opting for Wales. Represented Barbarians against Scotland at Murrayfield (drew 16–16, 7.9.91), Cork Constitution and Old Wesley. Ever-present in Wales' 1992 Five Nations campaign and was heading for a similar record in last season's Championship before losing his place for the final game in Paris. A member of Llanelli's League and Cup-winning side, he turned out against an Italy XV, Australia, England, Scotland and Ireland before losing Test place on summer tour to South Africa

Touchlines: Basketball, water-polo

Corcoran, I. Scotland

Full Name: Ian Corcoran
Club: Gala
Position: Hooker
Height: 5ft 10in (1.78m)
Weight: 12st 10lb (81kg)
Occupation: Carpet fitter with H A Gillies
Born: Edinburgh, 11.5.63
Family: Carrie (wife)
Family links with rugby: Two brothers play for Gala
International debut: Australia 27, Scotland 12, 1992
Five Nations' debut: None
Best moment in rugby: Coming on for full debut against Australia in Sydney
Worst moment in rugby: Being dropped from senior Scotland squad in 1989 (replacement v Fiji and Romania) after France B game
Most respected opponent: Kenny Lawrie (ex-Gala and Scotland)
Serious injuries: Damaged knee ligaments required operation

Scotland (1992)		
Last Season	1 cap	0 pts
Career	1 cap	0 pts

Caps (1): **1992** A(1R)

Points Nil

167

Other sporting achievements: Cricket for Gala

Best memory last season: Captaining Scotland to victory in Dubai Sevens

Suggestions to improve rugby: *On-field* – Touch judges must help/consult more with referees. *Off-field* – Players remunerated for working time lost to game although must guard against too much money coming in as that would spoil it

Notable landmarks in rugby career: With John Allan having departed to South Africa, Ian came through as Scotland's reserve hooker behind Lion Kenny Milne. He toured Australia in the summer of '92 (playing in four of the eight games), making his debut as a tenth minute replacement for Milne in the 27–12 first Test loss to the Wallabies in Sydney on 13 June. Thereafter he was consigned to the role of bench reserve throughout the 1993 Five Nations' Championship, with further opportunities under the spotlight being reserved for the abbreviated game. He skippered Scotland to victory in the Dubai Sevens, beating South African province Natal in 22–12 in the final, having accounted for England 19–17 in the previous round. He then appeared in the inaugural World Cup Sevens tournament at Murrayfield in April, though Scotland enjoyed little success there. A former Scotland Under-21 cap, he was promoted to Scotland B in 1989/90, playing against France B at Oyonnax in 1990. Captain of Gala for the past three seasons, he toured Japan with Scotland in 1989 (playing in two of the five games). Last season turned out for Scotland A in the wins over Spain (won 35–14, Madrid, 12.9.92) and Italy (won 22–17, Melrose, 19.12.92)

Touchlines: Squash, badminton, DIY

Ant Strachan feeds his line, watched by (from left to right) Martin Bayfield, Andy Reed, Paul Burnell, Zinzan Brooke, Ian Jones, Robin Brooke and Kenny Milne

Costello, R. A.   Ireland

Full Name: Richard Anthony Costello
Club: Garryowen
Position: Lock
Height: 6ft 7in (2.01m)
Weight: 17st (108kg)
Occupation: Publican at the Locke Bar, Limerick
Born: Limerick, 8.3.64
Family: Anna (wife), Tony (son), Richard (son), Kate (daughter)
Former clubs: Univ of Wellington (NZ), Palmerston North (NZ), Randwick (Aus), Old Crescent, Wanderers
International debut: Scotland 15, Ireland 3, 1993
Five Nations' debut: As above
Best moment in rugby: Winning 1991/92 All-Ireland League title with Garryowen; beating 1992 Wallabies with Munster
Worst moment in rugby: Losing Ireland place after one cap
Most respected opponent: Gary Whetton (New Zealand)

Ireland (1993)

Last Season	1 cap	0 pts
Career	1 cap	0 pts

Caps (1): 1993 S

Points Nil

Serious injuries: Broken hand, torn knee ligaments (required operation)
Best memory last season: Getting capped v Scotland
Suggestions to improve rugby: *On-field* – New laws are generally improving rugby, but not the one concerning the ruck and maul. Change it back please. *Off-field* – IRFU are improving all the time but more could still be done to help players
Notable landmarks in rugby career: One from the 'have boots, will travel' school, he spent two years playing club rugby in New Zealand before crossing the Tasman Sea to help Randwick (Campese, Ella, Poidevin et al.) win the 1989 Australian Club Championship and Sydney Premiership. Had previously made his Munster debut in 1985, after joining Old Crescent from school. Returned home in time to share in Garryowen's 1991/92 All-Ireland League triumph and to regain his provincial berth. His stock continued to rise and, after featuring in Ireland 13-22 defeat by Scotland in the 'A' International on 28 December 1992, he was invited to play in the main event, at Murrayfield on 16 January. However, the man he deposed, Lion-to-be Mick Galwey, returned the following game along with Neil Francis and Richard was squeezed out

169

Cronin, D. F.   Scotland

Full Name: Damian Francis Cronin
Club: London Scottish
Position: Lock
Height: 6ft 6in (1.98m)
Weight: 17st 10lb (112.5kg)
Occupation: Sales manager with
Walcot Reclamation Ltd (Bath)
Born: Wegberg, West Germany,
17.4.63
Family: Annie (wife)
Family links with rugby: Father is
a past-president of Ilford Wanderers
Former clubs: Ilford Wanderers,
Bath
International debut: Ireland 22,
Scotland 18, 1988
Five Nations' debut: As above
Best moment in rugby: Winning
1990 Grand Slam with Scotland
Worst moment in rugby: Being
dropped by Scotland during 1991
World Cup
Most respected opponent: Robert
Norster (Cardiff & Wales)
Serious injuries: Ligament damage
in both knees. Staple put in right
knee
Best memory last season: Getting
picked to tour with British Lions
Other sporting achievements:
Drove in celebrity race round Brands Hatch

Scotland (1988)

Last Season	5 caps	0 pts
Career	28 caps	8 pts
Lions 1993	Tour to New Zealand	

Caps (28): **1988** I, F, W, E, A **1989** W,
E, I, F, Fj, Ro **1990** I, F, W, E,
NZ(1,2) **1991** F, W, E, I, Ro wc-
Z **1992** A(2) **1993** I, F, W, E

Points (8 – 2t): **1989** I(1t) **1990** W(1t)

Suggestions to improve rugby: *On-field* – Do not change the lineout. It is a
lottery which is half the fun. Those who survive are technicians who learn to
survive. Better off working on keeping the game flowing more. Make people
stay on their feet more and referees more aware of players, especially flankers,
coming over the top. *Off-field* – Look seriously at commercialization of rugby
in support of players. Some sort of trust fund for international players. The
SRU needs to be more sympathetic and flexible towards the players
Notable landmarks in rugby career: Returned to rugby after fracturing base
of spine aged 22. Built reputation in Scotland with performances for Anglo-
Scots, having become eligible thanks to Lothian-based grandparents. Helped
1987 Anglo's beat French at Cupar and was included in Scottish XV which
achieved a similar feat. Toured with Scotland to Zimbabwe in 1988, captaining

them against Mashonaland District. Japan (1989) and New Zealand (1990). Ever-present alongside Chris Gray in Scotland second row during 1991 Five Nations' Championship after missing early season win (49–3) over Argentina through injury but was largely kept out of 1991 World Cup campaign and 1992 Championship by Doddie Weir and Neil Edwards. Lust for the game returned on moving from Bath to London Scottish. Helped them win promotion back to Courage League division one in 1991/92 before touring Australia with Scotland last summer and recapturing his Test place from fellow-Anglo Edwards. Ever-present since and capped comeback with Lions' selection last summer, during which he made six appearances but failed to make the Test team

Touchlines: DIY (restoring the house)

David Campese challenges for a loose ball with Irish centres Phil Danaher (left) and Vince Cunningham during Australia's 42–17 win in Dublin

Crowley, D. J.   Australia

Full Name: Daniel (Dan) James Crowley
Club: Southern Districts
State: Queensland
Position: Tighthead prop
Height: 5ft 8in (1.73m)
Weight: 16st 3lb (103kg)
Occupation: Police officer, Queensland Police Service
Born: 28.8.65
Family: Lisa (wife), Jessica (daughter)
Former clubs: None, Souths since 1972
International debut: Australia 30, British Lions 12, 1989
Best moment in rugby: First cap
Worst moment in rugby: Losing third Test (series decider) to 1989 British Lions
Most respected opponent: All of them
Serious injuries: None
Best memory last season: Scoring first, and probably last, try at Twickenham in 30-20 win over Barbarians (28.11.92)

Australia (1989)

Last Season	2 caps	0 pts
Career	6 caps	0 pts

Caps (6): **1989** BL(1,2,3) **1991** wc-WS **1992** I,W

Points Nil

Suggestions to improve rugby: *On-field* – No kicking out on the full from anywhere; make the backs do some work

Notable landmarks in rugby career: Dan was the man who presented Her Majesty the Queen with a miniature football prior to Australia's World Cup final win over England in 1991, having made just the one tournament appearance against Western Samoa. Indeed, his links with the United Kingdom stretch back to 1989 when he made his debut against the British Lions and retained his place through the three-Test series. That same year he toured Canada and France but was stood down for the 1990 trip across the Tasman Sea. With Tony Daly and Ewen McKenzie pretty much shoring up the Test propping duties Crowley's outings have been restricted to just three appearances since the 89' Lions left Oz in triumph. He was a reserve in all Tests in 1991. however, he ended 1992 on a high when, with Daly missing the tour to Ireland and Wales, he wore the loosehead' jersey in both internationals. Dan had himself been unavailable for the historic visit to South Africa in August, but once in Britain was one of the busiest players on duty: playing also against

Leinster, Munster, Ulster and Connacht on the Irish leg, and Wales B and Llanelli once the tourists switched their attentions to the Principality. Perhaps his proudest moment came with a try in the 30–20 defeat of the Barbarians at a packed Twickenham

Tours: 1989 – Canada and France. 1991 – New Zealand, World Cup. 1992 – Ireland and Wales
Touchlines: Work
Player to watch: Anyone after my position
Player of the Year: Too many great players in their own right

Cunningham, V. J. G.   Ireland

Full Name: Vincent John Gerald Cunningham
Club: St Mary's College
Position: Centre, outside-half
Height: 5ft 11in (1.81m)
Weight: 13st (82kg)
Occupation: Bank official with Allied Irish
Born: Dublin, 14.3.67
Family: Single
Family links with rugby: Father played for (and coached and selected) St Mary's
International debut: Ireland 10, England 21, 1988
Five Nations' debut: Scotland 15, Ireland 3, 1993
Best moment in rugby: Winning first cap in Millennium match
Worst moment in rugby: Breaking hand in training to miss Ireland's tour to North America (1989)
Most respected opponent: Serge Blanco (Biarritz & France)
Serious injuries: Broken hand
Other sporting achievements: Cricket for Irish Schoolboys
Best memories last season: Beating England and scoring two tries against All Blacks at Dunedin

Ireland (1988)

Last Season	7 caps	8 pts
Career	14 caps	14 pts
Lions 1993	Tour to New Zealand	

Caps (14): **1988** E(b), It **1990** Arg(R) **1991** Na(1,2) wc–Z, J(R) **1992** NZ(1,2), A **1993** S, F, W, E

Points (14 – 3t,1c): **1988** It(1c) **1991** Na(2:1t) **1992** NZ(1:2t)

Suggestions to improve rugby: *Off-field* – Broken time payments
Notable landmarks in rugby career: Outside-half in first Irish Schools team

173

to beat Wales. Played in Irish touring side which beat France four seasons ago. Amassed seven caps since debut against England in 1988 Dublin Millennium match. Toured Namibia with Ireland (1991), playing in both Tests (scoring try in second), and added a further couple of caps in World Cup. Scored Ireland U-25s' try in 12–10 defeat of US Eagles (Limerick, 10.3.90) and landed conversion in 36–17 defeat of Spain (Limerick, 8.9.90). Kicked penalty goal in Ireland B's 16–0 defeat of Scotland (Ravenhill, 22.12.90). Toured to New Zealand (1992) with Ireland and was very nearly responsible for one of the great shocks in the game's history. He scored two tries and 'no-hopers' Ireland led 12–0 in the first Test in Dunedin on 30 May before New Zealand edged home 24–21. Retained his place in the Irish midfield throughout the seven-Test campaign, sharing in wins over Wales and England. Also played major role as Irish VII came within a whisker of final in inaugural World Sevens tournament at Murrayfield in April 1993. When Scotland's Scott Hastings was forced to return home early from the British Lions' tour of New Zealand with a rearranged face, Vinnie was summoned and made three appearances against Taranaki (scored two tries), Hawke's Bay and Waikato

Touchlines: Enjoy horse-racing at Leopardstown and Phoenix Park, cricket, golf

Eric Elwood, the saviour of Irish rugby in 1993 – played 2, won 2. There were many who thought the Irish outside-half deserved a call-up for the Lions tour to New Zealand

Daly, A. J.   Australia

Full Name: Anthony (Tony) John
Daly
Club: Randwick
State: New South Wales
Position: Loosehead prop
Height: 5ft 10in (1.78m)
Weight: 16st 3lb (103kg)
Occupation: Sales consultant with
Carmin Office Furniture
Born: 7.3.66
Family: Shannon (wife)
Former clubs: Wests (1985–86),
Gordon (1987-90), Easts (1991–92)
International debut: New Zealand
24, Australia 12, 1989
Best moment in rugby: 1991
World Cup victory
Worst moment in rugby: Not
playing in 1991 Grand Final with
Easts
Most respected opponent: Olo
Brown (Auckland & New Zealand)
Serious injuries: Broken ankle
(1988); disc protrusion (1992)
Best memory last season:
Winning 1992 Bledisloe Cup and
beating South Africa
Suggestions to improve rugby:
Off-field – More investments for
players; more media for the game

Australia (1989)

Last Season	6 caps	0 pts
Career	25 caps	12 pts

Caps (25): **1989** NZ, F(1,2) **1990**
F(1,2,3), US, NZ(1,2,3) **1991**
W(a), E(a), NZ(a1,a2) wc–Arg,
W(b), I, NZ(b), E(b) **1992**
S(1,2), NZ(1,2,3), SA

Points (12 – 3t): **1990** F(3:1t), US(1t)
1991 wc-E(b:1t)

Notable landmarks in rugby career: Proudly holds the distinction of having
scored the only try of the 1991 World Cup final when Australia defeated
England 12–6. A breakaway wing-forward in his school days at St Joseph's
College, he was transformed into a prop when playing under former Wallaby
front-rower John Griffiths at Western Suburbs in Sydney. So well did he master
the art that he was plucked from the relative obscurity of club rugby in 1989
and asked to prop against Richard Loe in the All Black Test at Eden Park. He
has rarely taken a backwards glance since, amassing 25 caps of which six were
gained in 1992, even though he was not available to tour Ireland and Wales in
the autumn. Having teamed up with New South Wales front row cohorts Phil
Kearns and Ewen McKenzie to dispose of Scotland's summer challenge 2–0,
the trio remained in place to do a similar job on New Zealand, although, in
giving up the Bledisloe Cup, the All Blacks at least had the consolation of a third

Test scalp with which to return home. In South Africa Tony played in the 24–17 win over Northern Transvaal in Pretoria before, the following week, helping to inflict a record 26–3 loss on the Springboks themselves

Tours: 1989 – New Zealand, Canada and France. 1990 – New Zealand. 1991 – New Zealand, World Cup. 1992 – South Africa, Ireland and Wales
Touchlines: Tennis, movies, socializing
Player to watch: Mark Bell (Warringah)
Player of the Year: Paul Carozza (Australia)

Danaher, P. P. A.   Ireland

Full Name: Philip Paul Anthony Danaher
Club: Garryowen
Position: Fullback
Height: 5ft 11in (1.81m)
Weight: 13st 10lb (87kg)
Occupation: Insurance official with Norwich Union Life Insurance (Limerick)
Born: Limerick, 5.10.65
Family: Single
Former clubs: Abbeyfeale, Lansdowne
International debut: Ireland 22, Scotland 18, 1988
Five Nations' debut: As above
Best moments in rugby: Winning 1991/92 All-Ireland League with Garryowen; beating England (1993)
Worst moment in rugby: Being dropped second time round after 31–12 Paris loss (3.3.90)
Most embarrassing moment: Touching ball down behind line and conceding 5-yard scrum against Wales (ref was wrong!)
Most respected opponent: Jeremy Guscott (Bath & England)

Ireland (1988)

Last Season	6 caps	0 pts
Career	16 caps	6 pts

Caps (16): **1988** S, F, W, WS, It **1989** F, NZ(R) **1990** F **1992** S, F, NZ(1), A **1993** S, F, W, E

Points (6 – 2p): **1988** It(2p)

Biggest influence on career: Don Spring (Dublin Univ & Ireland No.8, 1978–81)
Serious injuries: Broken both ankles, serious hamstring injuries
Other sporting achievements: Badminton at national level while at school. Gaelic football for Limerick (helped them reach 1991 Munster Cup final)

Suggestions to improve rugby: *On-field* – Referees must be more universal in their interpretations. Improve coaching of schools and age-group levels. *Off-field* – More recognition from Unions for amount of time and commitment involved in playing. Allow players to benefit financially from rugby-related activities

Notable landmarks in rugby career: Succeeded Phil Matthews as Ireland captain for final game of 1992 Five Nations Championship, against France in Paris (21.3.92). Ireland lost 44–12 to complete whitewashed Wooden Spoon. Then led side to New Zealand for summer tour , having previously toured to France and North America. Skippered Irish to sensational 12–0 lead over All Blacks in first Test at Dunedin. After he had gone off injured in the 35th minutes, New Zealand recovered, just, to scrape home 24–21. Missed second Test but recovered fitness in time to lead side in 17–42 loss to Australia (31.10.92). Subsequently relinquished captaincy to Michael Bradley but retained his midfield berth throughout the 1993 Five Nations' Championship. Collected first international honours in 1982 when represented Ireland Schools (v E,W). Left Garryowen for Lansdowne in 1984 but returned four years later. The 1987/88 season brought his Munster debut and first full cap (at fullback) against Scotland (16.1.88). In and out of favour ever since – including missing out on appearance in 1991 World Cup – but came back in second half of 1992 Five Nations' campaign

Touchlines: Social golf

Davies, A. Wales

Full Name: Adrian Davies
Club: Cardiff
Position: Outside-half
Height: 5ft 10in (1.78m)
Weight: 12st 4lb (79kg)
Occupation: Surveyor
Born: Bridgend, 9.2.69
Family: Single
Family links with rugby: Brother (Graham) plays for Bridgend; brother (Lloyd) plays for Cambridge University
Former clubs: Pencoed Youth, Neath
International debut: Wales 24, Barbarians 31, 1990
Five Nations' debut: None
Best moment in rugby: Helping Neath beat the mighty Pontypool

side in the 1986/87 Schweppes Welsh Cup semi-finals

Worst moment in rugby: 1990 Varsity match

Most respected opponent: Aled Williams (Swansea)

Biggest influence on career: Ron Waldron (coach at Wales U-19s & Neath)

Serious injuries: Neck problem for one and a half years

Wales (1990)		
Last Season	2 caps	3 pts
Career	4 caps	3 pts

Caps (4): **1991** Ba(R), A **1993** Z(1,2)

Points (6 – 2dg): **1991** A(1dg) **1993** Z(1:1dg)

Other sporting achievements: Football Blue at Cambridge (offered trials with Leeds United and Sheffield Wednesday aged 16), having played for Wales U-15s

Best memory last season: Regaining Test place in Zimbabwe

Suggestions to improve rugby: *On-field* – Legalize lifting in line-out if it will make the set-piece less of a mess. Abandon idea of quick throw-ins at lineouts. Preserve kicking in rugby – it is an art. *Off-field* – For us to compete with Southern Hemisphere nations we must sort ourselves out. Players do not necessarily have to gain but they must certainly not lose out by playing top-level rugby. It is a joke when nations tour short-handed because certain players cannot afford time off work. Unions have accepted some kind of responsibility that people cannot train four or five times per week and then play purely for enjoyment. The players must not be ignored

Notable landmarks in rugby career: Captained Wales at U-18, U-19 and U-21 levels. Kicked four penalty goals for Wales B in 15–28 loss to France B at La Teste (12.11.89). Made full debut for Wales when coming on as 47th minute replacement for Mark Ring during 24–31 loss to Barbarians (6.10.91) and dropped a goal against Australia in Wales' 6–63 record reversal in Brisbane (21.7.91). Included in Welsh World Cup squad but talent was not utilised. Switched from Neath to Cardiff seeing 'a perfect opportunity, with their great back-division, to be in a position to take hold of a game and run the show'. Captained Cambridge to 17–11 win over Oxford in 110th Varsity Match (10.12.92), kicking nine points. Played also in 1990 and 1991 Varsity matches. Kicked one conversion and two penalty goals on one Wales A appearance last season, but still lost 28–29 loss to Ireland A at Newport (5.3.93). Landed dropped goal in 35–14 first Test win over Zimbabwe (Bulawayo, 22.5.93) but outside-half berth went to Neil Jenkins after second Test in Harare. Scored one of Wales' eight tries in 56–17 defeat of the South African Barbarians, in Windhoek on 9 June

Touchlines: Cricket, piano, trumpet

Davies, J. D.   Wales

Full Name: John David Davies
Club: Neath
Position: Tighthead prop
Height: 5ft 10in (1.78m)
Weight: 17st (108kg)
Occupation: Farmer
Born: Carmarthen, 1.2.69
Family: Single
Family links with rugby: Cousin
plays for Cwmgwrach
Former club: Cwmgwrach
International debut: Wales 21,
Ireland 21, 1991
Five Nations' debut: As above
Best moment in rugby: Making
Wales debut v Ireland
Worst moment in rugby: Neath's
1990/91 Welsh Cup semi-final
defeat by Llanelli
Most respected opponent: Wales
prop Brian Williams (in training)
Suggestions to improve rugby:
On-field – More consistent
refereeing. Scrap 90-degree scrum
wheel law as it slows game down.
Off-field – Keep game amateur but
look after players better

Wales (1991)		
Last Season	2 cap	5 pts
Career	4 caps	5 pts

Caps (4): **1991** I, F **1993** F(R), Z(2)

Points (5-1t): **1993** Z(2:1t)

Notable landmarks in rugby career: Picked up his third full cap 25 minutes
from end of last season, coming on as a 55th minute replacement for Llanelli
loosehead Ricky Evans in 10–26 loss to France at Parc des Princes (20.3.93).
First player from Crymych to represent Wales Youth, turning out against
Ireland, France and England in 1987 and the same three opponents the
following season. Joined Neath in 1987 and was included in Wales B squad in
his first senior season. An Under-21 cap against Scotland in 1989 was followed
by 'B' recognition against Holland, in 34–12 win (1990/91) and against North
of England last season (won 21–13, Pontypool, 14.10.92). Graduated to senior
side in 1991, playing against Ireland (drew 21–21) and France (lost 3–36) in
Five Nations' Championship. Bench reserve for senior side throughout
1992/93 season, until Paris chance materialised. Toured with Wales to
Zimbabwe and Namibia last summer, marking solitary Test appearance with
try in the 42–13 win over Zimbabwe (Harare, 29.5.95). Also turned out against
Zimbabwe B and South African Barbarians (scoring try)
Touchlines: Hunting, shooting

Davies, N. G.   Wales

Full Name: Nigel Gareth Davies
Club: Llanelli
Positions: Centre, wing
Height: 6ft 1in (1.86m)
Weight: 13st 10lb (87kg)
Occupation: Management consultant
Born: Llanelli, 29.3.65
Family: Married
Family links with rugby: Father played for Trimsaran
Former club: Trimsaran
International debut: New Zealand 54, Wales 9, 1988
Five Nations' debut: Scotland 23, Wales 7, 1989
Best moment in rugby: Scoring second of two tries for Wales in 24–6 win over Western Samoa (1988)
Worst moment in rugby: Being dropped after Samoan game (1986)
Most respected opponent: Simon Halliday (ex-Harlequins & England) – so hard to mark
Other sporting achievements: County tennis (member of Llanelli LTC)

Wales (1988)		
Last Season	1 cap	0 pts
Career	5 caps	8 pts

Caps (5): 1988 NZ(2),WS 1989 S,I 1993 F

Points (8 – 2t): 1988 WS(2t)

Best memory last season:
Returning to international fray against France
Suggestions to improve rugby: *Off-field* – Broken time payments. More consideration should be given to players' families
Notable landmarks in rugby career: Returned to the international arena last season after a four-year absence when selected in the Welsh midfield to play France in Paris on 20 March 1993 (lost 10–26). He followed that up by touring with Wales to Zimbabwe and Naimibia over the summer. Had originally graduated from Trimsaran Youth to Wales Youth and passed through national Student and B levels before breaking into the Test side in 1988 on the disastrous tour to New Zealand. His debut came in the second Test, a 54–9 thrashing in Auckland which clinched one of the most convincing 2–0 series results ever. On his return he ran in two tries as Wales defeated Western Samoa 28–6 at Cardiff. The following season he made his Five Nations' debut against Scotland at Murrayfield in a game Wales lost 23–7. But lost his place after the 19–13 home loss to Ireland that same season. Nigel, who toured Italy with Wales B in

1986/87, is very highly regarded on the club scene inside the Principality and has been one of the central figures in Llanelli's triumphant exploits of late – not least their League and Cup double and their 13–9 victory over Australia last season

Touchlines: Reading, music, motocross

Davies, P. T. Wales

Full Name: Philip Thomas Davies
Club: Llanelli
Position: No 8, lock, flanker
Height: 6ft 3in (1.90m)
Weight: 17st 3lb (109kg)
Occupation: Sales executive with Quasar Chemicals (Neath)
Born: Seven Sisters, 19.10.63
Family: Caroline (wife), Rebecca (daughter) and Danikka (daughter)
Family links with rugby: Wife Caroline is Jonathan Davies' sister
Former club: Sevens Sisters, South Wales Police
International debut: Wales 24, England 15, 1985
Five Nations' debut: As above
Best moments in rugby: Captaining Llanelli to three Schweppes Challenge Cup triumphs (1988, 1991 and 1992) against Neath, Pontypool and Swansea respectively
Worst moment in rugby: Wales' 1990 whitewash
Most embarrassing moment: Having ball knocked from grasp by Kenfig Hill centre while touching down in Cup last season
Most respected opponent: Laurent Rodriguez (Dax & France)
Biggest influence on career: Gareth Jenkins (Llanelli coach)
Serious injuries: Broken cheekbone, misplaced disc in neck, dislocated elbow
Other sporting achievements: Swam for West Wales Schools
Best memory last season: Llanelli's win over Australia
Suggestions to improve rugby: *On-field* – Allow handling in rucks when it

Wales (1985)

Last Season	3 caps	5 pts
Career	35 caps	21 pts

Caps (35): **1985** E, Fj **1986** E, S, I, F, Fj, T, WS **1987** F, E(a), I wc–T, C, NZ **1988** WS, Ro **1989** S, I, F, E, NZ **1990** F, E, S **1991** I, F(a), A(a), F(b) wc–WS, Arg, A(b) **1993** F Z(1), Na

Points (21 – 5t): **1985** Fj(2t) **1986** I(1t) **1990** E(1t) **1993** Z(1:1t)

181

improves continuity of game. Improve general organization from national viewpoint. *Off-field* – Remuneration for time spent away from work. Reduce number of games played in Wales

Notable landmarks in rugby career: Picked up his 33rd cap on final Five Nations weekend last season when recalled in place of clubmate Tony Copsey for trip to France, who won 26–10 (20.3.93). His return capped a fine season, which included Llanelli beating the touring Wallabies 13–9 at Stradey (14.11.92) and clinching the League and Cup double, and which ended on tour with Wales in Zimbabwe and Namibia. Be nch reserve for Wales XV against Italy XV(won 43–12, Cardiff, 7.10.92). First played for Wales at 16-Group. Former policeman. Broke into full Welsh squad in 1984. Marked second cap with two tries in 40-3 win over Fiji at the National Stadium (9.11.85). Had jaw broken by punch in controversial Five Nations' clash with England (Twickenham, 7.3.87). Dropped after playing in 1987 World Cup and became Wales B captain. Returned against Western Samoa in 1988 but missed that year's Champion-ship. Retired from international arena when left out of team to play the centenary Barbarians (6.10.90) but returned during 1991 Five Nations and held place through 1992 Australia tour and World Cup before being replaced by Swansea's Stuart Davies for 1992 Championship campaign. Llanelli's most-capped in ternational (33 at lock, blindside flanker and No 8) has also represented Crawshays and the Barbarians. Stepped down as Scarlets' captain at end of 1991/92 season after five years in the job (four Cup finals, three wins)

Touchlines: Golf

Davies, S. Wales

Full Name: Stuart Davies
Club: Swansea
Position: No 8
Height: 6ft 3in (1.90m)
Weight: 17st 4lb (110kg)
Occupation: Environmental Health Officer with Swansea City Council
Born: Swansea, 2.9.65
Family: Lorna (wife)
Family links with rugby: Father (Elwyn) played at centre for Swansea
Former club: South Glamorgan Institute
International debut: Ireland 15, Wales 16, 1992
Five Nations' debut: As above

Best moment in rugby: Whole debut weekend in Ireland

Worst moment in rugby: Losing two successive WRU Schweppes Challenge Cup semi-finals (1990–91) and the next two finals (1992–93)

Most embarrassing moment: Falling over when running out onto pitch for Swansea against All Blacks (21.10.89, lost 22–37)

Wales (1992)		
Last Season	7 caps	5 pts
v Italy XV	1 app	5 pts
Career	11 caps	9 pts

Caps (8): **1992** I, F, E, S, A **1993** E, S, I, Z(1R,2), Na

Points (4 – 1t): **1992** I(1t) 1993 Z(2:1t)

Most respected opponent: Wayne Shelford (Northampton & New Zealand)

Biggest influence on career: My father

Serious injuries: Cartilage operation on each knee, torn medial ligaments in left knee

Best memories last season: Beating England at Cardiff; Swansea beating Wallabies 21–6

Suggestions to improve rugby: *On-field* – More discussion between players and referees. Increase feedback from both sides can only improve on-field understanding. *Off-field* – Greater rewards for efforts put in by players

Notable landmarks in rugby career: Capped 1992/93 season by leading Swansea to a famous 21–6 win over Australia at St Helens on 4 November 1992. Began term well with try in Wales XV's 43–12 win over Italy at the National Stadium (7.10.92) although, internationally, the campaign ended in disap-pointment when he was dropped for the final Championship game in Paris (20.3.93). Represented Wales at Under-15, Under-16 and Under-18 levels and was an Under-21 squad member (1987). Attended South Glamorgan Institute, where represented Welsh Colleges, Students and Academicals. Selected for Wales B squad in 1989 but the match against France coincided with his wedding. Called into Wales squad post-1991 World Cup and played full 1992 Championship season at No 8. As vice-captain of Swansea, was particularly proud to collect 1992 Heineken Championship winners' medal, though missed out on Cup winners' medal when Llanelli triumphed at the National Stadium. Scarlets repeated feat last season before Stuart left with Wales for tour of Zimbabwe and Namibia, where he appeared in all three Tests (the first as a late replacement against Zimbabwe). Scored try against Zimbabweans in 42–13 win in Harare (29.5.93)

Touchlines: Golf (22-handicap), seeing my wife

De Glanville, P. R.   England

Full Name: Philip Ranulph de Glanville
Clubs: Bath
Position: Centre
Height: 6ft (1.83m)
Weight: 13st (82kg)
Occupation: Marketing executive with Cow & Gate, Trowbridge
Born: Loughborough, 1.10.68
Family: Single
Family links with rugby: Father played for Loughborough and Rosslyn Park. Now MD of Rhino scrum machines
Former clubs: Durham Univ, Oxford Univ
International debut: England 33, South Africa 16, 1992
Five Nations' debut: Wales 10, England 9, 1993
Best moment in rugby: Winning first cap as replacement against South Africa (November 1992)
Worst moment in rugby: English Students losing 16–6 to Welsh in Cardiff (1989)

England (1992)

Last Season	2 caps	0 pts
1993	Tour to Canada	
Career	2 caps	0 pts

Caps (2): **1992** SA(R) **1993** W(R)

Points Nil

Most embarrassing moment:
Losing match for Durham Univ on Canadian tour when dropped a goalbound penalty effort beneath posts, and Univ of Victoria scored try from resultant scrum
Most respected opponent: Fran Clough (Wasps & England)
Best memory last season: England caps and Bath's Championship win
Serious injuries: Broken arm, dislocated collarbone
Suggestions to improve rugby: Retain County Championship as a meaningful entity
Notable landmarks in rugby career: Won two full caps last season despite not appearing in any starting line-ups. Indeed his two outings as a replacement totalled just 26 minutes. He was a 55th minute substitute for Tony Underwood against South Africa at Twickenham (won 33–16, 14.11.92) and a final-minute replacement for Ian Hunter in the 10-9 Championship defeat in Cardiff (6.2.93). Played in all four England B wins (vSp,I,F,It) in 1991/92. Two caps at Under-21 level included two tries in the inaugural match against Romania U-21s (won 54–13, Bucharest 13.5.89) on debut. Following B debut as a 20-

minute replacement in Piacenza, (Italy 0, England 44, 19. 3.89), he turned out in wins against Namibia and Spain in 1990/91. Helped underdogs Oxford University to win 1990 Varsity match (21–12, 11.12.90) and favourites Bath to win 1991/92 Pilkington Cup (scoring first try in thrilling extra-time defeat of Harlequins). Toured New Zealand with England B in summer of '92, playing in both 'Test' losses to the All Black XV (lost 18–24, Hamilton, 28.6.92; lost 18–26, Pukekohe, 5.7.92) and scoring a try in the second. Also appeared in cracking B game against South Africa at Bristol – tenth B appearance – which ended in a 20–16 win for the Springboks (7.11.92). Concluded fine season by helping Bath to League title and then embarking on England A's tour to Canada
Touchlines: Windsurfing

Deslandes, C.   France

Full Name: Christophe Deslandes
Club: Racing Club
Position: Lock, No 8
Height: 6ft 6½in (1.99m)
Weight: 16st 5lb (104kg)
Occupation: Computer analyst
Born: Saint-Monde, 2.1.65
Former club: Grenoble
International debut: Australia 21, France 9, 1990
Five Nations' debut: France 36, Wales 3, 1991
Notable landmarks in rugby career: Appeared at No 8 in his solitary France B outing, when scoring one of six tries in a 35–16 win over England B at Leicester (3.3.89). Graduated to the senior side the following season, touring Australia and playing in the 9–21 first Test loss to the Wallabies in Sydney (9.6.90). Lost his Test place thereafter, though turned out against New South Wales and Queensland. Returned to the international arena five months later when, after impressing in the colours of Centre-

France (1990)

Last Season	3 caps	0 pts
Career	6 caps	0 pts

Caps (6): 1990 A(1), NZ(2) **1991** W(a) **1992** R, Arg(a1,a2)

Points Nil

Limousin, narrow 24–27 losers to the touring All Blacks at Brive (24.10.90), he was called in for the second Test at Parc des Princes (10.11.90), one of ten changes from the side well beaten at Nantes the previous week. Unhappily for him and France, New Zealand still won 30–12 and he was adjudged responsible for indiscretions leading to three of Grant Fox's six penalty successes. Still, he retained his place in the squad throughout the 1991 Championship, making his Five Nations' debut in France's record 36–3 win over Wales in Paris (2.3.91). But he was then omitted both from the tour party to the United States and the World Cup squad. Almost a year's exile ended with his return in France's 25–6 defeat of Romania at Le Havre in May 1992, followed by appearances in both Tests on the 1992 summer tour of Argentina

Devergie, T.   France

Full Name: Thierry Devergie
Club: Nimes
Position: Lock
Height: 6ft 6in (1.98m)
Weight: 17st 4lb (110kg)
Occupation: Public relations officer
Born: Marseille, 27.7.66
International debut: Romania 12, France 16, 1988
Five Nations' debut: Wales 19, France 29, 1990
Notable landmarks in rugby career: Only started rugby at the age of 16 after a childhood spent playing handball. Quickly acquired representative honours, graduating through Schools, Junior, Army and 'B' levels. Broke into the French team in 1988 but had to wait two years to make his Five Nations' Championship bow (against Wales in Cardiff) due to a broken jaw sustained in 1989. Happily, he recovered in time to tour New Zealand in 1989. Switched to No 8 for the second Test against Australia that same year before reverting to lock thereafter, including an

France (1988)		
Last Season	2 caps	0 pts
Career	15 caps	0 pts

Caps (15): **1988** Ro **1989** NZ(1,2), BL, A(2) **1990** W, E, S, I, Ro, A(1,2,3) **1991** US(2), W

Points Nil

appearance against the British Lions XV in the French Revolution Bicentennial match (4.10.89). After a full international diary in 1990, including the three-Test series against Australia, Thierry was overlooked for the 1991 Five Nations' Championship, returning for the North American tour, before playing the role of redundant member in the French World Cup squad.

Deylaud, C.   France

Full Name: Christophe Deylaud
Club: Toulouse
Position: Centre
Height: 5ft 9½in (1.76m)
Weight: 11st 11lb (75kg)
Occupation: Civil servant
Born: 2.10.64
International debut: France 25, Romania 6, 1992
Five Nations' debut: None
Notable landmarks in rugby career: Highly promising midfielder but one who failed to sustain his challenge for a Test place last season as winter approached. Having been initially blooded in the 25–6 defeat of Romania at Le Havre (28.5.92), he was retained for the summer tour to Argentina, contributing a try and conversion to the 27–12 first Test win in Buenos Aires (4.7.92), although he was later replaced by Christian Courveille, and retaining his berth alongside Courveille for the 33–9 second Test win the following week. Nevertheless, he returned home with the praise of Robert

France (1992)
Last Season	4 caps	7 pts
Career	4 caps	7 pts
France VII	1993 World Cup Sevens	

Caps (4): 1992 R, Arg(a1,a2), SA(1)

Points (7 – 1t,1c): 1992 Arg(a1:1t,1c)

Paparemborde ringing in his ears. 'Christophe is going to become a magnificent player in our back division,' forecast the then team manager. 'He is an excellent link-man and his fast hands make him a very good distributor of the ball.' Yet the visit of South Africa to Lyon (17.10.92) marked the beginning of the end of his season as France were downed 15–20 and Thierry Lacroix was drafted in to partner Franck Mesnel. Deylaud retained his place in the squad until Christmas, warming the bench against South Africa in Paris (24.10.92) and Argentina in Nantes (14.11.92), but was then excluded from the squad for France's victorious 1993 Five Nations' Championship campaign. Ended season on a high note when selected to represent France in the inaugural World Cup Sevens tournament at Murrayfield (April 1993)

Dooley, W. A.   England

Full Name: Wade Anthony Dooley
Club: Preston Grasshoppers
Position: Lock
Height: 6ft 8in (2.03m)
Weight: 17st 13lb (113kg)
Occupation: Police constable with
Lancashire Constabulary
Born: Warrington, 2.10.57
Family: Sharon (wife), Sophie
Helen (daughter) and Sara Eleanor
(daughter)
Family links with rugby: Father
(Geoff) played Rugby League.
Brother (Paul) also plays for
Grasshoppers
Former club: Fylde
International debut: England 22,
Romania 15, 1985
Five Nations' debut: England 9,
France 9, 1985
Best moments in rugby: Achieving
double Grand Slam (1991–92) with
England; 1991 World Cup final
Worst moment in rugby: England
losing Grand Slam match to
Scotland (1990)
Most embarrassing moment:
Being banned for one match for part
in unsavoury Wales–England match
at Twickenham (lost 12–19, 7.3.87)
Most respected opponents: Steve
Cutler (Australia)/Bob Norster
(Wales)/Gary Whetton (NZ)
Biggest influence on career: Dick
Greenwood (ex-Grasshoppers &
England coach)
Serious injuries: Torn medial
ligament (right knee)

England (1985)		
Last Season	5 caps	0 pts
Career	55 caps	12 pts
Lions 1986		
1989	2 Tests	0 pts
1993	Tour to New Zealand	

Caps (55): **1985** Ro, F, S, I, W,
NZ(2R) **1986** W, S, I, F **1987** F,
W wc-A, US, W **1988** F, W, S,
I(1,2), A(a1,a2), Fj, A(b) **1989** S,
I, F, W, Ro, Fj. Lions-A (2,3)
1990 I, F, W, S, Arg(a1,a2),
Arg(b) **1991** W, S, I, F wc-NZ,
US, F, S, A **1992** S, I, F, W, C,
SA **1993** W, S, I

Points (12 – 3t): **1986** F(1t) **1987** wc-
US(1t) **1992** W(1t)

Other sporting achievements: Blackpool police division volleyball champions
Best memory last season: Booking place on Lions tour
Suggestions to improve rugby: *On-field* – Repeal 90-degree scrummaging
law at international level. *Off-field* – Trust funds for International players. Relax

regulations on players earning money from promoting goods, sponsors for players etc. Clarification of what players can and cannot do. RFU must get act together

Notable landmarks in rugby career: Only the fourth Englishman to reach 50-cap milestone (Rory Underwood, Peter Winterbottom and Rob Andrew being the others). Celebrated feat with 77th minute try against Welsh (7.3.92). A Rugby League man at school, he met with considerable success in Union before retiring after returning home prematurely from the Lions tour in New Zealand last summer due to a family bereavement. Wade is England's most-capped lock (overtaking Bill Beaumont's previous best on the Argentina tour in July 1990). He also helped the Lions win the 1989 Test series 2–1 in Australia. Featured in both World Cup tournaments (1987 and 1991) and has been at the epicentre of all England's best work since his debut in 1985, though his effectiveness diminished a touch during 1992/93 season when new laws changed emphasis of game. His departure leaves a massive hole to be filled

Touchlines: All types of music except jazz. Watching old black and white movies. Fell walking. Eating out. Passion for gardening

Dowd, G. W. — New Zealand

Full Name: Graham William Dowd
Province: North Harbour
Position: Hooker
Height: 5ft 11in (1.81m)
Weight: 16st 8lb (105kg)
Occupation: Building estimator
Born: 17.12.63
Family: Raewyn (wife)
Former Province: Auckland (colts)
International debut: New Zealand 24, Ireland 21, 1992
Notable landmarks in rugby career: Enjoyed swift rise to prominence in 1991 after impressing in the All Black trial at Rotorua in the Possibles side beaten 22–40 by the Probables. He won his tighthead duel with Norm Hewitt 1–0. His next stop was the New Zealand XV which beat the touring Romanians (60–30 in Auckland) and USSR (56–6 in Hamilton). Then, after playing in Buck Shelford's New Zealand B side which defeated

New Zealand (1992)		
Last Season	1 cap	0 pts
Career	1 cap	0 pts

Caps (1): 1992 I(1R)

Points Nil

Australia B 21–15 in Brisbane, and warming the senior bench in the second and final leg of the Bledisloe Cup series against Australia in Auckland, Graham was selected as the back-up hooker to Sean Fitzpatrick in the All Blacks' World Cup squad. His luck ended there, as he was one of the few players not to feature in the tournament. But patience was rewarded in 1992 when, having been bench reserve throughout the centenary series, he unzipped his tracksuit and came on for loosehead prop Richard Loe 57minutes into New Zealand's 24–21 first Test victory over Ireland at Dunedin. Thereafter, he was taken on the tour of Australia and South Africa where, although unable to shift captain Fitzpatrick from the Test side, he was voted a considerable success in the seven midweek games, against South Australia, ACT, Victoria, Queensland B, Sydney, Orange Free State, Central Unions

Du Preez, R. J. South Africa

Full Name: Robert James Du Preez
Club: Harlequins (Durban)
Province: Natal
Position: Scrum-half
Height: 6ft (1.82m)
Weight: 14st 2lb (90kg)
Occupation: Insurance broker
Born: Potchefstroom, 19.7.63
International debut: South Africa 24, New Zealand 27, 1992
Former Provinces: Western Transvaal, Northern Transvaal
International debut: South Africa 24, New Zealand 27, 1992
Notable landmarks in rugby career: Much travelled since leaving Potchefstroom Technical High School in his home town, having followed his Provincial debut with Western Province in 1982, with a 78-match stint at Northern Transvaal, before moving on to Natal where last season (1992) he helped them to their second Currie Cup triumph in three years, by virtue of a 14–13 win over Transvaal at Ellis Park, Johannesburg (12.9.92).

South Africa (1992)		
Last Season	4 caps	0 pts
Career	4 caps	0 pts

Caps (4): **1992** NZ, A

Points Nil

His opposite number that day was Garth Wright, with whom he toured France and England in the autumn and who displaced him from the Test side for the three internationals. Prior to the tour Robert was a member of the Springbok side which marked South Africa's return to legitimate international competition. Having figured in Natal's 25–43 loss to the touring All Blacks in Durban (1.8.92), he partnered Naas Botha at half-back in the 24–27 Test loss to New Zealand in Johannesburg (15.8.92). The following week he was in the side annihilated 26–3 by world champions Australia in Cape Town. Despite his failure to make the Test team in Europe, he was twice honoured with the captaincy – in the 36–15 win over Languedoc–Roussillon (Beziers, 20.10.92), and in the 15–18 loss to French Universities (Tours, 28.10.92). In addition, he turned out against France B (lost 17–24, Bordeaux, 4.10.92), Provence–Cote D'Azur (won 41–12, Marseille, 13.10.92) and, at Elland Road, Leeds, the Northern Division (won 19–3, 10.11.92)

Eales, J. A. Australia

Full Name: John Anthony Eales
Club: Brothers
State: Queensland
Position: Lock
Height: 6ft 7in (2.00m)
Weight: 16st 7lb (107kg)
Occupation: Promotions manager with G&E Hotels
Born: 27.6.70
Family: Jack (father), Rosa (mother), Bernadette (sister), Damian (brother), Antoinette (sister), Rosaleen (sister)
Former clubs: None. Brothers since 1988
International debut: Australia 63, Wales 6, 1991
Best moments in rugby: First cap; 1991 World Cup; 1992 Bledisloe Cup
Worst moments in rugby: Injury vs Llanelli in 1992 defeat; losing Eden Park Test to New Zealand
Most respected opponent: Ian Jones (North Auckland & New Zealand)
Serious injuries: Right a/c joint v World XV (April 1992); left shoulder vs Llanelli (1992)

Australia (1991)

Last Season	7 caps	4 pts
Career	17 caps	4 pts

Caps (17): **1991** W(a), E(a), NZ(a1,a2). wc–Arg, WS, W(b), I, NZ(b), E(b) **1992** S(1,2), NZ(1,2,3), SA, I

Points (4 – 1t): **1992** S(2:1t)

Best memory last season: Bledisloe Cup win at Ballymore which clinched 1992 series

Suggestions to improve rugby: *Off-field* – If rugby is to continue to be as professional as it is, playing and training wise, where currently we are on call for virtually 11 months of the year, it needs to give players some financial security. Many players have to make big sacrifices to go on tours. Promotion of the game must also be given a high priority

Notable landmarks in rugby career: One of the world's foremost lineout men, John announced himself in 1990 when winning the coveted Rothmans Medal Best-and-Fairest Award in Brisbane club rugby. His skills were appreciated by a wider audience when he toured Europe with the Emerging Wallabies, playing in the 12–12 draw with England B at Wasps. From there he was included in the Aussies' World Cup training squad and, having made his debut in the record rout of Wales at Ballymore, he played all six matches in the Cup-winning side. His astonishing rise continued in 1992 when he was selected to play for the World XV in the Centenary Series against New Zealand. Unfortunately, he damaged a shoulder in the second Test. Started 1992 superbly when voted the Chivas Regal Man-of-the-Series against Scotland, having scored his first Test try in the 27–12 opening international win. Thereafter, toured South Africa – playing against Northern Transvaal and the Republic itself – and took his cap tally to 17 when appearing in the 42–17 win over Ireland on 31 October. His other tour outings came against Leinster, Ulster (scored try), Swansea, Neath and Llanelli

Tours: 1991 – New Zealand, World Cup. 1992 – South Africa, Ireland and Wales

Touchlines: Golf, cricket, reading

Rory Underwood tests John Timu's defence during the first Test in Christchurch. The All Black fullback shepherded his man into touch

Earl, A. T.　　　　　　　　　New Zealand

Full Name: Andrew Thomas Earl
Club: Glenmark
Province: Canterbury
Position: Flanker, No 8, lock
Height: 6ft 4in (1.93m)
Weight: 15st 12lb (101kg)
Occupation: Farmer
Born: Christchurch, 12.9.61
Family: Teressa (wife)
Family links with rugby: Chris (brother) played prop for Canterbury (1984-86), NZ Colts (1984) and NZ Emerging Players
Former province (club): Wairarapa-Bush (Tuhitangi, 1979–82)
International debut: New Zealand 18, France 9, 1986
Notable landmarks in rugby career: An impressive player since making his first-class debut as a 17-year old for Wairarapa–Bush, where represented New Zealand Colts in 1982. After four years he switched unions to Canterbury and was a fixture in the side which monopolized the Ranfurly Shield from late '82 to '85, when Auckland embarked on their as-yet unbeaten run with a 28–23 win at Christchurch.

New Zealand (1986)

Last Season	2 caps	0 pts
Career	14 caps	12 pts

Caps (14): **1986** F(a), A(1), F(b2R) **1987** wc–Arg **1989** W, I **1991** Arg(1R,2), A(a1). wc–E(R), US, S **1992** A(2,3R)

Points (12 – 3t): **1987** wc–Arg(1t) **1991** Arg(1R:1t). wc–US(1t)

Andy broke into the New Zealand Test side in 1986, while the Cavaliers were serving their ban. He turned out at lock on his debut against France, in the win at Lancaster Park, before switching to flanker for his second appearance against Australia, the 12–13 loss in Wellington. He lost his place for the next two Tests to fellow Cantabrian Jock Hobbs, he of Lancashire club Vale of Lune fame, but toured France at the end of the year, coming on as a second half replacement lock for Gary Whetton in the famous 16–3 second Test loss at Nantes. Andy was a member of the All Blacks' World Cup winning squad in 1987, selected as a flanker, though played just the one game: scoring a 67th minute try in the 46–15 defeat of Argentina at Carisbrook, Dunedin. Played eight games on the 1988 tour of Australia without being capped. Returned to the Test side during the 1989 tour of Wales and Ireland, after Alan Whetton sustained hamstring tear against Swansea. Enjoyed his most productive international year in 1991 when he collected six caps, two on the tour of Argentina, one in the opening Test of the Bledisloe Cup series, and three in the World Cup. Missed out on original selection for tour to Australia and South Africa but responded to injury SOS in time to play in the second and third (replacement) Tests against the Aussies. Scored try in the 33–14 win over Orange Free State

Edwards, N. G. B.   Scotland

Full Name: Neil George Barry Edwards
Club: Harlequins
Position: Lock
Height: 6ft 4in (1.93m)
Weight: 18st (114kg)
Occupation: Chartered surveyor with Furnitureland of Catford
Born: Carshalton, Surrey, 20.8.64
Family: Single
Family links with rugby: Father (Barry) played for Army and Richmond
Former club: Rosslyn Park
International debut: Scotland 7, England 25, 1992
Five Nations' debut: As above
Best moments in rugby: Scotland's pushover try against England on my debut; reaching semi-finals with Barbarians at 1989 Hong Kong Sevens
Worst moments in rugby: Captaining Harlequins to a 20–42 loss at the hands of Cambridge Univ the day before the 1991 World Cup final; losing Scotland place

Scotland (1992)		
Last Season	1 cap	0 pts
Career	5 caps	4 pts

Caps (5): **1992** E, I, F, W, A(1)

Points (4 – 1t): **1992** F(1t)

Most embarrassing moment: Singing 'Flower of Scotland' prior to Scottish debut I was smiling at someone in the crowd, totally lost my concentration, and started singing the wrong line
Most respected opponent: John Morrison (Bristol & England B)
Biggest influences on career: Father and Dick Best (Harlequins coach)
Serious injuries: Compressed vertebrae of neck (Nov 1990)
Other sporting achievements: Soccer trial for Crystal Palace FC, as a goalkeeper, when aged 18
Suggestions to improve rugby: *On-field* – Eliminate the wearing of long

Australian Rugby League studs, which are long, thin and much sharper, like stiletto heels. Easily able to severely damage someone's back at the bottom of a ruck. people forget that there are no rucks in RL and we have to go to work on Monday. *Off-field* – Greater involvement of wives and girlfriends by Unions. Easier to get blessing for periods away from them if they are made to feel special

Notable landmarks in rugby career: Lost Scotland place to fellow Anglo Damian Cronin during 1992 tour to Australia, having picked up fifth cap in first Test, which ended 27–12 in Wallabies' favour (Sydney, 13.6.92). Spent five years with Rosslyn Park on leaving school aged 17. Made debut against Newport aged 19 when Paul Ackford left to join Harlequins. Represented England Students and British Polys while studying at Oxford Polytechnic before being attending England's 1989 training camp in Portugal. The year previous he had helped Harlequins win the John Player Special Cup at Twickenham. Quins' coach Dick Best selected him for the London XV which beat the touring Wallabies, but with messrs Ackford and Dooley firmly ensconsed in the England set-up, Neil turned to his Scottish qualification (Dundonian grandparents). Impressed playing for the Anglo-Scots, Scotland B and the Junior Reds in the 1992 national trial and was consequently one of four newcomers to be blooded in the Calcutta Cup clash. Scored winning try against France at Murrayfield on third appearance, on an afternoon in which he cleaned out not only the French lineout but also a bookmaker (£1,500) who had offered 40/1 odds against his scoring the first try. The rumour is that said bookie now offers Neil at 4/1-on favourite for every game he plays

Touchlines: Skiing, cricket

Elwood, E. P.   Ireland

Full Name: Eric Paul Elwood
Club: Lansdowne
Position: Outside-half
Height: 6ft (1.83m)
Weight: 13st 4lb (84kg)
Occupation: Sales representative with Irish Distillers
Born: Galway, 26.2.69
Family: Single
Former club: Galwegians
International debut: Wales 14, Ireland 19, 1993
Five Nations' debut: As above
Best moment in rugby: Winning first cap
Worst moment in rugby: Lansdowne's relegation from

Division One of the 1991/92 All-Ireland League

Most respected opponent: Frano Botica (ex-New Zealand)

Biggest influences on career: Michael Casserely, Warren Gatland, Eddie O'Sullivan and Graham Taylor

Serious injuries: Chipped vertebrae in neck (1987)

Ireland (1993)		
Last Season	2 caps	23 pts
Career	2 caps	23 pts

Caps (2): **1993** W,E

Points (23 – 1c,5p,2dg): **1993** W(1c,3p), E(2p,2dg)

Other sporting achievements: Gaelic footballer

Best memory last season: Beating England

Suggestions to improve rugby: *On-field* – Like to see ruck/maul law reffed according to the spirit of the game and not to the letter of the law. But killing of the ball should always be penalized. *Off-field* – Too much strain on players to give required commitment and still satisfy employers. So many firms these days see rugby employees as liabilities rather than assets

Notable landmarks in rugby career: Having missed out on a Schools trial, first wore an Ireland jersey on 30 September 1989 when on the national U-21 side beaten 10–9 by their Italian counterparts in Treviso. Bench reserve for following match v New Zealand U-21s (D 13–13, 19.11.89). Connacht debut came in the same year, v Ulster. Progressed up international ladder last season after series of impressive displays for Connacht: v Australia and throughout Inter-Provincial Championship. Missed national trial but was drafted onto Ireland bench for the visit to Dublin of France, and subsequently succeeded Niall Malone as outside-half. Headlined in games v Wales and England, not least because Ireland won both. He contributed 23 of the 36 points scored by the men in green and was widely acclaimed. His omission from the Lions' squad, named 48 hours after England's defeat in Dublin, was contentious.

Touchlines: Gym, social golf

Grant Fox, the All Black's matchwinner, tags Lion's skipper Gavin Hastings during the first Test in Christchurch. Peter Winterbottom and Frank Bunce are in close attendance

Evans, I. C.   Wales

Full Name: Ieuan Cenydd Evans
Club: Llanelli
Position: Wing
Height: 5ft 10½in (1.79kg)
Weight: 13st 5lb (85kg)
Occupation: Leasing executive with
Autopia Contract Hire (Cwmbran)
Born: Pontardulais, 21.3.64
Family: Single
Family links with rugby: Father
(John) played for Aberavon
Former club: Carmarthen Quins
International debut: France 16,
Wales 9, 1987
Five Nations' debut: As above
Best moment in rugby: Scoring
tries that (i) clinched Test series for
1989 Lions in Australia and (ii) beat
England in Cardiff (1993)
Worst moment in rugby: New
South Wales 71, Wales 8, 1991
Most respected opponent: David
Campese (Mediolanum Milan &
Australia) – can never let him out of
your sight
Serious injuries: Recurring
dislocated shoulder, broken leg
Best memory last season: Scoring
decisive try against England at the
National Stadium – a very gratifying
score
Suggestions to improve rugby:
Off-field – Reimburse employers for
employees' time spent away from
work playing rugby. Employers are
indirectly the sponsors of the game.
Credit WRU for moving in right
direction

Wales (1987)		
Last Season	5 caps	10 pts
v Italy XV	1 app	5 pts
Career	36 caps	42 pts
Lions 1989	3 Tests	4 pts
1993	3 Tests	0pts

Caps (36): **1987** F, E(a),S, I(a)
wc–I(b), C, E(b), NZ,A **1988** E,
S, I, F, NZ(1,2) **1989** I, F, E.
Lions–A(1,2,3) **1991** E, S, I,
F(a), A(a), F(b) wc–WS, Arg,
A(b) **1992** I, F, E, S, A **1993** E, S,
I, F. Lions–NZ (1,2,3)

Points (42 – 10t): **1987** I(a:1t) wc–C(4t)
1988 S(1t), F(1t) **1989**
Lions–A(3:1t) **1991** wc-WS(1t)
1993 E(1t), I(1t)

Notable landmarks in rugby career: The *Rugby World & Post* 1992/93
Player of the Year, Ieuan was named Wales' 103rd captain when appointed
under the management of Robert Norster and Alan Davies prior to 1991 World
Cup. Playing career severely hampered by injury – five dislocations and two
operations. Played all three Tests in 1989 Lions series win (2–1) in Australia,

scoring series-clinching try in final Test in Sydney (won 19–18, 15.7.89). On return was forced to miss whole of 1989/90 season through injury. Played in five matches in 1987 World Cup, scoring four tries in 40–9 defeat of Canada, and contributed one (against Western Samoa) to Wales' 1991 Cup challenge. Scored six tries for Wales B in 1985 defeat of Spain (80–9) at Bridgend. National hero when running in winning try against England (6.2.93) last season. Also crossed against Ireland, in next Test at Arms Park (6.3.93) to account for two-thirds of Wales' entire try-tally in 1992/93 season. One of four Welshmen on 1993 Lions squad, making seven appearances (including all three Tests). Scored tries in each provincial match (v North Harbour, Maoris, Otago and Auckland). Domestically, scored winning try as Llanelli beat Australia 13–9 (14.11.92) and shared in Scarlets' 1992/93 League and Cup double
Touchlines: Tennis, cricket, squash, golf

Evans, R. L.   Wales

Full Name: Richard (Ricky) Lloyd Evans
Club: Llanelli
Position: Loosehead prop
Height: 6ft 2in (1.88m)
Weight: 17st 3lb (109kg)
Occupation: Fireman in the Dyfed-Powys Brigade
Born: Cardigan, 23.6.61
Family: Married with son and daughter
Former clubs: Cardigan, Army
International debut: Wales 10, England 9, 1993
Five Nations' debut: As above
Best moment in rugby: Beating England on debut in Cardiff
Worst moment in rugby: Not being included in Welsh squad for 1993 tour to Zimbabwe and Namibia
Most embarrassing moment: Coming on as replacement flanker for Llanelli and used hands to push ball back between legs at scrum
Most respected opponent: David Young (ex-Cardiff & Wales)
Serious injuries: Broken leg

Wales (1993)

Last Season	4 caps	0 pts
Career	4 caps	0 pts

Caps (4): **1993** E, S, I, F

Points Nil

198

Other sporting achievements: Long boat rowing for Aberporth LBC
Best memories last season: Wales debut and Llanelli's success
Suggestions to improve rugby: Referees must hold tighter disciplinary reins
Notable landmarks in rugby career: Spent nine years in Army (16–25) before playing for two years in Pembrokeshire League with Cardigan. Other causes represented are Army, Crawshays and both Wales and British Fire Brigades. Broke leg against Cambridge University in only his sixth game for Llanelli. Toured Canada with Wales B in 1989, making three appearances. Wore their colours again last season in 21–13 victory over North of England (Pontypool, 14.10.92) and 11–24 loss to Australia (Cardiff, 7.11.92). Gained revenge on Wallabies following weekend when helping Llanelli score 13–9 win at Stradey. Scarlets completed great season with League and Cup double. Ricky, who finished fourth in the televised 'Strongest Man' competition in 1992, made his Wales debut in 1993 Five Nations' Championship as a result of Mike Griffiths' freak cycling accident in Lanzarote, in which he broke a collarbone to put himself out for campaign. Ricky wore No 1 jersey in all four games but was then omitted from Welsh squad to tour Zimbabwe and Namibia

Farr-Jones, N. C. **Australia**

Full Name: Nicholas (Nick) Campbell Farr-Jones
Club: Sydney University
Position: Scrum-half
Height: 5ft 10in (1.78m)
Weight: 13st 3lb (84kg)
Occupation: Solicitor with Garland Hawthorn Brahe
Born: 18.4.62
Family: Angela (wife), Jessica (daughter)
Former clubs: None. Sydney University since 1980
International debut: England 3, Australia 19, 1984
Best moments in rugby: Winning 1991 World Cup; beating South Africa by record score (26–3) in August 1992
Worst moment in rugby: Losing to 1989 British Lions
Most embarrassing moment: Being photographed in the nude talking to British Prime Minister John Major
Most respected opponent: Gary Armstrong (Jed-Forest & Scotland)

Serious injuries: None
Other sporting achievements: Winning a chook in 1977 for the best back-nine at the Australia Golf Club
Best memories last season: Meeting ANC leader Nelson Mandela during 1992 tour of South Africa; winning 1992 Bledisloe Cup
Suggestions to improve rugby: *On-field* – Administrators to consult players, coaches and referees before making law changes. *Off-field* – administrators to leave running of game to professional marketing groups, providing the essence of rugby union is not lost
Notable landmarks in rugby career: Retired as Australia's captain after leading the side to a famous 26–3 win over South Africa in Cape Town. The defeat was the heaviest ever suffered by the Springboks and victory completed Nick's collection of scalps. The Wallabies' most-capped scrum-half, with 59 appearances to his name (though one came as a replacement wing), he also shared with Michael Lynagh the world record halfback partnership of 47 games together. The seeds of a proud career were sown in 1981 when he moved into senior grade rugby after only a year of Colts. He played for Australia Universities on tour in Britain before returning in 1984 as the Grand Slam scrum-half. An ever-popular Barbarians' invitee, he was first appointed as Australian captain against England in 1988 and remained in charge until leaving the Newlands pitch on 22 August 1992
Tours: 1984 – Fiji, United Kingdom and Ireland. 1985 – New Zealand. 1986 – New Zealand. 1987 – World Cup, South America. 1988 – Engl and, Scotland and Italy. 1989 – New Zealand, France and Canada. 1990 – New Zealand. 1991 – New Zealand, World Cup. 1992 – South Africa
Touchlines: Golf, tennis
Player to watch: Ben Clarke (Bath & England)
Player of the Year: John Eales (Australia)

Australia (1984)		
Last Season	6 caps	5 pts
Career	59 caps	37 pts

Caps (59): 1984 E, I, W, S 1985 C(1,2), NZ, Fj(1,2) 1986 It, F, Arg(1,2), NZ(1,2,3) 1987 SK. wc–E, I, F, W(R). NZ, Arg(2) 1988 E(a1,a2), NZ(1,2,3), E(b), S, It 1989 BL(1,2,3), NZ, F(1,2) 1990 F(1,2,3), US, NZ(1,2,3) 1991 W(a), E(b), NZ(a1,a2). wc–Arg, WS, I, NZ(b), E(b) 1992 S(1,2), NZ(1,2,3), SA

Points (37 – 9t): 1984 S(1t) 1985 C(1:1t), C(2:1t), Fj(1:2t) 1987 SK(1t) 1989 F(2:1t) 1990 US(1t) 1992 NZ(3:1t)

Fitzgibbon, M. J.   Ireland

Full Name: Michael Joseph
Fitzgibbon
Club: Shannon
Position: Openside flanker
Height: 6ft 1½in (1.87m)
Weight: 14st 7lb (92kg)
Occupation: Production manager
with Waterford Glass
Born: Askeaton, County Limerick,
2.4.66
Family: Single
Family links with rugby: Uncle
(Basil) played for Munster
Former club: Trinity
International debut: Ireland 15,
Wales 16, 1992
Five Nations' debut: As above
Other sporting achievements:
Represented Limerick at Gaelic
football (minor and U-21 levels)
**Notable landmarks in rugby
career:** Won six caps in two seasons
of representing Irish Schools. Also
played for Irish Universities, whilst
at Dublin University, before getting
Ireland B call-up for 24–10 win over

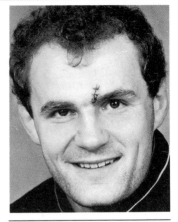

Ireland (1992)

Last Season	2 caps	0 pts
Career	6 caps	0 pts

Caps (6): 1992 W, E, S, F, NZ(1,2)

Points Nil

England (Old Belvedere, 1.3.91). Second B cap (Edinburgh 28.12.91) yielded
a Fitzgibbon try, in the 29–19 win over Scotland B. Won a Munster Senior Cup
medal with Shannon in 1986. Connacht regular who made debut for Ireland
Under-25s against Italy in 1987. Included in 44-man preliminary Ireland squad
for 1991 World Cup but was omitted from final selection. Broke into full side
in 1992 Five Nations' Championship when was an ever-present at openside
flanker (turning out against Wales, England, Scotland and France), and then
went on summer tour to New Zealand where he played in both Test defeats
(21–24 at Dunedin and 6–59 in Wellington). Has not reappeared since in
national team
Touchlines: Indoor soccer, all sport

Fitzpatrick, S. B. T.　　New Zealand

Full Name: Sean Brian Thomas Fitzpatrick
Club: University Province: Auckland
Position: Hooker
Height: 6ft (1.83m)
Weight: 14st 10lb (93kg)
Occupation: Marketing manager
Born: Auckland, 4.6.63
Family: Bronwyn (wife)
Family links with rugby: Brian (father) won three caps as All Black five-eighth (1953 W; 1954 I,F)
International debut: New Zealand 18, France 9, 1986
Notable landmarks in rugby career: Appointed New Zealand captain when a torn calf muscle in the final trial ruled out Mike Brewer prior to the 1992 centenary series, Sean was an everpresent throughout a nine-Test campaign which incorporated the tour to Australia and South Africa, as well as the visits of the World XV and Ireland. Captaincy rested well on his shoulders, taking nothing away from his performances as he took to 52 his tally as the country's most-capped hooker. What makes his achievement the more remarkable is the fact that his last 47 caps have come consecutively – a run which includes all New Zealand's 12 World Cup ties in 1987 and 1991. His total

New Zealand (1986)

Last Season	12 caps	5 pts
Career	52 caps	25 pts

Caps (52): **1986** F(a), A(1), F(b1,b2) **1987** wc-It, Fj, Arg, S, W, F. A **1988** W(1,2), A(1,2,3) **1989** F(1,2), Arg(1,2), A, W, I **1990** S(1,2), A(1,2, 3), F(1,2) **1991** Arg(1,2), A(a1,a2). wc-E, US, It, C, A(b), S **1992** Wd(1,2,3), I(1,2), A(1,2,3), SA **1993** BL(1,2,3)

Points (25 – 6t): **1987** A(2t) **1989** F(2:1t) **1990** A(1:1t),A(2:1t) **1993** BL(3:1t)

All Black appearances amount to 78. Sean, who is widely considered to be the world's premier lineout thrower, is the first Auckland hooker to pass the 100-appearance mark for the province, a total amassed since his debut in 1984. It was not until 1986 that he secured a regular provincial berth, a year which coincided with his Test debut, against France in Christchurch, while the Cavaliers were away in South Africa. He was displaced by the returning Hika Reid for the second and third Tests against the Wallabies later in the year but reversed the roles for the tour of France and has since resisted each and every pretender to his throne. Equalled NZ record for a hooker when scoring two tries in the 30–16 win over Australia in 1987. He was selected for New Zealand Schools in 1981, progressing to NZ Colts, whom he represented in 1983 (along with John Kirwan, Grant Fox and Murray Mexted) and captained the following year. His 1984 charges included Bernie McCahill, Frano Botica (now Wigan RL) and Paul Henderson. Captained the All Blacks on nine occasions during the 1992 tour to Australia (scoring two tries against NSW) and South Africa, in the process becoming the first New Zealander to captain a winning side in the Republic. Then added scalp of 1993 Lions

Fox, G. J. New Zealand

Full Name: Grant James Fox
Club: University
Province: Auckland
Position: Stand-off
Height: 5ft 9in (1.75m)
Weight: 11st 12lb (75kg)
Occupation: Sports marketing executive
Born: New Plymouth, Taranaki, 16.6.62
Family: Adele (wife), Kendall (daughter), Ryan (son)
International debut: Argentina 20, New Zealand 33, 1985
Serious injuries: Pelvis (1991)
Notable landmarks in rugby career: New Zealand's leading Test points scorer with 573 points – a total surpassed only by Australia's Michael Lynagh (760) – Grant is a

former captain of New Zealand Schools who represented NZ Colts in 1983 (along with Sean Fitzpatrick, John Kirwan and Murray Mexted). He first represented Auckland in 1982 when just 20 and has been a central figure in the Province's Ranfurly Shield monopoly since 1985, the year in which he marked his Test debut with a dropped goal against Argentina – opposite another scoring legend, Hugo Porta (605 points). First represented the All Blacks on the 1984 tour of Fiji, when turned out against a President's XV and an Eastern XV, scoring 27 points (3c,6p,1dg). With 126 points, Grant was the leading scorer in the 1987 World Cup, which New Zealand won. He kicked 17 points in the 29–9 final defeat of France on his home Eden Park pitch. Indeed, so impressive was his performance that, after the second World Cup, his 1987 records – total points (126), conversions (30) and penalty goals (21), as well as single match totals for cons (ten) and pens (six) remain supreme. His two-tournament total of 170 (126 + 44) betters second-best Lynagh by 22. If 1987 was his best scoring year, with an average of 20 points through his seven appearances, it was closely followed by 1989 (av: 17 points) and 1988 (av: 15 points). Needed 35 fewer games than Don Clarke to pass the Kiwi legend's 1964 All Black record of 781 points, amassed in 89 games. His tally of well over 3,000 first-class points constitutes another national best. Bitter at public criticism, he contemplated retirement at the end of a 1991 season undermined by a serious hip injury. Replaced by Walter Little after the first Test defeat by the World XV, he displayed great character to return after the Ireland series and excel against Australia and South Africa. Kicked All Blacks to series defeat of 1993 Lions

New Zealand (1985)

Last Season	9 caps	80 pts
Career	44 caps	605 pts

Caps (44): **1985** Arg(1) **1987** wc–It, Fj, Arg, S, W, F. A **1988** W(1,2), A(1,2,3) **1989** F(1,2), Arg(1,2), A, W, I **1990** S(1,2), A(1,2,3), F(1,2) **1991** Arg(1,2), A(a1,a2). wc–E, It, C, A(b) **1992** Wd(1,2R), A(1,2,3), SA **1993** BL(1,2,3)

Points (605 – 1t,116c,116p,7dg): **1985** Arg(1:1dg) **1987** wc–It(8c,2p), Fj(10c,2p), Arg(2c,6p), S(2c,6p), W(7c,1p), F(1c,4p,1dg). A(1c, 3p,1d g) **1988** W(1:6c), W(2:8c, 2p), A(1:3c,2p), A(2:2c,1p), A(3: 3c,4p) **1989** F(1:2c,3p), F(2:3c, 4p), Arg(1:7c,2p), Arg(2:6c,3p), A(2c,4p), W(3c,4p), I(1c,3p) **1990** S(1:1t,4c,1p), S(2:1c,5p), A(1:1c,1p), A(2:3c,2p,1dg), A(3: 2p,1dg), F(1:2c,3p,1dg), F(2:2c, 6p) **1991** Arg(1:1c,5p), Arg(2:4c, 4p), A(1:1c,2p), A(2:2p). wc-E (1c,4p), It(3c,3p), C(3c,1p), A (2p) **1992** Wd(1:2p), Wd(2:1c), A(1:1c,1p), A(2:2c,1p), A(3:2c, 3p,1dg), SA(3c,2p) **1993** BL(1:5p), BL(2:1c) BL(3:3c,3p)

Serge Blanco, the world's most-capped player, hugs Denis Charvet at the end of his farewell game on 31 October 1992, in which he captained the French Barbarians against South Africa

Francis, N. P.   Ireland

Full Name: Neil Patrick Francis
Club: Blackrock College
Position: Lock
Height: 6ft 6in (1.98m)
Weight: 16st 9lb (106kg)
Occupation: Banker with
Gatehouse Leasing
Born: Dublin, 17.3.64
Family: Single
Former clubs: London Irish, Manly
(Aus)
International debut: Ireland 32,
Tonga 9, 1987
Five Nations' debut: Scotland 37,
Ireland 21, 1989
Best moment in rugby: Winning
1981 Schools Cup final with
Blackrock

Worst moment in rugby: Being
dropped by Ireland on 1989 North
American tour
Most respected opponent: Laurent
Rodriguez (Dax & France)
Serious injuries: Broken vertebrae
(out for two years)
Other sporting achievements:
Javelin for Ireland (national junior
and senior champion)

Ireland (1987)		
Last Season	1 cap	0 pts
Career	20 caps	4 pts

Caps (20):	**1987** wc–T, A **1988** WS, It **1989** S **1990** E, F, W **1991** E, S, Na(1,2) wc–Z, J, S, A **1992** W, E, S **1993** F
Points (4 – 1t):	**1988** WS(1t)

**Notable landmarks in rugby
career:** Injury decimated his 1992/93 season, even if he did recover in time to
win 20th cap in 6–21 loss to France in Dublin (20.2.93). Represented Irish
Schools five times (1981–82), but back injury meant no representative rugby
for four years from the age of 19, by which time he had already won Leinster
Senior Cup medal with Blackrock. Did not represent Leinster until 1986.
Scored try for Ireland Under-25s against Canada in 1986. Rejoined Blackrock
from London Irish in 1989. Made full Ireland debut in 1987 World Cup but
not called upon again until October 1988 when scored only international try to
date against touring Western Samoans. Sole Irish representative in Home
Unions team which played Rest of Europe at Twickenham in 1990 Romania
Appeal match. Ever-present in 1991/92 season, including each 1991 World
Cup-tie, until final Five Nations' match in Paris when Brian Rigney returned,
thus breaking Neil's 11-game streak. Toured Namibia with Ireland in 1991 but
missed trip to New Zealand in summer of '92

Fuls, H. T. South Africa

Full Name: Heinrich Theodorus
Fuls
Club: RAU
Province: Transvaal
Position: Centre
Height: 6ft 3in (1.90m)
Weight: 14st 2lb (90kg)
Born: Bloemfontein, 8.3.71
International debut: South Africa
24, New Zealand 27, 1992
**Notable landmarks in rugby
career:** A product of Grey College,
Bloemfontein, he was one of the 17
players accorded the honour of
carrying the South African banner
back into international rugby. A
bench reserve for the historic visit of
New Zealand to Ellis Park,
Johannesburg on 15 August 1992,
Heinrich was brought into the fray
as a last-minute replacement for
Transvaal team mate James Small.
The previous week he had played on
the left wing as Junior South Africa
went down 10–25 to the All Blacks
in Pretoria. He missed out on the

South Africa (1992)

Last Season	3 caps	0 pts
Career	3 caps	0 pts

Caps (3): 1992 NZ(R) 1993 F(1,2)

Points Nil

action against Australia (22.8.92) but returned to Ellis Park for the Currie Cup
final on 12 September and scored Transvaal's only try in a 14–13 defeat by
Natal. His next stop was France where he appeared in five of the Springboks'
seven provincial engagements – against Aquitaine (won 29–22, Pau, 7.10.92),
Midi-Pyrenees (won 18–15, Toulouse, 15.10.92), Langedoc–Roussillon (won
36–15, Beziers, 20.10.92), French Universities (lost 13–18, Tours, 28.10.92)
and French Barbarians (lost 20–25, Lille, 31.10.92) – before crossing the
English Channel and turning out against England B (won 20–16, Bristol,
7.11.92), as a 70th minute replacement for Pieter Muller, and the Northern
Division (won 19–3, Leeds, 10.11.92). Partnered Pieter Müller in midfield for
both Tests against the French tourists last summer

Gallart, P.   France

Full Name: Philippe Gallart
Club: Beziers
Position: Prop
Height: 6ft ½in (1.85m)
Weight: 18st 1lb (115kg)
Occupation: International
computer company representative
Born: 18.12.62
Former club: Pezenas
International debut: France 6,
Romania 12, 1990
Five Nations' debut: Scotland 10,
France 6, 1992
**Notable landmarks in rugby
career:** Recalled in place of Philippe
Gimbert against Scotland (7.3.92),
for the first time since being sent-off
by Clive Norling for punching Tim
Gavin in the 48th minute of the
28–19 third Test win against
Australia in Sydney (30.6.90). For
that misdemeanour a four-month
suspension was meted out, ensuring
that he played no part in the 1991
Five Nations campaign when only
England stood between France and a
fifth Grand Slam. Despite touring to

France (1990)
Last season	6 caps	0 pts
Career	12 caps	0 pts

Caps (12): **1990** Ro, A(1,2R,3) **1992** S,
I, R, Arg(a1,a2), SA(1,2), Arg(b)

Points Nil

North America in summer of '91 he was no less redundant, and failed to make
the 26-man World Cup squad. However, the Paris debacle, which wrote
Gimbert and Lascube out of the international script, allowed Gallart to restore
a representative career which had begun, in Stade Patrice Brocas, Auch, with
defeat against Romania (24.5.90). Injury forced him from the field prematurely, to be replaced by Pascal Ondarts, although he returned Down Under to play
in two and a half Tests against the Wallabies. Doubled Test tally to 12 last
season when wearing the No 3 jersey in each of France's first half dozen
internationals: one against Romania, two against South Africa and three against
Argentina (two on tour in South America). Lost place to Merignac's Laurent
Seigne for 1993 Five Nations' Championship

Galthie, F.   France

Full Name: Fabien Galthie
Club: Colomiers
Position: Scrum-half
Height: 5ft 10½in (1.80m)
Weight: 12st 4lb (78kg)
Occupation: Student
Born: Cahors, 20.3.69
International debut: Romania 21,
France 33, 1991
Five Nations' debut: Wales 9,
France 12, 1992
**Notable landmarks in rugby
career:** Became the first player from
the Colomiers club (Parisien
suburb) to be capped when, to the
surprise of many, he succeeded
Pierre Berbizier at No 9. It was
widely anticipated that Henri Sanz, a
former France B captain and long-
standing understudy to 'le patron'
would step up but erstwhile coach
Daniel Dubroca thought differently,
and successor Berbizier, himself,
agreed. Consequently, Fabien was
given his debut in Bucharest
(22.6.91) and remained intact for
eight of the next ten internationals,

France (1991)

Last Season	2 caps	9 pts
Career	11 caps	9 pts

Caps (11): **1991** Ro, US(1) wc-Ro, Fj,
C, E **1992** W, E, S, R, Arg(b)

Points (9 – 2t): **1992** R(1t), Arg(b:1t)

before Toulon's Aubin Hueber took over for Ireland's Championship visit to
Paris (21.3.92) following mounting criticism of the incumbent. In his defence,
Fabien was unable to settle into a half-back understanding because of the
constantly changing identity of his stand-off, with Didier Camberabero,
Thierry Lacroix and Alain Penaud all given a shot. He even captained France
for part of the Five Nations' game against England (15.2.92) when Philippe
Sella was injured. Saw little Test action last season though was a try -scorer in
both games he did play – against Romania (won 25–6, Le Havre, 28.5.92) and
Argentina (lost 20–24, Nantes, 14.11.92). He was one of eight casualties after
the Pumas' historic first win on French soil. Bench reserve for both Tests
against South Africa

Galwey, M. J.   Ireland

Full Name: Michael Joseph Galwey
Club: Shannon
Position: Lock, flanker
Height: 6ft 4in
Weight: 17st
Occupation: Sales representative
with Hibernian Business Equipment
Born: County Kerry, 8.10.66
Family: Single
Former club: Castle Island
International debut: Ireland 13,
France 21, 1991
Five Nations' debut: As above
Best moments in rugby: Winning
first cap against French in Dublin
(2.2.91); scoring try in win against
England (20.3.93)
Worst moment in rugby: Losing
1988/89 Munster Cup final to
Constitution
Most respected opponent: Donal
Lenihan (Cork Constitution &
Ireland)
Serious injuries: Damaged Achilles
tendon
Other sporting achievements:
Winner of All-Ireland Gaelic
Football medal with Kerry in 1986

Ireland (1991)		
Last Season	6 caps	5 pts
Career	13 caps	5 pts
Lions 1993	1 Test	0 pts

Caps	(13): **1991** F, W, Na(2R) wc-J **1992** E, S, F, NZ(1,2), A **1993** F, W, E. Lions–NZ(1)
Points	(5 – 1t): **1993** E(1t)

Best memories last season:
Ireland's two Championship wins and Lions' selection
Notable landmarks in rugby career: Enjoyed memorable 1992/93 season,
culminating in his selection as one of only two first choice Irish Lions (Nick
Popplewell being the other). A campaign which began with two Tests in New
Zealand ended back in the Land of the Long White Cloud with the British
Lions last summer (as a flanker). Only disappointment came when he lost his
place to Richard Costello for the Five Nations' opener at Murrayfield. But
quickly rebounded to share in wins over Wales and England, scoring lone try
in latter game. Selected to play with Munster U-20 whilst a member of Castle
Island, he took possession of a Munster Senior Cup medal in three successive
seasons, and was awarded a Shannon RFC cap for the achievement. Played for
Ireland U-25s in wins over US Eagles (12–10, Limerick 10.3.90) and Spain
(36–17, Limerick 8.9.90). First called into Irish squad for 1988 tour of France
but did not break into the senior team until the 1991 Five Nations'

Championship, playing against France and Ireland having warmed bench in season-opener against Argentina. Made B debut in 1989 against Scotland at Murrayfield (drew 22–22, 9.12.89) and added caps against Argentina (scoring try), Scotland and England in 1990/91. Toured with Ireland to Namibia (1991) and New Zealand (1992)

Touchlines: Fishing the Kerry Lakes

Gavin, B. T. Australia

Full Name: Bryant Timothy (Tim) Gavin

Clubs: Eastern Suburbs (Aus), Mediolanum Milan (It)

State: New South Wales

Position: No 8, Lock

Height: 6ft 5in (1.96m)

Weight: 16st 12lb (107kg)

Occupation: Rugby development officer

Born: 20.11.63

Family: Single

Former clubs: None. Easts (Sydney) since 1983

International debut: Australia 19, New Zealand 19, 1988

Best moment in rugby: Beating England 40–15 at Sydney in 1991

Worst moment in rugby: Sustaining knee injury in club game before 1991 World Cup which forced me to miss tournament

Most embarrassing moment: Being sidestepped by a grey-haired Italian at least ten years older than me

Most respected opponent: Wayne Shelford (New Zealand)

Serious injuries: Knee reconstruction (1991), 1992 thigh injury

Australia (1988)

Last Season	5 caps	0 pts
Career	22 caps	20 pts

Caps (22): **1988** NZ(2,3), S, It(R) **1989** NZ(R), F(1,2) **1990** F(1,2,3), US, NZ(1,2,3) **1991** W(a), E(a), NZ(a1) **1992** S(1,2), SA, I, W

Points (20 – 5t): **1990** F(2:1t), US(1t) **1991** W(a:2t), NZ(a1:1t)

Best memory last season: Beating South Africa 26-3 in Cape Town

Suggestions to improve rugby: *On-field* – Change the tackle law as these days players are picked because of their ability to kill the ball. *Off-field* – There must be financial reward for the time players put in at international level. Gone are the days of twice-a-week training and playing on the Saturday with a few beers afterwards

Notable landmarks in rugby career: Made his debut against the All Blacks in 1988 but it was a further two years before the second row-turned No 8 (with more than a little help from national coach Bob Dwyer) shook off the challenge of Steve Tuynman to secure a regular berth. Once in the side he wasted little time attracting a host of admirers, not least the Australian Society of Rugby Writers who voted him their Player of the Year in 1990. Tim was a racing certainty for the Aussies' 1991 World Cup squad before sustaining a knee injury in club colours and having to watch the crowning glory via satellite in Oz. Injury continued to frustrate him in 1992 when a bruised thigh kept him out of the 2–1 Bledisloe Cup series-win. he recovered in time to tour South Africa and made a wonderful start in the Republic – scoring two tries as the Wallabies downed Western Transvaal 46–13 in Potchefstroom on 11 August. He did not reappear until the Test match, in Cape Town on 22 August, when the Wallabies handed the Springboks a frightful beating (26–3). From there he toured Ireland and Wales, playing in both internationals in addition to the wins over Leinster, Ulster (two tries), Wales B and the Barbarians, and the losses to Swansea and Llanelli

Tours: 1988 – England, Scotland and Italy. 1989 – New Zealand, Canada and France. 1990 – New Zealand. 1992 – South Africa, Ireland and Wales.

Touchlines: Fishing, skiing

Player to watch: Garrick Morgan (Souths)

Player of the Year: Tim Horan (Australia)

Geldenhuys, A.   South Africa

Full Name: Adri Geldenhuys
Club: Despatch
Province: Eastern Province
Position: Lock
Height: 6ft 6in (1.98m)
Weight: 17st (108kg)
Occupation: Clerk
Born: Clanwilliam, 11.7.64
Former club: Tarbes (Fr)
International debut: South Africa 24, New Zealand 27, 1992
Notable landmarks in rugby career: Hit the headlines for the wrong reasons during the 1992 tour of France when he was captured on television flattening Abdel Benazzi at a lineout in the first Test in Lyon

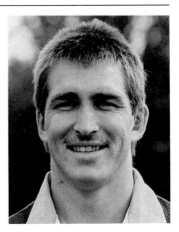

(17.10.92), which South Africa won 20–15. However, he was treated leniently by referee Brian Kinsey, who had been alerted to the incident by English touch judge Tony Spreadbury, and remained on the field. Despite the subsequent outcry in France, Adri retained his place in the

South Africa (1992)

Last Season	4 caps	0 pts
Career	4 caps	0 pts

Caps (4): **1992** NZ, A, F(1,2)

Points Nil

Springbok second row the following weekend in Paris when France tied up the series with an emphatic 29–16 win. However, by the time South Africa arrived at Twickenham on 14 November, Northern Transvaal's Drikus Hattingh had taken over as partner to fellow Blue Bull Adolf Malan. His only other tour outings came against France B (lost 17–24, Bordeaux, 4.10.92) and Provence-Cote d'Azur (won 41–12, Marseille, 13.10.92). Despite missing Eastern Province's match against Australia at Boet Erasmus Stadium, Port Elizabeth (18.8.92), which resulted in a 34–8 win for the tourists, Adri figured in both home Tests, packing down alongside Malan in the 24–27 loss to the All Blacks (15.8.92) and the 3–26 record loss to the Wallabies (22.8.92)

Genet, J. -P.   France

Full Name: Jean-Pierre Genet
Club: Racing Club de France
Position: Hooker
Height: 5ft 11½in (1.82m)
Weight: 14st (89kg)
Born: Chatellerault, 15.10.62
Former clubs: Espinay-sur-Orge, C.A.S.G.
International debut: Scotland 10, France 6, 1992
Five Nations' debut: As above
Notable landmarks in rugby career: Not much of a season internationally after collecting his third cap in 25–6 win over Romania at Le Havre on 28 May 1992. Subsequently toured Argentina but did not make the Test side. A combination of Bayonne's Jean-Marie Gonzalez and Nice's Jean-Francois Tordo divided up the national hooking duties thereafter. Had enjoyed two outings in 1992 Championship – upgraded from France A and B representative rugby following Vincent Moscato's indiscretion against England

(15.2.92). Participated in the FIRA Championship and the 27–18 win over Scotland B respectively, before making the 1992 Five Nations' trip to Murrayfield, where Lions' loosehead David Sole was his illustrious opponent. He at least had the comfort of packing down alongside prop Louis Armary, his captain and front row cohort at A and B level. A member of Racing's French Championship winning side of 1990, having previously experienced the dejection of defeat in the 1987 final to Toulon, Jean-Pierre retained his tighthead berth for the Paris match against Ireland, but failed to get his name on any of France's seven tries

France (1992)

Last Season	1 cap	0 pts
Career	3 caps	0 pts

Caps (3): **1992** S, I, R

Points Nil

Geoghegan, S. P. Ireland

Full Name: Simon Patrick Geoghegan
Club: London Irish
Position: Wing
Height: 6ft 1in (1.86m)
Weight: 13st (83kg)
Occupation: Articles clerk with Rosling King, Fleet Street
Born: Barnet, Herts, 1.9.68
Family: Single
Former club: Wasps (Colts)
International debut: Ireland 13, France 21, 1991
Five Nations' debut: As above
Best moment in rugby: Scoring try on second full international appearance for Ireland in 21–21 draw with Wales (16.2.91)
Worst moment in rugby: Seeing Australia's Michael Lynagh score last-gasp try to deny us victory in 1991 World Cup quarter-final
Most respected opponent: Eddie Saunders (Rugby)
Best memory last season: Defeat of England (20.3.93)
Suggestions to improve rugby: *On-field* – Alter amount of points

Ireland (1991)

Last Season	5 caps	0 pts
Career	16 caps	16 pts

Caps (16): **1991** F, W, E, S, Na(1) wc-Z, S, A **1992** E, S, F, A **1993** S, F, W, E

Points (16 – 4t): **1991** W(1t), E(1t), S(1t) wc-Z(1t)

awarded for penalty goals as this tends to devalue the worth of a try which is the essence of rugby union. *Off-field* – Players should be properly remunerated for time spent training at internationals quad sessions etc

Notable landmarks in rugby career: Missed Ireland's tour to New Zealand in 1992 but returned to side for visit of world champions Australia to Dublin. Failed to emulate his previous scoring exploits in that game or in his subsequent outings in the 1993 Five Nations' Championship. Represented Ireland at Under-25, Students, B and Full level. Quickly rose to prominence, with try-scoring debuts for Ireland U-25 (36–17 v Spain, Limerick 8.9.90) and Ireland B (27–12 v Argentina, Limerick 20.10.90). Quality Inter-Provincial performances for Connacht sped his progress into the senior national XV, for whom he opposed the Bayonne Express, Patrice Lagisquet, on his debut against France at Lansdowne Road (2.2.91). Scored tries in next three internationals, against Wales, Ireland and Scotland. Toured Namibia (1991), playing in first Test, and claimed fourth Ireland try in 55–11 World Cup defeat of Zimbabwe

Touchlines: Cinema, reading, swimming, tennis, cricket

Gerber, D. M. South Africa

Full Name: Daniel (Danie) Mattheus Gerber
Club: Northerns-Tygerberg-College
Province: Western Province
Position: Centre
Height: 6ft 2in (1.87m)
Weight: 14st 2lb (90kg)
Occupation: Representative
Born: Port Elizabeth, 14.4.58
Former club/province:
Despatch/Eastern Province
International debut: South America 13, South Africa 22, 1980
Notable landmarks in rugby career: South Africa's record Test try-scorer with 19 in just 24 internationals dating back to his debut against South America in Montevideo, Uruguay (18.10.80) when he popped over for his first.

Has displayed remarkable longevity, being every bit as potent 12 years on when claiming a try-brace against New Zealand in Johannesburg (15.8.92) and one in each of the two Tests against France in October. Such career stamina is no blessing from up above. He has had to work at it, and used to be famous for a two-hour daily training schedule which included a minimum 300 sit-ups. Since

214

his provincial debut in 1978 for Eastern Province (for whom he played 114 times), he has remained a persistent thorn in the flesh of opponents, helping himself to two tries against Ireland at Cape Town in 1981, and bagging a hat-trick against the unfortunate South American Jaguars in a 50–18 rout at Pretoria the following year. A powerfully built figure, Danie became a firm favourite of the Barbarians when he scored four dazzling tries against Cardiff in 1983 and two more against Scotland. England were not immune to his skills either, conceding three Gerber tries in 18 first-half minutes at Ellis Park (9.6.84), as England were thumped 35–9. Despite missing the two-Test series against the 1989 World XV he returned strongly in 1992, playing in all five Tests and additionally turning out against Aquitaine (won 29–22, Pau, 7.10.92) and, with a try apiece, against Midi-Pyrenees (won 18–15, Toulouse, 15.10.92) and the Midlands Division (won 32–9, Leicester, 4.11.92)

South Africa (1980)

Last Season	5 caps	20 pts
Career	24 caps	82 pts

Caps (24): **1980** SAm(b1,b2), F **1981** I(1,2), NZ(1,2,3), US **1982** SAm(1,2) **1984** E(1,2), SAm(1,2) **1986** Cv(1,2,3,4) **1992** NZ, A, F(1,2), E

Points (82 – 19t,1c): **1980** SAm(b1:1t), SAm(b2:1t) **1981** I(1:2t) **1982** SAm(1:3t), SAm(2:1t) **1984** E(1:1t), E(2:3t), SAm(1:1t,1c), SAm(2:1t) **1986** Cv(3:1t) **1992** NZ(2t), F(1:1t), F(2:1t)

Gibbs, I.S. Wales

Full Name: Ian Scott Gibbs
Club: Swansea
Position: Centre
Height: 5ft 10in (1.78m)
Weight: 13st 7lb (86kg)
Occupation: Self-employed sports consultant
Born: Bridgend, 23.1.71
Family: Single
Family links with rugby: None. Father (Graham) is a former pole vaulter and international gymnast
Former clubs: Pencoed, Bridgend, Neath
International debut: Wales 6, England 25, 1991
Five Nations' debut: As above
Best moment in rugby: Being picked to tour with 1993 British Lions

Worst moment in rugby: Losing to Western Samoa in the 1991 World Cup after improved second half performance
Most respected opponent: Philippe Sella (Agen & France)
Biggest influence on career: Father – kept me on the right track without ever pressuring me
Serious injuries: General wear and tear from playing 18 matches for Wales and 30-odd league games in 12-month period

Wales (1991)		
Last Season	5 caps	0 pts
v Italy XV	1 app	5 pts
Career	18 caps	0 pts
Lions 1993	2 Tests	5pts

Caps (18): **1991** E, S, I, F(a), A(a), F(b) wc-WS, Arg, A(b) **1992** I, F, E, S, A **1993** E, S, I, F. Lions–NZ(2,3)

Points Lions–NZ(3:1t)

Other sporting achievements: Play tennis for club in Bridgend
Best memory last season: Swansea's 21–6 win over Australia (scored try)
Suggestions to improve rugby: *Off-field* – In order to attain a better standard, players need a lot more time to train. Therefore, either players/employers need to be subsidised. I train as much as I can (all aspects) yet I still do not feel up to the standards of the Southern Hemisphere nations or even England
Notable landmarks in rugby career: Made full debut against England aged 19: first pupil of Ysgol Gyfun Llanharry to be capped by Wales. Switched to Swansea in January 1992 (scoring hat-trick of tries on debut at Cardiff) in time to share in Championship win, having previously played with Neath, Bridgend (toured USA with Brewery Field club in 1990) and Pencoed, with whom won seven Welsh Youth caps (over two seasons) and captained side in 1989/90. Quickly progressed up the representative ladder on joining Neath, marking Wales B debut in Holland with try in 34–12 win (Leiden, 2.12.90) before being called into the full side for the 1991 Five Nations' Championship. Voted youngest-ever Welsh Player of Year (1990/91). Toured Australia with Wales (1991), appearing in five of the six matches, and played throughout 1991 World Cup and 1992 and 1993 Five Nations' campaigns. Scott, who has twice rejected considered bids from Rugby League for his signature, started last season with one of Wales XV's seven tries in the 43–12 win over Italy at the National Stadium. He scored another important try as Swansea beat the touring Wallabies 21–6 (4.11.92), and ended the campaign as a member of the '93 Lions, playing in the last two Tests and claiming a try in the latter.
Touchlines: Boxing, music, golf, tennis

Gonzales, J. -M.   France

Full Name: Jean-Marie Gonzales
Club: Bayonne
Position: Hooker, prop
Height: 5ft 7½in (1.72m)
Weight: 13st 10lb (88kg)
Occupation: Salesman
Born: 10.7.67
International debut: Argentina 12, France 27, 1992
Five Nations' debut: None
Notable landmarks in rugby career: Until Jean-Francois Tordo's switch from flanker prior to the 1993 Five Nations' Championship, France seemed unsure as to who they wanted to perform their hooking duties. Jean-Pierre Genet, the Racing Club de France rake, lost the jersey on tour in Argentina, having done the honours against Romania at Le Havre in May, and coach Pierre Berbizier instead invited Jean-Marie to put in a bid. The Bayonne man played in both Tests in Bueons Aires against a poor Pumas side and kept the job through the two-Test series with South

France (1992)

Last Season	8 caps	5 pts
Career	8 caps	5 pts

Caps (8): **1992** Arg(a1,a2), SA(1,2), Arg(b) **1993** R, SA(1,2)

Points (5 – 1t): Arg(b:1t)

Africa, despite the 15–20 loss France suffered at Lyon on 17 October. But his time was nearly up. Had France not allowed Argentina, now themselves on tour, an historic first victory on French soil at Nantes on 14 November, he might have survived. As it was the Pumas won 24–20 and, in spite of the hooker scoring one of the home side's three tries, he was one of eight casualties as the selectors wielded the broom. He did not reappear again subsequently, although he was granted a place on the bench at Parc des Princes (20.3.93) to watch France beat Wales 26–10 and clinch the inaugural Five Nations' Cup. Returned to side at prop for 37–20 win over Romania in Bucharest before reverting to hooker throughout series win over South Africa

Graou, S.   France

Full Name: Stephane Graou
Club: Auch
Position: Prop
Height: 5ft 11in (1.80m)
Weight: 16st 10lb (106kg)
Occupation: Commercial officer
Born: Auch, 1.5.66
International debut: France 20,
Argentina 24, 1992
Five Nations' debut: None
**Notable landmarks in rugby
career:** As storming starts to Test
careers go, Stephane's must rate
somewhere down the list, which is a
pity because he worked hard to put
himself into the frame. A member of
the French squad which won the
1988 Students World Cup, he
waited two years before touring
Namibia with a French development
squad. Finally he got his shot at the
big time when selected to tour
Argentina in 1992 with the senior
squad, but rather than exploit the
opportunity he had himself sent-off
against Cuyo, having come on as a

France (1992)

Last Season	3 caps	0 pts
Career	3 caps	0 pts

Caps (3): **1992** Arg(b:R) **1993** SA(1,2)

Points Nil

replacement in the 30–32 loss in Mendoza on 30 June 1992. In all, he appeared
in four of the eight tour games but remained uncapped until the Pumas visited
Nantes on 14 November. At half-time in a Test which was to make history for
all the wrong reasons, as far as France was concerned, he entered the fray as
replacement for Philippe Gallart. But Argentina won 24–20 to register their
first ever victory on French soil and Stephane returned from whence he came,
with instead Merignac's Laurent Seigne presented with the No 3 jersey for the
1993 Five Nations' Championship. The Auch skipper had to make do with
replace-ment duties throughout the triumphant campaign to add to those he
carried out in South Africa's two-Test visit in October. Tripled his cap total
with appearances in both Tests against South Africa late summer

Griffiths, M.   Wales

Full Name: Michael Griffiths
Club: Cardiff
Position: Loosehead prop
Height: 5ft 11in (1.81m)
Weight: 16st 10lb (106kg)
Occupation: Self-employed builder with G D Griffiths, Rhondda (will go anywhere!)
Born: Tonypandy, 18.3.62
Family: Anne (wife), Joel Michael (son) and Luc Rhys (son)
Family links with rugby: Brother plays for Ystrad Rhondda
Former clubs: Ystrad Rhondda, Bridgend
International debut: Wales 24, Western Samoa 6, 1988
Five Nations' debut: Scotland 23, Wales 7, 1989
Best moment in rugby: Winning first Welsh cap against touring Samoans (12.11.88)
Worst moments in rugby: Wales losing 6–34 to England at Twickenham (18.2.90); breaking collarbone in freak cycling accident and missing 1992/93 international season
Most embarrassing moment: Twice having to change shorts against France (1991/92) in front of the Princess of Wales

Wales (1988)		
Last Season	4 cap	0 pts
v Italy XV	1 app	0 pts
Career	26 caps	0 pts
Lions 1989		

Caps (26): **1988** WS, Ro **1989** S, I, F, E, NZ **1990** F, E, Na(1,2), Ba **1991** I, F(a), F(b) wc–WS,Arg, A(b) **1992** I, F, E, S, A 1993 Z(1,2), Na

Points Nil

Most respected opponents: Jeff Probyn (Wasps & England: for his technique) and Iain Milne (Heriot's FP & Scotland: for his size and strength)
Biggest influence on career: Ian Stephens and Merideth James (Bridgend)
Serious injuries: Broken ribs, fractured arm, twisted shoulder muscles, damaged ankle and knee ligaments
Other sporting achievements: Accomplished soccer player (centre-back)
Suggestions to improve rugby: *On-field* – Abandon new ruck and mauling law. Good mauling is an art. *Off-field* – Look after players better. They are the people who draw the crowds
Notable landmarks in rugby career: Mike's penchant for mountain biking wrecked his international hopes last season when he suffered a broken

collarbone as a result of colliding with Anthony Clement and Colin Stephens in a freak accident on Lanzarote's mountain roads in January during Wales' preparations for the 1993 Five Nations' campaign. So having propped on the loosehead in the 6–23 loss to Australia in Cardiff on 21 November, not to forget against Italy on 7 October in a non-cap affair, his Test season was over until his return on last summer's tour of Zimbabwe and Namibia. Started career in back-row but moved to front of scrum shortly before joining Bridgend. Moved to Cardiff for new challenges and found them: playing for Crawshays, Wales B (in 12–18 loss to France B, Brecon 29.10.88), Wales and 1989 Lions. Despite failing to oust David Sole in Test side, he played in six of the Lions' 12 games, including the final game (as a replacement) against the ANZAC XV. Played at tighthead against Barbarians (6.10.90). Only Welsh representative in Home Unions' team which played Rest of Europe at Twickenham on behalf of Romania Appeal (won 43–18, 22.4.90). Missed the 1991 tour to Australia but was quickly recalled for the duration of the World Cup and 1992 Five Nations' Championship. Played all three Tests on last summer's tour of Africa
Touchlines: Mountain biking (!)

Guscott, J. C. England

Full Name: Jeremy Clayton Guscott
Club: Bath
Position: Centre
Height: 6ft 1in (1.86m)
Weight: 13st 5lb (85kg)
Occupation: Marketing co-ordinator with British Gas
Born: Bath, 7.7.65
Family: Jayne (wife) and child
International debut: Romania 3, England 58, 1989
Five Nations' debut: England 23, Ireland 0, 1990
Best moment in rugby: Try scored for 1989 Lions v Australia in second Test
Worst moment in rugby: Being dropped by Bath for semi-finals of 1989/90 Pilkington Cup
Most embarrassing moment: Any time I miss a tackle

Most respected opponent: All of them
Biggest influence on career: S J Halliday (Harlequins & England)
Best memory last season: Bath's Championship win and Lions' selection

Suggestions to improve rugby: *On-field* – Reduce the amount of offences in the lineout. There must be 100-odd, when there should be no more than five or six, and it is such an annoying part of the game. Scrap 90-degree scrum wheel law. *Off-field* – Allow players to earn money through off-field activities. The situation is im-proving but there remains no overall consensus: each Union applies the rules as they see fit. The International Board should insist the same applies worldwide, but they seem to back away from confrontation
Notable landmarks in rugby career: An automatic selection for the 1993 Lions (along with England

England (1989)		
Last Season	6 caps	18 pts
Career	28 caps	73 pts
Lions 1989	2 Tests	4 pts
1993	3 Tests	0pts

Caps (28): **1989** Ro, Fj. Lions–A(2,3) **1990** I, F, W, S, Arg(b) **1991** W, S, I, F, Fj, A(a) wc–NZ, It, F, S, A(b) **1992** S, I, F, W, C, SA **1993** F, W, S, I. Lions–NZ(1,2,3)

Points (73 – 16t,2dg): **1989** Ro(3t), Fj(1t). Lions–A(2:1t) **1990** I(1t), F(1t), S(1t), Arg(b:2t) **1991** A(a:1t) wc–It(2t) **1992** S(1dg), I(1t), C(1t), SA(1t) **1993** W(1dg), S(1t)

midfield partner Will Carling) after another top-notch international sea-son in which he claimed five-point tries against Canada, South Africa and Scotland and a dropped goal in defeat by Wales in Cardiff. For many, though, his most memorable contribution of the campaign was his part in the wonderful move which led to Rory Underwood's try against the Scots (6.3.93). Stuart Barnes' break and divine pass allowed Jerry to stretch his legs like the thoroughbred he is, leave the tartan defence for dead and then release Underwood. On a domestic note, he helped Bath win the 1992/93 Courage Championship. Started career with Bath's mini-section as a wing, aged seven. Meteoric rise in 1989 brought two caps for England B, three tries on full England debut in Bucharest, and one invitation from the British Lions (before capped by England). Scored crucial try in Brisbane (second Test: won 19–12, 8.7.89) to bring Lions back into the series which they went on to win 2–1. Ever-present throughout England's back-to-back Grand Slams (1991-92) and wore No 12 jersey in 1991 World Cup final, having previously toured Australia (1991). Toured New Zealand with World XV (April 1992), playing in first two Tests, including famous 28-14 first Test defeat of All Blacks. Collected fourth Pilkington Cup winners' medal in 1992 to add to those collected in '87, '89 and '90
Touchlines: Golf

Hall, M. R.   Wales

Full Name: Michael Robert Hall
Club: Cardiff
Positions: Centre, wing
Height: 6ft 1in (1.86m)
Weight: 15st 3lb (96kg)
Occupation: Chartered surveyor
with Cooke and Arkwright (Cardiff)
Born: Bridgend, 13.10.65
Family: Single
Former clubs: Bridgend, Maesteg,
Cambridge University
International debut: New Zealand
52, Wales 3, 1988
Five Nations' debut: Scotland 23,
Wales 7, 1989
Best moments in rugby: Selection
for 1989 British Lions. 1990 Hong
Kong Sevens with Barbarians
Worst moment in rugby: Every
time I go to Twickenham!
Most embarrassing moment:
England 34, Wales 6 (17.2.90,
record defeat at Twickenham)
Most respected opponent:
Philippe Sella (France)
Biggest influence on career: Brian
Nicholas (coach at Bridgend)
Serious injuries: Hamstring tears
Other sporting achievements:
Schoolboy honours at county level in
soccer, basketball and cricket
Suggestions to improve rugby:

Wales (1988)		
Last Season	4 caps	0 pts
v Italy XV	1 app	0 pts
Career	25 caps	8 pts
Lions 1989	1 Test	0 pts

Caps (25): **1988** NZ(R1,2), WS, Ro
1989 S, I, F, E, NZ. Lions–A(1)
1990 F, E, S **1991** A(a), F(b)
wc–WS, Arg, A(b) **1992** I, F, E,
S, A **1993** E, S, I

Points (8 – 2t): **1989** S(1t), E(1t)

On-field – Too many of the new rules are half-measures. The mauling rule
encourages players to kill the ball. The line-out shambles still needs addressing.
Off-field – Market game properly. Clear up ambiguities in laws on amateurism.
WRU are doing well (appointing marketing manager etc), but I would still like
to see players better looked after, with more sympathy from the unions with
regard to employers etc.
Notable landmarks in rugby career: 1989 Lion who failed to retain his place
on the 1993 tour, not helped by being dropped by Wales for their final Five
Nations' game in Paris. Prior to that had started season on wing against Italy
XV at Cardiff Arms Park (won 43–12, 7.10.92), before reverting to centre in
Wales B side beaten 24–11 by Australia (7.11.92). He was in the same position

when touring Wallabies met first-choice Welsh side, and retained his place through England, Scotland and Ireland games. Ended season on Wales' tour to Zimbabwe and Namibia. Past captain of British Universities, Welsh Students and Wales U-21s. Two Blues at Cambridge (1987,88). Wales B against France in 1987 (lost 0–26). 1989 Lions against Australia in first Test (lost 12–30). Toured to New Zealand (1988) and Australia (1991) with Wales, and to South Africa (1989) with World XV. Scored winning try against England (Cardiff, 18.3.89, won 12–9) to deny them 1989 Five Nations' Championship. Tore hamstring on first appearance in 1990/91 season and having recovered, promptly did it again. Returned to international duty Down Under '91 and was ever present thereafter until Paris match on 20 March 1993

Touchlines: Golf

Hamilton, G. F. Ireland

Full Name: Gordon Frederic Hamilton
Club: Ballymena
Position: Flanker
Height: 6ft (1.83m)
Weight: 14st 9lb (93kg)
Occupation: Shipping executive with Hamilton Shipping & Travel (Belfast)
Born: Belfast, 13.5.64
Family: Single
Family links with rugby: Father (Jimmy) played for NIFC
Former clubs: Blackheath, North of Ireland (NIFC)
International debut: Ireland 13, France 21, 1991
Five Nations' debut: As above
Best moment in rugby: Scoring my first try for Ireland
Worst moment in rugby: Losing to Australia in quarter-finals of 1991 World Cup
Most embarrassing moment: Fell over when running out for team photo prior to full debut. Cut thumb badly and needed stitches
Most respected opponent: John Jeffrey (Kelso & Scotland)
Biggest influence on career: My father

Ireland (1991)		
Last Season	1 cap	4 pts
Career	10 caps	4 pts

Caps (10): **1991** F, W, E, S(a), Na(2) wc–Z, J, S(b), A **1992** A

Points (4 – 1t): **1991** wc–A(1t)

Serious injuries: Prolapsed disc (ruled me out of 1992 New Zealand tour)
Suggestions to improve rugby: *On-field* – None, game is in good shape. *Off-field* – Compensation for time lost from work to rugby. Clarify what players can and cannot do. No-one knows where they stand
Notable landmarks in rugby career: Prolapsed disc injury playing for Ulster against Munster in 1991/92 Inter-Provincial Championship ruled him out of '92 Five Nations' Championship and summer tour to New Zealand. He returned in the 42–17 loss to touring Australia at Lansdowne Road on 31 October but did not figure in 1993 Championship. Prop at school and had final Ulster Schools trial. But was wrong shape for a prop. Played three seasons for Scottish Universities while at Dundee University. Also played for Blackheath (1986/87) and Kent before returning to join NIFC to become their first capped player for ten years when he was capped against France (2.2.91). Also represented Ulster (two years) and Ireland B, in 16–0 defeat of Scotland B (22.12.90) at Ravenhill (having withdrawn injured from team to play Argentina on 20.10.90). Ever-present throughout 1991 Five Nations' Championship, he then toured Namibia before returning to play in all four of Ireland's World Cup fixtures
Touchlines: Sailing (half-tonners), golf

Hastings, A. G. Scotland

Full Name: Andrew Gavin Hastings
Club: Watsonians
Position: Fullback
Height: 6ft 2in (1.88m)
Weight: 14st 7lb (92kg)
Occupation: Sports marketing executive with The Carnegie Partnership
Born: Edinburgh, 3.1.62
Family: Engaged to Diane
Family links with rugby: Clifford (father) played No8 for Edinburgh XV and Watsonians; Scott (brother) plays for Watsonians, Scotland and British Lions; Graeme (brother) plays centre for Melbourne RFC and Victoria State (Australia); Ewan (brother) plays on wing for Watsonians

Former clubs: Cambridge University, London Scottish
International debut: Scotland 18, France 17, 1986

Five Nations' debut: As above
Best moments in rugby: Winning 1990 Grand Slam; 1989 British Lions' 2–1 series win in Australia; taking part in the 1992 New Zealand Rugby Football Union Centenary celebrations; captaining Scotland (1992/93) and 1993 British Lions
Worst moment in rugby: Missing kick in front of posts against England in 1991 World Cup semi-final at Murrayfield (26.10.91)
Most embarrassing moment: Missing plane home from Ireland after B international
Most respected opponent: The All Blacks, because of their record – I've only beaten them once in nine attempts (first Test: NZ 14, World XV 28, 1992)
Biggest influence on career: Parents (Clifford and Isobel)
Other sporting achievements: Appearing on TV in Trail Blazers (1988) and Pro-Celebrity Golf (1990)
Best memory last season: Leading out Scotland at Murrayfield (16.1.93) for Test against Ireland
Suggestions to improve rugby: *On-field* – Pretty satisfied now that IRB have banned the scrum-half dummy pass and banned players from

Scotland (1986)		
Last Season	5 caps	40 pts
Career	45 caps	424 pts
Lions 1986		
1989	3 Tests	28 pts
1993	3 Tests	35pts

Caps (45): **1986** F, W, E, I, Ro **1987** I, F, W, E wc-F, Z, R, NZ **1988** I, F, W, E, A **1989** Fj, Ro. Lions–A(1,2,3) **1990** I, F, W, E, NZ(1,2), Arg **1991** F, W, E(a), I(a) wc–J, I(b), WS, E(b), NZ **1992** E, I, F, W, A(1) **1993** I, F, W, E. Lions-NZ(1,2,3)

Points (424 – 10t,60c,88p): **1986** F(6p), W(1t,1p), E(3c,5p), I(2p), Ro(3c,5p) **1987** I(1c), F(1c,4p), W(2c,2p), E(1c,2p) wc–F(4p), Z(1t,8c), Ro (2t,8c,1p), NZ(1p) **1988** I(2c,2p), F(1t,4p), W(4p), E(2p), A(1t,1c,1p) **1989** Fj(1t,4c,2p), Ro(3c,2p). Lions–A(1:2p), A(2:1t,1p), A(3:5p) **19 90** F(1p), NZ(1:2c), NZ(2:2c,2p), Arg(1t,5c,1p) **1991** W(1c,2p), I(a:1t,1p) wc–J(1t,5c,2p), I(b:2c,3p), WS(2c,4p), E(b:2p), NZ(2p) **1992** E(1p), I(2c,2p), F(2p), W(1p), A(1:1c,2p) **1993** I(1c,1p), F(1p), W(5p), E(3p). Lions–NZ(1:6p), NZ(2:4p), NZ(3:1c1p)

charging full-back immediately he has caught high ball; both of which I suggested in last year's edition. Get fit and stay fit. Practise your weaknesses. *Off-field* – Players should be looked after adequately – certainly not allowed to be disadvantaged for loss of earnings. You cannot differentiate between rugby related and non-related activities. We should all be playing on a level field – abuse of IRB regulations is widespread
Notable landmarks in rugby career: Enjoyed phenomenal 1992/93 season in that he was appointed to captain both Scotland and the British Lions. Missed second Test in Australia (Summer '92) due to injury but recovered in time to kick 32 points in Scotland's 1993 Five Nations' campaign. Won two Blues at Cambridge University (1984–85) and five caps for Scotland B before establishing Scottish record with six penalty goals on full debut (17.1.86). Holds Scottish points-scoring record with 424 in 45 internationals, and Scottish

record for most points scored in a Five Nations' season (52 in 1986). Toured with Scotland to North America (1985), the 1987 World Cup (where scored 62 points in four games), and New Zealand (1990). Scored go-ahead try in second Test for 1989 Lions and 15 points in victorious decider. Kicked penalty for 1986 British Lions in 7–15 defeat by The Rest at Cardiff in match to celebrate centenary of IRFB. Played in '1989 Home Unions' 29–27 win over France (scored 22 points) and for '1989 Barbarians' against All Blacks. Led London Scottish to 1989/90 Courage League division three title, and Watsonians to promotion (1990/91) to McEwan's League division one. Captained Barbarians at 1991 Hong Kong Sevens. Represented 1992 World XV in three-Test series against All Blacks (NZRFU centenary celebrations), kicking penalty in 28–14 first Test win and scoring try in second. Returned with 1993 Lions, playing in nine of the 13 games and scoring 101 points. Heralded as an outstanding skipper both on and off the park.

Touchlines: Playing golf with Sam Torrance against Ronan Rafferty and Peter Alliss – most nervous I've ever been in my life, including winning first cap at Murrayfield

---

Hastings, S.   Scotland

Full Name: Scott Hastings
Club: Watsonians
Positions: Centre, wing, fullback
Height: 6ft 1in (1.86m)
Weight: 14st 10lb (93kg)
Occupation: Advertising account manager with Barker's, Scotland
Born: Edinburgh, 4.12.64
Family: Jenny (wife)
Family links with rugby: Clifford (father) played No 8 for Edinburgh XV and Watsonians; Gavin (brother) plays for Watsonians and captains Scotland and British Lions; Graeme (brother) plays centre for Melbourne RFC and Victoria State (Australia); Ewan (brother) plays on wing for Watsonians
Former club: Newcastle Northern
International debut: Scotland 19, France 18, 1986
Five Nations' debut: As above
Best moment in rugby: 1989 Lions' Test series win; 1990 Grand Slam win with Scotland; playing in Hong Kong Sevens

Worst moment in rugby: Sustaining hamstring injury on first appearance in 1987 World Cup (55–28 win v Romania); facial injury which curtailed 1993 Lions tour

Most embarrassing moments: My 1987 World Cup injury and discovering I did not have any Y-fronts to change into after a match

Most respected opponent: Brendan Mullin (Blackrock & Ireland) – played opposite him ever since we captained our respective countries in a Schools international

Biggest influence on career: Family's involvement in rugby

Serious injuries: Torn hamstring, cartilage operation (1985), broken cheekbone (1987 v Wales)

Best memory last season: Selection for British Lions

Suggestions to improve rugby: *On-field* – Take all conversions in front of the posts. Put posts on dead-ball line so penalties cannot be kicked from the halfway line and teams will be more inclined to run the ball. Increase try-worth to six points. *Off-field* – Allow players to undertake any commercial activity. Why can we not wear and promote a certain brand of boots? It would not hurt anyone. Relax amateurism rules totally as IRB have no apparent jurisdiction

Notable landmarks in rugby career: Shares with Sean Lineen the world record for an international centre partnership of 28 games (Lineen retired after 1992 Australia tour). Along with Doddie Weir, Craig Chalmers and Tony Stanger, Scott was ever-present in 1992/93 campaign which started in Oz and concluded at Twickers. But unable to add to seven try-tally in those six games. Only Scotland try came in (shadow Scotland XV) 'A' team's 22–17 defeat of Italy at Melrose (19.12.92) Selected to tour with 1993 Lions to New Zealand, under captaincy of brother Gavin. Pair had become first Scottish brothers to play together in a Lions' Test back in 1989. Former Watsonians captain (1989/90) who helped Edinburgh to three Inter-District Championship 'grand slams' between 1986–88. Also ex-skipper of Scottish Schools. Played three times for Scotland U-21s and once for Scotland B (at fullback in 9–0 win over Italy B, Glasgow 7.12. 85). Also played at outside-half, for Anglo-Scots, during time at Newcastle Polytechnic. Key cog in Scotland's 1990 Grand Slam machine, making famous try-saving tackle on England's Rory Underwood in Murrayfield decider. Within five caps of joining Jim Renwick (51) as Scotland's most-capped centre

Touchlines: Underwater hockey refereeing; bandit golfer (18-handicap), watching films, viticulture

Scotland (1986)		
Last Season	6 caps	0 pts
Career	46 caps	28 pts
Lions 1989		2 Tests
1993		Tour to New Zealand

Caps (46): **1986** F, W, E, I, Ro **1987** I, F, W wc-Ro **1988** I, F, W, A **1989** W, E, I, F, Fj, Ro. Lions–A(2,3) **1990** I, F, W, E, NZ(1,2), Arg **1991** F, W, E(a), I(a) wc–J, Z, I(b), WS, E(b), NZ **1992** E, I, F, W, A(1,2) **1993** I, F, W, E

Points (28 – 7t): **1986** E(1t), Ro(1t) **1987** F(1t) **1988** I(1t) **1991** I(1t) wc–J(1t), Z(1t)

Hattingh, H.   South Africa

Full Name: Hendrikus (Drikus) Hattingh
Club: Normaal College Pretoria
Province: Northern Transvaal
Position: Lock
Height: 6ft 4½in (1.94m)
Weight: 18st 3lb (116kg)
Occupation: Market agent
Born: Rustenburg, 21.2.68
International debut: South Africa 3, Australia 26, 1992
Other sporting achievements: Former Junior Springbok athlete
Notable landmarks in rugby career: Rose to prominence in the Northern Transvaal side which completed a Currie Cup–Lion Cup double in his first season on the team. A product of Normaal College, Pretoria, Drikus had a busy time on South Africa's 1992 European tour. Having had made his Test bow as a 64th minute replacement for Adri Geldenhuys in the 3–26 loss to Australia (Cape Town, 22.8.92), he featured in eight

South Africa (1992)

Last Season	3 caps	0 pts
Career	3 caps	0 pts

Caps   (3): 1992 A(R), F(2R), E

Points Nil

of the ten non-internationals played in France and England – against France B (lost 17–24, Bordeaux, 4.10.92), Aquitaine (won 29–22, Pau, 7.10.92), Midi-Pyrenees (won 18–15, Toulouse, 15.10.92), Langedoc–Roussillon (won 36–15, Beziers, 20.10.92) , French Universities (lost 13–18, Tours, 28.10.92), the Midlands Division (won 32–9, Leicester, 4.11.92), England B (won 20–16, Bristol, 7.11.92) and the Northern Division (won 19–3, Leeds, 10.11.92) – scoring tries against France B, Languedoc–Roussillon and England B. In addition the former Junior Springbok athlete took his cap tally to three, coming on as a 49th minute replacement, again for Geldenhuys, in the 16–29 second Test defeat by France at the Parc des Princes, and then playing from start to finish against England at Twickenham (lost 16–33, 14.11.92)

Henderson, P. W.   New Zealand

Full Name: Paul William
Henderson
Province: Southland
Position: Flanker
Height: 6ft 2in (1.88m)
Weight: 15st (95kg)
Born: Bluff, South Island, 21.9.64
Former Province: Otago
International debut: Argentina 14,
New Zealand 21, 1991
Serious injuries: Damaged knee
ligaments (v Neath, 1989)
**Notable landmarks in rugby
career:** Announced himself as an
18-year old with a stirring
performance for Southland in their
41–3 loss to the 1983 British Lions
at Invercargill. After turning out for
the Province for four seasons he
moved to Dunedin in 1987 and
played for Otago until reverting back
to Southland at the start of 1992.
Paul's international career began
when he represented New Zealand
Secondary Schools and, in 1983–84,
NZ Colts. Team mates in 1983
included Sean Fitzpatrick, Grant

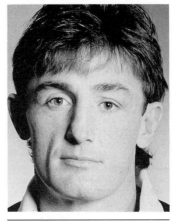

New Zealand (1991)

Last Season	4 caps	4 pts
Career	6 caps	4 pts

Caps (6): **1991** Arg(1). wc-C **1992**
Wd(1,2,3),I(1)

Points (4 – 1t): **1992** I(1:1t)

Fox and Murray Mexted, while Fitzpatrick captained the '84 side which
featured Bernie McCahill and Wigan Rugby League's former All Black Frano
Botica. Toured with New Zealand to Wales and Ireland in 1989 but a knee
ligament injury sustained against Neath forced him to return home after only
three games. Luck finally changed in 1991 when, during the All Blacks' tour of
Argentina he was awarded his first cap in the 28–14 win over the Pumas in
Buenos Aires. Still, he only made the 1991 World Cup squad when Otago's
Mike Brewer was withdrawn through injury. The trip allowed him to collect his
second cap, in the 29–13 quarter-final defeat of Canada in the pouring rain at
Lille's Stade du Nord. Despite missing the final trial in 1992 because of a calf
muscle strain, Paul made the All Black line-up for the centenary series, retaining
his place in each of the three Tests against the World XV. although he failed to
finish the second and third legs. It was not until Ireland's visit to Dunedin on
30 May that he finally made the scoresheet, crossing for the first of the Blacks'
four tries as Ireland, 100/1 no-hopers, had their remarkable 12–0 lead pegged
back; eventually losing 24–21. Injury robbed him of further caps when, two

games into the tour of Australia and South Africa – having taken his tally of All Black appearances to 19 with outings against Western Australia and New South Wales – he broke his thumb against the latter and was forced to return home. The fact that he only narrowly failed to recover his fitness before the party departed for the South African leg of the tour was little consolation

Hendriks, P. South Africa

Full Name: Pieter Hendriks
Club: Roodepoort
Position: Wing
Height: 6ft (1.82m)
Weight: 13st 8lb (86kg)
Occupation: Teacher
Born: Douglas, 13.4.70
International debut: South Africa 24, New Zealand 27, 1992
Other sporting achievements: Former South African junior hurdles champion
Notable landmarks in rugby career: Enjoyed a marvellous 1992 season, even if his form did taper off somewhat in the latter stages when Northern Transvaal wing Jacques Olivier took over his Test slot for the three Internationals in Europe. Back home, Pieter set a South African record for tries scored in a season with 33 in the 1992 campaign as Transvaal marched to the Currie Cup final. Unhappily, for his province, there was no No 34 in the Ellis Park final on 12 September and Natal

South Africa (1992)

Last Season	2 caps	0 pts
Career	2 caps	0 pts

Caps (2): 1992 NZ, A

Points Nil

won the Cup for the second time in three years, 14–13. By this time Pieter had already picked up his first two caps, playing in the defeats by New Zealand (24–27, Johannesburg, 15.8.92) and Australia (3–26, Cape Town, 22.8.92). His first tries for the Springboks came in France where, after failing to cross in the 17–24 loss to France Espoirs, he bagged a score in the 36–15 win over Languedoc-Roussillon at Beziers and the solitary South African try in Tours where French Universities triumphed 18–13. Unable to prevent Olivier hijacking his Test place, he had to content himself with appearances against the Midlands Division at Leicester and the North at Leeds

Herbert, A. G.   Australia

Full Name: Anthony Gerard
Herbert
Club: GPS
State: Queensland
Position: Centre, fullback
Height: 6ft (1.83m)
Weight: 13st 8lb (86kg)
Occupation: Sales and promotions
representative with Castlemaine
Perkins XXXX
Born: 13.8.66
Family: Suellen (wife), Rachael
(daughter), Justine (daughter),
James (son)
Former clubs: None
International debut: Australia 65,
South Korea 18, 1987
Best moment in rugby: Scoring try
after coming on as replacement in
third Test v New Zealand (1992)
Worst moment in rugby: Losing
the above game 23–26
Most embarrassing moment:
Acting as replacement breakaway in
third Test of Bledisloe series and
knowing when they were calling
Zinzan Brooke in the lineouts but
not capable enough to stop him

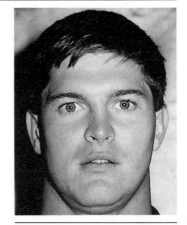

Australia (1987)		
Last Season	1 cap	5 pts
Career	8 caps	5 pts

Caps (8): **1987** SK(R). wc-F(R) **1990**
F(1R), US, NZ(2,3) **1991** wc-
WS **1992** NZ(3R)

Points (5 – 1t): **1992** NZ(3:1t)

Most respected opponent: Don't get to play against many, but anyone chosen
to play for his country deserves the utmost respect
Serious injuries: Damaged three transversus (abdominal) muscles (1992)
Other sporting achievements: Teamed up at golf with Jason Little in Fiji to
triumph against the odds and handicaps of Tim Horan and John Brass
Best memory last season: Winning the 1992 Bledisloe Cup and thrashing
South Africa
Suggestions to improve rugby: *On-field* – Reduce value of penalty to two
points. *Off-field* – Better compensation for elite players to enable them to
produce greater results more consistently
Notable landmarks in rugby career: In and out of the Wallabies' Test side
during the past six years, he gained his sixth cap in 1992 as a 42nd minute
replacement in the third Test against New Zealand in Sydney. A dead 'rubber'
it might have been, with Australia having already sewn up the series, but
Herbert seized his opportunity with both hands and claimed his first Test try.

Despite that the All Blacks won 26–23. Thereafter he failed to add to his Test match experience, the majority of which was obtained in 1990 when he made appearances against France, the United States and New Zealand (twice). Despite his shortage of Test action in 1992 he turned out in the wins over Western Transvaal, Northern Transvaal, and Eastern Province (scored try) in South Africa, and in the defeats by Munster and Swansea once the tour moved on to Britain

Tours: 1987 – World Cup. 1989 – Canada and France. 1990 – New Zealand. 1991 – New Zealand, World Cup. 1992 – South Africa, Ireland and Wales
Touchlines: Golf and work
Player to watch: Daniel Herbert (younger brother)
Player of the Year: Phil Kearns (Australia)

Stuart Barnes in action on his maiden Five Nations' start, against Scotland at Twickenham – nine years after making his Test debut

Hills, W. G.   South Africa

Full Name: Willem (Willie)
Gerhardus Hills
Club: Police
Province: Northern Transvaal
Position: Hooker
Height: 5ft 11in (1.80m)
Weight: 17st 5lb (110kg)
Occupation: Policeman
Born: Pretoria, 26.1.62
International debut: France 15,
South Africa 20, 1992
Other sporting achievements:
Provincial colours in softball and
weightlifting
**Notable landmarks in rugby
career:** Has made swift progress
since his provincial debut in 1990
for Northern Transvaal, no doubt
aided by the Blue Bulls' Currie Cup-
Lion Cup double in 1991. Educated
at the Gardens School in Pretoria, he
had played 30 matches for Northern
Transvaal but none for South Africa
before embarking on the Springboks'
tour of France and England. He came
close to a full debut against Australia

South Africa (1992)

Last Season	5 caps	0 pts
Career	5 caps	0 pts

Caps (5): **1992** F(1,2),E **1993** F(1,2)

Points Nil

(22.8.92) but, having represented his province against the Wallabies the
previous week (lost 17–24 in Pretoria), lost out to Blue Bulls team mate Uli
Schmidt in selection at Cape Town. Schmidt, who also hooked against New
Zealand, did not tour and Hills needed no second invitation to take over.
Appearances at prop against Aquitaine (won 29–22, Pau, 7.10.92), Midi-
Pyrenees (won 18–15, Toulouse, 15.10.92) and French Universities (lost
13–18, Tours, 28.10.92) preceded his Test debut in the number two jersey at
Lyon where the Springboks beat France 20–15. He again had the hooking res-
ponsibilities the following week in Paris when France rebounded with a 29–16
win and a busy season was completed in England with outings against the Midlands Division (won 32–9, Leicester, 4.11.92), England B (won 20–16, Bristol,
7.11.92) and, at Twickenham, England themselves (14.11.92, lost 16–33).

Hogg, C. D.   Scotland

Full Name: Carl David Hogg
Club: Melrose
Position: No 8, lock, flanker
Height: 6ft 4in (1.93m)
Weight: 15st 7lb (98kg)
Occupation: Graduate civil engineer with Crouch Hogg and Waterman
Born: Galashiels, 5.7.69
Family: Single
Family links with rugby: Jim Telfer (uncle) played for Scotland (25 caps, 1964–70) and Lions (8 Tests, 1966–68)
International debut: Australia 27, Scotland 12, 1992
Five Nations' debut: None
Best moment in rugby: Making Scotland debut on '92 Australian tour
Worst moment in rugby: Being well beaten by Randwick in 1990 Melrose Sevens
Most respected opponent: John Jeffrey (Kelso & Scotland)
Serious injuries: Back operation to remove disc

Scotland (1992)		
Last Season	2 caps	0 pts
1993	Tour to South Seas	
Career	2 caps	0 pts

Caps (2): 1992 A(1,2)

Points Nil

Best memory last season: Test debut in Sydney against Wallabies (13.6.92)
Suggestions to improve rugby: *Off-field* – Greater media coverage of club games. More sponsorship at club level
Notable landmarks in rugby career: Became 19th Melrose player to be capped by Scotland when appeared at blindside in Scotland's two Test defeats against Australia on 1992 tour (12–27 and 13–37). Played in shadow Scotland side (A team) which beat Italy 22–17 at the Greenyards on 19 December, and in Scotland A side which won well (22–13) in Dublin against Ireland counterparts on 28 December. But damaged ankle ligaments in latter match and was forced to miss first Trial, then Championship opener against Ireland. Selectors subsequently opted not to disturb Weir–Turnbull–Morrison back row combination and fit-again Carl remained on bench. Represented Scotland Schools (1986/87) and U-19s before breaking into Scotland Under-21 side (1989/90) and captained side in 10–24 loss to Wales at Ayr. Aged just 19 when appeared in 1989 Scottish Trial. Graduated to Scotland B during 1991/92 season, warming bench in Belfast before making debut in 10–31 home loss to France

in unaccustomed surroundings of second row. Member of Scotland squad at 1992 Students World Cup in Italy and toured Fiji, Tonga and Western Samoa last summer with senior party

Touchlines: Golf

Hontas, P. France

Full Name: Pierre Hontas
Club: Biarritz Olympique
Position: Wing
Height: 5ft 11in (1.80m)
Weight: 13st 4lb (84kg)
Occupation: PE teacher
Born: Biarritz, 19.7.66
Family: Single
International debut: Scotland 21, France 0, 1990
Five Nations' debut: As above
Notable landmarks in rugby career: A virtual stranger to the Home Unions, having turned out just the once, when France lost 21–0 to Grand Slam champions-elect Scotland (17.2.90) at Murrayfield on his debut. It was not a particularly auspicious performance, neither by France, who had Alain Carminati sent-off for stamping on John Jeffrey, nor Pierre, who failed to prevent opposite number Iwan Tukalo slipping through his defensive cover to score. A clubmate of Serge Blanco at Biarritz, he retained his place on the right wing

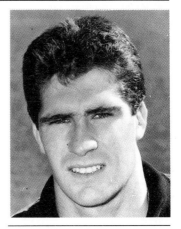

France (1990)

Last Season	5 caps	0 pts
Career	9 caps	0 pts

Caps (9): **1990** S,I,R **1991** R **1992** Arg(b) **1993** E,S,I,W

Points Nil

for the 31–12 Paris victory over Ireland but again failed score, as was the case on his two outings since, both against Romania. The last of which, as a left wing in the 33-21 win in Bucharest (22.6.91), preceded a spell in the international wilderness as Jean-Baptiste Lafond, Patrice Lagisquet, Philippe Saint-André and, latterly, Sebastien Viars carved up the wing duties. Pierre, who had toured New Zealand with France in 1989, scoring three tries in one match against Seddon Shield, returned to Test favour on 14 November 1992 when France suffered their first ever defeat by Argentina on home soil. In this case it was Nantes where the Pumas triumphed 24–20. Pierre kept his place throughout victorious Five Nations' championship campaign

Horan, T. J.   Australia

Full Name: Timothy (Tim) James
Horan
Club: Southern Districts
State: Queensland
Position: Centre, five-eighth
Height: 6ft (1.83m)
Weight: 13st 8lb (86kg)
Occupation: Sales representative
with Castlemaine Perkins XXXX
Born: 15.5.70
Family: Katrina (wife), Lucy
(daughter)
Former clubs: None. Souths since
1988
International debut: New Zealand
24, Australia 12, 1989
Best moment in rugby: Winning
1991 World Cup
Worst moment in rugby: Losing to
New Zealand at Eden Park in second
Test of 1991 Bledisloe Cup series
Most embarrassing moment:
Answering just one question on Sale
of the Century
Most respected opponent: Jerry
Guscott (Bath & England)
Serious injuries: Knee (1990)
Best memory last season: Beating
South Africa
Suggestions to improve rugby:
On-field – Improve standards of
refereeing

Australia (1989)

Last Season	8 caps	18 pts
Career	25 caps	50 pts

Caps	(25): **1989** NZ, F(1,2) **1990** F(1), NZ(1,2,3) **1991** W(a), E(a), NZ(a1,a2). wc–Arg, WS, W(b), I, NZ(b), E(b) **1992** S(1,2), NZ(1,2,3), SA, I, W
Points	(50 – 12t): F(1:2t) **1990** NZ(2:1t) **1991** W(a:1t). wc–Arg(2t), W(b:1t), NZ(b:1t) **1992** S(2:2t), NZ(1:1t), I(1t)

Notable landmarks in rugby career: For many, the outstanding player in
world rugby in 1992, Tim has proved a highly capable performer since being
given his debut as a teenager against New Zealand in 1989 – two years after
helping Australia Under-17s beat their New Zealand counterparts 16–3. In
tandem with Southern Districts and Queensland team mate Jason Little, who
also appeared in the aforementioned game, he has forged a midfield partnership
which compares favourably even alongside the likes of Bunce–Little,
Muller–Gerber and Guscott–Carling. A World Cup winner in 1991 and ever-
present for Australia in 1992, he bagged a try in the 16–15 first Test win over
New Zealand, in Sydney on 4 July, and another in the 42–17 defeat of Ireland,
at Lansdowne Road on 31 October. prior to those, he represented the World

XV against New Zealand in the first and third Tests of the '92 Centenary Series. On tour in South Africa he helped beat Northern Transvaal 24–17 in Pretoria as well as playing in the record 26–3 Test victory. The players of Leinster, Ulster, Swansea, Llanelli and the Barbarians encountered him during the Wallabies' visit to the United Kingdom

Tours: 1989 – New Zealand, Canada and France. 1990 – New Zealand. 1991 – New Zealand, World Cup. 1992 – South Africa, Ireland and Wales
Touchlines: Golf and family
Player to watch: Damien Smith (Queensland)
Player of the Year: Willy Ofahengaue (Australia)

Hueber, A. France

Full Name: Aubin Hueber
Club: Lourdes
Position: Scrum-half
Height: 5ft 8in (1.70m)
Weight: 12st (76kg)
Occupation: Communications officer with Var Regional Council
Born: Tarbes, 5.4.67
International debut: Australia 19, France 28, 1990
Five Nations' debut: France 44, Ireland 12, 1992
Notable landmarks in rugby career: France's first-choice scrum-half since making his Five Nations' debut in 44–12 rout of Ireland in Paris on 21 March 1992. Although rested for subsequent engagement against Romania at Le Havre, he played the next nine games thereafter – three against Argentina (two on tour in July 1992), two against South Africa and all four in France's triumphant 1993 Five Nations' campaign. Scored try and dropped goal in 33–9 second Test win over Pumas in Buenos Aires (11.7.92). Had succeeded Henri Sanz as France B scrum-half at Brecon (29.10.88)

France (1990)

Last Season	12 caps	8 pts
Career	16 caps	8 pts

Caps (16): **1990** A(3), NZ(1) **1991** US(2) **1992** I **1992** Arg(a1,a2), SA(1,2), Arg(b) **1993** E, S, I, W, R. SA(1,2)

Points (8 – 1t,1dg): **1992** Arg(a2:1t,1dg)

when Wales B were defeated 18-12. Again partnered Thierry Lacroix at half-back when the second string were undone 14–12 by Scotland B at Melrose

(18.2.89), and was captain when Wales B were beaten 28–15 in La Teste (12.1 1.89). A year earlier he had appeared at Auch in a non-cap match against Ireland and moved a step nearer cap-recognition when selected to represent the Rest of the Europe against the Four Home Unions (lost 43–18) at Twickenham in a match organ-ized to raise money for the Romania appeal (22.4.90). He again under-studied Sanz when France toured Australia in 1990 and was given his longawaited chance in the third Test, Jacques Fouroux's last match as coach, which the visitors won 28–19 (30.6.90), despite the dismissal of Philippe Gallart. He went on to play in the first Test against New Zealand (3.11.90) but was replaced by Sanz after France lost 3–24. A third cap followed, however, in the lightning-shortened second Test win over the United States on France's pre-World Cup tour before Fabien Galthie pipped him to 1991 World Cup selection

---

Hunter, I.   England

Full Name: Ian Hunter
Club: Northampton
Position: Fullback, wing, centre
Height: 6ft 2in (1.88m)
Weight: 14st 7lb (92kg)
Occupation: Commercial artist
Born: Harrow, London 15.2.69
Family: Single
Family links with rugby: Father played in New Zealand
Former clubs: Windermere, Carlisle, Nottingham
Best moment in rugby: England caps and Lions' selection
Worst moments in rugby: Losing to Harlequins in extra-time in 1990/91 Pilkington Cup final; dislocating shoulder in first match of '93 Lions tour and having to come home
Most embarrassing moment: Falling over for no reason in front of capacity crowd at Northampton just before kick-off
Best memory last season: Scoring two tries on debut against Canada
Suggestions to improve rugby:

England (1992)		
Last Season	3 caps	15 pts
Career	3 caps	15 pts
Lions 1993	Tour to New Zealand	

Caps (3): **1992** C **1993** F,W

Points (15 – 3t): **1992** C(2t) **1993** F(1t)

On-field: Play league games on a home and away basis. *Off-field* – RFU to sort out their amateur regulations, like every other nation has

Notable landmarks in rugby career: Educated in Windermere, Ian finally broke in England's senior squad at start of 1992/93 season when making his debut at Wembley on 17 October, when England beat Canada 26–13. To compound his joy, he scored two tries (his opener, England's first ever five-point score). A natural fullback, he won all his three caps on the right wing – other two coming in 1993 Five Nations' Championship against France and Wales. Selected for South Africa game but forced to withdraw with freak injury suffered in impromptu soccer match during club training. Interviewed by Des Lynam on *Sportsnight* as next star of English rugby, after scoring crucial try (off crossbar) in 16–15 defeat of French at Twickenham (16.1.93), he was then promptly dropped. Still, had made sufficient impression to earn Lions selection for 1993 summer tour to New Zealand. Fate then took over and he returned home prematurely having dislocated shoulder in 30–17 tour-opening win against North Auckland at Whangarei. Had appeared in New Zealand in summer of '92 when took England B cap-total to 11 with appearances at fullback in both losing Tests (lost 18–24, Hamilton, 28.6.92; lost 18–26, Pukekohe, 5.7.92). Scored two tries and a conversion in first Test. Celebrated winning 12th 'B' cap with try in 16–20 loss to Springboks at Bristol (7.11.92). In all, his dozen 'B' appearances yielded 42 points. Previous caps came against: Emerging Australians, Spain (twice: three tries and dropped goal), Italy B (twice: one try), Ireland B (twice: two tries) and France B (twice). Helped Northampton win promotion to first division (1989/90) and into 1990/91 Pilkington Cup final against Harlequins. Represented centenary Barbarians (1990/91) and toured Australia with England (1991)

England captain Will Carling sets alarm bells ringing in the South African defence, during the home side's 33–16 win at Twickenham

Jenkins, G. R.   Wales

Full Name: Garin Richard Jenkins
Club: Swansea
Position: Hooker
Height: 5ft 10in (1.78m)
Weight: 15st 2lb (96kg)
Occupation: Employed by
Rhondda Leisure Services, Rhondda
Borough Council
Born: Ynysybwl, 18.8.67
Family: Single
Family links with rugby: Father's
uncle played for Wales. Mother's
cousin propped for Wales and Lions
Former clubs: Ynysybwl,
Pontypridd, King Country (NZ),
Pontypool
Best moments in rugby: Winning
first Welsh cap; scoring try in win
over Wallabies (1992)
Worst moment in rugby: Losing
place in Welsh team before 1993
Five Nations' Championship
Most respected opponent: All of
them
Other sporting achievements:
Marbles champion at Treobart
Junior School
Best memory last season:
Swansea's 21–6 win over touring Australians

Wales (1991)		
Last Season	1 cap	0 pts
v Italy XV	1 app	0 pts
Career	9 caps	0 pts

Caps (9): **1991** F(b) wc-WS(R), Arg,
A(b) **1992** I, F, E, S, A

Points Nil

Notable landmarks in rugby career: Lost place in Welsh side last season
having performed hooking duties in 43–12 win over Italy XV at Cardiff
(7.10.92) and 6–23 loss to Australia (21.11.92) also in National Stadium.
Between two outings he helped Swansea to a famous win over Wallabies at St
Helens, scoring one of All Whites' two tries in 21–6 victory (4.11.92). But Five
Nations' Championship Pontypool's Nigel Meek had earned vote, with
Llanelli's Andrew Lamerton his bench deputy. Garin, a former coal miner,
represented Boys Clubs of Wales U-18s and Glamorgan U-23s. He started his
career with Ynysybwl, the birthplace of national coach Alan Davies, and in
1990 toured Kenya with Pontypool, having represented Pooler against 1989
All Blacks. Broke into Wales team at the start of 1991/92 season when Davies
was appointed coach following the 1991 Australia tour, and played in all eight
games spanning the French 'floodlit' game, the 1991 World Cup and 1992 Five
Nations' Championship (pack leader). Completed great season by securing

1991/92 Heineken League premier division honours with Swansea
Touchlines: Soccer, cricket, weightlifting

Jenkins, N. R. Wales

Full Name: Neil Roger Jenkins
Club: Pontypridd
Position: Outside-half
Height: 5ft 10in (1.78m)
Weight: 12st 7lb (80kg)
Occupation: PR consultant with
Just Rentals Ltd (Pontypridd)
Born: Church Village, Pontypridd,
8.7.71
Family: Single
International debut: Wales 6,
England 25, 1991
Five Nations' debut: As above
Best moment in rugby: Beating
England at Cardiff (1993)
Worst moment in rugby: Being
sent-off in 39th minute of 6–27
1991/92 Schweppes Cup semi-final
against Llanelli at Arms Park
Most respected opponents: Didier
Camberabero (Beziers & France)
and Philippe Sella (Agen & France)
Biggest influences on career:
Parents and two uncles
Best memory last season:
Atmosphere in Arms Park during
and after England game
Suggestions to improve rugby:
On-field – Award less points for
goals. *Off-field* – Unions should pay
players wages when rugby takes
them away from work, rather than expecting goodwill from employers

Wales (1991)

Last Season	7 caps	61 pts
1993	Tour to Zimbabwe/Namibia	
Career	15 caps	100 pts

Caps (15): **1991** E, S, I, F **1992** I, F, E,
S **1993** E, S, I, F, Z(1,2), Na

Points (100 – 2t,11c,22p,1dg): **1991**
E(1p), I(1t,1dg) **1992** I(3p),
F(3p), S(1c,3p) **1993** E(1c,1p),
I(3p), F(1c,1p), Z(1:3c,2p),
Z(2:1t,3c,2p), Na(2c,3p)

Notable landmarks in rugby career: An ever-present for Wales in last three
Five Nations' campaigns yet, remarkably, had appeared in no other Tests
(including 1991 World Cup) prior to Wales' 1993 tour to Africa. Last season,
he was idle as Llanelli's Colin Stephens wore sacred Welsh No 10 jersey against
Italy XV and Australia. Once in situ, continued to add to his career points tally.
His four appearances yielded 19 points, including five crucial points in 10–9
defeat of England (6.2.93). Represented Wales A team pre-Christmas in 21–13

win over North of England at Pontypool (14.10.92) in which he contributed 11 points (1c,3p). Played for East Wales Under-11s v West Wales, East Glamorgan and Wales Youth (1989/90). Having broken into Wales U-21s into 1990/91 – playing against New Zealand Under-21 XV (14pts:4c,2p) and Scotland U-21 (15pts: 1t,1c,3p) – added a second cap and ten points in 22–15 win over Ireland U-21 in 1991/92 (2c,2p). An eventful 1990/91 had also seen him graduate to Wales B where he scored 18 points in 34–12 win over Netherlands (1t,4c,2p) in Leiden

Touchlines: Golf

Johns, P. S.   Ireland

Full Name: Patrick Stephen Johns
Club: Dungannon
Position: Lock, No 8
Height: 6ft 6in (1.98m)
Weight: 16st (102kg)
Occupation: Dentist
Born: Portadown, 19.2.68
Family: Single
Former clubs: Newcastle Univ, Gosforth, Dublin Univ
International debut: Ireland 20, Argentina 18, 1990
Five Nations' debut: Scotland 15, Ireland 3, 1993
Best moments in rugby: First match for Ireland (Schools v Australia, 1988); wins over Wales and England (1993)
Most embarrassing moment: Getting my shorts ripped off aged 13
Most respected opponent: Alan Whetton (Auckland & New Zealand) – the best about
Serious injuries: Neck injury, broken wrist
Best memory last season: Beating England in Dublin

Ireland (1990)

Last Season	7 caps	0 pts
Career	8 caps	0 pts

Caps (8): **1990** Arg **1992** NZ(1,2), A **1993** S, F, W, E

Points Nil

Suggestions to improve rugby: *On-field* – Less emphasis on set-play. Encourage more open rugby
Notable landmarks in rugby career: Along with St Mary's Vince Cunningham and Greystones' Lion Nick Popplewell, he had distinction of playing in all eight Tests involving Ireland in 1992/93 (from New Zealand tour

through to triumph over England). During that period he was joined in Irish engine room by Mick Galwey, Brian Rigney, Richard Costello and Neil Francis. Represented Ulster against 1989 All Blacks (lost 3–21, Ravenhill 21.11.89) and helped them win record sixth Irish Inter-Provincial Championship. Last season they won it again. Represented Ireland Schools in 1986, against Japan (twice), Australia, England and Wales. Toured Canada with Dungannon (1989). Played for Ireland at Under-21 and Under-25 level (twice) in 1988/89 season. Also turned out for Irish Students and Universities while at Dublin University. Represented Ireland B in 22–22 draw with Scotland B at Murrayfield (9.12.89) and twice against England B – in 24–10 win at Old Belvedere (scoring try, 1.3.91) and at Richmond (No 8 in 15–47 loss, Richmond 31.1.92). First capped by Ireland against touring Argentina Pumas (27.20.90)

Touchlines: Cycling

Johnson, M. O.   England

Full Name: Martin Osborne Johnson
Club: Leicester
Position: Lock
Height: 6ft 7in (2.01m)
Weight: 17st 10lb (112kg)
Occupation: Bank officer with Midland Bank (Market Harborough)
Born: Solihull, 9.3.70
Family: Single
Former clubs: Wigston, College Old Boys (NZ)
International debut: England 16, France 15, 1993
Five Nations' debut: As above
Best moment in rugby: Making full debut against France at Twickenham (16.1.93)
Worst moment in rugby: Leicester's semi-final defeat by Harlequins in 1991/92 Pilkington Cup
Most respected opponent: Paul Ackford (Ex-Harlequins & England)
Serious injuries: Dislocated left shoulder (April 1991) playing for

England (1993)		
Last Season	1 cap	0 pts
1993		Tour to Canada
Career	1 cap	0 pts
Lions 1993	2 Tests	0pts

Caps (1): **1993** F. Lions–NZ(2,3)

Points Nil

Midlands U-21s v London U-21s. Required operation and out for four months
Best memories last season: England call-up and Leicester's Pilkington Cup final triumph
Suggestions to improve rugby: *On-field* – Beware not to alter too much of the game. If we try to make too many changes, in an attempt to pamper for television etc, we stand the chance of changing the face of the game, and that would be disastrous. *Off-field* – Use commonsense to resolve the amateurism question. Do what is fair.
Notable landmarks in rugby career: Spent 18 months playing out in New Zealand for College Old Boys (1990–91) and for King Country in Division Two of inter-Provincial Championship, during which time he also represented New Zealand Colts against Australia counterparts on a two-week tour. Team mates on tour included All Blacks Va'aiga Tuigamala, John Timu and Blair Larsen. Planned to remain only 12 months but niggling shoulder complaint prolonged his stay. Had previously represented England Schools (1987–88) and 1989 England Colts (along with Damien Hopley and Steve Ojomoh) prior to heading Down Under. On his return played for England U-21 – partnering Gloucester's David Sims in 94–0 rout of Belgium (Wolverhampton, 1.9.91), before turning out, again alongside Sims, in England B's wins against France B (Paris, 15.2.92) and Italy B (Rome, 7.3.92). But it was last season that he really hit the big-time. Expecting to play for England A against France A, at leicester on 15 January, he was diverted to Twickenham where Wade Dooley had withdrawn from senior side with thigh injury. At less than 24 hours notice Martin was thrust into 1993 Five Nations' opener and acquitted himself well, especially in second half. Returned to A-team thereafter, playing in wins over Italy A, Spain and Ireland A in February and March, and spent the first part of last summer on tour with them in Canada, playing in both legs of the 1–1 Test series. Preparing for home he was diverted to New Zealand as a replacement for Dooley, who returned home early from the Lions tour due to the death of his father. Martin took his chance with both hands, winning a berth in the second and third Test teams

Jones, I. D.   New Zealand

Full Name: Ian Donald Jones
Club: Kamo
Province: North Auckland
Position: Lock
Height: 6ft 6in (1.98m)
Weight: 15st 10lb (100kg)
Occupation: Builder
Born: Whangarei, 17.4.67
International debut: New Zealand 31, Scotland 16, 1990
Notable landmarks in rugby career: An outstanding player since his early days when he represented Whangarei Schools (1979) and North Island Under-18s. The teenage Jones broke into both the Kamo first XV and North Auckland Colts side in 1986, and two years later made his bow for North Auckland, whom he now captains. Having marked his inaugural season of provincial rugby (1988) with four tries in eight matches, he played in the 1989 All Black Trials and was included in the squad for their tour to Wales and Ireland. Failed to make the Test side but did make a lot of friends and consequently returned to Britain the following year as an invited guest of the centenary

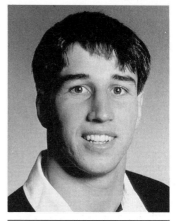

New Zealand (1990)

Last Season	12 caps	4 pts
Career	29 caps	12 pts

Caps (29): **1990** S(1,2), A(1,2,3), F(1,2) **1991** Arg(1,2), A(a1,a2). wc–E, US, It, C, A(b), S **1992** Wd(1,2,3), I(1,2), A(1,2,3), SA **1993** BL(1,2R,3)

Points (12 – 3t): **1990** S(1:1t) **1991** A(1:1t) **1992** I(2:1t)

Barbarians, playing against England, Wales and Argentina. By then he had made his Test debut against Scotland at Dunedin, following the retirement of Murray Pierce, and celebrated with a try in the 31–16 win. Ian appeared in all seven All Black Tests in 1990 and toured Argentina the following year, starting both Tests. A try in the 21–12 Bledisloe Cup first Test defeat by Australia. An everpresent in the World Cup he maintained his place throughout the nine-Test schedule in 1992, claiming his third international try in the second Test romp over Ireland. Enjoyed an impressive tour of Australia and South Africa last season, edging highly-rated Wallaby John Eales in the lineout. Made ten appearances on the tour, including one (a formidable display) as captain against Orange Free State at Bloemfontein, and is seen as a future New Zealand test skipper. Returned to Britain in November 1992 to reunite with his Barbarian colleagues for the match against Australia

Jones, M. N.   New Zealand

Full Name: Michael Niko Jones
Province: Auckland
Position: Flanker, No 8
Height: 5ft 11in (1.80m)
Weight: 15st 2lb (96kg)
Born: Auckland, 8.4.65
Former country: Western Samoa
International debut: Western
Samoa 14, Wales 32, 1986
International debut (NZ): New
Zealand 70, Italy 6, 1987
Serious injuries: Damaged knee
(1989)
**Notable landmarks in rugby
career:** Widely regarded as the
world's best flanker, Auckland-born
Michael first caught the eye playing
in the colours of Western Samoa
against Wales at Suva in 1986. By
the following year New Zealand had
snapped him up and he was
included in their World Cup-
winning squad, scoring a try against
Italy at Eden Park 30 minutes into
his debut and claiming the All
Blacks' first, after 17 minutes of their
29–9 World Cup final win over
France on the same Auckland field.
Had been marked out as something
special ever since his provincial
debut in 1985 when he scored three
tries against South Canterbury.
However, his climb to the very
pinnacle of the world game was
abruptly halted in 1989 when he

Western Samoa (1986)		
Career	1 cap	0 pts
New Zealand (1987)		
Last Season	9 caps	0 pts
Career	31 caps	36 pts

Caps (31): **1987** wc–It, Fj, S, F. A **1988**
W(1,2), A(2,3) **1989** F(1,2),
Arg(1,2) **1990** F(1,2) **1991**
Arg(1,2), A(1,2). wc–E, US, S
1992 Wd(1,3), I(2), A(1,3), SA
1993 BL(1,2,3)

Points (36 – 9t): **1987** wc–It(1t), F(1t)
1988 W(2:1t), A(2:1t) **1989**
Arg(1:2t) **1990** F(2:1t) **1991**
Arg(2:1t). wc–E(1t)

sustained a serious knee injury playing against Argentina, having scored two
tries in the 60–9 first Test defeat of the Pumas at Carisbrook, Dunedin. The
injury was described by his specialist as 'the equivalent of being hit by a truck
doing 60mph'. As a consequence he missed the tour to Wales and Ireland but
returned, 18 months later, for the 1990 tour of France, during which he crossed
for a try in the 30–12 second Test victory in Paris. Made headlines on and off
the paddock at the 1991 World Cup, scoring the only try of the tournament
opener as England were beaten 18–12 in their own Twickenham backyard,

before declining to play in the quarter-final and semi-final ties against Canada and Australia respectively as the games fell on a Sunday – a day of rest in his book. This refusal to compromise his religious beliefs led to him missing the Brisbane Test against Australia in the 1992 Bledisloe Cup series, as well as the outings against NSW and Queensland, but he still managed eight appearances on the Australia/South Africa tour during which he was in a class of his own as lineout tailgunner

Jones, R. N.   Wales

Full Name: Robert Nicholas Jones
Club: Swansea
Position: Scrum-half
Height: 5ft 8in (1.73m)
Weight: 11st 8lb (74kg)
Occupation: Business development executive with Swansea Building Society
Born: Trebanos, 10.11.65
Family: Megan (wife)
Family links with rugby: Father-in-law (Clive Rowlands) played for Wales and Lions. Brother (Rhodri) plays for Neath
International debut: England 21, Wales 18, 1986
Five Nations' debut: As above
Best moments in rugby: Captaining Wales. 1989 Lions winning decisive third Test against Australia
Worst moments in rugby: Captaining Wales in 1990 whitewash – very, very despondent. Defeat by New Zealand in 1987 World Cup
Most embarrassing moment: Attempted dropped goal for Wales against Ireland, hit ground before ball and sent it 3 yards. Paul Dean collected and initiated move which led to Irish try
Most respected opponents: Pierre Berbizier (ex-Agen & France) and

Wales (1986)		
Last Season	4 caps	0 pts
v Italy XV	1 app	0 pts
Career	46 caps	4 pts
Lions 1989	3 Tests	0 pts
1993	Tour to New Zealand	

Caps (46): **1986** E, S, I, F, Fj, T, WS **1987** F, E(a), S, I(a), US wc–I(b), T, E(b), NZ, A **1988** E, S, I, F, NZ(1), WS, Ro **1989** I, F, E, NZ. Lions–A(1,2,3) **1990** F, E, S, I **1991** E, S, F(b) wc–WS, Arg, A(b) **1992** I, F, E, S, A **1993** E, S, I

Points (4 – 1t): **1987** wc–E(1t)

Gary Armstrong (Jed-Forest & Scotland)
Biggest influence on career: Father (Cliff)
Other sporting achievements: Cricket for Wales at three age-groups
Best memories last season: Swansea's defeat of Wallabies and my late selection for Lions
Suggestions to improve rugby: *On-field* – England winning 1991 Grand Slam with hardly any tries made a mockery of old scoring system. However, increasing try value has only served to make for a greater disparity between the major and the developing nations, discouraging the latter. Better to have reduced penalty value for technical offenses. Take Wales' 63–6 loss to Australia. Under the new system that score would have been 75–7. *Off-field* – Greater depth of consideration for players. Re-consider amateur issue so that players can benefit away from play. Look after players' employers with tickets etc. WRU trying to be more forward looking than other Unions but they are governed by IRB. Moves still have to be made to improve situation because there are still very few player-benefits considering time put in. Commitments and time involved ever-increasing. Yet athletes are able to benefit from their amateur sport
Notable landmarks in rugby career: Most-capped Swansea player (46) and former captain of the St Helens club as well as of Wales. Within seven caps of joining rugby legend Gareth Edwards as Wales' most-capped scrum-half. But omission from final game of 1993 Five Nations' Championship in Paris (with Llanelli skipper Rupert Moon coming in) reduced the likelihood of him adding further to his tally. However, season ended on a high note when he was drafted into Lions squad for New Zealand tour, after his good friend and original selection, Scotland's Gary Armstrong, withdrew with a groin injury. He made six appearances but was unable to shift Dewi Morris from the Test berth. Robert first turned out for Swansea whilst still at Cwmtawe School, having already played for West Wales U-11s and Wales 12-Group. Represented Welsh Schools for two seasons before graduating, by way of Wales B in 1985, to senior XV for 1986 Five Nations' Championship. Enjoyed outstanding World Cup (1987) and equally magnificent tour, to Australia, with 1989 Lions. Partnered Jonathan Davies in 22 internationals before latter switched codes. Missed Welsh tour of Namibia in 1991 through injury but did go to Fiji, Tonga and Western Samoa (1986), New Zealand (1988) and Australia (1991). Scored only Wales try in 1987 World Cup quarter-final win (16–3) over England
Touchlines: Golf

Joseph, J. W.   New Zealand

Full Name: Jamie Joseph
Province: Otago
Position: Flanker
Height: 6ft 5in (1.96m)
Weight: 16st 8lb (105kg)
Born: Blenheim, 21.11.69
Family links with rugby: Jim (father) played for New Zealand Maoris in 1960s
International debut: New Zealand 54, World XV 26, 1992
Notable landmarks in rugby career: Made a controversial entrance onto the Test stage, when spotted stamping by television – for which he later received a four-week suspension from the Union's judiciary committee – on his debut against the World XV, in the second Test of the 1992 centenary series. However, he made news, for the right reasons, on the All Black tour of Australia and South Africa. Lost out in selection stakes to first Mike Brewer, his Provincial skipper, then Andy Earl in the first two tests against Australia, although he came

New Zealand (1992)

Last Season	8 caps	5 pts
Career	8 caps	5 pts

Caps (8): **1992** Wd(2), I(1), A(1R,3), SA. BL(1,2,3)

Points (5 – 1t): **1992** A(3:1t)

on as a 65th minute replacement for Brewer in Sydney. But he was awarded the start in the 'dead rubber' and scored a wonderful try. Against South Africa, too, he impressed. In all he made nine appearances on the trip, bagging a try in the 80–0 defeat of Western Australia. His other outings were against New South Wales, Victoria, Queensland, Natal, Junior South Africa. A latecomer to top-grade rugby, having completed only two seasons of First Division rugby at Otago, the 1991 national champions. He was acclaimed the Province's most improved player in 1992 and in the same year, excelled in two national trials at Napier, finishing on the winning side for Fitzpatrick's XV and the Saracens team which beat a New Zealand XV 20–15. Completed an excellent campaign by following in his father's studprints and representing the New Zealand Maoris on their tour of the Pacific Islands

Kahl, P. R.   Australia

Full Name: Paul Raymond Kahl
Club: Eastern Districts (Brisbane)
State: Queensland
Position: Five-eighth
Height: 6ft ½in (1.84m)
Weight: 14st 5lb (91kg)
Occupation: Officer with
Commonwealth Bank Finance
company
Born: 4.4.69
Family: The Beverley House family
(roomies Toni, Amanda and
Dalton)
Former clubs: None
International debut: Wales 6,
Australia 23, 1992
Best moment in rugby: Test debut
v Wales; helping Queensland win
1991 Dubai Sevens
Worst moments in rugby:
Queensland v Fiji (had a shocker);
Queensland v Canterbury (six
players, including me, got
hypothermia)
Most embarrassing moment:
Being flattened from behind by
punch from an Irish prop

Australia (1992)		
Last Season	1 cap	0 pts
Career	1 cap	0 pts

Caps   (1): 1992 W

Points Nil

Most respected opponent: Steffi Graf and any All Black forward
Serious injuries: Damaged ankle and acromio-clavicular shoulder joints
Other sporting achievements: Still trying to achieve in rugby
Best memory last season: Winning Super Six for Queensland
Suggestions to improve rugby: *On-field* – Take a close look at rules regarding
ruck possession. *Off-field* – My female room mates suggest shorter shorts and
a 'men of rugby' calendar with me as cover page and January Boy!
Notable landmarks in rugby career: A representative career restricted by the
fact that his position and State coincided with that of Michael Lynagh. The
outside-half from Queensland was finally given an extended chance to shine in
the '92 State team while Lynagh was playing with Treviso in Italy. Paul, who
made his Queensland debut in 1988, also had Lynagh's absence to thank for
his Test debut last season. Having served as his deputy throughout South
Africa, Ireland and Wales – 'dirt-tracking' against Western Transvaal, Eastern
Province (scored try), Munster, Connacht, Swansea and Monmouthshire – he
was drafted in to replace the injured Lynagh in the 23–6 Test defeat of Wales

on 21 November. The following week he helped Australia close their season with a 30–20 victory over the Barbarians at Twickenham
Tours: 1992 – South Africa, Ireland and Wales
Touchlines: Rock climbing, beach, music, gym, golf, reading, sleeping, eating
Player to watch: Ilie Tabua (Queensland)
Player of the Year: David Wilson (Australia)

Kearns, P. N. Australia

Full Name: Philip (Phil) Nicholas Kearns
Club: Randwick
State: New South Wales
Position: Hooker
Height: 6ft (1.83m)
Weight: 17st (108kg)
Occupation: Key account executive with Tooheys Ltd
Born: 27.6.67
Family: Keith, Nereda, Vicki (sister)
International debut: New Zealand 24, Australia 12, 1989
Best moment in rugby: Winning first cap; winning World Cup; 1992 Bledisloe series win
Worst moment in rugby: Losing second leg of 1991 Bledisloe Cup series 3–6, allowing New Zealand to retain trophy
Most embarrassing moment: Falling over as I moved in at a shot on goal
Serious injuries: Not enough room in this book
Best memories last season: Winning 1992 Bledisloe Cup; beating South Africa
Suggestions to improve rugby: *On-field* – Get rid of the new ruck/maul law. Change positional names back to the old way. *Off-field* – Pay players more
Notable landmarks in rugby career: Ended the 1992 season captaining Australia to a 23–6 win over Wales, at Cardiff on 21 November, having been a

Australia (1989)

Last Season	8 caps	0 pts
Career	28 caps	24 pts

Caps (28): **1989** NZ, F(1,2) **1990** F(1,2,3), US, NZ(1,2,3) **1991** W(a), E(a), NZ(a1,a2). wc–Arg, WS, W(b), I, NZ(b), E(b) **1992** S(1,2), NZ(1,2,3), SA, I, W

Points (24 – 6t): **1989** F(2:1t) **1990** US(1t), NZ(3:1t) **1991** W(a:2t). wc–Arg(1t)

Randwick reserve grade player only three years earlier. In 1989 he sprung from obscurity to hook against the All Blacks and has remained in the line-up ever since. The Test captaincy, in the absence of injured Michael Lynagh, capped another fine season in which he packed down alongside Randwick team mate Ewen McKenzie throughout. Like another Wallaby front row, Dan Crowley, his only came in the 30–20 win over the Barbarians at Twickenham on 28 November – a match in which he also carried out the captaincy duties. His other appearances on tour came against Northern Transvaal, Leinster, Ulster, Swansea, Wales B and Llanelli, at Stradey Park where the scarlets won 13–9 to spoil Phil's 100 per cent tour captaincy record

Tours: 1989 – New Zealand, France and Canada. 1990 – New Zealand. 1991 – New Zealand, World Cup. 1992 – South Africa, Ireland and Wales

Touchlines: Golf, surfing, reading

Player to watch: Willie Ofahengaue (New South Wales)

Player of the Year: Willie Ofahengaue (Australia)

Kelaher, T. P. Australia

Full Name: Timothy (Tim) Patrick Kelaher

Club: Randwick

State: New South Wales

Position: Fullback, centre

Height: 6ft (1.83m)

Weight: 12st 8lb (80kg)

Occupation: Trainee futures broker with All States Futures (Sydney)

Born: 24.7.70

Family: Michael (father), Lyn (mother), Andrew (brother), David (brother), Anthony (brother), Peter (brother), Elizabeth (sister)

Former clubs: None. Randwick since 1991

International debut: Australia 16, New Zealand 15, 1992

Best moment in rugby: Winning first cap in opening Test of 1992 Bledisloe Cup series

Worst moment in rugby: Seriously injuring my kidney at start of 1991 season which put me out for three months and ruled out my representative chances for that year

Australia (1992)		
Last Season	2 caps	5 pts
Career	2 caps	5 pts

Caps (2): 1992 NZ(1),I(R)

Points (5 – 1t): (I:1t)

Serious injuries: Torn kidney (1991)

Best memory last season: Winning Sydney Grand Final; scoring first Test try against Ireland

Notable landmarks in rugby career: A member of the Emerging Wallabies party which toured England and Europe in 1990, though he was not in the side held 12–12 by England B at Wasps (4.11.90). Fellow tourists included Jason Little, Peter Slattery, Willie Ofahengaue, David Nucifora, Dan Crowley and John Eales. Had represented Australian Schools in 1989 and broke into first grade with Eastwood the following season. Switched club allegiances to Randwick in 1991 and played at hooker for Australia's Sevens team in 1992, before touring New Zealand with New South Wales. Renewed acquaintances with the men in Black when given Test debut in the victorious 16–15 first leg of the 1992 Bledisloe Cup series (deputizing for injured fullback Marty Roebuck) in Sydney on 4 July. With Roebuck restored to rude health Kelaher fulfilled the role of back-up on the tours to South Africa, Ireland and Wales. He kicked eight points (1c,2p) in the 24-17 defeat of Northern Transvaal and 14 points (1c,4p) in the 34–8 win over Eastern Province, and continued his scoring exploits when the tourists arrived in Britain. He contributed all 19 points (1t,1c,4p) in the 19–22 loss to Munster, 11 points in the 16–8 win at Neath and shared the remaining 32 points amongst Connacht (3p), Swansea (2p) and Welsh Students (1t,4p). Llanelli were the only side to deny him as he even scored a try when coming on as a half-time replacement for Michael Lynagh in the 42–17 win over Ireland

Tours: – 1992 South Africa, Ireland and Wales

Touchlines: Training, beach

Player to watch: Kevin O'Kane (club hooker in Sydney)

David Campese in characteristic pose – goose-stepping away from Lions-to-be Nick Popplewell and Will Carling in Australia's 30–20 defeat of the Barbarians at Twickenham

Kenny, P.   Ireland

Full Name: Paddy Kenny
Club: Wanderers
Position: Flanker, No.8
Height: 6ft 3in (1.91m)
Weight: 15st (95kg)
Occupation: Investment banker
Born: Philippines, 28.4.60
Family: Married
Family links with rugby: Son-in-law of former Ireland international Jim McCarthy (1948-55)
Former club: University College Dublin
International debut: New Zealand 59, Ireland 6, 1992
Five Nations' debut: None
Best moment in rugby: Taking part in 1988 Hong Kong Sevens
Worst moment in rugby: Missing selection for Ireland v Fiji (1985)
Most respected opponent: Zinzan Brooke (Auckland & New Zealand)
Serious injuries: Damaged shoulder
Best memory last season: Winning Ireland cap on tour to New Zealand

Ireland (1992)		
Last Season	1 cap	0 pts
Career	1 cap	0 pts

Caps (1): 1992 NZ(2R)

Points Nil

Notable landmarks in rugby career: Played on 1992/92 Wanderers team which won promotion from second division of All-Ireland League (with seven wins from nine starts) behind champions Lansdowne. Season had began well for Paddy with his inclusion on Ireland's summer tour to New Zealand and it was there he made his long-awaited senior debut. Selected as bench reserve for second Test in Wellington on 6 June 1992, he was brought on after just 18 minutes as a replacement for Shannon's injured openside Mick Fitzgibbon. Unhappily, for Paddy and Ireland, there were to be no repeat of their first Test heroics (when leading 12–0 before finally succumbing 21–24) as they were handed easily their biggest ever defeat by the All Black machine, losing 59–6. That was the last he saw of Test action as Gordon Hamilton, who had not toured, took over at No 7 for the Wallaby visit to Dublin on October 31, and Malone's Denis McBride did the honours throughout 1993 Five Nations' Championship. Paddy's first taste of the big time had come in 1981 on University College Dublin's tour to the United States. Four years later he was included in the Ireland squad to tour Japan and, after representing Leinster against New Zealand in 1989, he scored one of Ireland B's two tries in 22–22 draw with Scotland B at Murrayfield on 9 December 1989

Kingston, T. J.   Ireland

Full Name: Terence John Kingston
Club: Dolphin
Position: Hooker
Height: 5ft 10in (1.78m)
Weight: 14st 9lb (93kg)
Occupation: Financial advisor with Lifetime Assurance
Born: Cork, 19.9.63
Family: Single
Former club: Lansdowne
International debut: Ireland 6, Wales 13, 1987
Five Nations' debut: Ireland 22, Scotland 18, 1988
Best moment in rugby: Selection for 1987 World Cup and gaining first cap against Wales during the tournament
Worst moment in rugby: Being dropped from Irish team and Dolphin's failure to qualify for National League in 1989/90 play-off match
Most respected opponent: All of them
Best memories last season: Beating England and captaining Munster to win over touring Wallabies

Ireland (1987)

Last Season	3 caps	0 pts
Career	13 caps	8 pts

Caps (13): **1987** wc-W, T, A **1988** S, F, W, E(a) **1990** F, W **1991** wc-J **1993** F, W, E

Points (8 – 2t): **1988** W(1t) **1990** W(1t)

Suggestions to improve rugby: *On-field* – An extra five metres should be added to all penalties as an increased deterrent and to encourage team benefiting to take fast, running ball while opposition is retreating

Notable landmarks in rugby career: Re-established himself as Ireland's premier hooker in 1993 Five Nations' Championship, taking over from Ballymena's Lion Steve Smith and Greystones' John Murphy who had divided up the duties earlier in the 1992/93 campaign. Terry, who was last a regular member of the side in the 1988 Championship, played in the home defeat by France before, as vice-captain, playing a full role in the famous wins over Wales and England. If those successes were not sufficient cause for celebration, he also

skippered Munster to a 22–19 victory over the touring Australians, in Cork on 21 October 1992. Had captained Ireland to a 32–16 World Cup win over Japan (Dublin, 9.10.91) in a 1991/92 season which he otherwise viewed from the bench, as Smith monopolised the No 2 jersey. In all, Terry has represented Irish Schools (1982), Ireland Under-21s (1984), Ireland Under-25s (1987, three caps), Ireland B (beat Argentina 27–12, Limerick 20.10.90) and, on 13 occasions since his debut in the 1987 World Cup (in place of injured Harry Harbisson), Ireland Full. Toured with Ireland to Namibia (1991) and New Zealand (1992), playing three of Ireland's eight games on the more recent trip
Touchlines: Golf

Kirwan, J. J. New Zealand

Full Name: John Joseph Kirwan MBE
Clubs: Marist (NZ), Treviso (It)
Province: Auckland
Position: Wing
Height: 6ft 3in (1.90m)
Weight: 14st 7lb (92kg)
Occupation: Public relations officer
Born: Auckland, 16.12.64
Family: Fiorella (wife)
International debut: New Zealand 10, France 9, 1984
Serious injuries: Ruptured achilles tendon (1984 and 1989)
Notable landmarks in rugby career: New Zealand's record try-scorer and second most-capped player (behind Gary Whetton – 58), with 34 in 56 Tests, John's exploits have been central to the success of

the All Blacks since breaking into the side in 19 84 against France at Lancaster Park. Only the previous season he had made his provincial debut in the Auckland centenary game against the President's XV, while a Marist third XV player. Dropped out of the 1986 rebel Cavaliers tour to South Africa and instead busied himself with three appearances against both Australia and France. His failure to score that year was corrected in 1987 when he collected a World Cup best of six tries (matched by compatriot Craig Green) as New Zealand surged to glory. Largely responsible for burying Wales on the Principality's disastrous 1988 tour, scoring four tries in the 52–3 first Test rout and adding another two as the second Test ended 54–9 in the hosts' favour. John maintained his record of at least a try-per-Test in 1988 with four in the three-match series against Australia before his playing career was put on hold the following season. Playing against Pontypool, he ruptured his Achilles tendon and was sidelined for six months. Quickly returned to his best with two tries on comeback in 31–16 first Test defeat of Scotland in 1990 while, on the 1991 tour of Argentina, he collected eight tries in five games. John, who spent a number of off-seasons playing for Treviso in Italy and is now with second division club Sienna, took his total of All Black outings to 87 with nine appearances (and another six tries) on the 1992 tour of Australia and South Africa, a trip in which he rallied from a decidedly shaky start in the first two Aussie Tests

New Zealand (1984)

Last Season	11 caps	18 pts
Career	56 caps	138 pts

Caps (56): **1984** F(1,2) **1985** E(1,2), A, Arg(1,2) **1986** F(a), A(1,2,3), F(b1,b2) **1987** wc-It, Fj, Arg, S, W, F. A **1988** W(1,2), A(1,2,3) **1989** F(1,2), Arg(1,2), A **1990** S(1,2), Arg(1,2,3), F(1,2) **1991** Arg(2), A(a1,a2). wc–E, It, C, A(b), S **1992** Wd(1,2,3), I(1,2), A(1,2,3), SA **1993** BL(2,3)

Points (138 – 34t): **1985** E(2:1t), Arg(1:2t), Arg(2:2t) **1987** wc–It(2t), Fj(1t), W(2t), F(1t). A(1t) **1988** W(1:4t), W(2:2t), A(1:2t), A(2:1t), A(3:1t) **1989** Arg(1:2t), Arg(2:1t) **1990** S(1:2t), A(1:1t) **1991** Arg(2:1t). wc–C(1t) **1992** Wd(3:1t), I(2:1t), A(2:1t), SA(1t)

Lacroix, T. France

Full Name: Thierry Lacroix
Club: Dax
Position: Outside-half, centre
Height: 6ft 1in (1.86m)
Weight: 13st 2lb (83kg)
Occupation: Physiotherapy student
Born: Nogaro, 2.3.67
International debut: France 15, Australia 32, 1989
Five Nations' debut: France 36, Wales 3, 1991
Notable landmarks in rugby career: Helps France win 1992 Students World Cup in Italy prior to touring out for France Espoirs in 24–17 win over touring Springboks in Bordeaux on 4 October '92. In that game Thierry accounted for most of the points – kicking four penalty goals and converting one of Pierre Hontas' two tries. His fortunes at senior level improved the longer the

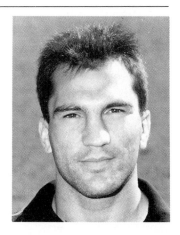

campaign lasted. A replacement in the first Test against South Africa, when France were beaten, he was brought in for the second Test to add some fire power and responded with 19 points (2c,5p) in 29–16 victory in Paris (24.10.92). Scored winning try against Scotland (6.2.93) three penalty goals against Wales (20.3.93), both games also played in the Parc des Princes, as France won 1993 Five Nations' Championship. Thierry burst onto the international scene with 17 points – five penalty goals and

France (1989)

Last Season	7 caps	63 pts
Career	14 caps	92 pts

Caps (14): **1989** A(1R,2) **1991** W(a:R). wc–R(b), C(R), E(b) **1992** SA(2), E, S, I, W, SA(1,2)

Points (92 – 1t,3c,26p,1dg): **1989** A(2:1c,5p) **1991** wc–C(2p), E(2p) **1992** SA(2:2c,5p) **1993** S(1t), W(3p), SA(1:5p), SA(2:4p,1dg)

a conversion – on his first start in France's 25–19 defeat of Australia in the second Test in Lille. His debut had come in the first Test as a replacement for Didier Camberabero. In spite of his prolific start he had to wait until the 1991 Five Nations Championship for his third cap, when replacing Philippe Sella in the 36–3 win over Wales (2.3.91). He again replaced Sella against Wales in the contest to celebrate the Arms Park's new flood lights (4.9.91) before further profiting from another's misfortune in the World Cup; injury to Camberabero allowing him three further caps and the opportunity to kick four penalty goals, two each against Canada and quarter-final opponents England. Did not feature in Pierre Berbizier's 1992 Five Nations' plans. Representing France B in 1988/89, he had kicked ten points (2c,2p) in the 18–12 defeat of Wales B in Brecon (29.10.88), and all 12 (4p) in the 14–12 loss to Scotland B at Melrose (18.2.89). Made an outstanding contribution to France's Series win in South Africa last summer, kicking five penalty goals in the 20–20 first Test draw and contributing another 15 points to the 18–17 second Test win

Ieuan Evans exploits a rare mistake by Rory Underwood to score for Wales against England in Cardiff. The home side won the match 10–9

Lafond, J.-B. France

Full Name: Jean-Baptiste Lafond
Club: Bègles-Bordeaux
Position: Fullback, wing
Height: 5ft 11in (1.80m)
Weight: 13st (83kg)
Occupation: Businessman in wine trade
Born: Neuilly-sur-Seine, 29.12.61
Family links with rugby: Grandfather, who played for Bayonne, played for France in 11–11 Twickenham draw with England in 1922
Former Club: Racing Club de France
International debut: France 15, Australia 15, 1983
Five Nations' debut: Scotland 18, France 17, 1986
Notable landmarks in rugby career: Finally established himself as a regular in the French team in 1991/92 season when appearing in 11 of the 12 matches, even if for the last of those, against Ireland, he was relegated to replacement and was only brought into the fray ten minutes from time. Spent much of the remainder of 1992 on Test sidelines. An absentee from the French summer tour to Argentina, he was picked as reserve for the first Test loss to South Africa before starting second game, in Paris, on right wing. Subsequently was ever-present at fullback as France won 1993 Five Nations' Championship;

France (1983)

Last Season	5 caps	7 pts
Career	36 caps	101 pts

Caps (36): **1983** A(1) **1985** Arg(1,2) **1986** S, I, W, E, Ro **1987** I(R) **1988** W **1989** I, W, E **1990** W, A(3R), NZ(2) **1991** S, I, W(a), E(a), Ro(a), US (1), W(b) wc–Ro(b:R), Fj, C, E(b) **1992** W, E, S, I(R), SA(2) **1993** E, S, I, W

Points (101 – 14t,7c,8p,2dg): **1983** A(1dg) **1985** Arg(1:1t) **1986** I(1dg),W(2t) **1988** W(2p) **1989** I(1t,2c,2p), W(3c,2p) **1990** W(1t) **1991** W(a:1t), US(1t), Ro(R:1t), Fj(3t), C(1t), E(1t) **1992** W(1c), S(2p) **1993** W(1t,1c)

contributing seven points (1t,1c) as they clinched title with a 26–10 win over Wales on 20 March 1993. Prior to 1991 injuries and selection restricted the outings of Jean-Baptiste, the most versatile and exciting of backs – he plays wing, centre and fullback with equal dexterity – and it was not until 1986 that he made his Championship debut. In seven years, from his debut (marked with a dropped goal) in the 15–15 draw with Australia at Clermont-Ferrand in 1983, he turned out just 16 times, with 1986 representing his only complete Five Nations' campaign prior to 1993. Yet he has always been a prolific scorer – claiming ten tries on the 1986 tour to Australia, having crossed for six in two non-cap Tests against Japan (four in the 50–0 win in Dax and two in Nantes when Japan were crushed 52–0) the previous year. Wales represent his favourite opponents, having scored in all seven Franco–Welsh Five Nations' contests (43 points) in which he has appeared

Lamerton, A. E. Wales

Full Name: Andrew Edwin Lamerton
Club: Llanelli
Position: Hooker
Height: 6ft (1.83m)
Weight: 15st 2lb (96kg)
Occupation: Machine operator with Dyfed Steel (Llanelli)
Born: Pontypridd, 28.5.70
Family: Single
Family links with rugby: Father (Roger) played for Llantrisant and Mid-District
Former clubs: Beddau, Neath
International debut: France 26, Wales 10, 1993
Five Nations' debut: As above
Best moment in rugby: Playing for Wales
Worst moment in rugby: Finding out Llanelli prop Ricky Evans had not been picked to tour Zimbabwe and Namibia (1993)
Most embarrassing moment: Ripping shorts playing at Cardiff and being brought out pair two sizes too small. To everyone's amusement they got stuck halfway up my legs

Wales (1993)

Last Season	4 caps	0 pts
1993	Tour to Zimbabwe/Namibia	
Career	4 caps	0 pts

Caps (1): 1993 F, Z(1,2), Na

Points Nil

Most respected opponent: Graham Dawe (Bath & England)
Best memory last season: Llanelli beat Australia at Stradey
Biggest influence on career: David Fox (Llanelli hooker) – for pushing me
Suggestions to improve rugby: *On-field* – New rules generally to Llanelli's liking as we like to play an open game. But referees should not blow too early when the ball gets tied up. Give it a chance to come out. Referees also need to

be more consistent in their officiating of the advantage law. It is very frustrating at present. *Off-field* – WRU must sort out their problems quickly as it reflects badly on all of Welsh rugby. No complaints as a Wales squad member in the way I am treated. In fact, we are treated like princes

Notable landmarks in rugby career: Wales' youngest hooker since 1947, having been capped in the final game of the 1993 Five Nations' Championship, against France in Paris, after excellent season which included helping Llanelli beat touring Australians 13–9 at Stradey on 14 November. While at Bryncelynnog County School he played four times for Wales U-18s (1986/87) and, having moved on to Beddau, picked up four Wales Youth caps(1987/88), scoring try v Canada. Represented Wales Under-21s twice v Scotland (1990–91), before which had featured in Llanelli side which gave 1989 All Blacks such a run for their money. Bench reserve for 1991 and 1992 Welsh Cup finals and, last season, against England, Scotland and Ireland

Touchlines: Golf (26-handicap)

Larsen, B. P.   New Zealand

Full Name: Blair Larsen
Province: North Harbour
Position: Lock
Height: 6ft 6in (1.98m)
Weight: 16st 12lb (107kg)
Born: 20.1.69
International debut: New Zealand 54, World XV 26, 1992
Notable landmarks in rugby career: Like Jamie Joseph, Blair's progress to the top has been swift. Voted North Harbour's most promising player in 1991, he went on to make a favourable impression in the 1992 national trials (after just 14 Provincial outings), from where a full debut in the second leg of the centenary series was his next stop. One of six changes to the side beaten 28–14 by the World XV in the first Test, he claimed one of the ten tries scored by the revived All Blacks in a 54–26 win. Blair retained his place for the next two Tests, the victorious centenary decider and New Zealand's decidedly uncomfortable

New Zealand (1992)		
Last Season	3 caps	4 pts
Career	3 caps	4 pts

Caps   (3): **1992** Wd(2,3), I(1)

Points (4 – 1t): **1992** Wd(2:1t)

24–21 first Test win over Ireland. The Irish, rated 100/1 no-hopers before the off at Carisbrook, having been demolished 62–7 by Auckland seven days earlier, led 12–0 and 18–12 before succumbing. As a result of such a close squeak the selectors made widespread alterations to the side for the second Test, with Blair one of the casualties. Nevertheless, he kept his spot in the squad for the tour to Australia and South Africa, and figured in seven of the 16 engagements. His one try came in the second match against South Australia, at Adelaide, where the visitors won 48–18, while he also turned out against Australian Capital Territory, Victoria, Queensland B and Sydney, before heading across to South Africa for the physical challenge of Orange Free State at Bloemfontein, and the less taxing 39–6 win over Central Unions

Lawlor, P. J.   Ireland

Full Name: Philip John Lawlor
Club: Bective Rangers
Position: No 8
Height: 6ft 5in (1.95m)
Weight: 16st 3lb (103kg)
Occupation: Farmer
Born: Kildare, 2.7.65
Family: Single
Former club: Naas
International debut: Ireland 20, Argentina 18, 1990
Five Nations' debut: Scotland 15, Ireland 3, 1993
Best moment in rugby: Getting capped against touring Pumas
Worst moment in rugby: Breaking ankle playing for Leinster against South West Division (Sept 1989)
Other sporting achievements: Gaelic football for Naas
Most respected opponent: Wayne Shelford (Northampton & New Zealand)
Best memory last season: Recall to Ireland side after two-year absence

Ireland (1990)

Last Season	2 caps	0 pts
Career	3 caps	0 pts

Caps (3): 1990 Arg 1992 A 1993 S

Points Nil

Notable landmarks in rugby career: Played international rugby at three levels in 1990/91: for Ireland Under-25s against Spain (won 36–17, Limerick 8.9.90), for Ireland B against Argentina (won 27–12, Limerick 20.10.90) and England (won 24–10, Old Belvedere 1.3.91), and for Ireland against Argentina

(Dublin, 27.10.90). Since then he has been rather less stretched: being called upon only to fulfil bench reserve duties in the 1992 Five Nations' matches against England, Scotland and France before, last season, adding to his single cap at No 8 (though he swapped positions mid-game with blindside flanker Brian Robinson) in the 17–42 loss to Australia in Dublin (31.10.92) and in the 3–11 defeat by Scotland at Murrayfield (16.1.93). Made Leinster debut against Llanelli (1989/90), scoring two tries. Broke ankle on second provincial appearance and missed remainder of season. Captained Bective for past two seasons but was forced to miss Ireland's summer tour to New Zealand in 1992 through injury

Touchlines: Gaelic football, horse racing, golf

Leahy, K. T.   Ireland

Full Name: Kelvin Tremaine Leahy
Club: Wanderers
Position: Flanker, No.8
Height: 6ft 3in (1.90m)
Weight: 16st (102kg)
Occupation: Manager with Norwich Irish Building Society
Born: Cork, 1.9.65
Family: Deidre (wife)
Family links with rugby: Father (Mick) played at lock (replacing Willie-John McBride) for Ireland in 6–15 loss to Wales in 1964
International debut: New Zealand 24, Ireland 21, 1992
Five Nations' debut: None
Best moment in rugby: Captaining Ireland B to 16–0 win over Scotland B (1990/91)
Most respected opponent: Philip Matthews (Wanderers & Ireland)
Best memory last season: Helping Ireland come so close to shock win over New Zealand in Dunedin
Serious injuries: Shoulder dislocation (required operation)

Ireland (1992)		
Last Season	1 cap	0 pts
Career	1 cap	0 pts

Caps (1): 1992 NZ(1)

Points Nil

Suggestions to improve rugby: *On-field* – Happy now try is worth five points. *Off-field* – Reimburse employers for lost working hours due to rugby

Notable landmarks in rugby career: They said Ireland had no chance yet the Boys in Green came within a whisker of pulling off one of the biggest shocks in rugby history. Kelvin made his debut that day in Dunedin (30.5.92) when 'no-hopers' Ireland led the mighty All Blacks 12–0 before ultimately being edged out 24–21. Indeed, when Kelvin was replaced (at half-time by Greystones' Brian Rigney) the Irishmen were in front. Injury sidelined Kelvin for second Test and although he was selected as a bench reserve for the visit of Australia to Dublin on 31 October 1992 he did not win another Irish cap. Represented 1984 Irish Schools and skippered Combined Provinces Under-21s for two seasons. Replacement for Ireland Under-25s against US Eagles (1989/90). Captained Leinster and Ireland Under-25s (against Spain) in 1990/91, scoring try for latter in 36–17 win (Limerick, 8.9.90). Captained Ireland B to 16–0 defeat of Scotland (Ravenhill, 22.12.90), having previously made debut in 27–12 win against touring Pumas (20.10.90). Won third B cap last season in 15–47 loss to England B (Richmond, 31.1.92) prior to touring New Zealand with Ireland

Touchlines: Swimming, fishing (fly/spinning)

Leonard, J.   England

Full Name: Jason Leonard
Club: Harlequins
Position: Loosehead prop
Height: 5ft 10in (1.78m)
Weight: 17st 2lb (109kg)
Occupation: Self-employed carpenter and joiner
Born: Barking, London, 14.8.68
Family: Single
Former clubs: Barking, Saracens
International debut: England 12, Fiji 20, 1989
Five Nations' debut: Wales 6, England 25, 1991
Best moments in rugby: Winning two Grand Slams and helping Harlequins win 1991 Pilkington Cup final
Worst moment in rugby: Losing World Cup final with England
Most embarrassing moment: Ball landing on my head during B match in France (1989/90)
Most respected opponent: Jeff Probyn (Wasps & England) – superb technique and physical abilities
Serious injuries: Ruptured disc in neck (1991/92)
Best memory last season: Being told I was able to play for Harlequins at start

of season at West Hartlepool long before doctors had thought I would be fit again

Suggestions to improve rugby: *On-field* – Law makers must consult players. That is rugby's biggest problem. I don't like ruck/maul law yet it was right to keep it for another year because game cannot being in a state of flux. Why don't they just leave laws alone? Still need to build more of an understanding with referees over interpretations. *Off-field* – If player loses out on pay because of rugby then reimburse him. It is an amateur game and players do not want to be paid but, equally, they do not want to lose out financially

England (1990)		
Last Season	6 caps	0 pts
Career	25 caps	0 pts
Lions 1993	3 Tests	0 caps

Caps (25): **1990** Arg(a1,a2), Arg(b) **1991** W, S(a), I, F(a), Fj, A(a) wc–NZ, It, US, F(b), S(b), A(b) **1992** S, I, F, W, C, SA **1993** F, W, S, I. Lions–NZ(1,2,3)

Points Nil

Notable landmarks in rugby career: Only England forward to play in last 24 Internationals, an unbroken run dating back to his debut against Argentina in July 1990. In that period he has played on two Grand Slam sides and in a World Cup campaign which culminated in a Final appearance against Australia. Yet the period has also included an injury which seriously threatened his playing career. After the 1992 Championship a neck injury required delicate surgery, including a muscle graft. He had experienced problems at Murrayfield against Scotland (18.1.92) and it finally ruptured against Wales (7.3.92). Surgeons replaced the ruptured disc with piece of bone, then waited for it to bond with existing vertebra. He was off work for three months but, with no England tour, was able to recover in good time before returning last season for opening Test against Canada at Wembley. Jason started his career at Barking, helping them win Essex Colts Cup before tasting success at Twickenham with Eastern Counties winning U-21 County Championship. Won 1989/90 Courage League division two title with Saracens and sat on England U-21 bench in Romania (1989). Broke into England B ranks in 1989/90, winning caps against Fiji and France and warming bench against USSR before being promoted to senior status on '90 tour of Argentina when he made his debut in Buenos Aires. Acclaimed major feat on 1993 Lions's tour when appearing in all three Tests on wrong side (tighthead) of front row

Lewis, E. W.   Wales

Full Name: Emyr Wyn Lewis
Club: Llanelli
Position: Flanker, No 8
Height: 6ft 4in (1.93m)
Weight: 16st 11lb (107kg)
Occupation: Police officer with Dyfed Powys Police Authority
Born: Carmarthen, 29.8.68
Family: Single
Former club: Carmarthen Athletic
International debut: Wales 21, Ireland 21, 1991
Five Nations' debut: As above
Best moment in rugby: Selection for first cap
Worst moment in rugby: Missing England game in 1992 due to food poisoning on eve of game. I had wanted to play in an England game since I was a little boy and had to wait until the following season. In the event, the wait proved worthwhile
Most embarrassing moment: Running down sidelines in support of attack, playing against Northampton (1990/91) and falling over, twisting ankle in process
Most respected opponent: Laurent Cabannes (Racing Club & France)

Wales (1991)		
Last Season	8 caps	10 pts
v Italy XV	1 app	0 pts
1993	Tour to Zimbabwe/Namibia	
Career	18 caps	10 pts

Caps (18): **1991** I, F(a), A(a),F(b) wc–WS, Arg, A(b) **1992** I, F, S, A **1993** E, S, I, F, Z(1,2) Na

Points (10 – 2t): **1993** Na(2t)

Biggest influence on career: Peter Herbert (fitness coach) and Gareth Jenkins (Llanelli coach)
Best memories last season: Landing dropped goal to win Swalec Cup for Llanelli
Suggestions to improve rugby: *On-field* – Any rule to speed game up is all right by me. *Off-field* – Reduce number of games being played. I reckon 35 Saturdays will be taken up with League, Cup or international matches this season. Market the game better
Notable landmarks in rugby career: Wales' 1991/92 Player-of-the-Year enjoyed a fruitful campaign last season, quite apart from playing in all five Internationals and the 43–12 Wales XV win over Italy at Cardiff (7.10.92). He also figured in Llanelli's 13–9 defeat of the touring Wallabies at Stradey (14.11.92) and in their League and Cup double. In the case of the latter victory

over Neath in the Swalec final he emerged as an improbable hero when he dropped a late goal to clinch victory. Emyr wore the Welsh No 6 in all games except the Paris finale when he moved to No 8 to accommodate clubmate Mark Perego on the blindside. Previously had missed playing for Welsh Schools because he was too old by two days. Could not play for Wales Youth either because still at school, but on leaving represented Wales at Under-20, Under-21 and B (for two minutes as replacement in 34–12 defeat of the Netherlands at Leiden, 2.12.90) before graduating to senior level. Emerged from disastrous 1991 (tour to Australia and World Cup) with reputation enhanced. Having played for less than a minute of Llanelli's 1989 Schweppes Cup final loss to Neath (after coming on as a replacement), he embarked on a hat-trick of Cup wins with the Scarlets in 1990/91 (scoring a try in defeat of Pontypool), 1991/92 and last season. Toured with Wales to Zimbabwe and Namibia last summer, scoring two tries in 38–23 defeat of the Namibians.

Touchlines: Fishing (river spinning), shooting

Lineen, S. R. P.   Scotland

Full Name: Sean Raymond Patrick Lineen
Club: Boroughmuir
Position: Centre
Height: 6ft 1½in (1.87m)
Weight: 13st 5lb (85kg)
Occupation: Sales and Marketing manager with ScotRun Publications
Born: Auckland, New Zealand, 25.12.61
Family: Lynne (wife)
Family links with rugby: Terry (father) played twelve times for New Zealand (1957–60); Troy (brother) represented Auckland at junior level
Former clubs: Pakuranga, Papakura, Counties (all NZ), Bombay, Pontypool
International debut: Scotland 23, Wales 7, 1989
Five Nations' debut: As above
Best moment in rugby: First Scotland cap against Wales and winning 1990 Grand Slam
Worst moment in rugby: Losing to England in semi-finals of 1991 World Cup

Most embarrassing moment: Over-indulging on beverages at Gatwick on trip to join Boroughmuir after arriving early from New Zealand on 28-hour flight. When collected and taken straight to training with new team mates I brought everything up. So much for Muir's great New Zealand hope!

Most respected opponent: Philippe Sella (Agen & France)

Biggest influence on career: My father

Scotland (1989)

Last Season	2 caps	4 pts
Career	29 caps	8 pts

Caps (29): **1989** W, E, I, F, Fj,Ro **1990** I, F, W, E, NZ(1,2), Arg **1991** F, W, E, I, Ro wc–J, Z, I, E, NZ **1992** E, I, F, W, A(1,2)

Points (8 – 2t): **1990** NZ(1:1t) **1992** A(2:1t)

Serious injuries: Knee-cap popped off (required operation)

Other sporting achievements: Auckland junior badminton

Suggestions to improve rugby: *On-field* – Standards of refereeing have improved but still nowhere near as good as the Southern Hemisphere officials. Problem is that nowadays we all have to go to university for four years just to understand the rules. *Off-field* – Clear cut definition of what players can and cannot do regarding rugby-related activities away from the field. At present 90% of earning opportunities for rugby union players have been taken away. Our responsibility is to leave the game, on and off the field, in a ship-shape condition for the next generation

Notable landmarks in rugby career: Shares, with Scott Hastings (save his best man), the distinction of being one half of the world's most-capped centre partnership (28 appearances in tandem). Boroughmuir's most-capped player, he qualified for Scotland through grandfather who came from the Hebrides. Helped Counties win first New Zealand National Sevens in 1985 and returned to New Zealand on tour with Scotland (1990). Also toured Japan (1989) and Australia (1992). Ever-present throughout Scotland's four Championship campaigns, from 1989–92, having missed only one international (World Cup quarter-final v Western Samoa – injured) between his debut against Wales in 1989 and his retirement after second Test in Australia 21 June 1992; a game in which he scored his second Test try. Helped Boroughmuir win first McEwan's League Championship in 1990/91

Touchlines: Racket sports, especially squash

Little, J. S. **Australia**

Little, J. S.   Australia

Full Name: Jason Sidney Little
Club: Southern Districts
State: Queensland
Position: Centre, wing
Height: 6ft 1in (1.86m)
Weight: 14st 2lb (90kg)
Occupation: Marketing officer with Queensland Cotton Corp.
Born: 26.8.70
Family: Roy (father), Pat (mother), Jonelle (sister), Ashley (brother), Steven (brother)
Former clubs: None. Souths since 1988
International debut: France 15, Australia 32, 1989
Best moment in rugby: Test debut v France
Worst moment in rugby: Breaking ankle v United States prior to 1990 New Zealand tour
Most embarrassing moment: Accused of enhancing a potential moustache whilst playing in Japan
Most respected opponent: Frank Bunce (North Harbour & New Zealand)
Serious injuries: Broken ankle (1990)
Other sporting achievements: Limited!
Best memory last season: 1992 Bledisloe Cup series win
Suggestions to improve rugby: *On-field* – Correct the ruck and maul rule

Australia (1989)

Last Season	7 caps	0 pts
Career	21 caps	17 pts

Caps (21): **1989** F(1,2) **1990** F(1,2,3), US **1991** W(a),E(a), NZ(a1,a2). wc–Arg, W(b), I, NZ(b), E(b) **1992** NZ(1,2,3), SA, I, W

Points (17 – 4t): **1990** F(2:1t), US(1t) **1991** W(a:1t) **1992** I(1t)

Notable landmarks in rugby career: Like club and state colleague Tim Horan, with whom he has formed arguably the world's best midfield partnership, his rise to prominence was helped in no small measure by a strong showing for Australia Under-17s in their 16–3 over New Zealand in 1987. Two years later he was in Britain with the Emerging Wallabies – playing in the 12–12 draw with England B at Wasps – and the same year he broke into the Test side at Strasbourg in the first match against France during a Wallabies' tour which also took in Canada. He has since picked up a World Cup winners' medal, after playing five times in the 1991 tournament, and played an equally full role in the 1992 Bledisloe Cup triumph over holders New Zealand. Jason, who was reared in the Darling Downs region of Queensland, was an ever-present in the '92

Wallabies XV, scoring his fourth Test try in the 42–17 rout of Ireland, in Dublin on 31 October, and also fitting in tour appearances against northern Transvaal, Leinster, Ulster (one try), Swansea, Neath (one try), Llanelli and the Barbarians

Tours: 1989 – Canada and France. 1991 – New Zealand, World Cup. 1992 – South Africa, Ireland and Wales.

Touchlines: Golf, movies, reading

Player to watch: Brett Johnstone (Queensland reserve half-back)

Player of the Year: John Eales/David Wilson (both Australia)

Little, W. K. New Zealand

Full Name: Walter Kenneth Little
Club: Glenfield
Province: North Harbour
Position: Centre, wing, outside-half
Height: 5ft 10½in (1.79m)
Weight: 12st (76kg)
Occupation: Mechanic
Born: Takapuna, 14.10.69
Former province: Auckland
International debut: New Zealand 31, Scotland 16, 1990
Notable landmarks in rugby career: Mr Versatile in the New Zealand set-up, having appeared at outside-half, centre and wing in consecutive Tests last season. Walter was seen as the heir apparent to Grant Fox's No10 jersey until the Auckland man decided his career was far from over. When Fox was dropped after New Zealand's first test beating at the hands of the World XV, Walter moved from centre into the vacant half-back berth and guided the team to a centenary series win. He retained his job description for the 2–0 series defeat of Ireland before being selected again at centre for the tour

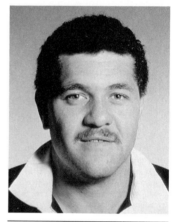

New Zealand (1990)

Last Season	10 caps	5 pts
Career	22 caps	9 pts

Caps (22): **1990** S(1,2), A(1,2,3), F(1,2) **1991** Arg(1,2), A(a1). wc–It, S **1992** Wd(1,2,3), I(1,2), A(1,2,3), SA **1993** BL(1)

Points (9 – 2t): **1991** wc–S(1t) **1992** A(3:1t)

of Australia and South Africa as Fox returned to conduct affairs at first-five. During the trip he played in nine of the 16 matches, scoring tries against South Australia, Queensland, Junior South Africa and, best of all, Australia in the third

Test. That score in Sydney was a classic, as he looped around Tuigamala and bolted through the opening to set New Zealand on their way to a 26–23 win. His excellent 1992 was a far cry from 1991 when he was replaced in the Test side by Bernie McCahill, following the 21–12 Bledisloe Cup loss to Australia, after a run of ten consecutive Tests. He made only two appearances in the World Cup, scoring the winning try as the All Blacks clinched third place in Cardiff at the expense of Scotland, whom Walter had come up against on his international debut at Dunedin in 1990. Such an impression did he make that he figured in all seven Tests that season. Walter, who plays in the same North Harbour back division as fellow All Blacks Frank Bunce and Ant Strachan, was introduced to British audiences on New Zealand's 1989 tour of Wales and Ireland when, as the youngest member of the touring party, just 20, he was picked for bench duties at Cardiff and featured against the Barbarians at Twickenham. Three months earlier he had helped New Zealand Colts beat their Australian counterparts 38–15 in Auckland

Llewellyn, G. O.   Wales

Full Name: Gareth Owen Llewellyn
Club: Neath
Position: Lock
Height: 6ft 6in (1.98m)
Weight: 16st 8lb (105kg)
Occupation: Fitter with British Steel (Port Talbot)
Born: Cardiff, 27.2.69
Family: Single
Family links with rugby: Brother (Glyn) plays for Neath and Wales; father (David), who was in Army with Will Carling's dad, is a qualified WRU coach
Former club: Llanharan
International debut: Wales 9, New Zealand 34, 1989
Five Nations' debut: England 34, Wales 6, 1990
Best moment in rugby: Winning first Wales cap

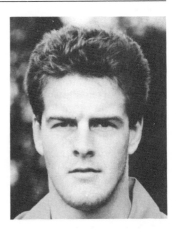

Worst moment in rugby: Twice being dropped by Wales
Most embarrassing moment: Almost tripping over when running out at Cardiff for first cap
Most respected opponent: Bob Norster (ex-Cardiff & Wales)
Biggest influence on career: Llanharan RFC as a whole

Serious injuries: Dislocated collar-bone, damaged pelvis

Best memory last season: Being asked to captain Wales on summer tour to Zimbabwe and Namibia

Suggestions to improve rugby: *On-field* – Greater consistency in refereeing interpretations. Ridiculous discrepancies exist at present. *Off-field* – Take better care of players

Notable landmarks in rugby career: Outstanding 1992/93 season

Wales (1989)

Last Season	5 caps	0 pts
v Italy XV	1 app	0 pts
1993	Tour to Zimbabwe/Namibia	
Career	16 caps	4 pts

Caps (16): **1989** NZ **1990** E, S, I **1991** E, S, A(a:R) **1992** I, F, E, S, A **1993** E, S, I, F, Z(1,2), Na

Points (14 – 3t): **1990** I(1t) **1993** Z(2:2t)

for Gareth culminated in his appointment to captain Wales on summer tour to Zimbabwe and Namibia during which he played in all three Tests, scoring two tries in the 42–13 second Test win over Zimbabwe in Harare. The Neath skipper's performance was central in the famous 10–9 victory over England at Cardiff on 6 February 1993 and his line-out exploits, in particular, took him to the threshold of Lions' selection. He was an ever-present throughout the five-Test campaign and also played in the 43–12 non-cap win over Italy in Cardiff (7.10.92). Capped three times by Wales Youth. Toured New Zealand with Welsh U-19 team (1987), playing at No 8. Also played for Crawshays and Barbarians. Represented Wales against England and Scotland in 1990/91 before losing place to Paul Arnold. Has previously partnered brother Glyn in second row both for Neath and Wales. Toured Australia with Wales in 1991, coming on as a 20th minute replacement for Phil Davies in 6–63 Test defeat to Wallabies. Omitted from Wales' World Cup squad in 1991 but recalled for 1992 Five Nations' Championship, as lock partner for Llanelli's Tony Copsey, and has remained ever since

Touchlines: Golf, squash, weights

At the Parc des Princes, Aubin Hueber, the French scrum-half, is about to be engulfed by Welsh flanker Mark Perego. But Hueber had the last laugh as France triumphed 26–10

Loe, R. W.   New Zealand

Full Name: Richard Wyllie Loe
Club: Fraxer-Tech
Province: Waikato
Position: Prop
Height: 6ft 1in (1.85m)
Weight: 17st (108kg)
Occupation: Farmer
Born: Christchurch, 6.4.60
Family: Felicity (wife) and Jessica (daughter)
Family links with rugby: Nephew of former New Zealand coach Alex 'Grizz' Wyllie
Former club/province: Lyon (France), Canterbury (1980), Marlborough (1982)
International debut: New Zealand 70, Italy 6, 1987
Notable landmarks in rugby career: The bad boy of world rugby, having been banned for nine months (reduced on appeal to six) for eye-gouging Otago's New Zealand fullback Greg Cooper 15 minutes into the National Championship final which Waikato, fourth at the end of the regular season, won 40–5. The suspension cost him the chance to accept a player/coach post with French club Vichy. If that was not bad enough publicity for a genuinely talented

New Zealand (1987)

Last Season	8 caps	12 pts
Career	38 caps	20 pts

Caps (38): 1987 wc–It, Arg 1988 W(1,2), A(1,2,3) 1989 F(1,2), Arg(1,2), A, W, I 1990 S(1,2), A(1,2,3), F(1,2) 1991 Arg(1,2), A(a1,a2). wc–E, It, C, A(b), S 1992 Wd(1,2,3), I(1), A(1,2,3), SA

Points (20 – 5t): 1989 A(1t) 1990 S(2:1t) 1992 Wd(2:2t),Wd(3:1t)

player, who had successfully adapted to the loosehead propping role after more than an 50 All Black outings and 34 Tests on the other side, he seriously incurred the wrath of Australia during the 1992 Bledisloe Cup series. During the second Test Richard was seen to break Wallaby match-winning wing Paul Carozza's nose with an elbow smash, having been accused of inflicting damage to Sam Scott-Young's head in the first Test. A member of the world's most-capped front row combination (with McDowell and Fitzpatrick), his international career began out of the blue in 1986 when he was recruited from Lyon, where he was playing club rugby, to bolster an injury-plagued All Black touring side in France. His test debut came the following year in the 1987 World Cup rout of Italy and in the ensuing tour of Japan he succeeded John Drake as regular tighthead. Played for centenary Barbarians against England in 1990 and in eight of New Zealand's nine Tests in 1992, the exception being the second match against Ireland when the calf muscle he had aggravated in the Dunedin opener failed to recover in time to prevent Olo Brown taking over. The highlight of his season was his two-try display in the second Test victory over the World XV

Logan, K. M.   Scotland

Full Name: Kenneth (Kenny) McKerrow Logan
Club: Stirling County
Position: Fullback, wing
Height: 6ft 1in (1.85m)
Weight: 13st 8lb (86kg)
Occupation: Farmer at Powis Mains Farm, Stirling
Born: 3.4.72, Stirling
Family: Single
International debut: Australia 37, Scotland 13, 1992
Five Nations' debut: England 26, Scotland 12, 1993
Best moment in rugby: Winning first cap in Australia
Worst moment in rugby: 1992 Scotland Trial when Scott Hastings charged down my clearance kick and scored a try
Most embarrassing moment: Gregor Townsend dummying me in the Gala-Stirling game. Every time he is shown on TV that moment is replayed
Most respected opponent: Michael Lynagh (Australia)

Scotland (1993)

Last Season	2 caps	0 pts
1993	Tour to South Seas	
Career	2 caps	0 pts

Caps (2): 1992 A(2) 1993 E(R)

Points Nil

Biggest influence on career: Hamish Logan (cousin) who played ten years for West of Scotland
Other sporting achievements: Turned down soccer trials (goalkeeper) with Dundee United and Hearts to pursue rugby career
Best memory last season: Coming on at Twickenham against England
Suggestions to improve rugby: *On-field* – New rules have changed game for the better. Allow fullbacks to 'mark' on the run. *Off-field* – Players must be reimbursed for loss of earnings. If I did not work for a family concern I could

never take so much time off for rugby

Notable landmarks in rugby career: First Stirling County player to be capped when selected at fullback in place of the injured Gavin Hastings for 13–37 second Test defeat by Australia during 1992 summer tour on which he played in seven of the eight games (four as wing, three as fullback). Thoroughly enjoyed the experience, his confidence high after making a try/match-saving tackle on Paul Carozza in the 15–15 draw with Queensland and earning widespread media acclaim. Represented Scotland U-18, U-19 (fullback v '91 Aussie Schools) and U-21 level and captained Glasgow to 1991/92 U-21 Championship. Picked to tour Oz before playing in any national trial. 1993 Championship bench reserve before coming on at HQ as 60th minute replacement for Scott Hastings. Found time also for three Scotland A caps last season and scored a try in each game, v Spain (Madrid, won 35–14), Ireland (Dublin, won 22–13) and France (lost 19–29, Aberdeen). Toured with Scotland last summer to Fiji, Tonga and Western Samoa

Touchlines: Squash, weights, running 400-acre farm

Lynagh, M. P. **Australia**

Full Name: Michael Patrick Lynagh
Clubs: Queensland Univ (Aus), Benetton Treviso (It)
State: Queensland
Position: Five-eighth
Height: 5ft 10in (1.78m)
Weight: 12st 8lb (80kg)
Occupation: Commercial Real Estate manager
Born: 25.10.63
Family: Single
Former clubs: None
International debut: Fiji 3, Australia 16, 1984
Best moments in rugby: 1984 Grand Slam tour; 1991 World Cup victory
Worst moment in rugby: 1987 World Cup
Most embarrassing moment:
Running into the goalposts whilst trying to catch a kick in an under-age match
Most respected opponent: Grant Fox (Auckland & New Zealand)
Serious injuries: Broken collarbone (1983), dislocated shoulder (1992)
Other sporting achievements: Cricket for Queensland Schoolboys
Best memory last season: Winning the 1992 Bledisloe Cup and being named

Australia captain

Notable landmarks in rugby career: Australia's captain and the world's leading points scorer with 760 points. His total comprises 12 tries, 125 conversions, 145 penalty goals and nine dropped goals. With the gifted Mark Ella superglued to the Wallaby No 10 jersey, Michael started International life as a centre on in Suva on 9 June 1984. He marked the occasion with three penalty goals and has been popping them over ever since. He missed the Bledisloe Cup series that year but toured Great Britain and Ireland where he appeared at centre in all four Tests of the Aussies' Grand Slam. His 21-point haul in the defeat of Scotland equalled the Wallaby single-match record held by Paul McLean. He upped it a couple of notches on his first Test appearance at outside-half against Canada on 15 June 1985 when he registered 23 points (7c,3p) and by the end of 1990 he had twice enjoyed 24-point afternoons. Michael, who spends his Australian summers playing with Treviso in Italy, passed the 100-point barrier playing against the Italians on 1 June 1986. Has bagged 148 points in two World Cup tournaments, the second of which yielded a winners' medal. Helped Australia regain Bledisloe Cup from New Zealand in 1992 and succeeded Nick Farr-Jones as national skipper after the historic 26–3 rout of South Africa in Cape Town on 22 August. First Test in charge saw him last only 40 minutes against Ireland (won 42–17, Dublin, 31.10.92) before dislocating left shoulder. Subsequently missed Cardiff Test

Australia (1984)

Last Season	7 caps	71 pts
Career	60 caps	760 pts

Caps (60): **1984** Fj, E, I, W, S **1985** C(1,2), NZ **1986** It, F, Arg(1,2), NZ(1,2,3) **1987** wc–E, US, J, I, F, W. Arg(1,2) **1988** E(a1,a2), NZ(1,3R), E(b), S, It **1989** BL(1,2,3), NZ, F(1,2) **1990** F(1,2,3), US, NZ(1,2,3) **1991** W(a), E(a), NZ(a1,a2). wc–Arg, WS, W(b), I, NZ(b), E(b) **1992** S(1,2), NZ(1,2,3), SA, I

Points (760 – 12t,125c,145p,9dg): **1984** Fj(3p), E(1t,2c,1p), I(1p,1dg), W(1t), S(3c,5p) **1985** C(1:7c,3p), C(2:3c,2p,1dg), NZ(1c,1p) **1986** I t(6c,1p), F(1c,6p,1dg), Arg(1:4c,5p), Arg(2:1c,4p), NZ(1:1c,1p), NZ(2:3p,1dg), NZ(3:1c,4p) **1987** wc–E(1c,3p), US(6c,1p), J(5c), I(4c,3p), F(2c,3p,1dg), W(2c,2p,1dg). Arg(1:1t,2c,1p), Arg(2:1c,3p) **1988** E(a1:6p), E(a2:1t,3c,2p), NZ(1:1p), NZ(3:1c), E(b:2c,1p), S(3c,2p), It(1t,8c,1p) **1989** BL(1:4c,1p,1dg), BL(2:1c,2p), BL(3:1c,4p), NZ(1c,2p), F(1:2c,4p), F(2:1c,3p) **1990** F(1:1c,5p), F(2:6c,4p), F(3:1c,2p,1dg), US(2t,8c), NZ(1:2p), NZ(2:2p,1dg), NZ(3:1c,5p) **1991** W(a:2t,6c,1p), E(a:4c,4p), NZ(a1:2c,3p), NZ(a2:1p). wc–Arg(3c,2p), WS(3p), W(b:1t,4c,2p), I(1t,2c,1p), NZ(b:1c,2p), E(b:1c,2p) **1992** S(1:1t,1c,3p), S(2:1c,5p), NZ(1:2p), NZ(2:3p), NZ(3:2c,3p), SA(1c,3)

Tours: 1983 – Italy and France. 1984 – Fiji, United Kingdom and Ireland. 1985 – New Zealand. 1986 – New Zealand. 1987 – World Cup, South America. 1988 – England, Scotland and Italy. 1989 – Canada and France. 1990

– New Zealand. 1991 – New Zealand, World Cup. 1992 – South Africa, Ireland and Wales.
Touchlines: Surfing, golf, fishing, music, films
Player to watch: Ben Clarke (Bath & England)
Player of the Year: John Eales (Australia)

McBride, W. D.   Ireland

Full Name: William Denis McBride
Club: Malone
Position: Flanker
Height: 5ft 10in (1.80m)
Weight: 13st 10lb (87kg)
Occupation: Mechanical engineer with Ballylumford Power Ltd
Born: Belfast, 9.9.64
Family: Catrina (wife)
Family links with rugby: Brother also plays
Former club: Queen's University Belfast
International debut: Ireland 9, Wales 12, 1988
Five Nations' debut: As above
Best moments in rugby: Ireland XV beating France XV 19–18 at Auch (1988) in non-cap tour match and 1993 defeat of England
Worst moment in rugby: Second half of Ireland's 3–35 defeat by England in 1988 when we conceded 35 points without reply
Most embarrassing moment: Ireland v England (1988)
Most respected opponents: Wayne Shelford (Northampton & New Zealand) and Laurent Rodriguez (Dax & France)

Ireland (1988)

Last Season	4 caps	0 pts
Career	12 caps	8 pts

Caps (12): **1988** W, E, WS, It **1989** S **1990** F, W, Arg **1993** S, F, W, E

Points (8 – 2t): **1988** WS(1t) **1990** W(1t)

Other sporting achievements: Completed the 1982 Belfast City Marathon
Best memory last season: Captaining Ulster to Inter-Provincial title
Suggestions to improve rugby: *On-field* – Reduce value of penalty goal. Scrap 90-degree scrummage wheel law. *Off-field* – Better marketing of the sport. All countries should send teams to Hong Kong Sevens. Permit players to benefit from off-field activities
Notable landmarks in rugby career: Malone and Ulster captain who

returned to the Test arena after a three-year gap in last season's Five Nations' Championship. He might have re-emerged earlier but having flown out to New Zealand with Ireland for the 1992 summer tour, he was on his way home after just one game – the victim of a freak training accident when he broke a toe after catching a stud in Kelvin Leahy. Having skipped Ulster to Cara Inter-Provincial Championship triumph before Christmas, he played all four matches in the 1993 Five Nations' afterwards, including wins over Wales (19–14, Cardiff, 6.3.93) and England (17–3, Dublin, 20.3.93). First representative honours came for Ulster and Irish Schools sides in 1983. Graduated to Ulster Under-20s and Combined Provinces Under-21s in 1984/85 before making his senior Ulster bow against Connacht in 1987. Having impressed on summer tour to France, which featured a 19–18 non-cap victory against the French, he was given his Test debut in the '88 Championship against Wales. Collected his first try third-time out against Western Samoa but lost his place after win over Italy. In and out of favour for next four years before firmly taking possession of the No 7 jersey last season

Touchlines: Athletics (400 metres)

McCall, C. M. Ireland

Full Name: Con Mark McCall
Club: Bangor
Position: Centre, outside-half
Height: 5ft 10in (1.78m)
Weight: 12st 6lb (79kg)
Occupation: Public servant
Born: Bangor, 29.11.67
Family: Single
Family links with rugby: Peter (brother) plays for QUB
International debut: New Zealand 24, Ireland 21, 1992
Five Nations' debut: None
Best moment in rugby: Winning Ulster Bank Schools Cup with Bangor GS
Worst moment in rugby: Ireland's 24–58 to New Zealand second division side Manawatu. We were hammered. Losing 7–62 to Auckland was bad but they were so good that it did not feel as embarrassing
Most respected opponent: Michael Lynagh (Australia)

Ireland (1992)		
Last Season	2 caps	0 pts
1993	Dev. tour to Africa	
Career	2 caps	0 pts
Caps (2): **1992** NZ(1R,2)		
Points Nil		

Biggest influence on career: Bangor coach Ashley Armstrong – changed me from outside-half to centre when I was 23

Other sporting achievements: Irish Schools cricket with Vince Cunningham and Ciaran Clarke. Also played for Irish Universities and Irish U-23s

Best memory last season: Getting capped in New Zealand

Suggestions to improve rugby: *On-field* – Ruck and maul law should be seriously looked at. Too many sides are kicking and killing the ball. And it is not being refereed properly. *Off-field* – More should be done for players who make such a massive commitment to the sport. I had to take special leave for half the New Zealand tour and whenever I'm needed in Dublin for training I am faced with a four-hour drive south. We should not lose out financially

Notable landmarks in rugby career: Fleeting visit to the international arena, touring New Zealand with Ireland in the summer of '92 ('because a lot of other guys pulled out') and playing in both Test defeats at the hands of the All Blacks, though his debut came as a 35th minute replacement for injured skipper Philip Danaher. Played five games in all, kicking penalty goal in the Auckland landslide defeat. Returned home to represent Ulster against Australia at Ravenhill (13 provincial apps in all) but then contracted a viral infection which put him out of rugby for two months. Recovered, he closed the season by adding Ireland A caps against Wales (won 29–28, Newport, 5.3.93) and England (lost 18–22, Donnybrook, 19.3.93) to those won in 1991/92 against Scotland and England. Prior to that played six times for Ireland Schools, captaining the side four times

Touchlines: Cricket (for Bangor CC)

McCall, R. J. Australia

Full Name: Roderick (Rod) James McCall

Club: Brothers (Brisbane)

State: Queensland

Position: Lock

Height: 6ft 6in (1.98m)

Weight: 17st 5lb (110kg)

Occupation: Sales director with Walmac Printing Ltd

Born: 20.9.63

Family: Lorelle (wife), Maegan (daughter)

Former clubs: None. Brothers since 1980

International debut: France 15, Australia 32, 1989

Best moment in rugby: Winning

1987 Brisbane Grand Final and 1991 World Cup

Worst moment in rugby: Losing 3–6 to New Zealand at Eden Park in 1991 which cost us Bledisloe Cup

Most respected opponent: Paul Ackford (Harlequins, England and BBC)

Serious injuries: Left knee dislocation (1988), left shoulder a/c (1991)

Other sporting achievements: Several centuries in golf

Australia (1989)

Last Season	8 caps	5 pts
Career	26 caps	5 pts

Caps (26): **1989** F(1,2) **1990** F(1,2,3), US, NZ(1,2,3) **1991** W(a), E(a), NZ(a1,a2). wc-Arg, W(b), I, NZ(b), E(b) **1992** S(1,2), NZ(1,2,3), SA, I, W

Points (5 – 1t): **1992** W(1t)

Best memory last season: 1992 Bledisloe Cup win; scoring first try v Wales

Suggestions to improve rugby: *On-field* – Lose new maul law. *Off-field* – Get rid of archaic rugby administrators who change rules without asking players and who uphold those which need changing (i.e. the ones who have no idea which direction the game is taking)

Notable landmarks in rugby career: Waited three years for his Test debut after first touring with Australia in 1986 to New Zealand. His call finally came in 1989 when he was given a chance in the first Test victory over France in Strasbourg. He needed no second invitation and has since been a Test regular, since 1991 alongside John Eales. His honours have included a 1991 World Cup winners' medal and a share in the 1992 Bledisloe Cup series win over the All Blacks. A full schedule last season saw him play all eight Tests – scoring his maiden international try in the 23–6 defeat of Wales in Cardiff – in addition to appearances against Northern Transvaal, Leinster, Ulster, Wales B, Neath, Llanelli, Monmouthshire (as a replacement) and the Barbarians

Tours: 1986 – New Zealand. 1988 – England, Scotland and Italy. 1989 – Canada and France. 1990 – New Zealand. 1991 – New Zealand, World Cup. 1992 – South Africa, Ireland and Wales

Touchlines: Spending time with family

Player to watch: Tim Kelaher (NSW) – he could be anything!

Player of the Year: Jason Little (Australia)

McCarthy, P.D.   Ireland

Full Name: Paul David McCarthy
Club: Cork Constitution
Position: Tighthead prop
Height: 6ft (1.83m)
Weight: 17st 12lb (113kg)
Occupation: Service engineer for Hotpoint
Born: Cork, 27.8.63
Former club: Dolphin
International debut: New Zealand 24, Ireland 21, 1992
Five Nations' debut: Scotland 15, Ireland 3, 1993
Best moments in rugby: Winning first cap in Dunedin; helping Ireland B beat England B 24–10 (1991), and Cork Con winning inaugural All-Ireland League (1990/91)
Worst moment in rugby: Losing Ireland place in 1993 to Peter Clohessy
Most respected opponent: Staff Jones (ex-Pontypool & Wales)
Best memory last season: Coming so close to beating All Blacks on my Ireland debut

Ireland (1992)

Last Season	4 caps	0 pts
Career	4 caps	0 pts

Caps (4): **1992** NZ(1,2),A **1993** S

Points Nil

Suggestions to improve rugby: *On-field* – Improve refereeing of scrum
Notable landmarks in rugby career: A 1992/93 season which began with such promise ended disappointingly for Paul as he lost the Irish tighthead berth to Young Munster's Peter Clohessy during the 1993 Five Nations' Championship. The change of mind by the selectors followed Ireland's bad defeat at the hands of Scotland in Edinburgh on 16 January. It was Paul's fourth consecutive Test appearance, having made his debut against the All Blacks in Dunedin on 30 May 1992 during summer tour. On that day Ireland led 12–0 before eventually being reeled in and losing 24–21. He played also in the 59–6 second Test loss in Wellington the following week and then against world champions Australia in a similarly heavy defeat (17–42) at Lansdowne Road on 31 October. Prior to his international call-up he had won Schools Junior and Senior Cup medals, represented Munster in Irish Inter-Provincial Championships and Ireland B against Scotland B (won 16–0, Ravenhill 22.12.90), England B (won 24–10, Old Belvedere 1.3.91) and Scotland B (won 29–19, Edinburgh 28.12.91), scoring a try in the latter. An Irish World Cup triallist as far back as 1987, Paul shared in Cork Constitution's All-Ireland League

triumph in 1991, having moved from Dolphin four years previously. Last season turned out for Munster in the loosehead position
Touchlines: Shooting, fishing

McDowell, S. C.   New Zealand

Full Name: Steven Clark McDowell
Club: Suburbs
Province: Auckland
Position: Prop
Height: 5ft 11in (1.80m)
Weight: 16st 14lb (103kg)
Occupation: Hotelier
Born: Rotorua, 27.8.61
Family: Alease (daughter)
Other sporting achievements:
Black Belt in Judo – Western boycott prevented him from representing NZ in the 1980 Moscow Olympics
Former province/clubs: Bay of Plenty (1982–84), St Michaels, Kahukura, Pakuranga
International debut: Argentina 20, New Zealand 33, 1985
Notable landmarks in rugby career: New Zealand's most-capped prop, his reputation as the world's finest loosehead prop was diminished on New Zealand's 1992 tour of Australia and South Africa where he was given just one weekend engagement (against Queensland) and failed to make the test side, Richard Loe moving across from tighthead. Less dynamic than usual, he had to make do with just seven outings in all, and included in that was the dubious privilege of skippering the midweek side in the 40–17 hammering by Sydney at Penrith. However, recent form must not overshadow a marvellous Test career dating back to 1985, when he succeeded Gary Knight in the All Blacks team. Having switched provincial allegiance to Auckland in 1984 after 44 matches for Bay of Plenty he made his international debut against Hugo Porta's Pumas on the tour of Argentina. Despite missing

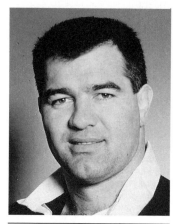

New Zealand (1985) ·

Last Season	5 caps	0 pts
Career	46 caps	12 pts

Caps (46): **1985** Arg(1,2) **1986** A(2,3), F(2,3) **1987** wc–It, Fj, S, W, F. A **1988** W(1,2), A(1,2,3) **1989** F(1,2), Arg(1,2), A, W, I **1990** S(1,2), A(1,2,3), F(1,2) **1991** Arg(1,2), A(a1,a2). wc–E, US, It, C, A(b), S **1992** Wd(1,2,3), I(1,2)

Points (12 – 3t): **1987** wc–It(1t) **1988** W(2:1t), A(1:1t) two games, as punishment for touring South Africa with the unsanctioned New Zealand Cavaliers in 1986, he went on to become a member of the world's most-capped front row combination (with Fitzpatrick and Loe). His place remained unchallenged until a poor first Test in Argentina in 1991 almost cost him his place for the second game. He remained first choice, however, throughout the World Cup, the centenary series and the for the visit of Ireland. Not exactly a prolific scorer – he has not scored a Test try for five years – Steve crossed for one of a dozen tries against Italy in the 1987 World Cup and added two further scores the following season, against the hapless Welsh, and Australia

---

McKenzie, E. J. A. Australia

Full Name: Ewen James Andrew McKenzie
Clubs: Randwick (Aus: since 1985), Paris Univ (Fr: since 1993)
State: New South Wales
Position: Tighthead prop
Height: 6ft (1.82m)
Weight: 17st 5lb (110kg)
Occupation: Trainee waste management engineer with CGEA (France) and its affiliate COLLEX (Australia). Responsible for activities in industrial and domestic waste collection, transfer and recycling
Born: 21.6.65
Family: Sally (wife)
Former clubs: Harlequins (Melbourne, 1984),
International debut: France 9, Australia 21, 1990
Best moments in rugby: Beating NZ in 1991 World cup semi-final; beating NZ in Wellington (1990); beating South Africa (1992); winning Bledisloe Cup (1992)
Worst moment in rugby: Losing Grand Final to Parramatta (1986); missing selection for 1986 Scotland Test; being dropped by NSW selectors in 1989; injury during British Lions

Australia (1990)

Last Season	8 caps	5 pts
Career	24 caps	9 pts

Caps (24): **1990** F(1,2,3), US, NZ(1,2,3) **1991** W(a), E(a), NZ(a1,a2). wc–Arg, W(b), I, NZ(b), E(b). **1992** S(1,2), NZ(1,2,3), SA, I, W

Points (9 – 2t): **1990** US(1t) **1992** I(1t)

Most embarrassing moment: Tony Daly and I doing our Fat Percentage tests prior to the 1991 World Cup. P.S – I should also mention that Phil Kearns managed, with Tony Daly alongside, to lose a tighthead in a sixth grade trial match in 1993. Just in case they forget to mention it!

Most respected opponent: Normally it's the next one. The following opponents' attributes I have admired: Entertainer – Tony Daly; story telling – Peter Fatialofa; scrummaging – Frederico Mendez; athleticism – Steve McDowell; demeanor/ornament to the position – David Sole; dancing – Olo Brown; drinking games – Jeff Probyn; singing – Pascal Ondarts/Geoff Didier; most like to have a drink with – Jason Leonard (our paths have not crossed post-match despite two games against him)

Serious injuries: Posterior cruciate tear left knee (1987), medial ligament strain (1989), numerous other arthritic-causing ailments that medicine has been unable to cure

Best memory last season: Watching a drunken Phil Kearns attempt to impersonate Winston Churchill during his Baa-Baas after-dinner speech

Suggestions to improve rugby: *On-field* – Exotic sevens tournament for tight-five only. More Barbarian-type fixtures. Regular Northern Hemisphere v Southern Hemisphere fixtures. Reduce dropped goal value to one point. Universal trial by video. Standardized eligibility for national teams. Improve refereeing standards. Get rid of the new maul turnover rule as it encourages negative play. *Off-field* – More efforts to improve situations for wives and children. They suffer more from the effects of time given up to rugby

Notable landmarks in rugby career: The first born and bred Victorian since 1932 to represent Australia, Ewen moved to Sydney club Randwick in 1985 to further his rugby career and, five years later, was rewarded with his first cap on the tour to France. Since those early days – a knee injury in 1989 had delayed his Test debut – he has built one of the most respected front row partnerships in world rugby with fellow New South Walians Phil Kearns and Tony Daly. A measure of the esteem in which he is held was that the World XV included him in their side to play the All Blacks in the 1992 Centenary Series, a year after he had picked up a World Cup winners' medal at Twickenham. A test ever-present in 1992, scoring his second international try in the 42–17 win over Ireland in Dublin, he also appeared against Northern Transvaal, Leinster, Munster, Ulster (scored try), Wales B, Llanelli and the Barbarians

Tours: 1988 – England, Scotland and Italy. 1989 – Canada and France. 1990 – New Zealand. 1991 – New Zealand, World Cup. 1992 – South Africa, Ireland and Wales

Touchlines: Trying to find ways to spend more time with my wife

Player to watch: Talented and crazy Franco/Portuguese Paris University winger Arthur Gomez

Players of the Year: David Campese/Rod McCall (Aus), John Timu/Ian Jones (NZ)

MacDonald, I.   South Africa

Full Name: Ian Macdonald
Club: Roodespoort
Province: Transvaal
Position: Flanker
Height: 6ft 5in (1.95m)
Weight: 17st 5lb (110kg)
Occupation: Teacher
Born: Pretoria, 22.2.68
International debut: South Africa 24, New Zealand 27, 1992
Notable landmarks in rugby career: Educated at Rhodesfield Technical High in Kemptonpark, Ian quickly proved himself a thoroughbred by breaking into the Transvaal side in 1989 and teaming up with Springbok back row legend Jannie Breedt. Both men were selected by South Africa for their historic return to Test rugby against New Zealand at Ellis Park (15.8.92), a match which ended 24–27 in favour of the All Blacks, and again the following week in the heavy loss to Australia (23–26, Cape Town). Completing the back row trio was

South Africa (1992)

Last Season	3 caps	0 pts
Career	3 caps	0 pts

Caps (3): 1992 NZ,A 1993 F(1)

Points Nil

Natal skipper Wahl Bartmann but he turned on his colleagues the following month, leading Natal to a 14–13 win over Transvaal in a poor Currie Cup final (Johannesburg, 12.9.92). Ian's disappointment was compounded when he lost his breakaway Test place to Northern Transvaal's Adriaan Richter in France and to Western Province giant Frederik Smit at Twickenham against England. However, he still made six appearances for the Springboks: against France B (lost 17–24, Bordeaux, 4.10.92), Provence–Cote d'Azur (won 41–12, Marseille, 13.10.92), Langedoc-Roussillon (won 36–15, Beziers, 20.10.92), French Universities (lost 13–18, Tours, 28.10.92), the Midlands Division (won 32–9, Leicester, 4.11.92), and the Northern Division (won 19–3, Leeds, 10.11.92). His one try came at the Velodrome in Marseille against Provence–Cote d'Azur

Malan, A. W.   South Africa

Full Name: Adolf Weich Malan
Club: Harlequins (Pretoria)
Province: Northern Transvaal
Position: Lock
Height: 6ft 8½in (2.04m)
Weight: 17st 5lb (110kg)
Occupation: Attorney
Born: Germiston, 6.9.61
International debut: South Africa
20, World XV 19, 1989
**Notable landmarks in rugby
career:** In his tenth year of
provincial rugby with Northern
Transvaal, Adolf had mixed three
Currie Cup triumphs with the Blue
Bulls (1987–88–91) into the 159
appearances which preceded his
departing for Europe with the
Springboks in October 1992. So
highly has he been regarded since
South Africa's return to the Test
arena that he was one of only five
ever-presents through the five-match
programme in 1992 – Naas Botha,
Danie Gerber, James Small and
Pieter Müller being the others. In
addition to his Test outings against

South Africa (1989)

Last Season	5 caps	0 pts
Career	7 caps	0 pts

Caps (7): **1989** Wd(1,2) **1992** NZ, A,
F(1,2), E

Points Nil

New Zealand, Australia, France (twice) and England, he turned out against
Aquitaine (won 29–22, Pau, 7.10.92), Midi-Pyrenees (won 18–15, Toulouse,
15.10.92), French Barbarians (lost 20–25, Lille, 31.10.92) and England B
(won 20–16, Bristol, 7.11.92)

Malone, N. G.   Ireland

Full Name: Niall Gareth Malone
Clubs: Oxford University & London
Irish
Position: Outside-half
Height: 5ft 11in (1.81m)
Weight: 13st (82kg)
Occupation: Social studies student
Born: Leeds, 30.4.71
Family: Single
Former clubs: Collegians (Belfast),
Loughborough Students
International debut: Scotland 15,
Ireland 3, 1993
Five Nations' debut: As above
Best moments in rugby: Winning
first cap at Murrayfield; winning
1989 Schools Cup with Methodists
(Belfast) against Wallace HS
Worst moments in rugby: Losing
Ireland place after two caps; 1992
Varsity match defeat by Cambridge
Most embarrassing moment:
Missing kick in front of posts in
1989 Schools Cup final
Most respected opponent: Tony
Underwood (Leicester, Cambridge
Univ, England and Lions)
Serious injury: Dislocated elbow

Ireland (1993)		
Last Season	2 caps	9 pts
Career	2 caps	9 pts

Caps (2): 1993 S, F

Points (9 – 3p): 1993 S(1p), F(2p)

Other sporting achievements: Soccer for Belfast Primary Schools
Best memory last season: Running out at Lansdowne Road for French game
Suggestions to improve rugby: More feedback from selectors. They should
be obliged to tell a player why he has been dropped
Notable landmarks in rugby career: Selected by Ireland for 1993 Five
Nations' Championship after eight-point (1c,2p) haul on B debut against
Scotland (lost 13–22, Dublin, 28.12.92) and super 18-point, two-try
performance for the Probables in the Irish Trial. Suffered in strong wind at
Murrayfield on his debut against Scotland on 16 January and although he
landed a second-half penalty it was not enough to stop the Scots running out
convincing winners, by more than the 15–3 scoreline suggested. Kept his place
for Dublin match against France on 20 February and kicked another two
penalties, but Ireland lost again (6–21) and Lansdowne's Eric Elwood was
brought in for the next two games, against Wales and England. The Irish won
both. Niall had made a favourable impression in the 111th (1992) Varsity

Match even though he again finished on the losing side. Underdogs Cambridge won 19–11, despite the Keble College student landing a penalty and a dropped goal in the first half-hour to put the Dark Blues 6–3 ahead. Has also represented Ulster Schools, Ulster U-19s, Ulster U-20s, 1989 Irish Schools, Irish Exiles Under-21s, Irish Exiles, Ireland U-21s (24 points in four games) and England Universities. In 1991 he turned out for an International Select XV against the Irish President's XV (one of Ireland's World Cup build-up matches) and dropped a goal in the 18–10 win over England U-21s. Prior to that he had landed a penalty goal on his Under- 21 debut against the Netherlands (lost 7–21) and kicked five penalty goals and a dropped goal against England (won 22–16, Moseley, 2 9.10.90)

Mannion, N. P. S. Ireland

Full Name: Noel Patrick Stephen Mannion
Club: Lansdowne
Position: No 8, flanker
Height: 6ft 4in (1.93m)
Weight: 16st 3lb (103kg)
Occupation: Sales representative with Dubarry Shoes and Pony sportswear
Born: Ballinasloe, 12.1.63
Family: Single
Family links with rugby: Brother (Jack) played for Galwegians and Connacht
Former clubs: Ballinasloe, Drumoyne (Aus), Corinthians
International debut: Ireland 49, Western Samoa 22, 1988
Five Nations' debut: Ireland 21, France 26, 1989
Best moment in rugby: Intercepting Welsh kick on own 22 and running ball back for Ireland try in 19–13 win (Cardiff, 4.2.89)
Worst moment in rugby: Running a quick penalty for Connacht against Ulster, tripping for no apparent reason, and knocking ball forwards
Most embarrassing moment: As above

Ireland (1988)

Last Season	1 cap	0 pts
Career	16 caps	12 pts

Caps (16): **1988** WS, It **1989** F, W, E, S, NZ **1990** E, S, F, W, Arg **1991** Na(1R,2) wc-J **1993** S

Points (12 – 3t): **1989** W(1t) **1991** wc-J(2t)

Most respected opponent: Wayne Shelford (Northampton & New Zealand)
Biggest influence on career: Oliver Burke (Connacht U-20 coach) – way ahead of his time
Serious injuries: Broken collarbone, wrist. Twisted knee
Other sporting achievements: Played one season of Gaelic football for Galway. Came on as replacement during 1987 All-Ireland semi-final replay defeat by Cork
Best memory last season: Winning All-Ireland League division two title with Lansdowne
Suggestions to improve rugby: *On-field* – Standardize refereeing in southern and northern hemispheres. Presently too many different interpretations. Conformity is desperately needed. *Off-field* – Clarify laws regarding amateurism. What, exactly, are we entitled to do? No-one is clear. If problem is not sorted, the other sports will start attracting the best players in Ireland
Notable landmarks in rugby career: It was ironic that he owed his one Test outing last season to London Irish's Brian Robinson, the man whose form had stood between Noel and a headful of caps. When Robinson withdrew from the side selected to open the 1993 Five Nations' Championship against Scotland, at Murrayfield on 16 January, Noel was drafted in as the solitary Connacht representative. But Scotland won (15–3) and he was lost his place in the resultant shake-up – not to Robinson but to Mick Galwey who was moved to No 8 with Neil Francis filling the Shannon Lion's second row berth. Noel represented Connacht at Schools and U-20 level before making his senior Provincial debut in 1985. Played for Ireland U-25s against Canada following season. Made 12 straight appearances for senior side between 1988 and the Argentina match in 1990. First Corinthians player to be capped by Ireland. Scored famous try in second full appearance against Wales (1989) when he intercepted and ran virtually the full length of Cardiff Arms Park. Toured with Ireland to Canada (1989) and was an ever-present. Made Barbarians bow against Newport in 1989/90. Switched clubs from Corinthians to Lansdowne at start of 1990/91, having won Connacht Senior Cup medal with former in 1988. Toured with Ireland to North America (1989), Namibia (1991) and New Zealand (1992)
Touchlines: Music, reading

Full Name: Nigel Meek
Club: Pontypool
Position: Hooker
Height: 5ft 10in (1.78m)
Weight: 15st 2lb (96kg)
Occupation: Builder
Born: Blaina, 20.10.64
Family: Natasha (daughter)
Family links with rugby: Various
cousins play for Blaina
Former clubs: Blaina, Ebbw Vale,
Blaena Gwent
International debut: Wales 10,
England 9, 1993
Five Nations' debut: As above
Best moment in rugby:
Representing Barbarians v Australia
at Twickenham (28.11.92)
Worst moment in rugby: Getting
dropped after third cap v Ireland
(1993)
Most embarrassing moment: Too
numerous to mention
Most respected opponent: All of
them – not much to choose between
the top international hookers

Wales (1993)		
Last Season	3 caps	0 pts
Career	3 caps	0 pts

Caps (3): 1993 E, S, I

Points Nil

Biggest influences on career: Bob Smith (Blaina youth coach), father
(Norman), Mike Ruddock (when Blaina coach) – all equally
Best memory last season: Final whistle of debut v England
Suggestions to improve rugby: *On-field* – Leave new laws alone. They have
sped game up and made it more attractive. You've got to be a better player to
prosper these days. you have got to be able to make the ball available. To be fair
most try; there are very few intent on killing it. But lineout is still shamble area
They've tried their best to improve it but to no avail. *Off-field* – Like to think
players at the top could make money from advertising products if companies
felt they were worthy of their investment. Allow them to exploit their fame
Notable landmarks in rugby career: A real mixed bag was 1992/93 for Nigel.
Given his Wales A debut v North of England (won 21–13, 14.10.92) he
promptly lost his place after a disappointing team performance. Touch of
fortune then when coming on as 19th minute replacement for Llanelli's David
Fox in the next A game against Australia. He was reunited with the Wallabies
soon after when chosen as the non-cap in the Barbarians side which went down
30–20 to the tourists at Twickenham. 'If I had not played in that game I would

have never have made the Wales side. it was a wonderful opportunity for me and I will remember it forever.' Having been on the bench for Wales' non-cap win over Italy at start of season, he was upgraded for the Five Nations' Championship, playing in the first three games before being one of many to fall from favour as a result of the loss to Ireland. Season ended with him being omitted from Wales' tour squad for Zimbabwe and Namibia. Started out with hometown club of Blaina, where he won a Monmouthshire cap. Switched to Ebbw Vale where he took up the reins of captaincy in 1990/91, and was then again on the move to Pontypool. Has also skippered the Welsh Counties
Touchlines: Guitar (three-chord wonder)

Milne, K. S. Scotland

Full Name: Kenneth Stuart Milne
Club: Heriot's FP
Position: Hooker
Height: 6ft (1.83m)
Weight: 15st 12lb (101kg)
Occupation: Sales manager with P.E.C. Barr, Printers of Leith
Born: Edinburgh, 1.12.61
Family: Eleanor (wife), Stuart (son) and Jenny (daughter)
Family links with rugby: Iain (brother) played for Heriot's, Scotland and British Lions. David (brother) plays for Heriot's and Scotland
International debut: Scotland 23, Wales 7, 1989
Five Nations' debut: As above
Best moment in rugby: 1990 Grand Slam
Worst moment in rugby: Being dropped at any level
Most embarrassing moment: Accidentally flooring the referee when the front rows of Heriot's and Jed-Forest squared up. He let me off
Most respected opponents: Gary Callender (Kelso & Scotland) and Brian Moore (Harlequins & England)
Biggest influence on career: Brothers Iain and David

Scotland (1989)		
Last Season	5 caps	0 pts
Career	25 caps	12 pts
Lions 1993	1 Test	0 caps

Caps (25): **1989** W, E, I, F, Fj, Ro **1990** I, F, W, E, NZ(2), Arg **1991** F, W, E wc–Z **1992** E, I, F, W, A(1) **1993** I, F, W, E

Points (12 – 3t): **1989** Fj(1t) **1990** Arg(2t)

Best memory last season: Lions' selection

Suggestions to improve rugby: *On-field* – Stop changing the rules. Scottish Inter-District Championship should be broadened to include likes of Bath and Leicester. A British League of sorts, with stronger opposition, must be the way forward. *Off-field* – Clarification of amateurism issue desperately needed. More could be done for the players. Rewards are very minimal, especially in Scotland

Notable landmarks in rugby career: Although he still has some way to go to match the 52-cap haul of Scotland's most-capped hooker Colin Deans (1978–87), Kenny is developing into one of the best the nation has produced. Last summer he toured New Zealand with the British Lions appearing in the first Test following an international season when he had been consistently outstanding. With former Edinburgh Academical John Allan having emigrated to South Africa his long-time rival for the No 2 jersey was out of the picture and Kenny, who had been restricted to just one outing during the 1991 World Cup, was free from distraction. Scored first international try against Fiji in October 1989 and became the first Scotland hooker to score two tries in an International when bagging a brace in the 49–3 defeat of Argentina, at Murrayfield on 10 November 1990, the year in which he had been ever-present through the triumphant Grand Slam campaign. Toured with Scotland to North America (1985 & 1991), New Zealand (1990) and Australia (1992). On the latter trip he lasted just ten minutes in the 12–27 first Test defeat in Sydney before injury forced him out of the fray, to be replaced by Gala's Ian Corcoran. He was an absentee the following week as the Aussies completed a 2–0 series win at Ballymore and was again missing when a shadow Scotland side warmed up for the 1993 Five Nations' campaign with a 22–17 win over Italy at Melrose. However he was in situ when the Championship got underway the following January. The youngest of the three-capped Milne brothers, Kenny has six Scotland B appearances to his name

Touchlines: Fly fishing (salmon & trout)

Lions outside-half Rob Andrew evades All Black flanker Michael Jones before planting a clearance kick upfield during the first Test in Christchurch

Moon, R. H. St J. B.   Wales

Full Name: Rupert Henry St John
Barker Moon
Club: Llanelli
Position: Scrum-half
Height: 5ft 11in (1.81m)
Weight: 13st 7lb (86kg)
Occupation: TV
researcher/production manager with
Rugby Vision (Cardiff)
Born: Birmingham, 1.2.68
Family: Single
Family links with rugby: Brother
(Richard) plays scrum-half for
Rosslyn Park. Sister (Estelle) plays
scrum-half/back row for Wasps
Ladies. All three of us have got
winners' medals in national
competitions
Former clubs: Walsall, Abertillery,
Neath
International debut (England):
England B 12, Emerging Australians
12, 1990
International debut (Wales):
France 26, Wales 10, 1993
Five Nations' debut: As above
Best moments in rugby: Kicking
conversion from each touchline playing for Barbarians at 1991 Hong Kong
Sevens; captaining Barbarians against Cork Constitution on centenary tour;
selection to Wales team (1993)

Wales (1993)

Last Season	4 caps	10 pts
1993	Tour to Zimbabwe/Namibia	
Career	4 cap	10 pts

Caps (4): **1993** F, Z(1,2), Na

Points (10-2t):**1993** Z(1:It), Na(1t)

Worst moment in rugby: Head-high tackle by Gloucester's Dave Sims which
dislocated my shoulder
Most embarrassing moments: Saying my full name on national television;
losing kicking competition to Llanelli club mates Phil Davies and Gary Jones
Most respected opponents: David Bishop (ex-Pontypool & Wales) and
brother Richard (Rosslyn Park & England B)
Biggest influence on career: Alfie 'the fruitbat' Brickell (Abertillery coach) –
inspired to me go further at age of 18
Serious injuries: Popped rib cartilage, shoulder dislocation
Other sporting achievements: Cricket for Walsall. Soccer for Midlands
Schools
Best memory last season: Captaining Llanelli to 13–9 win over Australia and
then to League and Cup double

Suggestions to improve rugby: *On-field* – Only allow kicking inside 22. Scrap farcical 90-degree scrum wheel law. Clarify interpretation of tackle law. Can you pass ball on ground or not? *Off-field* – Give all Student rugby players free food vouchers (but never money). Organize cheap nose jobs for people with big noses, when finished playing career

Notable landmarks in rugby career: Enjoyed magnificent 1992/93 season both for club and country. On the domestic front he was shouldered off Stradey Park after captaining Llanelli to a 13–9 defeat of the touring Wallabies (14.11.92). By the end of the campaign the Scarlets had also taken delivery of the Heineken League and Swalec Cup double. Declaring his allegiance to Wales in 1991/92 – having sat on bench for England Schools and stood on pitch for England Colts, Under-21s (scored try in inaugural match: Romania 13, England 54, Bucharest 13.5.89), Students (as captain and in 1988 Students World Cup) and B grades – led to his Test debut on 20 March 1993 when displacing British Lion Robert Jones for the match against France in Paris (lost 10–26). Had been everpresent bench reserve prior to that. Ended season on tour with Wales in Zimbabwe and Namibia. Joined Llanelli in 1990/91 and was promptly selected for four England B games against Emerging Australians, Ireland B, France B and Spain. Scored two tries in Kingsholm defeat of Spain. Picked up Man-of-the-Match awards in both 1990/91 and 1991/92 Schweppes Challenge Cup finals when Llanelli beat Pontypool and Swansea respectively. Captained England Students against pre-World Cup England XV. Selected to England's development squad but then switched to Wales, saying: 'After six years of living in Wales I have found myself being deeply affected by the passion for, and commitment to the game as shown by the whole community.' Bench reserve for Wales throughout 1992 Five Nations' Championship. Rupert, who has also represented Saltires, Public School Wanderers, Crawshays and Barbarians, captained Wales A in 1992/93 against North of England (won 21–13, Pontypool, 14.10.92) and Australia (lost 11–24, Cardiff, 7.11.92)

Touchlines: Watching educational videos, eating out, ballet, theatre

Moore, B. C.   England

Full Name: Brian Christopher Moore
Club: Harlequins
Position: Hooker
Height: 5ft 9in (1.76m)
Weight: 14st 3lb (90kg)
Occupation: Commercial litigation partner with Edward Lewis & Co.
Born: Birmingham, 11.1.62
Family: Dr Penny Sowden (wife)
Former clubs: Old Crossleyans, Nottingham
International debut: England 21, Scotland 12, 1987
Five Nations' debut: As above
Best moment in rugby: 1991 Grand Slam decider against France
Worst moment in rugby: Wales 16, England 3, (1987 World Cup quarter-final)
Most embarrassing moment: Being forced to watch pre-match team talks on video
Most respected opponent: Kenny Milne (Scotland)
Biggest influence on career: Alan Davies (Nottingham coach)
Serious injuries: Fractured ego v Scotland, Murrayfield 17.3.90
Other sporting achievements: Intermediate swimming certificate
Best memory last season: Quins' Pilkington Cup semi-final win over Wasps

England (1987)		
Last Season	5 caps	0 pts
Career	45 caps	4 pts
Lions 1989	3 Tests	0 pts
1993	2 Tests	0pts

Caps (45): **1987** S wc–A, J, W(b) **1988** F, W, S, I(1,2), A(a1,a2), Fj, A(b) **1989** S, I, F, W, Ro, Fj. Lions–A(1,2,3) **1990** I, F, W, S, Arg(a1,a2) **1991**W, S(a), I, F(a), Fj, A(a) wc–NZ, It, F(b), S(b), A(b) **1992** S, I, F, W, SA **1993** F, W, S, I. Lions–NZ(2,3)

Points (4 – 1t): **1989** I(1t)

Suggestions to improve rugby: *On-field* – More consistent refereeing and, even more importantly, more consistent refereeing selections so that experienced officials always handle big matches and so that referees serve their time going up a proper ladder. What we have at present are referees taking charge of Pilkington Cup semi-finals, then Old Haberdashers, then a school game, then an International. That shouldn't happen. The refereeing this year has been awful, with or without the new laws. It is too important at a time when so much is expected of the players and the game which has to function as well. If they are not good and entertaining no-one will watch them. I do not like the ruck/maul law. Any rule which means the ball is in play less often, for less amount of time, and encourages more kicking, is not going to be a good rule. It was supposed to encourage more tries and more play. We've seen less of both. And the evidence for that has come from New Zealand where, allegedly, they're supposed to be able to play these new rules to the best and fullest advantage. The old law didn't need changing if refs refereed the tackle law properly. I still maintain that referees should consult players pre-season to discuss rule changes and interpretations. *Off-field* – Parity between northern and southern hemisphere in what is allowed under the amateur regulations. No uniform interpretation of off-field activities. Why not? We should all be treated the same, irrespective of which hemisphere we are located. I don't necessarily think the Aussies and New Zealanders are receiving broken time payments but their earnings out of sponsorship for off the field activities is far more liberally interpreted than ours. They are asking for compensation for time lost – strict broken time payments, which I am not adverse to either. Automatic retirement from RFU Committee at 55. Major revision of amateurism laws, along with those concerning foul play, line-outs and kickable penalties. Player representation on all major decision and law-making committees. The latest rule changes were not made in any co-ordinated fashion, rather picked out of a hat. Administrators must learn to consult those who matter before making decisions. Until we step onto the field we do not which rules will work. Proper lines of communication are absolutely vital to the future of the game. After all, you cannot run a successful company without consulting people

Prospects for 1995 World Cup: If Rugby World Cup Ltd haven't got a contingency plan for South Africa they want shooting. It's one of the less stable countries around. Who knows what state, politically, it will be in two years. The World Cup is too important for sentimentality to encroach on proper decision making, and although everyone, including myself, wanted it to be played in South Africa, there is no doubt it can be held there in 1999 if the situation is stabilised. But if the World Cup is a disaster or doesn't happen at all because of inadequate planning and inadequate or non-existent contingency plans it will be an absolute tragedy. There is no excuse at all. We all know that South Africa is delicately poised. Why then jeopardise the most important world event in the sport when you could wait? It is by no means certain whether the political situation in two years will be stable enough in two years to even allow them to compete.

Notable landmarks in rugby career: England's most-capped hooker, overtaking John Pullin's 42-cap mark (1966–76) in the defeat by Wales in Cardiff last season. Omitted from England team for only fourth time in England's last 49 internationals when John Olver stood in against Canada at Wembley on 17 October 1992 but a strong performance for England B against South Africa at Bristol (lost 16–20, 7.11.92) prompted his recall for the South Africa game the following week. Former captain of Nottingham and England B (on first appearance) who represented England Students in 1982 and toured Romania and Spain with England U-23s. First played for Nottingham in 1981 and left them for Quins prior to 1990/91 season. Voted 1990/91 Whitbread/

Rugby World 'Player of Year'. Ever-present in 1989 Lions' 2–1 series win over Australia and visited New Zealand with the Lions' class of 1993 last summer. Toured with England to Australia/Fiji (1988), Argentina (1990) and Fiji/Australia (1991)

Touchlines: Opera, theatre, cooking, training, tennis, golf

Morgan, G. J.   Australia

Full Name: Garrick Jay Morgan
Club: Southern Districts
State: Queensland
Position: Flanker, No 8
Height: 6ft 6in (1.98m)
Weight: 17st (108kg)
Occupation: Sales representative with Castlemaine Perkins XXXX
Born: 25.1.70
Family: Monique (mother), John (father), Evette (sister)
Family links with rugby: Father (John 'Pogo' Morgan) played rugby league for Australia
Former clubs: None. Souths since 1989
International debut: Australia 16, New Zealand 15, 1992
Best moment in rugby: Scoring two tries for Queensland v 1992 All Blacks
Worst moment in rugby: Going off injured v Monmouthshire at Ebbw Vale (1992)

Australia (1992)

Last Season	3 caps	0 pts
Career	3 caps	0 pts

Caps (3): 1992 NZ(1R,3R), W

Points Nil

Most embarrasssing moment: being wrongly sent-off during match with Munster on 1992 Irish tour
Most respected opponent: Michael Jones (Auckland & New Zealand)
Serious injuries: Groin-pelvis (Wales Test 1992)
Other sporting achievements: Basketball for Queensland Country
Best memory last season: Cardiff Arms Park Test (1992)
Suggestions to improve rugby: *On-field* – Get representative players to go to schools etc. We need to get to grass rugby of rugby and fertilize. *Off-field* – Compensate players for lost revenue due to heavy representative commitments
Notable landmarks in rugby career: Chosen for Queensland in 1990 without having played a first grade match, he made a name for himself in the

Australian Sevens team that same year. In 1991 he toured with the Wallabies to New Zealand, as a replacement for Tim Gavin, and played against Counties. And in 1992, again as a replacement (in the 77th minute for Sam Scott-Young), he made his international bow in the 16–15 Test defeat of New Zealand in Sydney. A second cap followed in the third Test loss, this time as a 33rd minute replacement for John Eales before he was granted the luxury of the entire match against Wales, at Cardiff, in the final Test of the season. Other appearances on tour in 1992 came against Western Transvaal (scored try), Eastern Province, Munster, Connacht, Wales B (scored try) and Monmouthshire

Tours: 1990 – New Zealand. 1992 – South Africa, Ireland and Wales
Touchlines: Surfing, basketball, golf, swimming
Players to watch: Barry Lea, Brett Johnson (both Souths)
Player of the Year: Tim Horan (Australia)

Morris, C. D. England

Full Name: Colin Dewi Morris
Club: Orrell
Position: Scrum-half
Height: 6ft (1.83m)
Weight: 13st 7lb (86kg)
Occupation: Promotions manager with Hallbridge of Warrington
Born: Crickhowell, Wales, 9.2.64
Family: Single
Former clubs: Brecon, Crewe & Alsager College, Winnington Park, Liverpool St Helens
International debut: England 28, Australia 19, 1988
Five Nations' debut: England 12, Scotland 12, 1989
Best moments in rugby: Scoring try on England debut and winning. Scoring winning try for North in 15–9 defeat of Australia (Oct 1988). Winning 1992 Grand Slam. 1993 Lions selection
Worst moment in rugby: Losing 9–12 to Wales at Cardiff (March 1989) and being dropped thereafter
Most embarrassing moment: Being dropped by North for match against US Eagles after five

England (1988)

Last Season	6 caps	5 pts
Career	15 caps	21 pts
Lions 1993	3 Tests	0pts

Caps (15): **1988** A **1989**: S, I, F, W **1992** S, I, F, W, C, SA **1993** F, W, S, I. Lions–NZ(1,2,3)

Points (21 – 5t): **1988** A(1t) **1992** S(1t), I(1t), F(1t), SA(1t)

consecutive international caps and five consecutive divisional caps

Most respected opponent: Richard Hill (Bath & England)

Biggest influence on career: Mickey Skinner (Blackheath & England) – for his team talks

Serious injuries: Broken nose (three times), serious ligament damage to left shoulder, both knees and right ankle, dislocated finger

Other sporting achievements: Gwent Schools Under-19 County cricket finalists

Best memories last season: Lions' selection

Suggestions to improve rugby: *On-field* – More consistency among referees. Just getting used to new rules now so right not to reppeal them. Give the turnover law another season – if referees interpret law correctly there is no problem. Refereeing must get better as discipline becomes an ever-greater factor. Immediate action for serious offences. Reduce value of penalties to two points. Scrap 90-degree scrummaging law

Notable landmarks in rugby career: Stormed back into international picture in 1991/92, despite sitting out World Cup on bench. Replaced Richard Hill for Five Nations' Championship and was big hit: scoring tries in first three games, against Scotland, Ireland and France. Went from strength to strength in 1992/93: everpresent in England jersey, scoring fifth Test try against South Africa (won 33–16, Twickenham, 14.11.92) and ended campaign by touring with British Lions to New Zealand making the No 9 jersey his in all three Tests. Previously, disappeared as quickly as he rose when dropped by England after 1989 Five Nations' loss in Wales. Dewi had graduated from junior rugby to international level in six months, via Winnington Park, Liverpool St Helens, Lancashire, the North and England B (whom he first represented against 1988 touring Wallabies). Scored three tries to inspire Lancashire to 32–9 victory over Middlesex in 1990 County Championship final. Toured with England to Argentina (1990) and Australia (1991)

Touchlines: Motocross, holidays spent on lazy beaches

Morrison, I. R.   Scotland

Full Name: Iain Robert Morrison
Club: London Scottish
Position: Flanker
Height: 6ft 1in (1.86m)
Weight: 15st 7lb (98kg)
Occupation: Money broker,
Director of Bond Sales with Swiss
Corporation
Born: Linlithgow, 14.12.62
Family: Courtenay (child)
Family Links with rugby: Father
captain Melville College FP
Former clubs: Linlithgow,
Cambridge Univ
International debut: Scotland 15,
Ireland 3, 1993
Five Nations' debut: As above
Best moment in rugby: Winning
1991 Middlesex Sevens
Worst moment in rugby: Breaking
leg in 1988 during qualifying for
Middlesex Sevens
Most respected opponent: Stuart
Barnes (Bath & England)
Biggest influence on career: Tony
Rodgers (Cambridge Univ coach)

Scotland (1993)		
Last Season	4 caps	0 pts
Career	4 caps	0 pts
Caps (4): **1993** I, F, W, E		
Points Nil		

Serious injuries: Broken right leg (plate attached with ten screws); Knee
cartilage operation (1993)
Best memory last season: Earning selection for Scotland
Suggestions to improve rugby: *On-field* – Keep faith with new regulations for
time being as players are still adapting. *Off-field* – Top players should be
compensated for time given up to rugby. There will soon come a time when
international players will not have a decent job. I am losing out dramatically. A
large part of my salary is performance-related bonus. If I am away I am losing
out
Notable landmarks in rugby career: A latecomer to international rugby, Iain
had turned 30 when making his first appearance for Scotland A, in the 22–13
win over Ireland A on 28 December 1992. He then played in his first Scotland
Trial and was promptly given his full debut, on 16 January 1993, in the 15–3
defeat of Ireland. He retained his openside berth for the duration of the
Championship. Yet during his formative days at Glenalmond School he had
represented Scotland 16-Group at Sevens and toured with them to Zimbabwe.
Joined Linlithgow aged 16. Varsity appearances ensued for Cambridge in 1983

and 1984, during which time he also toured to Japan and the USA. Regular for London Scottish and Anglo-Scots since 1985. Scored try in Anglo Scots' 19–16 win over touring French in 1987. Helped London Scottish to five London Floodlit Sevens titles in addition to twice being on winning sides at Dubai Sevens, most recently last season with Scotland. Unfortunate to miss out on 1993 Lions selection

Touchlines: Collect antique glasses

Mougeot, C.   France

Full Name: Christophe Mougeot
Club: Bègles-Bordeaux
Position: Lock
Height: 6ft 5in (1.96m)
Weight: 16st 7lb (105kg)
Occupation: PE teacher
Born: Dijon, 22.11.63
Former club: Is-sur-Tille
International debut: Wales 9, France 12, 1992
Five Nations' debut: As above
Notable landmarks in rugby career: Brought into the French team when new coach Pierre Berbizier began his tenure of office in the 1992 Tournoi des Cinq Nations. Started games against Wales and England yet completed neither. In the first there were allegations of a 'tactical substitution' as he made way for Olivier Roumat midway through the contest, with France getting cleaned out in the line-out, but against England there was little doubt he had torn a thigh muscle. Christophe first caught the

France (1992)

Last Season	1 cap	0 pts
Career	3 caps	0 pts

Caps (3): 1992 W, E, Arg(b)

Points Nil

eye when scoring a try in Begles–Bordeaux's 1991 French Club Championship final win over Toulouse (won 19–10). Also in the 1990/91 season he helped France B humiliate Scotland B 31–10 at Hughenden. Prior to that he played junior rugby near Dijon and impressed playing at No 8 for France A against the touring All Blacks at La Rochelle, despite being on the wrong end of a 22–15 scoreline. Missed out on the World Cup when Jean-Marie Cadieu took preference. Picked up third Test cap last season when chosen to partner Roumat against Argentina at Nantes on 14 November. Unhappily for

Christophe, and French rugby in general, the Pumas broke their duck on French soil (winning 24–20) and the selectors reached for the guillotine

Muller, L. South Africa

Full Name: Lood Muller
Province: Natal
Position: Tighthead prop
Height: 6ft (1.83m)
Weight: 16st 9lb (105kg)
Age: 34 years
Occupation: Policeman
International debut: South Africa 24, New Zealand 27, 1992
Notable landmarks in rugby career: Earned his place at tighthead for the historic international comeback match against New Zealand, in Johannesburg on 15 August 1992, following an exceptional performance against Richard Loe when his province Natal entertained the tourists at Durban's Kings Park on 1 August. New Zealand won 43–25 in front of 40,000 witnesses, having led 16–6 at half-time, but Lood did enough to get the Test nod ahead of Transvaal rival Heinrich Rodgers and Orange Free State's Piet Bester. He kept his slot in spite

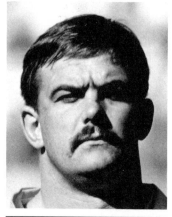

South Africa (1992)		
Last Season	2 caps	0 pts
Career	2 caps	0 pts

Caps (2): **1992** NZ, A

Points Nil

of the 27–24 Johannesburg loss and packed down against Tony Daly the following week on a painful afternoon for South African rugby at Newlands. The sunshine of Ellis Park was replaced with wet and heavy conditions in Cape Town where the visitors handed the Springboks their heaviest ever defeat, by 26–3, after pulling away in the second half with 20 unanswered points. Lood did not tour to France and England, the tighthead duties being shared by Rodgers, Western Province's Keith Andrews, Northern Transvaal's Andries Truscott and even Willie Hills, the Blue Bulls' hooker. However, he did play on the Natal side which captured the Currie Cup for the second time in three years, in Johannesburg on 12 September 1992, when beating Transvaal 14–13. That day he packed down alongside former Edinburgh Academicals and Scotland hooker John Allan and against his Test rival Rodgers

Müller, P. G.   South Africa

Full Name: Pieter Gysbert Müller
Club: College Rovers
Province: Natal
Position: Centre
Height: 6ft 3in (1.90m)
Weight: 14st 2lb (90kg)
Occupation: Sales executive
Born: Bloemfontein, 5.5.69
Family links with rugby: Brother
(Helgard) played for Orange Free
State and won two caps – 1986
Cv(4R) 1989 Wd(1R)
Former Province: Orange Free
State
International debut: South Africa
24, New Zealand 27, 1992
**Notable landmarks in rugby
career:** Reckoned to be the best
player in South African rugby in
1992, Pieter has size and the pace to
go with it. Born and educated in
Bloemfontein he represented South
African Schools before making his
Provincial bow for Orange Free
State in 1990. After 27 matches for
OFS he switched allegiances to
Natal, with whom he picked up a

South Africa (1992)

Last Season	7 caps	5 pts
Career	7 caps	5 pts

Caps (7): **1992** NZ, A, F(1,2), E 1993
F(1,2)

Points (5 – 1t): **1992** NZ(1t)

Currie Cup winners' medal in '92, following the 14–13 final win over Transvaal
at Ellis Park, Johannesburg on 12 September. It was in the same arena that he
had made his international debut a month earlier, in the 24–27 defeat by New
Zealand. His place in the XV which took the Springboks back into genuine Test
rugby for the first time in 11 years was won with a fine performance for Natal
in the 25–43 loss to the All Blacks at Kings Park, Durban on 1 August. He
marked his debut in South African colours with a try to go with the two bagged
by fellow centre Danie Gerber. The following week he was required at
Newlands in Cape Town for the visit of Australia, who ran riot with an historic
26–3 win. Pieter retained his berth alongside Gerber throughout the tour of
France and England, playing in all three Tests. In addition he turned out against
France B (lost 17–24, Bordeaux, 4.10.92), Midi-Pyrenees (a replacement in
18–15 win, Toulouse, 15.10.92), Provence-Cote d'Azur (scored try in 41–12
win, Marseille, 13.10.92), French Barbarians (scored try in 20–25 loss, Lille,
31.10.92) England B (won 20–16, Bristol, 7.11.92)

Murphy, J. N.   Ireland

Full Name: John Noel Murphy
Club: Greystones
Position: Hooker
Height: 6ft (1.78m)
Weight: 15st 7lb (98kg)
Occupation: Sales representative with Batchelor Ltd (Dublin)
Born: Dublin, 8.2.63
Family: Single
Former clubs: South Brisbane (Aus)
International debut: Ireland 17, Australia 42, 1992
Five Nations' debut: Not applicable
Best moment in rugby: Getting capped against Wallabies
Worst moment in rugby: Getting hammered by Wallabies
Most respected opponent: Phil Kearns (Australia)
Best memory last season: Beating Shannon away
Suggestions to improve rugby: *On-field* – Work on refereeing standards, especially in Ireland. Hold development courses for officials. Keep ruck/maul turnover law 'a bit longer before weighing up its merits. *Off-field* – None. Ireland is now getting its act together

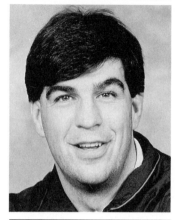

Ireland (1992)

Last Season	1 cap	0 pts
Career	1 cap	0 pts

Caps (1): 1992 A

Points Nil

Notable landmarks in rugby career: A member of the 1981 Ireland Schools team, he captained Ireland B to 29–19 win over Scottish counterparts at Murrayfield on 28 December 1991. Has also captained Leinster and last season skippered Greystones, with whom he had toured to Canada way back in 1982. After that, represented Leinster U-20s in 1982/83 season before leaving the country to spend two seasons with South Brisbane in Australia. Replaced Steve Smith as Ireland hooker for visit of world champions Australia on 31 October 1992 before roles were again reversed for the start of 1993 Five Nations' Championship. When Terry Kingston came in for Smith after the opening loss in Scotland, John was selected for bench reserve duty where he remained throughout the remainder of the campaign
Touchlines: Golf

Murphy, K. J.   Ireland

Full Name: Kenneth John Murphy
Club: Cork Constitution
Position: Fullback
Height: 6ft (1.83m)
Weight: 12st 7lb (80kg)
Occupation: Family garage business
Born: Cork, 31.7.66
Family: Single
Family links with rugby: Grandfather (Noel: 11 caps between 1930–33) and father (Noel Jnr: 41 caps between 1958–69) both played for Ireland
International debut: England 23, Ireland 0, 1990
Five Nations' debut: As above
Best moment in rugby: Winning 1990/91 All-Ireland League with Cork Con
Worst moment in rugby: Missing penalty which cost Christian Brothers College Junior Schools Cup; Losing 1992/93 championship to Young Munster on points difference
Most respected opponents: Gavin Hastings (Watsonians & Scotland) and Serge Blanco (ex-Biarritz & France)

Ireland (1990)		
Last Season	1 cap	0 pts
Career	11 caps	0 pts

Caps	(11): **1990** E, S, F, W, Arg **1991** F, W(R), S(R) **1992** S, F, NZ(2R)

Points Nil

Notable landmarks in rugby career: Unique family record – father and grandfather also having played for Ireland. Played Irish Schools against Junior All Blacks (1985). Represented Combined Provinces on internal tour and was a replacement for Ireland U-25s against Italy (1989). Toured France with Irish squad (1988) and, in December 1989, won first Ireland B cap against Scotland (drew 22–22, Murrayfield 9.12.89). Two months later was promoted to senior side for 1990 Five Nations' Championship, and played in each of the four games. Lost No 15 jersey to Jim Staples for bulk of 1991 Five Nations' Championship, but still made three appearances, twice replacing the unfortunate Staples. A non-playing member of the Irish World Cup squad, he was recalled for duty in 1992 Championship against Scotland and France. Helped Cork Constitution win 1990/91 All-Ireland League title. Toured with Ireland to New Zealand in the summer of 1992 where he picked up his 11th cap, coming on as a 38th minute replacement for Staples in the 59–6 loss to the All Blacks (Wellington, 6.6.92)

Nicol, A. D.   Scotland

Full Name: Andrew Douglas Nicol
Club: Dundee High School FP
Position: Scrum-half
Height: 5ft 11½in (1.82m)
Weight: 13st 4lb (84kg)
Occupation: Business Studies
student at Dundee Institute of
Technology
Born: Dundee, 12.3.71
Family: Single
Family links with rugby: Alastair
(brother) plays for Scotland U-18s,
Army, and Dundee HSFP. George
Ritchie (grandfather) played for
Scotland against England at
Twickenham (1932: lost 3–16)
Former club: Heriot's FP
International debut: Scotland 7,
England 25, 1992
Five Nations' debut: As above
Best moments in rugby: Winning
first cap against England; scoring try
against Ireland; representing World
XV in New Zealand
Worst moment in rugby:
Dislocating collarbone in Scotland
B's 19–29 loss to Ireland B

Scotland (1992)		
Last Season	2 caps	0 pts
1993	Tour to South Seas	
Career	6 caps	4 pts

Caps (6): **1992** E, I, F, W, A(1,2)

Points (4 – 1t): I(1t)

(28.12.91) and thus missing 1992 Scotland Trial
Most embarrassing moment: Ripping shorts open in a club game against
Perthshire. Trying to change them and the ball coming back to me
Most respected opponents: Gary Armstrong (Jed-Forest & Scotland) and
Nick Farr-Jones (NSW & Australia)
Biggest influence on career: Sandy Hutchison (Dundee High School PE
teacher and coach)
Serious injuries: Sprung collarbone (five weeks out), medial ligament, dislo-
cated elbow, concussion
Other sporting achievements: Cricket for Dundee High School CC
Best memory last season: Appointed Scotland captain for summer tour to
South Seas
Suggestions to improve rugby: *On-field* – Should be able to alter new laws
immediately should they be seen not to work, rather than having to wait a year…
and more. Greater consistency in appreciation of laws from referees. *Off-field*
– Allow players to benefit from rugby-related activities. IRB must clarify what

players can and cannot do

Notable landmarks in rugby career: Something had to give last season when Gary Armstrong returned to full fitness. Scotland found herself with arguably the two best scrum-halves in Europe in direct competition. Gary Armstrong drew the selectorial nod (and was subsequently outstanding) and Andy, who had anyway struggled with injury for much of the campaign, warmed the bench. However, his time came again when Armstrong again departed the scene (first called into the Lions squad then ruled out through injury). He was appointed to captain an inexperienced Scotland party bound for the South Seas. Played three seasons for Scotland Schools. Captained Schools and Scotland Under-19s (great honour). One game for Scotland Under-21s (concussed against Combined Services) before earning Scotland B call-up in 1990/91 for 10–31 loss to France B at Hughenden (2.3.91). Scored Scots' solitary try that day. Toured North America with Scotland (1991), scoring a try on each of three appearances (v Alberta, Rugby East and Ontario). Not included in World Cup squad but good performances for Scottish Students (against Oxford University) and Scotland B (against Ireland B: another try) prompted selection for 1992 Five Nations' Championship in place of knee-ligament victim Armstrong. Scored try against Ireland on second outing. Concluded amazing season (also helped Dundee HSFP gain promotion) with selection to World XV for Test series in New Zealand to celebrate centenary of NZRFU. Also represented Barbarians in 1992 Hong Kong Sevens and toured Australia (1992) with Scotland, playing in both Tests

Touchlines: Golf, cricket

Ofahengaue, V. Australia

Full Name: Viliame (Willie) Ofahengaue (O)
Club: Manly
State: New South Wales
Position: Flanker, No 8
Height: 6ft 4in (1.93m)
Weight: 16st 7lb (105kg)
Occupation: Pile driver for Emanon Pty Ltd (Manly, NSW)
Born: 3.5.68
Family: Heleni (wife), Lavinia (mother), Sione (father), Sione Kata (brother), Epalahame (brother), Talia (sister)
Former clubs: Manly since 1989
International debut: New Zealand 21, Australia 6, 1990

Best moments in rugby: Being picked to play for Wallabies and winning 1991 World Cup

Worst moment in rugby: Being left in Australia by the New Zealand team when I toured Oz with them in in 1988

Most respected opponent: Everyone

Serious injuries: Knee (1989)

Best memory last season: Winning against Wales

Australia (1990)		
Last Season	5 caps	0 pts
Career	17 caps	16 pts

Caps (17): **1990** NZ(1,2,3) **1991** W(a), E(a), NZ(a1,a2). wc–Arg, W(b), I, NZ(b), E(b) **1992** – S(1,2), SA, I, W

Points (16 – 4t): **1990** NZ(2:1t) **1991** W(a:1t), E(a:2t)

Suggestions to improve rugby: *On-field* – Improve discipline

Notable landmarks in rugby career: Without doubt one of the characters of 1992, developing a sizeable fan club during Australia's tour to Ireland and Wales. Missed the Bledisloe Cup series win over New Zealand due to a knee injury but came back strongly (very strongly) in the Tests against South Africa, Ireland and Wales. Other appearances on tour came against Western Transvaal, Eastern Province, Leinster, Ulster, Wales B, Llanelli and the Barbarians. Tongan born and Auckland educated, Willie O toured New Zealand in 1990 as a late inclusion for Jeff Miller. Two years earlier he had been in the New Zealand Schools side but because of visa difficulties he was refused re-entry into the land of the Kiwi and headed back to Oz to live with his uncle. New Zealand's loss was Australia's gain as he has quickly amassed 17 caps and developed a fearsome reputation as an explosive runner and bone-crunching defender. Represented the World XV against New Zealand in the 1992 Centenary Series and helped Australia reach the 1993 World Cup Sevens final in Edinburgh

Tours: 1990 – New Zealand. 1991 – New Zealand, World Cup. 1992 – South Africa, Ireland and Wales

Touchlines: Music, movies

Player to watch: David Campese (Randwick & Milan)

Player of the Year: Tim Horan (Australia)

O'Hara, P. T.   Ireland

Full Name: Patrick Thomas O'Hara
Club: Cork Constitution
Position: Flanker
Height: 6ft 2in (1.88m)
Weight: 15st (95kg)
Occupation: Sales director with Architectural and Metal Systems Ltd (Cork)
Born: Essex, England, 4.8.61
Family: Maire (wife), Darren (son) and Grian (son)
Former club: Sunday's Well
International debut: Ireland 49, Western Samoa 22, 1988
Five Nations' debut: Ireland 21, France 26, 1989
Best moment in rugby: First full cap against France

Worst moment in rugby: Getting concussed against England 1989 (lost 3–16)
Most embarrassing moment: Playing in front of provincial selectors in 1984/85, ended up in centre and attempted long pass to wing that was intercepted for try
Most respected opponent: Finlay Calder (Stewart's-Melville & Scotland) – great reader of game, very street wise, and always willing to advise
Biggest influence on career: Father (Tom)
Serious injuries: Two years of foot and shoulder ligament damage. Torn groin muscle
Other sporting achievements: Won a number of cross-country races when in Essex
Best memory last season: Coming through spell of injury to regain Ireland place and share in wins over Wales and England
Suggestions to improve rugby: *On-field* – Stopping messing about with the rules. Leave game alone. Allow playing ball on ground, with in reason. *Off-field* – Greater financial support for tourists. Not looking to make money, just do not want to lose out
Notable landmarks in rugby career: Made Sunday's Well debut in 1979, aged 18, and the following year helped them win Cork Charity Cup. Won first Munster provincial cap in 1983 and went on to represent them against 1984

Ireland (1988)

Last Season	3 caps	0 pts
Career	14 caps	4 pts

Caps (14): **1988** WS(R) **1989** F, W, E, NZ **1990** E, S, F, W **1991** Na(1) wc-J **1993** F, W, E

Points (4 – 1t): **1991** wc-J(1t)

309

Wallabies and 1989 All Blacks. Toured with Ireland to France (1988), North America (1989) and Namibia (1991). Had to wait until 15 minutes from end of 1988 game against Western Samoa to replace Phil Matthews and win first cap. Voted 1989/90 Irish Player of the Year. Foot and shoulder injuries forced him to miss the entire 1991 Championship though he recovered in time to make Ireland B debut at Old Belvedere (1.3.91) when England B were beaten 24–10. Solitary appearance in 1991/92 came in the 32–16 World Cup-tie against Japan in Dublin (9.10.91), an occasion he marked with his first international try. Further injury again sidelined him thereafter before he was granted respite in February 1993. He wasted little time returning to the international fray at blindside and played a key role in Ireland's late-season resurgence, when they upset the odds by beating Wales and England

Touchlines: Built garden shed all by myself

Olivier, J. South Africa

Full Name: Jacques Olivier
Club: Tukkies
Province: Northern Transvaal
Position: Wing
Height: 5ft 10½in (1.79m)
Weight: 13st 3lb (84kg)
Occupation: Law student
Born: Pretoria, 13.11.68
Family links with rugby: Nephew of Springbok legend Jan Ellis
International debut: France 15, South Africa 20, 1992
Notable landmarks in rugby career: When the name J H Ellis appears on your family tree rugby is always going to be a likely pastime. Jan won 38 caps at flanker between 1965–76 – a figure which remains unsurpassed by any of his compatriots. So it is with Jacques, a former Junior Springbok, who made his provincial bow in 1991 and has since reeled off 38 appearances for Northern Transvaal. In that short time he convinced the selectors he was worthy of international

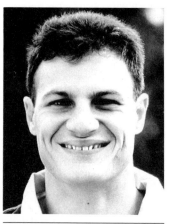

South Africa (1992)

Last Season	5 caps	0 pts
Career	5 caps	0 pts

Caps (5): **1992** F(1,2), E **1993** F(1,2)

Points Nil

recognition and was included in the party for the 1992 tour to France and England. On that trip he developed into the first-choice left wing, playing in all three Tests – two against France (won 20–15, Lyon, 17.10.92; lost 16–29, Paris, 24.10.92) and the 16–33 loss to England at Twickenham (14.11.92). In the other games he scored four tries in five games with only the French Barbarians (lost 20–25, Lille, 31.10.92) denying him. His touchdowns came against Aquitaine (won 29–22, Pau, 7.10.92), Midi-Pyrenees (won 18–15, Toulouse, 15.10.92), Provence-Cote d'Azur (won 41–12, Marseille, 13.10.92) and, on the British leg of the tour, England B in the Springboks' thrilling 20–16 victory at Bristol on 7 November. The other big game of 1992 for Jacques came for the Blue Bulls against the world champion Wallabies at Loftus Versfeld, Pretoria (14.8.92), which the tourists won 24–17

Olver, C. J.   England

Full Name: Christopher John Olver
Club: Northampton
Position: Hooker
Height: 5ft 9in (1.76m)
Weight: 13st 2lb (83kg)
Occupation: Head of Department at Northampton GS
Born: Manchester, 23.4.62
Family: Sue (wife) and Lisa (daughter)
Former clubs: Sandbach, Harlequins
International debut: England 51, Argentina 0, 1990
FIve Nations' debut: None
Best moments in rugby: Lifting John Player Cup after captaining Harlequins to 28–22 win over Bristol in 1988 final. Winning first England cap against Argentina (3.11.90)
Worst moment in rugby: Losing two JP Cup semi-finals with Quins
Most embarrassing moment: Every time I lose a strike against head
Most respected opponents: Phil Keith-Roach and Peter Wheeler
Biggest influence on career: Bev

England (1990)		
Last Season	1 cap	0 pts
1993	Tour to Canada	
Career	3 caps	0 pts

Caps (3): **1990** Arg(b) **1991** wc–US **1992** C

Points Nil

Risman (ex-Loughborough College & England) – my lecturer at Borough Road College who advised me to switch from flanker to hooker
Serious injuries: Achilles tendon (operation). Dislocated shoulder (twice)

Other sporting achievements: Hit Australian cricket captain Allan Border for three consecutive sixes. 7-handicap golfer

Best memory last season: Winning third cap in 26–23 win over Canada at Wembley

Suggestions to improve rugby: *On-field* – Recruit referees who have actually played in front row. All referees seem to be backs who have no idea what is going on in the scrum. Structure season so that all League rugby is conducted on consecutive Saturdays (Sept–Nov). Then play divisionals (Dec) and then, after Christmas, Internationals. This would remove present ludicrous dilemma of players having to play major league games seven days before Internationals. *Off-field* – Compensate employers for loss of employees to rugby

Notable landmarks in rugby career: Holds England record for most matches watched from the bench – 32, but was rewarded for his loyalty to the cause last season when appointed captain of England party to tour Canada over the summer. Previously toured with England to Argentina (1990) and Australia (1991), winning long-awaited first full cap in between, in defeat of touring Pumas (3.11.90). Won second cap in 37–9 World Cup win over the United States at Twickenham (11.10.91) and third last season (17.10.92) when displacing Brian Moore for hooking berth in 26–13 defeat of Canada at Wembley Stadium (Twickenham was under reconstruction). Also represented England XV in 33–15 win over Italy XV (1.5.90) and in 18–16 win over centenary Barbarians (29.9.90). Captained England B in 12–9 win over Italy (Waterloo, 27.3.91)

Touchlines: Fly fishing and shooting

Ougier, S. France

Full Name: Stephane Ougier
Club: Toulouse
Position: Fullback, wing, centre
Height: 6ft 3in (1.90m)
Weight: 14st 7lb (92kg)
Occupation: Student
Born: Toulouse, 5.10.67
International debut: France 25, Romania 6, 1992
Five Nations' debut: England 16, France 15, 1993
Notable landmarks in rugby career: Utility back whose rise to prominence was helped by the form of his club side, Toulouse, with whom he won a French club championship runners-up medal in

1989. A bright lad, he is studying for a doctorate in electronics, Stephane has worked his way up the representative ladder, wearing the colours of France at Under-19, Students and B levels. Last season he took the final step when selected at fullback for the match against Romania at Le Havre

France (1992)

Last Season	3 caps	4 pts
Career	3 caps	4 pts

Caps (3): **1992** R, Arg(a1) **1993** E(R)

Points (4 – 2c): **1992** R(2c)

on 28 May. A 25–6 result, which helped France retain the FIRA Championship, was swelled by his two conversions. Included in the party for the summer tour of Argentina, he played at fullback in the 27–12 first Test victory in Buenos Aires on 4 July but lost his place to Colomiers' Jean-Luc Sadourny the following weekend. He remained out of favour throughout the two-Test series with South Africa back home and the return with Argentina in Nantes, which ended with disastrous defeat for the French. However, he was required for bench duties in each of the four Five Nations' Championship matches in 1993 and played a part in France's triumph, albeit only 28 minutes as replacement for Thierry Lacroix in the 15–16 loss to England at Twickenham on 16 January

Penaud, A. France

Full Name: Alain Penaud
Club: Brive
Position: Outside-half
Height: 5ft 11in (1.81m)
Weight: 14st 2lb (90kg)
Born: Juillac, 19.7.69
Former club: Objat
Occupation: Student
International debut: Wales 9, France 12, 1992
Five Nations' debut: As above
Notable landmarks in rugby career: First-choice outside-half for France in 1992, Alain drew admiration from Robert Paparemborde for his performances on the summer tour of Argentina. 'Penaud confirmed his status as the best fly-half in France,' said the team manager. He continued to shine in

the home series against South Africa; scoring two tries in the 15–20 defeat at Lyon (17.10.92) and another the following week as France gained her revenge by winning 29–16 in Paris. Was then moved to centre for the visit to Nantes of

Argentina (14.11.92) and when the Pumas recorded their first ever win on French soil, Alain was caught in the clearout. Didier Camberabero returned for the 1993 Championship which France won. Alain had made a strong impression after being given his chance out of the blue by new coach Pierre Berbizier in the '92 Championship. Having dropped a goal in France's three-point defeat of Wales in Cardiff on his debut (1.2.92), he managed a try against

France (1992)

Last Season	9 caps	18 pts
Career	13 caps	33 pts

Caps (13): **1992** W, E, S, I, R, Arg(a1,a2), SA(1,2), Arg(b) **1993** R,SA(1,2)

Points (33 – 6t,2dg): **1992** W(1dg), E(1t), I(2t), Arg(a1:1dg), SA(1:2t), SA(2:1t) **1993** SA(2:1dg)

England in a 31–13 losing cause next time out (15.2.92), after charging down Will Carling's attempted clearance in the 66th minute. He drew a blank in Edinburgh, but ended the season with a two-try flourish against Ireland: starting and finishing the seven-try rout with touchdowns in the second and 85th minutes. Originally made a name for himself when guiding French Schools to the 1987 'Triple Crown' with 18 points in wins against Scotland, Wales and England. From there he graduated to France A and the 1989/90 FIRA Championship, in which he tasted triumph when scoring the try that inspired a 22–14 victory over the Soviet Union and gave France A the title on try-difference

Pene, A. R. B.   New Zealand

Full Name: Arran Pene
Province: Otago
Position: No 8
Height: 6ft 3in (1.91m)
Weight: 16st 5lb (104kg)
Born: 26.10.67
International debut: New Zealand 14, World XV 28, 1992
Notable landmarks in rugby career: A member of Otago's outstanding All Black back row, which took Otago to the National Championship final, Arran ironically owed his Test selection to Mike Brewer, his Provincial captain and fellow back rower, whose calf injury ruled him out of selection and the national captaincy. Arran grabbed

his chance with both hands and, after coming on as a 35th replacement for Michael Jones in the 14–28 first Test defeat by the World XV, monopolised the No 8 berth throughout the rest of the centenary series and two-Test visit of Ireland. Involved with two winning sides in the national Trials at Napier, he showed himself to be a prolific scorer: bagging four tries

New Zealand (1992)

Last Season	8 caps	16 pts
Career	8 caps	16 pts

Caps (8): **1992** Wd(1R,2,3), I(1,2), A(1,2R) **1993** BL(3)

Points (16 – 4t): **1992** Wd(2:1t), Wd(3:1t), I(2:2t)

in as many Test appearances. It was little surprise that he won selection to the All Black squad touring Australia and South Africa, however injuries – in particular a broken hand – led to him losing his first-choice spot to Zinzan Brooke for the second Test against Australia. Despite coming on as a replacement for Kevin Schuler in that game, he failed to win back his place for the third 'dead' leg of the Bledisloe Cup series or for the victory over South Africa in Johannesburg. In all, he played in only eight of the 16 tour engagements; the others being Western Australia, New South Wales, Queensland B, Orange Free State, Junior South Africa and Central Unions. On the domestic front he was an integral part of the Otago side which reached the final of the National Championship (where they lost to Waikato) and finished runners-up (again to Waikato) in the CANZ tournament. Recalled in place of Zinzan Brooke at No 8 for decisive third Test in 1993 Lions in Auckland

Perego, M. A. Wales

Full Name: Mark Angelo Perego
Club: Llanelli
Position: Flanker
Height: 6ft (1.83m)
Weight: 14st 7lb (92kg)
Occupation: Fireman with Dyfed Powys Brigade
Born: Winchester, Hants, 8.2.64
Family: Married
Family links with rugby: Father played for Llanelli, Army and Wales Youth
Former club: South Wales Police
International debut: Wales 9, Scotland 13, 1990
Five Nations' debut: As above
Best moment in rugby: Llanelli's 1992/93 campaign

Worst moment in rugby: Llanelli losing to Cardiff in 1989/90 Cup (first Cup-tie defeat with club)
Most respected opponent: Jonathan Griffiths (ex-Llanelli & Wales)
Serious injuries: Torn neck muscles, concussion (twice)
Other sporting achievements: Golf (8-handicap)

Wales (1990)		
Last Season	2 caps	0 pts
1993	Tour to Zimbabwe/Namibia	
Career	3 caps	0 pts

Caps (3): **1990** W **1993** F, Z(1)

Points Nil

Best memory last season: Returning to Wales side for Paris match
Suggestions to improve rugby: Increase emphasis on schoolboy rugby
Notable landmarks in rugby career: English-born Mark returned to his best form last season as part of the Llanelli 'red machine' who monopolised the honours in the Principality, winning the League and Cup double. Mark, who had also collected a Cup winners' medal in 1988 when Neath succumbed 28–13, was a member of the Wales B side beaten 11–24 by Australia at Cardiff on 7 November 1992 but gained quick revenge the following weekend when Llanelli beat the tourists 13–9 at Stradey. He retained his place in the second-string side, by now rechristened Wales A, for the 57–12 win over Holland in Den Bosch on 6 February 1993 and was then upgraded onto the senior bench for the 14–19 defeat at the hands of Ireland in Cardiff (6.3.93). That result prompted changes and Mark, who had previously represented Wales at U-15, U-16, U-18 and Youth levels, came in on the blindside (instead of Emyr Lewis, who switched to No 8) for the 10–26 loss to France (20.3.93). The player who had started career at Llanelli and returned after a two-year spell at South Wales Police, ended the season in Africa where he toured with Wales to Zimbabwe and Namibia, playing in the 35–14 first Test defeat of Zimbabwe in Bulawayo
Touchlines: River and mountain running, golf

Franck Mesnel executes a copybook tackle on Welsh centre Nigel Davies in the Parc des Princes. Richard Webster and Laurent Cabannes offer admiring glances

Popplewell, N. J.   Ireland

Full Name: Nicholas James Popplewell
Club: Greystones
Position: Loosehead prop
Height: 5ft 10in (1.78m)
Weight: 16st 7lb (105kg)
Occupation: Warehouse manager with Argus Furniture
Born: Dublin, 6.4.64
Family: Single
Former club: Gorey
International debut: Ireland 6, New Zealand 23, 1989
Five Nations' debut: Ireland 15, Wales 16, 1992
Best moment in rugby: Winning first cap against 1989 All Blacks; selection for 1993 Lions
Worst moment in rugby: Only lasting 20 minutes on debut before cracking a rib
Most respected opponent: Des Fitzgerald (DLSP & Ireland)
Serious injuries: Broken ribs (twice)
Other sporting achievements: Hockey for Irish Schools (three caps)
Best memories last season: Beating England

Ireland (1989)

Last Season	7 caps	0 pts
Career	18 caps	8 pts
Lions 1993	3 Tests	0 pts

Caps (18): **1989** NZ **1990** Arg **1991** Na(1,2) wc–Z, S, A **1992** W, E, S, F, NZ(1,2), A **1993** S, F, W, E. Lions–NZ(1,2,3)

Points (8 – 2t): **1991** wc–Z(2t)

Suggestions to improve rugby: *On-field* – Decrease value of penalty goal to two points. Scrap 90-degree scrum wheel law. *Off-field* – Compensate players for time lost away from work – not payments, just reduced hassle in claiming legitimate expenses

Notable landmarks in rugby career: In only second full season as first-choice loosehead prop in Ireland side Nick gained selection for the 1993 British Lions and spent his second successive summer in New Zealand (along with Shannon's Mick Galwey). Had taken over the Irish No 1 jersey during 1991/92 season following 1991 tour to Namibia where he played in both both Tests. Made great start to 1991 World Cup when scoring two tries in 55–11 Pool win over Zimbabwe in Dublin (6.10.91). With exception of Japan game, when John Fitzgerald took his turn, he retained his slot for remainder of tournament and then throughout 1992 Five Nations' Championship, before touring with Ireland

to Kiwi land. Returned with his reputation enhanced and was one of only three permanent fixtures (Vince Cunningham and Paddy Johns being the others) throughout seven-Test Irish programme. That meant he experienced the lows – heavy defeats by New Zealand (second Test), Australia and, to a lesser extent, Scotland – and the highs – a great first Test show against the All Blacks and the wins over Wales and England. Previously, Nick had been a member of Irish party which toured France (May 1988) and North America (1989: playing in 24–21 defeat of Canada). Retired injured after 20 minutes of full debut against 1989 All Blacks and lost place for 1990 Championship. Redundant thereafter, except for 1990 Argentina (won 20–18) game, before heading off to Namibia. Helped train Presentation Juniors Bray U-15s to two Leinster Junior Cups in three years. Represented Ireland U-25s v US Eagles (1990). Scored one of Ireland B's four tries in 24–10 win over England B (Old Belvedere, 1.3.91)
Touchlines: Golf, tennis, squash

Preston, J. P. New Zealand

Full Name: Jon Paul Preston
Club: Burnside
Province: Canterbury
Position: Stand-off, scrum-half, centre
Height: 5ft 10in (1.78m)
Weight: 12st 2lb (77kg)
Born: 15.11.67
International debut: New Zealand 46, USA 6, 1991
Serious injuries: Dislocated shoulder (1992)
Notable landmarks in rugby career: Jon's 1992 tour of Australia and South Africa was a tale of two shoulder dislocations. Sustaining the injury in the opening tour fixture against Western Australia (having scored a try, two conversions and a penalty), he was sidelined for four games before marking his return against a Victorian XV with three conversions in the 53–3 win. However, he was unable to recover his best form then, and in the missions against Queensland B, Sydney, Orange Free State and

New Zealand (1991)

Last Season	3 caps	0 pts
Career	5 caps	28 pts

Caps (5): 1991 wc–US, S **1992** SA(R) 1993 BL(2,3)

Points (28 – 1t,4c,5p): **1991** wc–US(4c,2p), S(3p) **1993** BL(3:1t)

Central Unions. Just when hope appeared lost first-choice scrum-half Ant Strachan dislocated his shoulder 16 minutes into the Test against South Africa in Johannesburg. Enter Mr Preston for a mighty impressive afternoon's work in tandem with half-back partner Grant Fox. Jon was first seen in Britain with the 1984 New Zealand Schools touring party and, after visiting Canada on the 1990 development tour and helping a New Zealand XV stroll past the Soviet Union 56–6 in 1991, returned to the United Kingdom for the World Cup – selected as reserve half-back in preference to Simon Mannix and Paul McGahan. He was employed at outside-half for the 46–6 pool win over the United States, kicking 14 points, and returned in the third place play-off game against Scotland in Cardiff, slotting three penalty goals in a 13–6 victory. Jon, who had played on the 1991 New Zealand B team which beat Australia B 21–15 in Brisbane, was missing from the Canterbury side which crushed Ireland 38–13 last season, but was back in time to claim a New Zealand record of 20 conversions in a single match as West Coast were routed 128–0. Replaced Strachan for last two Tests v 1993 Lions, scoring try in 30–13 Auckland decider

Probyn, J. A. — England

Full Name: Jeffrey Alan Probyn
Club: Wasps
Position: Tighthead prop
Height: 5ft 10in (1.78m)
Weight: 15st 10lb (100kg)
Occupation: Director of Probros Ltd (family furniture firm)
Born: London, 27.4.56
Family: Jennifer (wife), Jeffrey Paul (son), Steven James (son) and Rebecca (daughter)
Family links with rugby: Brother (Chris) plays for Redbridge (ex-Surrey and London Counties)
Former clubs: Old Albanians, Ilford Wanderers, Streatham/Croydon, Richmond, Askeans
International debut: France 10, England 9, 1988
Five Nations' debut: As above
Best moment in rugby: Winning second Grand Slam with England
Worst moment in rugby: Leaving field concussed in Ireland (1989)
Most embarrassing moment: Getting lifted by Welsh prop Staff Jones for trying to be clever (Twickenham, 1988)

Most respected opponent: Paul Rendall (Wasps & England: technically brilliant) and Jason Leonard (Harlequins & England)

Biggest influence on career: Dennis Bedford (hooker/coach at Streatham/Croydon) – convinced me my future was at tighthead

Serious injuries: Damaged ligaments in left knee. Ear stitches

Best memory last season: Winning back England place for Five Nations' campaign

England (1988)

Last Season	4 caps	0 pts
Career	37 caps	12 pts

Caps (37): **1988** F, W, S, I(1,2), A(a1,a2), A(b) **1989** S, I, Ro(R) **1990** I, F, W, S, Arg(a1,a2), Arg(b) **1991** W, S, I, F, Fj, A(a) wc–NZ, It, F, S, A(b) **1992** S, I, F, W **1993** F, W, S, I

Points (12 – 3t): **1989** Ro(1t) **1990** I(1t) **1991** Fj(1t)

Suggestions to improve rugby: *On-field* – Refereeing is still a major problem which the authorities have got to recognise. There are only five capable of refereeing internationals to a proper standard. Never mind the players, the professionalising of rugby must start with the referees. Hold seminars for officials to sort out common strategy. Get touch judges more involved in running of game. As for the rule changes, far too much tinkering goes on by people who do not understand what is going on in the scrum. Unions should get player representatives involved in law-making and not pretend they are administering for the whole game rather than for a select few. The need to be 100 per cent fitter to accommodate the new rule changes is taking away from the average player. That is not what I went into the game for and I have played at every level. I am sad to see the way things have changed. For example, none of the young players knew the words to our rugby songs on the Barbarians tour. Endemic of the problem – we have lost the social aspect. *Off-field* – I would like to think players could progress hand-in-hand with RFU into modern era. Allow players to benefit from off-field activities; after all, RFU market themselves on fame of players

Notable landmarks in rugby career: First England cap (January 1988) came at the age of 31. An occasional centre in junior rugby before moving to Wasps. Outside club rugby, has represented Hertfordshire and Surrey county clubs, Hertfordshire, Surrey, Middlesex, London Counties, London, Barbarians, Public School Wanderers, England B (four games), World XV (1989 against South Africa), and Home Unions (1989 v France). Scored tries in England's wins over Romania (1989), Ireland (1990), Fiji (1991) and Queensland on 1988 tour of Australia. Returned Down Under on tour with England (1991) having attended Argentina the previous summer. Ever present throughout England's back-to-back Grand Slams and played in 1991 World Cup final. Rates the 1991 World Cup quarter-final against France in Paris as the most difficult game he ever played in. 'There was such mental pressure on us and the overall intensity of the game was awesome.' England career looked to be at an end when Bath's Victor Ubogu took over at tighthead last season for the two autumn Tests against Canada and South Africa. But Jeff powered back and come the 1993 Five Nations' Championship was back alongside Jason Leonard and Brian Moore in the 'traditional' front row. Final international of the campaign – the 3–17 defeat by Ireland in Dublin – allowed him to win his 37th cap and so overtake Gary Pearce as England's most-capped prop

Touchlines: Sailing, shooting, fishing, watching children grow up and play sport

---

Proctor, W. T.   Wales

Full Name: Wayne Thomas Proctor
Club: Llanelli
Position: Wing, fullback
Height: 6ft (1.83m)
Weight: 12st 2lb (77kg)
Occupation: Student at Swansea Institute of Higher Education
Born: Bridgend, 12.6.72
Family: Single
Former club: Cardigan Youth
International debut: Wales 6, Australia 23, 1992
Five Nations' debut: Wales 10, England 9, 1993
Best moment in rugby: Beating England on Five Nations' debut (6.2.93)
Worst moment in rugby: Missing out on a Welsh Schools cap
Most embarrassing moment: Being interviewed by the BBC for the first time
Most respected opponent: Tony Underwood (England & Lions)
Other sporting achievements: Represented Wales 11 times at athletics; third in 1988 British Schools 400m hurdles

Wales (1992)

Last Season	6 caps	10 pts
1993	Tour to Zimbabwe/Namibia	
Career	6 caps	10 pts

Caps (6): 1992 A 1993 E, S, Z(1,2), Na

Points (10 – 2t):1993 Z(1:1t), Na(1t)

Best memory last season: Breaking into Wales side; Llanelli's win over Australia
Suggestions to improve rugby: *On-field* – Introduce alternative to the scrum to help quicken up the game. *Off-field* – Sell the game better. Televise more live games at different levels
Notable landmarks in rugby career: Rapidly progressed into Wales senior side last season, only seven months after having made debut for Welsh Under-21s in 28–19 win over Scotland at Stirling on 18 April 1992. And he got to know

the touring Wallabies well in the process as he followed an outing for Wales B against them (Australia won 24–11 at Cardiff, 7.11.92) with another the following weekend as Llanelli won 13–9 at Stradey. Seven days later and he made his Test debut in the 6–23 loss to the men from Down Under at the National Stadium. Wayne, who had previously won four Welsh Youth caps and three Wales Under-19 caps (touring with the latter to Canada), kept his place for the first two matches of the 1993 Five Nations' Championship, sharing in the euphoria which surrounded the 10–9 defeat of England at Cardiff and then the dejection which followed their 0–20 shutout at Murrayfield. It was then that the selectors turned to the pace of Olympic hurdler Nigel Walker, though Wayne was asked to tour with the national side to Zimbabwe and Namibia in the summer of '92, by which time he had experienced Llanelli's League and Cup double. The Cup final win over Neath gave him his second medal as he had figured in the 16–7 Final defeat of Swansea the previous season

Touchlines: Athletics, tennis, badminton

Rayer, M. A.   Wales

Full Name: Michael Anthony Rayer
Club: Cardiff
Position: Fullback
Height: 5ft 10in (1.78m)
Weight: 13st 3lb (78kg)
Occupation: Sales representative with Dimex Ltd
Born: Cardiff, 21.7.65
Family: Married
Family links with rugby: Father (Alec) played for Penarth, Cardiff Athletic and Llandudno
Former club: Llandudno
International debut: Wales 13, Western Samoa 16, 1991
Five Nations' debut: England 24, Wales 0, 1992
Best moment in rugby: Landing

dropped goal in extra-time of 1987 Schweppes Cup final against Swansea to put Cardiff in winning position
Worst moment in rugby: Being dropped by Wales (1993) which scuppered Lions chances
Most embarrassing moment: Aqua-planing 20 feet with ball in sodden conditions at St Helen's playing for Cardiff against Swansea
Most respected opponent: Jean-Baptiste Lafond (Begles & France)
Serious injuries: Dislocated elbow (1988), sprung shoulder joint, damaged

ribs, torn hamstring, ankle and knee ligaments

Other sporting achievements: Captained Wales B baseball team (1990/91)

Best memory last season: Victory over England

Suggestions to improve rugby: Develop more professional attitude. Disband 'old school tie' committees and stop living in past

Notable landmarks in rugby career: Bizarre and sad end to last season for Mike who had established himself as one of the world's premier fullbacks when he was dropped for the final International of the Five Nations' campaign against France, with Tony Clement returning. Considered a very likely lad for Lions selection his chances were blown straight out of the window. Instead Clement was picked and Mike spent summer with Wales in Zimbabwe and Namibia, playing in two of the three Tests. A regular fixture in the Wales side from the 68th minute of the non-cap International with Italy on 7 September 1992, when he came on for Scott Gibbs and scored a great try, Mike also turned in an accomplished performance for the Barbarians against Australia at Twickenham on 28 November and for Wales in the 10–9 victory over England on 6 February 1993. Captained Wales Youth (1983–85) at fullback prior to joining Cardiff in 1984/85, he played twice for Wales B, as a replacement against France B at Begles (lost 0–26, 17.10.87) and then from the start against the same opposition at La Teste two years later (won 28–15, 12.11.89). Toured Namibia with Wales (1990) but was unable to shift Paul Thorburn from fullback slot, despite scoring 28 points in 67–9 defeat of North Region (Tsumeb, 6.6.90). Top scored on tour with 64 points in three appearances. Knee surgery in August 1991 further delayed his entry into big time, but day finally arrived when replacing Clement during World Cup defeat by Western Samoa. Third and fourth Wales B appearances came last season against the North of England (scoring try in 21–13 win at Pontypool, 14.10.93) and Australia (7.11.92)

Wales (1991)		
Last Season	6 caps	0 pts
v Italy XV	1 app	5 pts
1993	Tour to Zimbabwe/Namibia	
Career	10 caps	3 pts

Caps (10): **1991** wc–WS(R), Arg, A(R) **1992** E(R), A **1993** E, S, I, Z(1), Na

Points (3 – 1p): **1991** wc–Arg(1p)

Reece-Edwards, H.   South Africa

Full Name: Hugh Reece-Edwards
Club: Crusaders
Province: Natal
Position: Fullback
Height: 6ft 2½in (1.89m)
Weight: 15st 2lb (96kg)
Occupation: Representative
Born: Johannesburg, 5.1.61
International debut: France 15,
South Africa 20, 1992
**Notable landmarks in rugby
career:** Possesses one of the most
prolific boots in South African
rugby, having scored over 1,000
points in first class rugby. He holds
the Natal record of 887 points, nine
of which came in the 1992 Currie
Cup final when his three penalty
goals contributed mightily to the
province's 14–13 victory over
Transvaal (Ellis Park, Johannesburg,
12.9.92) – their second Cup success
in three years. New Zealand also
experienced his potency when they
visited Kings Park, Durban on 1
August. Hugh landed six penalty

South Africa (1992)

Last Season	2 caps	0 pts
career	2 caps	0 pts

Caps (2): **1992** F(1,2)

Points Nil

goals and the conversion of a penalty try for a 20-point haul but the All Blacks
still won 43–25. Educated at Northlands in Durban he made his provincial
debut for Natal in 1982, 147 matches ago. He went on to represent the Junior
Springboks before earning Test recognition at the age of 31 during the
Springboks' tour of France and England. He played in both internationals
against the French – the 20–15 win in Lyon on 17 October and the 16–29
reversal in Paris the following weekend – before losing the No 15 jersey to
Transvaal's Theo van Rensburg (who had occupied the berth in the home
Tests against New Zealand and Australia) for the final international against
England at Twickenham on 14 November. His other tour appearances came
against France B (lost 17–24, Bordeaux, 4.10.92), Provence-Cote d'Azur
(kicked 16 points – 5c,2p – in 41–12 win, Marseille, 13.10.92), the French
Barbarians (lost 20–25, Lille, 31 .10.92) and the Northern Division (landed 14
points – 1c,4p – in 19–3 win, Leeds, 10.11.92)

Reed, A. I. Scotland

Full Name: Andrew Ian Reed
Club: Bath
Position: Lock
Height: 6ft 7in (2.01m)
Weight: 17st 10lb (112kg)
Occupation: Energy consultant with Pro-Eco Energy Econmists
Born: St Austell, Cornwall, 4.5.69
Family: Sarah (wife)
Family links with rugby: Father played in Royal Navy. Brother (Alec) played for Hong Kong Islanders
Former clubs: Bodmin, Camborne, Plymouth Albion
International debut: Scotland 15, Ireland 3
Five Nations' debut: As above
Best moment in rugby: Winning first cap
Worst moment in rugby: Cornwall's two County Championship final defeats v Durham (1988/89) and Lancashire (1991/92)
Most embarrassing moment: Dropping ball in front of clubhouse, playing for Bath United, when over for try

Scotland (1993)		
Last Season	4 caps	0 pts
Career	4 caps	0 pts
Lions 1993	Tour to New Zealand	

Caps (4): 1993 I, F, W, E

Points Nil

Most respected opponent: Olivier Roumat (France)
Biggest influence on career: The whole Bath experience
Serious injuries: Torn ankle ligaments, a/c shoulder joint
Best memory last season: Being informed of selection to Scotland and British Lions
Other sporting achievements: Goalkeeper for Cornwall Schools
Suggestions to improve rugby: *On-field* – Leave the lineout to the discretion of the referees. *Off-field* – A realistic appreciation of how much time and effort is put into playing top-level rugby. I don't want to make money from rugby – I just enjoy playing and building friendships through the sport – but it was to see that our commitment was appreciated. It takes me more than six hours to get to Murrayfield for training, and I still have to get home
Notable landmarks in rugby career: Meteoric rise up representative ladder in 1992/93 season – from second-choice club player to British Lion. A regular in Cornwall's County Championship side, playing in three Twickenham finals

325

in four years from 1989–92 (beating Yorkshire 29–20 in 1990/91), his only international experience had come in the colours of England Colts. All that changed last season when a series of impressive televised displays for Bath alerted first the Anglo-Scots, whom he turned out for in the Inter-District Championship, then Scotland. His switch of allegiances came courtesy of an Edinburgh-born mother and a Hearts football scarf which a Scottish spy spotted him wearing watching a rugby match in Plymouth. The news was relayed back up north and on 16 January 1993, having played in Scotland A's 22–13 win in Dublin, the former Bodmin Town goalkeeper (South Western League), made his debut in the 15–3 win over Ireland at Murrayfield, a 1,200-mile round trip from his home. A member of Bath, whom he joined for their 1990 tour to Australia, Andy was one of six Scottish Lions (though eight were originally selected) in New Zealand last summer

Touchlines: Watersports

Reynolds, A. D. Wales

Full Name: Alan David Reynolds
Club: Swansea
Position: Flanker
Height: 6ft 1in (1.86m)
Weight: 15st 3lb (97kg)
Occupation: Plasterer
Born: 24.1.66
Family: Single
Family links with rugby: Brother-in-law David Jacobs played for Neath and Wales B
Former clubs: Whitland, Laugharne
International debut: Namibia 9, Wales 18, 1990
Five Nations' debut: None
Best moment in rugby: Making Welsh debut in first Test against Namibia
Worst moment in rugby: Being dropped for second Test
Notable landmarks in rugby career: Alan ended two years without a Test appearance last season when he came on as a 64th minute replacement for Llanelli's

Wales (1990)

Last Season	1 cap	0 pts
Career	3 caps	0 pts

Caps (3): **1990**: Na(1,2R) **1992** A(R)

Points Nil

Emyr Lewis in the 6–23 loss to Australia, at Cardiff Arms Park on 21 November

326

1992. His bench selection had been prompted by a series of outstanding displays, most notably in Swansea's crushing 21–6 defeat of the Wallabies, at St Helens on 4 November. By him coming on at blindside wing-forward in Cardiff alongside Richard Webster and Stuart Davies, Australia were again faced with the Swansea back row. Alan, who had also been a bench reserve when Wales B beat North of England 21–13 at Pontypool (14.10.92) played the full 80 minutes against Ireland A at Newport on 5 March 1993; a match the Irish edged by the odd point in 57. He returned to reserve duty in the '93 Five Nations' Championship at Cardiff against England (6.2.93) and at Murrayfield a fortnight later. Represented Wales at Youth level against England in 1985 (while with Whitland Youth) and Pembrokeshire against the touring United States Eagles in 1987. Two years later he played for Swansea against New Zealand. Alan, who had Wales Under-21 trials and who has played for Wales at the Hong Kong Sevens, toured Namibia in 1990, turning out in five of the six games (scoring a try against Central Districts) including the two Tests (the second as replacement for Mark Jones)

Richards, D. England

Full Name: Dean Richards
Club: Leicester
Position: No 8
Height: 6ft 3½in (1.92m)
Weight: 17st 5lb (111kg)
Occupation: Police officer
Born: Nuneaton, 11.7.63
Family: Nicky (wife)
Family links with rugby: Father (Brian) played for Nuneaton
Former club: Roanne (France)
International debut: England 25, Ireland 20, 1986
Five Nations' debut: As above
Best moment in rugby: Winning decisive third Test with 1989 Lions
Worst moments in rugby: Losing four front teeth whilst in action; England losing to Wales in Cardiff (1989)
Most respected opponent: Brian Moore (Harlequins & England)
Biggest influence on career: My work
Serious injuries: Recurring dislocated shoulder
Best memory last season: Being picked for Lions after being omitted by England

Suggestions to improve rugby: *On-field* – Home Unions must guard against taking on new laws just because they suit the Southern Hemisphere nations. *Off-field* – Reduce maximum age of committee men to 55. Allow players to prosper from non-rugby related activities, as they do everywhere else in the world
Notable landmarks in rugby career: Selected to tour with 1993 British Lions despite not figuring in England's plans for Five Nations' Championship, Dean commands enormous worldwide respect. A powerhouse of a player and a wonderful driving influence who is nigh impossible to dispossess, he nonetheless had the England No 8 jersey wrestled from his grasp by Bath's young gun Ben Clarke whose ultra-mobile style of play was perfectly suited to the new laws. Clarke also toured to New Zealand last summer. Dean's one cap last season came at Wembley Stadium where Canada were beaten 26–13 (17.10.92). Test appearance number 34 firmed up his position as the nation's most-capped No 8. He joined Leicester in 1982 after season playing in France. Played for England Schools at lock, before graduating to England U-23s (against Romania). Has also represented Leicestershire and Midlands Division. Scored two tries on international debut against Ireland 'but it was one of my worst performances'. Played in 1987 World Cup and returned to Australia with 1989 Lions, playing in all three Tests of 2–1 series win. Shoulder injury ruled out 1989/90 season. Lynchpin of England's 1991 Grand Slam success. Scored one of England XV's two tries in 18–16 defeat of centenary Barbarians at Twickenham (29.9.90). Voted 1990/91 Whitbread/Rug by World Player of Year. Toured Fiji/Australia (1991) and played in three World Cup Pool games before Mike Teague took over at No 8 for knock-out stages. Returned in 1992 Five Nations' Championship, helping England to second Grand Slam. Scored try in England A's 66–5 defeat of Spain at Richmond on 5 March 1993
Touchlines: Squash, five-a-side soccer

England (1986)		
Last Season	1 cap	0 pts
Career	34 caps	24 pts
Lions 1989	3 Tests	0 pts
1993	3 Tests	0 pts

Caps (34): **1986** I, F **1987** S wc–A, J, US, W **1988** F, W, S, I(1), A(a1,a2), Fj, A(b) **1989** S, I, F, W, Ro. Lions–A(1,2,3) **1990** Arg It, US **1991** W, S, I, F, F j, A(a) wc–NZ, It, US **1992** S(R), F, W, C. Lions–NZ(1,2,3)

Points (24 – 6t): **1986** I(2t) **1987** wc–J(1t) **1988** A(a2:1t) **1989** I(1t), Ro(1t)

Richter, A.   South Africa

Full Name: Adriaan Richter
Club: Harlequins (Pretoria)
Province: Northern Transvaal
Position: No 8
Height: 6ft 5in (1.96m)
Weight: 15st 6lb (98kg)
Occupation: Accountant
Born: Roodepoort, 10.5.66
Former Province: Transvaal
International debut: France 15,
South Africa 20, 1992
**Notable landmarks in rugby
career:** Started the Springboks' tour
to France and England as a flanker,
had a game at lock, and finished up
as No 8 in the Test against England.
During the course of the trip he
developed into a first-choice player,
deposing Transvaal's Ian
Macdonald as breakaway wing-
forward in the two internationals
against France – the 20–15 win in
Lyon on 17 October and the 16–29
loss in Paris' Parc des Princes the
following weekend. His other tour
appearances came against Aquitaine

South Africa (1992)

Last Season	3 caps	0 pts
Career	3 caps	0 pts

Caps (3): 1992 F(1,2), E

Points Nil

(won 29–22, Pau, 7.10.92), Midi-Pyrenees (won 18–15, Toulouse, 15.10.92),
French Universities (lost 13–18, Tours, 28.10.92) the French Barbarians (lost
20–25, Lille, 31.10.92), the Midlands Division (won 32–9, Leicester, 4.11.92)
and England B (scored try in 20–16 win, Bristol, 7.11.92). Although he missed
out on selection for the two home Tests against New Zealand and Australia in
August, he did captain Northern Transvaal against the All Blacks (lost 17–24)
at Loftus Versfeld, Pretoria on 14 August. Four years earlier (1988) he had
made his provincial debut for rivals Transvaal, with whom he played 27 times,
before switching to the Blue Bulls, for whom he has thus far made 21
appearances

Rigney, B. J. Ireland

Full Name: Brian Joseph Rigney
Club: Greystones
Position: Lock
Height: 6ft 4in (1.93m)
Weight: 17st 8lb (112kg)
Occupation: Brewers representative
Born: Portlaoise, 22.9.63
Family: Single
Family links with rugby: Four
brothers play for Portlaoise
Former clubs: Portlaoise,
Highfield, Bective Rangers
International debut: Ireland 13,
France 21, 1991
Five Nations' debut: As above
Best moment in rugby: Winning
first senior cap against French
Worst moment in rugby: Being
sent-off after 14 minutes playing for
Ireland B against Scotland B in
Belfast (22.12.90) for throwing a
silly punch; knee ligament injury
sustained in Namibia '91
Most embarrassing moment:
Belfast dismissal
Most respected opponent: Donal
Lenihan (Cork Constitution & ex-
Ireland) – tremendous dedication and application

Ireland (1991)

Last Season	2 caps	0 pts
Career	8 caps	0 pts

Caps (8): **1991** F, W, E, S, Na(1) **1992** F, NZ(1R,2)

Points Nil

Serious injuries: Broken ankle (missed 1987 Munster Cup final as a result);
torn knee ligaments (1991)
Other sporting achievements: Won honours for Gaelic football and hurling
with Portlaoise. Various swimming achievements as boy
Best memory last season: Returning to Ireland side against New Zealand
Suggestions to improve rugby: *Off-field* – Standardize northern and southern
hemisphere unions' attitudes towards amateurism. Reimburse employers for
time lost to rugby. Form a players committee at top level
Notable landmarks in rugby career: Severe knee-ligament injury during
1991 Namibia tour put him out of World Cup and three-quarters of 1992 Five
Nations' Championship. Returned for 12–44 loss to France, in Paris on 21
March '92, and then toured New Zealand, taking his cap-tally to eight with
appearances in both Tests. At Dunedin in the first match (30.5.92) he came on
as a half-time replacement for Wanderers' Kelvin Leahy as Ireland narrowly
lost 24–21. The following weekend in Wellington he played from the start as

Ireland went down 6–59. Brian did not begin playing rugby until the age of 19, preferring Gaelic and hurling. Joined Bective Rangers before settling down with Greystones. Capped in third season by Leinster. Picked for Ireland XV against Wales and the United States Eagles during 1989 North American tour. Although no caps were awarded by the Irish both opponents received caps. Made Ireland B debut in 22–22 draw with Scotland (1989/90) and won second cap in ill-fated match against same opponents the following season when he was dismissed. Called into Ireland's 1991 Five Nations' squad and played full campaign

Robinson, B. F.   Ireland

Full Name: Brian Francis Robinson
Club: London Irish
Position: No 8
Height: 6ft 4in (1.94m)
Weight: 15st (95kg)
Occupation: PE teacher
Born: Belfast, 20.3.66
Family: Single
Former club: Ballymena
International debut: Ireland 13, France 21, 1991
Five Nations' debut: As above
Best moment in rugby: Breaking Irish single-match try-scoring record with four against Zimbabwe in 1991 World Cup
Worst moment in rugby: Tearing cruciate and medial ligaments in first match after touring Zimbabwe with Ulster (1986/87) and missing next 18 months
Most respected opponent: Zinzan Brooke (Auckland & New Zealand)
Serious injuries: As above
Best memory last season: Scoring try against Wales
Suggestions to improve rugby:

Ireland (1991)

Last Season	5 caps	5 pts
Career	18 caps	25 pts

Caps (18): 1991 F, W, E, S, Na(1,2) wc–Z, S, A 1992 W, E, S, F, NZ(1,2), A 1993 W, E

Points (25 – 6t): 1991 S(1t) wc–Z(4t) 1993 W(1t)

On-field – Pleased to see more points awarded for tries. *Off-field* – Relax amateur rules to allow players to earn money away from rugby. Reimburse employers for time lost
Notable landmarks in rugby career: Holds world record for most tries scored by a forward in a single International with the four he bagged against

Zimbabwe in the 55–11 World Cup defeat of Zimbabwe, at Lansdowne Road on 6 October 1991. It also represented a record for any Irish player, surpassing the hat-tricks claimed by half a dozen names including Keith Crossan (v Romania, 1986) and Brendan Mullin (v Tonga, 1987). Switched clubs in 1992/93 season from Ballymena to London Irish but his injury problems followed him across the Irish Sea and, having played both Tests in New Zealand over the summer and against Australia (31.10.92), he then missed the Five Nations' losses to Scotland and France. Made an immediate impact on his return, however, bagging Ireland's try in the 19–14 win at Cardiff (6.3.93) and also figuring in the famous 17–3 defeat of England (Dublin, 20.3.93). Brian played for Combined Irish Provinces as a 20-year old, the Irish Wolfhounds seven in Sicily (1989/90), for Ireland U-25s against US Eagles (1989/90) and for Ulster against 1989 All Blacks. He made his Ireland B debut in 22–22 draw with Scotland B (1989/90) and in the 16–0 Ravenhill return the following season (22.12.90). Scored his first international try in 25–28 loss to Scotland at Murrayfield (16.3.91)

Touchlines: Sub-aqua diving, keep-fit

Rodgers, P. H. South Africa

Full Name: Pieter Heinrich Rodgers
Club: Germiston–Simmer
Province: Transvaal
Position: Prop
Height: 6ft (1.82m)
Weight: 16st 7lb (105kg)
Occupation: Import/export businessman
Born: Harrismith, 23.6.62
Former Province: Northern Transvaal
International debut: South Africa 20, World XV 19, 1989
Notable landmarks in rugby career: One of seven over-30s selected to carry the South African banner back into international rugby when New Zealand visited the Republic on 15 August 1992, his

day was marred by a 51st minute injury which forced him out of the fray, to be replaced by Johann Styger. His Orange Free State rival never relinquished the No 1 jersey thereafter – playing in each of the four remaining international assignments – but instead of moping, Heinrich returned to full fitness and booked himself into the tighthead berth for the two Tests against France – the 20–15 win in Lyon on 17 October and the 16–29 reversal in Paris on the 24th. His other outings on the European tour came against France B (lost 17–24, Bordeaux, 4.10.92), Aquitaine (a replacement in the 29–22 win, Pau, 7.10.92), Midi-Pyrenees (won 18–15, Toulouse, 15.10.92), Provence–Cote d'Azur (won 41–12, Marseille, 13.10.92), the English Midlands Division (won 32–9, Leicester, 4.11.92) and the Northern Division (won 19–3, Leeds, 10.11.92). He was honoured with the captaincy against Provence–Cote d'Azur and the North. Formerly with Northern Transvaal, for whom he made his bow in 1984 and played 94 times, Heinrich played in the two Tests against the World XV in 1989 before moving to Transvaal, with whom he appeared in the 1992 Currie Cup final, alongside former Scotland B hooker Harry Roberts. Natal triumphed 14–13 in the final, at Ellis Park on 12 September

South Africa (1989)

Last Season	3 caps	0 pts
Career	5 caps	0 pts

Caps (5): **1989** Wd(1,2) **1992** NZ, F(1,2)

Points Nil

Roebuck, M. C.   Australia

Full Name: Martin (Marty) Clive Roebuck
Club: Eastwood
State: New South Wales
Position: Fullback, five-eighth, centre
Height: 5ft 10in (1.77m)
Weight: 12st 8lb (80kg)
Occupation: Marketing executive with Linfox Distribution Group
Born: 10.1.65
Family: Su (wife), Kiah (daughter), Mary (mother), Pat (father), Louise (sister), Anne (sister), Mike (brother), Tim (brother)
Former clubs: None. Eastwood since 1983

International debut: Australia 63, Wales 6, 1991
Best moment in rugby: Winning 1991 World Cup
Worst moment in rugby: Any loss to New Zealand
Most embarrassing moment: Being told my haircut has 'given inspiration to

people with bad haircuts all over the world!'

Most respected opponents: John Kirwan/Grant Fox (both Auckland & New Zealand)

Serious injuries: Ankle reconstructions (right–1990, left–1991), fractured left ankle (1993)

Other sporting achievements: Once sat through half an hour of motor racing

Best memory last season: Winning 1992 Bledisloe Cup and beating Wales

Australia (1991)

Last Season	7 caps	25 pts
Career	17 caps	41 pts

Caps (17): **1991** – W(a), E(a),NZ(a1,a2). wc-Arg,WS,W(b), I, NZ(b), E(b) **1992** – S(1,2), NZ(2,3), SA, I, W

Points (41 – 4t,5c,5p): **1991** W(a:1t), E(a:1t). wc–W(b:2t) **1992** I(4c,3p), W(1c,2p)

Suggestions to improve rugby: *On-field* – Award 'mark' for any catch – in the air or not – to discourage over-kicking. Limit line-out to five. *Off-field* – Remove 'men only' culture when organizing social/official functions. Give more thought to providing for player compensation for tours and time off work generally

Notable landmarks in rugby career: Dodgy ankles have restricted his representative career (missing virtually all of 1990) but since his debut against the hapless Welsh tourists in 1991, when opened his scoring account with a try, he has been ranked among the world's very best fullbacks. He toured Canada and France in 1989, appearing four times for the Wallabies in provincial games. Having won New South Wales' player of the year award in 1991 he embarked on a splendid 1992 campaign. Injury robbed him of a place in the first Test defeat of New Zealand in Sydney but he returned for the second and third legs of what turned out to be a triumphant Bledisloe Cup series. In South Africa he kicked 16 points (2c,4p) as Western Transvaal were routed 46–13 and also played in the historic Test with the Republic, before turning his attentions towards Great Britain. In addition to the two Test wins, in which he scored 25 points – 17 (4c,3p) against Ireland and eight (1c,2p) against Wales – he also kept the scoreboard ticking over at the expense of Leinster (13 points: 2c,3p), Ulster (10: 5c), Wales B (14: 1c,4p), Monmouthshire (14:1c,4p) and the Barbarians (15: 3c,3p). Only Llanelli denied him

Tours: 1989 – France and Canada. 1991 – New Zealand, World Cup. 1992 – South Africa, Ireland and Wales

Touchlines: Playing with Kiah

Player to watch: Matt Burke/Graeme Thompson (both NSW)

Player of the Year: Willie Ofahengaue (Australia)

Roumat, O.   France

Full Name: Olivier Roumat
Club: Dax
Position: Lock
Height: 6ft 6in (1.98m)
Weight: 17st 5lb (111kg)
Occupation: Surveyor
Born: Mont-de-Marsan, 16.6.66
Family links with rugby: Father played in Mont-de-Marsan back row
International debut: New Zealand 34, France 20, 1989
Five Nations' debut: Wales 19, France 29, 1990
Notable landmarks in rugby career: Became the first French forward to score a five-point try when touching down against South Africa in Paris on 24 October 1992. It helped France salvage a share of the series and cemented Olivier's place for the triumphant 1993 Five Nations' campaign. His 1992 summer had been spoiled by the dismissal he incurred playing against New Zealand for a World XV at Athletic Park, Wellington. It was the second Test and the Dax surveyor lasted only nine minutes before Kiwi referee David Bishop dismissed him for illegal use of the shoe. He was banned for four weeks and did not

France (1989)

Last Season	9 caps	5 pts
Career	36 caps	13 pts

Caps (36): **1989** NZ(2R), BL **1990** W, E, S, I, Ro, A(1,2,3), NZ(1,2) **1991** S, I, W, E, Ro, US(1), W wc-Ro, Fj, C, E **1992** W(R), E(R), S, I, SA(1,2), Arg(b)**1993** E, S, I, W, SA(1,2)

Points (13 – 3t): **1991** W(1t) wc–Ro(1t) **1992** SA(2:1t)

tour to Argentina with the French side. However, he did play in the return match at Nantes, when Argentina (14.11.92) won on French soil for the first time, and was one of the few players not to be dropped as a result. Partnered Agen's Abdel Benazzi in the second row throughout 1993 Championship campaign. That was in marked contrast to the previous season when, despite being France's only genuine quality lineout jumper, he lost out to Begles' Christophe Mougeot in the selection stakes for the 1992 Tournoi des Cinq Nations. It did not cost him a cap, though, as Mougeot failed to last the course against Wales and England and Olivier was sent into the fray in the 40th and 64th minutes respectively. Thereafter, he started the games against Scotland and Ireland. Formerly a flanker, his position against the British Lions XV who helped celebrate the bicentenary of the French Revolution in 1989, he built himself an impressive reputation in the 1988 Student World Cup and helped France B beat Wales B 28–15 in La Teste (12.11.89), four months after replacing Marc Cecillon against New Zealand in Auckland for his first cap. Captained France to 1993 series win in South Africa

Russell, P. Ireland

Full Name: Peter Russell
Club: Instonians
Position: Outside-half
Height: 5ft 9in (1.75m)
Weight: 12st (76kg)
Occupation: Bank official with Northern Bank Ltd
Born: Belfast, 22.2.62
Family: Married
Family links with rugby: Father captained Instonians in 1950s
International debut: England 23, Ireland 0, 1990
Five Nations' debut: As above
Best moment in rugby: Winning first full cap at Twickenham
Worst moment in rugby: Being left out after above game
Other sporting achievements: Tennis for Ulster Schools. Cricket for Instonians
Best memory last season: Returning to Ireland side two years after winning first cap
Notable landmarks in rugby career: Looked destined to go down in history as a one-cap wonder when

Ireland (1990)

Last Season	3 caps	23 pts
Career	4 caps	23 pts

Caps (4): 1990 E **1992** NZ(1,2), A

Points (23 – 4c,5p): **1992** NZ(1:3c,1p), NZ(2:1c), A(4p)

dropped after debut against England, at Twickenham on 20 January 1990. But Peter returned to the senior squad for the 1992 tour to New Zealand, succeeding Ralph Keyes and fellow Ulsterman Derek McAleese, and appeared in four games, including both Test matches. His 38-point tally included 11 in the Internationals. First time up, against the All Blacks in Dunedin on 30 May, he landed a penalty goal and converted Ireland's three tries (scored by Vince Cunningham 2 and Jim Staples) as New Zealand were given the fright of their lives by the supposed no-hopers before edging the contest 24–21. The following week, although he again converted all Ireland's tries, it was a different matter. The Irish only scored one (through wing Neville Furlong), while the men in black ran-up a record 59 points. Retained his place on return home, kicking four penalty goals in the 17–42 loss to Australia (Dublin, 31.10.92), but was replaced for the start of the 1993 Five Nations' Championship by Oxford University's Niall Malone. Peter first came to light playing for Ulster Schools. He won two Irish Schools caps against England and Wales (1979/80) and toured with them to Australia, playing four games. Represented Ulster U-20s and won first full provincial cap in 1986 against an International XV. Toured Zimbabwe with Ulster (1987), playing in three games. Broke into Ireland team in Jan 1990, having scored 12 points for Ireland B in 22–22 draw with Scotland, but after England game was consigned to bench for game in France

---

Ryan, D.   England

Full Name: Dean Ryan
Club: Wasps
Position: Flanker, No 8
Height: 6ft 6in (1.98m)
Weight: 16st 13lb (107kg)
Occupation: Manager with DHL, the couriers
Born: Tuxford, 22.6.66
Family: Wendy (wife)
Former club: Saracens
International debut: Argentina 12, England 25, 1990
Five Nations' debut: None
Best moment in rugby: London 21, Australia 10, 1988
Worst moment in rugby: Fractured arm for second time in 1989 v Cardiff
Most embarrassing moment: Trying to stop Australian wing David Campese
Most respected opponent: Dean Richards (Leicester, England & Lions)
Serious injuries: Fractured left arm (twice)

England (1990)		
Last Season	1 caps	0 pts
Career	3 caps	4 pts

Caps (3): **1990** Arg(a1,a2) **1992** C

Points (4 – 1t): **1990** Arg(a1:1t)

Best memory last season: Winning third cap against Canada
Suggestions to improve rugby: *Off-field* – Relax amateur laws
Landmarks in rugby career: It is not many footballers who get the opportunity to experience the 'Wembley roar' as they run out onto the hallowed turf in front of a partisan England crowd. Even fewer rugby men get the opportunity

so Dean was indeed honoured to do so on 17 September 1992 when England played Canada at Wembley Stadium (because Twickenham was under reconstruction). Wearing the No 6 jersey he helped the home side to a 26–13 win yet did not appear subsequently as Moseley's Mike Teague returned. Wasps' 1992/93 club captain made his England B debut in 9–37 loss to 1988 touring Wallabies and, despite having to withdraw through injury from the 1989 B game against France, he returned to make four appearances in 1990/91 season (v Emerging Australians, Spain, Ireland and France), scoring try in 50–6 win over Spain. Missed Wasps' crowning glory in 1989/90, having left for New Zealand when the London club clinched English League title on final day of season against Saracens. Toured Argentina with England in 1990, picking up two full caps and scoring try on his Test debut in Buenos Aires (28.7.90). A previous tourist with London in Australia, Dean was unavailable for England B's trip to New Zealand in 1992, but did go to Canada with England A last summer
Touchlines: Squash

Sadourny, J.-L. France

Full Name: Jean-Luc Sadourny
Club: Colomiers
Position: Wing, fullback
Height: 6ft 1in (1.86m)
Weight: 13st 9lb (86.5kg)
Occupation: Sales representative
Born: Toulouse, 26.8.66
International debut: Wales 9, France 22, 1991
Five Nations' debut: France 13, England 31, 1992
Notable landmarks in rugby career: One of four fullbacks employed by France during 1992/93 season, he deposed Stephane Ougier on the 1992 summer tour of Argentina, after coming on as a 42nd minute replacement for the Toulouse played in the 27–12 first Test win in Buenos Aires (4.7.92). Retained his place for second Test the following week and took his captally to nine with appearances in both legs of the drawn series with South Africa back home in October. However, Sebastien Viars was then

France (1991)		
Last Season	7 caps	0 pts
Career	12 caps	4 pts

Caps (12): **1991** W(R) wc–C(R) **1992** E(R), S, I, Arg(a1R,a2), SA(1,2) **1993** R,SA(1,2)

Points (4 – 1t): **1992** I(1t)

selected to wear the No 15 jersey against Argentina in Nantes and Jean-Baptiste Lafond took over after that humiliating loss. Being dropped was not the first knock-out blow Jean-Luc had suffered in his Test career. For he suffered concussion in the 10–6 win over England B at Bristol in 1991, having previously marked his B debut with a try in the 31–10 win over Scotland at Hughenden. Lightning struck twice for the unfortunate player as he lasted just nine minutes on his Five Nations' debut against England in Paris (15.2.92). Having replaced injured captain Philippe Sella in the 55th minute he was then involved in a head-on collision with outside-half Alain Penaud attempting a scissors movement and was led groggily from the arena. His first cap (following the 1991 US tour during which he scored two tries against USA B) came as a 76th minute replacement for Serge Blanco in the floodlit international against Wales at the Arms Park (4.9.91) and it was yet again as a replacement, this time against Canada in the vital World Cup Pool game, that he made his second appearance, given 30 minutes after Sella retired from the fray. It was a novelty for Jean-Luc to start the following game at Murrayfield and then in Paris where he scored a try in the 44–12 win over Ireland

Saint-André, P.   France

Full Name: Philippe Saint-André
Club: Montferrand
Position: Wing
Height: 5ft 11in (1.80m)
Weight: 13st 6lb (85kg)
Occupation: Self-employed sponsorship agent
Born: Romans, 19.4.67
Former clubs: Romans, Clermont-Ferrand
International debut: France 6, Romania 12, 1990
Five Nations' debut: Ireland 13, France 21, 1991
Notable landmarks in rugby career: Philippe has become one of Europe's most potent finishers with 13 Test tries in the past two years and if for nothing else he will forever be remembered for the try he scored against England in the 1991 Grand Slam decider at Twickenham on 16 January 1991. The move was initiated by Serge Blanco and fed, via Jean-Baptiste Lafond, Didier Camberabero, Philippe Sella and then Camberabero's boot behind enemy lines where the Philippe, who has clocked 10.9s over 100m,

scorched through to apply the coup de grace. His dozen touchdowns have come in the 22-game period bridging the 1991 and 1993 Five Nations' Championship campaigns. Wales, though they declined last season, have otherwise donated a try-per-game to Philippe's collection. Last season it was England (two) and Ireland who were the generous benefactors as France won the inaugural Five Nations' Cup. He also toured to Argentina with the French side, crossing in the 33–9 second Test win in Buenos Aires (11.7.92), and turned out on both occasions against South Africa (in Lyon and Paris). A prolific try-scorer in French club rugby for Montferrand, he also represented France A and B before stepping into the top flight at Stade Patrice Brocas, Auch (24.5.90) as a centre for the visit of Romania, who triumphed (12–6) on French soil for the first time

France (1990)		
Last Season	12 caps	29 pts
Career	30 caps	57 pts

Caps (30): **1990** Ro, A(3), NZ(1,2) **1991** I(R), W, E, US(1,2), W wc–Ro, Fj, C, E **1992** W, E, S, I, R, Arg(a1,a2), SA(1,2) **1993** E, S, I, W, R, SA(1,2)

Points (57 – 13t): **1991** W(1t), E(1t), US(1:1t), W(1t) wc–Ro(1t), C(1t) **1992** W(1t), R(1t), Arg(a2:1t) **1993** E(2t), I(1t), SA(1:1t)

Schmidt, U. L.   South Africa

Full Name: Uli Schmidt
Province: Northern Transvaal
Position: Hooker
Height: 5ft 11in (1.81m)
Weight: 14st 8lb (92kg)
Occupation: Doctor
Age: 32 years
International debut: South Africa 21, NZ Cavaliers 15, 1986
Notable landmarks in rugby career: One of South Africa's really classy players, he did not not tour France or England in 1992 which was a great shame given the fact that his age may prevent him from doing so too much in the future. According to John Allan, the Edinburgh Academicals and Scotland hooker now reinstalled in the Republic, Uli has been the world's best hooker for

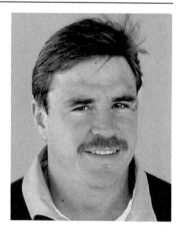

a considerable time. That was why the Springboks asked him to perform the honours for them when they returned to the international fold against the touring All Blacks following 11 years of isolation. He packed down between Heinrich Rodgers and Lood Muller at Ellis Park, Johannesburg, on 15 August but unhappily for them, New Zealand won 27–24. A week later, inside Cape Town's Newlands stadium, he was unable to prevent the

South Africa (1986)		
Last Season	4 caps	5 pts
Career	10 caps	9 pts

Caps (10): **1986** Cv(1,2,3,4) **1989** Wd(1,2) **1992** NZ,A **1993** F(1,2)

Points (9 – 2t): **1986** Cv(3:1t) **1993** F(1:1t)

Wallabies running riot and inflicting a world record defeat on South Africa. That was Uli's eighth cap although his first six were won against controversial opposition. He was an ever-present through the four-Test series against the rebel New Zealand Cavaliers in 1986, scoring a try in the 33–18 third Test victory in Pretoria (24.5.86) as the springboks headed towards a 3–1 series win. Three years later, when the First National Bank XV toured as part of the SARB's centenary celebrations, he played in each of the Republic's two wins: (1) won 20–19, Cape Town, 26.8.89; (2) won 22–16, Johannesburg, 1.9.89

Scott, M. W.   Scotland

Full Name: Martin William Scott
Club: Edinburgh Academicals
Position: Hooker
Height: 6ft (1.83m)
Weight: 15st 7lb (98kg)
Occupation: Civil servant
Born: Falkirk, 5.7.66
Family: Karen (wife), Robyn (daughter) and Ashley (daughter)
Former clubs: Rosyth and District, Dunfermline
International debut: Australia 37, Scotland 13, 1992
Five Nations' debut: None
Best moments in rugby: Making Test debut at Brisbane (1992). Scoring try for Edinburgh Borderers against Scotland XV at Murrayfield (1990/91)

Worst moment in rugby: Tearing ankle ligaments against Watsonians in 1990
Most respected opponent: Kenny Milne (Heriot's FP & Scotland)
Biggest influence on career: Ian McNeill (Dunfermline fitness coach)

341

Serious injuries: Torn ankle ligaments

Best memory last season: Winning first cap in Brisbane (21.6.92)

Suggestions to improve rugby: *On-field* – Sceptical about new maul law. *Off-field* – Sort out trust funds, especially for self-employed players who really stand to lose out from increased commitments to rugby

Scotland (1992)

Last Season	1 cap	0 pts
1993	Tour to South Seas	
Career	1 cap	0 pts

Caps (1): 1992 A(2)

Points Nil

Notable landmarks in rugby career: One of the few North & Midlands players to be recognised at international level, Martin was selected to tour Australia in 1992 as a result of the decision taken by Edinburgh Academicals' John Allan to return to South Africa permanently. A member of Dunfermline at the time, He was the third hooker in the tour party but still earned a cap. First-choice Kenny Milne was injured early in the first Test in Sydney (13.6.92) and Gala's Ian Corcoran deputised. But the following week at Ballymore the selectors opted to go with Martin who played the full 80 minutes in a 13–37 loss to the world champions. No such highlights on hi s return from Down Under, despite switching club allegiances to Edinburgh Accies. His one international outing came for Scotland A in their 19–29 defeat by France A, in Aberdeen on 20 March 1993. Martin, who took up rugby at the age of 15, and turned out at lock f or North and Midlands Under-21s had previously represented Scotland Under-21s, in 19–39 loss to Wales (Wrexham, 1987) and Scotland B against Ireland B (lost 19–29, Edinburgh 28.12.91) and France B (lost 18–27, Albi 3.2.92)

Touchlines: Golf, football

Springbok outside-half Naas Botha exhibits his very best form against England at Twickenham. Opposite number Rob Andrew can only watch and admire

Scott-Young, S.   Australia

Full Name: Samuel (Sam) Joseph
Norman Scott-Young
Club: Southern Districts
State: Queensland
Position: No 8, flanker
Height: 6ft 3½in (1.92m)
Weight: 16st 3lb (103kg)
Occupation: Consultant with
Sports Marketing and Management
Born: 7.4.67
Family: Donna (wife), Devil
(German Shepherd), Ely (German
Shepherd)
International debut: France 31,
Australia 48, 1990
Best moment in rugby: Winning
1992 Bledisloe Cup
Worst moment in rugby: Being
knocked-out in third Test v All
Blacks (1992). Losing to Toulouse
in 1990 World Provincial
Championship
Most embarrassing moment:
Putting in a chip in the Australia-
North Harbour game and the ball
coming off the side of my boot
straight to Walter little who ran it
back 60 metres

Australia (1990)		
Last Season	3 caps	0 pts
Career	7 caps	0 pts

Caps (7): **1990** F(2,3R), US, NZ(3)
           1992 NZ(1,2,3)

Points Nil

Most respected opponent: Mike Teague (England)
Serious injuries: Broken collarbone, thumb, ribs, arm, toe, nose. Torn medial
knee ligaments (left and right)
Best memory last season: Beating the All Blacks twice; winning club grand
final
Suggestions to improve rugby: *On-field* – Take the game to the people
Notable landmarks in rugby career: Broke into the Wallaby side in 1990 on
the tour of Canada and France. Selected in place of the injured Jeff Miller for
the extraordinary second Test with France which ended in a 48–31 victory.
Came on as a replacement in the third Test and, by the time he had helped
Australia win the dead rubber against the Bledisloe Cup-winning All Blacks
later that year, his tally of caps had reached five. Missed out on selection for the
1991 World Cup but returned in 1992 playing a full part (at No 8) as Australia
gained their Bledisloe Cup revenge on New Zealand. Although he toured to
both South Africa and Britain – playing against Northern Transvaal, Eastern

Province (as lock), Munster, Connacht, Swansea, Neath, Monmouthshire, Welsh Students and the Barbarians – he was considered surplus to Test match requirements as Tim Gavin had recovered from the badly bruised thigh that had sidelined him during the All Black series

Tours: 1989 – Canada and France. 1990 – New Zealand. 1991 – New Zealand. 1992 – South Africa, Ireland and Wales
Touchlines: Enjoying my wife's company
Player to watch: Barry Lea (Souths)
Player of the Year: Ieuan Evans (Wales)

Seigne, L. France

Full Name: Laurent Seigne
Club: Merignac
Position: Prop
Height: 5ft 10in (1.78m)
Weight: 16st 9lb (106kg)
Occupation: Commercial officer
Born: Tulle, 12.8.60
International debut: France 27, British Lions 29, 1989
Five Nations' debut: England 16, France 15, 1993
Notable landmarks in rugby career: Laurent was an ever-present in the French front row during the 1993 Five Nations' Championship – in marked contrast to the rest of his Test career which has been a stop-start affair. Selected for his debut four years earlier against the British Lions XV in the Parc des Princes on 4 October 1989 in a match staged to celebrate the bicentenary of the French Revolution, he packed down in an eight which included Olivier Roumat, Philippe Benetton, Thierry Devergie and the outstanding Laurent Rodriguez. But the Lions, sorry the Home Unions XV, had the last roar, winning a thriller 29–27. Laurent retained his place for the next International, the first Test against Australia in Strasbourg (4.11.89), but when France lost a match they were red-hot favourites to win (15–32), heads rolled, among them his. Still, he returned in Nantes the following season when New Zealand were the visitors for the first

France (1989)		
Last Season	5 caps	0 pts
Career	8 caps	0 pts

Caps (8): **1989** BL, A(1) **1990** NZ(1) **1993** E, S, I, W, R

Points Nil

of two Tests (3.11.90). A match for which the French front row allegedly prepared by head-butting each other, ended in 3–24 defeat and Laurent was again sent packing. This time it was two and a half years before he re-emerged but when he did – called into the squad as a replacement for calf injury-victim Philippe Gallart – he hung around long enough to share in France's Championship triumph, for which they received the inaugural Five Nations' Cup, and to share in 37–20 win over Romania in Bucharest

Sella, P.   France

Full Name: Philippe Sella
Club: Agen
Position: Centre
Height: 5ft 11in (1.80m)
Weight: 13st 4lb (84kg)
Occupation: Businessman
Born: Clairac, 14.2.62
International debut: Romania 13, France 9, 1982
Five Nations' debut: England 15, France 19, 1983
Notable landmarks in rugby career: Appointed French captain when Pierre Berbizier retired to become national coach (first match in charge was against Wales, 1.2.92) but lost honour when dropped for Romania's visit to Le Havre (28.5.92) and subsequently for '92 tour to Argentina. However, reclaimed midfield berth on 14 November for disastrous return against Pumas in Nantes. His only consolation in a game which saw Argentina secure their first ever win on French soil was his 26th Test try. The 27th and most recent came in the 21–6 win over Ireland in Dublin (20.2.93) as France completed the third leg of their 1993 Championship win. Philippe is the world's most-capped centre three-quarter. Indeed, only Serge Blanco's 93-cap haul exceeds his own tally of 91 (including six caps at wing and one at fullback), amassed since his debut in the 1982 defeat by Romania. On his next appearance, in the first Test against Argentina, he scored the first two of his 27 international tries. He played 45 consecutive Tests until injury ruled him out of the 49–3 win over Romania, a match played on his own Agen pitch (11.11.87). It was but a temporary blip for a man who had also represented France at Schools, Juniors and Universities grade. In 1986 he scored a try in every Championship match, equalling a feat achieved only by compatriot Patrick Esteve (1983), Johnny Wallace (Scotland, 1925) and Carston Catcheside (England, 1924). That same year he was a lone

in playing all 12 French internationals and represented the Five Nations in a 13–32 defeat by the Overseas Unions in the IRB Centenary match at Twickenham (19.4.86). The next season he played a key role in France's run to the 1987 World Cup final. A torn thigh muscle accounted for his absence from the 1991 World Cup opener against Romania but, typically, he returned with two dazzling tries in the following match against Fiji. Moved to within two of Blanco's world record cap tally during summer of '93 with outings against Romania, in Bucharest, and South Africa (twice), in the Republic

France (1982)

Last Season	8 caps	10 pts
Career	91 caps	110 pts

Caps (91): **1982** Ro, Arg(1,2) **1983** E, S, I, W, A(1,2), Ro **1984** I, W, E, S, NZ(1,2), Ro **1985** E, S, I, W, Arg(1,2) **1986** S, I, W, E, Ro(a), Arg(1,2), A, N Z, Ro(b), NZ(1,2) **1987** W, E, S, I wc–S, Ro, Z(R), Fj, A, NZ **1988** E, S, I, W, Arg(a1,a2), Arg(b1,b2), Ro **1989** I, W, E, S, NZ(1,2), BL, A(1,2) **1990** W, E, S, I, A(1,2,3) **1991** W, E, Ro, US(1,2), W, Fj, C, E **1992** W, E, S, I, Arg(b) **1993** E, S, I, W, R, SA(1,2)

Points (110 – 27t): **1982** Arg(1:2t) **1983** E(1t) **1984** I(1t), W(1t), E(1t), Ro(1t) **1986** S(1t), I(1t), W(1t), E(1t), Ro(a:1t), Arg(2:1t), A(1t), NZ(1:1t) **1987** E(1t),wc–S(1t), Ro(1t), A(1t) **1988** I(1t), Arg(4:1t) **1990** W(1t) **1991** W(1t), Fj(2t) **1992** Arg(b:1t) **1993** I(1t)

Shiel, A. G. Scotland

Full Name: Andrew Graham Shiel
Club: Melrose
Position: Outside-half, centre
Height: 5ft 10lb (1.78m)
Weight: 12st 10lb (81kg)
Occupation: Stonemason with Historic Scotland (Melrose)
Born: Galashiels, 13.8.70
Family: Single
Family links with rugby: Father (Andrew) played for Melrose GS
Former club: Manly (Aus)
International debut: Scotland 24, Ireland 15, 1991
Five Nations' debut: Scotland 15, Ireland 3, 1993
Best moment in rugby: Scoring

winning try against Ireland on Scotland debut after coming on as 43rd minute replacement in 1991 World Cup match at Murrayfield

Worst moment in rugby: Not making the Scottish Schools XV to play New Zealand in 1988

Most embarrassing moment: Ball toppled over in front of posts before I kicked it during 1990 Hawick Sevens

Scotland (1991)		
Last Season	4 caps	0 pts
Career	6 caps	4 pts

Caps (6): 1991 wc–I(R),WS **1993** I,F,W,E

Points (4 – 1t): **1991** wc–I(R:1t)

Most respected opponent: Sean Lineen (Boroughmuir & Scotland)

Biggest influences on career: Ian McGeechan and Jim Telfer

Serious injuries: Straining inner and exterior quadriceps and adductor muscle (1988/89) and missing over four months rugby. Pelvic strain (Nov 1990) – three months out

Other sporting achievements: Athletics for Borders Schools and Borders AAA

Best memory last season: Winning McEwan's Championship for third time in four seasons with Melrose

Suggestions to improve rugby: *On-field* – Playing standards need to be improved at club level in Scotland – inferior to England and Wales. Still too forward orientated in Scotland (lack of running ability). *Off-field* – Treat players better for all they put into the game

Notable landmarks in rugby career: Missed Scotland's 1993 tour to the South Seas (after straining his left knee's anterior cruciate ligament in training) at the end of a season in which he had established himself as the successor to Sean Lineen alongside Scott Hastings in the Scottish midfield. He played in all four legs of the 1993 Five Nations' Championship after a Trial in which he started for the Possibles and finished with the Probables. Represented Scottish Schools three times, Scotland U-19s and U-21s (twice). Scored six points in 1989/90 defeat (10–24) by Wales Under-21 and played in 15–23 loss to same opposition (1990/91). Toured with Scotland to New Zealand (1990), North America and Canada (1991) and Australia (1992): made four appearances in New Zealand (Wellington, Nelson Bays/Marlborough, Southland and Manawatu) and five games out of six (including non-cap Tests against US Eagles and Canada) in North America. Represented European Saltires against South Pacific Barbarians in XVs prior to 1991 Hong Kong Sevens. Having been included in Scotland's 1991 World Cup squad, he was given debut against Ireland as a 43rd minute replacement for outside-half Craig Chalmers. A fairytale scenario saw him score a try as Scotland came from behind to win. Seven days later he won second cap (as centre) in quarter-final against Western Samoa when knee injury ruled out Lineen. Reverted to bench reserve thereafter. Remained in Australia after 1992 tour to spend summer playing with Manly. Played in Scotland A's 22–13 win over Ireland A (Dublin, 28.12.92)

Touchlines: Social golf, cricket, swimming

Slattery, P. J.   Australia

Full Name: Peter John Slattery
Club: Queensland University
State: Queensland
Position: Scrum-half
Height: 5ft 9in (1.76m)
Weight: 12st 4lb (78kg)
Occupation: Sales representative with Rugby Products of Australia
Born: 6.6.65
Family: Single
Former clubs: Wests (1983–86). Queensland Univ since 1987
International debut: Australia 67, USA 9, 1990
Best moment in rugby: Winning 1991 World Cup; beating Wales (1992)
Worst moment in rugby: Pre-season training
Most embarrassing moment: Driving to training in my car
Serious injuries: Broken arm (1987)
Best memory last season: Queensland winning Super Six
Suggestions to improve rugby: *On-field* – Ban kicking ball out on full inside your own 22
Notable landmarks in rugby

Australia (1990)		
Last Season	2 caps	0 pts
Career	8 caps	8 pts

Caps (8): **1990** US(R) **1991** W(aR), E(aR). wc–WS(R),W(b),I(R) **1992** I,W

Points (8 – 2t): **1990** US(1t) **1991** wc–W(b:1t)

career: Assigned the considerable task of filling the Wallaby No 9 jersey worn by Nick Farr-Jones, after the long-time skipper and inspiration hung up his boots having claimed the scalp of South Africa. He helped the Aussies beat Ireland and Wales, partnering Queensland outside-half colleagues Michael Lynagh and Paul Kahl in the process. Peter is an experienced player in his own right, having been a Test reserve on and off since 1985. He bagged a try on his international debut in 1990 after coming on as a replacement for Farr-Jones in the 67–9 defeat of the United States Eagles. The following year he replaced the injury-prone Farr-Jones on a further four occasions, twice during the Wallabies' triumphant World Cup campaign. In 1992 he captained Queensland to victory in the prestigious Super Six Championship and skippered the Aussies twice on tour in South Africa, against Western Transvaal and Eastern Province. When the tour moved on to Britain he figured in the matches with Leinster, Ulster, Swansea, Neath, Llanelli and the Barbarians

Tours: 1989 – France and Canada. 1990 – New Zealand. 1991 – New Zealand, World Cup. 1992 – South Africa, Ireland and Wales
Touchlines: Sleeping, eating and surfing

Small, J. T. South Africa

Full Name: James Terence Small
Club: Wits
Province: Transvaal
Position: Wing
Height: 6ft (1.82m)
Weight: 13st 3lb (84kg)
Occupation: Representative
Born: Cape Town, 10.2.69
Family links with rugby: None.
Son of former Springbok soccer
player Vernon Small
International debut: South Africa
24, New Zealand 27, 1992
**Notable landmarks in rugby
career:** A part-time male model who
certainly looks impressive when on
the attack, if not to such an extent in
defence. Formerly a superb soccer
player, which he inherited from his
father, James was included in the
first Springbok side selected after the
ending of the international boycott.
Not only did he play against New
Zealand but Australia also the
following week before turning out
for his province Transvaal in the
1992 Currie Cup final. Unhappily

South Africa (1992)

Last Season	7 caps	10 pts
Career	7 caps	10 pts

Caps (7): 1992 NZ, A, F(1,2), E **1993**
F(1,2)

Points (10 – 2t): 1992 F(1:1t) **1993**
F(2:1t)

for the player, victory went to Natal by the odd point in 27 (at Ellis Park,
Johannesburg on 12 September), but his smile was restored when he scored one
of South Africa's two tries in their 20–15 victory over France, in Lyon on 17
October. in addition to retaining his place for the next two Test engagements,
against France (lost 16–29, Paris, 24.10.92) and England (lost 16–33,
Twickenham, 14.11.92) he also turned out against Aquitaine (scoring a try in
29–22 win, Pau, 7.10.92), Midi-Pyrenees (won 18–15, Toulouse, 15.10.92),
French Barbarians (bagging try in 20–25 loss, Lille, 31.10.92), and England B
(won 20–16, Bristol, 7.11.92). A former South African Schools player, he had
made 59 appearances for Transvaal prior to embarking on the 1992 European
Tour

Smit, F. C.   South Africa

Full Name: Frederik Smit
Club: St Claude (Fra)
State: Western Province
Position: Flanker
Height: 6ft 7in (2.0m)
Weight: 17st 7lb (111kg)
Born: 13.8.66
International debut: England 33,
South Africa 16, 1992
**Notable landmarks in rugby
career:** Not originally selected to
tour France and England with the
Springboks but called up from his
base in France, where he plays for St
Claude, after injury put paid to
Botha Rossouw's trip. He was just in
time to play against the French
Barbarians in the last match before
the itinerary switched across the
English Channel and, though that
was not a happy occasion for neither
player nor team, with the Baa-baas
winning 25–20 in Lille (31.10.92),
happier days were just around the
corner. For Smit this meant 14
November when he made his Test

South Africa (1992)

Last season	1 cap	5 pts
Career	1 cap	5 pts

Caps (1): **1992** E

Points (5 – 1t): **1992** E(1t)

bow against England at No 8 and celebrated with the Springboks' solitary try
on the half-hour. Prior to his Twickenham date Frederik had come on as a 19th
minute replacement for Northern Transvaal lock Phillip Schutte in the 32–9
defeat of the Midlands Division, at Leicester on 4 November, and played
throughout the thrilling 20–16 win over England B at Bristol's Memorial
ground three days later. Prior to embarking for his European rugby, he had
come on as a replacement for Johannes Styger in the 20th minute of the Junior
Springboks' 10–25 loss to New Zealand at Pretoria's Loftus Versfeld stadium

Smith, I. R. Scotland

Full Name: Ian Richard Smith
Club: Gloucester
Position: Flanker
Height: 6ft (1.83m)
Weight: 14st (89kg)
Occupation: Civil engineering technician with Gloucestershire Design
Born: Gloucester, 16.3.65
Family: Karen (wife)
Family links with rugby: Father (Dick) was an England trialist who played for (and captained) Gloucester and Barbarians
Former club: Longlevens
International debut (England): Spanish Select 15, England B 32, 1989
International debut (Scotland): Scotland 7, England 25, 1992
Five Nations' debut: As above
Best moment in rugby: Running out at Murrayfield for first Scotland cap against England
Worst moment in rugby: Losing 1989/90 Pilkington Cup final 6–48 to Bath

Scotland (1992)

Last Season	2 caps	0 pts
1993	Tour to South Seas	
Career	5 caps	0 pts

Caps (5): **1992** E, I, W, A(1,2)

Points Nil

Most embarrassing moment: Above match – we were humiliated
Most respected opponent: Lyn Jones (Neath)
Biggest influences on career: Father and Derek Cook (coach at Longlevens)
Suggestions to improve rugby: *On-field* – More consistency in refereeing. Perhaps set up refereeing seminars where they can get together with players and coaches to work things out. *Off-field* – Reimburse employers for employee's time lost to rugby. It's not that we want to profit from rugby, it's that we, and our bosses, don't want to be out of pocket. Relax amateur laws
Notable landmarks in rugby career: Toured to Australia with Scotland in the summer of 1992 and appeared at openside in both Test defeats at Sydney and Brisbane. A former England 18-Group trialist, who played 200th game for Gloucester in the 1990 Pilkington Cup final, Ian spent the 1988 Australian season playing in Wollongong. Toured Spain with England B (1990) and was selected to England's 1991 World Cup squad, having spent 1990 off-season on standby for Argentina tour, but then decided to switch allegiances to Scotland (Scottish grandparents on father's side) and played twice for Scotland B in

1990/91 (v Ireland and France) before leading side in 19–29 home loss to Ireland in 1991/92, a season in which also captained Gloucester (as in 1992/93) and broke into Scotland team for Five Nations' Championship. He missed only the French visit to Murrayfield, due to a badly cut hand, but was absent throughout 1993 Championship, displaced by another Anglo-Scot, London Scottish's Iain Morrison. Ian, prior to losing place, had been tipped in some quarters as a successor to national captain David Sole; after all he did skipper Scotland against New South Wales (lost 15–35, Sydney, 6.6.92). But a place in the shadow Scotland XV which struggled to beat Italy at Melrose on 19 December 1992 was as near as he came to the national side in any capacity
Touchlines: Shooting, squash, trout fishing

Smith, S. J.   Ireland

Full Name: Stephen James Smith
Club: Ballymena
Position: Hooker
Height: 6ft 1in (1.86m)
Weight: 16st (102kg)
Occupation: Sports representative with Edge Sports (Ballymena)
Born: Belfast, 18.7.59
Family: Single
Family links with rugby: Brother (Oliver) plays for Ballymena
International debut: Ireland 10, England 21, 1988
Five Nations' debut: Ireland 21, France 26, 1989
Best moment in rugby: Selection for 1989 Lions
Worst moment in rugby: Losing to Australia in last seconds of 1991 World Cup quarter-final in Dublin
Most respected opponent: Sean Fitzpatrick (Auckland & New Zealand)
Biggest influence on career: Sid Millar (ex-Ballymena, Ireland & Lions)
Serious injuries: Damaged rib cartilage (1990)
Suggestions to improve rugby:
On-field – Welcome any laws which

Ireland (1988)		
Last Season	3 caps	0 pts
Career	25 caps	8 pts
Lions 1989		

Caps (25): **1988** E(b), WS, It **1989** F, W, E, S, NZ **1990** E **1991** F, W, E, S, Na(1,2) wc–Z, S, A **1992** W, E, S, F, NZ(1,2) **1993** S

Points (8 – 2t): **1988** E(b:1t) **1991** F(1t)

speed up game. However, success of new rules will depend on the referees' interpretations. *Off-field* – More professional approach away from field to match greater commitment being made by players. Pace of change is moving faster on pitch than off it

Notable landmarks in rugby career: The season 1992/93 was not a vintage for Steve by any means, as he lost his place after playing in both Tests on the summer tour of New Zealand. Greystones' John Murphy came in for the Australian Test (31.10.92) and although Steve regained the berth for the 1993 Five Nations' opener at Murrayfield (lost 3–16, 16.1.93), he promptly lost it again thereafter, this time to Dolphin's Terry Kingston. Steve had been called out to 1987 World Cup as Ireland's second replacement hooker but did not feature. Following season broke into Ireland team and became first Irishman to mark debut with a try since Hugo MacNeill in 1981. Represented Barbarians against 1988 Wallabies, 1989 Home Unions against France, and 1989 Lions in Australia, playing five games and scoring two tries. Toured South Africa with 1989 World XV and found experience awe-inspiring – 'a real eye-opener'. Helped Ballymena win 1989/90 Ulster League and Cup double for second consecutive season (first team to achieve feat since 1907). Although only bench reserve for Ireland B against Argentina in early 1990/91, was a regular for Ireland in ensuing Five Nations' Championship, scoring try in loss to France. Toured Namibia in summer of 1991 and played in all but the Japan World Cup-tie last in 1991/92 campaign

Touchlines: Golf (15-handicap)

Sole, D. M. B. Scotland

Full Name: David Michael Barclay Sole
Club: Edinburgh Academicals
Position: Prop
Height: 5ft 11in (1.81m)
Weight: 16st 4lb (103kg)
Occupation: Grain buyer for United Distillers
Born: Aylesbury, 8.5.62
Family: Jane (wife), Jamie (son) and Gemma (daughter)
Former clubs: Exeter University, Toronto Scottish, Bath
International debut: Scotland 18, France 17, 1986
Five Nations' debut: As above
Best moment in rugby: Captaining Scotland to 1990 Grand Slam

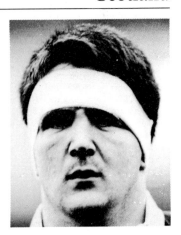

Worst moments in rugby: Coming so close to winning second Test against New Zealand (Auckland, 23.6.90) before losing 18–21

Most respected opponents: Iain Milne (Heriot's FP & Scotland) and Jean-Pierre Garuet (Lourdes & France) – two of the world's strongest scrummagers, who don't bend the rules, but use their immense strength to succeed

Biggest influence on career: Four years spent at Bath RFC

Serious injuries: Broken nose and cheekbone playing in Bath's 12–3 win against Moseley in 1987 John Player Cup quarter-final

Scotland (1986)		
Last Season	2 caps	4 pts
Career	44 caps	12 pts
Lions 1989	3 Tests	0 pts

Caps (44): **1986** F, W **1987** I, F, W, E wc–F, Z, Ro, NZ **1988** I, F, W, E, A **1989** W, E, I, F, Fj, Ro. Lions–A(1,2,3) **1990** I, F, W, E, NZ(1,2), Arg **1991** F, W, E, I, Ro wc–J, I, WS, E, NZ **1992** E, I, F, W, A(1,2)

Points (12 – 3t): **1989** Ro(1t) **1990** NZ(1:1t) **1992** A(2:1t)

Suggestions to improve rugby: *On-field* – Pleased to see more points awarded for a try. Hopefully that will have the effect of taking the emphasis off kicking. *Off-field* – The question of amateurism needs urgent attention. For a start where is the line drawn between rugby-related and non rugby-related activities? Surely there is no difference. Players' commitment to international rugby is becoming ever greater but at our own expense. Yet the set-up is totally different for the Southern Hemisphere nations. The IRB must make and enforce universal regulations.

Notable landmarks in rugby career: Won 1987 John Player Cup winners' medal with Bath (won 19–12 v Wasps, 2.5.87). Made Scotland debut as one of six newcomers against France (won 18–17, Murrayfield, 17.1.86). Appointed Scotland captain for Scotland 38, Fiji 17 (Murrayfield, 28.10.89) and went on to become Scotland's most capped leader with 25 games in charge (prior to his retirement after 1992 tour to Australia), including the 1990 Grand Slam decider when he memorably led Scotland slowly onto the field prior to beating England. Also captained Lions against New South Wales B (won 39–19, Dubbo 27.6.89) and the Anzacs (won 19–15, Queensland 23.7.89) during 1989 tour of Australia, Barbarians against 1989 All Blacks (lost 10–21, Twickenham 25.11.89) and Home Unions against Europe in aid of the Romanian Appeal (won 43–18, Twickenham 22.4.90). Recalls with great affection the £2 fine he imposed on anyone who kicked to touch during 1991 Barbarians' Easter Tour match at Cardiff

Stanger, A. G. Scotland

Full Name: Anthony George Stanger
Club: Hawick
Position: Wing
Height: 6ft 2in (1.88m)
Weight: 15st 2lb (96kg)
Occupation: Sales representative with Roxburgh Windows (Hawick)
Born: Hawick, 14.5.68
Family: Single
Family links with rugby: Peter (brother) plays for Hawick and Scotland U-18s
Former club: Warringah (Aus)
International debut: Scotland 38, Fiji 17, 1989
Five Nations' debut: Ireland 10, Scotland 13, 1990
Best moment in rugby: Scoring winning try in 1990 Grand Slam decider against England
Worst moment in rugby: Getting dropped by Hawick in 1986/87 as an 18-year old
Most respected opponents: Keith Crossan (Instonians & Ireland) and Patrice Lagisquet (Bayonne & France)
Biggest influence on career: Girlfriend Bid Butterfield
Other sporting achievements: Hawick High School athletics champion (three times)

Scotland (1989)		
Last Season	6 caps	5 pts
Career	30 caps	61 pts

Caps (30): **1989** Fj, Ro **1990** I, F, W, E, NZ(1,2), Arg **1991** F, W, E, I, Ro wc–J, Z, I, WS, E, NZ **1992** E, I, F, W, A(1,2) **1993** I, F, W, E

Points (61 – 15t): Fj(2t), Ro(3t) **1990** E(1t), NZ(2:1t), Arg(2t) **1991** I(1t) wc–J(1t), Z(1t), WS(1t) **1992** I(1t) **1993** I(1t)

Best memory last season: Enjoying playing rugby again. The past few seasons had been a bit of a struggle, a grind. The fun was not there
Suggestions to improve rugby: *On-field* – Reduce value of the penalty goal. Pleased that they did not change all the new rules again at the end of last season, as we were just becoming familiar with them. *Off-field* – Do not try to bring about too much change too quickly. The SRU are doing very well, but they must ensure that everyone is treated equally when it comes to peripheral benefits. Not much money in Scottish game
Notable landmarks in rugby career: Scored six tries in first six internationals (two on debut against Fiji, three against Romania and one against England in 1990 Grand Slam decider). Toured with Scotland to Japan (1989), New

355

Zealand (1990), North America (1991) and Australia (1992). Made debut for Hawick while 17-year-old student. Earned five caps for Scottish Schools at centre in 1985/86, followed by two for Scotland U-21s. Began 1990/91 season with two tries in 49–3 defeat of Argentina, taking try-tally to nine in as many games. Could not sustain that prolific pace through 1991/92 season's 11-game schedule but did not do badly. Ever-present (including playing in 16–16 draw with Barbarians at Murrayfield), he managed four tries: three in the World Cup tournament and one against Ireland in Championship for second consecutive season. Also turned out for Scotland A in 36–16 win over Spain (Murrayfield, 28.12.91). Made second A-team appearance last season in 22–13 win over Ireland (28.12.92), scoring two tries to book his Five Nations' place. Celebrated with great try in the Championship opener against Ireland to join Iwan Tukalo as Scotland's second top try scorer (15). Extended his unbroken run in the side to 30 Tests. Injury cost him a place in Scotland's World Cup seven.

Touchlines: Social golf

Staples, J. E. Ireland

Full Name: James (Jim) Edward Staples
Club: London Irish
Position: Fullback, wing
Height: 6ft 2in (1.88m)
Weight: 13st 9lb (86kg)
Occupation: Commercial property agent with Richard Ellis Chartered Surveyors
Born: London, 20.10.65
Family: Single
Family links with rugby: Younger brother (David) plays for Westcombe Park
Former clubs: St Mary's, Bromley, Sidcup
International debut: Wales 21, Ireland 21, 1991
Five Nations' debut: As above
Best moment in rugby: Making Ireland debut in Cardiff (1991)

Worst moments in rugby: Michael Lynagh's last-gasp try for Australia in our World Cup quarter-final. Missing out on promotion to English First Division with London Irish in 1988/89 after losing 22–21 to last-minute dropped goal by Blackheath, having led 21–0 at half-time

Most embarrassing moment: Missing flight home from Spain on first county senior trip

Most respected opponent: Gavin Hastings (Watsonians & Scotland) – strong, fast and always a threat

Biggest influence on career: John O'Driscoll (Connacht: got me involved in the provincial scene)/Roy White (schoolteacher: took me along to Sidcup where he was captain)

Ireland (1991)		
Last Season	3 caps	5 pts
Career	14 caps	21 pts
Caps	(14): **1991** W, E, S, Na(1,2) wc–Z, J, S, A **1992** W, E, NZ(1,2), A	
Points	(21 – 4t,2c): **1991** W(1t), Na(2:1t,2c) wc–J(1t) **1992** NZ(1:1t)	

Serious injuries: Prolapsed disc in back, broken nose

Other sporting achievements: Played in same forward line as Arsenal and England striker Ian Wright for Greenwich Borough

Suggestions to improve rugby: *On-field* – No kicks to be allowed into touch on full, even those taken inside own 22. By increasing try value I fear the ball just won't come out and there will be a lot more penalties conceded. *Off-field* – Act to compensate players from losing out in terms of career development

Notable landmarks in rugby career: Missed 1993 Five Nations' campaign due to knee injury sustained in the Trial, having been first-choice fullback before Christmas. He toured with Ireland to New Zealand over the summer of 1992, weighing in with one of the three tries which so nearly proved good enough to beat the All Blacks in the first Test at Dunedin on 30 May. Also played in second Test in Wellington and against Australia, at Lansdowne Road on 31 October. Took over from former Ireland fullback Hugo MacNeill at No 15 in London Irish team. Represented Connacht against 1989 All Blacks and Irish Wolfhounds in 1988/89 Hong Kong Sevens. Played twice for Ireland Under-25s before reaching B grade in 1989/90 with appearance in 22–22 draw with Scotland. Selected for senior bench against France in 1991 Five Nations' opener before playing in next three games, scoring try in 21–21 draw with Wales. Toured with Ireland to Namibia (1991) and New Zealand (1992)

Touchlines: Soccer, most other sports

Stark, D. K.   Scotland

Full Name: Derek Alexander Stark
Club: Boroughmuir
Position: Wing
Height: 6ft 2in (1.88m)
Weight: 13st 12lb (88kg)
Occupation: Chef in Foxbar Hotel, Kilmarnock
Born: Johnstone, 13.4.66
Family: Single
Former clubs: Kilmarnock, Ayr
International debut: Scotland 16, Ireland 3, 1993
Five Nations' debut: As above
Best moment in rugby: Scoring try nine minutes into Scotland debut
Worst moment in rugby: Not playing in Hong Kong Sevens for Barbarians due to injury
Most embarrassing moment: Having shorts ripped off playing for Kilmarnock with nothing underneath to spare my blushes. Ran straight off the pitch
Most respected opponent: Matt Duncan (West of Scotland & Scotland)

Scotland (1993)

Last Season	4 caps	5 pts
Career	4 caps	5 pts

Caps (4): **1993** I, F, W, E

Points (5 – 1t): **1993** I(1t)

Biggest influence on career: Matt Duncan – great help to me showing me the ropes
Serious injuries: Broken collarbone, fingers, ribs; ripped ear; displaced vertebrae in back
Other sporting achievements: Athletics – Scottish international sprinter (100m in 10.6s, 200m in 21.5s)
Best memory last season: Debut score against Ireland
Suggestions to improve rugby: *On-field* – Reduce points worth of kicks. Too often an average side with a good kicker win games. *Off-field* – reimbursement for loss of earnings
Notable landmarks in rugby career: Burst onto Test scene last season when scoring a great try with first touch in international rugby. Playing against Ireland at Murrayfield, on 16 January 1993, he tore inside Simon Geoghegan to cross for a score which set Scotland up for an emphatic 15–3 result. Retained his place throughout Championship although was not as effective thereafter. Aged 18 before played rugby yet represented Scotland Under-21s in 1987, scoring two tries in 19–39 loss to Wales Under-21s at Wrexham. Played football

whilst training for hotel business in London, taking two years away from rugby. Continued athletics with good friend Brian Whittle (British Olympic runner). Made Scotland B debut in 18–12 defeat of France (Chalon-sur-Saone) and added to B tally with appearances against France B (won 14–12, Melrose 18.2.89), Italy B (won 26–3, L'Aquila 4.12.88), Ireland B (lost 19–29, scored try, Murrayfield 28.12.91) and France B (lost 18–27, Albi 3.2.92). When second-string was relabelled the A-team last season Derek played against Spain (won 35–14, Madrid, 12.9.92) and Italy (won 22–17, Madrid, 19.12.92). Toured with Scotland to Zimbabwe (1988) and Australia (1992)

Touchlines: Golf (10-handicap), cooking (recommends his Italian carbonara)

Stephens, C. J.   Wales

Full Name: Colin John Stephens
Club: Llanelli
Position: Outside-half
Height: 5ft 7½in (1.72m)
Weight: 11st 10lb (74kg)
Born: Morriston, 29.11.69
Occupation: Area manager with Clean-Shine Industrial & Domestic Cleaning Company (Llanelli)
Family: Single
International debut: Ireland 15, Wales 16, 1992
Five Nations' debut: As above
Best moment in rugby: Being picked for Wales in 1992 Five Nations' Championship
Worst moment in rugby: Being dropped three-quarters of way through above Championship
Most respected opponent: Paul Turner (ex-Newport & Wales)
Biggest influences on career: Llanelli club coaches over last four years
Serious injuries: Hamstring tears
Other sporting achievements:
Cricket for Wales (six games in Minor Counties) and Llanelli. Opening bowler. Had trials with Worcestershire 2nd XI against Gloucestershire and took four wickets

Best memory last season: Dropping two goals as Llanelli beat Australia 13–9

Suggestions to improve rugby: *On-field* – make game more exciting. Place

Wales (1992)		
Last Season	1 cap	6 pts
Career	4 caps	9 pts

Caps (4): 1992 I, F, E, A

Points (9 – 2p,1dg): 1992 I(1dg), A(2p)

greater emphasis on running with the ball. *Off-field* – Make sure players do not lose out for time away from work playing rugby. At present rewards are considerably lower than time put in

Notable landmarks in rugby career: Cracking 1992/93 season at domestic level for Colin who played an inspirational role as Llanelli beat the touring Wallabies 13–9 at Stradey Park on 14 November 1992. He landed two dropped goals and converted Ieuan Evans' try. Also shared in Scarlets' League and Cup double triumph. Like clubmate Wayne Proctor, Colin appeared three times against the Australians in a three-week spell. Seven days before Llanelli's win, he kicked two penalty goals in Wales B's 11–24 loss at the National Stadium (7.11.92), and the following weekend he repeated the feat as the Test side lost 6–23. Lost No 10 jersey to Pontypridd's Neil Jenkins before 1993 Championship campaign. He had played two seasons for Welsh Schools (1986–87), touring New Zealand, and went on to represent Welsh Universities and Colleges. Scored 14 points on U-21 debut at Murrayfield in 20–13 defeat of Scots U-21s (1988). Toured Canada with Wales B (1989), playing against Nova Scotia, Saskatchewan, British Columbia and Canada. Scored try in latter (Edmonton, 3.6.89) as Wales B won 31–29. Represented centenary-celebrating Barbarians in last two minutes of 16–16 draw with Scotland in 1991. Broke into senior Welsh squad in 1992 Five Nations' Championship, playing against Ireland, France and England

Strachan, A. D.   New Zealand

Full Name: Anthony (Ant) Strachan
Province: North Harbour
Position: Scrum-half
Height: 5ft 9in (1.75m)
Weight: 13st (82kg)
Born: Te Awamutu, 7.6.66
Former Provinces: Otago, Auckland
International debut: New Zealand 54, World XV 26, 1992
Serious injuries: Dislocated shoulder (1992)
Notable landmarks in rugby career: Made the All Black scrum-half position his own with a brilliant 1992 campaign. His prodigious clearance speed earned him a national call-up after just eight first-class games for Auckland, where he

was back-up to Jason Hewett. It was an injury to Hewett which gave him his ticket to the big time, ahead of Paul McGahon and Kevin Putt. And although his squad selection was as second string scrum-half, he was given his Test debut as early as the second leg of the centenary series, following New Zealand's 14–28 first

New Zealand (1992)		
Last Season	9 caps	8 pts
Career	9 caps	8 pts
Caps (9): **1992** Wd(2,3), I(1,2), A(1,2,3), SA **1993** BL(1)		
Points (8 – 2t): **1992** Wd(2:1t), I(2:1t)		

Test defeat in Christchurch. Brought in for Graeme Bachop he responded with a try in the 54–26 Wellington win. A product of Auckland Grammar School, Ant kept his place as New Zealand completed their come-from-behind series win in Auckland and through the two-Test Ireland visit, contributing another try in the 59–6 second Test victory in Wellington. So to Australia and South Africa, New Zealand's three-month, 16-match mega-tour. No-one surpassed Ant's tally of ten appearances, nor his consistent high standard of performance. Outings against Western Australia (as a replacement), South Australia, New South Wales (scored try), Queensland, Natal (scored try) and Junior South Africa were mixed with four more Test caps, although in the last, New Zealand's 27–24 defeat of South Africa at Ellis Park, Johannesburg, he lasted just 16 minutes before dislocating his shoulder and making way for Jon Preston. A member of New Zealand's Student World Cup-winning squad in 1988, he has enjoyed remarkably little Provincial action. His search for action last season took him across the bridge from Auckland to North Harbour, having started out with Otago in 1987. Lost scrum-half berth to Jon Preston after first Test win over British Lions in Christchurch

Scotland scrum-half Gary Armstrong carves an opening between Jeremy Guscott and Ben Clarke at Twickenham. England won 26–12

Strauss, C. P.   South Africa

Full Name: Christiaan (Tiaan)
Petrus Strauss
Club: Northerns-Tygerberg-College
Province: Western Province
Position: No 8
Height: 6ft 1in (1.86m)
Weight: 15st 6lb (98kg)
Occupation: Articled clerk with
Cape Town law firm
Born: Upington, 28.6.65
International debut: France 15,
South Africa 20, 1992
**Notable landmarks in rugby
career:** Captain of the Junior
Springboks side which played
against both Namibia and New
Zealand (lost 15–20) in 1992.
Widely seen as the future Springbok
skipper, Tiaan made a favourable
impression on the tour of France
and England last season when he
played in all three Tests and five
other games besides: against France
B (lost 17–24, Bordeaux, 4.10.92),
Aquitaine (won 29–22, Pau,
7.10.92), Midi-Pyrenees (won 18–

South Africa (1992)

Last Season	5 caps	0 pts
Career	5 caps	0 pts

Caps (5): **1992** F(1,2), E **1993** F(1,2)

Points Nil

15, Toulouse, 15.10.92), French Barbarians (lost 20–25, Lille, 31.10.92) and
England B (won 20–16, Bristol, 7.11.92). A powerful man, the legacy of his
days on the family farms in the Kalahari and Namibia, he was pulled from the
under-20 ranks to make his senior debut for Western Province in 1986. He was
capped 120 times by his union before Jannie Breedt retired and there was finally
room in the back row for him to make his Test bow in the 20–15 defeat of
France in Lyon on 17 October 1992. Not that he had sat around idly waiting
for his chance. He had spent the late 1980s and early 1990s in Italy playing
with Noceto, a second division outfit to be found near Parma. Such experience stood
him in good stead during the Springboks' long stay in Europe and his form
remained solid through the second Test against France in Paris and the
Twickenham loss to England. Turned out in both home Tests against France
last summer (1993)

Styger, J. J.   South Africa

Full Name: Johannes (Johann) Jakobus Styger
Club: Oud-Studente
Province: Orange Free State
Position: Prop
Height: 6ft (1.82m)
Weight: 16st 7lb (105kg)
Occupation: Dentist
Born: Bloemfontein, 31.1.62
Former Province: Northern Transvaal
International debut: South Africa 24, New Zealand 27, 1992
Notable landmarks in rugby career: An aggressive dentist is bad news for everyone other than Springbok fans. Johann, who tends to teeth by profession, is a tough customer in the colours of both Orange Free State and South Africa, with whom he quickly graduated from the replacements' bench, where he started the 1992 international campaign against New Zealand, to first-choice loosehead prop. His cause was helped by the

South Africa (1992)

Last Season	5 caps	0 pts
Career	5 caps	0 pts

Caps (5): **1992** NZ(R), A, F(1,2), E

Points Nil

51st minute injury suffered by Transvaal's Heinrich Rodgers against the All Blacks which allowed Johann into the fray at Ellis Park. But once in the spotlight he never departed. Indeed, when Rodgers returned to the side fully fit, for the two Tests in France, he did so on the other side of the scrum. Born and educated (at Grey College) in Bloemfontein, Johann played 13 matches for Northern Transvaal, following his debut in 1983, before switching to Free State where he has since made over 60 appearances. One of those came on Wednesday 5 August, in front of 25,000 supporters at Free State Stadium, where the touring All Blacks recovered from an 11–10 half-time deficit to win 33–14. His other Springbok outings on tour in Europe came against Aquitaine (won 29–22, Pau, 7.10.92), Languedoc–Roussillon (won 36–15, Beziers, 20.10.92), French Barbarians (lost 20–25, Lille, 31.10.92) and England B (won 20–16, Bristol, 7.11.92)

Teague, M. C.   England

Full Name: Michael Clive Teague
Club: Moseley
Position: No 8, flanker
Height: 6ft 3in (1.91m)
Weight: 16st 7lb (105kg)
Occupation: Self-employed builder
Born: Gloucester, 8.10.59
Family: Lorraine (wife)
Family links with rugby:
Grandfather played for
Gloucestershire
Former clubs: Cardiff, Gloucester
Old Blues, Gloucester
International debut: France 32,
England 18, 1984
Five Nations' debut: As above
Best moment in rugby: 1989
Lions winning decisive third Test
against Australia (15.7.89)
Worst moment in rugby: England
losing 1990 Grand Slam decider to
Scotland
Most embarrassing moment:
Giving Wales three seconds of hell at
Cardiff in 1989 and then being
carried off
Most respected opponent: Murray
Mexted (Wellington & New
Zealand)
Serious injuries: Torn shoulder,
knee ligaments
Suggestions to improve rugby:

England (1985)		
Last Season	5 caps	0 pts
Career	27 caps	12 pts
Lions 1989	2 Tests	0 pts
1993	Tour to New Zealand	

Caps (27): **1985** F(R), NZ(1,2) **1989** S, I, F, W, Ro. Lions–(2,3) **1990** F, W, S **1991** W, S(a), I, F(a), Fj, A(a) wc–NZ, It, F(b), S(b), A(b) **1992** SA **1993** F, W, S, I

Points (12 – 3t): **1985** NZ(1:1t) **1991** W(1t), I(1t)

On-field – Cannot improve the game that much, it's improving itself. Pleased about five points for a try; perhaps less for a penalty goal too

Notable landmarks in rugby career: Returned last season after one of his not uncharacteristic lay-offs to regain the England blindside berth against South Africa at Twickenham (14.11.92). His previous cap had come in the World Cup final on 2 November 1991. Mike played throughout '93 Five Nations' campaign before leaving on his second tour of duty with the British Lions. On his first, in 1989, he was voted 'Player of the Series' as the Lions came from behind to win 2–1 in Australia. Having represented England at U-23 and B levels he spent four years in the international wilderness, on moving from Gloucester to Cardiff, after gaining his first three caps in 1985. Returned in

1989 and at the end of that season won his Lions place, though failed to make the Test line-up. Again lost England slot in 1990, for the Argentina game (3.11.90) when John Hall came in, but regained it throughout 1991 Five Nations' Grand Slam campaign, and contributed vital tries against Wales and Ireland. Also represented England B in 12–12 draw with Emerging Australians. Toured with England to South Africa (1984), New Zealand (1985) and Fiji/Australia (1991). Played in 1991 World Cup final at No 8 having begun tournament at blindside wing-forward

Touchlines: Motocross

Timu, J. K. R.   New Zealand

Full Name: John Kahukura Raymond Timu
Club: University
Province: Otago
Position: Wing, fullback
Height: 5ft 10½in (1.80m)
Weight: 13st 10lb (87kg)
Occupation: PE student
Born: Dannevirke, Hawke's Bay, 8.5.69
International debut: Argentina 14, New Zealand 28, 1992
Notable landmarks in rugby career: Hailed as the new John Gallagher following his spectacularly successful switch from wing to fullback in 1991. Indeed, John has been one of New Zealand's most prized assets ever since making the Otago team in 1988 in his first year out of school and immediately shattering the Province's try-scoring record. His tally of 16 bettered the previous mark established back in 1948 and won him a place on the 1988 NZ Maoris' world tour. By the age of 22 he had become Otago's all-time leading try-scorer, with 54 tries in 63 games, and quickly showed he

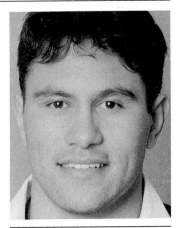

New Zealand (1991)

Last Season	9 caps	9 pts
Career	16 caps	21 pts

Caps (16): **1991** Arg(1), A(1,2). wc–E, US, C, A **1992** Wd(2), I(2), A(1,2,3), SA 1993 BL(1,2,3)

Points (21 – 5t): **1991** wc–US(1t), C(2t) **1992** I(2:1t), A(2:1t)

---

was not afraid to cross the International try-line either. The year before he toured Australia with New Zealand Colts (with Va'aiga Tuigamala, Blair Larsen and Craig Innes), and helped beat the Wallabies 24–21, John had been flown to Britain to join the New Zealand senior squad's 1989 tour of Wales and Ireland as a replacement. Characteristically, he bagged a try on his All Black debut against Newport and two more next time out against Leinster. In 1990 he also visited France with the national squad but it was not until the 1991 tour of Argentina that he picked up his first cap, standing in for the injured John Kirwan. He failed to score in that first Test but crossed nine times in the seven tour games he appeared in. Such prolific form brought him back to Britain for the World Cup and four more caps, the pick being his two-try display from fullback in the 29–12 quarter-final defeat of Canada in Lille. Scored further tries in the second Tests against Ireland and Australia in 1992, the latter on a tour in which he began with four tries against Western Australia. Played ten times in all, three times on the South African leg, and scored one of the triumphant All Blacks' three Test tries in Johannesburg.

Toombs, R. C. Australia

Full Name: Richard Craig Toombs
Club: Northern Suburbs
State: New South Wales
Position: Centre, wing
Height: 5ft 10in (1.78m)
Weight: 13st 1lb (83kg)
Occupation: Sales representative with Southern Pacific Hotels
Born: 4.1.68
Family: Peter (father), Helen (mother), Marc (brother), Brett (brother), Geoffery (brother)
Former club: Souths (Brisbane: 1988–89)
International debut: Australia 27, Scotland 12, 1992
Best moment in rugby: First cap v Scotland

Worst moment in rugby: Losing three consecutive Grand Finals in 1987–89
Most respected opponent: John Eales (Brothers & Australia)
Serious injuries: Dislocated finger
Best memories last season: The final whistle of the second Test

Australia (1992)		
Last Season	2 caps	0 pts
Career	2 caps	0 pts

Caps (2): **1992** S(1,2)

Points Nil

against the All Blacks, which signalled that we had won the Bledisloe Cup. Beating South Africa

Suggestions to improve rugby: *On-field* – Cut down the demands on international players, so as the local competitions do not suffer through a lack of profile names. Even Test players enjoy club competitions, and not just the finals! *Off-field* – Daily tour allowance is not sufficient remuneration – player should be reimbursed at least complete loss of wages
Tours: 1988 – England, Scotland and Italy. 1991 – New Zealand, World Cup. 1992 – South Africa, Ireland and Wales
Touchlines: Girlfriend Carissa, beach
Player to watch: Matt Burke (NSW)
Player of the Year: John Eales (Australia)

Tordo, J. -F.   France

Full Name: Jean-Francois Tordo
Club: Nice
Position: Flanker, hooker
Height: 6ft 1in (1.86m)
Weight: 14st 10lb (93kg)
Occupation: Building foreman
Born: Nice, 1.8.64
Former club: Toulon
International debut: United States 9, France 41, 1991
Five Nations' debut: Wales 9, France 12, 1992
Notable landmarks in rugby career: Succeeded Marc Cecillon as French captain following the 1992 summer tour to Argentina, on which he played both Tests at breakaway. But not before he had been dropped from the side following the 16–29 defeat by South Africa in Lyon, a game in which he appeared at blindside. His debut as captain coincided with Argentina's first ever win on French soil, In Nantes (14.11.92). However, coach Pierre Berbizier keeps faith with the Nice man while moving him to hooker for the 1993 International

France (1991)

Last Season	9 caps	0 pts
Career	14 caps	0 pts

Caps (14): **1991** US(1R) **1992** W, E, S, I, R, Arg(a1,a2), SA(1), Arg(b), **1993** E, S, I, W

Points Nil

Championship. Four games later and France collect the inaugural Five Nations' Cup. At home in either front or back row Jean-Francois hooked France B to a 28–15 win over Wales B at La Teste (12.11.89), reverted to back row for France B's 31–10 defeat of Scotland B at Hughenden (2.3.91), but then went reclaimed the No 2 jersey for the 10–6 win over England B a fortnight later. Promoted to the senior XV on the 1991 tour of the United States and made his debut as a 73rd minute replacement for Michel Courtiols in the 41–9 win at Denver (13.7.91). Although excluded from the French World Cup squad, he returned for the 1992 Tournoi des Cinq Nations, occupying the No 6 jersey throughout the campaign. Tasted the high life as a teenager when, aged 18, he won a runners-up medal after coming on as a second half replacement for Nice in the 1983 French Club Championship final. Thereafter, joined Toulon but returned to the French Riviera and Nice in September 1990, having toured New Zealand with France in 1989, hooking against Manawatu and flanking in the wins over Bay of Plenty and a Seddon Shield XV. Jean-Francois has also hooked for France A in the FIRA Championship. Brutally injured on 1993 summer tour to South Africa, ruling him out of the two Test matches

Townsend, G. P. J.　　　Scotland

Full Name: Gregor Peter John Townsend
Club: Gala
Position: Outside-half, centre
Height: 5ft 11in (1.81m)
Weight: 12st 7lb (80kg)
Occupation: History/politics student at Edinburgh University
Born: Edinburgh, 26.4.73
Family: Single
Family links with rugby: Father (Peter) played twice for South of Scotland
International debut: England 26, Scotland 12, 1993
Five Nations' debut: As above
Best moment in rugby: Coming on as a replacement for debut at Twickenham
Worst moment in rugby: Having a nightmare against Ireland on Scotland B debut – being intercepted and dropping ball for try
Most embarrassing moment: Dropping first four passes in Gala-Melrose League game (7.12.91)
Most respected opponent: Craig

Scotland (1993)		
Last Season	1 cap	0 pts
1993	Tour to South Seas	
Career	1 cap	0 pts

Caps (1): 1993 E(R)

Points Nil

368

Chalmers (Melrose & Scotland)
Biggest influence on career: My father (Peter)
Serious injuries: Sprung ribs at 1992 Hong Kong Sevens, damaged knee ligaments in 1993 Scotland Trial
Best memory last season: Scotland debut
Suggestions to improve rugby: *On-field* – Greater integration between top and bottom level of game (massive difference between club and international level in terms of facilities etc). *Off-field* – Pump more money into Scottish game
Notable landmarks in rugby career: Having played in eight of Scotland's tour games in Australia (1992) Gregor appeared set to succeed the retired Sean Lineen in the tartan midfield. All went according to plan before Christmas: he helped Scotland win the Dubai Sevens and turned out for Scotland A in the 35–14 defeat of Spain, kicking three conversions and three penalty goals (Madrid, 12.9.92). In the full Scotland side masquerading as a Scotland A XV, he bagged a try in the 22–17 win over Italy at Melrose (19.12.92). A week later there was a Townsend conversion in Scotland A's 22–13 Dublin win over Ireland. But in the Scotland Trial it all went wrong. Gregor sustained knee-ligament damage and was ruled out of Test contention. Melrose's Graham Shiel received the call. However, Gregor recovered in time to earn his first cap as a 26th minute replacement for arm-break victim Craig Chalmers in the 12–26 Twickenham loss to England (6.3.93). He subsequently toured with Scotland to Fiji, Tonga and Western Samoa last summer. Gregor has always been wary of the hyperbole which has painted him as the new Jonathan Davies. But his progress up the representative ladder has been swift. He turned out for Irish Wolfhounds at 1992 Hong Kong Sevens, having quickly progressed through Gala U-14, U-15 and U-16 ranks and, in 1991/92, played for Scotland U-21 in 19–28 loss to Wales U-21 (Stirling, 18.4.92) and Scotland B, against Ireland B (landed two penalty goals in 19–29 loss, Murrayfield 28.12.91) and France B (kicked conversion and two penalty goals in 18–27 loss, Albi 3.2.92)
Touchlines: Golf (10-handicap)

Tuigamala. V. L.   New Zealand

Full Name: Va'aiga Lealuga
Tuigamala
Club: Ponsonby
Province: Auckland
Position: Wing
Height: 5ft 10½in (1.79m)
Weight: 15st 9lb (99kg)
Occupation: Travel consultant
Born: Faleasiu, 4.9.69
International debut: New Zealand
46, USA 6, 1991
**Notable landmarks in rugby
career:** Samoan-born Va'aiga
graduated to the New Zealand squad
in 1989 after a five-try display for
Auckland against Mid-Canterbury,
and three tries in the All Black Trial.
Although unable to command a
regular Provincial place, due to the
presence of John Kirwan and Terry
Wright, his performances for New
Zealand Colts against Australia
Under-21s in 1988 (one try in 19–24
defeat) and 1989 (three tries in
38–15 win) prompted his national
call-up for the '89 tour to Canada,
Wales and Ireland. His All Black
debut against British Columbia in
Vancouver, where he scored the
second of his side's three tries in the

New Zealand (1991)

Last Season	11 caps	5 pts
Career	15 caps	21 pts

Caps (15): **1991** wc–US, It, C, S **1992**
Wd(1,2,3), I(1), A(1,2,3), SA
1993 BL(1,2,3)

Points (21 – 5t): **1991** wc–US(1t), It(1t)
1992 Wd(1:1t), Wd(2:1t),
A(1:1t)

48–3 win, was followed by outings against Pontypool (one try), Neath,
Leinster, Connacht (one try) and Ulster (one try) Injury at The Gnoll cost him
further appearances, but he had long since built a formidable reputation as a
battering ram. A third year of New Zealand Colts in 1990, when he contributed
seven tries in the three games in Oz, and a good tour to France the same year
(playing against Languedoc, French Barbarians and France A), did him no
harm but it was not until the following year, back in the Britain for the World
Cup, that he was capped. Having helped New Zealand B beat their Aussie
counterparts 21–15 in Brisbane, Va'aiga marked his full debut against the
United States with a try in the 46–6 win, notched another next time out against
Italy. He retained his place for the knock-out games against Canada and
Scotland and, last season, played an unbroken role in the centenary series,
weighing in with tries in each of the first two Tests. Fullback for the NZ Maoris,

he was one of six players axed after the All Blacks' first Test defeat of Ireland but he reclaimed his spot for the Bledisloe Cup series (scoring in the first Test) and the Ellis Park showdown on the tour of Australia and South Africa

---

Tukalo, I. Scotland

Full Name: Iwan Tukalo
Club: Selkirk
Position: Left wing
Height: 5ft 9in (1.76m)
Weight: 13st 4lb (85kg)
Occupation: Senior engineer with British Gas, Scotland
Born: Edinburgh, 5.3.61
Family: Wife (Susan)
Former club: Royal High
International debut: Scotland 15, Ireland 18, 1985
Five Nations' debut: As above
Best moment in rugby: Beating England to win 1990 Grand Slam
Worst moment in rugby: First Test against New Zealand in 1990 – I had a shocker
Most embarrassing moment: Running to listen to captain's instructions in Scotland's match v Fiji (1989) and arriving too late
Most respected opponent: David Campese (Mediolanum Milan & Australia) – electrifying pace over five yards and excellent side-step
Biggest influence on career: John Rutherford (Selkirk & Scotland)
Serious injuries: Torn ligaments, ankle, elbow and knee. Torn hamstring
Suggestions to improve rugby:
On-field – To make it more competitive, reduce size of Scottish first division to eight clubs and play matches on home and away basis. Also, Scotland desperately needs a national cup competition to bring an element of competitiveness lacking in club rugby at present. *Off-field* – Let events take their natural course. Sad for game when people just look to it for making a bit of extra money

Scotland (1985)

Last Season	2 caps	0 pts
Career	37 caps	60 pts

Caps (37): **1985** I **1987** I,F(a), W, E wc–F(b), Z, Ro, NZ **1988** F, W, E, A **1989** W, E, I, F, Fj **1990** I, F, W, E, NZ(1) **1991** I, Ro wc–J, Z, I(b), WS, E(b), NZ **1992** E, I, F, W, A(1,2)

Points (60 – 15t): **1987** I(1t) wc–Z(2t), Ro(1t) **1988** F(1t) **1989** I(3t), Fj(1t) **1990** F(1t) **1991** Ro(1t) wc–J(1t), Z(3t)

Notable landmarks in rugby career: Became Scotland's most-capped wing when succeeding Arthur Smith (33 caps, 1955–62) with 34th appearance in 10–6 win over France at Murrayfield (7.3.92). Had privilege of meeting Arthur's widow later in the 1991/92 season. Four tries in the 1991 World Cup (three v Zimbabwe, 9.10.91) lifted him into joint second place on Scotland's all-time try-scoring list with 15 – nine behind Ian Smith (24t in 32 games, 1924–33) and equal with Tony Stanger. Played three times at scrum-half for Scottish Schools in 1978–79, captaining side against France; toured with Scotland to Romania (1984), North America (1985), Spain and France (1986), Japan (1989), New Zealand (1990) and Australia (1992). Scored three tries for Scotland A XV in 39–7 defeat of Spain (Seville, 22.12.90). Retired from Test rugby after 1992 Scotland tour

Touchlines: Squash, social golf

Turnbull, D. J.   Scotland

Full Name: Derek James Turnbull
Club: Hawick
Position: Flanker
Height: 6ft 4in (1.93m)
Weight: 15st 6lb (98kg)
Occupation: Police Officer with Lothians and Borders Police
Born: Hawick, 2.10.61
Family: Angie (wife)
Family links with rugby: Father (Jim) is past president of Hawick Trades RFC
Former clubs: Hawick PSA, Hawick Trades
International debut: New Zealand 30, Scotland 3, 1987 (World Cup)
Five Nations' debut: Scotland 23, France 12, 1988
Best moment in rugby: Coming on as a replacement in the 1990 Grand Slam decider against England at Murrayfield
Worst moment in rugby: Missing 1992 Five Nations' Championship due to broken jaw
Most embarrassing moment: Leading a Hawick Sevens side out at Gala Sports on 1 April, 1989. The

Scotland (1987)

Last Season	4 caps	5 pts
Career	14 caps	9 pts

Caps (10): **1987** wc–NZ **1988** F, E **1990** E(R) **1991** F, W, E, I, Ro wc–Z **1993** I, F, W E

Points (9 – 2t): **1991** wc–Z(1t) **1993** W(1t)

rest of the side stayed in the dressing room until I was out onto the pitch myself – all by myself!

Most respected opponent: Willie Duggan (Blackrock College & Ireland) – he knew how to cheat well

Biggest influences on career: Derrick Grant (Hawick & ex-Scotland coach), my father and Norman Suddon

Other sporting achievements: Completed London Marathon in 1982

Best memory last season: Scoring try in win over Wales

Suggestions to improve rugby: *On-field* – New mauling law is too negative for my liking. Don't allow anyone to kick the ball outside their own 22. Teams then would have to run and rugby would demand a more mobile approach. More liberal interpretations by referees, like in southern hemisphere. *Off-field* – Have got to have means of earning a living. SRU must compensate employers for the time their employees give up to rugby. Not just monetary aspect; you lose your holidays too

Notable landmarks in rugby career: Derek, who has toured with Scotland to North America (1985), France and Spain (1986), World Cup (1987), Zimbabwe (1988), Japan (1989) and New Zealand (1990) made his Hawick debut as a 17-year-old against Alnwick (December 1978) and nine years later came on as replacement for John Jeffrey for first cap in 1987 World Cup quarter-final against New Zealand. He scored his first international try in 55–12 defeat of Zimbabwe (Murrayfield, 9.10.91) and added another in 1993 Five Nations' Championship as Wales were routed 20–0 at Murrayfield (20.2.93). He has picked up six B caps (including his debut match in 1989) and helped Hawick win the 1992 Gala Sevens. After turning out for Scotland A last season in 35–14 defeat of Spain in Madrid (12.9.92) he regained his blindside berth in Test side and held onto it through 1993 Championship before finishing season at Murrayfield in World Cup Sevens action for Scotland

Touchlines: Enjoy golf – especially the 19th hole

Ubogu, V. E. England

Full Name: Victor Eriakpo Ubogu
Club: Bath
Position: Loose-head prop
Height: 5ft 9in (1.76m)
Weight: 16st 2lb (102.5kg)
Occupation: London-based company director with family-owned security firm
Born: Lagos, Nigeria, 8.9.64
Family: Single
Former clubs: Moseley, Richmond
International debut: England 26, Canada 13, 1992
Five Nations' debut: None
Best moments in rugby: Being capped by England; Bath beating Toulouse in 1989/90
Worst moment in rugby: Not reaching last four with England in 1988 Student World Cup after losing to Soviet Union and New Zealand
Best memory last season: Winning first cap
Suggestions to improve rugby: There should be more regard for players. We tend to be ignored – not listened to enough

England (1992)		
Last Season	2 caps	0 pts
1993	'A' Tour to Canada	
Career	2 caps	0 pts

Caps (2): 1992 C,SA

Points Nil

Notable landmarks in rugby career: Wembley debuts are few and far between but Victor, a member of Oxford's beaten Varsity team in 1987, made his in the shadow of the twin towers when selected ahead of Jeff Probyn against Canada on 17 September 1992 (Twickenham was unavailable due to reconstruction). England won the game 26–13 and your man, who had impressed on England B's 1992 summer tour to New Zealand (playing in the 18–24 first 'Test' loss at Hamilton, 28.6.92), kept his place for the visit of the Springboks to Twickenham on 14 November. But he lost his place to Probyn for the 1993 Five Nations' campaign. Adept on either side of the scrum, he won a Pilkington Cup winners' medal with Bath in 1990 after helping demolish arch-rivals Gloucester 48–6 at Twickenham. Scored two tries for England B in 50–6 defeat of Spain in 1991/92, having made his second-string debut in the 12–12 draw with the Emerging Australians, at Wasps on 4 November 1990. Helped Bath win 1992/93 Courage Championship before embarking with England A on summer tour to Canada

Underwood, R.   England

Full Name: Rory Underwood
Club: Leicester & RAF
Position: Wing
Height: 5ft 9in (1.76m)
Weight: 13st 7lb (86kg)
Occupation: RAF pilot
Born: Middlesbrough, 19.6.63
Family: Wendy (wife), Rebecca (daughter) and Alexandra (daughter)
Family links with rugby: Brother (Tony) plays for Leicester, England and British Lions
Former club: Middlesbrough
International debut: England 12, Ireland 9, 1984
Five Nations' debut: As above
Best moment in rugby: Winning first (1991) Grand Slam with England
Worst moment in rugby: England's 9–12 loss to Wales at Cardiff (1989)
Most embarrassing moment: Making error which led to Wales scoring crucial try against England in above match
Most respected opponent: Patrice Lagisquet (Bayonne & France)
Biggest influence on career: Geoff Cooke (England manager)
Other sporting achievements: Swam and played cricket for Barnard Castle School, which England team-mate Rob Andrew also attended
Best memory last season: Try scored against Scotland (move sparked by Stuart Barnes and Jeremy Guscott inside England 22)
Suggestions to improve rugby:
On-field – RFU Committee working more with players in the future. At present some do, some do not. *Off-field* –

England (1984)		
Last Season	5 caps	5 pts
Career	60 caps	145 pts
Lions 1986		
1989	3 Tests	0 pts
1993	3 Tests	5 pts

Caps (60): **1984** I, F, W, A **1985** Ro, F, S, I, W **1986** W, I, F **1987** I, F, W, S wc–A, J, W **1988** F, W, S, I(1,2), A(a1,a2), Fj, A(b) **1989** S, I, F, W. Lions–A(1,2,3). Ro, Fj **1990** I, F, W, S, Arg(b) **1991** W, S, I, F, Fj, A wc–NZ, It, US, F, S, A **1992** S, I, F, W, SA **1993** F, W, S, I. Lions–NZ(1,2,3)

Points (145 – 36t): **1984** F(1t) **1985** I(1t) **1987** wc–J(2t) **1988** I(1:2t), I(2:1t), A(a1:1t), A(a2:1t), Fj(2t), A(b:2t) **1989** Fj(5t) **1990** I(1t), F(1t), W(2t), Arg(b:3t) **1991** I(1t), F(1t), Fj(1t) wc–It(1t), US(2t), F(1t) **1992** S(1t), I(1t), F(1t) **1993** S(1t). Lions–NZ(2:1t)

Continued improvement by Unions in looking after players and wives. International Board must make unambiguous rulings concerning amateurism. Only reward should be in playing for natural enjoyment

Notable landmarks in rugby career: England's most-capped player (60) and record try-scorer (36). Scored two tries for Leicester against Barbarians in 1983 and, three months later, was in England team. Missed tour to Argentina in summer of 1990, due to RAF commitments, having already become England's most-capped back and highest try-scorer during 1989/90 season. RAF duties also took precedence over tours to South Africa (1984) and New Zealand (1985). Equalled Dan Lambert's 1907 England record of five tries in an international, against Fiji (won 58–23, Twickenham 4.11.89). Previously played for England Colts, U-23 and B teams. Toured Australia with 1989 Lions, playing in all three Tests. Try scored in 16–7 defeat of Ireland during 1991 Grand Slam was most important of career (No 26) as it kept the dream alive. Also scored in 21–19 win over France (1991 Grand Slam decider). In 1991/92 he notched a further eight tries: including four en route to World Cup final and three in 1992 Grand Slam campaign. Retired from international arena once back-to-back Grand Slams were safely in the bag but did a Frank Sinatra and returned last season after missing the Wembley opener against Canada. Ever present from then onwards, scoring glorious try against Scotland at Twickenham on 6 March 1993. It was his 36th but first to be worth five points. Three times last season played on same England team as brother Tony – the first brothers to appear in same England championship side since the Wheatley brothers packed down against Scotland in 1938. Clocked up 60th cap and shared in Leicester's Pilkington Cup triumph before embarking on second tour of British Lions duty in New Zealand. Provided highlight of trip with match-clinching try in 20–7 second Test win in Wellington

Touchlines: Crosswords, reading

Mick Galwey struggles to resist the clutches of Welsh flanker Emyr Lewis and wing Mike Hall during Ireland's 19–14 win in Cardiff

Underwood, T.   England

Full Name: Tony Underwood
Clubs: Leicester, Cambridge Univ
Position: Wing
Height: 5ft 9in (1.76m)
Weight: 12st 10lb (81kg)
Occupation: Investment banker
with Lehman Brothers
Born: Ipoh, Malaysia, 17.2.69
Family: Single
Family links with rugby: Brother
Rory is England's record try-scorer
and most-capped player (60 caps –
36 tries, 145 points)
International debut: England 26,
Canada 13, 1992
Five Nations' debut: England 26,
Scotland 12, 1993
Best moments in rugby: 1993
Lions' selection; Playing for
Barbarians against 1989 All Blacks,
for Irish Wolfhounds in Hong Kong
Sevens, and for Cambridge in 1991
Varsity match
Worst moments in rugby:
Cambridge's 1990 Varsity match
loss (12–21) to Oxford. England's
1990 Tour to Argentina

England (1992)

Last Season	4 caps	10 pts
Career	4 caps	10 pts
Lions 1993	Tour to New Zealand	

Caps (4): **1992** C, SA **1993** S, I

Points (10 – 2t): **1992** SA(1t) **1993** S(1t)

Most embarrassing moment: Post-try behaviour following my late score in
1991 Varsity match
Most respected opponents: Ian Hunter (Northampton & England B) and
David Campese (Mediolanum Milan & Australia)
Biggest influence on career: My mother (Anne)
Serious injuries: Broken jaw, torn hamstring and damaged knee cartilage – all
in second half of 1989/90 season
Best memory last season: Scoring England tries against South Africa and
Scotland
Suggestions to improve rugby: *On-field* – Expansion of League programme
to home and away. National training guidelines to filtrate down to club rugby.
Off-field – Take necessary steps to prevent player drain to rugby league. Greater
representation of players' views in Union
Notable landmarks in rugby career: Played for England Schools (18-
Group) before graduating to England team for inaugural Student World Cup
(1988). Played for Barbarians in 10–21 defeat by 1989 All Blacks at

Twickenham and for England in 18–16 win over Barbarians (1990/91). Represented Irish Wolfhounds in 1989 Hong Kong Sevens. Gone on to represent Combined Students, England B, North of England and, latterly, England in 1990 summer tour of Argentina (v Tucuman, Cuyo and Cordoba Selections). Having made his England B debut in 12–20 loss to Fiji in 1989, he went to represent second-string XV in 1990/91 against Emerging Australians (12–12) and Ireland (lost 10–24), and scored four tries in Barbarians' Easter Tour match at Cardiff. In 1991/92 Tony scored five tries in four England B games: three against Ireland B (won 47–15, Richmond 31.1.92) and one apiece against Spain and France B. Not surprisingly, he was selected to tour with England B to New Zealand (1992), where he played in both 'Tests', scoring a try in the 18–26 second leg defeat in Pukekohe (5.7.92). Returned home to take his tally of B caps to 12 with outings against South Africa (scored try in 16–20 loss at Bristol, 7.11.92), France B (scored try in 29–17 win at Leicester, 15.1.93) and against Italy B (scored two tries in 59–0 rout at Bath (3.2.93). In among these prolific exploits, Tony fitted in his Test debut against Canada, at Wembley on 17 October 1992 and his first top-level try in the 33–16 defeat of South Africa (Twickenham, 14.11.92). Lost place for first two games of 1993 Championship but returned (on opposite flank to brother Rory) to score try against Scotland (Twickenham, 6.3.93). Helped Leicester win 1992/93 Pilkington Cup before touring New Zealand with 1993 British Lions
Touchlines: Cricket, squash, golf, tennis

Wainwright, R. I. — Scotland

Full Name: Robert Iain Wainwright
Club: Edinburgh Academicals
Position: Flanker
Height: 6ft 5in (1.95m)
Weight: 15st 4lb (97kg)
Occupation: Army doctor
Born: Perth, 22.3.65
Family: Single
Family links with rugby: Father (J. F. Wainwright) a 1956 Cambridge Blue
Former club: Cambridge University
International debut: Ireland 10, Scotland 18, 1992
Five Nations' debut: As above
Best moment in rugby: Replacing Neil Edwards against Ireland (1992) to win first cap
Worst moment in rugby: Cam-

bridge Univ v Durham Univ (Jan 1988)

Most respected opponent: John Jeffrey (Kelso & ex-Scotland)

Other sporting achievements: Boxing Blue at Cambridge Univ

Serious injuries: Broken cheekbone (Jan 1990), ankle (Sept 1990)

Scotland (1992)

Last Season	2 caps	4 pts
Career	4 caps	4 pts

Caps (4): **1992** I(R), F, A(1,2)

Points (4 – 1t): **1992** A(1:1t)

Best memory last season: Scoring try against Australia in Sydney

Notable landmarks in rugby career: Representative career really took off in 1991/92 season when he captained Scotland B, broke into senior side and toured Australia in summer, playing in both Tests and claiming Scotland's only try in 12–27 Sydney loss (13.6.92). First cap had come four months earlier when replacing Neil Edwards for the last two minutes against Ireland in Dublin (15.2.92). He then played the full 80 minutes in the 10–6 win over France (7.3.92). Injury deprived him of a run in the Scotland side on his return from Down Under last season. Having appeared in three consecutive Varsity matches (1986–88), he made his Scotland B debut in 26–3 win over Italy at L'Aquila. Won further B caps against Ireland (lost 0–16, 22.12.90) and, as captain, against France (lost 18–27, Albi 3.2.92). He scored a try in the latter contest. Other career landmarks include participation on Barbarians Easter tour (1988), Hong Kong Sevens (1988, 89) and 1989 tour to Japan with Scotland (two games, two tries)

Touchlines: Wildlife, fishing, photography, whisky

Walker, N. K.   Wales

Full Name: Nigel Keith Walker

Club: Cardiff

Position: Wing

Height: 5ft 11in (1.81m)

Weight: 12st 9lb (80kg)

Occupation: Development officer with Sports Council of Wales

Born: Cardiff, 15.6.63

Family: Mary (wife)

International debut: Wales 14, Ireland 19, 1993

Five Nations' debut: As above

Best moment in rugby: Scoring try v France (1993)

Worst moment in rugby: First five minutes of my comeback game when I gave away 14 points v

Cardiff HSOB

Most respected opponent: Ieuan Evans (Llanelli & Wales)

Serious injuries: Torn ankle ligaments, sprained wrist

Other sporting achievements: 110m hurdles semi-finalist in 1984 Los Angeles Olympics having clocked 14.07s in heat

Wales (1993)		
Last Season	2 caps	5 pts
Career	2 caps	5 pts

Caps (2): **1993** I,F

Points (5 – 1t): **1993** F(1t)

Best memory last season: Scoring first try in Heineken League v Newbridge

Suggestions to improve rugby: *On-field* – Greater dialogue between referees and players, especially regarding new laws; interpretations of the laws vary greatly

Notable landmarks in rugby career: Olympic hurdler who reached the top in a second sport when capped against Ireland on 6 March 1993 at Cardiff. The following Test, against France, he became the first Welshman to cross the try-line at Parc des Princes since Jeff Squire ten years earlier. Returned to rugby at the age of 29, following conversation with Cardiff's Mark Ring, having gained a Welsh Schools trial in 1981. Made an immediate impression last season, getting among the try leaders in the Heineken Championship, appearing in the East-West match at Cardiff in December and scoring a try hat-trick in Den Bosch on 6 February as Wales A walloped Holland 57–12. Ambition is 'to maximize my potential and to become an automatic choice in the Wales side.'

Touchlines: No time

Wallace, R. M.   Ireland

Full Name: Richard Michael Wallace

Club: Garryowen

Position: Wing

Height: 5ft 11in (1.80m)

Weight: 13st 7lb (86kg)

Occupation: Associate partner with K Walshe & Associates

Born: Cork, 16.1.68

Family: Single

Former club: Cork Constitution

International debut: Namibia 15, Ireland 6, 1991

Five Nations' debut: Ireland 15, Wales 16, 1992

Best moment in rugby: 1993 Lions call-up and defeat of England

Most respected opponent: Tony

Underwood (Leicester, England and Lions)

Other sporting achievements: Sailed (Laser class) for Ireland at 1990 European Championships (France)

Notable landmarks in rugby career: Spent last two summers in New Zealand, each trip providing a tale of the unexpected. In 1992 he had only just overcome the jet-lag following the trip out with Ireland when he was punched, playing against Canterbury, sustained a hair-line fracture of the jaw, and was flown home. In 1993 he was minding his own business in Moscow when Ian Hunter was injured in the British Lions' first engagement against North Auckland and he was summoned post haste as a replacement – taking to three the number of Irish representatives (Mick Galwey and Nick Popplewell being the others). Richard took his first step up the representative ladder when appearing for Munster Under-18s and Under-21s (1988). A member of the 1987/88 Irish Colleges XV, he scored a try in the 24–10 defeat of England B at Old Belvedere on only his second outing for Ireland B (1.3.91). Added third B cap in 29–19 win at Murrayfield (28.12.91). Broke into Ireland senior XV on 1991 tour of Namibia, when replacing Simon Geoghegan in 74th minute of first Test (Windhoek, 20.7.91). Scored tour-high five tries in Namibia. Marked Five Nations' debut with try in Dublin loss to Wales (18.1.92), and retained place throughout Championship (also crossing against Scotland) before ill-fated trip to the land of the All Black. Added third Test try last season in 17–42 loss to Australia (Dublin, 31.10.92) and helped Ireland reach semi-finals of inaugural World Cup Sevens (Murrayfield, April 1993)

Touchlines: Flying (hold private licence), sailing, reading, music

Ireland (1991)		
Last Season	5 caps	5 pts
Career	10 caps	13 pts
Lions 1993	Tour to New Zealand	

Caps (10): **1991** Na(1R) **1992** W, E, S, F, A **1993** S, F, W, E

Points (13 – 3t): **1991** W(1t), S(1t) **1992** A(1t)

Watt, A. G. J.   Scotland

Full Name: Alan Gordon James Watt
Club: Glasgow High/Kelvinside
Position: Prop, lock
Height: 6ft 5in (1.96m)
Weight: 19st (121kg)
Occupation: Student at Jordanhill College
Born: Glasgow, 10.7.67
Family: Single
Family links with rugby: Father (Gordon) played for Jordanhill FP, grandfather (Jimmy Cairney) played for Hutchesons'
International debut: Scotland 51, Zimbabwe 12, 1991
Five Nations' debut: Scotland 15, Ireland 3, 1993
Best moment in rugby: Winning first cap
Worst moment in rugby: Injury forcing withdrawl from Scotland side to play France in Paris (6.2.93)
Most embarrassing moment: Sprinting into a goalpost in training and knocking myself out
Most respected opponent: Stewart Hamilton (Stirling County)
Best memories last season: Making Five Nations' debut against Ireland at Murrayfield (16.1.93)
Suggestions to improve rugby: *On-field* – New mauling rule is a nonsense. Use scrummage to restart game. Bring back double-banking in lineout, second rows would be then left alone and the whole set-piece would be a lot tidier
Notable landmarks in rugby career: Omission from Scotland party to tour Fiji, Tonga and Western Samoa last summer represented a sad end to a season which had begun so brightly for big Wattie. Having turned out for Scotland A against Spain (won 35–14, Madrid, 12.9.92) and Ireland A (won 22–13, Dublin, 28.12.92), he was selected as loosehead for the Possibles in the Scotland Trial but, when Bristol's former England B prop Alan Sharp pulled out of the national side picked to play Ireland in the 1993 Five Nations' curtain-raiser, Alan was drafted in for his debut (though typical of his luck it was too late to get a mention in the matchday programme). After a satisfactory performance he was retained for the trip to Paris three weeks later but pulled out six days before suffering with the ubiquitous 'mystery virus'. Missed the

Scotland (1991)		
Last Season	1 cap	0 pts
Career	2 caps	0 pts

Caps (1): **1991** wc-Z 1993 S

Points Nil

remainder of the campaign and was then overlooked for the South Seas trip, with manager Alan Hosie explaining that Alan 'appears to be in the process of going back to playing in the second row' (which was the position he occupied most competently before the selectors decided to turn him into a prop). He previously represented Scotland Schools, scoring try against Wales in 1987, and Scotland U-21s (twice v Wales, 1987–88). Called into Scotland A team as prop for 39–7 defeat of Spain in Seville (1990) despite club position being lock. Also given Scotland B debut, in 10–31 defeat by France at Hughenden (2.3.91), before touring North America with Scotland (1991) and playing against US Eagles (won 41–12) and Canada (lost 19–24) in non-cap Tests. Also scored two tries in 76–7 win over Alberta and one in 24–12 defeat of Rugby East. Included in Scottish World Cup squad and played against Zimbabwe (9.10.91), as well as being bench reserve on four occasions, including semi-final against England. Toured Australia with Scotland (1992)
Touchlines: Waterskiing

Webb, J. M.   England

Full Name: Jonathan Mark Webb
Club: Bath
Position: Fullback
Height: 6ft 2in (1.88m)
Weight: 13st 8lb (86kg)
Occupation: Surgeon
Born: London, 24.8.63
Family: Amanda (wife), Harriet (daughter) and Sophie (daughter)
Family links with rugby: Uncle (Ken Reid) played for Richmond and Barbarians
Former clubs: Bristol Univ, Northern, Bristol
International debut: England 6, Australia 19, 1987
Five Nations' debut: France 10, England 9, 1988
Best moments in rugby: Scoring

first England try in 1991 World Cup win over Italy (won 36–6); winning 1992 Grand Slam; becoming England's most-capped fullback and leading points-scorer
Worst moments in rugby: Wales 12, England 9 (18.3.89); missing 1993 Lions selection
Most respected opponent: Michael Lynagh (Queensland & Australia)
Biggest influences on career: Bob Reeves (Univ of Bristol) and Jack Rowell

(Bath coach)

Serious injuries: Knee cartilage operation (before 1989 season)

Other sporting achievements: Golf (18-handicap)

Suggestions to improve rugby: *On-field* – All conversions should be taken from in front of the posts (perhaps from 35 metres). I don't see why a try in the corner, which so often is a more skilful score, should be effectively penalized by a reduced chance of the extra two points. It is illogical. Greater consistency between northern and southern hemisphere referees is still required. *Off-field* – Clarify financial side of game (relating to amateurism). There are still niggling confusions as to what is allowed to be done off the field

Notable landmarks in rugby career: Educated in Newcastle and played for Northern before medical studies forced move to West Country. Represented England B before making England debut as replacement for concussed Marcus Rose in 1987 World Cup. Returned to Australia on 1988 England tour. Lost England fullback slot to Simon Hodgkinson in May 1989. Moved to Bath at tail-end of 1989/90 season to revitalize career and was recalled to full England squad in 1990/91. Having graduated from doctor (Dr) to surgeon (Mr) status and become Fellow of Royal College of Surgeons (FRCS), he toured with England to Fiji/Australia in 1991 (playing in both Tests) before enjoying a record-breaking 1991/92 season. Quite apart from helping Bath win the League and Cup double, he became England's most-capped fullback (now 33 appearances) and England's leading points scorer (now 296), in the process establishing a Five Nations' record for the most points in a single campaign (67) and national bests for most points in a match (24 against Italy at Twickenham in World Cup) and a Championship encounter (22 v Ireland, Twickenham 1.2.92). Ever-present last season, kicking 50 points in England's six Tests. Helped Bath win 1992/93 League title but was overlooked for Lions tour to New Zealand

Touchlines: Playing oboe, golf

England (1987)

Last Season	5 caps	50 pts
Career	32 caps	296 pts

Caps (32): **1987** wc–A, J, US, W **1988** F, W, S, I(1,2), A(a1,a2), A(b) **1989** S, I, F, W **1991** Fj, A wc–NZ, It, F, S, A **1992** S, I, F, W, C, SA

Points (296 – 4t,41c,66p): **1987** wc–A(1c), J(7c,2p), US(3c,4p), W(1p) **1988** F(2p), W(1p), S(2p), I(1:1c,1p), I(2:2c,3p), A(a1:1c,2p), A(b:3c,2 p) **1989** S(2p) **1991** Fj(2c,2p), A(1c,3p) wc–NZ(3p), It(1t,4c,4p), F(1c,3p), S(2p), A(2p) **1992** S(1c,4p), I(2t,4c,2p), F(1t,3c,3p), W(3c,2p), C(2p), SA(2c,3p) **1993** F(1c,3p), W(2p), S(1c,3p), I(1p)

Webster, R. E.   Wales

Full Name: Richard Edward
Webster
Club: Swansea
Position: Flanker
Height: 6ft 2in (1.88m)
Weight: 14st 7lb (92kg)
Occupation: Sales representative
with The Brickyard (Swansea)
Born: Morriston, 9.7.67
Family: Kelly (daughter)
Former club: Bonymaen
International debut: Australia 21,
Wales 22, 1987 (World Cup)
Five Nations' debut: Ireland 15,
Wales 16, 1992
Best moments in rugby: Winning
first Wales cap in World Cup third
place play-off; being selected for
1993 Lions
Worst moment in rugby: Getting
injured
Most respected opponent: Alan
Reynolds (Swansea & Wales)
Biggest influence on career: My
father (Phil) – always been there for
me
Serious injuries: Six operations on
knee, two broken bones in hand
Best memory last season:
Swansea's 21–6 defeat of Wallabies
(4.11.92)

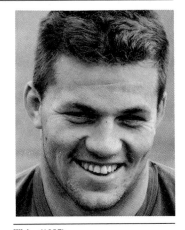

Wales (1987)		
Last Season	5 caps	0 pts
v Italy XV	1 app	5 pts
Career	13 caps	4 pts
Lions 1993	Tour to New Zealand	

Caps (13): **1987** wc-A **1990** Ba **1991**
wc-Arg, A(b) **1992** I, F, E, S, A
1993 E, S, I, F

Points (4 – 1t): **1992** S(1t)

Suggestions to improve rugby: *On-field* – More sympathetic refereeing in
rucks/mauls. Less club games in between league matches. *Off-field* – All
committee members to retire at 35. Clubs to be more sympathetic to players
and players' needs
Notable landmarks in rugby career: Set tone for great 1992/93 season with
try in Wales' 43–12 non-cap win over Italy at the Arms Park (7.10.92). The
following month he helped Swansea beat Australia 21–6 at St Helens (4.11.92).
Subsequently, was ever present through out Wales' international season,
playing in the 6–23 loss to Australia and the 1993 Five Nations' campaign.
Capped term with selection for 1993 British Lions. Won six caps for Welsh
Youth (1984–86) whilst playing for Bonymaen before spending the summer of
1987 in Australia, primarily representing Canberra but also Wales against the

Aussies in the World Cup third/fourth place play-off (Rotorua, 18.6.87), having been called up as an emergency replacement. Persistent knee problems kept him out of the international limelight until 1990 when he turned against the centenary Barbarians but another injury, this time a broken hand, meant that he missed the 1991 Five Nations' Championship. At last fit, he toured Australia (1991), though he was not fielded in the Test, and rose to prominence first in the World Cup and then the 1992 Five Nations' Championship, during which he scored his first Test try, in the 15–12 defeat of Scotland

Touchlines: Horse riding, weightlifting, DIY

Weir, G. W. Scotland

Full Name: George Wilson (Doddie) Weir
Club: Melrose
Position: No 8, lock
Height: 6ft 6in (1.98m)
Weight: 15st 6lb (98kg)
Occupation: Farmer with John W Weir
Born: Edinburgh, 4.7.70
Family: Single
Family links with rugby: Father (John) played for Gala. Brother (Thomas) plays for Scottish Schools. Brother (Christopher) plays for Melrose
International debut: Scotland 49, Argentina 3, 1990
Five Nations' debut: Scotland 7, England 25, 1992
Best moment in rugby: Getting capped against Argentina
Most embarrassing moment: Trying to kick clear and then dive on a loose ball, and missing it both times, in 1991 Melrose Sevens first round loss to Hawick
Most respected opponents: John Jeffrey (Kelso & ex-Scotland) and David Sole (Edinburgh Acads & ex-Scotland)
Biggest influence on career: Jim Telfer (Melrose coach) – told me what to do, when and how

Scotland (1990)

Last Season	6 caps	0 pts
1993	Tour to South Seas	
Career	18 caps	4 pts

Caps (18): **1990** Arg **1991** Ro wc-J, Z, I, WS, E, NZ **1992** E, I, F, W, A(1,2) **1993** I, F, W, E

Points (4 – 1t): **1991** wc–Z(1t)

386

Other sporting achievements: Stow sprint champion. Completing Thirlestone cross-country (horses)
Best memory last season: Melrose winning League title
Suggestions to improve rugby: *On-field* – Sort out lineout. There is supposed to be a one-metre gap but no-one bothers with it. Better education of referees to allow game to flow better. Abolish conversions and instead increase worth of tries. *Off-field* – Allow players to benefit from rugby-related activities. Make beer cheaper so we can have a better time after rugby
Notable landmarks in rugby career: Toured New Zealand with Scottish Schools (1988) and Scotland (1990). Represented South of Scotland in Inter-District Championship, Scotland U-19, Scotland U-21s (v Wales, 1990 and 1991) and Scotland B, becoming the youngest forward to represent them (at 19) in 22–22 draw with Ireland B (Murrayfield, 9.12.89). Has also played in the annual Scotland A game against Spain for the past three years (1990–93) and last season also turned out against Italy (19.12.92) for the full Scotland side masquerading as the A-team. Made full debut against touring Pumas (10.11.90). Toured North America with Scotland (1991), playing in all six matches (including two non-cap Tests against US Eagles and Canada), and Australia (1992), appearing at lock in both Tests. Ever present for Scotland on his return home. Helped Melrose win McEwan's Scottish Club Championship for third time in four seasons in 1992/93, and retain Border League for fourth consecutive season
Touchlines: Horse riding (one-day eventing), clay pigeon shooting, training six days per week

Wilkinson, C. R.   Ireland

Full Name: Colin Robert Wilkinson
Club: Malone
Position: Fullback, outside-half, centre
Height: 5ft 11in (1.81m)
Weight: 12st 4lb (79kg)
Occupation: Solicitor with James Murlend & Son
Born: Belfast, 4.4.61
Family: Claire (wife) and Ben (son)
Family links with rugby: Brother-in-law (John Martin) is the Ireland physio
International debut: Scotland 15, Ireland 3, 1993
Five Nations' debut: As above
Best moment in rugby: Selection to Ireland's 1991 World Cup squad as an over-30 – big thrill

Worst moment in rugby: Captaining Malone to defeat by Ballymena in 1989/90 Ulster Senior Cup final
Most respected opponent: Keith Crossan (Instonians & Ireland)
Biggest influence on career: Chuck Evans (schoolteacher) – converted me from No 8 to centre
Best memory last season: Making Ireland debut at Murrayfield

Ireland (1993)		
Last Season	1 cap	0 pts
Career	1 cap	0 pts

Caps (1): 1993 S

Points Nil

Suggestions to improve rugby: *On-field* – More consistency in refereeing. *Off-field* – Reimbursement for time lost to rugby

Notable landmarks in rugby career: Played for Ulster at Schools, Under-19, Under-20, Under-21, Under-23 and senior levels, his debut in the top-grade coming in 1985. Made the first of his seven Ireland A appearances in 1990 against Argentina (27–12, Limerick 20.10 .90). Landed conversion and penalty goal for Ireland B in 24–10 defeat of England B at Old Belvedere (1.3.91) and added a try in the corresponding fixture at Richmond in 1991/92 (31.1.92) when England won 47–15. Figured also in three B wins over Scotland (16–0, Ravenhill 22.12.90; 29–19, Murrayfield 28.12.91; 13–22, Dublin 28.12.92). Included in Ireland's preliminary squad for 1991 World Cup but omitted from final 26. Selected as replacement for the first time when Australia visited Dublin on 31 October 1992. Finally got his chance on 16 January 1992 when turning out at fullback against Scotland at Murrayfield (lost 3–15)
Touchlines: Golf (18-handicap)

Williams-Jones, H.   Wales

Full Name: Hugh Williams-Jones
Club: South Wales Police
Position: Prop
Height: 5ft 11in (1.81m)
Weight: 16st 6lb (104.5kg)
Occupation: Police sergeant with South Wales Constabulary
Born: Bryncethin, 10.1.63
Family: Karyn (wife), Lloyd (son) and Nia (daughter)
Family links with rugby: Brother (Richard) in Grade III WRU referee
Former clubs: Bryncethin Youth, Bridgend, Llanelli, Pontypridd
International debut: Scotland 23, Wales 7, 1989
Five Nations' debut: As above

Best moment in rugby: Winning first full cap

Worst moment in rugby: Australia tour 1991 – being thrashed by New South Wales (8–71) and Australia (6–63)

Most embarrassing moment: South Wales Police's Welsh Cup quarter-final defeat against Llanharan in 1988/89

Most respected opponent: David Sole (Edinburgh Academicals & Scotland)

Biggest influence on career: Brian Nicholas (my coach at Bryncethin and Bridgend) – sorted my head out

Other sporting achievements: Glamorgan County Cricket U-15 cap

Best memory last season: Wales' win over England

Suggestions to improve rugby: *On-field* – Abolish 90-degree wheel law altogether as it is too negative. *Off-field* – IRB must clarify regulations relating to amateurism and then insist on worldwide adherence. Things are slowly moving in the right direction

Notable landmarks in rugby career: Four years on from his debut Hugh finally made it through a Five Nations' campaign as first-choice player. Indeed, he was an ever-present in the Welsh side throughout the 1992/93 campaign, and also turned out in the 43–12 non-cap defeat of Italy (Cardiff, 7.10.92). Capped twice by Welsh Youth in 1982 (v England Colts and France Juniors) whilst with Bryncethin. Toured to Italy (1986) and Canada (1989) with Wales B. Capped in 15–28 loss to France B (La Teste, 12.11.89). Also toured to New Zealand (1988) with Combined Services and Australia (1991) with Wales. Missed 1990 trip to Namibia due to family commitments. Past captain of Glamorgan County and representative of Crawshays and British Police. Toured with Wales to Zimbabwe and Namibia over summer of 1993, playing in two out of the three Tests

Touchlines: Cricket for Police divisional side, social golf

Wales (1989)

Last Season	7 caps	0 pts
v Italy XV	1 app	0 pts
1993	Tour to Zimbabwe/Namibia	
Career	12 caps	0 pts

Caps 12): **1989** S(R) **1990** F(R), I **1991** A(a) **1992** S, A **1993** E, S, I, F, Z(1), Na

Points Nil

Wilson, D. J.   Australia

Full Name: David John Wilson
Club: Eastern Districts
State: Queensland
Position: Flanker
Height: 6ft 2in (1.88m)
Weight: 14st 11lb (94kg)
Occupation: Area manager with BP Oil
Born: 4.1.67
Family: June (mother), Keith (father), Peter (brother) and Paul (brother)
Former clubs: None. Easts since 1986
International debut: Australia 27, Scotland 12, 1992
Best moment in rugby: Second Test win over All Blacks which secured 1992 Bledisloe Cup series
Worst moment in rugby: Missing the 1990 tour to New Zealand due to broken ankle
Most respected opponent: Michael Jones (Auckland & New Zealand)
Serious injuries: Knee reconstruction (1987), broken ankle (1990), broken collarbone (1992)

Australia (1992)

Last Season	8 caps	5 pts
Career	8 caps	5 pts

Caps (8): 1992 S(1,2), NZ(1,2,3), SA, I, W

Points (5 – 1t): 1992 W(1t)

Other sporting achievements: Bettering 105 for a round of golf
Best memory last season: Bledisloe series win and beating South Africa in historic one-off Test in Cape Town
Suggestions to improve rugby: *On-field* – Penalty and dropped goal should be worth only two points. *Off-field* – Players at representative level should be financially rewarded
Notable landmarks in rugby career: Another of the current crop of Wallabies who emerged on the 1989 tour to Canada and France, David 's progress was slowed by a fractured ankle which kept him out of the 1990 tour to New Zealand. However, he had recovered in time to tour Europe with the Emerging Wallabies later that year, along with the likes of Jason Little, John Eales and Willie Ofahengaue. A highly valued member of the Test side, since his debut against Scotland in 1992, he featured in all eight Tests last season, scoring a try in the final engagement: a 23–6 win over Wales at Cardiff Arms Park. In addition David, a dual winner in 1989 and 1991 of the Queensland

Rothmans Medal, turned out against Western Transvaal (scored try), Northern Transvaal, Leinster (scored try), Ulster, Connacht, Llanelli and Wales B
Tours: 1989 – France and Canada. 1992 – South Africa, Ireland and Wales
Touchlines: Surfing, golf, fishing
Player to watch: Garrick Morgan (Souths)
Player of the Year: Paul Carozza (Australia)

Winterbottom, P. J.   England

Full Name: Peter James Winterbottom
Club: Harlequins
Position: Flanker
Height: 6ft (1.83m)
Weight: 14st 9lb (92kg)
Occupation: Inter-dealer Eurobond broker with Tullett and Tokyo
Born: Horsforth, Leeds, 31.5.60
Family: Single
Family links with rugby: Father played for Headingley and is secretary and past president
Former clubs: Fleetwood, Headingley, Exeter, Napier HS OBs (NZ), Hawke's Bay (NZ), Durban HS OBs (SA), Merolomas (Vancouver, Can)

International debut: England 15, Australia 11, 1982
Five Nations' debut: Scotland 9, England 9, 1982
Best moment in rugby: Playing in 1991 World Cup final
Worst moments in rugby: Losing 1991 World Cup final. Losing to Bath with last kick of extra-time in 1992 Pilkington Cup final
Most embarrassing moment: Being caught from behind by Gareth Chilcott, playing touch rugby
Most respected opponent: Former French flanker Jean-Pierre Rives
Biggest influence on career: My father

England (1982)		
Last Season	6 caps	5 pts
Career	58 caps	13 pts
Lions 1983	4 Tests	0 pts
1993	3 Tests	0 pts

Caps (58): **1982** A, S, I, F, W **1983** F, W, S, I, NZ. Lions–NZ(1,2,3,4) **1984** S, F, W, SA(1,2) **1986** W, S, I, F **1987** I, F, W wc–A, J, US, W **1988** F, W, S **1989** Ro, Fj **1990** I, F, W, S, Arg(a1,a2), Arg(b) **1991** W, S, I, F, A wc–NZ, It, F, S, A **1992** S, I, F, W, C, SA **1993** F, W, S, I. Lions–NZ(2,3)

Points (13 – 3t): **1987** wc–US(2t) **1992** C(1t)

Serious injuries: My brain
Other sporting achievements: School U-16 tennis champion
Best memory last season: Tour selection for British Lions
Suggestions to improve rugby: Consult players before introducing rules. I cannot understand why the new rules were brought in. There is nothing wrong with the ruck/maul law before. If a side has the ball you know they have to release it
Notable landmarks in rugby career: England's most-capped forward (58 since debut in 1982) and second-most capped player behind Rory Underwood (60). Remarkable durability, having toured with Lions last summer ten years after last visiting New Zealand with them. Much travelled player who shot up the representative ranks following impressive displays for Yorkshire, and England against France in 1981 B International. Represented England Colts at No 8, before switching to flanker, where played for Yorkshire. Tours include New Zealand with 1983 Lions, and South Africa (1984), World Cup (1987, scoring two tries against USA), Argentina (1990) and Fiji/Australia (1991) with England. Played club rugby all over world, including for Hawke's Bay in New Zealand. Ever-present during back-to-back Grand Slams (1991–92), making 50th appearance in 38–9 win over Ireland at Twickenham (1.2.92). Harlequins captain between 1990–93, leading team to 1991 and 1992 Pilkington Cup finals (winning in 1991 against Northampton). Scored third Test try of career on 17 October 1992 when England beat Canada 26–13 at Wembley Stadium
Touchlines: Golf, squash

Wright, G. D. South Africa

Full Name: Garth Derick Wright
Club: Wanderers
Province: Transvaal
Position: Scrum-half
Height: 6ft (1.83m)
Weight: 14st 2lb (90kg)
Occupation: Financial advisor
Born: East London, 9.9.63
Former Province: Eastern Province
International debut: South Africa 33, NZ Cavaliers 18, 1986
Notable landmarks in rugby career: Unfortunate not to have played in the two home Tests against New Zealand and Australia in 1992 as he was poised for selection before

a calf muscle injury, a fortnight before the All Blacks' arrival, let in Natal rival Robert du Preez. The pair had come face to face in the 1992 Currie Cup final, at Ellis Park on 12 September, when du Preez again finished in the driver's seat as Natal won 14–13 to secure their second Cup win in three seasons. However, Garth had the last laugh as he leapfrogged du Preez in the pecking order during the Springboks' tour to France and England, and appeared in all three Test matches on the trip. In addition he played five other games against Aquitaine (at outside-half in 29–22 win, Pau, 7.10.92), Midi-Pyrenees (won 18–15, Toulouse, 15.10.92), French Barbarians (lost 20–25, Lille, 31.10.92), the Midlands Division (won 32–9, Leicester, 4.11.92) and England B (won 20–16, Bristol, 7.11.92). Prior to last season he had picked up four caps – two against the rebel New Zealand Cavaliers in the third and fourth Tests of the Game's most controversial ever series, and two against the First National Bank (World) XV in 1989

South Africa (1986)

Last Season	3 caps	0 pts
Career	7 caps	4 pts

Caps (7): **1986** Cv(3,4) **1989** Wd(1,2) **1992** F(1,2), E

Points (4 – 1t): **1986** Cv(4:1t)

Wright, P. H. Scotland

Full Name: Peter Hugh Wright
Club: Boroughmuir
Position: Prop
Height: 6ft (1.83m)
Weight: 17st 2lb (109kg)
Occupation: Blacksmith with MacDonald & Ross Structural Engineers
Born: Bonnyrigg, 30.12.67
Family: Audrey (wife)
Family links with rugby: Graham (brother) and David (brother) play for Lasswade
Former club: Lasswade
International debut: Australia 27, Scotland 12, 1992
Five Nations' debut: France 11, Scotland 3, 1993
Best moment in rugby: Being told I was in the British Lions squad
Worst moment in rugby: Tearing medial and cruciate knee ligaments
Biggest influence on career: Bruce Hay (Boroughmuir coach)
Serious injuries: Torn medial and cruciate knee ligaments

Best memory last season: Running out at Murrayfield against Wales

Notable landmarks in rugby career: The seventh player to be capped from the Boroughmuir club, Peter appeared on both sides of the Scottish front row last season – making his debut on the tour to Australia in the first Test defeat in Sydney on

Scotland (1992)		
Last Season	5 caps	0 pts
Career	5 caps	0 pts
Lions 1993	Tour to New Zealand	

Caps (5): **1992** A(1,2) **1993** F, W, E

Points Nil

13 June. He retained his place the following week at Ballymore when the world champion Wallabies ran out 37–13 winners, but was deposed by Paul Burnell for the 1993 Five Nations' Championship. That would have been that but for the fact that the Scots were having something of a crisis at loosehead in the wake of David Sole's retirement. Bristol's Alan Sharp was picked but withdrew injured and after one cap his replacement, GHK's Alan Watt, also pulled out of contention. Peter was offered the job and did so well against France, Wales and England that he was picked to tour New Zealand with the British Lions last summer. Although he failed to make the Test side, Peter did turn out against North Auckland, the NZ Maoris, Southland, Taranaki, Hawke's Bay and Waikato. During the previous Lions tour in 1989 he was to be found in Japan with Scotland, where he made appearances against Kanto and Japan Under-23. Indeed, Peter is no stranger to representative rugby, having played for Scotland at Under-15, Under-18, Under-19 and Under-21 levels. He also skippered Edinburgh Under-21s. He played his first senior game for Boroughmuir at the age of 18 and his Scotland B bow in the 14–12 win over France B at Melrose in 1989. He added to his A/B tally last season with an appearance at tighthead in the 22–13 win over Ireland A in Dublin (28.12.92)

Touchlines: Golf, all sports

The moment of triumph for Wales captain Ieuan Evans as he dives on the ball for the winning try against England in the Arms Park

APPENDIX

APPLESON, Mark Edward. **Status:** Scotland A. **Position:** Wing, fullback. **Club:** London Scottish. **Debut:** Scotland B 19, Ireland B 29, 1991. **Caps:** 2B,2A. **Points:** 7B(2c,1p). **1992/93:** 2A. **Born:** London, 26.2.68. **Height:** 5ft 10in. **Weight:** 13st 5lb. **Occupation:** PE teacher. **Notes:** Helped Scotland win 1992 Dubai Sevens

ATHERTON, Stephen. **Status:** South Africa squad. **Position:** Lock. **Province:** Natal. **Club:** Pinetown. **Caps:** 0. **Provincial debut:** 1988. **Born:** England, 17.3.65. **Height:** 6ft 7in. **Weight:** 18st 8lb. **Notes:** Made six appearances on Springboks' 1992 tour to France and England

BACK, Neil Antony. **Status:** England A. **Position:** Flanker. **Club:** Leicester. **Debut:** England B 12, Emerging Australians 12, 1990. **Caps:** 1xv,4A,8B,3u/21. **Points:** 10A(2t),8B(2t),12u/21(3t). **1992/93:** 4A,1B. **Born:** Coventry, 16.1.69. **Height:** 5ft 10in. **Weight:** 13st 10lb. **Notes:** Two tries in 59–0 rout of Italy A (3.2.93)

BALDWIN, David Neil. **Status:** England A. **Position:** Lock. **Club:** Sale. **Debut:** England A 18, USSR 10, 1989. **Caps:** 3A. **Points:** 0. **1992/93:** 1A. **Born:** Leeds, 3.9.64. **Height:** 6ft 6in. **Weight:** 17st 8lb. **Occupation:** Screen printer. **Notes:** Played in A-team's 24–18 first Test defeat v New Zealand XV (28.6.92)

BALDWIN, Graham Paul Samuel. **Status:** England A. **Position:** Prop. **Club:** Northampton. **Debut:** Spain 3, England A 34, 1992. **Caps:** 5B,2u/21. **Points:** 0. **1992/93:** 1A. **Born:** 6.12.68. **Height:** 6ft 1in. **Weight:** 17st. **Occupation:** Health/fitness instructor. **Notes:** B-team prop in 24–18 first Test loss to New Zealand (28.6.92)

BATES, Steven Michael. **Status:** England bench. **Position:** Scrum-half. **Club:** Wasps. **Debut:** Romania 3, England 58, 1989. **Caps:** 1xv,1F,6A. **Points:** 0. **1992/93:** 1A. **Born:** Merthyr Tydfil, 4.3.63. **Height:** 5ft 10in. **Weight:** 13st. **Occupation:** Teacher. **Notes:** 1992/93 back-up to Dewi Morris; 'A' v South Africa (7.11.92)

BLACKMORE, Andrew George. **Status:** England A. **Position:** Lock. **Club:** Bristol. **Debut:** England A 16, South Africa 20, 1992. **Caps:** 7A. **Points:** 0. **1992/93:** 7A. **Born:** Bristol, 1.11.65. **Height:** 6ft 7in. **Weight:** 17st 4lb. **Notes:** Career injury man who returned last season to play v SA,F,It,S,I,C(1,2)

BRIAL, Michael. **Status:** Australia squad. **Position:** Flanker, No 8. **Club:** Eastern Suburbs. **State:** NSW. **Debut:** Munster 22, Australia 19, 1992. **Caps:** 0. **Age:** 21. **Height:** 6ft 3in. **Weight:** 16st 7lb. **Occupation:** Futures trader. **Notes:** Ex-Aus u/21s (1990–91) who played four times on 1992 tour to Ireland/Wales

BUCKETT, Ian. **Status:** Wales A. **Position:** Prop. **Club:** Swansea. **Debut:** Netherlands 12, Wales A 34, 1990. **Caps:** 3A. **Points:** 0. **1992/93:** 2A (v N,I). **Born:** Hollywell, 23.12.67. **Height:** 6ft 1in. **Weight:** 16st. **Occupation:** Student. **Note:** Toured with Wales to Namibia (1990) and Zimbabwe/Namibia (1993); played for Oxford in '92 Varsity match

BUCKTON, John Richard. **Status:** England A. **Position:** Centre. **Club:** Saracens. **Debut:** England 28, Australia 19, 1988. **Caps:** 1xv,3F,1A,4 B. **Points:** 4xv(1t). **1992/93:** 1A. **Born:** Hull, 22.12.61. **Height:** 6ft 2in. **Weight:** 13st. **Occupation:** Travel company manager. **Notes:** 1992/93 'A' outing v France A.

BUZZA, Alan Jan. **Status:** England A. **Position:** Fullback. **Club:** Wasps. **Debut:** France A 15, England A 15, 1990. **Caps:** 5A. **Points:** 9A(2t). **1992/93:** 3A. **Born:** Beverley, Yorks, 3.3.66. **Height:** 6ft. **Weight:** 13st. **Notes:** Nine points (1t,2c) in 59–0 defeat of Italy A (3.2. 93); replacement v South Africa (7.11.92)

CAZALBOU, Jerome. **Status:** France bench. **Position:** Scrum-half. **Club:** Toulouse. **Debut:** None. **Caps:** 5A. **Points:** 20 (5t). **1992/93:** 1A. **Born:** Toulouse, 30.4.69. **Height:** 5ft 8½in. **Weight:** 11st 12lb. **Occupation:** Bank official. **Notes:** Captained France Espoirs to 24–17 win over South Africa in Bordeaux (4.10.92)

CHALLINOR, Andrew Paul. **Status:** England A. **Position:** Outside-half. **Club:** Harlequins. **Debut:** England A 29, France A 17, 1992. **Caps:** 6A. **1992/93:** 6A (v F,It,Sp,C1,2). **Points:** 45 (3t,3c,8p). **Born:** Wolverhampton, 5.12.69. **Height:** 6ft. **Weight:** 13st 2lb. **Note:** 14pts v France, 10pts v Italy, 5pts v Spain, 16pts v Canada (1,2)

CLARK, Christopher. **Status:** England A. **Position:** Prop. **Club:** Swansea. **Debut:** England A 59, Italy A 0, 1993. **Caps:** 3A,2u/21. **Points:** 0. **1992/93:** 3A. **Height:** 6ft. **Weight:** 16st. **Notes:** Combined England u/21 duties in 1992/93 with 'A' team outings v France, Italy and Spain

DAWE, Richard Graham Reed. **Status:** England A. **Position:** Hooker. **Club:** Bath. **Debut:** Ireland 17, England 0, 1987. **Caps:** 4F,10A. **Points:** 0. **1992/93:** 2A. **Born:** Plymouth, 4.9.59. **Height:** 5ft 11in. **Weight:** 13st 10lb. **Note:** Capped four times in 1987 (I,F,W,wc-US); played in both Tests on A-tour to New Zealand

DAWSON, Matthew. **Status:** England A. **Position:** Scrum-half. **Club:** Northampton. **Debut:** England A 29, France A 17, 1993. **Caps:** 4A,1u/21. **Points:** 15A(3t),4u/21 (1t). **Height:** 5ft 10in. **Weight:** 13st. **Notes:** Great 1992/93 campaign for club and England A. 1 try v Italy A (3.2.93), 2 v Ire A (19.3.93). Tour to Canada (injured first match)

DUNN, Kevin Anthony. **Status:** England A. **Position:** Hooker. **Club:** Wasps. **Debut:** England A 9, Australia 37, 1988. **Caps:** 8A (also: 89:F, It,Fj; 93:F,It,Sp,I). **Points:** 9(2t). **Height:** 5ft 9in. **Weight:** 13st 10lb. **Notes:** Tries v France (1989) and Spain (1993)

EKERT, Anthony. **Status:** Australia squad. **Position:** Scrum-half. **Club:** Gordon. **State:** NSW. **Debut:** None. **Age:** 24. **Height:** 5ft 10in. **Weight:** 12st. **Occupation:** Student. **Notes:** Played v Munster, Connacht, Wales B, Monmouthshire and Welsh Students during 1992 Ireland/Wales tour

ETHERIDGE, John. **Status:** Ireland A. **Position:** Lock. **Club:** Northampton. **Debut:** Wales A 28, Ireland A 29, 1993. **Caps:** 2A. **Points:** 0. **1992/93:** 2A. **England A caps:** 2 (1989 It,USSR). **Points:** 0. **Born:** Gloucester, 8.6.65. **Height:** 6ft 6in. **Weight:** 16st 7lb. **Note:** Played v Wales A and England A in 1992/93.

FORD, Stephen Paul. **Status:** Wales A. **Position:** Wing. **Club:** Cardiff. **Debut:** Ireland 14, Wales 8, 1990. **Caps:** 8F,4A. **Points:** 8F(2t),22 A(5t). **1992/93:** 2A(2t). **Born:** 15.8.65. **Height:** 6ft. **Weight:** 12st 7lb. **Occupation:** Carpet fitter. **Notes:** Record 7 tries for Wales A v Saskatchewan (1989). 2 v Holland (6.2.93)

FOX, David. **Status:** Wales A. **Position:** Hooker. **Club:** Llanelli. **Debut:** Wales A 11, Australia 24, 1992. **Caps:** 1A. **Points:** 0. **1992/93:** 1A. **Born:** 4.12.59. **Height:** 5ft 9in. **Weight:** 13st 7lb. **Occupation:** Fireman. **Notes:** Permanent reserve through 1992 Five Nations' campaign. A debut v Aussies (7.11.92)

FURLONG, Neville. **Status:** Ireland Full. **Position:** Wing. **Club:** Garryowen. **Debut:** New Zealand 24, Ireland 21, 1992. **Caps:** 2F,2A. **Points:** 4F(1t). **Height:** 6ft 2in. **Weight:** 14st 5lb. **Occupation:** Army officer. **Born:** 10.7.68. **Notes:** Scored lone Irish try in 6–59 loss to All Blacks (second Test, Wellington, 6.6.92)

GARFORTH, Darren James. **Status:** England A. **Position:** Prop. **Club:** Leicester. **Debut:** England A 66, Spain 5, 1993. **Caps:** 2A. **Points:** 0. **Born:** 9.4.66. **Height:** 5ft 10in. **Weight:** 16st 10lb. **Occupation:** Tubular technician. **Notes:** Toured with England A to Canada (1993); other A appearance against Ireland

GRAY, Christopher Andrew. **Status:** Scotland A. **Position:** Lock. **Club:** Nottingham. **Debut:** Scotland 23, Wales 7, 1989. **Caps:** 22F,4B,2A. **Points:** 12F (3t). **1992/93:** 2A (as captain). **Born:** Haddington, 11.7.60. **Height:** 6ft 5in. **Weight:** 16st 12lb. **Occupation:** Dental surgeon. **Notes:** 1990 Grand Slam lock

GREENWOOD, Matthew James. **Status:** England A. **Position:** Flanker. **Club:** Wasps. **Debut:** Spain 3, England A 34, 1992. **Caps:** 7A (92: v Sp,I,F,It ; 93: NZ1,It,I). **Points:** 0. **Born:** 25.9.64. **Height:** 6ft 6in. **Weight:** 16st 8lb. **Occupation:** Quantity surveyor. **Notes:** Toured with England A to NZ(1992) and Canada (1993)

HAAG, Martin. **Status:** England A. **Position:** Lock. **Club:** Bath. **Debut:** Spain 3, England A 34, 1992. **Caps:** 3A. **Points:** 4(1t). **Born:** 28.7 .68. **Height:** 6ft 5½in. **Weight:** 16st 7lb. **Occupation:** Financial advisor. **Notes:** Helped Bath win 1991/92 League & Cup double. Scored try in 47–15 win over Ireland A (1992)

HACKNEY, Stephen Thomas. **Status:** England A. **Position:** Wing. **Club:** Leicester. **Debut:** England B 9, Australia 37, 1988. **Caps:** 6A. **Points:** 24 (5t). **1992/93:** 4A (4t:vSp). **Born:** 13.6.68. **Height:** 5ft 11in. **Weight:** 13st 4lb. **Notes:** Scored four tries in England A's 66–5 win over Spain (Richmond, 5.3.93)

HALL, Jonathan Peter. **Status:** England A. **Position:** Flanker, No 8. **Club:** Bath. **Debut:** Scotland 18, England 6, 1984. **Caps:** 20F,8A. **Points:** 8F(2t),4A(1t). **1992/93:** 6A(1t:vI). **Born:** 15.3.62. **Height:** 6ft 3½in. **Weight:** 16st 7lb. **Occupation:** Lloyds underwriter. **Notes:** Full debut aged 21; '92/93 England A captain

HALPIN, Garrett Francis. **Status:** Ireland A. **Position:** Prop. **Club:** London Irish. **Debut:** England 23, Ireland 0, 1990. **Caps:** 5F,2A. **Points:** 0. **1992/93:** 1A. **Born:** 14.2.66. **Height:** 5ft 11in. **Weight:** 17st 4lb. **Notes:** Irish international hammer thrower at 1987 World Championships (Rome)

HESLOP, Nigel John. **Status:** England A. **Position:** Wing. **Club:** Orrell. **Debut:** Argentina 12, England 25, 1990. **Caps:** 10F,3A. **Points:** 12 F(3t). **1992/93:** 1A (vSA). **Born:** 4.12.63. **Height:** 5ft 10in. **Weight:** 12st 7lb. **Notes:** Scored England's two tries v Leicester (5.9.92) but switched codes to R Oldham when dropped

HILL, Richard, John. **Status:** England bench. **Position:** Scrum-half. **Club:** Bath. **Debut:** South Africa 33, England 15, 1984. **Caps:** 29F. **Points:** 8F(2t). **Born:** 4.5.61. **Height:** 5ft 7in. **Weight:** 12st 11lb. **Occupation:** Financial consultant. **Notes:** Played in England's 18–11 win over Leicester (5.9.92)

HOPLEY, Damian Paul. **Status:** England A. **Position:** Centre. **Debut:** England A 12, Emerging Australians 12, Nov 1990. A **Caps:** 10A. **Points:** 9A(2t). **1992/93:** 9A(2t). **Club:** Wasps. **Born:** 12.4.70. **Height:** 6ft 2in. **Weight:** 14st 10lb. **Notes:** Only A-team everpresent in '92/93. Cambridge Blue (1992) in 19–11 Varsity win

HOWLEY, Robert. **Status:** Wales A. **Position:** Scrum-half. **Club:** Bridgend. **Debut:** Holland 12, Wales A 57, 1993. **Caps:** 2A. **Points:** 5A(1t) . **1992/93:** 2A(1t). **Born:** 13.10.70. **Height:** 5ft 10½in. **Weight:** 12st 5lb. **Notes:** Scored try on A-team debut in Den Bosch (6.2.93). Toured Zimbabwe/Namibia (1993) with Wales

HYNES, Martin, Peter. **Status:** England A. **Position:** Prop. **Club:** Orrell. **Debut:** New Zealand 26, England A 18, 1992. **Caps:** 3A,1u/21. **Points:** 0. **1992/93:** 3A. **Born:** 23.8.68. **Height:** 5ft 9in. **Weight:** 15st 4lb. **Occupation:** Electrician. **Notes:** Bench reserve through 1992 Five Nations'. Eng XV v Leicester (5.9.92)

ISAAC, Gary Ronald. **Status:** Scotland bench. **Position:** Prop. **Club:** Gala. **Debut:** Spain 7, Scotland A 39, 1990. **Caps:** 2xv,1A,1u/21. Points: 0. **1992/93:** 2xv,3F(R). **Born:** Dufftown, 15.2.66. **Height:** 5ft 10in. **Weight:** 15st 8lb. **Occupation:** Surveyor. **Notes:** Benchman three times last season (v France, Wales & England). Scotland XV v Fiji and Tonga (1993)

JARDINE, Ian Carrick. **Status:** Scotland A. **Position:** Centre. **Club:** Stirling County. **Debut:** Scotland B 22, Ireland B 22, 1990. **Caps:** 3 B,3A. **Points:** 4B (1t). **1992/93:** 3A. **Born:** Dunfermline, 20.10.64. **Height:** 6ft 1in. **Weight:** 13st 7lb. **Occupation:** Teacher. **Notes:** Regular A centre in 1992/93. On 1993 tour played against Fiji, Tonga, W. Samoa

JONES, Ian Wyn. **Status:** Wales A. **Position:** Wing, fullback. **Club:** Llanelli. **Debut:** Wales A 11, Australia 24, 1992. **Caps:** 3A,1u/21. **Points:** 5A. **1992/93:** 3A(1t). **Born:** Carmarthen, 12.5.71. **Height:** 5ft 10in. **Weight:** 12st 4lb. **Occupation:** Sheet worker. **Note:** Try v I (Lost 28–29, 5.3.93). Toured to Zimbabwe/Namibia (1993)

JONES, Peter Martin. **Status:** Scotland A. **Position:** Prop. **Club:** Gloucester. **Debut:** Wales 15, Scotland 12, 1992. **Caps:** 1F,2A,2B. **Points:** 0. **1992/93:** 1A. **Born:** 28.12.64. **Height:** 5ft 11in. **Weight:** 15st 8lb. **Occupation:** Engineer. **Notes:** A-team prop v Italy (19.12.92).

JORGENSEN, Peter. **Status:** Australia Full. **Position:** Wing, fullback. **State:** NSW. **Debut:** Australia 27, Scotland 12, 1992. **Caps:** 2 (also: 37–13 v S, 1992). **Points:** 0. **Born:** 30.4.73. **Height:** 5ft 11in. **Weight:** 12st 7lb. **Occupation:** Futures market trainee. **Notes:** Toured Britain with Australia U-19s in 1991/92

KARDOONI Aadel. **Status:** England A. **Position:** Scrum-half. **Club:** Leicester. **Debut:** New Zealand 24, England A 18, 1992. **Caps:** 2 (also: NZ 26, England A 18, 1992). **Points:** 0. **Born:** 17.5.68 (Tehran, Iran). **Height:** 5ft 8in. **Weight:** 11st 8lb. **Notes:** Pilkington Cup winner with Leicester in 1993, runner-up in 1988

KNOETZE, Francois (Faffa). **Status:** South Africa squad. **Position:** Centre. **Province:** Western Province. **Debut:** South Africa 20, World XV 19, 1989. **Caps:** 2F (also: 22–16 v World XV). **Points:** 4(1t). **Born:** 18.1.63. **Height:** 5ft 6in. **Weight:** 12st 2lb. **Occupation:** Actuary. **Notes:** Try on debut at Cape Town (26.8.89)

LANDREAU, Fabrice. **Status:** France Espoirs. **Position:** Hooker. **Club:** Grenoble. **Debut:** France B 18, England B 22, 1992. **Caps:** 1B. **Points:** 0. **Born:** 1.8.68. **Height:** 5ft 10in. **Weight:** 15st. **Occupation:** French electricity official. **Notes:** France benchman since 1992 Arg tour. Helped Espoirs bt SA 24–17 (4.10.92)

LEGGE, Sean, **Status:** Wales A. **Position:** No 8. **Club:** SW Police. **Debut:** Wales A 11, Australia 24, 1992. **Caps:** 4A. **Points:** 0. **1992/93:** 4A. **Born:** 21.8.68. **Height:** 6ft 5in. **Weight:** 16st 10lb. **Occupation:** Police officer. **Notes:** Everpresent for Wales A during '92/93. Welsh benchman in 1992 Championship

LE ROUX, Hendrik Pieter (Hennie). **Status:** South Africa full. **Position:** Outside-half. **Province:** Transvaal. **Debut:** South Africa 20 France 20, 1993. **Caps:** 2. **Points:** 0. **Born:** 10.7.67. **Height:** 5ft 10in. **Weight:** 12st 8lb. **Occupation:** Student. **Notes:** Junior Springbok; six apps on 1992 tour to France and England (try v Provence-Cote d'Azur, 13.10.92)

McINTOSH, Dale Lynsay Manawa. **Status:** Scotland A. **Position:** Flanker. **Club:** Pontypridd. **Debut:** Scotland A 19, Ireland B 29, 1991. **Caps:** 1A,2B,1u/21. **Points:** 0. **1992/93:** 1A. **Born:** Turangi (NZ), 23.11.69. **Height:** 6ft 3in. **Weight:** 16st. **Occupation:** Labourer. **Notes:** Scotland Trial injury robbed him of Test cap

MACDONALD, Andy. **Status:** Scotland A. **Position:** Lock/flanker. **Club:** Heriot's FP. **Debut:** Scotland B 22, Ireland B 22, 1989. **Caps:** 4A,5 B. **Points:** 4A(1t). **1992/93:** 3A. **Born:** Nairn, 17.1.66. **Height:** 6ft 8in. **Weight:** 17st 10lb. **Occupation:** Surveyor. **Notes:** 1992/93 lock v Spain & Ireland, flanker v France

MELVILLE, Eric. **Status:** France bench. **Position:** No 8, flanker. **Club:** Toulon. **Debut:** France 31, Ireland 12, 1990. **Caps:** 6F. **Points:** 0. **1992/93:** 4(R). **Born:** Cape Town, 27.6.61. **Height:** 6ft 5in. **Weight:** 17st. **Occupation:** Computer programmer. **Notes:** Permanent French benchman in 1993 Five Nations' campaign

MILLAR, Peter. **Status:** Ireland A. **Position:** Tighthead prop. **Club:** Ballymena. **Debut:** England A 47, Ireland A 15, 1992. **Caps:** 4. **Points:** 0. **1992/93:** 3A. **Born:** 8.6.62. **Height:** 6ft 1in. **Weight:** 16st 6lb. **Occupation:** Bank official. **Notes:** 1992/93 A-team appearances v Scotland (70th min rep), Wales and England

MILLARD, David Bruce. **Status:** Scotland bench. **Position:** Scrum-half. **Club:** London Scottish. **Debut:** Scotland A 19, France A 29, 1993. **Caps:** 1A. **Points:** 0. **1992/93:** 1F(R),1A. **Born:** 19.9.64. **Height:** 6ft 1½in. **Weight:** 14st 4lb. **Occupation:** Osteopath. **Notes:** Led Scotland in 1988 Students World Cup and 1993 World Cup Sevens

MILLIGAN, Kenneth R. **Status:** Scotland A. **Position:** Wing, centre. **Club:** Stewart's-Melville FP. **Debut:** Scotland A 19, France A 29, 1993. **Caps:** 1A. **Points:** 0. **1992/93:** 1A. **Born:** 19.7.72. **Height:** 5ft 10in. **Weight:** 12st 7lb. **Notes:** Helped Stewart's-Melville win McEwan's Scottish Division II title. Toured with Scotland to South Seas (1993)

MONCRIEFF, Mark. **Status:** Scotland A. **Position:** Wing. **Club:** Gala. **Debut:** Spain 14, Scotland 35, 1992. **Caps:** 2A,3B. **Points:** 4A(1t). **Born:** 19.12.68. **Height:** 5ft 10in. **Weight:** 11st 10lb. **Notes:** Only unused member of 1991 World Cup squad; scored try v Spain in Madrid (12.9.92); toured South Seas (1993), playing against Fiji, Tonga and W. Samoa

MONTLAUR, Pierre. **Status:** France bench. **Position:** Outside-half. **Club:** Agen. **Debut:** France 13, England 31, 1992. **Caps:** 1F. **Points:** 0. **1992/93:** 1F(R:Wales). **Born:** Castelsarrasin, 7.2.63. **Height:** 5ft 8in. **Weight:** 11st 12lb. **Note:** Solitary bench appearance in 1992/93, having been valued squad man in 1991/92

MORRIS, Martyn Stuart. **Status:** Wales A. **Position:** Flanker. **Club:** Neath. **Debut:** Scotland 21, Wales 25, 1985. **Caps:** 3A,11F - 1985:S,I, F 1990:I,Na(1,2),Ba 1991:I,F,wc-WS(R) 1992:E. **Points:** 0. **1992/93:** 1F(R),1A. **Born:** 23.8.62. **Height:** 6ft 3in. **Weight:** 15st. **Note:** Wales XV bench v Italy (7.10.92); A v Aus (7.11.92)

MULLINS, Andrew Richard. **Status:** England A. **Position:** Prop. **Club:** Harlequins. **Debut:** England 58, Fiji 23, 1989. **Caps:** 1F,13A/B. **Points:** 0. **1992/93:** 2A,2B. **Born:** London, 12.12.64. **Height:** 5ft 11in. **Weight:** 16st 1lb. **Occupation:** Accountant. **Note:** Played both A Tests in NZ (1992) and 1993 A games v F,It

MUNRO, Donald Shade. **Status:** Scotland A. **Position:** Lock. **Club:** Glasgow H/K. **Debut:** France A 12, Scotland A 18, 1988. **Caps:** 5A. **Points:** 0. **1992/93:** 2A. **Born:** 19.11.66. **Height:** 6ft 6in. **Weight:** 17st. **Notes:** Returned to rugby in 1992, two years after shattering knee. Toured with Scotland to South Seas (1993), played v W. Samoa

MUSTOE, Lyndon. **Status:** Wales A. **Position:** Prop. **Club:** Pontypool. **Debut:** Netherlands 12, Wales A 57, 1993. **Caps:** 2A,1u/21. **Points:** 0 . **1992/93:** 2A. **Born:** Newport, 30.1.69. **Height:** 5ft 11in. **Weight:** 15st. **Occupation:** Bricklayer. **Note:** Capped also v Ireland A (1993) and Scotland u/21 (1990)

NUCIFORA, David Vincent. **Status:** Australia bench. **Position:** Hooker. **Club:** Queensland. **State:** Queensland Univ. **Debut:** Australia 32, Argentina 19, 1991. **Caps:** 1F. **Points:** 0. **Born:** 15.1.62. **Height:** 6ft. **Weight:** 15st. **Occupation:** Auctioneer. **Notes:** 5 apps on '92 Ireland/ Wales tour; capt v Munster & Welsh Students

OJOMOH, Stephen Oziegbe. **Status:** England A. **Position:** Flanker, No 8. **Club:** Bath. **Debut:** New Zealand 26, England A 18, 1992. **Caps:** 7A,2u/21. **Points:** 4A(1t). **1992/93:** 7A(1t). **Born:** 25.5.70. **Height:** 6ft 2in. **Weight:** 16st. **Notes:** Try on England A debut (5.7.92). Member of Bath's '92/93 title-winning side. Eng A summer tourist v Canada (1,2)

OLIVER, Greig Hunter. **Status:** Scotland A. **Position:** Scrum-half. **Club:** Hawick. **Debut:** Scotland 60, Zimbabwe 21, 1987. **Caps:** 3F,3A,2B. **Points:** 4F(1t),4A(1t). **1992/93:** 1A. **Born:** Hawick, 12.9.64. **Height:** 5ft 8½in. **Weight:** 12st 8lb. **Occupation:** Newspaper sub-editor. **Notes:** 'A' scrum-half v Spain (12.9.92)

OOSTHUYSEN, Deon Eugene. **Status:** South Africa squad. **Position:** Wing. **Province:** Northern Transvaal. **Debut:** None. **Born:** 4.12.63. **Height:** 5ft 8½in. **Weight:** 11st 10lb. **Occupation:** Bank official. **Notes:** Blue Bulls' record try-scorer; Six apps on '92 tour to France and England (try v Midlands, 4.11.92)

PATTON, Michael Brian. **Status:** Ireland A. **Position:** Hooker. **Club:** Oxford Univ. **Debut:** Ireland A 13, Scotland A 22, 1992. **Caps:** 1A,2u/21. **Points:** 0. **1992/93:** 1A. **Born:** 15.7.69. **Height:** 6ft. **Weight:** 15st 2lb. **Notes:** Captained Oxford to 11–19 Varisty loss (1992) and Ireland u/21s twice (1990/91)

PEARS, David. **Status:** England XV. **Position:** Fullback, outside-half. **Club:** Harlequins. **Debut:** Argentina 12, England 25, 1990. **Caps:** 3 F,8A,1u/21. **Points:** 59A,2u/21. **1992/93:** 2A(4pts). **Born:** 6.12.67. **Height:** 5ft 10in. **Weight:** 12st 5lb. **Notes:** Kicked 14pts (4p,1c) in 2-test series v Canada (1993)

POTTER, Stuart. **Status:** England A. **Position:** Centre. **Club:** Leicester. **Debut:** England A 59, Italy A 0, 1993. **Caps:** 5A. **Points:** 10A(2t). **1992/93:** 5A(2t). **Born:** 11.11.67. **Height:** 5ft 11in. **Weight:** 13st 8lb. **Occupation:** Insurance broker. **Notes:** Two tries on debut v Italy (Bath, 3.2.93). Also played v Sp, I, C(1,2)

POTTS, Kevin. **Status:** Ireland A. **Position:** Lock, flanker. **Club:** St Mary's College. **Debut:** Scotland A 19, Ireland A 29, 1991. **Caps:** 3 A. **Points:** 4(1t). **1992/93:** 2A. **Born:** 6.11.66. **Height:** 6ft 4in. **Weight:** 16st 12lb. **Occupation:** Accountant. Captained Ireland development squad tour to Zim/Nam/SA (1993)

PRETORIUS, Petrus (Piet) Ingenas Lourens. **Status:** South Africa squad. **Position:** Flanker, lock. **Club:** Pretoria. **Province:** Northern Transvaal. **Debut:** None. **Born:** 17.8.64. **Height:** 6ft 3½in. **Weight:** 16st 1lb. **Occupation:** Technician. **Notes:** Six apps on '92 tour to France and England

REDMAN, Nigel Charles. **Status:** England A. **Position:** Lock. **Club:** Bath. **Debut:** Scotland 33, England 6, 1986. **Caps:** 13F. **Points:** 4(1t). **1992/93:** 1A. **Born:** 16.8.64. **Height:** 6ft 4in. **Weight:** 17st 2lb. **Occupation:** Electrician. **Notes:** Rep England v Leicester (5.9.92) and England A v South Africa (7.11.92)

REID, Stuart James. **Status:** Scotland A. **Position:** No 8, flanker. **Club:** Boroughmuir. **Debut:** USA 12, Scotland 41, 1991. **Caps:** 2xv,2A,3 B,2u/21. **Points:** 12xv(3t). **1992/93:** 1A. **Born:** Kendal, 31.1.70. **Height:** 6ft 3 1/2in. **Weight:** 15st 11lb. **Occupation:** Bank officer. **Notes:** 3 tries for '91 Scotland XV v USA(2) and Canada(1)

RIDGE, Martin Patrick. **Status:** Ireland A. **Position:** Centre. **Club:** Blackrock College. **Debut:** Scotland A 19, Ireland A 29, 1991. **Caps:** 3A,2u/21. **Points:** 8A(2t). **1992/93:** 1A. **Born:** 8.10.70. **Height:** 6ft 1½in. **Weight:** 13st 3lb. **Notes:** Toured NZ (1992); 'A' tries v S,I ('91/92); 54th min 'A' rep v E (19.3.93)

ROBERTS, Harry. **Status:** South Africa bench. **Position:** Hooker. **Province:** Transvaal. **Debut:** None. **Born:** 3.12.60. **Height:** 5ft 10in. **Weight:** 14st 13lb. **Occupation:** Network technician. **Notes:** Ex-Scotland B hooker (1991 v Ireland), who returned home (like John Allan). Six apps on '92 tour to France/England

RODBER, Timothy Andrew Keith. **Status:** England A. **Position:** No 8. **Club:** Northampton. **Debut:** Scotland 7, England 25, 1992. **Caps:** 2F,5A,1u/21. **Points:** 8A(2t). **1992/93:** 1A. **Born:** 2.7.69. **Height:** 6ft 6in. **Weight:** 16st 8lb. **Notes:** Regular England benchman in 1992/93 though played for A-team v South Africa (7.11.92)

ROY, Stuart. **Status:** Wales A. **Position:** Lock. **Club:** Cardiff. **Debut:** Wales A 21, North of England 13, 1992. **Caps:** 4A,1u/21. **Points:** 0. **1992/93:** 4A. **Born:** Ely, 25.12.68. **Height:** 6ft 6in. **Weight:** 17st 4lb. **Occupation:** Medical practitioner. **Landmark:** Everpresent in 1992/93 Wales A side (vNoE,A,N,I)

SAUNDERS, Rob. **Status:** Ireland A. **Position:** Scrum-half. **Club:** London Irish. **Debut:** Ireland 13, France 21, 1991. **Caps:** 11F,2A,1u/21. **Points:** 0. **1992/93:** 1A. **Born:** 5.8.68. **Height:** 5ft 10in. **Weight:** 13st. **Occupation:** Marketing executive. **Notes:** Captained Ireland on debut but dropped after 11 straight apps

SCHUTTE, Phillip. **Status:** South Africa squad. **Position:** Lock. **Province:** Northern Transvaal. **Debut:** None. **Age:** 24. **Height:** 6ft 7½in. **Weight:** 19st 9lb. **Notes:** Pulled off SA development tour in Western Samoa to join Springboks in England (1992) when Adri Geldenhuys withdrew. Played v Midlands and North

SMITH, Damian. **Status:** Australia bench. **Position:** Wing. **Club:** Souths. **State:** Queensland. **Debut:** Munster 22, Australia 19, 1992. **Born:** 1.2.69. **Height:** 6ft 2in. **Weight:** 14st 9lb. Bank official. **Notes:** Played in eight of Wallabies' 13 games on 1992 tour to Ireland and Wales, scoring tries in three of the outings

SODEN, Philip Joseph. **Status:** Ireland A. **Position:** Loosehead prop. **Club:** Cork Constitution. **Debut:** Ireland A 16, Scotland A 0, 1990. **Caps:** 5A,2u/21. **Points:** 0. **1992/93:** 3A. **Born:** 6.9.69. **Height:** 6ft. **Weight:** 16st 10lb. **Occupation:** Owns dry-cleaning business. **Notes:** Everpresent in No 1 jersey for '92/93 A-team

STEELE, John. **Status:** England A. **Position:** Outside-half. **Club:** Northampton. **Debut:** England A 31, Namibia 16, 1990. **Caps:** 2A. **Points:** 0. **1992/93:** 1A. **Born:** 9.8.64. **Height:** 5ft 10in. **Weight:** 13st. **Occupation:** Army officer. **Notes:** 76th minute replacement for Ian Hunter in 16–20 loss to Australia (7.11.92)

THOMPSON, Gavin John. **Status:** England A. **Position:** Centre. **Club:** Harlequins. **Born:** 30.8.69. **Height:** 6ft. **Weight:** 13st 6lb. **Debut:** England A 12, Emerging Australians 12, 1990. **Caps:** 6A,3u/21. **Points:** 12u/21(3t). **1992/93:** 1A. **Notes:** Capt England U-21s twice (1989/90 v R,Neth); toured Arg with England ('90)

THORNEYCROFT, Harvey Spencer. **Status:** England A. **Position:** Wing. **Club:** Northampton. **Debut:** England A 29, France A 17, 1993. **Caps:** 4A,3u/21. **Points:** 15A(3t),12u/21(3t). **Born:** 22.2.69. **Height:** 6ft. **Weight:** 14st. **Notes:** Tries in three of four 1993 A-team apps, v France, Italy and Spain. Ireland alone escaped

TOLAND, Liam Thomas. **Status:** Ireland A. **Position:** Flanker. **Club:** Old Crescent. **Debut:** Wales A 29, Ireland A 28, 1993. **Caps:** 2A,2u/21. **Points:** 0. **Born:** 18.6.72. **Height:** 6ft 2in. **Weight:** 14st 7lb. **Notes:** Turned out for A-team v Wales (5.3.93) and England (19.3.93). U/21 caps also v Wales and England (1991)

TRUSCOTT, Jan Andries. **Status:** South Africa squad. **Position:** Hooker. Province: Northern Transvaal. **Debut:** France Espoirs 24, South Africa 17, 1992. **Caps:** None. **Born:** 22.7.68. **Height:** 6ft. **Weight:** 16st 3lb. **Occupation:** Engineering student. **Notes:** Played in '92 Students World Cup and in 4 games on Fra/Eng tour

WAKEFORD, John Donald Marshall. **Status:** Wales A. **Position:** Lock. **Club:** SW Police. **Debut:** Wales 24, Western Samoa 6, 1988. **Caps:** 2F. **Points:** 4F(1t). **Born:** 29.9.66. **Height:** 6ft 7in. **Weight:** 17st. **Occupation:** Policeman. **Notes:** Try on full debut v Samoans (12.11.88); A-team v Australia (7.11.92)

WALKER, Lloyd Frederick. **Status:** Australia squad. **Position:** Centre. **Club:** Randwick. **State:** NSW. **Debut:** Australia 19, New Zealand 19, 1988. **Caps:** 8. **Points:** 8(2t). **Born:** 7.3.59. **Height:** 6ft 1in. **Weight:** 13st 5lb. **Notes:** Everpresent v 1989 Lions; four apps on Aussie tour of Ireland and Wales (1992)

WILSON, Grant Douglas. **Status:** Scotland A. **Position:** Prop. **Club:** Boroughmuir. **Debut:** Scotland B 22, Ireland B 22, 1989. **Caps:** 2A,3B. **Points:** 0. **1992/93:** 2A. **Born:** Edinburgh, 10.11.66. **Height:** 5ft 11in. **Weight:** 16st 7lb. **Occupation:** Police officer. **Notes:** 'A' games v Ireland and France. Toured with Scotland to South Seas (1993)

WOODS, Niall. **Status:** Ireland A. **Position:** Left wing. **Club:** Blackrock College. **Debut:** Ireland A 13, Scotland A 22, 1992. **Caps:** 3A,2u/21. **Points:** 0A,19u/21. **Born:** 21.6.71. **Height:** 5ft 11in. **Weight:** 11st 8lb. **Notes:** A-team apps v S,W,E (1992/93). Toured Zim/Nab/SA in 1993 with Ireland's development squad

WYLLIE, Douglas, Stewart. **Status:** Scotland A. **Position:** Outside-half/Centre. **Club:** Stew-Mel. **Debut:** Scotland 12, Australia 37, 1984. **Caps:** 13F,4A,3B. **Points:** 3F(1dg),9A(2t). **1992/93:** 2A(5pts:1t). **Born:** 20.5.63. **Height:** 6ft 1in. **Weight:** 13st 10lb. **Notes:** 1992/93 'A' outings v Spain and France. Capt Scotland XV to 21–5 defeat of Tonga Pres XV (2.6.93)

REFEREES

INTERNATIONAL REFEREES 1992/93

W D Bevan (Wales)	NZ v Wd(1,3),F v S
D J Bishop (New Zealand)	NZ v Wd(2),SA v A
F Burger (South Africa)	Arg v F(1,2)
O E Doyle (Ireland)	F v W
J Dume (France)	W v E, S v W
J M Fleming (Scotland)	A v NZ(1), E v F
C J Hawke (New Zealand)	A v S(2)
S R Hilditch (Ireland)	E v SA, SA v F(1)
B Kinsey (Australia)	F v SA(1,2),NZ v BL(1)
D Leslie (Scotland)	I v F
K W McCartney (Scotland)	F v R
A R MacNeill (Australia)	NZ v I(1,2), SA v NZ, W v I, I v E
L McLachlan (New Zealand)	A v S(1)
R J Megson (Scotland)	F v Arg
E Morrison (England)	I v A, S v I, SA v F(2)
P Robin (France)	A v NZ(2,3), NZ v BL(2,3)
G Simmonds (Wales)	E v C
A J Spreadbury (England)	W v A
B Stirling (Ireland)	E v S

Irish referee Stephen Hilditch lays down the law to England skipper Will Carling

BEVAN, Derek. **Apps:** 18. **Test debut:** England 22, Romania 15, 1985. **Five Nations' debut:** France 29, England 10, 1986. **Dismissals:** 0. **Note:** Refereed 1991 World Cup final.

    Record: 1985 E v R **1986** F v E, NZ v A(1,2) **1987** wc-NZ v Fj, F v Z. A v NZ **1988** I v WS **1990** NZ v S(2) **1991** I v F. wc-F v Fj, S v WS, E v A. **1992** S v E, E v I, NZ v Wd(1), NZ v Wd(3) **1993** FvS

BISHOP, David. **Apps:** 17. **Test debut:** Fiji 15, Wales 22, 1986. **Five Nations' debut:** Scotland 13, England 7, 1990. **Dismissals:** 0. **Note:** Refereed 1990 Grand Slam decider; assaulted in tunnel after 1991 France-England World Cup quarter-final.

    Record: 1986 Fj v W, R v F, I v R **1987** wc-W v T, W v C **1988** A v E(1,2), E v A, S v A **1990** S v E, I v W **1991** S v W, W v I. wc-A v Arg, F v E **1992** NZ v Wd(2), SA v A

BURGER, Frederick (Freek). **Apps:** 7. **Test debut:** France 25, Australia 19, 1989. **Five Nations' debut:** Scotland 10, France 6, 1992. **Dismissals:** 0. **Note:** refereed 1980 British Lions, Ireland (1981), South America and World XV (1982–4), NZ Cavaliers (1986) and South Sea Barbarians (1987) before Test debut.

    Record: 1989 F v A(1,2) **1990** S v Arg **1992** S v F, F v I, Arg v F(1,2)

DOYLE, Owen Edward. **Apps:** 14. **Test debut:** Wales 9, Scotland 15, 1984. **Five Nations' debut:** ditto. **Dismissals:** 1 – 1988 Arg v F: A Lorieux (F). **Note:** Five Nations' debut coincided with first leg of Scotland's 1984 Grand Slam.

    Record: 1984 W v S, R v S, W v A **1987** E v S **1988** F v E, Arg v F(1,2), W v WS **1989** F v S **1990** F v E **1991** wc-It v US, Fj v R **1992** W v F **1993** F v W

DUME, Joel. **Apps:** 2. **Test debut:** Wales 10, England 9, 1993. **Five Nations' debut:** ditto. **Dismissals:** 0. **Notes:** Test debut aged just 33, having impressed in 1992 at Students' World Cup and with handling of England B-South Africa.

    Record: 1993 W v E, S v W

FLEMING, James (Jim) Mathieson. **Apps:** 16. **Test debut:** Ireland 13, England 10, 1985. **Five Nations' debut:** ditto. **Dismissals:** 2 – 1991 wc-WS v Arg: M Keenan (WS), P Sporleder (Arg). **Note:** Controlled five games in 1991 World Cup, including England-New Zealand opener, Ireland–Australia quarter-final and Wallabies-New Zealand semi.

    Record: 1985 I v E **1986** A v Arg(1,2) **1987** E v F. wc-A v J, Fj v Arg. F v R **1989** F v W **1990** NZ v A(1) **1991** W v F. wc-E v NZ, Arg v WS(R), I v A, NZ v A **1992** A v NZ(1) **1993** E v F

HAWKE, Colin J. **Apps:** 3. **Test debut:** Ireland 20, Argentina 18, 1990. **Five Nations' debut:** None. **Dismissals:** 1 – 1990 E v Arg: Federico Mendez (Arg). **Note:** Responsible for first sending-off in Argentina's Test history.

    Record: 1990 I v Arg, E v Arg **1992** A v S(2)

HILDITCH, Stephen R. **Apps:** 14. **Test debut:** Scotland 12, Australia 37, 1984. **Five Nations' debut:** England 3, Wales 11, 1988. **Dismissals:** 2 – 1992 F v E: G Lascube (F), V Moscato (F). **Note:** Only the fourth ref to mete out two sendings-off in a Test.

    Record: 1984 S v A **1985** W v Fj **1987** wc-R v Z, S v R **1988** E v W **1989** E v F, NZ v A, S v R **1991** E v S. wc-F v C, S v NZ **1992** F v E, E v SA **1993** SA v F(1)

KINSEY, Brian. **Apps:** 7. **Test debut:** Tonga 7, Wales 15, 1986. **Five Nations' debut:** None. **Dismissals:** 0. **Note:** Officiated both South African Tests in France last season but yet to make Five Nations' bow seven years after debut.

    Record: 1986 T v W **1990** Arg v E(1,2) **1991** Fj v E **1992** F v SA(1,2) **1993** NZ v BL(1)

LESLIE, David. **Apps:** 2. **Test debut:** England 34, Wales 6, 1990. **Five Nations' debut:** ditto. **Dismissals:** 0. **Note:** International debut coincided with Wales' heaviest ever defeat

against England.
Record: 1990 E v W **1993** I v F

McCARTNEY, Ken W. **Apps:** 3. **Test debut:** France 31, Ireland 12, 1990. **Five Nations' debut:** ditto. **Dismissals:** 0. **Note:** Awarded 32 penalties during the second Test of the 1991 Bledisloe Cup series in Auckland when New Zealand beat Auistralia 6–3 to retain the trophy.
Record: 1990 F v I **1991** NZ v A(2) **1992** F v R

MACNEILL, Sandy A R. **Apps:** 12. **Test debut:** France 29, Argentina 9, 1988. **Five Nations' debut:** Wales 14, Ireland 19, 1993. **Dismissals:** 0. **Note:** Busiest Test referee in 1992/93 with five appointments. Ireland will welcome him any time for Five Nations' duty.
Record: 1988 F v Arg(1,2) **1989** W v NZ, I v NZ **1990** F v NZ(1,2) **1991** wc-C v R **1992** NZ v I(1,2), SA v NZ **1993** W v I, I v E

McLACHLAN, L. **Apps:** 1. **Test debut:** Australia 27, Scotland 12, 1992. **Five Nations' debut:** None. **Dismissals:** 0. **Note:** A newcomer on the international scene, having made his bow in Sydney in the summer of '92.
Record: 1992 A v S(1)

MEGSON, Ray J. **Apps:** 7. **Test debut:** Wales 19, England 12, 1987. **Five Nations' debut:** same match. **Dismissals:** 0. **Note:** Drew short straw with Test debut when assigned now-infamous 1987 Wales–England clash at Cardiff.
Record: 1987 W v E **1988** I v W, I v It **1991** W v E, A v NZ **1992** E v W, F v Arg(b)

MORRISON, Ed. **Apps:** 7. **Test debut:** France 15, Scotland 9, 1991. **Five Nations' debut:** ditto. **Dismissals:** 1 – 1991 R v F: C Cojocariu (R). **Note:** One of 16 Test referees with dismissals to their name, courtesy of '91 Bucharest clash.
Record: 1991 F v S, R v F. wc-S v J, A v WS **1992** I v A **1993** S v I, SA v F(2)

ROBIN, Patrick. **Apps:** 8. **Test debut:** Italy 6, Australia 55, 1988. **Five Nations' debut:** England 23, Ireland 0, 1990. **Dismissals:** 0. **Note:** Man in the middle when Western Samoa stunned Wales in '91 World Cup.
Record: 1988 It v A **1989** S v Fj **1990** E v I **1991** wc-W v WS **1992** A v NZ(2,3) **1993** NZ v BL(2,3)

SIMMONDS, Gareth. **Apps:** 1. **Test debut:** England 26, Canada 13, 1992. **Five Nations' debut:** None. **Dismissals:** 0. **Note:** Holds distinction of having refereed England's only International played at Wembley Stadium
Record: 1992 E v C

SPREADBURY, Tony. **Apps:** 3. **Test debut:** Australia 21, France 9, 1990. **Five Nations' debut:** Ireland 10, Scotland 18, 1992. **Dismissals:** 0. **Note:** Proved a talisman for away sides in 1992 with both Scotland and Australia doing the business.
Record: 1990 A v F(1) **1992** I v S, W v A

STIRLING, Brian W. **Apps:** 4. **Test debut:** England 58, Fiji 23, 1989. **Five Nations' debut:** England 26, Scotland 12, 1993. **Dismissals:** 2 – 1989 E v Fj: T Vonolagi (Fj), N Nadruku (Fj). Notes: Marked debut with double sending-off; one of only four refs to have sent two off in a Test.
Record: 1989 E v Fj **1991** Arg v NZ(1,2) **1993** E v S

THE YEAR IN REVIEW

Your comprehensive review of the 1992/93 International season begins here, chronicling the matches that mattered between May 1992 and July 1993, a 14-month span which constitutes the *RUWW's* '92/'93 season. In the case of tours, the playing party is listed, along with (in most cases) their clubs and the tour matches in which they appeared (by way of numbers which correspond to those given to each fixture in the results section). New caps are denoted by a ', and individual match captains by a *. Points scored are abbreviated to t (try), c (conversions), p (penalty) and dg (dropped goal). In the case of the Five Nations' Championship, numbers bracketed after the scorers' name indicate time of score.

France (9) 25, Romania (0) 6
Le Havre, 28 May 1992

Less a case of shuffling the pack than the backs as France introduce a new midfield division (Michel Marfaing and Christophe Deylaud) and fullback (Stephane Ougier) in favour of captain Philippe Sella, Franck Mesnel and Jean-Luc Sadourny respectively. A match of traditional significance to the FIRA Championship sees other changes at scrum-half where Fabien Galthie returns for Aubin Hueber, and at lock where Racing Club's Christophe Deslandes comes in for the suspended Olivier Roumat. The expected upshot of such change is a close affair yet, in the event, France have little trouble in accounting for the Romanians, winning four-nil on the try-count.

France: S Ougier' (Toulouse); P Saint-André (Montferrand), M Marfaing' (Toulouse), C Deylaud' (Toulouse), S Viars (Brive); A Penaud (Brive), F Galthie (Colomiers); L Armary (Lourdes), J-P Genet (Racing Club), P Gallart (Beziers), C Deslandes (Racing Club), J-M Cadieu (Toulouse), J-F Tordo (Nice), L Cabannes (Racing Club), M Cecillon (Bourgoin, capt). *Repl:* D Berty (Toulouse) for Viars, 37 mins; T Devergie (Nimes) for Deslandes, 53 mins.
Scorers – *Tries:* Saint-Andre, Cadieu, penalty try, Galthie. *Conversions:* Ougier 2, Viars. *Penalty goal:* Viars.

Romania: Brici; Dumitru, Lungu, Racean, Solomie; Ignat, Coman; Leonte, Ion, Vlad, Cojocariu, Constantin, Dinu, Seceleanu, Dumitras (capt).
Scorer – *Penalty goals:* Racean 2.

Referee: K McCartney (Scotland).

Series score: Played 38, France 28, Romania 8, Drawn 2.

IRELAND TO NEW ZEALAND
May-June 1992: P8 W3 D0 L5 F153 A287

For Ireland to embark on a tour to New Zealand with their whitewashed wooden spoon appears as sensible as lighting up in a petrol station, probably less so as many of their established names cry off prior to departure. Sure enough, there are some grotesque beatings – 13–38 to Canterbury, 24–58 to lowly Manawatu, 6–59 to New Zealand in the second Test and, worst of all, 7–62 to mighty Auckland. Yet in amongst the thrashings is the most extraordinary result, one that allows Ireland to return home with some hope. It is a loss (21–24), but a remarkably narrow one, just seven days on from the Auckland debacle. Dunedin is the venue, 30 May the date, 26,000 are in attendance, the first Test is the occasion and the All Blacks are in opposition. But Ireland lead 12–0 in as many minutes, through tries by Vinnie Cunningham and Jim Staples. New Zealand are level at 18–18 come the changeround, but Ireland again pull clear with a Peter Russell penalty. Frank Bunce, with his second score of the game, saves New Zealand's blushes, but barely. 'We set out to break their pattern, upset their rhythm,' says skipper Phil Danaher. 'If you allow them to settle into a rhythm, you're in trouble.' Unhappily for Ireland, New Zealand recover their rhythm the following week in Wellington and rip the tourists to shreds, with fullback Matthew Cooper's 23-point haul representing a world record tally for a Test debutant.

PARTY: F Aherne (Lansdowne – 2*,4R,5,7); **M Bradley** (Cork Constitution – 1,3*,4*,6,8*); **R Carey** (Dungannon – 3,5,6,8); **T Clancy** (London Irish – 1,3,5,7); **J Clarke** (Dolphin – 2,4,7,8R); **R Costello** (Garryowen – 2,5,7); **V Cunningham** (St Mary's College – 1R,2,3,4,5,6,8); **P Danaher** (Garryowen, capt – 1*,6*); **J Etheridge** (Northampton – 1,3,4,7); **M Fitzgibbon** (Shannon – 2,3,4,6,8); **N Furlong** (UC Galway – 1,3,4,6,8); **M Galwey** (Shannon – 1,2R,3,4,6,8); **G Halpin** (London Irish – 2,4R,5,7); **P Johns** (Dungannon – 3,4,6,7,8); **P Kenny** (Wanderers – 5,7,8R); **T Kingston** (Dolphin – 3,4,7*); **K Leahy** (Wanderers – 3,5*,6); **D McAleese** (Ballymena – 2,3R,4R,5,7); **D McBride** (Malone – 1); **M McCall** (Bangor – 3,4,6R,7,8); **P McCarthy** (Cork Constitution – 3,4,6,8); **N Mannion** (Lansdowne – 1,2,5,7); **K Murphy** (Cork Constitution – 1,2R,3,4R,5,7,8R); **N Popplewell** (Greystones – 1,2,4,6,8); **M Ridge** (Blackrock College – 1,2,5,7); **B Rigney** (Greystones – 2,5,6R,8); **B Robinson** (Ballymena – 1,2,4,6,7R,8); **P Russell** (Instonians – 1,3,6,8); **S Smith** (Ballymena – 1,2,5,6,8); **J Staples** (London Irish – 2,4,5,6,8); **R Wallace** (Garryowen – 1,2).

Results: (1) South Canterbury 16, Ireland 21 (Timaru, 13 May); (2) Canterbury 38, Ireland 13 (Christchurch, 16 May); (3) Bay of Plenty 23, Ireland 39 (Rotorua, 20 May); (4) Auckland 62, Ireland 7 (Auckland, 23 May); (5) Poverty Bay-East Coast 7, Ireland 22 (Gisborne, 26 May); (6) **first Test: New Zealand 24, Ireland 21** (Dunedin, 30 May); (7) Manawatu 58, Ireland 24 (Palmerston North, 2 June); (8) **second Test: New Zealand 59, Ireland 6** (Wellington, 6 June).

Scorers (153 – 21t,15c,12p,1dg) – Russell 38 (10c,5p,1dg); McAleese 26 (4c,6p); Murphy 10 (2t,1c); Aherne 8 (2t); Cunningham 8 (2t); Furlong 8 (2t); Galwey 8 (2t); Mannion 8 (2t); Wallace 8 (2t); Bradley 4 (1t); Carey 4 (1t); Clarke 4 (1t); Popplewell 4 (1t); Ridge 4 (1t); Rigney 4 (1t); Staples 4 (1t); McCall 3 (1p).

New Zealand (18) 24, Ireland (18) 21
first Test: Dunedin, 30 May 1992

New Zealand: G Cooper (Otago); V Tuigamala (Auckland), F Bunce (North Harbour), J Kirwan (Auckland), E Clarke (Auckland); W Little (North Harbour), A Strachan (Auckland); R Loe (North Harbour), S Fitzpatrick (Auckland, capt), S McDowell (Auckland), B Larsen (North Harbour), I Jones (North Auckland), J Joseph (Otago), P Henderson (Southland), A Pene (Otago). *Repl:* G Dowd⁺ (North Harbour) for Loe, 58 mins;
Scorers – *Tries:* Bunce 2, Clarke, Henderson. *Conversions:* Cooper 4.

Ireland: Staples; Carey⁺, Danaher (capt) (McCall⁺ 37), Furlong⁺, Cunningham; Russell,

410

Bradley; Popplewell, Smith, McCarthy*, Johns, Galwey, Leahy* (Rigney 40), Fitzgibbon, Robinson.
Scorers – *Tries:* Cunningham 2, Staples. *Conversions:* Russell 3. *Penalty goal:* Russell.

Referee: A MacNeill (Australia)

Series score: Played 11, New Zealand 10, Ireland 0, Drawn 1.

New Zealand (15) 59, Ireland (6) 6
second Test: Wellington, 6 June 1992

New Zealand: M Cooper* (Waikato); J Timu (Otago), F Bunce (North Harbour), J Kirwan (Auckland), E Clarke (Auckland); W Little (North Harbour), A Strachan (Auckland); O Brown* (Auckland), S Fitzpatrick (Auckland, capt), S McDowell (Auckland), R Brooke* (Auckland), I Jones (North Auckland), M Brewer (Otago), M Jones (Auckland), A Pene (Otago).
Scorers – *Tries:* Cooper 2, Bunce 2, Penne 2, Timu, Kirwan, Clarke, I Jones, Strachan. *Conversions:* Cooper 6. *Penalty goal:* Cooper.

Ireland: Staples (Murphy 38); Carey, McCall, Furlong, Cunningham; Russell (Clarke 46), Bradley (capt); Popplewell, Smith, McCarthy, Johns, Rigney, Galwey, Fitzgibbon (Kenny* 18), Robinson.
Scorers – *Try:* Furlong. *Conversion:* Russell.

Referee: A MacNeill (Australia).

Series score: Played 12, New Zealand 11, Ireland 0, Drawn 1.

SCOTLAND TO AUSTRALIA
May–June 1992: P8 W2 D2 L4 F150 A177

Even for the promise of a television series and a best-selling book, Michael Palin would not have undertaken the itinerary presented to Scotland. Eight games in 24 days, across the length and breadth of Australia, home of the world champions, is ambitious to say the least. Foolhardy is probably nearer the mark. But in the name of experience Scotland head Down Under and no sooner have they arrived than they are playing catch-up, beaten 17–16 by a Northern Territory Invitation XV in Darwin's Rugby Park. To respond by sharing the spoils with Super Six winners Queensland and then with the Emerging Wallabies, merits a degree of optimism ahead of the upcoming Test series. New South Wales have other ideas though and, with both David Sole and Gavin Hastings missing, the try-less Scots crash 15–35. The only good news is that Australia are installed as overwhelming favourites for the Sydney Test, when Peter Wright, Carl Hogg and Ian Corcoran are to debut. Written off, Scotland respond by taking a 9–7 lead at half-time, thanks chiefly to a Rob Wainwright try. The Scots are still reflecting on that interval scoreline on return home which indicate the remainder of the tour is not up to much. The Wallabies leapfrog over their guests in the second period, winning 27–12, and are even more convincing a week later at Ballymore, chalking up a 37–13 decision – an occasion on which Kenny Logan and Martin Scott both make their Test bows.

PARTY: D Bain (Melrose – 1,3,5,7); **C Chalmers** (Melrose – 2,4,6, 8); **I Corcoran** (Gala – 1,3,5,6R); **D Cronin** (London Scottish – 1,3,5,7,8); **P Dods** (Gala – 1*,3*,5*,7*); **N Edwards** (Harlequins – 2,4,6); **C Gray** (Nottingham – 1,3,5,7); **G Hastings** (Watsonians – 2,6); **S Hastings** (Watsonians – 2,4,6,8); **C Hogg** (Melrose – 2,3,5,6,7R,8); **P Jones** (Gloucester – 1,3,4,5,7); **S Lineen** (Boroughmuir – 2,4,6,8); **K**

411

Logan (Stirling County – 1,2R,3,4,5R,7,8); **A Macdonald** (Heriot's FP – 5,7; **D McIvor** (Edinburgh Academicals – 1,3,4,7); **D Millard** (London Scottish – 1,3,5,7); **K Milne** (Heriot's FP – 2,3R,4,6); **A Nicol** (Dundee HSFP – 2,4,6,8); **S Reid** (Boroughmuir – 1,3); **J Robertson** (Heriot's FP – 1,5,7); **M Scott** (Dunfermline 7,8); **G Shiel** (Melrose – 1,3,5,7); **I Smith** (Gloucester – 2,4*,6,8); **D Sole** (Edinburgh Academicals, capt – 2*,3R,6*,8*); **T Stanger** (Hawick – 1,4,5,6,7R,8); **D Stark** (Ayr – 2,3,5,7); **G Townsend** (Gala – 1,3,5,7); **I Tukalo** (Selkirk – 2,4,6,8); **R Wainwright** (Edinburgh Academicals – 2,4,6,8); **A Watt** (Glasgow H/K – 1,3,5,7); **G Weir** (Melrose – 2,4,6); **P Wright** (Boroughmuir – 2,4,6,7R,8).

Results: (1) Northern Territory 17, Scotland 16 (Darwin, 28 May); (2) Queensland 15, Scotland 15 (Brisbane, 31 May); (3) Emerging Wallabies 24, Scotland 24 (Hobart, 3 June); (4) New South Wales 35, Scotland 15 (Sydney, 6 June); (5) NSW Country 10, Scotland 26 (Newcastle, 9 June); (6) **first Test: Australia 27, Scotland 12** (Sydney, 13 June); (7) Queensland Country 12, Scotland 29 (Toowoomba, 17 June); (8) **second Test: Australia 37, Scotland 13** (Brisbane, 21 June).

Scorers (150 – 20t,11c,12p,4dg) – Dods 29 (7c,5p); Chalmers 23 (1c,5p,2dg); Townsend 14 (2t,2dg); G Hastings 12 (3c,2p); Stark 12 (3t); Lineen 8 (2t); Millard 8 (2t); Cronin 4 (1t); Gray 4 (1t); Hogg 4 (1t); Milne 4 (1t); Reid 4 (1t); Robertson 4 (1t); Shiel 4 (1t); Sole 4 (1t); Stanger 4 (1t); Wainwright 4 (1t); Watt 4 (1t).

Australia (7) 27, Scotland (9) 12
first Test: Sydney, 13 June 1992

Australia: M Roebuck (NSW); D Campese (NSW), R Tombs[+] (NSW), T Horan (Queensland), P Carozza (Queensland); M Lynagh (Queensland), N Farr-Jones (NSW, capt); A Daly (NSW), P Kearns (NSW), E McKenzie (NSW), R McCall (Queensland), J Eales (Queensland), V Ofahengaue (NSW), D Wilson[+] (Queensland), T Gavin (NSW). *Repl:* P Jorgensen[+] (NSW) for Carozza, 65 mins.
Scorers – *Tries:* Campese 2, Lynagh, Carozza. *Conversion:* Lynagh. *Penalty goals:* Lynagh 3.

Scotland: G Hastings; Stanger, S Hastings, Lineen, Tukalo; Chalmers, Nicol; Sole (capt), Milne (Corcoran[+] 10), Wright[+], Edwards, Weir, Hogg[+], Smith, Wainwright.
Scorers – *Try:* Wainwright. *Conversion:* G Hastings. *Penalty goals:* G Hastings 2.

Referee: L McLachlan (New Zealand).

Series score: Played 13, Australia 6, Scotland 7.

Australia (16) 37, Scotland (3) 13
second Test: Brisbane, 13 June 1992

Australia: M Roebuck (NSW); D Campese (NSW), R Tombs (NSW), T Horan (Queensland), P Carozza (Queensland); M Lynagh (Queensland), N Farr-Jones (NSW, capt); A Daly (NSW), P Kearns (NSW), E McKenzie (NSW), R McCall (Queensland), J Eales (Queensland), V Ofahengaue (NSW), D Wilson (Queensland), T Gavin (NSW). *Repl:* P Jorgensen (NSW) for Campese, 79 mins.
Scorers – *Tries:* Carozza 2, Horan 2, Eales. *Conversion:* Lynagh. *Penalty goals:* Lynagh 5.

Scotland: Logan[+]; Stanger, S Hastings, Lineen, Tukalo; Chalmers, Nicol; Sole (capt), Scott[+], Wright, Cronin, Weir, Hogg, Smith, Wainwright.
Scorers – *Tries:* Lineen, Sole. *Conversion:* Chalmers. *Penalty goal:* Chalmers.
Referee: C Hawke (New Zealand).
Series score: Played 14, Australia 7, Scotland 7.

United States (6) 9, Canada (22) 32
(16th CanAm International)
Denver, Colorado, 13 June 1992

Canada score their biggest win in the history of the CanAm fixture but it is little wonder as the Eagles are obliged to cover their own travel expenses and arrive in Denver with only six of their World Cup squad. The Canucks, with a dozen, collect 19 points in as many minutes and are 22–6 up at the interval. Outside-half Gareth Rees bags 20 points in all on an afternoon when Gord and debutant Scott MacKinnon make history by becoming the first brothers to appear in a Canadian Test team. Scott, the Ontario wing, is one of two new caps (British Columbia No 8 Colin McKenzie being the other), while the USA introduce five.

USA: P Sheahy; R Schurfield, J Burke, M Waterman*, B Tofaeono (V Anatoni 75); M Gale*, G Goodman*; L Manga, P Johnston, N Mottram, K Swords (capt), J Keller (M Vander Molen 20), R Farley, D Steinbauer*, B Smoot*.
Scorer – *Penalty goals:* Gale 2. *Dropped goal:* Gale.

Canada: D Lougheed; P Palmer, S Gray, J Graf, S MacKinnon*; G Rees, C Tynan; E Evans, K Svoboda, D Jackart, N Hadley (capt), I Gordon, A Charron, G MacKinnon, C McKenzie*.
Scorers – *Tries:* Rees, Tynan, Gray, Palmer. *Conversions:* Rees 2. *Penalty goals:* Rees 4.

Referee: D Reardon (United States).

Series score: Played 16, United States 4, Canada 11, Drawn 1.

ENGLAND B TO NEW ZEALAND
June–July 1992: P8 W6 D0 L2 F273 A127

The success of a tour is measured on Test results so, while Stuart Barnes' England win all six of their other games against assorted opposition, their defeats in both Internationals takes the shine off the trip. The New Zealand XV is, in fact, a third XV as the leading 30 players are away on Bledisloe Cup business in Australia. Retaining the old laws, although the rest of New Zealand has already switched over, England B have little trouble in overcoming two third division sides, two second division outfits and New Zealand Universities. Only North Auckland, to lose their first division status come the season's end, put up a real fight before going down 27–31. Barnes accepts his goalkicking cost the chance of victory in the first Test (lost 18–24), but is equally forthright in his condemnation of the refereeing of Colin Hawke in the second Test (18–26) at Pukekohe after New Zealand recover a 9–18 deficit. Crucially, Wellington's Simon Mannix lands five goals from five attempts.

PARTY: N **Back** (Leicester); D **Baldwin** (Sale); G **Baldwin** (Northampton); **S Barnes** (Bath, capt); M **Bayfield** (Northampton); J **Cassell** (Saracens); G **Childs** (Wasps); B **Clarke** (Bath); G **Dawe** (Bath); P **de Glanville** (Bath); K **Dunn** (Gloucester); M **Greenwood** (Nottingham); M **Haag** (Bath); A **Harriman** (Harlequins); D **Hopley** (Wasps); I **Hunter** (Northampton); M **Hynes** (Orrell); A **Kardooni** (Leicester); N **Matthews** (Gloucester); A **Mullins** (Harlequins); S **Ojomoh** (Bath); M **Russell** (Harlequins); D **Ryan** (Wasps); D **Scully** (Wakefield); D **Sims** (Gloucester); J **Steele** (Northampton); G **Thompson** (Harlequins); H **Thorneycroft** (Northampton); V

Ubogu (Bath); **T Underwood** (Leicester).

Results: (1) North Otago 4, England B 68 (Oamaru, June 10); (2) Southland 16, England B 31 (Invercargill, June 13); (3) NZ Universities 15, England B 32 (Wellington, June 17); (4) Wairarapa-Bush 6, England B 40 (Masterton, June 20); (5) Wanganui 9, England B 35 (Wanganui, June 24); (6) **New Zealand XV 24, England B 18** (Hamilton, June 28; (7) North Auckland 27, England B 31 (Whangarei, July 1); (8) **New Zealand XV 26, England B 18** (Pukekohe, July 5).

Scorers (273 – 45t,27c,12p,1dg): Barnes 74 (2t,15c,11p,1dg), Steele 25 (11c,1p), Harriman 24 (6t), Underwood 24 (6t), Back 12 (3t), Bayfield 12 (3t), de Glanville 12 (3t), Hackney 12 (3t), Ojomoh 12 (3t), Thorneycroft 12 (3t), Hunter 10 (2t,1c), Thompson 8 (2t), Ubogu 8 (2t), Cassell 4 (1t), Childs 4 (1t), Dunn 4 (1t), Hopley 4 (1t), Kardooni 4 (1t), Russell 4 (1t), penalty try.

New Zealand XV 24, England B 18
first 'Test': Hamilton, 28 June 1992

New Zealand XV: G Cooper (Otago); E Rush (North Harbour), S Pierce (North Harbour), M Berry (Wairarapa-Bush), T Tagaloa (North Harbour); L Stensness (Manawatu), S Crabb (Waikato); M Allen (Taranaki), W Gatland (Waikato, capt), P Coffin (King Country), S Gordon (Waikato), C Tregaskis (Wellington), G Taylor (North Auckland), D Seymour (Canterbury), R Turner (North Harbour).
Scorers – *Tries:* Crabb, Tagaloa. *Conversions:* Cooper 2. *Penalty goals:* Cooper 2. *Dropped goals:* Cooper 2.

England B: Hunter; Hackney, de Glanville, Hopley, Underwood; Barnes (capt), Kardooni; G Baldwin, Dawe, Ubogu (Mullins 4), D Baldwin, Bayfield, Greenwood, Back, Clarke.
Scorers – *Tries:* Hunter 2, Hopley, Underwood. *Conversion:* Hunter.

Referee: L McLachlan (Otago).

New Zealand XV 26, England B 18
second 'Test': Pukekohe, 5 July 1992

New Zealand XV: M Berry (Wairarapa-Bush); A McCormick (Canterbury), S Pierce (North Harbour), L Stensness (Manawatu), T Tagaloa (North Harbour); S Mannix (Wellington), S Crabb (Waikato); M Allen (Taranaki), W Gatland (Waikato, capt), G Walsh (North Harbour), S Gordon (Waikato), C Tregaskis (Wellington), G Taylor (North Auckland), D Seymour (Canterbury), R Turner (North Harbour).
Scorers – *Tries:* Stensness, Turner. *Penalty goals:* Mannix 5. *Dropped goal:* Stensness.

England B: Hunter; Hackney, de Glanville (Thompson 52), Hopley, Underwood; Barnes (capt), Kardooni; Hynes, Dawe, Mullins, Haag, Bayfield, Ojomoh, Back, Clarke.
Scorers – *Tries:* Ojomoh, de Glanville. *Conversions:* Barnes 2. *Penalty goals:* Barnes 2.

Referee: C Hawke (New Zealand).

WESTERN SAMOA TO NEW ZEALAND
June 1992: P3 W2 D0 L1 F122 A77

Western Samoa, who made countless friends en route to the 1991 World Cup quarter-finals, are popular visitors to New Zealand and, despite having since donated Frank Bunce,

Stephen Bachop, Pat Lam and Timo Tagaloa to the All Black cause, provide dogged opposition for national champions-to-be Waikato (in the inaugural first-class fixture under the new laws), Bay of Plenty and Manawatu. In the case of the latter, the tourists win 35–22, only five days after Manawatu had beaten Ireland 58–24.

Results: (1) Waikato 39, Western Samoa 29 (Hamilton, 1 June); (2) Bay of Plenty 16, Western Samoa 58 (Rotorua, 4 June); (3) Manawatu 22, Western Samoa 35 (Palmerston, 7 June).

Scorers (17t,11c,5p) – A Aiolupo 31 (1t,7c,4p); T Vaega 15 (3t); V Ala'alatoa 10 (2t); A Ieremia 10 (2t); B Lima 10 (2t); J Paramore 10 (2t); K Seinafo 10 (2t); M Vaea 9 (3c,1p); D Kaleopa 5 (1t); M Keenan 5 (1t); K Sio 5 (1t); F Saena 2 (1c).

TONGA TO NEW ZEALAND
June-July 1992: P5 W2 D0 L3 F65 A105

Tonga struggle to come to terms with the new laws on their five-match tour of New Zealand, suffering heavy defeats at the hands of King Country and North Harbour but keeping a handle on the scoreline against high-flying Taranaki, setting out on a campaign that is to later yield the second division title.

Results: (1) Horowhenua 9, Tonga 20 (Levin, 28 June); (2) King Country 30, Tonga 8 (Taumaranui, 1 July); (3) Taranaki 33, Tonga 25 (New Plymouth, 4 July); (4) Thames Valley 3, Tonga 5 (Paeroa, 8 July); (5) North Harbour 30, Tonga 7 (Takapuna, 12 July).

Scorers (65 – 9t,4c,4p) – C Schaumkel 18 (3c,4p); T Latailakepa 10 (2t); T Tuineau 10 (2t); T Kakato 5 (1t); F Masila 5 (1t); H Nisa 5 (1t); M Vea 5 (1t); M Vunipola 5 (1t); B Tasi 2 (1c).

FRANCE TO ARGENTINA
June-July 1992: P8 W5 D0 L2 Ab1 F241 A136

Bigger headlines are made to prior to departure than in the Land of the Puma itself, where France breeze to a 2–0 series win over poor opposition by Argentina's standards. Coach Pierre Berbizier and general manager Robert Paperemborde decide they do not require captain Philippe Sella, centre partner Franck Mesnel and utility back Jean-Baptiste Lafond. Each is allegedly asked to 'take a break from the game', a request which goes down like a cup of cold you-know-what. The Management reckon it is time to blood France's promising youth – players like Toulouse centres Michel Marfaing and Christophe Deylaud, Colomiers' Laurent Mazas, Pau's Philippe Bernat-Salles and Agen's Christian Coeurveille. With Argentina's rugby at a low ebb, it is impossible to measure the success of the French policy. France return home with their first series shutout of the Pumas since 1974, although they do register defeats against Tucuman (their first by Argentine provincial opposition in 18 matches), Cuyo (who had beaten England in 1990) and Rosario (after a half-time power-cut causes the game's abandonment). The first Test, which France win 27–12, is adjudged the worst International ever played in Argentina. The result (33–9) the following week is even more conclusive, once the superb Aubin Hueber has broken the 9–9 tie on 53 minutes.

PARTY: L Armary (Lourdes); P Benetton (Agen); P Bernat-Salles (Pau); X Blond (Racing Club); L Cabannes (Racing Club); J-M Cadieu (Toulouse); M Cecillon (Bourgoin, capt); C Coeurveille (Agen); C Deslandes (Racing Club); T Devergie

(Nimes); **C Deylaud** (Toulouse); **P Gallart** (Beziers); **F Galthie** (Colomiers); **J-P Genet** (Racing Club); **J-M Gonzalez** (Bayonne); **S Graou** (Auch); **A Hueber** (Toulon); F Landreau (Angouloeme); **M Marfaing** (Toulouse); **H Miorin** (Toulouse); **S Ougier** (Toulouse); **A Penaud** (Brive); **C Reigt** (Lourdes); **J-L Sadourny** (Colomiers); **P Saint-André** (Montferrand); **J-F Tordo** (Nice); **S Viars** (Brive).

Results: (1) Cordoba 20, France 62 (Cordoba, 16 June); (2) Buenos Aires 12, France 28 (Buenos Aires, June 20); (3) Tucuman 25, France 23 (San Miguel, June 23); (4) Argentina B 18, France 32 (San Juan, June 27); (5) Cuyo 32, France 30 (Mendoza, June 30); (6) **first Test: Argentina 12, France 27** (Buenos Aires, July 4); (7) * Rosario 8, France 6 (Rosario, July 7); (8) **second Test: Argentina 9, France 33** (Buenos Aires, July 11). * Abandoned at half-time due to power cut.

Scorers (241 – 25t,16c,23p,5dg) – Viars 112 (5t,9c,23p), Saint-André 30 (6t), Ougier 17 (1t,6c), Bernat-Salles 15 (3t), Penaud 13 (2t,1dg), Benetton 10 (2t), Marfaing 10 (2t), Reigt 9 (3dg), Hueber 8 (1t,1dg), Deylaud 7 (1t,1c), Gonzales 5 (1t), Sadourny 5 (1t).

Argentina (6) 12, France (14) 27
first Test: Buenos Aires, 4 July 1992

Argentina: L Criscuolo*; G Jorge (Pucara), S Meson (Tucuman), H Garcia-Simon (Pueyrredon), D Cuesta Silva (San Isidro); L Arbizu (Belgrano Athletic), G Camardon (Alumni); F Mendez (Mendoza), M Bosch (Olivos), D Cash (San Isidro), R Perez* (Rosario), G Llanes (La Plata), P Sporleder (Curupayti), P Garreton (Circulo Universitario, capt), M Carreras (Olivos).
Scorers – *Penalty goals:* Meson 3. *Dropped goal:* Arbizu.

France: Ougier; Saint-Andre, Marfaing, Deylaud, Viars; Penaud, Hueber; Armary, Gonzales*, Gallart, Tordo, Cadieu, Deslandes, Benetton, Cecillon (capt). *Repl:* Sadourny for Ougier, 48 mins; Coeurveille* for Deylaud, 78 mins.
Scorers – *Tries:* Deylaud, Viars. *Conversion:* Viars. *Penalty goals:* Viars 4. *Dropped goal:* Penaud.

Referee: F Burger (South Africa).

Series score: Played 24, Argentina 3, France 20, Drawn 1.

Argentina (6) 9, France (9) 33
second Test: Buenos Aires, 11 July 1992

Argentina: L Criscuolo; M Teran (Tucuman), D Cuesta Silva (San Isidro), S Meson (Tucuman), G Jorge (Pucara); L Arbizu (Belgrano Athletic), G Camardon (Alumni); F Mendez (Mendoza), M Bosch (Olivos), D Cash (San Isidro), R Perez (Rosario), G Llanes (La Plata), P Sporleder (Curupayti), P Garreton (Circulo Universitario, capt), J Santamarina (Tucuman). *Repl:* De La Pena* for Teran, 41 mins.
Scorers – *Penalty goals:* Meson 2. *Dropped goal:* Arbizu.

France: Sadourny; Saint-Andre, Coeurveille, Deylaud, Viars; Penaud, Hueber; Armary, Gonzales, Gallart, Tordo, Cadieu, Deslandes, Cabannes, Cecillon (capt). *Repl:* Benetton for Cadieu, 65 mins; Devergie for Tordo, 75 mins.
Scorers – *Tries:* Hueber, Viars, Saint-Andre. *Conversions:* Viars 3. *Penalty goals:* Viars 3. *Dropped goal:* Hueber.

Referee: F Burger (South Africa).

Series score: Played 25, Argentina 3, France 21, Drawn 1.

NEW ZEALAND COLTS TO AUSTRALIA
July 1992: P3 W3 D0 L0 F139 A17

New Zealand Colts cap an unbeaten tour with their fourth consecutive victory over the Auld Enemy. The young Blacks recover an 8–10 deficit at Ballymore to triumph 20–10, with wing Glen Osborne, who is to excel in the inaugural World Cup Sevens at Murrayfield in April '93, weighing in with two tries.

PARTY: L Barry (North Harbour, capt), **T Blackadder** (Canterbury), **J Daniel** (Wellington), **M Filipo** (Auckland), **V Going** (Waikato), **M Hammett** (Canterbury), **C Izatt** (Manawatu), **S Lancaster** (Auckland), **M Leslie, B McCormack** (Otago), **D Matthews** (King Country), **M Mayerhofler** (North Harbour), **A Miller** (Bay of Plenty), **E Moncrieff** (Wellington), **G Osborne** (North Harbour), **M Paewai** (Hawke's Bay), **K Rolleston** (Wellington), **S Simpkin** (Bay of Plenty), **G Simpson** (North Harbour), **G Slater** (Taranaki), **R Taimalietane** (Auckland), **K Todd** (Auckland), **D Watts** (Hawke's Bay). **Coach:** P Thorburn. **Assistant coach:** S Going. **Manager:** G Atkin.

Results: (1) Gold Coast 7, New Zealand Colts 83 (Brisbane, 12 July); (2) Darling Downs 0, New Zealand Colts 36 (Toowoomba, 16 July); (3) **Australia Under-21 10, New Zealand Colts 20.**

Scorers (139 – 23t,6c,4p) – Osborne 33 (5t,4c); Miller 21 (1t,2c,4p); Going 10 (2t); Mayerhoffler 10 (2t); Rolleston 10 (2t); Simpson 10 (2t); Blackadder 5 (1t); Filipo 5 (1t); Hammett 5 (1t); Izatt 5 (1t); Leslie 5 (1t); Matthews 5 (1t); Paewai 5 (1t); Slater 5 (1t); Todd 5 (1t).

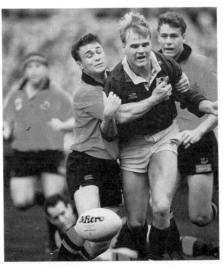

Wallaby wing Paul Carozza forces Simon Geoghegan to spill the ball during Ireland's 17–42 loss in Dublin

Australia U-21 (10) 10, New Zealand Colts (8) 20
Brisbane, 19 July 1992

Australia U-21: M Burke; B Lea, R Constable, R Maher, M O'Connor; D Emtage (capt),
B Free; C Blades, T Colley, G Panaho, M Murray, T Hornibrook, A Innes, G Hislop, M
Connors.
Scorers – *Try:* Lea. *Conversion:* Emtage. *Penalty goal:* Emtage.

NZ Colts: Rolleston; Osborne, Mayerhofler, Matthews, Paewai; Miller, McCormack;
Slater, Hammett, Filipo, Blackadder, Lancaster (Watts), Daniel, Simpson, Barry (capt).
Scorers – *Tries:* Osborne 2, Filipo. *Conversion:* Miller. *Penalty goal:* Miller.

Referee: I Anderson (South Africa).

NEW ZEALAND TO AUSTRALIA AND SOUTH AFRICA
June-August 1992: P16 W13 D0 L3 F567 A252

Much water has flown under Auckland Bridge since New Zealand's semi-final defeat by
Australia in the 1991 World Cup signalled the end of a remarkably successful All Black
era. Now there are places to be won in the side and the toughest places of all to visit.
Australia are the world champions and South Africa think they should be. New Zealand
tour both and on a mammoth 16-match tour add weight to the Wallaby claim before
helping to expose the returning Springboks as International novices. On top of this
punishing schedule is the small matter of embracing a new set of rules. Despite the 2–1
Bledisloe Cup series defeat in Australia, newly appointed coach Laurie Mains is generally
reckoned to have laid solid foundations on which to build the next All Black dynasty.
Outstanding contributions come from former Western Samoa World Cup centre Frank
Bunce, who has since jumped camp, John Timu, who completes a highly successful switch
from wing to fullback, and backrower Zinzan Brooke, who relishes the new law changes.
New captain Sean Fitzpatrick should also take a bow for his performances on and off the
paddock. There is disappointment – the first two 'Bledisloe' Test defeats and the crushing
40–17 reversal suffered at the hands of Sydney at Penrith; there is controversy – Richard
Loe's alleged dirty tactics; but overall, there is renewed optimism instilled in the proudest
of rugby nations.

PARTY: G Bachop (Canterbury – 4); **S Bachop** (Otago – 1,4,6,8,10,13,15); **M Brewer**
(Otago – 2*,4*,5); **R Brooke** (Auckland – 1,3,5,7,9,11,14,16); **Z Brooke** (Auckland –
2,4,6*,7,9,11,12,14,15R,16); **O Brown** (Auckland – 1,3,5,7,9,11,12,14,16); **F Bunce**
(North Harbour – 1,3,5,7,9,11,12,13,14,16); **E Clarke** (Auckland – 1,4,6,8,10,12,14,15);
M Cooksley (Counties – 1,4,6,8,10,12,15); **M Cooper** (Waikato – 1,3,6,8,10,13, 15); **G
Dowd** (North Harbour – 2,4,6,8,10,13,15); **A Earl** (Canterbury – 9,10,11R,13,14R,15);
M Ellis (Otago – 2,4,6,8,10,13R,15); **S Fitzpatrick** (Auckland, capt – 1*,3*,5*,7*,9*,
11*,12*,14*,16*); **G Fox** (Auckland – 2,3,5,7,9,11,12,14,16); **P Henderson** (Southland
– 1,3); **I Jones** (North Auckland – 2,3,5,7,9,11,12,13*,14,16); **M Jones** (Auckland –
2,5,6,8,11,12,14,16); **J Joseph** (Otago – 1,3,5R,6,7,11, 12,14,16); **J Kirwan** (Auckland –
2,3,5,7,9,11,12,14,16); **P Lam** (Auckland – 10); **B Larsen** (North Harbour – 2,4,6,8,10,
13,15); **W Little** (North Harbour – 2,3,5,7,9,11,13,14,16); **R Loe** (Waikato – 1,3,5,8*,9,
11,12,14,16); **S McDowell** (Auckland – 2,4,6,7,10*,13*,14,16); **A Pene** (Otago – 1,3,5,8,
9R,13,14R,15); **J Preston** (Canterbury – 1,6,8,10,13,15,16R); **G Purvis** (Waikato – 2,4,
6,8,10,13,15); **E Rush** (North Harbour – 4,6,8,10,13,15); **K Schuler** (North Harbour –
3R,4,7,8,9); **D Seymour** (Canterbury – 10,13,15); **A Strachan** (Auckland) 1R,2,3,5,7,9,
11,12,14,16); **G Taylor** (North Auckland – 10R); **J Timu** (Otago – 1,3,4,5,7,9,11,12,

14,16); **V Tuigamala** (Auckland – 1,2,3R,5,7,9,11,12,13,16); **T Wright** (Auckland – 2,4,6,8,10,15). **Coach:** L Mains. **Assistant coach:** E Kirton. **Manager:** N Gray.

Results: (1) Western Australia 0, All Blacks 80 (Perth, 21 June); (2) South Australia XV 18, All Blacks 48 (Adelaide, 24 June); (3) New South Wales 9, All Blacks 41 (Sydney, 28 June); (4) Australian Capital Territory 13, All Blacks 45 (Canberra, 1 July); (5) **first Test: Australia 16, New Zealand 15** (Sydney, 4 July); (6) Victorian XV 3, All Blacks 53 (Melbourne, 8 July); (7) Queensland 19, All Blacks 26 (Brisbane, 12 July); (8) Queensland B 13, All Blacks 32 (Cairns, 15 July); (9) **second Test: Australia 19, New Zealand 17** (Brisbane, 19 July); (10) Sydney 40, All Blacks 17 (Penrith, 22 July); (11) **third Test: Australia 23, New Zealand 26** (Sydney, 25 July); (12) Natal 25, All Blacks 43 (Durban, 1 August); (13) Orange Free State 14, All Blacks 33 (Bloemfontein, 5 August); (14) Junior South Africa 10, All Blacks 25 (Pretoria, 8 August); (15) Central Unions 6, All Blacks 39 (Witbank, 10 August); (16) **Test: South Africa 24, New Zealand 27** (Johannesburg, 15 August).

Scorers (567 – 75t,45c,33p,1dg): Fox 118 (23c,23p,1dg); Cooper 71 (4t,15c,7p); Wright 40 (6t,2c,2p); Timu 35 (7t); Kirwan 30 (6t); Bunce 25 (5t); Rush 25 (5t); Tuigamala 20 (4t); Little 20 (4t); Clarke 20 (4t); Ellis 20 (4t); Preston 18 (1t,5c,1p); Loe 15 (3t); Bachop 15 (3t); Schuler 15 (3t); Z Brooke 10 (2t); Strachan 10 (2t); Joseph 10 (2t); Fitzpatrick 10 (2t); I Jones 5 (1t); M Jones 5 (1t); Larsen 5 (1t); Cooksley 5 (1t); Earl 5 (1t); Seymour 5 (1t); Brewer 5 (1t); G Bachop 5 (1t).

BLEDISLOE CUP
July 1992: Australia win series 2–1

Australia (8) 16, New Zealand (12) 15
first Test: Sydney, 4 July 1992

Australia: T Kelaher[+] (NSW); P Carozza (Queensland), J Little (Queensland), T Horan (Queensland), D Campese (NSW), M Lynagh (Queensland), N Farr-Jones (NSW, capt); T Daly (NSW), P Kearns (NSW), E McKenzie (NSW), J Eales (Queensland), R McCall (Queensland), T Coker (Queensland), D Wilson (Queensland), S Scott-Young (Queensland). *Repl:* G Morgan[+] (Queensland) for Scott-Young, 77 mins.
Scorers – *Tries:* Campese, Horan. *Penalty goals:* Lynagh 2.

New Zealand: Timu; Kirwan, Bunce, Little, Tuigamala; Fox, Strachan; Loe, Fitzpatrick (capt), Brown, I Jones, R Brooke, Brewer (Joseph 65), M Jones, Pene.
Scorers – *Tries:* Tuigamala, Bunce. *Conversion:* Fox. *Penalty goal:* Fox.

Referee: J Fleming (Scotland).

Series score: Played 94, Australia 25, New Zealand 64, Drawn 5.

Australia (11) 19, New Zealand (7) 17
second Test: Brisbane, 19 July 1992

Australia: M Roebuck (NSW); P Carozza (Queensland), J Little (Queensland), T Horan (Queensland), D Campese (NSW), M Lynagh (Queensland), N Farr-Jones (NSW, capt); T Daly (NSW), P Kearns (NSW), E McKenzie (NSW), J Eales (Queensland), R McCall (Queensland), T Coker (Queensland), D Wilson (Queensland), S Scott-Young (Queensland).
Scorers – *Tries:* Carozza 2. *Penalty goals:* Lynagh 3.

New Zealand: Timu; Kirwan, Bunce, Little, Tuigamala; Fox, Strachan; Loe, Fitzpatrick (capt), Brown, I Jones, R Brooke, Schuler (Pene 7), Earl, Z Brooke.
Scorers – *Tries:* Timu, Kirwan. *Conversions:* Fox 2. *Penalty goal:* Fox.

Referee: P Robin (France).

Series score: Played 95, Australia 26, New Zealand 64, Drawn 5.

Australia (13) 23, New Zealand (13) 26
third Test: Sydney, 25 July 1992

Australia: M Roebuck (NSW); D Campese (NSW), J Little (Queensland), T Horan (Queensland), P Carozza (Queensland); M Lynagh (Queensland), N Farr-Jones (NSW, capt); T Daly (NSW), P Kearns (NSW), E McKenzie (NSW), J Eales (Queensland), R McCall (Queensland), D Wilson (Queensland), T Coker (Queensland), S Scott-Young (Queensland). *Repl:* G Morgan (Queensland) for Eales, 33 mins; A Herbert (Queensland) for Scott-Young, 42 mins.
Scorers – *Tries:* Farr-Jones, Herbert. *Conversions:* Lynagh 2. *Penalty goals:* Lynagh 3.

New Zealand: Timu; Kirwan, Bunce, Little, Tuigamala; Fox, Strachan; Loe, Fitzpatrick (capt), Brown, I Jones, R Brooke (Earl), M Jones, Joseph, Z Brooke.
Scorers – *Tries:* Little, Joseph. *Conversions:* Fox 2. *Penalty goals:* Fox 3. *Dropped goal:* Fox.

Referee: P Robin (France).

Series score: Played 96, Australia 26, New Zealand 65, Drawn 5.

South Africa (0) 24, New Zealand (10) 27
Johannesburg, 15 August 1992

South Africa: T van Rensburg[+] (Transvaal); P Hendricks[+] (Transvaal), P Muller[+] (Natal), D Gerber (Western Province), J Small[+] (Transvaal); N Botha (Northern Transvaal, capt), R du Preez[+] (Natal); H Rodgers (Transvaal), U Schmidt (Northern Transvaal), L Muller[+] (Natal), A Geldenhuys[+] (Eastern Province), A Malan[+] (Northern Transvaal), W Bartmann (Natal), I Macdonald[+] (Transvaal), J Breedt (Transvaal). *Repl:* J Styger[+] (Orange Free State) for Rodgers, 51 mins; H Fuls[+] (Transvaal) for Small, 80 mins.
Scorers – *Tries:* Gerber 2, P Müller. *Conversions:* Botha 3. *Penalty goal:* Botha.

New Zealand: Timu; Tuigamala (M Cooper 80), Little, Bunce, Kirwan; Fox, Strachan (Preston 15); Loe, Fitzpatrick (capt), Brown, I Jones, R Brooke, Joseph, M Jones, Z Brooke.
Scorers – *Tries:* Z Brooke, Kirwan, Timu. *Conversions:* Fox 3. *Penalty goals:* Fox 2.

Referee: A MacNeill (Australia).

Series score: Played 38, South Africa 20, New Zealand 16, Drawn 2.

AUSTRALIA TO SOUTH AFRICA
August 1992: P4 W4 D0 L0 F130 A41

When you are the world champions everybody is out to knock you off your perch. Every game is a 'Cup Final', every opponent sees themselves as heir apparent to your throne. So it is with Australia in 1992, but the Wallabies can take the heat. Having seen off New Zealand's advances, and in so doing relieved them of the Bledisloe Cup, the men in gold set about South Africa. Remember the banner 'You are not World Champions until you have beaten the Springboks' which was unfurled during the 1991 World Cup? How those cocky South African fans must have wished they had kept their own counsel. Despite the eventual narrow margin of defeat against New Zealand the previous week, the Springboks are singularly ill-equipped to cope with Test rugby at the summit. Australia underscore the point with a stunning 26–3 win in Cape Town – the heaviest Test defeat ever suffered by the shellshocked host nation.

PARTY: A Blades (NSW – 1,3); **D Campese** (NSW – 1,2,3R,4); **P Carozza** (Queensland – 2,3,4); **T Coker** (Queensland – 2,3); **A Daly** (NSW – 2,4); **J Eales** (Queensland – 2,4); **N Farr-Jones** (NSW, capt – 2★,4★); **T Gavin** (NSW – 1,4); **A Herbert** (Queensland – 1,2R,3); **T Horan** (Queensland – 2,4); **D Junee** (NSW – 1,3); **P Kahl** (Queensland – 1,3); **P Kearns** (NSW – 2,4); **T Kelaher** (NSW – 2,3); **T Lawton** (Queensland – 1,3); **J Little** (Queensland – 2,4); **M Lynagh** (Queensland – 2,4); **R McCall** (Queensland – 2,3R,4); **E McKenzie** (NSW – 2,4); **G Morgan** (Queensland – 1,3); **V Ofahengaue** (NSW – 1,3,4); **M Roebuck** (NSW – 1,4); **M Ryan** (Queensland – 1,3); S **Scott-Young** (Queensland – 2,3); **P Slattery** (Queensland – 1★,3); **R Tombs** (NSW – 1,3); **W Waugh** (NSW – 1,3); **D Wilson** (Queensland – 1,2,4).

Results: (1) Western Transvaal 13, Wallabies 46 (Potchefstroom, 11 August); (2) Northern Transvaal 17, Wallabies 24 (Pretoria, 14 August); (3) Eastern Province 8, Wallabies 34 (Port Elizabeth, 18 August); (4) **Test: South Africa 3, Australia 26** (Cape Town, 22 August).

Scorers (130 – 15t,5c,15p) – Kelaher 22 (2c,6p), Lynagh 17 (1c,5p), Roebuck 16 (2c,4p), Campese 15 (3t), Carozza 10 (2t), Gavin 10 (2t), Blades 5 (1t), Herbert 5 (1t), Junee 5 (1t), Kahl 5 (1t), Morgan 5 (1t), Slattery 5 (1t), Waugh 5 (1t), Wilson 5 (1t).

South Africa (3) 3, Australia (8) 26
Cape Town, 22 August 1992

South Africa: T van Rensburg (Transvaal); P Hendricks (Transvaal), P Müller (Natal), D Gerber (Western Province), J Small (Transvaal); N Botha (Northern Transvaal, capt), R du Preez (Natal); J Styger (OFS), U Schmidt (Northern Transvaal), L Muller (Natal), A Geldenhuys (Eastern Province), A Malan (Northern Transvaal), W Bartmann (Natal), I Macdonald (Transvaal), J Breedt (Transvaal). *Repl:* D Hattingh⁺ (Northern Transvaal) for Geldenhuys, 64 mins.
Scorer – *Penalty goal:* Botha.

Australia: M Roebuck (NSW); D Campese (NSW), J Little (Queensland), T Horan (Queensland), P Carozza (Queensland); M Lynagh (Queensland), N Farr-Jones (NSW, capt); T Daly (NSW), P Kearns (NSW), E McKenzie (NSW), J Eales (Queensland), R McCall (Queensland), D Wilson (Queensland), V Ofahengaue (NSW), T Gavin (Queensland).
Scorers – *Tries:* Carozza 2, Campese. *Conversion:* Lynagh. *Penalty goals:* Lynagh 3.

Referee: D Bishop (New Zealand).

Series score: Played 29, South Africa 21, Australia 8.

Leicester (3) 11, England XV (7) 18
Leicester, 5 September 1992

English rugby gives a decidedly cool welcome to the new laws in a mess of a match at Leicester, to mark the club's centenary. The change whereby 'when the ball becomes unplayable, or the ruck/maul becomes stationary, the team not in possession at the start of the ruck/maul will put the ball into an ensuing scrum', causes as much mayhem as had been expected. What should have been a grand spectacle, comparable with the annual Tigers-Barbarians Christmas duel, resembles more an eyesore for the 15,000 onlookers. What should be celebratory occasion is tarnished by a series of unpleasant outbreaks of nastiness up front; a bi-product of the frustration caused by the new laws, no doubt. There are a brace of tries for Orrell winger Nigel Heslop, one for opposite number Steve Hackney and a shoulder dislocation for Leicester openside Neil Back, who is playing for England. Confused? Everyone else seems to be.

Leicester: J Liley; S Hackney, S Potter, I Bates, R Underwood; J Harris, A Kardooni; G Rowntree, R Cockerill; D Garforth, M Poole, D Richards, J Wells (capt), N Richardson, S Povoas.
Scorers – *Try:* Hackney. *Penalty goals:* Liley 2.

England XV: J Webb (Bath); N Heslop (Orrell), W Carling (Harlequins, capt), J Guscott (Bath), T Underwood (Leicester); R Andrew (Toulouse), R Hill (Bath); M Hynes (Orrell), B Moore (Harlequins), J Probyn (Wasps), N Redman (Bath), M Bayfield (Northampton), S Ojomoh (Bath), N Back (Leicester), B Clarke (Bath). *Repl:* M Pepper (Nottingham) for Back, 15 mins; P de Glanville (Bath) for Heslop, 45 mins; D Pears (Harlequins) for Webb, 55 mins.
Scorers – *Tries:* Heslop 2. *Conversion:* Webb. *Penalty goal:* Webb. *Dropped goal:* Andrew.

Referee: E Morrison (Bristol).

Spain (0) 14, Scotland A (14) 35
Madrid, 12 September 1992

Alan Watt, who at somewhere in the neighbourhood of 20 stones was the heaviest player to participate in the 1991 World Cup, makes an excellent start to the season in the intense heat of Madrid's University Stadium where he has a hand in two of Scotland's three second-half tries. The final try-count is 4–2 in favour of the visitors, with Kelso flanker Adam Roxburgh capping a super debut display with one. Others to stand out are Stirling County centre Ian Jardine and Gala's exciting Gregor Townsend. Spain's cause is not aided by their failure (using four kickers) to convert six penalty attempts.

Spain: F Puertas; P Martin, J Azkargorta, G Rivero, J Hermosilla; O Garcia, J Diaz; J Alvarez (capt), F Castro, X Alducin, M Auzmendi, A Malo, J Etxeberria, E Illaregui, J Gutierrez.
Scorers – *Tries:* Gutierrez, Azkargorta. *Conversions:* Puertas 2.

Scotland A: K Logan (Stirling County); D Stark (Boroughmuir), G Townsend (Gala), I Jardine (Stirling County), M Moncrieff (Gala); D Wyllie (Stewart's-Melville FP), G Oliver (Hawick); P Burnell (London Scottish), I Corcoran (Gala), A Watt (Glasgow High/Kelvinside), C Gray (Nottingham, capt), A Macdonald (Heriot's FP), D Turnbull (Hawick), A Roxburgh (Kelso), G Weir (Melrose).
Scorers – *Tries:* Wyllie, Roxburgh, Moncrieff, Logan. *Conversions:* Townsend 3. *Penalty goals:* Townsend 3.

Referee: C Rouve (France).

Series score: Played 5, Scotland A/XV 5, Spain 0.

Wales XV (17) 43, Italy (0) 12
Cardiff, 7 October 1992

If the Welsh Rugby Union have arranged this fixture as a getting-to-know-you exercise with the try-line it has the desired effect. But the achievement of a full-strength Wales side in scoring seven tries, to Italy's two, will regrettably be quickly forgotten as the campaign unfurls and just three Welsh touchdowns are diluted into five Test matches. Still, Wales delight in making hay while the sun briefly shines. A match sold on the line that Italy troubled England and New Zealand in the 1991 World Cup quickly becomes a no-contest as Wales, laden with purpose and uncharacteristically dressed in green, run amok, with centre Scott Gibbs to the fore. The Italians' decision to banish the spoiling game which served them well in the global tournament, though won few admirers, adds to Wales' comfort. The Arms Park scoreboard shows a 17–0 half-time score and it is not until 29 unanswered points have been bagged that Italy are allowed to open their account.

Wales XV: A Clement (Swansea); I Evans (Llanelli, capt), R Bidgood (Newport), S Gibbs (Swansea), M Hall (Cardiff); C Stephens (Llanelli), R Jones (Swansea); M Griffiths (Cardiff), G Jenkins (Swansea), H Williams-Jones (South Wales Police), G Llewellyn (Neath), A Copsey (Llanelli), E Lewis (Llanelli), R Webster (Swansea), S Davies (Swansea). *Repl:* M Rayer (Cardiff) for Bidgood, 68 mins.
Scorers – *Tries:* Clement, Evans, Stephens, Gibbs, Davies, Webster, Rayer, *Conversions:* Stephens 4.

Italy: P Vaccari (Calvisano); E Venturi (Rovigo), S Zorzi (Treviso), S Barba (Milan), Marcello Cuttita (Milan); M Bonomi (Milan), I Francescato (Trevisium); Massimo Cuttita (Milan), G Pivetta (San Dona, capt), G Grespan (Treviso), C Checchinato (Rovigo), M Giacheri (Treviso), A Bottacchiari (L'Aquila), R Cassina (Casale), J Gardner (Rovigo).
Scorers – *Tries:* Francescato, Marcello Cuttita. *Conversion:* Bonomi.

Referee: F Howard (England).

Wales B (3) 21, North of England (3) 13
Pontypool, 14 October 1992

Only three weeks before they entertain Australia at the National Stadium, Wales B are made to work hard for the spoils against the North of England. Ultimately, a three-minute spell midway through the second half, which yields tries for the impressive duo of wing Wayne Proctor and fullback Mike Rayer, tips the scales towards the hosts, whose attacks have lacked punch during the first hour of play. The dependable Neil Jenkins converts all three penalty attempts to maintain Welsh spirits until messrs Proctor and Rayer take over. The visitors at least finish with a flurry, hooker Simon Mitchell crossing in the corner for Paul Grayson to add a conversion to his two penalty goals.

Wales B: M Rayer (Cardiff); S Davies (Swansea), N Boobyer (Llanelli), N Davies (Llanelli), W Proctor (Llanelli); N Jenkins (Pontypridd), R Moon (Llanelli, capt); R Evans (Llanelli), N Meek (Pontypool), J Davies (Neath), P Davies (Llanelli), S Roy (Cardiff), I Davies (Swansea), L Jones (Llanelli), S Legge (South Wales Police).
Scorers – *Tries:* Proctor, Rayer. *Conversion:* Jenkins. *Penalty goals:* Jenkins 3.

North of England: J Mallinder (Sale); J Eagle (Leeds), B Barley (Wakefield), K Simms, (Liverpool St Helens, capt), S Bromley (Rugby); P Grayson (Waterloo), D Scully (Wakefield); P Lancaster (West Hartlepool), B Mitchell (West Hartlepool), M Whitcombe (Sale), N Allott (Waterloo), K Westgarth (West Hartlepool), M Greenwood (Wasps), A Ireland (Waterloo), A MacFarlane (Sale)
Scorers – *Try:* Mitchell. *Conversion:* Grayson. *Penalty goals:* Grayson 2.

Referee: C B Muir (Scotland).

Series score: Played 1, Wales B 1, North of England 0.

England (16) 26, Canada (6) 13
Wembley, 17 October 1992

Home is where the heart is, and Wembley, dress it up as you will, is no Twickenham. Much blame for England's tepid showing is given to their absence from HQ, which is under reconstruction, and the whole truth only manifests itself later on, when Wales and Ireland score shock wins. Canada, it should be said, are no mugs. Anyone who witnessed the World Cup will know that. Yet they are under-strength and not at one with the new laws. Only once debutant Ian Hunter, the Northampton fullback-cum England wing, has plundered his second try in the game's final minute can the sitting tenants and the 40,000 crowd finally breathe that ubiquitous sigh of relief. The first five-point try in England's Test history goes to Hunter on 17 minutes, a bullish effort to overhaul Canada's three-point lead, gained by way of a Gareth Rees penalty goal a dozen or so minutes earlier. When Jeremy Guscott pops up for his 14th international try shortly afterwards, England appear set fair. Instead they tread water for the best part of the next hour, save only for Peter Winterbottom's third try in 53 Tests. The Canucks claim a try of their own through scrum-half John Graf and, as in the World Cup, their back row take the plaudits against an England side giving debuts to wingers Hunter and Tony Underwood and tighthead prop Victor Ubogu.

England: J Webb (Bath); I Hunter⁺ (Northampton), W Carling (Harlequins, capt), J Guscott (Bath), T Underwood⁺ (Leicester); R Andrew (Wasps), D Morris (Orrell); J Leonard (Harlequins), J Olver (Northampton), V Ubogu⁺ (Bath), M Bayfield (Northampton), W Dooley (Preston Grasshoppers), D Ryan (Wasps), P Winterbottom (Harlequins), D Richards (Leicester).
Scorers – *Tries:* Hunter 2, Guscott, Winterbottom. *Penalty goals:* Webb 2.

French lock Olivier Roumat outjumps Welshmen Gareth Llewellyn and Emyr Lewis in the 26–10 Paris win which assured France of the inaugural Five Nations' Cup

Canada: S Stewart (British Columbia); S Gray (British Columbia), M Williams⁺ (British Columbia), I Stuart (British Columbia), D Lougheed (Ontario); G Rees (British Columbia), J Graf (British Columbia); E Evans (British Columbia), K Svoboda (Ontario), D Jackart (British Columbia), I Gordon (British Columbia), J Knauer⁺ (British Columbia), N Hadley (British Columbia, capt), G MacKinnon (British Columbia), C McKenzie (British Columbia). *Repl:* K Wirachowski⁺ (British Columbia), for Evans, 48 mins.
Scorers – *Try:* Graf. *Conversion:* Rees. *Penalty goals:* Rees 2.

Referee: G Simmonds (Wales).

Series score: Played 1, England 1, Canada 0.

SOUTH AFRICA TO FRANCE AND ENGLAND
October-November 1992: P13 W9 D0 L4 F297 A236

South Africa win their first Test match since their official return to the international sporting fold when they defeat a lacklustre France side 20–15, in Lyon on 17 October. But while that victory gives cause for celebration it cannot disguise the fact that the Springboks are a shadow of their former self. This European tour exposes deficiencies in a nation's game denied legitimate international competition for 11 years. Players with no experience of touring, with no experience of playing for the good of the country rather than rival provinces, are asked to grow up quickly and to learn to live together before they can win together. The Lyon win rewards their effort but it is neither repeated in the second Test in Paris or against England once the tourists hop across the Channel. The 'Bok's, who leave France with a record of five wins and four defeats, feel more comfortable in England, not least because they can speak the lingo. Only the Twickenham International ends in defeat and the win over England B at Bristol comes in for rave reviews. However, it comes to late to save coach John Williams from being given the order of the boot on his return home.

PARTY: K Andrews (Western Province – 1,4,6,8,9,10,11,13); **S Atherton** (Natal – 3R, 4,6,8,9,12); **W Bartmann** (Natal – 2★,3,5,7,10); **H E Botha** (Northern Transvaal – 1★, 3★,5★,7★,9★,10★,11★,13★); **R du Preez** (Natal – 1,4,6★,8★,12); **H Fuls** (Transvaal – 2,3,6, 8,9,11R,12); **A Geldenhuys** (Eastern Province – 1,4,5,7); **D Gerber** (Western Province – 2,3,5,7,10,11,13); **D Hattingh** (Northern Transvaal – 1,2,3,6,7R,8,10,11,12,13); **P Hendriks** (Transvaal – 1,6,8,10,12); **W Hills** (Northern Transvaal – 2,3,5,7,8,10,11,13); **F Knoetze** (Western Province – 1,4,6,8,10,12); **H le Roux** (Transvaal – 1R,2,4,6,8,12); **I Macdonald** (Transvaal – 1,4,6,8,10,12); **A Malan** (Northern Transvaal – 2,3,5,7,9,11, 13); **P Müller** (Natal – 1,3R,4,5,7,9,11,13); **J Olivier** (Northern Transvaal – 2,3,4,5,7,9, 11,13); **D Oosthuysen** (Northern Transvaal – 1,4,6,8,10,12); **P Pretorius** (Northern Transvaal – 1,4,6,8,10R,12); **H Reece-Edwards** (Natal – 1,4,5,7,9,12); **A Richter** (Northern Transvaal – 2,3,5,7,8,9,10,11,13); **H Roberts** (Transvaal – 2,3,6,8R,9,12); **H Rodgers** (Transvaal – 1,2R,3,4★,5,7,10,12★); **B Rossouw** (Western Transvaal – 4,6); **J Small** (Transvaal – 2,3,5,7,9,11,13); **T Strauss** (Western Province – 1,2,3,5,7,9,11,13); **J Styger** (Orange Free State – 2,5,6,7,9,11,13); **T van Rensburg** (Transvaal – 1R,2,3,6,8, 10,11,13); **G Wright** (Transvaal – 2,3,5,7,9,10,11,13).

Results: (1) France B 24, South Africa 17 (Bordeaux, 4 October); (2) Aquitaine 22, South Africa 29 (Pau, 7 October); (3) Midi-Pyrenees 15, South Africa 18 (Toulouse, 15 October); (4) Provence-Cote D'Azur 12, South Africa 41 (Marseille, 13 October); (5) **first Test: France 15, South Africa 20** (Lyon, 17 October); (6) Languedoc-Roussillon 15, South Africa 36 (Beziers, 20 October); (7) **second Test: France 29, South Africa 16** (Paris, 24 October); (8) French Universities 18, South Africa 13 (Tours, 28 October); (9) French Barbarians 25, South Africa 20 (Lille, 31 October); (10) Midlands Division 9,

South Africa 32 (Leicester, 4 November); (11) England B 16, South Africa 20 (Bristol, 7 November); (12) Northern Division 3, South Africa 19 (Leeds, 10 November); (13) **Test: England 33, South Africa 16** (Twickenham, 14 November).

Scorers – Botha 74 (10c,11p,7dg), van Rensburg 48 (1t,5c,11p), Reece-Edwards 30 (6c,6p), Gerber 20 (4t), Olivier 20 (4t), Hattingh 15 (3t), Small 15 (3t), Hendriks 10 (2t), Knoetze 10 (2t), Müller 10 (2t), Bartmann 5 (1t), du Preez 5 (1t), le Roux 5 (1t), Macdonald 5 (1t), Oosthuysen 5 (1t), Richter 5 (1t), Roberts 5 (1t), Rossouw 5 (1t), Smit 5 (1t).

France Espoirs (6) 24, South Africa (8) 17
Bordeaux, 4 October 1992

France B: O Campan (Agen); P Hontas (Biarritz), T Lacroix (Dax), F Mesnel (Racing Club), D Berty (Toulouse); C Reigt (Lourdes), J Cazalbou (Toulouse, capt); L Benezech (Racing Club), F Landreau (Grenoble), S Graou (Auch), D Sanoko (Biarritz), H Chaffardon (Graulhet), X Blond (Racing Club), L Loppy (Toulouse), J-J Alibert (Begles-Bordeaux). *Repl:* M Courtiols (Begles-Bordeaux) for Blond, 40 mins; F Mandick for Alibert, 69 mins.
Scorers – *Tries:* Hontas 2. *Conversion:* Lacroix. *Penalty goals:* Lacroix 4.

South Africa: Reece-Edwards; Oosthuysen (van Rensburg 49), Knoetze, Müller, Hendricks; Botha (capt), du Preez; Rodgers, Truscott, Andrews, Hattingh, Geldenhuys, Pretorius, Macdonald, Strauss.
Scorers – *Try:* Hattingh. *Penalty goals:* Botha 3. *Dropped goal:* Botha.

Referee: E Morrison (England).

France (0) 15, South Africa (13) 20
first Test: Lille, 17 October 1992

Sebastien Viars, who could do no wrong when bursting onto the Five Nations' scene in the first part of the year, misses six out of eight kicks at goal as France hand a South Africa side, complete with five new caps, their maiden Test triumph since returning to the international fold. France manager Robert Paparemborde attributes the loss to his charges 'taking opponents too lightly' but the truth is that Viars' failure to come even close to emulating Naas Botha's kicking performance is pivotal. The South African skipper lands a dropped goal and a penalty and converts both tries, scored by the indefatigable Danie Gerber and James Small. Adding to French unhappiness is the facial injury suffered by replacement Abdel Benazzi, who is flattened at a line-out, allegedly by South African lock Adri Geldenhuys. The French are no pussy cats themselves but have been taking steps of late to put their own house in order. Ironically, Benazzi himself was one of several players omitted from the summer tour of Argentina for disciplinary reasons, and when All Black Richard Loe was found guilty of eye-gouging in New Zealand, he was denied a work permit to coach in France. Bernard Lapasset, the French Federation president, says: 'As far as discipline is concerned, the match is a victory for us.'

France: J-L Sadourny (Colomiers); P Saint-André (Montferrand), F Mesnel (Racing Club), C Deylaud (Toulouse), S Viars (Brive); A Penaud (Brive), A Hueber (Toulon); L Armary (Lourdes), J-M Gonzalez (Bayonne), P Gallart (Beziers), O Roumat (Dax), J-M Cadieu (Toulouse), J-F Tordo (Nice), L Cabannes (Racing Club), M Cecillon (Bourgoin, capt). *Repl:* A Benazzi (Agen) for Cadieu, 50 mins; P Benetton (Agen) for Tordo, 65 mins.
Scorers – *Tries:* Penaud 2. *Conversion:* Viars. *Penalty goal:* Viars.

South Africa: Reece-Edwards[*]; Small, Gerber, Müller, Olivier[*]; Botha (capt), Wright; Styger, Hills[*], Rodgers, Malan, Geldenhuys, Bartmann, Richter[*], Strauss[*].
Scorers – *Tries:* Gerber, Small. *Conversions:* Botha 2. *Penalty goal:* Botha. *Dropped goal:* Botha.

Referee: B Kinsey (Australia).

Series score: Played 20, France 3, South Africa 13, Drawn 4.

France (6) 29, South Africa (6) 16
second Test: Paris, 24 October 1992

All week long the guillotine has been prepared for French coach Pierre Berbizier. It is not needed. France's first ever Test victory over South Africa on home soil keeps the blade at bay. Stirred by four changes to the previous week's beaten XV, France clean out the South African lineout, where Abdel Benazzi is in inspirational fettle, and Laurent Cabannes reigns supreme in the loose. Add to that the about-turn in goalkicking form, with 17-point Thierry Lacroix mastering everything Viars failed to in Lille, and the characterless Springboks are buried.

France: J-L Sadourny (Colomiers); J-B Lafond (Begles), F Mesnel (Racing Club), T Lacroix (Dax), P Saint-André (Montferrand); A Penaud (Brive), A Hueber (Toulon); L Armary (Lourdes), J-M Gonzales (Bayonne), P Gallart (Beziers), A Benazzi (Agen), O Roumat (Dax), P Benetton (Agen), L Cabannes (Racing Club), M Cecillon (Bourgoin, capt). *Repl:* S Viars (Brive) for Lafond, 55 mins.
Scorers – *Tries:* Roumat, Penaud. *Conversions:* Lacroix 2. *Penalty goals:* Lacroix 5.

South Africa: Reece-Edwards; Small, Gerber, P Müller, Olivier; Botha (capt), Wright; Styger, Hills, Rodgers, Malan, Geldenhuys (Hattingh 49), Bartmann, Richter, Strauss.
Scorers – *Try:* Gerber. *Conversion:* Botha. *Penalty goals:* Botha 2. *Dropped goal:* Botha.

Referee: B Kinsey (Australia).

Series score: Played 21, France 4, South Africa 13, Drawn 4.

England B (5) 16, South Africa (8) 20
Bristol, 7 November 1992

England B: I Hunter (Northampton); N Heslop (Orrell), P de Glanville (Bath), D Hopley (Cambridge Univ & Wasps), T Underwood (Leicester); S Barnes (Bath, capt), S Bates (Wasps); M Hynes (Orrell), B Moore (Harlequins), J Probyn (Wasps), N Redman (Bath), A Blackmore (Bristol), T Rodber (Northampton), N Back (Leicester), B Clarke (Bath). *Repl:* A Buzza (Wasps) for Heslop, 64 mins; J Steele (Northampton) for Hunter, 76 mins.
Scorers – *Tries:* Hunter, Underwood. *Penalty goals:* Barnes 2.

South Africa: Van Rensburg; Small, Gerber, P Müller, Olivier; Botha (capt), Wright; Styger, Hills, Andrews, Hattingh, Malan, Strauss, Smit, Richter. *Repl:* Fuls for Müller, 70 mins.
Scorers – *Tries:* Hattingh, Olivier, Richter. *Conversion:* Botha. *Dropped goal:* Botha.

Referee: J Dume (France).

England (11) 33, South Africa (16) 16
Twickenham, 14 November 1992

England rouse themselves to win an enthralling contest on their return to HQ yet for much

427

of the match they are required to play catch-up. The Springboks, who have improved with each outing in England, lead 16-11 at half-time with skipper Naas Botha in majestic form. What England lack in the first period is control, as given South Africa by Botha's unerring boot. However, they reassert themselves in the new half with Martin Bayfield becoming a towering presence in the lineout and debutant Ben Clarke a powerful backrow force. Given the ball there are tries for Jerry Guscott, Dewi Morris and Will Carling but, although victory is ultimately convincing, England know deep down that all is not hunky dory, that they remain uncomfortable with the new regulations.

England: J Webb (Bath); T Underwood (Leicester), W Carling (Harlequins, capt), J Guscott (Bath), R Underwood (Leicester & RAF); R Andrew (Wasps), D Morris (Orrell); J Leonard (Harlequins), B Moore (Harlequins), V Ubogu (Bath), M Bayfield (Northampton), W Dooley (Preston Grasshoppers), M Teague (Moseley), P Winterbottom (Harlequins), B Clarke⁺ (Bath). *Repl:* P de Glanville (Bath) for T Underwood, 58 mins.
Scorers – *Tries:* T Underwood, Guscott, Morris, Carling. *Conversions:* Webb 2. *Penalty goals:* Webb 3.

South Africa: van Rensburg; Small, Gerber, P Müller, Olivier; Botha, Wright; Styger, Hills, Andrews, Hattingh, Malan, Strauss, Smit, Richter.
Scorers – *Try:* Smit. *Conversion:* Botha. *Penalty goals:* Botha 2. *Dropped goal:* Botha.

Referee: S Hilditch (Ireland).

Series score: Played 10, England 3, South Africa 6, Drawn 1.

France 20, Argentina 24
Nantes, 14 November 1992

France lose to Argentina on home soil for the first time as their dodgy autumn form continues. Coach Pierre Berbizier pays the price for a number of experimental selections and manager Robert Paparemborde promptly gives him the order of the boot. However, when French Federation president Bernard Lapasset returns from holiday he reinstates Berbizier and disciplining Paparemborde, who resigns his post as manager in protest. Berbizier, le Petit General, reveals that he had wanted to 'identify a group of 30-35 players

Llanelli captain Rupert Moon in classic pose on his Test debut against France in Paris. Despite Wales' best intentions France triumphed 26–10

428

I could use in the next World Cup campaign.' But the scenario is paifully reminiscent of the first Test loss to South Africa the previous month. Sebastien Viars missing five penalty attempts, while 24-year old counterpart Santiago Meson lands seven from seven, and it matters not that France rule the try-count three-nil. A late dropped goal by Lisandro Arbizu settles the issue.

France: S Viars (Brive); P Bernat-Salles (Paloise), P Sella (Agen), A Penaud (Brive), P Hontas (Biarritz); L Mazas (Colomiers), F Galthie (Colomiers); L Armary (Lourdes), J-M Gonzales (Bayonne), P Gallart (Beziers), O Roumat (Dax), C Mougeot (Begles), J-F Tordo (Nice, capt), P Benetton (Agen), A Benazzi (Agen).

Scorers – *Tries:* Galthie, Gonzales, Sella. *Conversion:* Viars. *Penalty goal:* Viars.

Argentina: S Meson (Tucuman); M Teran (Tucuman), D Cuesta-Silva (San Isidro), S Salvat (Alumni), G Jorge (Pucara; L Arbizu (Belgrano, capt), G Camardon (Alumni); F Mendez (Mendoza), R Le Fort (Tucuman), P Noriega (Hindu), G Llanes (La Plata), P Sporledor (Curupayti), G Garcia (Rosario), J Santamarina (Tucuman), R Perez (Rosario).

Scorers – *Penalty goals:* Meson 7. *Dropped goal:* Arbizu.

Referee: R J Megson (Scotland).

Series score: Played 26, France 21, Argentina 4, Drawn 1.

AUSTRALIA TO IRELAND AND WALES
October-November 1992: P13 W10 D0 L3 F312 A161

Australia complete an arduous Test season unbeaten with comfortable wins over Ireland and Wales, adding to the series win over New Zealand and the rout of South Africa. Nobody can accuse the world champions of taking the title and running, except back at their most dangerous rivals. Only three times do they slip in the entire season and each occasion is included in this tour, with Munster, Swansea and Llanelli boasting the most prized scalp of them all. But despite Munster's latest triumph over a touring side – they beat the All Blacks in 1978 – Ireland are no match. Memories of the 1991 World Cup quarter-final classic are briefly evoked as the teams run out but subsequently exists not the slightest danger of a repeat of that nailbiter. David Campese, who has slagged off most aspects of the Irish game in the build-up, needs only 17 minutes to open the floodgates (42–17). Ciaran Fitzgerald later quits as Irish coach. Wallaby counterpart Bob Dwyer maintains that his charges are inhibited by the new laws – 'You can't play a controlled, precise game when the laws legislate against you doing that...everything's off the cuff under the new laws' – and indeed they twice stumble in Wales, at Swansea, where the Mike Ruddock-inspired All Whites are emphatic 21–6 winners, and at Llanelli, where two late dropped goals by Colin Stephens lifts the Scarlets to a dramatic 13–9 victory. Optimism is high that the national side will indulge in a spot of pay-back – goodness knows they owe the Wallabies a few points – but even without injured skipper Michael Lynagh the Aussies win (23–6) with plenty in hand.

PARTY: A Blades (Gordon & NSW – 6,8,10,12); **M Brial** (Easts & NSW – 2,8,10,12); **D Campese** (Randwick & NSW – 1,3,4R,5,11,13); **P Carozza** (Wests & Queensland – 1,3,5,6,11,13); **T Coker** (Souths & Queensland – 2,4,6,8,9R,10,11R,13); **D Crowley** (Souths & Queensland) 1R,2,3R,4,5,7,9,11,13); **A Daly** (Easts & NSW – 1); **D Dix** (NSW – 12); **J Eales** (Brothers & Queensland – 1,3,5,6,8,9); **A Ekert** (Gordon & NSW – 2,4,7,10,12); **T Gavin** (Easts & NSW – 1,3,5,6,7,9,11,13); **A Herbert** (GPS & Queensland – 2,4); **T Horan** (Souths & Queensland – 1,3,5,6,9,11,13); **D Junee**

(Randwick & NSW – 2,4,7,8,9,10,12); **P Kahl** (Easts & Queensland – 2,4,6,10,11,13); **P Kearns** (Randwick & NSW – 1,3,5,6,7,9*,11*,13*); **T Kelaher** (Randwick & NSW – 2,4,5R,6,8,9,12); **C Lillicrap** (Queensland Univ & Queensland – 2,3); **J Little** (Souths & Queensland – 1,3,5,6,8,9,11,13); **M Lynagh** (Queensland Univ & Queensland, capt – 1*,3*,5*); **R McCall** (Brothers & Queensland – 1,3,5,7,8,9,10R,11,13); **E McKenzie** (Randwick & NSW – 1,2R,3,5,7,9,11,13); **G Morgan** (Souths & Queensland – 2,4,7,10,11); **D Nucifora** (Queensland Univ & Queensland – 2*,4,8,10,12*); **V Ofahengaue** (Manly & NSW – 1,3,5,7,9,11,13); **S Poidevin** (Randwick & NSW – 12); **M Roebuck** (Eastwood & NSW – 1,3,5,7,9,10,11,13); **M Ryan** (Brothers & Queensland – 4,6,8,10,12); **S Scott-Young** (Souths & Queensland – 2,4,6,8,10,12,13); **P Slattery** (Queensland Univ & Queensland – 1,3,5,6,8,9,11,13); **D Smith** (Souths & Queensland – 2,4,6,7,8,9,10,12); **R Tombs** (Norths & NSW – 2,4,7,10,12); **L Walker** (Randwick & NSW – 7,8,12); **T Wallace** (Gordon – 7,8,12); **W Waugh** (Randwick & NSW – 2,4,6,10,12); **D Wilson** (Easts & Queensland – 1,3,4,5,7,9,11).

Results: (1) Leinster 11, Australia 38 (Dublin, 17 October); (2) Munster 22, Australia 19 (Cork, 21 October); (3) Ulster 11, Australia 35 (Belfast, 24 October); (4) Connacht 6, Australia 14 (Galway, 27 October); (5) **Test: Ireland 17, Australia 42** (Dublin, 31 October); (6) Swansea 21, Australia 6 (St Helens, 4 November); (7) Wales B 11, Australia 24 (Cardiff, 7 November); (8) Neath 8, Australia 16 (The Gnoll, 11 November); (9) Llanelli 13, Australia 9 (Stradey Park, 14 November); (10) Monmouthshire 9, Australia 19 (Ebbw Vale, 17 November); (11) **Test: Wales 6, Australia 23** (Cardiff, 21 November); (12) Welsh Students 6, Australia 37 (Bridgend, 24 November); (13) Barbarians 20, Australia 30 (Twickenham, 28 November).

Scorers (312 – 32t,19c,38p): Roebuck 100 (17c,22p), Kelaher 67 (3t,2c,16p), Campese 20 (4t), Little 15 (3t), Ryan 15 (3t), Smith 15 (3t), Gavin 10 (2t), Horan 10 (2t), Lynagh 10 (2t), McKenzie 10 (2t), Wilson 10 (2t), Crowley 5 (1t), Eales 5 (1t), Kearns 5 (1t), McCall 5 (1t), Morgan 5 (1t), Nucifora 5 (1t).

Ireland (6) 17, Australia (19) 42
Dublin, 31 October 1992

Ireland: J Staples (London Irish); S Geoghegan (London Irish), P Danaher (Garryowen, capt), V Cunningham (St Mary's College), R Wallace (Garryowen); P Russell (Instonians), F Aherne (Lansdowne); N Popplewell (Greystones), J Murphy* (Greystones), P McCarthy (Cork Constitution), M Galwey (Shannon), P Johns (Dungannon), B Robinson (London Irish), G Hamilton (Ballymena), P Lawlor (Bective Rangers).
Scorers – *Try:* Wallace (59). *Penalty goals:* Russell 4 (24,40,50,63).

Australia: Roebuck; Carozza, Little, Horan, Campese; Lynagh (capt, Kelaher 40), Slattery; Crowley, Kearns, McKenzie, McCall, Eales, Ofahengaue, Wilson, Gavin.
Scorers – *Tries:* Campese (17), McKenzie (21), Little (36), Kelaher (74), Horan (79). *Conversions:* Roebuck 4 (17,21,74,79). *Penalty goals:* Roebuck 3 (45,54,56).

Referee: E Morrison (England).

Series score: Played 14, Ireland 6, Australia 8.

Wales B (3) 11, Australia (3) 24
Cardiff, 7 November 1992

Wales B: M Rayer (Cardiff); I Jones (Llanelli), M Hall (Cardiff), N Davies (Llanelli), W

Proctor (Llanelli); C Stephens (Llanelli), R Moon (Llanelli, capt); R Evans (Llanelli), D Fox (Llanelli), H Williams-Jones (South Wales Police), S Roy (Cardiff), J Wakeford (South Wales Police), M Perego (Llanelli), M Morris (Neath), S Legge (South Wales Police). *Repl:* N Boobyer (Llanelli) for Jones, 14 mins; N Meek (Pontypool) for Fox, 19 mins.
Scorers – *Try:* Davies. *Conversions:* Stephens 2.

Australia: Roebuck; Smith, Tombs, Walker, Junee; Wallace, Ekert; Crowley, Kearns (capt), McKenzie, McCall, Morgan, Ofahengaue, Wilson, Gavin.
Scorers – *Tries:* Smith, Morgan. *Conversion:* Roebuck. *Penalty goals:* Roebuck 4.

Referee: B E Stirling (Ireland).

Series score: Played 2, Wales B 0, Australia 2.

Wales (3) 6, Australia (5) 23
Cardiff, 21 November 1992

Wales: M Rayer (Cardiff); I Evans (Llanelli, capt), M Hall (Cardiff), S Gibbs (Swansea), W Proctor' (Llanelli); C Stephens (Llanelli), R Jones (Swansea); M Griffiths (Cardiff), G Jenkins (Swansea), H Williams-Jones (SW Police), G O Llewellyn (Neath), A Copsey (Llanelli), E Lewis (Llanelli), R Webster (Swansea), S Davies (Swansea). *Repl:* A Reynolds (Swansea) for Lewis, 74 mins.
Scorer – *Penalty goals:* Stephens 2 (32,53).

Australia: Roebuck; Campese, Little, Horan, Carozza; Kahl', Slattery; Crowley, Kearns (capt), McKenzie, McCall, Morgan, Ofahengaue, Wilson (Coker 56), Gavin.
Scorers – *Tries:* Wilson (37), McCall (44), Campese (80). *Conversion:* Roebuck (44). *Penalty goals:* Roebuck 2 (48,63).

Referee: A J Spreadbury (England).

Series score: Played 16, Wales 8, Australia 8.

Barbarians (8) 20, Australia (13) 30
Twickenham, 28 November 1992

Barbarians: M Rayer (Wales); I Hunter (England), W Carling (England, capt), S Gibbs (Wales), T Underwood (England); S Barnes (England), R Jones (Wales); N Popplewell (Ireland), N Meek (Pontypool), J Probyn (England), I Jones (New Zealand), N Hadley (Canada), M Skinner (England), I Smith (Scotland), B Clarke (England).
Scorers – *Tries:* Hunter (20), I Jones (54), Probyn (74). *Conversion:* Barnes (74). *Penalty goal:* Barnes (7).

Australia: Roebuck; Carozza, Little, Horan, Campese; Kahl, Slattery; Crowley, Kearns (capt), McKenzie, McCall, Coker, Ofahengaue, Scott-Young, Gavin.
Scorers – *Tries:* Horan (13), Crowley (60), Kearns (75). *Conversions:* Roebuck 3. *Penalty goals:* Roebuck 3 (24,39,57).

Referee: J Fleming (Scotland).

111th Varsity Match
Oxford (6) 11, Cambridge (6) 19
Twickenham, 8 December 1992

Lloyd Davies, the youngest of three Welsh brothers to represent Cambridge, lands four out of five kicks at goal (including a dropped goal) as the Light Blues, splendidly marshalled by Eric Peters, twice come from behind to beat favourites Oxford and register their 51st victory in a series dating back 120 years. Ireland outside-half Niall Malone kicks six points for the Dark Blues.

Oxford: M T Joy; A E Lumsden (D S Currie 79), K P Street, D P O'Mahony, D O Spence; N G Malone, S F du Toit; I M Buckett, M B Patton (capt), A D Williams, D R Evans, J B B Daniell, B P Nasser, C C Lion-Cachet, B G O'Mahony.
Scorers – *Try:* Spence. *Penalty goal:* Malone. *Dropped goal:* Malone.

Cambridge: L Davies; S A Burns, J P Flood, D P Hopley, G R D Batstone; K L Price, M W de Maid; D R Perrett, A J G read, P G Callow, D J Bickle, D P A Dix, M B Duthie, R H J Jenkins, E W Peters (capt).
Scorers – *Try:* Batstone. *Conversion:* Davies. *Penalty goals:* Davies 2. *Dropped goals:* Davies, Flood.

Referee: E F Morrison (Bristol).

Series score: Played 111, Oxford 47, Cambridge 51, Drawn 13.

Scotland A (9) 22, Italy (9) 17
Melrose, 19 December 1992

Scotland, without an autumn international, opt to field what at the time they consider to be their first-choice XV against Italy at Melrose. The result provides cold comfort for the selectors, and for new skipper Gavin Hastings, less than a month before Ireland are due at Murrayfield to raise the curtain on the 1993 Five Nations' Championship. The Scots are profligate, both in goal kicking (Craig Chalmers lands only four of nine attempts), punting, and in choice of options, though the uncapped Boroughmuir wing Derek Stark has a super game in front of a 6,000 crowd. Second half tries by Scott Hastings and Gregor Townsend save home blushes, before Carlo Checchinato bags a late consolation for the dogged visitors.

Scotland A: G Hastings (capt); D Stark, G Townsend, S Hastings, M Appleson; C Chalmers (Melrose), G Armstrong (Jedforest); P Jones (Gloucester), I Corcoran (Gala), P Burnell (London Scottish), D Cronin (London Scottish), G Weir (Melrose), C Hogg (Melrose), I Smith (Gloucester), S Reid (Boroughmuir).
Scorers – *Tries:* S Hastings, Townsend. *Penalty goals:* Chalmers 4.

Italy: L Troiani (L'Aquila); P Vaccari (Calvisano), S Barba (Milano), I Francescato (Treviso), Marcello Cuttitta (Milano); D Dominguez (Milano), U Casellato (Treviso); Massimo Cuttitta (Milano), C Orlandi (Treviso), G Grespan (Rovigo), C Checchinato (Rovigo), P Reale (Rovigo), S Rigo (Treviso), J Gardner (Rovigo), M Giovanelli (Milano, capt) *Repl:* R Cassino (Milano) for Reale, 74 mins.
Scorers – *Try:* Checchinato. *Penalty goals:* Dominguez 3. *Dropped goal:* Dominguez.

Referee: R McDowell (Ireland).

Series score: Played 1, Scotland A 1, Italy 0.

Ireland A (10) 13, Scotland A (0) 22
Dublin, 28 December 1992

Scotland register their first victory over Ireland at second-string level since 1983 when responding to a 13-point deficit early in the second half with 22 unanswered points, including four tries. No-one is more relieved than Gala centre Gregor Townsend, having missed seven goal kicks out of eight. The Scots, fielding seven full caps to Ireland's two, trail to Ben Cronin's try and eight points from the boot of Niall Malone, but a rally which hails from a strong back row performance from messrs McIntosh, Morrison and Hogg, produces tries for Tony Stanger (2), skipper Andy Nicol and fullback Kenny Logan.

Ireland A: C Wilkinson (Malone); C Leahy (Wanderers), B Walsh (Cork Constitution), B Glennon (Lansdowne), N Woods (Blackrock Coll); N Malone (Oxford Univ), R Saunders (London Irish); P Soden (Cork Constitution), M Patton (Oxford Univ, capt), G Halpin (London Irish), D Tweed (Ballymena), R Costello (Garryowen), L Dineen (Cork Constitution), K McKee (Bangor), B Cronin (Garryowen). *Repl:* P Millar (Bangor) for Halpin, 66 mins.
Scorers – *Try:* Cronin. *Conversion:* Malone. *Penalty goals:* Malone 2.

Scotland A: K Logan (Stirling County); A Stanger (Hawick), G Townsend (Gala), I Jardine (Stirling County), M Appleson (London Scottish); G Shiel (Melrose), A Nicol (Dundee HSFP, capt); A Watt (Glasgow High/Kelvinside), K Milne (Heriot's FP), P Wright (Boroughmuir), A Reed (Bath), S Munro (Glasgow High/Kelvinside), D McIntosh (Pontypridd), I Morrison (London Scottish), C Hogg (Melrose). *Repl:* A Macdonald (Heriot's FP) for Hogg, 62 mins; G Wilson (Boroughmuir) for Watt, 68 mins.
Scorers – *Tries:* Stanger 2, Nicol, Logan. *Conversion:* Townsend.

Referee: D Matthews (England).

Series score: Played 8, Ireland A 4, Scotland A 3, Drawn 1.

England A (3) 29, France A (10) 17
Leicester, 15 January 1993

England are well-served by half-back debutants Matt Dawson and Paul Challinor as they overturn a 10–3 half-time deficit to beat a highly capable French side at Welford Road. The visitors are upset by a number of refereeing interpretations and become increasingly frustrated as England wipe out France's lead (earned with a well-worked try rounded off by David Berty and five of Olivier Campan's seven-point contribution) with touchdowns of their own from home favourite Tony Underwood, Harvey Thorneycroft and Damian Hopley. Challinor's boot accounts for 14 points.

England A: A Buzza (Wasps); T Underwood (Leicester), D Hopley (Cambridge University), J Buckton (Saracens), H Thorneycroft (Northampton); P Challinor (Harlequins), M Dawson (Northampton); M Hynes (Orrell), K Dunn (Wasps), A Mullins (Harlequins), D Ryan (Wasps), A Blackmore (Bristol), J Hall (Bath, capt), N Back (Leicester), S Ojomoh (Bath).
Scorers – *Tries:* Underwood, Thorneycroft, Hopley. *Conversion:* Challinor. *Penalty goals:* Challinor 4.

France A: O Campan (Agen); P Bernat-Salles (Pau), H Couffignal (Colomiers), M Marfaing (Toulouse), D Berty (Toulouse); A Penaud (Brive), G Accocebery (Tyrosse, capt); L Benezech (Racing Club), E Dasalmartini (Toulon), L Verge (Begles), H Chaffardon (Graulhet), Y Lemeur (Racing Club), L Loppy (Toulon), J-M Lhermet (Montferrand), J-L Alibert (Begles).
Scorers – *Tries:* Berty, Penaud. *Conversions:* Campan 2. *Penalty goal:* Campan.

Referee: J Bacigalupo (Scotland).

Series score: Played 9, England A 5, France A 3, Drawn 1.

After a gap of two years the Five Nations' Championship returns to being a competitive entity. Gone is the predictability of 1991 and 1992 when England carried all before them to achieve the first back-to-back Grand Slams since 1924. The new laws have been to England what a pair of scissors was to Samson. The change in the game's emphasis has sapped England's strength. As Will Carling explains on page 11: 'We had developed a very successful gameplan around keeping a hold of the ball and taking it forward. Suddenly, with the new laws, it was not particularly important to be taking the ball forward. You have got to keep recycling and recycling. But we had built our strength up on set-pieces and we were very good at working ourselves into the area of the field that we wanted to be in. In one fell swoop that was taken away from us.'

Instead of Carling it is Jean-Francois Tordo who hoists the inaugural Five Nations' Cup aloft in celebration. France, who had been alone in losing a Test to South Africa before Christmas and who had granted Argentina their first ever win on Gallic soil in November, are transformed into European kingpins. They are denied the Grand Slam only by England who, somewhat fortuitously, sneak the Championship opener 16–15 at Twickenham. England win that game thanks to what manager Geoff Cooke terms 'a deep-seated self-belief'. He cannot use that one three weeks later as Wales triumph 10–9 in Cardiff, though Carling insists: 'One defeat doesn't make us a bad team.' He is right, of course, but he knows deep down that the all-white machine is not running smoothly. Even against Scotland at HQ, when the visitors concede three glorious tries in the Championship's best 23-minute spell, England cannot sustain a performance for the full 80 minutes and the Scots' are relieved to escape a mighty good thumping. However, it is only when Ireland spring the biggest surprise in many a year – beating England 17–3 at a throbbing Lansdowne Road – that England's demise, however temporary, is confirmed.

France, meanwhile, have put behind them their loss to England and won their next two games against Scotland and Ireland. The Scots, who go down 11–3, know they have missed a magnificent opportunity to end 24 years without a win in Paris, but Ireland can have few complaints. So the destiny of the Championship hinges on the visit of Wales to Parc des Princes. The Dragon has not recovered from beating up on St George's mob first time up. Wales, having been crushed by Scotland 20–0 and upset by the resurgent Irishmen inside the National Stadium in the interim, make seven changes for the end-of-term visit to Paris, but to no avail. Wales finish with a whitewashed Wooden Spoon.

England (13) 16, France (12) 15
Twickenham, 16 January 1993

England, who draft in Martin Johnson as an 11th hour replacement for Wade Dooley (aggravated thigh injury during final run-out), win a tale of two rebounds at Twickenham. The first, after 36 minutes, sees Jon Webb's penalty attempt cannon off a post into the grateful, if surprised midriff, of Ian Hunter who scores under the posts to give England the most improbable of half-time leads. The second, inside the last ten minutes, is Jean-Baptiste Lafond's attempted dropped-goal which rebounds off the crossbar to keep England's single-point lead intact.

England: J Webb (Bath); I Hunter (Northampton), W Carling (Harlequins, capt), J Guscott (Bath), R Underwood (Leicester & RAF); R Andrew (Wasps), D Morris (Orrell); J Leonard (Harlequins), B Moore (Harlequins), J Probyn (Wasps), M Bayfield (Northampton), M Johnson' (Leicester), M Teague (Moseley), P Winterbottom (Harlequins), B Clarke (Bath).
Scorers – *Try:* Hunter (36). *Conversion:* Webb. *Penalty goals:* Webb 3 (1,9,53).

France: J-B Lafond (Begles); P Saint-André (Montferrand), P Sella (Agen), T Lacroix (Dax), P Hontas (Biarritz); D Camberabero (Beziers), A Hueber (Toulon); L Armary (Lourdes), J-F Tordo (Nice, capt), L Seigne (Merignac), A Benazzi (Agen), O Roumat (Dax), P Benetton (Agen), L Cabannes (Racing Club), M Cecillon (Bourgoin). *Repl:* S Ougier (Toulouse) for Lacroix, 52 mins; F Mesnel (Racing Club) for Sella, 31 mins.
Scorers – *Tries:* Saint-André 2 (6,16). *Conversion:* Camberabero (6). *Penalty goal:* Camberabero (59).

Referee: J M Fleming (Scotland).

Series score: Played 69, England 38, France 24, Drawn 7.

Scotland (15) 15, Ireland (0) 3
Edinburgh, 16 January 1993

Billed as the Wooden Spoon decider, this contest serves to distance Scotland from such derogatory talk. Ireland, though, are clueless and fully deserve nothing. Gavin Hastings' first team talk as Scotland skipper inspires an electric start from his charges. Derek Stark, the 10.6sec 100m man, turns his first possession in Test rugby into a try, cutting inside Simon Geoghegan on nine minutes with contemptuous ease. The Boroughmuir flier then releases fellow wing Tony Stanger for his 15th international try, a mark which puts him joint second with Iwan Tukalo on Scotland's all-time try-scoring list, and Scotland have the match wrapped up by half-time.

Scotland: G Hastings (Watsonians, capt); A Stanger (Hawick), S Hastings (Watsonians), G Shiel (Melrose), D Stark⁺ (Boroughmuir); C Chalmers (Melrose), G Armstrong (Jed-Forest); A Watt (Glasgow High/Kelvinside), K Milne (Heriot's FP), P Burnell (London Scottish), A Reed⁺ (Bath), D Cronin (London Scottish), D Turnbull (Hawick), I Morrison⁺ (London Scottish), G Weir (Melrose).
Scorers – *Tries:* Stark (9), Stanger (38). *Conversion:* G Hastings (9). *Penalty goal:* G Hastings (2).

Ireland: C Wilkinson (Malone); S Geoghegan (London Irish), V Cunningham (St Mary's College), P Danaher (Garryowen), R Wallace (Garryowen); N Malone (Oxford University), M Bradley (Cork Constitution, capt); N Popplewell (Greystones), S Smith (Ballymena), P McCarthy (Cork Constitution), P Johns (Dungannon), R Costello (Garryowen), P Lawlor (Bective Rangers), D McBride (Malone), N Mannion (Lansdowne).
Scorer – *Penalty goal:* Malone (59).

Referee: E Morrison (England).

Series score: Played 105, Scotland 55, Ireland 45, Drawn 4, Abandoned 1.

Wales (10) 10, England (9) 9
Cardiff, 6 February 1993

England have never been comfortable playing in Cardiff and here is no exception, even with two Grand Slams behind them. Wales, though devoid of attacking nouse, ironically score the game's only try on the stroke of halftime when Emyr Lewis' hurried clearance unwittingly releases Ieuan Evans for a famous try. A sprint here, a controlled fly-hack there and the Welsh captain arrives at the try line ahead of the ponderous Rory Underwood. Neil Jenkins converts to add to his early penalty goal and heroic defence from thereonin frustrates the old enemy. To cap a marvellous day for the Principality, Welsh rugby earns £1.8 million from the match, from a combination of gate receipts (51,700), corporate hospitality, TV rights, merchandising and perimeter advertising.

Wales: M Rayer (Cardiff); I Evans (Llanelli, capt), M Hall (Cardiff), S Gibbs (Swansea), W Proctor (Llanelli); N Jenkins (Pontypridd), R Jones (Swansea); R Evans (Llanelli), N Meek (Pontypool), H Williams-Jones (South Wales Police), G O Llewellyn (Neath), A Copsey (Llanelli), E Lewis (Llanelli), R Webster (Swansea), S Davies (Swansea).
Scorers – *Try:* I Evans (40). *Conversion:* Jenkins. *Penalty goal:* Jenkins (11).

England: J Webb (Bath); I Hunter (Northampton), W Carling (Harlequins, capt), J Guscott (Bath), R Underwood (Leicester & RAF); R Andrew (Wasps), D Morris (Orrell); J Leonard (Harlequins), B Moore (Harlequins), J Probyn (Wasps), M Bayfield (Northampton), W Dooley (Preston Grasshoppers), M Teague (Moseley), P Winterbottom (Harlequins), B Clarke (Bath). *Repl:* P de Glanville (Bath) for Hunter, 78 mins.
Scorers – *Penalty goals:* Webb 2 (4,28). *Dropped goal:* Guscott (38).

Referee: J Dume (France).

Series score: Played 99, Wales 48, England 39, Drawn 12.

France (3) 11, Scotland (3) 3
Paris, 6 February 1993

Back in 1969 Scotland beat France in Paris at Stade Colombes. They have not repeated the feat since. Four years later the French leg of the series had moved to Parc des Princes and 11 attempts on, Scotland are still looking to lower the French Tricolour there. This day should have seen the ending of that jinx. Scotland were superior in so many facets, but they were incapable of translating pressure into points. Gavin Hastings misses five out of six penalty attempts and numerous passes are dropped in promising positions. The game's one try comes from French centre Thierry Lacroix just after the hour. Scotland will try again in 1995. Twelfth time lucky?

France: J-B Lafond (Begles); P Saint-André (Montferrand), P Sella (Agen), T Lacroix (Dax), P Hontas (Biarritz); D Camberabero (Beziers), A Hueber (Toulon); L Armary (Lourdes), J-F Tordo (Nice, capt), L Seigne (Merignac), A Benazzi (Agen), O Roumat (Dax), P Benetton (Agen), L Cabannes (Racing Club), M Cecillon (Bourgoin).
Scorers – *Try:* Lacroix (63). *Penalty goals:* Camberabero 2 (13,52).

Scotland: G Hastings (Watsonians, capt); A Stanger (Hawick), S Hastings (Watsonians), G Shiel (Melrose), D Stark (Boroughmuir); C Chalmers (Melrose), G Armstrong (Jed-Forest); P Wright (Boroughmuir), K Milne (Heriot's FP), P Burnell (London Scottish), A Reed (Bath), D Cronin (London Scottish), D Turnbull (Hawick), I Morrison (London Scottish), G Weir (Melrose).
Scorer – *Penalty goal:* G Hastings (39).

Referee: W D Bevan (Wales).

Series score: Played 64, France 31, Scotland 30, Drawn 3.

Scotland (14) 20, Wales 0
Edinburgh, 20 February 1993

The Dragon to go from strength to strength – that is what 20,000 Welsh fans who flock north of the Border fully expect. The reality could not be further from truth. Wales, offensively impotent in spite of beating England, are, as they say, lucky to get nothing. Only their near water-tight defence saves a rout but, when the opposition has a goalkicker of the calibre of an in-form Gavin Hastings offering long-range options, it is immaterial. Hastings senior has a huge game, kicking five penalty goals in a nightmare of a swirling wind, and generally provides astute tactical leadership from the back. It is a fitting Murrayfield swansong for soon-to-retire Scotland coach Ian McGeechan. The only controversy centres around Derek Turnbull's try, which young French referee Joel Dume gives only after blowing up and peeling the outer layer of bodies from a maul on the Welsh line.

Scotland: G Hastings (Watsonians, capt); A Stanger (Hawick), S Hastings (Watsonians), G Shiel (Melrose), D Stark (Boroughmuir); C Chalmers (Melrose), G Armstrong (Jed-Forest); P Wright (Boroughmuir), K Milne (Heriot's FP), P Burnell (London Scottish), A Reed (Bath), D Cronin (London Scottish), D Turnbull (Hawick), I Morrison (London Scottish), G Weir (Melrose).
Scorers – *Try:* Turnbull (38). *Penalty goals:* G Hastings 5 (5,23,28,51,63).

Wales: M Rayer (Cardiff); I Evans (Llanelli, capt), M Hall (Cardiff), S Gibbs (Swansea), W Proctor (Llanelli); N Jenkins (Pontypridd), R Jones (Swansea); R Evans (Llanelli), N Meek (Pontypool), H Williams-Jones (South Wales Police), G O Llewellyn (Neath), A Copsey (Llanelli), E Lewis (Llanelli), R Webster (Swansea), S Davies (Swansea).

Referee: J Dume (France).

Series score: Played 97, Scotland 42, Wales 53, Drawn 2.

Ireland (6) 6, France (6) 21
Dublin, 20 February 1993

Ireland slip to their 11th successive Test defeat despite a heroic defensive effort generally and a valiant display from their pack. 'We won more ball in the first ten minutes than in the whole game against Scotland,' says coach Gerry Murphy who refuses to dwell on the negative. 'It could be argued that we deserved to win.' Really? True, France only score their two tries in the last ten minutes, through the two Philippes, Saint-André and Sella, but the tactically-limited Irish do not time deserve to win.

Ireland: C Clarke* (Terenure); S Geoghegan (London Irish), V Cunningham (St Mary's College), P Danaher (Garryowen), R Wallace (Garryowen); N Malone (Oxford University), M Bradley (Cork Constitution, capt); N Popplewell (Greystones), T Kingston (Dolphin), P Clohessy (Young Munster), P Johns (Dungannon), N Francis (Blackrock), P O'Hara (Cork Constitution), D McBride (Malone), M Galwey (Shannon).
Scorer – *Penalty goals:* Malone 2 (24,33).

France: J-B Lafond (Begles); P Saint-André (Montferrand), P Sella (Agen), T Lacroix (Dax), P Hontas (Biarritz); D Camberabero (Beziers), A Hueber (Toulon); L Armary (Lourdes), J-F Tordo (Nice, capt), L Seigne (Merignac), A Benazzi (Agen), O Roumat (Dax), P Benetton (Agen), L Cabannes (Racing Club), M Cecillon (Bourgoin).
Scorers – *Tries:* Saint-André (72), Sella (79). *Conversion:* Camberabero (79). *Penalty goals:* Camberabero 2 (40,48). *Dropped goal:* Camberabero (34).

Referee: D Leslie (Scotland).

Series score: Played 66, Ireland 25, France 36, Drawn 5.

England (11) 26, Scotland (6) 12
Twickenham, 6 March 1993

England have had a month to banish the painful memories of Cardiff and it proves long enough. Scotland, despite their failure to win at Twickenham since 1983, have come south determined to complete their 11th Triple Crown, but are sent home Tae Think Again by the resurgent English, though only after the visitors, leading 6–3, lose Craig Chalmers with a shattered right forearm. It is no coincidence that the all whites strike a rich attacking seam on the day Stuart Barnes is given his first Five Nations' start nine years after making his Test debut against Australia in 1984. Barnes ignites the previously under-utilized English back division with breathtaking speed of thought and sleight of hand. Jeremy Guscott and Tony Underwood cross as England floor the Scots with three tries in an exhilirating 23-minute spell, but it is Rory Underwood's try on 47 minutes, rounding off an 80-metre move initiated by Barnes' shimmy, burst of speed and delicious pass to the motoring Guscott, which brings the house down. A combination of stout Scottish defending and loss of concentration by the home side reprieves the visitors from a serious whipping in the last 20 minutes. Still, it is hardly the exit from the international arena Scotland coach Ian McGeechan would have scripted.

England: J Webb (Bath); T Underwood (Leicester), W Carling (Harlequins, capt), J Guscott (Bath), R Underwood (Leicester & RAF); S Barnes (Bath), D Morris (Orrell); J Leonard (Harlequins), B Moore (Harlequins), J Probyn (Wasps), M Bayfield (Northampton), W Dooley (Preston Grasshoppers), M Teague (Moseley), P Winterbottom (Harlequins), B Clarke (Bath).
Scorers – *Tries:* Guscott (28), R Underwood (49), T Underwood (54). *Conversion:* Webb (54). *Penalty goals:* Webb 3 (13,31,72).

Scotland: G Hastings (Watsonians, capt); A Stanger (Hawick), S Hastings (Watsonians), G Shiel (Melrose), D Stark (Boroughmuir); C Chalmers (Melrose), G Armstrong (Jed-Forest); P Wright (Boroughmuir), K Milne (Heriot's FP), P Burnell (London Scottish), A Reed (Bath), D Cronin (London Scottish), D Turnbull (Hawick), I Morrison (London Scottish), G Weir (Melrose). *Repl:* G Townsend (Gala) for Chalmers, 24 mins; K Logan (Stirling County) for S Hastings, 65 mins.
Scorers – *Penalty goals:* G Hastings 3 (6,71,80). *Dropped goal:* Chalmers (16).

Referee: S Hilditch (Ireland).

Series score: Played 110, England 54, Scotland 39, Drawn 17.

Wales (6) 14, Ireland (13) 19
Cardiff, 6 March 1993

There is something about Ireland at Cardiff which gives Wales all sorts of problems. Even an Irish side who have lost their last 11 internationals manage to sustain an unbeaten record at the Arms Park dating back to 1983. Wales, wholly incapable of reproducing the passionate performance that accounted for England in their last home game, owe their defeat largely to a newcomer to the Irish ranks by the name of Eric Elwood. The Lansdowne outside-half kicks 11 points and, in so doing, helps restore some long-lost Irish self-belief. Wales, for whom Ieuan Evans scores yet another super try, react by making seven changes to the side for the Championship closer in Paris.

Wales: M Rayer (Cardiff); I Evans (Llanelli, capt), M Hall (Cardiff), S Gibbs (Swansea), N Walker⁺ (Cardiff); N Jenkins (Pontypridd), R Jones (Swansea); R Evans (Llanelli), N Meek (Pontypool), H Williams-Jones (South Wales Police), G O Llewellyn (Neath), A Copsey (Llanelli), E Lewis (Llanelli), R Webster (Swansea), S Davies (Swansea). *Repl:* A Clement (Swansea) for Evans, 58 mins.
Scorers – *Try:* Evans (57). *Penalty goals:* Jenkins 3 (10,34,53).

Ireland: C Clarke (Terenure College); R Wallace (Garryowen), V Cunningham (St Mary's College), P Danaher (Garryowen), S Geoghegan (London Irish); E Elwood

(Lansdowne), M Bradley (Cork Constitution, capt); N Popplewell (Greystones), T Kingston (Dolphin), P Clohessy (Young Munster), P Johns (Dungannon), M Galwey (Shannon), P O'Hara (Cork Constitution), D McBride (Malone), B Robinson (London Irish).

Scorers – *Try:* Robinson (30). *Conversion:* Elwood. *Penalty goals:* Elwood 3 (39,45,61). *Dropped goal:* Clarke (13).

Referee: A MacNeill (Australia).

Series score: Played 96, Wales 57, Ireland 33, Drawn 6.

Ireland (3) 17, England (3) 3
Dublin, 20 March 1993

Dublin's fair city is in partisan mood after this one. Unexpected, would be a staggering understatement. Yes, Ireland had beaten Wales in Cardiff but all through their darkest hour they had avoided defeat there. Yes, England are a shadow of their Grand Slam greatness, but they had given Scotland a frightful seeing to at Twickers last time out. All that is in the home side's favour is that they have everything to gain, whereas Albion have rather a lot to lose. After all, the Lions squad for New Zealand is to be announced 48 hours after the game. In the game of mind warfare such a psychological weapon is handy indeed. It is hard to reconcile the fact that Eric Elwood is only winning his second cap, so accomplished is he at this level. Two caps, two wins – an utterly unthinkable success ratio

Martin Bayfield, with a little help from Mike Teague, gets the tap during England's 16–15 win over France at Twickenham

for any Irishman a couple of months back. Two penalty goals and two dropped goals from his boot get the strains of Cockles and Muscles underway, and Mick Galwey's late try sends the city into raptures.

Ireland: C Clarke (Terenure College); R Wallace (Garryowen), V Cunningham (St Mary's College), P Danaher (Garryowen), S Geoghegan (London Irish); E Elwood (Lansdowne), M Bradley (Cork Constitution, capt); N Popplewell (Greystones), T Kingston (Dolphin), P Clohessy (Young Munster), P Johns (Dungannon), M Galwey (Shannon), P O'Hara (Cork Constitution), D McBride (Malone), B Robinson (London Irish).
Scorers – *Try:* Galwey (79). *Penalty goals:* Elwood 2 (28,45). *Dropped goals:* Elwood 2 (41,75).

England: J Webb (Bath); T Underwood (Leicester), W Carling (Harlequins, capt), J Guscott (Bath), R Underwood (Leicester & RAF); S Barnes (Bath), D Morris (Orrell); J Leonard (Harlequins), B Moore (Harlequins), J Probyn (Wasps), M Bayfield (Northampton), W Dooley (Preston Grasshoppers), M Teague (Moseley), P Winterbottom (Harlequins), B Clarke (Bath).
Scorer – *Penalty goal:* Webb (33).

Referee: A MacNeill (Australia).

Series score: Played 106, Ireland 37, England 61, Drawn 8.

France (16) 26, Wales (3) 10
Paris, 20 March 1993

Wales score their first try at Parc des Princes in ten years, for all the good it does them. Nigel Walker, Cardiff's Olympic hurdler who had been drafted in for the previous match against Ireland, comes up with the five-pointer but France are 21–3 up at the time and set fair for the inaugural Five Nations' Cup. The Welsh selectors had come in for criticism for dropping national icon Robert Jones and Lions-tip Mike Rayer but debutant Rupert Moon and Tony Clement are no mugs either. Still, the bottom line is that Wales lose – with more than a little help from Philippe Benetton's try brace – and finish bottom of the Championship table. As coach Alan Davies concedes: 'Welsh rugby still has a long way to go.'

France: J-B Lafond (Begles); P Saint-André (Montferrand), P Sella (Agen), T Lacroix (Dax), P Hontas (Biarritz); F Mesnel (Racing Club), A Hueber (Toulon); L Armary (Lourdes), J-F Tordo (Nice, capt), L Seigne (Merignac), A Benazzi (Agen), O Roumat (Dax), P Benetton (Agen), L Cabannes (Racing Club), M Cecillon (Bourgoin).
Scorers – *Tries:* Benetton 2 (17,80), Lafond (72). *Conversion:* Lafond (17). *Penalty goals:* Lacroix 3 (7,37,39).

Wales: A Clement (Swansea); I Evans (Llanelli, capt), N Davies (Llanelli), S Gibbs (Swansea), N Walker (Cardiff); N Jenkins (Pontypridd), R Moon+ (Llanelli); R Evans (Llanelli), A Lamerton+ (Llanelli), H Williams-Jones (South Wales Police), G O Llewellyn (Neath), P Davies (Llanelli), M Perego (Llanelli), R Webster (Swansea), E Lewis (Llanelli). *Repl:* J Davies (Neath) for R Evans, 55 mins; P Arnold (Swansea) for Perego, 64 mins.
Scorers – *Try:* Walker (75). *Conversion:* Jenkins. *Penalty goal:* Jenkins (31).

Referee: O E Doyle (Ireland).

Series score: Played 67, France 28, Wales 36, Drawn 3.

THE 1993 FIVE NATIONS' CHAMPIONSHIP TABLE
(1992 positions in brackets)

	P	W	D	L	F	(t, c, p,dg)	A	(t, c, p,dg)	Pts
France (2)	4	3	0	1	73	8, 3, 8, 1	35	2, 2, 7, 0	6
Scotland (3)	4	2	0	2	50	3, 1,10, 1	40	4, 1, 6, 0	4
England (1)	4	2	0	2	54	4, 2, 9, 1	54	4, 2, 7, 3	4
Ireland (5)	4	2	0	2	45	2, 1, 8, 3	53	5, 2, 7, 1	4
Wales (4)	4	1	0	3	34	3, 2, 5, 0	74	5, 2,13, 2	2

Scorers (256 – 20t,9c,40p,6dg): 32 – G Hastings (Scotland) 1c, 10p. 31 – J Webb (England) 2c,9p. 23 – E Elwood (Ireland), 1c,5p,2dg. 22 – D Camberabero (France) 2c,5p,1dg. 19 – N Jenkins (Wales) 2c,5p. 15 – P Saint-André (France) 3t. 14 – T Lacroix (France) 1t,3p. 10 – P Benetton (France) 2t; I Evans (Wales) 2t. 9 – N Malone (Ireland) 3p. 8 – J Guscott (England) 1t,1dg. 7 – J-B Lafond (France) 1t,1c. 5 – M Galwey (Ireland) 1t; I Hunter (England) 1t; B Robinson (Ireland) 1t; P Sella (France) 1t; T Stanger (Scotland) 1t; D Stark (Scotland) 5; D Turnbull (Scotland) 1t; R Underwood (England) 1t; T Underwood (England) 1t; N Walker (Wales) 1t. 3 – C Chalmers (Scotland) 1dg; C Clarke (Ireland) 1dg.

England A 59, Italy A 0
Bath, 3 February 1993

Italy include six caps in their side but could do with a few more as England's A-team run riot at the Recreation Ground, scoring nine unanswered tries through Stuart Potter (2), Harvey Thorneycroft, Tony Underwood (2), Matthew Dawson, Alan Buzza and Neil 'too small' Back (2).

England A: A Buzza (Wasps); T Underwood (Leicester), S Potter (Leicester), D Hopley (Cambridge University), H Thorneycroft (Northampton); P Challinor (Harlequins), M Dawson (Northampton); C Clark (Swansea), K Dunn (Wasps), A Mullins (Harlequins), M Johnson (Leicester), A Blackmore (Bristol), J Hall (Bath, capt), N Back (Leicester), S Ojomoh (Bath). *Repl:* M Greenwood (Wasps) for Ojomoh, 68 mins.

Scorers – *Tries:* Potter (2), Thorneycroft, Underwood 2, Dawson, Buzza, Back 2. *Conversions:* Challinor 2, Buzza 2. *Penalty goals:* Challinor 2.

Italy A: P Dotto (Treviso); L Perziano (Treviso), M Tommasi (Milan), S Bordon (Rovigo), L Manteri (Treviso); M Bonomi (Milan), G Faltiba (San Dona); M Dal-Sie (San Dona), A Marengoni (Milan), F Properzi-Curti (Treviso), R Favaro (Treviso), M Giacheri (Treviso), R Cassina (Casale), D Beretta (Milan), F Coppo (Treviso). *Repl:* A Piazza (San Dona) for Marengoni, 56 mins.

Referee: G Black (Ireland).

Series score: Played 7, England A 6, Italy A 0, Drawn 1.

Netherlands 12, Wales A 57
's-Hertogensboch, 6 February 1993

For a nation whose senior side is less than regular in its try scoring, the nine visits across the Dutch line by the A-team is welcome indeed. Moreover, as Nigel Walker, Cardiff's former Olympic hurdler, claims a hat-trick on his international debut, there is further ground for optimism. Fellow Cardiff wing Steve Ford bags a brace and Swansea outside-half Aled Williams pockets 17 points.

Netherlands: A Marcker (Castricum); M Nagtegaal (RCH), G Bos (Diok), B Wisser (Diok), J Esseveld (Eamland); M Michelsen (HRC), W Hanekom (Diok); M Tielrooy (RCH), Y Kummer (Diok, capt), V Dubbeldam (DSR-C), P Koenen (Diok), M van Loom (Diok), R Broers (Diok), A Seijbel (Oemoemenoe), T Suring (ARC). *Repl:* M Geelhoed (HRC) for Broers, 4 mins.
Scorers – *Tries:* Koenen 2. *Conversion:* Bos.

Wales A: I Jones (Llanelli); S Ford (Cardiff), R Bidgood (Newport), N Davies (Llanelli, capt), N Walker (Cardiff); A Williams (Swansea), R Howley (Bridgend); I Buckett (Swansea), R McBryde (Swansea), L Mustoe (Pontypool), S Roy (Cardiff), P Arnold (Swansea), H Stone (Cardiff), M Perego (Llanelli), S Legge (SW Police). *Repl:* A Thomas (Neath) for McBryde.
Scorers – *Tries:* Bidgood, Howley, Williams, Walker 3, Davies, Ford 2. *Conversions:* Williams 6.

Referee: H Rohr (Germany).

Series score: Played 2, Netherlands 0, Wales A 2.

England A 66, Spain 5
Richmond, 5 March 1993

The rain on Spain is of the try variety as rampant England run in no fewer than 11 in this record romp. The chief beneficiary is Tigers wing Steve Hackney who bags a four-timer, while Bristol fullback Paul Hull includes two in his 21-point haul. England skipper Dean Richards also gets in on the act though the honour of scoring the day's final try goes to the battered Spaniards and their scrum-half Jeronimo Hernandez-Gil.

England A: P Hull (Bristol & RAF); S Hackney (Leicester), S Potter (Leicester), D Hopley (Cambridge University), H Thorneycroft (Northampton); P Challinor (Harlequins), M Dawson (Northampton); C Clark (Swansea), K Dunn (Wasps), D Garforth (Leicester), M Johnson (Leicester), A Blackmore (Bristol), M Greenwood (Wasps), S Ojomoh (Bath), D Richards (Leicester, capt).
Scorers – *Tries:* Dunn, Johnson, Hull 2, Hackney 4, Thorneycroft, Richards, Challinor. *Conversions:* Hull 4. *Penalty goal:* Hull.

Spain: F Puertas (capt); J Torres, G Rivero (J Diaz 67), A Mino, P Gutierrez; M Sanchez, J Hernandez-Gil; J Gutierrez, F de la Calle, R Lizarza, A Malo, V Esnaola, J Gutierrez, J Etxeberria, M Auzmendi (A Beloki 49).
Scorer – *Try:* Hernandez-Gil.

Referee: D R Davies (Wales).

Series score: Played 5, Spain 0, England A/B 5.

Wales A (3) 28, Ireland A (14) 29
Newport, 5 March 1993

Ireland edge a high-scoring affair by the odd point in 57 basically because they deny the talented Welsh backs sufficient possession…just. And in 19-point hero David Humphreys, the Queen's University Belfast outside-half, they unearth a player with almost as bright a future as Eric Elwood. Not only does he score one of Ireland's three tries, but lands a conversion, two penalty goals and two dropped goals. There is probably something he cannot do but Wales, despite edging the try-count 4–3, are not let in on the secret.

Wales A: I Jones (Llanelli); S Ford (Cardiff), R Bidgood (Newport), N Davies (Llanelli,

capt), W Proctor (Llanelli); A Davies (Cardiff), R Howley (Bridgend); I Buckett (Swansea), R McBryde (Swansea), L Mustoe (Pontypool), P Kawulok (Cardiff), S Roy (Cardiff), A Reynolds (Swansea), M Budd (Cardiff), S Legge (SW Police).
Scorers – *Tries:* Bidgood 2, Jones, Proctor. *Conversion:* A Davies. *Penalty goals:* A Davies 2.

Ireland A: J Staples (London Irish); R Carey (Dungannon), B Walsh (Cork Constitution), M McCall (Bangor), N Woods (Blackrock College); D Humphreys (Queen's University, Belfast), F Aherne (Lansdowne, capt); P Soden (Cork Constitution), B Mulcahy (Skerries), P Millar (Ballymena), J Etheridge (Northampton), D Tweed (Ballymena), K Potts (St Mary's College), L Toland (Old Crescent), N Mannion (Lansdowne).
Scorers – *Tries:* Walsh, Humphreys, Staples. *Conversion:* Humphreys. *Penalty goals:* Humphreys 2. *Dropped goals:* Humphreys 2.

Referee: S Piercy (England).

Ireland A 18, England A 22
Donnybrook, 19 March 1993

England's A-men complete their second consecutive Grand Slam with Northampton centre-turned-scrum half Matt Dawson in cracking form. He scores England's first and last try, with John Hall's close range effort splitting the two, and it is only Ireland's dedication to defensive duty that prevents a big loss. So sturdy are the hosts in that department that they not only avoid such a scenario but come close to pipping England, with a late try by Ronnie Carey, adding to the earlier score by Brian Walsh, closing the gap to a modest four points.

Ireland A: A White (St Mary's College); R Carey (Dunganno), B Walsh (Cork Constitution), M McCall (Bangor), N Woods (Blackrock College); D Humphreys (Queen's University, Belfast), F Aherne (Lansdowne, capt); P Soden (Cork Constitution), B Mulcahy (Skerries), P Millar (Ballymena), J Etheridge (Northampton), D Tweed (Ballymena), K Potts (St Mary's College), L Toland (Old Crescent), N Mannion (Lansdowne). *Repl:* S McKinty (Bangor) for Mannion, 25 mins; M Ridge (Blackrock College) for Woods, 54 mins.
Scorers – *Tries:* Walsh, Carey. *Conversion:* Humphries. *Penalty goal:* Humphries. *Dropped goal:* Humphries.

England A: P Hull (Bristol & RAF); S Hackney (Leicester), S Potter (Leicester), D Hopley (Cambridge University), H Thorneycroft (Northampton); P Challinor (Harlequins), M Dawson (Northampton); C Clark (Swansea), K Dunn (Wasps), D Garforth (Leicester), M Johnson (Leicester), A Blackmore (Bristol), D Hall (Bath, capt), S Ojomoh (Bath), M Greenwood (Wasps). *Repl:* N Beal (Northampton) for Hopley, 80 mins.
Scorers – *Tries:* Dawson 2, Hall. *Conversions:* Hull 2. *Penalty goal:* Hull.

Referee: R Yeman (Wales).

Scotland A (0) 19, France A (19) 29
Aberdeen, 20 March 1993

David McIvor, nicknamed 'Grandad' by various opponents because of his shock of grey hair, is the life and soul of Scotland's performance in a defeat by five tries to one at Rubislaw. Unhappily, for the home side, McIvor's high-profile display is not matched by team-mates as France encounter little defensive resistance, especially in the midfield area. Scotland's solitary try, from fullback Kenny Logan, arrives in the final minute.

Scotland A: K Logan (Stirling County); K Milligan (Stewart's-Melville FP), I Jardine (Stirling County), D Wyllie (Stewart's-Melville FP), J Kerr (Haddington); A Donaldson (Currie), D Millard (London Scottish); G Wilson (Boroughmuir), M Scott (Edinburgh Academicals), S Ferguson (Peebles), C Gray (Nottingham, capt), S Munro (Glasgow High/Kelvinside), A Macdonald (Heriot's FP), I Smith (Gloucester), D McIvor (Edinburgh Academicals).
Scorers – *Try:* Logan. *Conversion:* Donaldson. *Penalty goals:* Donaldson 4.

France A: J-L Sadourny (Colomiers); F Bertranck (Montferrand), P Arletaz (Perpignan), J-C Larran (Tarbes), L Arbot (Perpignan); B Bellot (Graulhet), F Galthie (Colomiers, capt); L Benezech (Racing Club), S Morizot (Perpignan), P Gallart (Bezier), Y Lemeur (Racing Club), O Merle (Grenoble), L Llopy (Toulon), J-M Lhermet (Montferrand), S Dispagne (Narbonne). *Repl:* L Labit (Castres) for Bellot, 40 mins.
Scorers – *Tries:* Larran, Bertranck 2, Arbot, Galthie. *Conversion:* Bellot 2.

Referee: B Campsall (England).

Series score: Played 21, Scotland A 8, France A 13.

CATHAY PACIFIC/HONG KONG BANK INVITATION SEVENS
Hong Kong, 3–4 April 1993

Scotland, their reputation enhanced following victory in the Dubai Sevens, join Ireland and a Welsh President's VII in the quarter-finals of the unofficial World Cup Sevens, but each loses out to Southern Hemisphere opposition. The Scots had led Western Samoa 7–0, while the Irish forced extra-time against Australia when Richard Wallace outsprinted David Campese to touch down. Each to no avail. For their part, the Welsh are blitzed by those masters of the abbreviated discipline, Fiji. With Waisale Serevi in full flow, Fiji are expected to complete their eighth win in the tournament, but the Samoans, having delighted in beating neighbours New Zealand in the semis, have other ideas. Inspired by Lolani Koko, who had turned down an invitation to represent the All Blacks, the Samoans run out 14–12 winners.

Pool matches: A – Fiji 49, Malaysia 0; Namibia 38, Malaysia 7; Fiji 40, Namibia 7. **B** – Canada 28, Papua New Guinea 10; Welsh President's VII 35, Papua New Guinea 12; Welsh President's VII 40, Canada 0. **C** – Ireland 7, Italy 5; Italy 19, Hong Kong 7; Ireland 24, Hong Kong 0. **D** – Australia 47, Singapore 5; US Eagles 42, Singapore 0; Australia 45, US Eagles 0. **E** – Western Samoa 35, Thailand 0; Japan 40, Thailand 0; Western Samoa 40, Japan 7. **F** – Scotland 28, Romania 5; Tonga 31, Romania 14; Scotland 10, Tonga 7. **G** – South Africa 49, Sri Lanka 0; Argentina 19, Sri Lanka 7; South Africa 28, Argentina 0. **H** – New Zealand 28, Taiwan 5; Taiwan 14, South Korea 7; New Zealand 34, South Korea 0.

Quarter-finals: Fiji 33, Welsh President's VII 7; Australia 17, Ireland 12; Western Samoa 28, Scotland 14; New Zealand 20, South Africa 12. **Semi-finals:** Fiji 17, Australia 14; Western Samoa 24, New Zealand 14. **Final:** Western Samoa 14, Fiji 12.

RUGBY WORLD CUP SEVENS
Murrayfield, Edinburgh 16-18 April 1993

Scotland spend mega bucks preparing for the inaugural World Cup Sevens, in places like Dubai, Australia and Fiji; England turn up at Murrayfield almost unannounced, their furthest trip being to, um, well Edinburgh probably. Guess who wins the Melrose Cup? Not Scotland. Nor, for that matter, favourites Fiji, nor Western Samoa, Australia or even the All Blacks. In a repeat of the 1991 XV-a-side World Cup final, utterly unfancied England meet the Wallabies and this time get the result right. Inspired by skipper Andrew Harriman – a one-cap wonder back in 1988, who scores a tournament record 12 tries – the English give the Northern Hemisphere a notable success over its more vaunted Southern counterpart. And it would have been an all Home Unions final had not semi-finalists Ireland again been denied at the last-gasp by Australia. England lead the final 21–0, before those Wallabies jump back into contention to make for an exciting climax. In many ways the final epitomizes the tournament itself. Lop-sided early on, with too many meaningless matches (the event must fall into line with Hong Kong's two-day format), the closing stages save the tournament's reputation as the quarter-finalists (though not New Zealand, Scotland, Wales, France and South Africa, who fail to reach the last eight) turn on the style.

Quarter-finals

Pool E: Ireland 17, Western Samoa 0; Fiji 21, Tonga 7; Fiji 14, Western Samoa 12; Ireland 14, Tonga 12; Western Samoa 42, Tonga 7; Fiji 31, Ireland 7.

Pool E	P	W	D	L	F	A	Pts
Fiji	3	3	0	0	66	26	9
Ireland	3	2	0	1	38	43	7
Western Samoa	3	1	0	2	54	38	5
Tonga	3	0	0	3	26	77	3

Pool F: Australia 7, South Africa 5; England 21, New Zealand 12; England 14, South Africa 7; New Zealand 42, Australia 0; South Africa 31, New Zealand 12; Australia 21, England 12.

Pool F	P	W	D	L	F	A	Pts
Australia	3	2	0	1	28	59	7
England	3	2	0	1	47	40	7
South Africa	3	1	0	2	43	35	5
New Zealand	3	1	0	2	68	52	5

Semi-finals
England 21, Fiji 7; Australia 21, Ireland 19.

Plate final
Argentina 19, Spain 12

Bowl final
Japan 33, Scotland 19

Final
England 21, Australia 17

England: Harriman, Adebayo, Beal, Scully; Sheasby, Rodber (Cassell 15), Dallaglio.
Scorers – *Tries:* Harriman, Dallaglio, Rodber. *Conversions:* Beal 3.

Australia: Campese, Constable, Lynagh, Taupeaafe; Fenwicke, Burke, Ofahengaue.
Scorers – *Tries:* Lynagh, Campese, Taupeaafe. *Conversion:* lynagh.

Referee: P Robin (France).

Romania 20, France 37
Bucharest, 20 May 1993

France introduce eight newcomers to the side which won the inaugural Five Nations' Cup two months previously and score a handsome win in Bucharest. Pau winger Philippe Bernat-Salles, on only his second Test appearance, scores a hat-trick of tries to bring a smile to the face of coach Pierre Berbizier. Le petit general had been left wincing on Bernat-Salles' last appearance as France crashed at home to Argentina in Nantes. Marc Cecillon claims the fourth try and there are 17 points from the boot of Sebastien Viars, who had been a spectator during the Championship season.

Romania: V Brici; M Dumitru, M Fulina, N Racean, J Solomie; N Nichitean, D Neaga; G Leonte, G Ion, D Popa, C Cojocariu, C Tudor, I S ecelenu, H Dumitras (capt), T Brinza. *Repl:* C Georghe for Ion; V Ionescu for Popa, T Oroin for Cojocariu.
Scorers – *Tries:* Neaga, Leonte. *Conversions:* Nichitean 2. *Penalty goals:* Nichitean 2.

France: J-L Sadourny (Colomiers); P Bernat-Salles (Pau), P Sella (Agen), H Couffignal (Colomiers), S Viars (Brive); A Penaud (Brive), A Hueber (Toulon); J-M Gonzalez (Bayonne), J-F Tordo (Nice, capt), L Seigne (Merignac), Y Lemeur (Racing Club), O Roumat (Dax), L Cabannes (Racing Club), J-M Lhermet (Montferrand), M Cecillon (Bourgoin). *Repl:* J Verge (SBUC) for Tordo.
Scorers – *Tries:* Bernat-Salles 3, Cecillon. *Conversions:* Viars 4. *Penalty goals:* Viars 3.

Referee: B Stirling (Ireland).

ENGLAND A TO CANADA
May-June 1993: P5 W4 D0 L1 F123 A57: (no caps awarded)

England, minus 16 British Lions, still include nine full internationals in their 30-man squad for the short tour to Canada. The cancellation of the proposed leg in the United States, because the USA Rugby Union cannot not afford to host a tour, prompts the decision not to award caps for the two 'Tests' against the Canucks, a series which is squared in Ottawa after England had fallen behind in Vancouver. John Olver, England's reserve hooker since 1989, is awarded the captaincy ahead of A team skipper John Hall and leads the side in each International. The biggest selectorial suprise is the inclusion of Tynedale centre John Fletcher, who plays his rugby in North Division One, equivalent to a fifth division nationally. But the most crucial pick turns out to be Harlequins outside-half Paul Challinor who contributes 16 points, including both tries, to the 19–14 second 'Test' victory. Paul Grayson, his rival for the No 10 jersey, leads the tour scoring charts with 26 points from his two non-Test appearances.

PARTY: A Adebayo (Bath – 1R,2,4,5); **N Back** (Leicester – 1,3,5); **N Beal** (Northampton – 1,3R,4); **A Blackmore** (Bristol – 1,3,5); **K Bracken** (Bristol – 1R,3,5); **A Buzza** (Wasps – 2,3); **P Challinor** (Harlequins – 1,3,5); **G Childs** (Wasps – 2); **M Dawson** (Northampton – 1); **P de Glanville** (Bath – 1); **S Douglas** (Newcastle Gosforth – 2,4); **K Dunn** (Wasps – 2,4); **J Fletcher** (Tynedale – 2,4); **D Garforth** (Leicester – 2,4); **P Grayson** (Waterloo – 2,4); **M Greenwood** (Wasps – 2,4); **S Hackney** (Leicester – 2,4); **J Hall** (Bath – 1,3,5); **D Hopley** (Wasps – 1,2R,3,5); **M Hynes** (Orrell – 2, 4); **M Johnson** (Leicester – 1,3,5); **R Langhorn** (Harlequins – 2,4); **S Ojomoh** (Bath– 1,3,5); **J Olver** (Northampton, capt – 1*,3*,5*); **C Oti** (Wasps – 1,3,5); **D Pears** (Harlequins – 1,3,5); **S Potter** (Leicester – 3,4,5); **N Redman** (Bath 2*,4*); **M Rennell** (Bedford – 2,4); **T Rodber** (Northampton); **G Rowntree** (Leicester – 1,3,5); **A Snow** (Harlequins – 2,4); **V Ubogu** (Bath – 1,3,5). **Coach:** M Slemen. **Assistant coach:** K Richardson. **Manager:**

P Rossborough.

Results: (1) British Columbia 10, England A 26 (Victoria, 22 May); (2) British Columbia XV 11, England A 26 (Vancouver, 26 May); (3) **first 'Test': Canada 15, England A 12** (Vancouver, 29 May); (4) Ontario 7, England A 40 (Toronto, 2 June); (5) **second 'Test': Canada 14, England A 19** (Ottawa, 5 June).

Scorers (123 – 13t,5c,15p,1dg) – Grayson 26 (4c,6p), Pears 23 (1c,7p), Challinor 19 (2t,2p,1dg), Adebayo 10 (2t), Potter 10 (2t), Be al 5 (1t), Bracken 5 (1t), Douglas 5 (1t), Greenwood 5 (1t), Hackney 5 (1t), Hopley 5 (1t), Rennell 5 (1t).

Canada 15, England A 12
first 'Test': Vancouver, 29 May 1993

Canada: S Stewart (UBC Old Boys); J Loveday (Calgary Irish), S Gray (Vancouver Kats), G Rees (Oak Bay Castaways), D Lougheed (Toronto Welsh); J Graf (UBC Old Boys), C Tynan (Vancouver Meralomas); E Evans (IBM Tokyo), K Svoboda (Ajax Wanderers, capt), D Jackart (UBC Old Boys), A Charron (Ottawa Irish), J Knauer (Vancouver Meralomas), G Ennis (Suntory Tokyo), B Breen (Vancouver Meralomas), C MacKenzie (UBC Old Boys)
Scorers – *Penalty goals:* Rees 4. *Dropped goal:* Graf.

England: Pears; Buzza (Beal 4), Potter, Hopley, Oti; Challinor, Bracken; Rowntree, Olver (capt), Ubogu, Johnson, Blackmore, Hall, Back, Ojomoh.
Scorer – *Penalty goals:* Pears 4.

Referee: S MacNeill (Australia).

Canada 14, England A 19
second Test: Ottawa, 5 June 1993

Canada: S Stewart (UBC Old Boys); J Loveday (Calgary Irish), S Gray (Vancouver Kats), G Rees (Oak Bay Castaways), D Lougheed (Toronto Welsh); J Graf (UBC Old Boys), C Tynan (Vancouver Meralomas); E Evans (IBM Tokyo), K Svoboda (Ajax Wanderers, capt), D Jackart (UBC Old Boys), J Knauer (Vancouver Meralomas), N Hadley (UBC Old Boys, capt), A Charron (Ottawa Irish), G MacKinnon (Ex Brittania Lions), G Ennis (Suntory Tokyo). *Repl:* J Hutchinson (York Yeomen) for MacKinnon, 77 mins.
Scorers – *Try:* MacKinnon. *Penalty goals:* Rees 3.

England: Pears; Adebayo, Potter, Hopley, Oti; Challinor, Bracken; Rowntree, Olver (capt), Ubogu, Johnson, Blackmore, Hall, Back, Ojomoh.
Scorers – *Tries:* Challinor 2. *Penalty goals:* Challinor 2, Pears.

Referee: S MacNeill (Australia).

SCOTLAND TO FIJI, TONGA AND WESTERN SAMOA
May–June 1993: P7 W6 D0 L1 F174 A66 (no caps awarded)

Scotland take 11 capped players with them to the South Seas, though only one, George 'Doddie' Weir had been a '93 Five Nations' regular. The consequence is widely expected to be a torrid trip but the inexperienced party surprise their critics by equipping themselves well. Indeed, going into the final match of a tour which features non-cap Internationals against Fiji, Tonga and Western Samoa, the Scots boast a 100 per cent record. Although they bow to the Samoans (11–28), who gain a measure of revenge for their 1991 World Cup quarter-final loss at Murrayfield, Scotland return home with the scalps of Fiji (21–10) and Tonga (23–5), and with the comfort of knowing that the pool of talent from which the international squad can draw is perhaps not as shallow as had been previously thought.

PARTY: K Armstrong (Jed-Forest – 2,4); **I Corcoran** (Gala – 6); **A Donaldson** (Currie – 1,3,4R,6); **S Ferguson** (Peebles – 2,3,5,7); **C Glasgow** (Heriot's FP – 6); **C Gray** (Nottingham – 1,3,5,6*); **N Grecian** (London Scottish – 2,3,6,7); **J Hay** (Hawick – 1,3,4R,5,7); **C Hogg** (Melrose – 2,4,6); **G Isaac** (Gala – 1,3,5,7); **I Jardine** (Stirling County – 1,3,5,7); **J Kerr** (Haddington – 1,4,6); **K Logan** (Stirling County – 1,3,4R,5,7); **A Macdonald** (Heriot's FP – 2,6); **R MacNaughton** (Northampton – 1,4,6); **D McIvor** (Edinburgh Academicals – 1,3,5,6,7); **K Milligan** (Stewart's-Melville FP – 2,4); **M Moncrieff** (Gala – 1,3,5,7); **S Munro** (Glasgow H/K – 2,4,7); **S Nichol** (Selkirk – 2,3,5,7); **A Nicol** (Dundee HSFP, capt – 2 *,3*,5*,6R,7*); **B Redpath** (Melrose – 1,4,6); **C Redpath** (Melrose – 2,4,6); **M Scott** (Edinburgh Academicals – 2,4); **R Scott** (London Scottish – 1,3,4,5,7); **I Smith** (Gloucester – 1*,3,5,7); **G Townsend** (Gala – 2,4,5,7); **M Wallace** (Glasgow H/K – 2,4,6); **G Weir** (Melrose – 1,3,5,6R,7); **G Wilson** (Boroughmuir – 1,4,6); **D Wyllie** (Stewart's-Melville FP – 2,4*,6). **Coach:** D Johnston. **Assistant coach:** R Dixon. **Manager:** A Hosie. **Originally selected:** M Appleson (London Scottish), D McIntosh (Pontypridd), D Millard (London Scottish), A Sharp (London Scottish), D Stark (Boroughmuir).

Results: (1) Fiji B 7 Scotland 14 (Nadi, 22 May); (2) Fiji Juniors 3, Scotland 15 (Suva, 26 May); (3) Fiji 10, Scotland 21 (Suva, 29 May); (4) Tongan President's XV 5, Scotland 21 (Nuku'alofa, 2 June); (5) Tonga 5, Scotland 23 (Nuku'alofa, 5 June); (6) Western Samoan President's XV 8, Scotland 33 (Apia, 9 June); (7) **Test: Western Samoa 28, Scotland 11** (Apia, 12 June).

Scorers (174 – 22t,8c,15p,1dg) – Townsend 30 (1t,2c,7p), Donaldson 25 (2c,7p), Nicol 20 (4t), Grecian 16 (1t,4c,1p), Hogg 15 (3t), penalty tries 15 (3t), Kerr 10 (2t), Logan 10 (2t), Wallace 10 (2t), Weir 10 (2t), Gray 5 (1t), Hay 5 (1t), Wyllie 3 (1dg).

Fiji B 7, Scotland 14
Nadi, 22 May 1992

Fiji B: I Saukuru; J Vatubua, J Wainibuli, I Nabewa, T Baleinaval; J Waqa, K Vuira; O Turua, A Sasse, J Low, R Uluilakeba, T Waqairawai, J Banuve, I Kunaqio, T Winiqolo (capt).
Scorers – *Try:* Kunaqio. *Conversion:* Saukuru.

Scotland: Logan; Moncrieff, Jardine, MacNaughton, Kerr; Donaldson, B Redpath; Isaac, Hay, Wilson, Gray, R Scott, McIvor, Smith (capt), Weir.
Scorers – *Try:* Kerr. *Penalty goals:* Donaldson 3.

Referee: B Kinsey (Australia).

Fiji 10, Scotland 21
'Test': Suva, 29 May 1993

Fiji: T Vonolagi; W Waisea, V Rauluni, E Nauga, T Lovo; E Rokowailoa, W Serevi; M Taga (capt), A Rabitu, I Naituku, P Naruma, A Nadolo, I Tanake, S Vonolagi, E Tuvunivono.
Scorers – *Try:* Rokowailoa. *Conversion:* Serevi. *Penalty goal:* Serevi.

Scotland: Logan; Grecian, Nichol, Jardine, Moncrieff; Donaldson, Nicol (capt); Isaac,

Hay, Ferguson, Gray, R Scott, McIvor, Smith, Weir.
Scorers – *Tries:* Hay, Logan. *Conversion:* Donaldson. *Penalty goals:* Donaldson 3.

Series score: Played 2, Fiji 0, Scotland 2.

Tongan President's XV 5, Scotland 21
Nuku'alofa, 2 June 1993

President's XV: T Vave; A Vasi, L Fotu, M Lavaka, T Va'enuku; T Kolo, E Tulikaki; T Lavaki, M Kite, T Lutua, V Taumoepeau, T Loto'ahea, T Tulikaki, F Fakaongo, M Manukia.
Scorer – *Try:* E Tulikaki.

Scotland: C Redpath; Milligan (Logan 28), MacNaughton (Donaldson 49), Wyllie (capt), Kerr; Townsend, B Redpath; Jones, M Scott (Hay 26), Wilson, Munro, R Scott, Armstrong, Wallace, Hogg.
Scorers – *Tries:* Penalty try, Townsend. *Conversion:* Townsend. *Penalty goals:* Townsend 3.

Referee: T Marshall (New Zealand).

Tonga 5, Scotland 23
'Test': Nuku'alofa, 5 June 1993

Tonga: I Tapueluelu; A Uasi, T Tu'ineau, M Lavaka, T Va'enuku; E Vuniploa, A Tulikaki; V Moa, F Masila, E Talaki, T Loto'ahea, I Fatani, I Fenukitau, M Manukia (capt), F Fakaongo.
Scorer – *Try:* Lavaka.

Scotland: C Redpath; Moncrieff, Nichol, Jardine, Logan; Townsend, Nicol (capt); Isaac, Hay, Ferguson, Gray, R Scott, McIvor, Smith, Weir.
Scorers – *Tries:* Weir, Logan, penalty try. *Conversion:* Townsend. *Penalty goals:* Townsend 2.

Referee: L McLachlan (New Zealand).

Series score: Played 2, Tonga 0, Scotland 2.

Western Samoan President's XV 8, Scotland 33
Apia, 9 June 1993

President's XV: A Leaupepe; T Vaeau, V Petu, M Vaeono, S Tupuola; J Kelemete, F Fetineiae; P Solaese, F Faasua, P Lilomaiava, N Siu, S Lemamea, P Paulo, S Tuilaepa, F Lalomilo.
Scotland: Grecian; Glasgow, MacNaughton, Wyllie, Kerr; Donaldson, B Redpath; Jones, Corcoran, Wilson, Gray (capt), Macdonald, McIvor, Wallace (Nicol), Hogg (Weir).
Scorers – *Tries:* Gray, penalty try, Weir, Nicol, Kerr. *Conversion:* Donaldson. *Penalty goal:* Donaldson. *Dropped goal:* Wyllie.

Referee: T Marshall (New Zealand).

Western Samoa (12) 28, Scotland (8) 11
'Test': Apia, 12 June 1993

Western Samoa: A Aiolupo; L Koko, T Vaega, A Ieremia, B Lima; D Kellet, J Tonuu; P Fatialofa (capt), T Leiasamaivao, A Leuu, P Leonasa, L Falanko, S Vaifale, M Iupeli,

D Kaleopa.

Scorers – *Tries:* Vaega, Kaleopa, Lima. *Conversions:* Kellett 2. *Penalty goals:* Kellett 3.

Scotland: Grecian; Moncrieff, Nichol, Jardine, Logan; Townsend, Nicol (capt); Isaac, Hay, Ferguson, Munro, R Scott, McIvor, Smith, Weir.
Scorers – *Try:* Nichol. *Penalty goals:* Townsend 2.

Referee: L McLachlan (New Zealand).

Series score: Played 2, Western Samoa 1, Scotland 1.

WALES TO ZIMBABWE AND NAMIBIA
May-June 1993: P6 W6 D0 L0 F282 A90

Wales come out of Africa feeling pretty good after winning all six matches in Zimbabwe and Namibia. For a team handed the Wooden Spoon in the Five Nations' Championship it is an encouraging effort. Gareth Jenkins, the assistant coach, declares: 'If we can't compete with the rest of the world in terms of size, then we have to compensate by being innovative, and what the tour has achieved has been to turn those sentiments into reality.' Llanelli centre Neil Boobyer and Cardiff wing Simon Hill are among the tour's major successes, making their Test debuts along with Llanelli flanker Lyn Jones. Zimbabwe (twice) and Namibia are well beaten in the Test arena, and there is another notable result in the 56–17 win over the South African Barbarians.

PARTY: P Arnold (Swansea – 2,3,4); **R Bidgood** (Swansea – 1,3,5); **N Boobyer** (Llanelli – 2,3,4,5,6); **I Buckett** (Swansea – 2,4); **A Copsey** (Llanelli – 2,4); **A Davies** (Cardiff – 1,3,4R,6); **J Davies** (Neath – 2,3,6); **P Davies** (Llanelli – 1,4R,5,6); **S Davies** (Swansea – 1R, 2*,3,4*,5,6); **M Griffiths** (Cardiff – 1,3,5,6); **S Hill** (Cardiff – 1,2,3,4,5,6R); **R Howley** (Bridgend – 2,4); **N Jenkins** (Pontypridd – 1 ,2,3,4,5,6); **I Jones** (Llanelli – 2,6); **L Jones** (Llanelli – 1,3,5); **A Lamerton** (Llanelli – 1,3,5,6); **E Lewis** (Llanelli – 1,3,5,6); **G O Llewellyn** (Neath, capt – 1*,3*,5*,6*); **R McBryde** (Swansea – 2,4); **R Moon** (Llanelli – 1,3,5,6); **M Perego** (Llanelli – 1,2,4,6); **W Proctor** (Llanelli – 1,3,4,5,6); **M Rayer** (Cardiff – 1,2,4,5,6); **A Williams** (Maesteg – 2,4,6R); **H Williams-Jones** (South Wales Police – 1 ,4,5); **H Woodland** (Neath – 2,4). **Coach:** A Davies. **Assistant coach:** G Jenkins. **Manager:** R Norster. **Originally selected:** N Davies (Llanelli), M Hall (Cardiff), N Walker (Cardiff).

Results: (1) **first Test: Zimbabwe 14, Wales 35** (Bulawayo, 22 May); (2) Zimbabwe B 13, Wales 64 (Harare, 25 May); (3) **second Test: Zimbabwe 13, Wales 42** (Harare, 29 May); (4) Namibia B 10, Wales 47 (Windhoek, 2 June); (5) **Test: Namibia 23, Wales 38** (Windhoek, 5 June); (6) South African Barbarians 17, Wales 56 (Windhoek, 9 June).

Scorers (282 – 40t,26c,9p,1dg) – Jenkins 89 (2t,26c,9p), Proctor 25 (5t), I Jones 20 (4t), Boobyer 15 (3t), Hill 15 (3t), Rayer 15 (3t), J Davies 10 (2t), P Davies 10 (2t), S Davies 10 (2t), Howley 10 (2t), Lewis 10 (2t), Llewellyn 10 (2t), Moon 10 (2t), A Davies 8 (1t,1dg), Arnold 5 (1t), Bidgood 5 (1t), Buckett 5 (1t), McBryde 5 (1t), Perego 5 (1t).

Zimbabwe 14, Wales 35
first Test: Bulawayo, 22 May 1993

Zimbabwe: I Noble (Old Miltonians); D Nash (Mat Busters), D Walters (Old Miltonians, capt), M Letcher (Old Hararians), V Olonga (Old Miltonians); C Brown (Harare Sports Club), S Day (Old Miltonians); G Snyder (Harare Sports Club), B Beattie (Old Miltonians), A Garvey (Old Miltonians), R Demblon (Old Hararians), T Tabvuma

(Old Miltonians), S Landman (Harare Sports Club), B Dawson (Old Miltonians), E Fargnoli (Old Miltonians).
Scorers – *Try:* Olonga. *Penalty goals:* Walters 3.

Wales: Rayer; Hill, Bidgood, Jenkins, Proctor; A Davies, Moon; Griffiths, Lamerton, Williams-Jones, P Davies, Llewellyn (capt), Perego, L Jones, Lewis (S Davies 77).
Scorers – *Tries:* Moon, Hill, Proctor, P Davies. *Conversions:* Jenkins 3. *Penalty goals:* Jenkins 2. *Dropped goal:* A Davies.

Referee: I Rogers (South Africa).

Zimbabwe B 13, Wales 64
Harare, 25 May 1993

Zimbabwe B: T Tambo; A Jani, D Maidza, G Whittal, D Nash; W Veltman, E MacMillan; D Johnstone, P Albasini, T Erlank, B Chivendire, M Fick, G Cheromo, D Kirkman, M Malaniphy.
Scorers – *Tries:* Chivendire, Kirkman. *Penalty goal:* Veltman.

Wales: I Jones; Hill, Boobyer, Woodland, Rayer; Jenkins, Howley; Buckett, McBryde, J Davies, Arnold, Copsey, Williams, Perego, S Davies (capt).
Scorers – *Tries:* I Jones 2, Rayer 2, Howley, Buckett, Boobyer, Hill, Arnold, Jenkins. *Conversions:* Jenkins 7.

Referee: K Shadwick (Zimbabwe).

Zimbabwe 13, Wales 42
second Test: Harare, 29 May 1992

Zimbabwe: I Noble (Old Miltonians); W Schultz (Karoi), D Walters (Old Miltonians, capt), M Letcher (Old Hararians), V Olonga (Old Miltonians); C Brown (Harare Sports Club), E MacMillan (Old Hararians); G Snyder (Harare Sports Club), B Beattie (Old Miltonians), A G arvey (Old Miltonians), R Demblon (Old Hararians), T Tabvuma (Old Miltonians), S Landman (Harare Sports Club), B Dawson (Old Miltonians), D Kirkman (Old Miltonians). *Repl:* E Chimbima (Old Hararians) for Schultz, 33 mins; B Chivendire (Old Hararians) for Landman, 53 mins.
Scorers – *Try:* Olonga. *Conversion:* Noble. *Penalty goals:* Noble 2.

Wales: Jenkins; Hill, Bidgood, Boobyer, Proctor; A Davies, Moon; Griffiths, Lamerton, J Davies, Arnold, Llewellyn, S Davies, L Jones, Lewis.
Scorers – *Tries:* Llewellyn 2, Bidgood, J Davies, Jenkins, S Davies. *Conversions:* Jenkins 3. *Penalty goals:* Jenkins 2.

Referee: I Anderson (South Africa).

Series score: Played 2, Zimbabwe 0, Wales 2.

Namibia B 10, Wales 47
Windhoek, 2 June 1993

Namibia B:

Wales: Rayer; Hill (A Davies 44), Boobyer, Woodland, Proctor; Jenkins, Howley, Buckett, McBryde, Williams-Jones, Arnold, Copsey, S Davies (capt), Perego, Williams (P Davies 53). *Sent-off:* McBryde.

Scorers – *Tries:* Proctor 2, Rayer, McBryde, Boobyer 2, Howley. *Conversions:* Jenkins 6.

Referee: F Theunissen (Namibia).

Namibia 23, Wales 38
Test: Windhoek, 5 June 1993

Namibia: J Coetzee; G Mans, H Smyman, M Marais, E Meyer; M Booysen, B Buitendag; C Derks, S Smith, A von Wyk, D Kotze, B Malgas, J Bernard, K Goosen, H Brink.
Scorers – *Tries:* Coetzee, Kotze. *Conversions:* Coetzee 2. *Penalty goals:* Coetzee 3.

Wales: Rayer; Hill, Bidgood, Boobyer, Proctor; Jenkins, Moon; Griffiths, Lamerton, Williams-Jones, P Davies, Llewellyn (capt), S Davies, L Jones, Lewis.
Scorers – *Tries:* Lewis 2, Hill, Proctor, Moon. *Conversions:* Jenkins 2. *Penalty goals:* Jenkins 3.

Referee: K McCartney (Scotland).

SA Barbarians 17, Wales 56
Windhoek, 9 June 1993

SA Barbarians: C Dirks (Transvaal); G Mans (Namibia), H Muller (OFS), H Snyman (Namibia), A Alexander (Border); J Stransky (Natal), J Roux (Transvaal); G Kebble (Natal), J Allan (Natal, capt), M Hurter (Western Transvaal), R Kruger (OFS), H Strydom (Transvaal), R Opperman (OFS), J Barnard (Namibia), G Teichman (Natal). *Repl:* C Derks (Namibia) for for Kebble, 40 mins; J Coetzee (Namibia) for Mans, 76 mins.
Scorers – *Tries:* Barnard, Stransky. *Conversions:* Stransky 2. *Penalty goal:* Stransky.

Wales: Rayer; I Jones, Boobyer, Jenkins, Proctor (Hill 39); A Davies, Moon; Griffiths, Lamerton, J Davies, S Davies, P Davies, Llewellyn (capt), Perego (Williams 66), Lewis.
Scorers – *Tries:* I Jones 2, Proctor, Perego, P Davies, J Davies, S Davies, A Davies. *Conversions:* Jenkins 5. *Penalty goals:* Jenkins 2.

Referee: F Burger (South Africa).

1993 SUPER-10 TOURNAMENT
April-May 1993

Transvaal bring a smile to the face of South African rugby with victory in the inaugural Super-10 tournament, contested by the premier club sides in the Southern Hemisphere, plus Western Samoa. Transvaal advance unbeaten through Pool B before accounting for Auckland 20–7 in the final in Johannesburg's packed Ellis Park stadium.

Pool A: Western Samoa 27, Queensland 19 (3.4.93); Otago 22, Auckland 63 (10.4.93); Queensland 21, Auckland 22 (17.4.93); Natal 56, Western Samoa 13 (17.4.93); Auckland 18, Western Samoa 10 (24.4.93); Otago 13, Natal 35 (25.4.93); Auckland 22, Natal 6 (30.4.93); Queensland 20, Otago 8 (1.5.93); Natal 32, Queensland 15 (8.5.93); Western Samoa x, Otago x (8.5.93).

Pool B: Waikato 29, North Harbour 24 (3.4.93); Transvaal 42, Northern Transvaal 22 (3.4.93); New South Wales 17, Waikato 13 (17.4.93); Transvaal 39, North Harbour 13 (17.4.93); Northern Transvaal 45, New South Wales 20 (23.4.93); Transvaal 30, Waikato 15 (24.4.93); Waikato 18, Northern Transvaal 28 (1.5.93); North Harbour 16, New South Wales 17 (1.5.93); North Harbour x, Northern Transvaal x (7.5.93); New South Wales 3, Transvaal 10 (8.5.93).

Final: Transvaal (10) 20, Auckland (7) 7 Ellis Park, Johannesburg, 22 May 1993

Transvaal: T van Rensburg; C Dirks, J Mulder, B Fourie, P Hendriks; H Le Roux, J Roux; B Swart, U Schmidt, J Le Roux, K Weise, H Strydom, I Macdonald, D Lotter, F Pienaar (capt).
Scorers – *Tries:* Pienaar, Schmidt. *Conversions:* van Rensburg 2. *Penalty goals:* van Rensburg 2.

Auckland: S Howarth; V Tuigamala, E Clarke, L Stensness, T Wright; G Fox, T Nu'uali'ta; C Dowd, S Fitzpatrick (capt), O Brown, R Brooke, R Fromont, B Jackson (Z Brooke 60), M Jones, M Carter.
Scorers – *Tries:* Tuigamala, Stensness. *Conversions:* Fox 2. *Penalty goal:* Fox.

Referee: F Burger (Western Province).

WELSH DEVELOPMENT SQUAD TO FRANCE
May 1993: P3 W2 D0 L1 F83 A59

Wales' winning summer ends on a losing note when the Welsh Development XV go down 12–22 to Selection d'Aquitain on the final leg of their three-match tour. They had look likely to emulate the 100 per cent record of the senior side in Africa and the Under-21 team in the Netherlands and France when defeating the world champion French Students (30–29) and Selection Cote des Basques 41–8.

PARTY: J Apsee (SW Police – 2,3); **B Atkins** (Abertillery – 2,3); **M Back** (Pontypridd – 1,3); **I Boobyer** (Neath – 1,3); **B Childs** (Tenby – 1,3); **A Dibble** (Newport – 2); **D Earland** (Pontypridd – 2); **M Evans** (Aberavon – 2,3R); **J Humphreys** (Cardiff – 1*,3*); **S Jenkins** (Bridgend – 1,2,3); **R Jones** (Neath – 1); **A Lewis** (Newport – 1,2,3); **S Lewis** (Pontypridd – 1,3); **D Llewellyn** (Newport – 3); **K Matthews** (Cardiff – 1,2R,3); **A Moore** (Cardiff – 2*); **S Parfitt** (SW Police – 1,2); **B Phillips** (Gloucester – 2); **P Pook** (Newbridge – 1,2); **C Raymond** (Bath – 2); **M Rowley** (Pontypridd – 1,3); **R Shaw** (Bridgend – 1,3); **A Thomas** (Neath – 2); **J Westwood** (Newport – 2,3); **G Wilkins** (Bridgend – 1,2); **S Williams** (Neath – 1,3).

Results: (1) French Students 29, Welsh Development XV 30 (Bayonne, 20.5.93); (2) Selection Cotes des Basques 8, Welsh Development XV 41 (Dax, 23.5.93); (3) Selection d'Aquitain 22, Welsh Development XV 12 (Mimizan, 25.5.93).

Scorers – Childs 32 (1t,3c,7p), Raymond 16 (5c,2p), Atkins 15 (3t), Humphreys 5 (1t), Moore 5 (1t), Westwood 5 (1t), Wilkins 5 (1t).

BRITISH LIONS TO NEW ZEALAND
May–July 1993: P13 W7 D0 L6 F314 A285

So the Lions again succumb in the toughest arena in world rugby but, heck, what an effort. With no thanks to whoever agreed to the itinerary, the most demanding on record, the best of British and Irish made friends at every turn and earned the respect of the New Zealanders – no mean feat. On paper their won seven–lost six record is disappointing, especially after such a tremendous start, and indeed the midweek XV do not really do themselves justice. But the weekend warriors frighten the life out of the All Blacks. The first Test is wrenched from the visitors' grasp by the referee, who awards an All Black try which leaves room aplenty for doubt, and a last-minute penalty, for goodness knows what, which Grant Fox pops over from long-range to wipe out the effect of Gavin Hastings' six penalty goals. Hastings, indeed, is an heroic captain, equal to every task save conjuring up the first Lions' series win in New Zealand since 1971. It is a close call, mind. The most complete performance thinkable produces a record victory in the fixture, by 20–7, in the second Test, with Rory Underwood haring away gleefully for the clinching score. But the All Blacks have the last laugh. T'was ever thus? In the space of a week they dismantle their machine, tune each individual component, and adroitly reassemble it. The confident Lions lead 10–0 early on in the decider at Eden Park, yet are then swept aside. The match is lost 30–13 and with it the series. Still, the Lions return home with heads held high, not least Englishman Ben Clarke, who enjoys a splendid campaign.

PARTY: **R Andrew** (Wasps & England – 2,4,6,7,9,11,13), **S Barnes** (Bath & England – 1,3,4R,5,6R,8,10,12), **M Bayfield** (Northampton & England – 2,4,5,7,9,11,13), **P Burnell** (London Scottish & Scotland – 2,4,5,9,12), **W Carling** (Harlequins & England – 2,3,5,7,9R,10,12*), **B Clarke** (Bath & England – 1,3,4,7,8R,911,13), **A Clement** (Swansea & Wales – 1,4,5R,6,8,10,12), **D Cronin** (London Scottish & Scotland – 1,3,6,8,10,12), **V Cunningham**[3] (St Mary's College & Ireland – 8,10,12), **W Dooley** (Preston Grasshoppers & England – 2,3,5), **I Evans** (Llanelli & Wales – 2,3,5,7,9,11,13), **M Galwey** (Shannon & Ireland – 1,4,5R,6,7,8,10,12), **S Gibbs** (Swansea & Wales – 2,4,6,8,9,11,13), **J Guscott** (Bath & England – 1,3R,4,5,6R,7,9,11,13), **G Hastings** (Watsonians & Scotland, capt – 1R,2*,3*,5*,6*,7*,9*,11*,13*), **S Hastings** (Watsonians & Scotland – 1,3,5R), **I Hunter** (Northampton & England – 1), **M Johnson**[4] (Leicester & England – 8,9,11,13), **R Jones**[1] (Swansea & Wales – 1,4,6,8,10,12); **J Leonard** (Harlequins & England – 1,3R,4,6,7,8,10,11,13), **K Milne** (Heriot's FP & Scotland – 2,4,5,7,8R,10,12), **B Moore** (Harlequins & England – 1,3,6,8,9,11,13), **D Morris** (Orrell & England – 2,3,5,6R,7,9,11,13), **A Nicol**[5] (Dundee HSFP & Scotland – 8R), **N Popplewell** (Greystones & Ireland – 2,3,5,7,9,11,13), **A Reed** (Bath & Scotland – 1,4,6,7,10,12), **D Richards** (Leicester & England – 2,4*,5,7,11,13), **M Teague** (Moseley

New Zealand wing Eroni Clarke is devoured by two hungry Lions in the first Test in Christchurch on 12 June

& England – 2,3,5,6,8,10,12), **R Underwood** (Leicester, RAF & England – 1,3,5,7,9,11,13), **T Underwood** (Leicester & England – 2,4,6,8,10,12), **R Wallace**[2] (Garryowen & Ireland – 4,6,8,10,12), **R Webster** (Swansea & Wales – 1,2R,6,8,9,10,12), **P Winterbottom** (Harlequins & England – 2,3,5,9,11,13), **P Wright** (Boroughmuir & Scotland – 1,3,6,8, 10,12). **Coach:** I McGeechan (Scotland). **Assistant coach:** R Best (England). **Manager:** G Cooke (England).

[1] Gerry Armstrong originally selected; [2] replaced Hunter; [3] replaced S Hastings; [4] replaced Dooley; [5] temporary replacement

Results: (1) North Auckland 17, Lions 30 (Whangarei, 22 May); (2) North Harbour 13, Lions 29 (Auckland, 26 May); (3) NZ Maoris 20, Lions 24 (Wellington, 29 May); (4) Canterbury 10, Lions 28 (Christchurch, 2 June); (5) Otago 37, Lions 24 (Dunedin, 5 June); (6) Southland 16, Lions 34 (Invercargill, 8 June); (7) **first Test: New Zealand 20, British Lions 18** (Christchurch, 12 June); (8) Taranaki 25 , Lions 49 (New Plymouth, 16 June); (9) Auckland 29, Lions 17 (Auckland, 19 June); (10) Hawke's Bay 29, Lions 17 (Napier, 22 June); (11) **second Test: New Zealand 7, British Lions 20** (Wellington, 26 June); (12) Waikato 38, Lions 10 (Hamilton, 29 June); (13) **third Test: New Zealand 30, British Lions 13** (Auckland, 3 July).

Scorers (314 – 33t,19c,33p,4dg) – G Hastings 101 (1t,12c,24p), Barnes 33 (6c,7p), Andrew 24 (2t,1c,2p,2dg), Evans 20 (4t), R Underwood 15 (3t), Clement 13 (2t,1dg), Guscott 10 (2t), T Underwood 10 (2t), Webster 10 (2t), Cunningham 10 (2t), Gibbs 10 (2t), penalty tries 10 (2t), Carling 8 (1t,1dg), S Hastings 5 (1t), Galwey 5 (1t), Richards 5 (1t), Reed 5 (1t), Cronin 5 (1t), Teague 5 (1t), Jone s 5 (1t), Wallace 5 (1t).

North Auckland 17, Lions 30
Whangarei, 22 May 1993

North Auckland: W Johnston; T Going, C Going, M Seymour, D Manako; A Monaghan, R Le Bas; L Davies, D Te Puni, C Barrell, I Jones (capt), E Jones, G Taylor, A Going, K Tuipolotu. *Repl:* R Hilton-Jones for Tuipolotu, 58 mins; L Sigley for Te Puni, 77 mins. **Scorers** – *Tries:* Te Puni, Seymour, T Going. *Conversion:* Johnston.

Lions: Clement; Hunter (G Hastings 38), Guscott, S Hastings, R Underwood; Barnes (capt), Jones; Leonard, Moore, Wright, Cronin, Reed , Galwey, Webster, Clarke. **Scorers** – *Tries:* Guscott, S Hastings, Clement, R Underwood. *Conversions:* Barnes, G Hastings. *Penalty goals:* Barnes, G Hastings.

Referee: L McLachlan (Dunedin).

Series score: Played 8, North Auckland 0, Lions 8.

North Harbour 13, Lions 29
Auckland, 26 May 1993

North Harbour: I Calder; E Rush, F Bunce, W Little, R Kapa; J Carter, A Strachan; R Williams, G Dowd, K Boroevich, B Larsen, D Mayhew, A Perelini, L Barry, R Turner (capt). *Repl:* D George for Larsen, 79 mins. **Scorers** – *Try:* Perelini. *Conversion:* Carter. *Penalty goals:* Carter 2.

Lions: G Hastings (capt); Evans, Gibbs, Carling, T Underwood; Andrew, Morris; Popplewell, Milne, Burnell, Dooley, Bayfield, Teague, Winterbottom, Richards (Webster 55). **Scorers** – *Tries:* T Underwood, Andrew, Evans, Webster. *Conversions:* G Hastings 3. *Penalty goal:* G Hastings.

Referee: A Riley (Waikato).

Series score: Played 1, North Harbour 0, Lions 1.

NZ Maoris 20, Lions 24
Wellington, 29 May 1993

Maoris: S Doyle (Manawatu); E Rush (North Harbour), G Konia (Hawke's Bay), R Ellison (Waikato), A Prince (Nelson Bays); S Hirini (We llington), S Forster (Otago); G Hurunui (Horowhenua), N Hewitt (Hawke's Bay), K Boroevich (North Harbour), J Coe (Counties), M Cooksley (Counties), J Joseph (Otago), Z Brooke (Auckland), A Pene (Otago, capt).
Scorers – *Tries:* Prince, Hirini. *Conversions:* Hirini 2. *Penalty goals:* Hirini 2.

Lions: G Hastings (capt); Evans, S Hastings, Carling (Guscott 73), R Underwood; Barnes, Morris; Popplewell (Leonard 50), Moore, Wright, Cronin, Dooley, Teague, Winterbottom, Clarke.
Scorers – *Tries:* Evans, R Underwood, G Hastings. *Conversions:* G Hastings 3. *Penalty goal:* G Hastings.

Referee: G Lempriere (Palmerston North).

Series score: Played 7, NZ Maoris 0, Lions 6.

Canterbury 10, Lions 28
Christchurch, 2 June 1993

Canterbury: A Lawry; P Bale, S Philpott, K Hansen, S Cleave; G Coffey, G Bachop; G Halford, M Hammett, S Loe, C England, M McAtamney , T Blackadder, G Smith, R Penney (capt). *Repl:* W Maunsell for Hansen, 4 mins; T Kelle for for Halford, 62 mins.
Scorers – *Try:* Smith. *Conversion:* Coffey. *Penalty goal:* Coffey.

Lions: Clement; Wallace, Guscott, Gibbs, T Underwood; Andrew (Barnes 76), Jones; Leonard, Milne, Burnell, Reed, Bayfield, Galwey, Clarke, Richards (capt).
Scorers – *Tries:* Guscott, Galwey, T Underwood, Andrew. *Conversion:* Andrew. *Penalty goal:* Andrew. *Dropped goal:* Andrew.

Referee: J Taylor (Counties).

Series score: Played 8, Canterbury 3, Lions 5.

Otago 37, Lions 24
Dunedin, 5 June 1993

Otago: J Timu; A Bell, M Ellis, J Leslie, P Cooke; S Bachop, S Forster; N Moore, D Latta (capt), M Mika, A Rich, G MacPherson, J Kronfield, J Joseph, A Pene.
Scorers – *Tries:* Cooke 2, Leslie, Latta, Timu. *Conversions:* Bell 3. *Penalty goal:* Bell. *Dropped goal:* Bachop.

Lions: G Hastings (capt); Evans, Carling (S Hastings 9, Clement 50), Guscott, R Underwood; S Barnes, D Morris; Popplewell, Milne, Burnell, Dooley, Bayfield (Galwey 79), Teague, Winterbottom, Richards.
Scorers – *Tries:* Richards, Evans. *Conversion:* G Hastings. *Penalty goals:* G Hastings 4.

Referee: C Hawke (South Canterbury).

Series score: Played 7, Otago 3, Lions 4.

Southland 16, Lions 34
Invercargill, 8 June 1993

Southland: S Forrest; P Johnston, A James, G Beardsley, J Cormack; S Culhane, R Murrell; R Palmer, D Heaps (S Hayes 70), C Corbett, M Tinnock (R Bekhuis 74), W Millar, B Morton, P Henderson (capt, D Henderson 40), R Smith.
Scorers – *Tries:* Cormack Johnston. *Penalty goals:* Culhane 2.

Lions: G Hastings (capt); Wallace, Gibbs (Guscott 69), Clement, T Underwood; Andrew (Barnes 67, Morris 79), Jones; Leonard, Moore, Wright, Cronin, Reed, Teague, Webster, Galwey.
Scorers – *Tries:* Penalty try, Reed, Clement. *Conversions:* G Hastings 2. *Penalty goals:* G Hastings 4. *Dropped goal:* Clement.

Referee: M Fitzgibbon (Canterbury).

Series score: Played 7, Southland 2, Lions 5.

New Zealand (11) 20, British Lions (9) 18
first Test: Christchurch, 12 June 1993

New Zealand: J Timu (Otago); E Clarke (Auckland), F Bunce (North Harbour), W Little (North Harbour), V Tuigamala (Auckland); G Fox (Auckland), A Strachan (North Harbour); C Dowd (Auckland), S Fitzpatrick (Auckland, capt), O Brown (Auckland), I Jones (North Auckland), R Brooke (Auckland), J Joseph (Otago), M Jones (Auckland), Z Brooke (Auckland). *Repl:* M Cooper (Waikato).
Scorers – *Try:* Bunce. *Penalty goals:* Fox 5.

British Lions: G Hastings (capt); Evans, Guscott, Carling, R Underwood; Andrew, Morris; Popplewell, Milne, Leonard, Bayfield, Reed, Galwey, Clarke, Richards.
Scorers – *Penalty goals:* G Hastings 6.

Referee: B Kinsey (Australia).

Series score: Played 29, New Zealand 22, Lions 5, Drawn 2.

Taranaki 25, Lions 49
New Plymouth, 16 June 1993

Taranaki: K Crowley; D Murfitt, K Mahon, K Eynon, A Martin; J Cameron, W Dromboski; M Allen (capt), S McDonald, G Slater, B O'Sullivan, J Roache, A Slater, F Mahoni, N Hill.
Scorers – *Tries:* O'Sullivan, A Slater, McDonald. *Conversions:* Crowley 2. *Penalty goals:* Crowley 2.

Lions: Clement; Wallace, Cunningham, Gibbs, T Underwood; Barnes (capt), Jones (Nicol 77); Wright, Moore, Leonard, Cronin, Johnson, Teague (Milne 77), Webster, Galwey (Clarke 33).
Scorers – *Tries:* Cronin, Teague, Cunningham 2, Jones, Wallace, Gibbs. *Conversions:* Barnes 4. *Penalty goals:* Barnes 2.

Series score: Played 7, Taranaki 1, Lions 6.

Hawke's Bay 29, Lions 17
Napier, 22 June 1993

Hawke's Bay: J Cunningham; A Hamilton, G Konia, M Paenai, P Davis; S Kerr, N Weber; T Taylor, N Hewitt (capt), O Crawford, J Fowler, W Davison, D Watts, G Falcon, S Tremain.
Scorers – *Tries:* Hewitt, Weber, Tremain. *Conversion:* Kerr. *Penalty goals:* Cunningham 2, Kerr. *Dropped goal:* Kerr.

Lions: Clement; Wallace, Cunningham, Carling, T Underwood; Barnes (capt), Jones; Wright, Milne, Leonard, Cronin, Reed, Teague, Webster, Galwey.
Scorers – *Try:* Webster. *Penalty goals:* Barnes 3. *Dropped goal:* Carling.

Referee: P O'Brien (North Otago).

Series score: Played 8, Hawke's Bay 1, Lions 6, Drawn 1.

New Zealand (7) 7, British Lions (9) 20
second Test: Wellington, 26 June 1993

New Zealand: J Timu (Otago); J Kirwan (Auckland), F Bunce (North Harbour), E Clarke (Auckland), V Tuigamala (Auckland); G Fox (Auckl and), J Preston (Wellington); C Dowd (Auckland), S Fitzpatrick (Auckland, capt), O Brown (Auckland), R Brooke (Auckland), M Cooksley (Counties), J Joseph (Otago), M Jones (Auckland), Z Brooke (Auckland). *Repl:* I Jones (North Auckland) for Cooksley, 40 mins.
Scorers – *Try:* Clarke. *Conversion:* Fox.

British Lions: G Hastings (capt); Evans, Gibbs, Guscott, R Underwood; Andrew, Morris; Popplewell, Moore, Leonard, Johnson, Bayfield, Clarke, Winterbottom, Richards.
Scorers – *Try:* R Underwood. *Penalty goals:* G Hastings 4. *Dropped goal:* Andrew.

Referee: P Robin (France)

Series score: Played 30, New Zealand 22, Lions 6, Drawn 2.

Waikato 38, Lions 10
Hamilton, 29 June 1993

Waikato: M Cooper; D Wilson, A Collins, R Ellison, W Warlow; I Foster, S Crabb; C Stevenson, W Gatland, C Stevenson, S Gordon, B Anderson (M Russell 71), R Jerram, D Monkley, J Mitchell (capt).
Scorers – *Tries:* Wilson, Monkley 2, Collins, Gatland. *Conversions:* Cooper 2. *Penalty goals:* Cooper 3.

Lions: Clement; Wallace, Cunningham, Carling (capt), T Underwood; Barnes, Jones; Wright, Milne, Burnell, Cronin, Reed, Teague, Webster, Galwey.
Scorers – *Try:* Carling. *Conversion:* Barnes. *Penalty goal:* Barnes.

Referee: T Marshall (Canterbury).

Series score: Played 8, Waikato 1, Lions 7.

New Zealand (14) 30, British Lions (10) 13
third Test: Auckland, 3 July 1993

New Zealand: J Timu (Otago); J Kirwan (Auckland), F Bunce (North Harbour), L Stensness (Auckland)*, V Tuigamala (Auckland); G Fox (Auckland), J Preston (Wellington); C Dowd (Auckland), S Fitzpatrick (Auckland, capt), O Brown (Auckland), I Jones (North Auckland), R Brooke (Auckland), J Joseph (Otago), M Jones (Auckland), A Pene (Otago). *Repl:* M Cooksley (Counties) for I Jones, 20 mins; Z Brooke (Auckland)

for M Jones, 73 mins.
Scorers – *Tries:* Bunce, Fitzpatrick, Preston. *Conversions:* Fox 3. *Penalty goals:* Fox 3.

British Lions: G Hastings (capt); Evans, Gibbs, Guscott, R Underwood; Andrew, Morris; Popplewell, Moore, Leonard, Johnson, Bayfield, Clarke, Winterbottom, Richards.
Scorers – *Try:* Gibbs. *Conversion:* G Hastings. *Penalty goal:* G Hastings.

Referee: P Robin (France).

Series score: Played 31, New Zealand 23, Lions 6, Drawn 2.

FRANCE TO SOUTH AFRICA
June–July 1993: P8 W4 D2 L2 F169 A159

France salvage some European honour and pride from the Southern Hemisphere by beating South Africa. Considering the lack of success in their provincial matches France have no right to expect much from the two internationals, the more so after they lose lock Abdelatif Benazzi and inspirational hooker Jean-François Tordo early on in the trip. Tordo, the French skipper, is raked in the face by Western Province's Garry Pagel and requires 50 stitches to his mouth, nose and cheek in a plastic surgery operation lasting two hours. Olivier Roumat takes over the captaincy duties and does a cracking job. The Springboks are held 20–20 in an ill-tempered first Test in Durban but the following week, at Ellis Park, Johannesburg, are edged out 18–17, despite their right wing James Small claiming the game's only try. Thierry Lacroix kicks 15 points to swing the pendulum towards the visitors.

Springbok lock Adolf Malan tussles with French rival Olivier Roumat at Lyon where South Africa register their first win (20–15) since returning to the international fold

PARTY: L Armary (Lourdes); A Benazzi (Agen); P Benetton (Agen); L Benezech (Racing Club); P Bernat-Salles (Pau); D Berty (Toulouse); X Blond (Racing Club); P Bondouy, L Cabannes (Racing Club); O Campan (Agen); J Cazalbou (Toulouse); M Cecillon (Bourgoin); H Couffignal (Colomiers); J-M Gonzales (Bayonne); S Graou (Auch); P Hontas (Biarritz); A Hueber (Toulon); T Lacroix (Dax); Y Lemeur (Racing Club); J-M Lhermet (Montferrand); L Loppy (Toulouse); O Merle (Grenoble); P Montlaur (Agen); A Penaud (Brive); O Roumat (Dax); J-L Sadourny (Colomiers); P Saint-André (Montferrand); L Seigne (Merignac); P Sella (Agen); J-F Tordo (Nice, capt).

Results: (1) Eastern Province 8, France 18 (Port Elizabeth, 9 June); (2) Western Province 6, France 12 (Cape Town, 12 June); (3) South Africa B 35, France 22 (East London, 15 June); (4) Free State x, France x (Blemfontein, 19 June); (5) Northern Transvaal 38, France 19 (Pretoria, 22 June); (6) **first Test: South Africa 20, France 20** (Durban, 26 June); (7) South African Development XV 13, France 38 (Welkom, 29 June); (8) **second Test: South Africa 17, France 18** (Johannesburg, 3 July).

South Africa (11) 20, France (14) 20
first Test: Durban, 26 June 1993

South Africa: T van Rensburg; J Small, P Müller, H Fuls, J Olivier; H le Roux, R du Preez; W Hills, U Schmidt, K Andrews, K Wiese, R Visagie, F Pienaar (capt), I Macdonald, C Strauss.
Scorers – *Try:* Schmidt. *Penalty goals:* van Rensburg 5.

France: Sadourny; Bernat-Salles (Campan 50), Lacroix, Sella, Saint-André; Penaud, Hueber; Armary, Gonzalez, Graou, Merle, Roumat (capt), Benetton, Cabannes, Cecillon.
Scorers – *Try:* Saint-André. *Penalty goals:* Lacroix 3. *Dropped goals:* Hueber, Penaud.

Referee: S Hilditch (Ireland).

Series score: Played 20, South Africa 12, France 3, Drawn 5.

South Africa (8) 17, France (9) 18
second Test: Johannesburg, 3 July 1993

South Africa: T van Rensburg; J Small, P Müller, H Fuls, J Olivier; H le Roux, R du Preez; W Hills (J Styger 8), U Schmidt, K Andrews, H Strydom, N Wegner, F Pienaar (capt), D Lotter, C Strauss.
Scorers – *Try:* Small. *Penalty goals:* van Rensburg 4.

France: Sadourny (Campan 50); Bernat-Salles, Sella, Lacroix, Saint-André; Penaud, Hueber; Armary, Gonzalez, Graou, Merle, Roumat (capt), Benetton, Cabannes, Cecillon.
Scorers – *Penalty goals:* Lacroix 4. *Dropped goals:* Penaud, Lacroix.

Referee: E Morrison (England).

Series score: Played 21, South Africa 12, France 4, Drawn 5.

Australia (24) 52, Tonga (0) 14
Brisbane, 3 July 1993

David Campese takes his world record haul to 54 tries as Australia easily account for plucky Tonga at Ballymore. Campo claims two of the Aussies' seven tries, with replacement scrum-half Brett Johnstone marking his Test debut with one. The other tries come from Paul Carozza, Jason Little, Tim Gavin and Garrick Morgan. Marty Roebuck kicks 15 points, and Michael Lynagh lands one conversion. The bad news for the Wallabies is that scrum-half Peter Slattery sustains broken ribs, after taking a knee to the back. Former captain and No 9, Nick Farr-Jones, agrees to make himself available for the Bledisloe Cup series.

Australia: M Roebuck; P Carozza, J Little, T Horan, D Campese; M Lynagh (capt), P Slattery (B Johnstone, 20 mins); T Daly, P Kearns, E McKenzie, R McCall, G Morgan, T Coker, D Wilson, T Gavin.
Scorers – *Tries:* Campese 2, Morgan, Gavin, Little, Carozza, Johnstone. *Conversions:* Roebuck 3, Lynagh. *Penalty goals:* Roebuck 3.

Tonga: T Vave; A Taufa, T Tu'ineau, M Lavaka, T Va'enuku; E Vunipola (T Kolo 75), M Vunipola; S Latu, R Kapeli, F Masila, F Mafi, I Fatani, I Fenukitau, F Mahoni, M Manukia.
Scorers – *Tries:* I Fenukitau, penalty try. *Conversions:* T Vave 2.

Referee: B Leask (Australia)

Series score: Played 3, Australia 2, Tonga 1.

BLEDISLOE CUP
July93: New Zealand win 1–0 and regain trophy

New Zealand (9) 25, Australia (3) 10
Dunedin, 17 July 1993

World champions Australia hand the Bledisloe Cup over to arch rivals New Zealand in this one-off encounter, and with it their label of invincibility. The wizards from Oz are unable to conjure up anything the previously retired Nick Farr-Jones, though that is a neat trick in itself. And even the experienced scrum-half's customary polished performance cannot inspire a victory at Carisbrook. The All Blacks, feeling good after their series win over the Lions, triumph through a combination of Grant Fox's accurate boot, which claims five penalty goals, and uncharacteristic errors of the unforced variety by Australia. New Zealand cement their advantage with two tries early in the second period. Skipper Sean Fitzpatrick powers onto a pass from John Kirwan to decisive effect two minutes before centre Lee Stensness adroitly chips ahead for Auckland team-mate Va'aiga Tuigamala to collect and tear into the Wallabies' defence. David Campese holds onto the rampaging bull but cannot prevent him slipping the scoring pass to Frank Bunce. Australia's Tim Horan, collecting a kick by 19-year old debutant Pat Howard (standing in for the injured Michael Lynagh), crosses to reduce the arrears but the damage to New Zealand's authority is superficial.

New Zealand: J Timu (Otago); J Kirwan (Auckland), F Bunce (North Harbour), L Stensness (Auckland), V Tuigamala (Auckland); G Fox (Auckland), J Preston (Wellington); C Dowd (Auckland), S Fitzpatrick (Auckland, capt), O Brown (Auckland), M Cooksley (Southland), R Brooke (Auckland), J Joseph (Otago), M Jones (Auckland), A Pene (Otago).
Scorers – *Tries:* Fitzpatrick, Bunce. *Penalty goals:* Fox 5.

Australia: T Kelaher (NSW); P Carozza (Queensland), J Little (Queensland), T Horan (Queensland), D Campese (NSW); P Howard' (Queensland), N Farr-Jones (NSW); A Daly (NSW), P Kearns (NSW), E McKenzie (NSW), R McCall (Queensland), G Morgan (Queensland), T Coker (Queensland), D Wilson (Queensland), T Gavin (NSW). *Repl:* A Herbert (Queensland) for Carozza.
Scorers – *Try:* Horan. *Conversion:* Kelaher. *Penalty goal:* Kelaher.

Series score: Played 94, New Zealand 65, Australia 24, Drawn 5.

461

MAJOR FIXTURES FOR SEASON 1993/94

SEPTEMBER 1993

29 Wales A v Japan (Llanelli)

OCTOBER

2 Dunvant v Japan (Dunvant)
6 East Wales v Japan (Abertillery)
9 CANADA v AUSTRALIA
   West Wales v Japan (Narberth)
12 Combined Divs 3/4 v Japan (Pontypridd)
13 Wales A v North of England (Pontypool)
16 WALES v JAPAN (Cardiff)
   French Selection v Australia (Dax)
19 Gloucester v SA Barbarians (Gloucester)
20 French Selection v Australia (Agen)
21 Leicester v SA Barbarians (Leicester)
23 London & SE Division v New Zealand
   (Twickenham)
   French Selection v Australia (Narbonne)
25 Newport v SA Barbarians (Newport)
26 Midland Division v New Zealand
   (Leicester)
   French Selection v Australia (Grenoble)
27 Llanelli v SA Barbarians (Llanelli)
30 FRANCE v AUSTRALIA (first Test:
   Strasbourg)
   South West Division v New Zealand
   (Redruth)

NOVEMBER

1 Bridgend v SA Barbarians (Bridgend)
2 Northern Division v New Zealand
   (Liverpool FC)
   French Selection v Australia (Toulon)
6 FRANCE v AUSTRALIA (second Test:
   Paris)
   Scottish Exiles v Auckland
   Bath v SA Barbarians (Bath)
7 England A v New Zealand (Gateshead)
8 Edinburgh v Auckland (Meggatland,
   Edinburgh)
10 South of Scotland v New Zealand
   (Galashiels)
11 French Barbarians v Australia (Clermont-
   Ferrand)
13 IRELAND v ROMANIA (Dublin)
   Scotland A v New Zealand (Old
   Anniesland, Glasgow)
14 District Selection v Auckland (Hawick)
16 Scotland Development XV v New
   Zealand (Myreside, Edinburgh)

20 SCOTLAND v NEW ZEALAND
   (Edinburgh)
23 England Emerging Players v New Zealand
   (Gloucester)
27 ENGLAND v NEW ZEALAND
   (Twickenham)
30 Combined Services v New Zealand
   (Devonport)

DECEMBER

4 Barbarians v New Zealand (Cardiff)
7 Varsity Match: Oxford v Cambridge
   (Twickenham)
18 Italy v Scotland A
28 Scotland A v Ireland A (Hughenden,
   Glasgow)

JANUARY 1994

4 Scotland A v Spain
14 Wales Under-21 v Scotland U-21
   (Cardiff)
15 FRANCE v IRELAND (Paris)
   WALES v SCOTLAND (Cardiff)

FEBRUARY

4 Ireland A v Wales A (Dublin)
   Ireland U-21 v Wales U-21
5 SCOTLAND v ENGLAND (Edinburgh)
   IRELAND v WALES (Dublin)
   Italy A v England A
18 England A v Ireland A (Richmond)
19 ENGLAND v IRELAND (Twickenham)
   WALES v FRANCE (Cardiff)
20 France A v Scotland A (Paris)

MARCH

4 Ireland U-21 v Scotland U-21 (Dublin)
5 FRANCE v ENGLAND (Paris)
   IRELAND v SCOTLAND (Dublin)
   France A v England A (Paris)
18 England A v South Africa B (Leicester)
   Scotland U-21 v France U-21 (Inverleith)
   Wales A v France A
19 ENGLAND v WALES (Twickenham)
   SCOTLAND v FRANCE (Edinburgh)

APRIL

2 Italy U-21 v Scotland U-21

JUNE

4 French Championship final (Paris)